PENGUIN CLASSICS

DIVINE RIGHT AND DEMOCRACY

David Wootton has carried out research on the history of Renaissance Venice at Balliol College, Oxford. He has been a research fellow at Peterhouse, Cambridge; a lecturer in the history of political thought at Westfield College, University of London; and a visiting professor in the department of politics of McGill University. He is now an associate professor at Dalhousie University, Canada, where he teaches early modern English history. He is the author of *Paolo Sarpi: Between Renaissance and Enlightenment* (1983), a study in the intellectual origins of atheism.

DIVINE RIGHT AND DEMOCRACY

An Anthology of Political Writing
in Stuart England

EDITED BY DAVID WOOTTON

PENGUIN BOOKS

Penguin Books Ltd, Harmondsworth, Middlesex, England
Viking Penguin Inc., 40 West 23rd Street, New York, New York 10010, U.S.A.
Penguin Books Australia Ltd, Ringwood, Victoria, Australia
Penguin Books Canada Limited, 2801 John Street, Markham, Ontario, Canada L3R 1B4
Penguin Books (N.Z.) Ltd, 182–190 Wairau Road, Auckland 10, New Zealand

—

First published 1986

—

—

Made and printed in Great Britain by
Richard Clay (The Chaucer Press) Ltd,
Bungay, Suffolk
Typeset in Monophoto Garamond

CONTENTS

Contents

Contents

ACKNOWLEDGEMENTS

I should like to thank John Crowley, John Dunn, Andrew Franklin, Ed Hundert and Michael Hunter for reading and commenting upon the Introduction, and Peter Phillips and Anthony Turner for their assistance in seeing the text through to press. The errors that remain are mine alone. I am indebted to Westfield College, University of London, for allowing me to employ the facilities of its computer unit for the final preparation of the typescript of this book.

PREFACE

The seventeenth century was England's 'century of revolution'.*
The revolution of 1642–9, which culminated in the execution of the
king and the declaration of a republic, saw the formation of the first
secular political party defending the inalienable rights of man, the
Levellers. It gave rise to the first communist movement with a strategy for effective social action, the Diggers. And it led to the formulation of the first materialist theory of historical change, in the
writings of James Harrington. The arguments of the American, the
French and even the Russian revolutions can be traced back to the
debates during England's mid-century crisis, while the arguments of
the radicals were directed against moderate defences of tradition and
royalist defences of authority that were to provide the foundations
on which Hume and Burke could construct modern conservatism.

The revolution of 1688 was a much more controlled and limited
affair. Precisely for this reason it became the key event in the Whig
interpretation of English history as a story of compromise and
constitutional adaptation, through which liberty had been established
in practice more securely than if it had always been defended in
abstract principle. But 1688 was the outcome of a prolonged crisis
which had begun with the attempts to exclude James from succession
to the throne in 1679. The political thought of the first Whigs was
shaped, not by the compromise of 1688, but by the fierce debates and
illegal plots of the preceding years.

The history of political thought in Stuart England is inseparable
from these periods of revolutionary crisis, periods when political
writers hoped to directly influence the outcome of events by the
force of their arguments. To read the major political theorists of
Stuart England, whether revolutionaries like Lilburne, Winstanley
and Sidney, or advocates of obedience as diverse as Filmer or Ascham,

---

* For two contrasting views of 'the century of revolution' see C. Hill, *The Century
of Revolution* (Edinburgh, 1961) and P. Laslett, *The World We Have Lost* (London, 1965;
rev. edn, 1983). I have found the following general introductions to the period
particularly helpful, and have drawn freely upon them in my own introduction: C.
Russell, *The Crisis of Parliaments, 1509–1660* (Oxford, 1971); C. Cross, *Church and People,
1450–1660* (London, 1976); K. Wrightson, *English Society, 1580–1680* (London, 1982);
C. Wilson, *England's Apprenticeship, 1603–1763* (London, 1965; rev. edn., 1985).
    There are general introductions to the political theory of the first half of our period
in J. P. Sommerville, *Politics and Ideology in England, 1603–1640* (London, 1986) and P.
Zagorin, *A History of Political Thought in the English Revolution* (London, 1954).

is to be plunged into a world in which many of our modern conceptions of political rights and social change are in process of construction.

Of course, when we think of seventeenth-century English political thought the names that first occur to mind are those of Hobbes and Locke, the first an advocate of obedience, the second of revolt. One of the purposes of this collection of texts is to facilitate the comprehension of Hobbes and Locke by placing them in a context of contemporary debate. To read them in isolation, without attention to the views of their contemporaries, is to lose sight of the arguments they were trying to overcome and the causes they were trying to assist. It is comparable to listening to the prosecution or the defence in a criminal trial without hearing the other side's case: without some sense of the strengths and weaknesses of the opponent it is impossible to grasp why apparently promising lines of argument are never pursued, while at other times what seem to be trivial distinctions and secondary issues are subjected to lengthy examination.

It may seem a counsel of perfection to appeal to a larger context when few people read the second book of *Leviathan* or the first of the *Two Treatises*, but a respect for the text as a whole is, in fact, inseparable from an attention to its context. Someone who steps into the court-room from outside to hear the defence's summing-up is likely to find it long-winded and beside the point, while those who have heard the evidence and listened to the prosecution will see how every word has its part to play in an effort to ensure the defendant's acquittal.

Putting political thinkers in their context involves recognizing that, like lawyers, they have very immediate and practical objectives to which their arguments are subordinated. Only one of the texts selected here was written by a university teacher, and even it was an official response to a political event and had nothing to do with the disinterested pursuit of truth. Nearly all the arguments presented here were contentious: indeed, one of the historian's problems is that issues on which everyone is agreed are rarely the subject of discussion, just as open-and-shut cases rarely come to trial. History, of course, delivers its own verdict on certain arguments. Since there are few hereditary monarchs exercising real power left, scarcely anyone now appeals to the divine right of kings. What is more, democracy is now seen as so evidently admirable that there is scarcely a country in the world which does not claim either to be a democracy or to have the intention of becoming one. But the fact that an argument eventually becomes extinct does not mean that – like some ancient dinosaur – it was not once well-adapted and successful; nor does it mean, as strict

Darwinians never tire of pointing out, that its successors, better adapted to new circumstances as they were, were necessarily more sophisticated or better engineered. The survival of the fittest cannot automatically be identified with progress.

The history of political thought has often been studied as a series of 'classic' texts: Plato, Aristotle, Augustine, Aquinas, Hobbes, Locke, Rousseau and so forth. In order to make this presentation persuasive the authors are generally presented as being in dialogue – a dialogue sometimes seen as imaginary, often as authentic, if somewhat one-sided – with each other. Of course, Hobbes and Locke were familiar with Aristotle. But their social values, their intellectual assumptions, their political institutions were fundamentally different from those of Alexander's Greece. The Aristotle with whom they entered into debate was a contemporary, the Aristotle of seventeenth-century university education, not an ancient Greek. It has become commonplace to insist on this sort of point, and the work of scholars such as A. W. H. Adkins on Plato and Aristotle or Felix Gilbert on Machiavelli has been directed at the recovery of the true cultural context of classic texts.* Seventeenth-century English political thought in particular has indeed been intensively studied by the new 'contextualist' historians of ideas, especially by what is sometimes termed the 'Cambridge school' of Skinner, Dunn, Pocock and their students. It is therefore worth separating, for a moment, the case for contextualism from the particular arguments of a school or schools.

The last two decades, it is generally agreed, have seen major changes in the study of the history of political thought, and there has been much talk of a 'revolution' inaugurated by Quentin Skinner's 1969 essay on 'Meaning and Understanding in the History of Ideas'.† In large part, however, these changes are the result of lengthy evolution, rather than of the heroic deeds of a vanguard party guided by correct theory. They represent merely the application

---

* A. W. H. Adkins, *Merit and Responsibility* (Oxford, 1960); F. Gilbert, *Machiavelli and Guicciardini* (Princeton, 1965).

† *History and Theory*, VIII (1969), pp. 3–53. The extensive writings by and about Skinner have been reviewed by J. H. Tully in 'The Pen is a Mighty Sword: Quentin Skinner's Analysis of Politics', *British Journal of Political Science*, XIII (1983), pp. 489–509. Two more recent contributions are D. Boucher, 'The Denial of Perennial Problems: The Negative Side of Quentin Skinner's Theory', *Interpretation*, XII (1984), pp. 287–300, and the first chapter of F. Oakley, *Omnipotence, Covenant and Order* (Cornell, 1984). Some of Pocock's work is collected in *Politics, Language and Time* (New York, 1971), and all but the most recent is reviewed in I. Hampsher-Monk, 'Political Languages in Time: The Work of J. G. A. Pocock', *British Journal of Political Science*, XIV (1984), pp. 89–116. Some of John Dunn's work is collected in *Political Obligation in Its Historical Context* (Cambridge, 1980).

of the methods and values of professional history to the history of ideas. The search for new sources, for a more detailed narrative, for a more exact sense of the complexity and inner logic of events, was bound to produce a new intellectual as it had already produced new political and new economic histories. The new history of political thought closely parallels, for example, the new history of science associated with the name of Thomas Kuhn.* In both disciplines what has been involved can be described as the application to new fields of Herbert Butterfield's attack upon anachronism in *The Whig Interpretation of History* (1931).

Butterfield addressed himself to an audience primarily concerned with English political history and so his attack was directed against the myths of English politics. If Skinner and Kuhn have defended their approaches in very different terms from those adopted by Butterfield the explanation lies in large part in the fact that the one has tried to wrest the history of political thought from the hands of contemporary political philosophers, while the other has tried to rescue the history of science from experimental scientists. The first has therefore addressed himself to the philosophical analysis of how one communicates meaning through texts, in order to meet linguistic philosophers on their own ground, while the second has striven to demonstrate that experimental evidence is not the sole factor determining the advance of science, by analysing the role of conceptual paradigms in directing research.

Good contextualist accounts of political theory were bound to appear as history became increasingly professionalized in the fifties: Pocock's *Ancient Constitution*, for example, was published in 1957, Sirluck's introduction to Milton's *Complete Prose Works*, volume two, in 1959, and Laslett's introduction to Locke's *Two Treatises* in 1960. All three remain models of their kind, and they pre-date by a decade the theoretical writings of Skinner, Dunn and Pocock himself. The basic case for contextualism had, in any case, been long established and remains a simple one. It is, to paraphrase Collingwood, an obvious fact that you cannot make sense of an answer until you know to what question it is a reply. In Collingwood's view this was not a principle peculiar to the history of ideas. His favourite example was the Roman wall between Tyne and Solway, which could not be made sense of, he maintained, until it was seen that the wall itself was not a defensive fortification, but merely the support for an elevated

* T. S. Kuhn, *The Structure of Scientific Revolutions* (2nd edn., Chicago, 1970); I. Lakatos and A. E. Musgrave (eds.), *Criticism and the Growth of Knowledge* (Cambridge, 1970).

sentry-walk.* In the Introduction that follows I suggest that early-seventeenth-century references to 'absolute monarchy' are defensive structures that are as liable to misinterpretation as the Roman wall.

Collingwood held that the problem of the Roman wall could be solved once one asked what it was meant to do. But it would be a mistake to think that all that is required for the understanding of an argument about the state or rights is a grasp of the problem its author meant to address when he wrote it, for texts are often comprehensible only when they are seen to betray the influence of wider developments in intellectual life, in politics or in society, just as the Roman wall has to be seen against the wider background of the military resources and strategic concerns of the late Roman empire. Hobbes's writing is from beginning to end an attack upon the Aristotelian philosophy of the universities. One might be able to follow his argument, but one could scarcely understand its impact, without some reference to the intellectual orthodoxies it was designed to undermine and with which Hobbes assumed his reader to be familiar. The writings of the Levellers owe much of their originality to their origins in religious disputes about toleration and freedom of worship. To read them without realizing that the first right they sought to defend was that of freedom of worship is to miss one of the central respects in which they sought to reshape the political life of their day. Filmer maintained that all authority derives from the authority of a father over his children: his argument cries out to be related to the family structure of his day. The authors themselves would often have admitted the relevance of contexts such as these, had they been asked, but reference to such contexts involves studying much more than the practical political objectives they pursued or the arguments of other political theorists which they were seeking to refute.

It has been a characteristic of Skinner's work that it has tended narrowly to define the context of political theories in terms of political objectives and political arguments. In doing so it has been seeking to present interpretations whose relevance could not be disputed even by contemporary political philosophers. Historians, however, are bound to recognize that the success of an argument depends partly upon social and economic, and not merely upon political or intellectual, factors. They are also bound to stress that arguments in the political arena are often deeply influenced by developments in theology, philosophy and natural science. The effort to avoid anachronistic assumptions about social and intellectual contexts, an

* R. G. Collingwood, *Autobiography* (Oxford, 1941).

effort which turned the founders of the Cambridge school against the social interpretations of a Macpherson on the one hand and the intellectualist analyses of a Strauss on the other, need not preclude a study of political theory within a broad range of cultural and social contexts.* Both Hobbes and Locke were largely dependent during much of their lives upon the patronage of members of the aristocracy. This simple fact does not, at first sight, tell us much about their political philosophies, for one defended authority, the other revolution. But, as Keith Thomas and John Dunn have shown, their social background is highly relevant to an understanding of their social attitudes and moral values, both of which have consequences for their views of politics.† It is thus necessary to take into account contexts that cannot be identified merely in terms of the immediate intentions of an author, but involve reference also to his unspoken assumptions and unconscious commitments.

The professional historian's commitment to the contextual study of the classic texts of political theory presents its own problems, no matter what language is employed to defend that commitment and no matter what particular context is identified as relevant. Professional history is generally written to be read only by professional historians, while the audience for the history of political thought has always been much wider than this. The classic texts were texts to be read, and no liberal education was complete without some reference to them. As a consequence they were liked and disliked, argued over and reinterpreted, in the same way as works of literature are, on the basis of personal acquaintance. The professional historian, arguing that Hobbes should be read in the light of Grotius, or Locke in the light of Filmer, is in danger of making the history of ideas something to be studied at second hand. It is worth remembering that the intellectual vigour and literary quality of the classic texts makes them of continuing interest in and of themselves. A number of the texts selected here – *Killing Noe Murder*, for example – are similarly capable of provoking and entertaining in their own right.

---

* C. B. Macpherson, *The Political Theory of Possessive Individualism* (Oxford, 1962); L. Strauss, *Persecution and the Art of Writing* (Glencoe, Ill., 1952). Foremost among Macpherson's critics has been K. V. Thomas: see 'The Social Origins of Hobbes's Political Thought', in K. C. Brown (ed.), *Hobbes Studies* (Oxford, 1965), pp. 185–236, and 'The Levellers and the Franchise', in G. E. Aylmer (ed.), *The Interregnum* (London, 1972), pp. 57–78. For a critical survey of Strauss's work, see M. F. Burnyeat's review of L. Strauss, *Studies in Platonic Political Philosophy*, in *The New York Review of Books*, XXXII, no. 9 (30 May 1985), pp. 30–6.

† K. V. Thomas, 'The Social Origins of Hobbes's Political Thought'; J. Dunn, 'Individuality and Clientage in the Formation of Locke's Social Imagination', in R. Brandt (ed.), *John Locke, Symposium Wolfenbüttel 1979* (Berlin, 1981), pp. 43–73.

This book represents the first occasion on which an attempt has been made to present in one volume a broad anthology of seventeenth-century English political thought. No one would question the assumption on which it is based, that there is a wide range of seventeenth-century English political thinkers who are of historical importance and who deserve to be read and not simply referred to; many would further agree that a knowledge of these authors enriches our understanding of classics such as *Leviathan* and the *Two Treatises*. Like all anthologists, I have had difficulty in deciding what to include and what to exclude. In the chapters which follow you will find some pages of Hobbes and of Locke, but none of *Leviathan* or the *Two Treatises*. This is because I have assumed some familiarity with those works, and because I have not wanted to sacrifice limited space to texts which are widely and cheaply accessible. The same thinking has led to the exclusion of Milton's *Areopagitica* and Locke's *Letter Concerning Toleration*.* Instead, I have tried in each chapter to focus upon one of the main debates of the century, debates to which Milton, Hobbes and Locke sought to contribute. The book is thus intended to provide a survey of the main issues in Stuart political thought and, consequently, to provide an introduction at first hand to authors who are normally encountered only in the summary accounts of secondary authorities. I have sought for the most part to select texts which have already been widely discussed, rather than to seek to advance to prominence unknown authors. At the same time I have preferred wherever possible to publish complete (and therefore necessarily short) texts, or, failing that, complete chapters or sections of texts, rather than to give numerous short extracts torn out of context. This has encouraged me on occasion to turn from great tomes to short essays: from Harrington's *Oceana*, for example, to his *Art of Lawgiving*. The result, I hope, is a bowl of distinct apples and oranges rather than a salad of chopped fruit.

I must admit to adopting two other criteria which some scholars will find unreasonable, but to which most readers will not, I think, take exception. The first is that I have confined this book to English political thought. Seventeenth-century political thought was only partly shaped by national boundaries. Both James I and Hobbes, for example, attacked the Italian Catholic Bellarmine. Both Hobbes and Locke spent long periods in exile. Nevertheless, to have included Bellarmine and Grotius, Bayle and Pufendorf would have necessarily

---

* Convenient editions of the texts I have excluded are T. Hobbes, *Leviathan*, ed. C. B. Macpherson (Harmondsworth, 1968); J. Locke, *Two Treatises*, ed. P. Laslett (Cambridge, 1960); ibid., *A Letter Concerning Toleration*, ed. J. H. Tully (Indianapolis, 1983); J. Milton, *Selected Prose*, ed. C. A. Patrides (Harmondsworth, 1974).

meant covering the whole of Europe and publishing not a volume but a library. Moreover English political thought did focus around certain national political issues, and I have tried to give coherence to my selection by isolating a particular issue in each chapter: in each case an issue which both formed a perennial subject for debate and at a particular moment lay at the very centre of national concern. In the Introduction which follows I have tried to give some indication of the relationships between English political theory and the intellectual life of Europe. Readers who wish to pursue this question further will find J. H. M. Salmon's *The French Religious Wars in English Political Thought* (1959) and J. G. A. Pocock's *The Machiavellian Moment: Florentine Political Thought and the Atlantic Republican Tradition* (1975) of particular interest.

Secondly, I have confined myself to texts written in English, or (in the case of *De Cive*) translated by a contemporary. This decision has reduced Selden, for example, to a paragraph where he deserved more. But I have not wanted to mix my own translations with texts in which contemporaries speak for themselves, and I have felt that the texts of greatest importance were those aimed at a wide audience of Englishmen rather than a far-flung community of scholars. It should be stressed, however, that the texts selected here were written by authors of very varying backgrounds and aimed at widely differing audiences.

In the seventeenth century, political philosophy had a recognized existence as an academic discipline. The study of politics, it was generally agreed, was based upon two key texts. The first was Aristotle's *Politics*, especially as interpreted by a lengthy series of scholastic philosophers. The second was the Bible, which provided in the Old Testament an account of a divinely ordained political order, and gave in the New the guiding principles of a Christian view of authority in church and state. Authors such as James I and Richard Hooker saw themselves as arguing on the basis of a philosophical and theological culture which they shared with many of their opponents, whether Jesuit priests or Puritan divines. A few intellectuals outside the universities, such as Filmer and Hobbes, held the leading intellectual traditions within this culture to be largely misconceived and set out to create a theory of politics which involved either radically reinterpreting Aristotle and the Bible or rejecting their authority, but even during the Civil War the majority of polemicists, whether parliamentary or royalist, sought to lay claim to a common culture and an established intellectual tradition.

Apart from Aristotle and the Bible, it was sometimes maintained that politics could be studied as a practical art in the pages of Roman historians and their humanist disciples, such as Machiavelli. Republicans like Harrington and Sidney sought to maintain that it was this tradition, rather than the scholarship of philosophers and theologians, which could alone explain what happened in politics and which must therefore be studied by those who wished to engage in effective political action. They too, for all their hostility to scholastic learning, addressed themselves to the educated and laid claim to an intellectual heritage whose authority was generally recognized.

The Civil War, however, saw the appearance of a quite new type of political theorizing. With the breakdown of central authority men such as Lilburne, Walwyn and Winstanley, none of whom had much formal education, sought to address a new political audience of craftsmen, apprentices and common soldiers. Writing at speed, often when in prison, and printing on hastily organized clandestine presses, the pamphlets and broadsheets they produced were crudely printed and coarsely illustrated. Their language was as far as possible that of their audience, a plain English which seems now (when it is not dense with Biblical imagery) much more modern than that of their Latinizing contemporaries. Since many of those they hoped to reach were illiterate they relied on their words being read aloud and discussed and debated in taverns and market-places. It would be wrong to read their writings as if they were directed at the same audience, or were intended to be read in the same manner, as those of Hooker, Hobbes or Harrington.

One of the particular difficulties in assessing the significance of the Civil War radicals is that they rarely refer to the books they have read or the arguments they have been influenced by. This, of course, does not mean that they were free of intellectual debts or detached from contemporary culture. An interesting parallel exists here between the writings of the radicals and those of Hobbes, who also avoided referring to the works of others. Recent work has begun to show Hobbes as seeking, like Descartes, to respond to the sceptical crisis provoked by Montaigne and Charron, although at the same time he adopted much from the sceptics' treatment of religion. If French scepticism is a central part of Hobbes's intellectual inheritance, then so it is too of William Walwyn's.* Walwyn, perhaps the most

* There is a fine, but as yet unpublished, paper on Hobbes's response to the sceptics' attack on knowledge by Richard Tuck, entitled 'Optics and Sceptics'. In the meantime there are valuable indications in P. F. Grendler, 'Pierre Charron: Precursor to Hobbes', *Review of Politics*, xxv (1963), pp. 212–24 and R. Tuck, 'Grotius, Carneades and Hobbes', *Grotiana*, iv (1983), pp. 43–62. Hobbes's place in the tradition of the sceptical discussion of religion which runs from Montaigne to Hume deserves study. Walwyn discusses Montaigne and Charron in *Walwyn's Just Defence* (1649), reprinted in W. Haller and G. Davies (eds.), *The Leveller Tracts* (New York, 1944).

radical of the Levellers, tells us his favourite reading was Montaigne's *Essays* and Charron's *Of Wisdom*. Hobbes may have written much of his work in Latin and had intellectual acquaintances across Europe, while Walwyn was confined to the English language, but they shared, at least in part, a common culture, and agreed on two key principles derived from the sceptical tradition: that the Bible could not be proved to be the word of God, and that men were by nature equal, social hierarchy being an artificial construct.

Hobbes and Walwyn were at opposite ends of the political spectrum, but drew their differing conclusions from certain common premises. Other radicals, too, seem to have drawn a direct inspiration from an intellectual inheritance which they shared with the educated elite. Particularly interesting in this regard is *Killing Noe Murder*, in which Sexby, who would otherwise be thought of as an uneducated agitator relying on his natural wit, demonstrates an ironic mastery not only of Biblical references but also of humanist sources. It would be wrong therefore to assume that the radicals were out of touch with the intellectual culture of their day. In the Introduction which follows I suggest that their transformation of previous theories of popular sovereignty was cogent and original. Their achievement in this respect has not been properly recognized by historians of political philosophy, despite the fact that their beliefs have become our own, simply because their arguments were never presented in the form of an academic treatise.

In recent years historians have expressed grave doubt as to whether the English Civil War was the first of modern revolutions, and many of them have preferred to regard the parliamentary leaders as conservative figures trying to preserve a sixteenth-century polity in the face of a modernizing absolutism, comparing the Great Rebellion in England to contemporary revolts against Bourbon and Habsburg rule.* There is, however, no European parallel to the Putney Debates, no French Lilburne or Spanish Walwyn, and the English Civil War can properly be described as having called forth a revolution in political thought. The brief crisis of the 1640s, however, took place within a long-term transformation in political thinking. In the early seventeenth century nearly all English people saw the king as an absolute ruler governing a nation of Christians by divine right. By the end of the century it was generally recognized that one could argue about politics without relying on religious premises; it was widely maintained that tyrants were answerable to their subjects; and it was even proposed that rulers and constitutions should be assessed

---

* R. C. Richardson, *The Debate on the English Revolution* (London, 1977).

in terms of their ability to ensure prosperity rather than godliness.

Historians of science have argued as to whether the scientific revolution carried out by Copernicus, Galileo, Boyle and Newton was the consequence of Plato supplanting Aristotle as a philosophical mentor, or of scientists seeking to help seamen locate themselves on the surface of the earth, soldiers master the new opportunities presented by the invention of gunpowder, and miners drain and ventilate their mines.* The transformation in political thinking with which we are concerned has similarly been explained in terms on the one hand of the application to politics of the theology of the Puritan sects, and on the other of the political needs of an emerging market society.† The one approach stresses the extensive implications of changing intellectual convictions, the other the practical purposes that ideas were designed to serve. Neither approach is satisfactory in isolation, nor should either approach be allowed to distract attention from those problems which were discovered by scientists in the pursuit of purely scientific questions, and by political theorists in the effort to construct coherent political philosophies.

Faced, therefore, with an inexhaustible range of topics to discuss, I have tried in the Introduction which follows to give only some preliminary indication, however cursory, of why the questions political theorists tackled took the form they did. I have concentrated on three problems which seem to me to be of central importance: Why did most English people in the early seventeenth century believe that they were ruled by an absolute monarch, and when and why did they stop believing this? When and how did the doctrine of popular sovereignty, the foundation of any democratic theory, become established? When and how did people come to believe that the purpose of political society was not so much to create a god-fearing community as to provide the framework within which individuals could compete in the pursuit of private wealth, and, in so doing, cooperate in creating national prosperity? The answers to these three questions are, I think, to be sought amongst the texts which follow, texts which represent a crucial period in the formation of our modern political and social theories.‡

* A. Koyré, *Metaphysics and Measurement* (London, 1968); L. T. Hogben, *Columbus, the Cannon Ball and the Common Pump* (London, 1974).

† A. S. P. Woodhouse (ed.), *Puritanism and Liberty* (London, 1938); MacPherson, *The Political Theory of Possessive Individualism*, op. cit.

‡ There is an indispensable account of the foundations that had been already laid by the time James I came to the English throne in Q. Skinner, *The Foundations of Modern Political Thought* (2 vols., Cambridge, 1978).

INTRODUCTION

And if any gilded or varnished Scribe or Pharisee ... find themselves aggrieved, I desire to let them know that *fiat justitia ruat coelum* is my motto, and if I perish, it shall be in the following of justice for justice' sake.

John Lilburne, *Jonah's Cry from the Whale's Belly* (1647)

Manus haec inimica tyrannis
Algernon Sidney's inscription in the visitors' book of Copenhagen University at the time of the restoration of Charles II (1660)

Titus, ouvre les yeux.
Quel air respires-tu? N'es-tu pas dans ces lieux
Où la haine des rois, avec le lait sucée,
Par crainte ou par amour ne peut être effacée?

Jean Racine, *Bérénice* (1670)

These people were extremely fond of liberty; but seem not to have understood it very well.

David Hume, *Political Discourses* (1752)

But unheroic as bourgeois society is, it nevertheless took heroism, sacrifice, terror, civil war, and battles of peoples to bring it into being.

Karl Marx, *The Eighteenth Brumaire of Louis Bonaparte* (1851)

Absolutism and the Ancient Constitution

Sir Charles Cornwallis, the king's ambassador at Madrid, when pressed by the Duke of Lerma to enter into a league with Spain, said to that minister: 'Though his Majesty was an absolute king, and therefore not bound to give an account to any of his actions, yet that so gracious and regardful a prince he was of the love and contentment of his own subjects, as I assured myself he would not think it fit to do anything of so great consequence without acquainting them with his intention.' Sir Walter Raleigh has this passage in the preface to his *History of the World*: 'Philip II, by strong hand and main force, attempted to make himself, not only an absolute monarch over the Netherlands, like unto the kings and monarchs of England and France, but Turk-like to tread under his feet all their natural and fundamental laws, privileges and ancient rights.' We may infer from these passages, either that the word *absolute* bore a different sense from what it does at present, or that men's ideas of the English government were then different. This latter inference seems juster. The word, being derived from the Latin and French, bore always the same sense as in these two languages. An absolute monarchy, in Charles I's Answer to the Nineteen Propositions, is opposed to a limited: and the king of England is acknowledged not to be absolute. So much had matters changed even before the Civil War.

David Hume, *The History of Great Britain* (1754)

Anyone seeking to define what political thought is about would probably quickly feel obliged to employ two key phrases: 'the state', and 'the rights of citizens'. In approaching the study of seventeenth-century English political thought, therefore, it is worth commencing by considering what these phrases would have meant to an Englishman in the reign of James I.

When we think of the state we think of a number of institutions: in particular Parliament, the civil service, the armed forces, the police and the law courts. We also associate the state with a number of key social programmes: old-age pensions, unemployment benefit and health care. We expect to support the state through taxation, and we expect it to recognize and protect our rights: our rights to political representation, freedom of expression and assembly, freedom of movement, to the presumption of innocence, to legal representation and to trial by jury. We are encouraged to exercise our freedoms by joining political parties and trades unions, and expect to learn about the policies of the government through a free press. It would scarcely be exaggerating to say that none of these institutions, none of these programmes, and none of these rights existed in a recognizable form in early-seventeenth-century England.

Parliament was a body that met irregularly for brief periods. It represented perhaps one-sixth of the adult males in the country.[1]* The fear was often expressed that, like many similar institutions on the Continent, it might soon cease to meet at all – and indeed, for eleven years, from 1629 to 1640, that prediction appeared to have been confirmed by events. Parliament in 1640 looked like an outdated institution, an institution whose support lay among the old, not the young. This was partly because when Parliament did meet during the first three decades of the century it often seemed to accomplish nothing of substance. Anything it did accomplish, of course, it was able to achieve solely because it had the king's approval; and when the king dissolved it, it disappeared, leaving behind no standing committees or continuing officers, until he should choose to re-convene it. There were no organized political parties, and parliamentary proceedings were carried on under a shroud of official secrecy: not until the mid eighteenth century (apart from a brief period of freedom during the Civil War) did journalists establish the right to report debates. Meanwhile, Members of Parliament whose speeches had displeased the king were liable to imprisonment without trial on Privy Council warrant. As James said: 'The Parliament not sitting, the[ir] liberties are not sitting.'[2]

If Parliament was weak, so was the civil service. Royal government still betrayed its origin as a system for the administration of the king's own household affairs. Offices in the royal administration were customarily bought and sold, being regarded as franchises for the extraction of fees from the public. The government was too poor to pay proper salaries to its own officials: James I's annual ordinary revenue at the beginning of his reign was around £400,000, or less than 2 shillings per head of population, at a time when a labourer might expect to earn £9 per year. The state was obviously absorbing only a tiny proportion of national income, and this was because the vast bulk of its revenue came not from taxes but from customs dues, the income on royal estates, and feudal dues such as wardship and purveyance. Charles I managed to raise royal income to £900,000 p.a. by the late 1630s. He did so not only by maximizing his income

* See 'Notes', page 78 below.

from feudal dues, and by raising customs dues (Bate's case in 1606 had given the Crown the right to set customs' rates as it chose), but also by pioneering a regular national tax, ship money, whose legality was upheld by the courts in 1637, despite the fact that most Englishmen continued to believe that direct taxation should be levied only in emergencies, and never without parliamentary approval. Even so his income was now only marginally better, in real terms, than the Crown's income in 1510: and in the meantime the population of the nation had doubled.

A government with so small a revenue could do little. Local administration was almost entirely in the hands of unpaid amateur officials, the justices of the peace. What influence Parliament did have derived in large part from the fact that members of the House of Commons were often also justices of the peace, and the king could not afford indefinitely to ignore the views of his own volunteer bureaucracy, particularly as he had only a limited capacity to compel obedience. He had no professional army to call upon, only a local militia organized by the same local gentry who became justices of the peace and Members of Parliament. Just as there was no army there was scarcely a police force: constables were part-time officials elected by their parishes. It was the parish too, not the nation, which was increasingly taking on the task of relieving the poor and of ministering to those too old or sick to work. To most Englishmen and women central government must have seemed distant and irrelevant: they were more immediately aware of the manor court, which concerned itself with their rents and property transactions; the parish, which raised taxes to pay for poor relief; and the county, which organized the militia and provided the courts at which malefactors were brought to justice. All this might happen within the framework of the king's law, but the king and his government played little direct part in it.

If the early-seventeenth-century state was highly decentralized and underfunded, the result was not that citizens had more rights and freedoms. In criminal cases trials were rarely allowed to run for more than a day. The accused had no automatic right to legal counsel: Sir John Davies thought the law could take pride in the fact that no lawyer would ever be called on to defend a rapist. He had no right to know the charge before the trial, and thus limited opportunity to organize a defence. Witnesses called on his behalf did not take the oath and their testimony was given less weight than that of witnesses for the prosecution. Punishments were normally corporal (only debtors were regularly imprisoned for long periods of time, and that at their own expense), and often capital: theft over 2 shillings was in principle punishable by death, although juries were often reluctant to convict, or else undervalued the goods, and the accused (if male) could often escape punishment for a first offence by pleading benefit of clergy, which involved establishing literacy by reciting the 'neck-verse': 'Have mercy upon mc, O God . . .' (Ps. 51: 1). Nevertheless, there were seventy executions a year in London between 1607 and 1616, out of a population of some quarter of a million. There were no opportunities to appeal.

It would be possible to compile a long list of rights which we take for granted that were denied to people in the early seventeenth century, rights, some of them, as important as the right to a fair trial. Travelling in search of work, for example, was illegal: vagabonds were to be whipped and sent back to their parish of origin, and lodgers could not be taken in without a licence. Wages were fixed by law: Sir Edward Coke, as Attorney-General, upheld the view that combinations to obtain higher wages were treasonous. The same man, famous for his defences of the liberties of Englishmen, employed a battering-ram to break down his daughter's door in order to take her to church to marry a man who was repugnant to her. Nor was there freedom to buy and sell: quite apart from government-granted monopolies in the production of goods like window glass and soap, monopolies whose legality was disputed, selling could take place only under carefully controlled conditions. Guilds exercised a monopoly control over many trades. Grain was supposed to be brought to market and sold retail: forestalling (selling before market), engrossing (hoarding) and regrating (wholesaling) were all illegal. It need not surprise us that even the clothes one wore were in principle controlled by law: only Knights of the Garter could wear crimson, for example. The law touched even the dead: from 1622 they were required to be dressed for burial in woollen cloth. Finally, attendance at church was, of course, compulsory.

Nevertheless, the English were convinced they had rights, and important ones at that. When Sir Walter Raleigh contrasted the absolute monarchies of France and England with the tyranny of the Turks he took it for granted that the English had 'fundamental laws, privileges and ancient rights': above all, the rights to have legislation and taxation approved by Parliament and to be tried by the common law and not be imprisoned without charge.[3] In England suspected criminals could feel secure in the knowledge that they would not be tortured unless they were under investigation for crimes against the state; on the Continent Roman legal traditions required the routine use of torture to establish the truth. Aside from these rights, however, it was accepted that the king could lay claim to a free hand: the choice of councillors, the command of the army, the marriages of the king and his family, foreign policy, coinage, and the pardoning of criminals were areas where royal prerogative was agreed to be unchecked. (Attempts to add religion to this list were bitterly disputed.)

Yet in the early seventeenth century the privileges of the English were coming to seem increasingly uncertain and the prerogatives of government increasingly burdensome. Royal proclamations threatened to supplant the statute law approved by Parliament. Prerogative courts such as the Star Chamber were popular because they provided speedy justice, but they were not bound by the rules of the common law. The Five Knights' case of 1627 had threatened to give the king the right to imprison without charge, a right which justices of the peace had long exercised against suspicious characters, but from which they had believed themselves to be immune. The Ship Money case of 1637 established the king's right to tax at times of national emergency, and made the king the sole judge of when such an emergency existed.

While what were thought to be established privileges were eroded, recognized prerogatives came to seem burdensome. In 1623 it seemed that Buckingham, the royal favourite, was going to arrange for the heir to the throne to marry a Spanish princess, and there were widespread rumours that, as a consequence, England was to become Catholic once more: royal control of the marriage of the heir to the throne and of foreign policy appeared to endanger the souls of Englishmen and women. In Ireland James had used his control over the coinage to write off part of his debts by devaluing the money in which they were repaid. He had also employed his prerogative of mercy for dubious purposes. In 1615 the Earl of Somerset, the king's favourite, was convicted of murdering Sir Thomas Overbury, but pardoned. There were suspicions that he had won his pardon by blackmailing the king. Each and every aspect of the prerogative was potentially offensive. In 1617 James was trying to raise a loan from the City of London, 'but some citizens were reluctant to contribute. James dealt with one of them by exercising his undoubted right to command his subjects to attend him in the uncharitable form of making the man walk behind the royal progress from London to Carlisle.'[4]

What we have at this point is a picture of a central government that was weak and yet was capable of acting in an arbitrary and tyrannical fashion. It is in explaining this seeming paradox that we need for the first time to turn from questions of the power of the state and the rights of citizens to questions more directly of political philosophy. What offset the fundamental weakness of the monarchy and ensured that it met only token resistance was an almost universally accepted conviction that order had to be maintained, and that order could only be maintained by unity in obedience to the monarchy. Precisely the weakness of central government ensured that the gentry of Tudor and early Stuart England would be preoccupied with the need to maintain order and unity.

When questions of order arose, people in seventeenth-century England immediately thought in Biblical terms. Political authority and private property, they were told from the pulpits, had been established as a result of the Fall. Because men were sinful order had to be imposed upon them, and all authority must be accepted as divinely ordained. Since over two thirds of adult men were illiterate in 1642, it was from the pulpit that most people derived their political philosophy. At the beginning of the century probably somewhat less than half the clergy were considered sufficiently well educated to be licensed to preach. As a consequence what their parishioners heard from the pulpit were government-authorized homilies calculated to inspire an unquestioning obedience. As more of the clergy received a university education it became harder for the government to 'tune the pulpits': the signal for civil war was given as much by the university-trained Puritan ministers of London as by the House of Commons.

Thus both the defence and the subversion of authority were naturally conducted in language drawn from the Bible. Before returning to the theme of order let me give an example of the way in which Biblical knowledge was taken for granted in political debate. When Strafford was impeached in May 1641, article 2 of the bill charged him with having said 'that the king's little finger should be thicker than the loins of the law'. Maynard expounded the charge as follows: 'Your Lordships may consider what a transcendent speech this was, out of whose mouth it came, what sad accidents happened upon it; nothing could move this Lord to utter: but his will and violence must out though he burnt a kingdom in pieces for it.' As Conrad Russell has pointed out – but as no one would have needed to explain to the House of Lords in 1641–

> No sad accidents had happened upon Strafford's speaking these words. But very sad accidents had happened upon the speaking of these words in I Kings 12, by the young counsellors to Rehoboam: 'thus shalt thou speak unto this people: – my little finger shall be thicker than my father's loins. And now whereas my father did lade you with a heavy yoke, I will add to your yoke: my father hath chastised you with whips, but I will chastise you with scorpions.' When Rehoboam repeated these words to the people, they replied: 'What portion have we in David? neither have we inheritance in the son of Jesse: to your tents, O Israel: now see to thine own house, David.'[5]

By reminding his audience of the counsellors of Rehoboam, Maynard had not only hoped to persuade the Lords of the novel doctrine that Strafford, though a faithful servant of the king, could be guilty of treason because he had sought to undermine the constitution, he also indirectly threatened the king with civil war if he did not dissociate himself from Strafford: a 'transcendent speech' indeed, and one best not uttered but alluded to.

Second after the Bible in dominating men's thinking on political questions was the imagery of the Great Chain of Being. According to this theory the universe consisted of a series of hierarchies. In heaven there was God and below him a descending series of angelic beings. In the skies there was the sun, and below it a descending series of planets. In the animal kingdom the king of beasts, the lion, stood atop a descending series of beasts. In the political order the king ruled over a descending series of authorities reaching down to village constables and churchwardens. In the microcosm of man's body the head ruled over the hierarchy of organs. Everywhere, order was associated with hierarchy, and each ordered system was comparable so that a network of correspondences could be drawn, establishing a more than metaphorical link between God, the sun, the king, the head and the lion. Within this universal hierarchy man held a central place. His rational soul placed him between the angels and the beasts; his body, the microcosm, recapitulated the order of the universe, the macrocosm; and his social order recapitulated the divine hierarchy of heaven.

The conceptual framework of the Great Chain of Being was an ambiguous one. It gave the king an unquestioned position of superiority, but at the same time it confined him within a framework which he must not seek to undermine and implied that his authority was limited by the obligation to preserve harmony. The sun might be the most important body in the heavens, but the planets all exercised an independent influence over men's lives. The head might be the organ of command in the body, but its power was sharply limited by the humours, which had to be maintained in a healthy balance, or reason would be swept away by passion. It was impossible to conclude from the theory of the Great Chain of Being that any one creature should exercise an arbitrary and unchecked authority unless one could successfully manipulate the theory of correspondences to argue that some creatures could hold an absolute and arbitrary power comparable to that of God himself. It was this that James I sought to do when he argued that one could discuss what God was going to do (cause the sun to rise in the heavens tomorrow morning, for example), but that it was blasphemy to try to set a limit to what God *could* do. So in countries with settled laws one could presume the king would rule by law; but just as God retained the power to set aside the ordinary course of nature with a miracle, so the king must retain the power to act outside the ordinary system of law. The king's power must be as unlimited in his sphere as was God's in the universe as a whole.[6] There was something to be said for this doctrine of an unlimited prerogative, but only, of course, if one could trust the king to employ his power wisely, and only if the normal course of law appeared to recognize the privileges and ancient rights of the subject.

The doctrine of the Great Chain of Being was one of the building blocks out of which was constructed the theory of the divine right of kings. The key to this theory was the claim that the king was answerable to no earthly authority, and that he was, in this sense at least, 'absolute'. This theory of absolute monarchy was almost universally acknowledged in the England of James I, but it was none the less something of a novel theory. In the Tudor period it had often been maintained that England had a mixed constitution, and that final authority lay with statute law as approved by Parliament: king, Lords and Commons. In James's reign there were two sufficient reasons why this theory was no longer articulated. The first was that James's succession, which was universally approved, was directly contrary to the will of Henry VIII, which named the line of his younger sister Mary to succeed should his children die without issue; it was arguably contrary to common law, which said that no alien could inherit estates in England; and it was contrary to the Act of Succession of 1543, and to the Act of 1584 debarring Mary Queen of Scots, James's mother, from the throne. In these circumstances to assert the supremacy of statute was to question James's title to the throne.[7]

Secondly, any theory of a mixed constitution, which based royal authority upon a contract between king and people, opened the way to the king's being held to account by his people, and so might be employed to justify tyrannicide. But in James's reign, particularly after the Gunpowder Plot of 1605, tyrannicide was a doctrine that only Catholics dared defend: to deny the absolute authority of the king appeared to open the way to the legitimation of Catholic plotting. The old doctrine of a mixed constitution and a limited monarchy thus disappeared – albeit temporarily – from view, and the Jesuits were allowed to establish a monopoly in constitutionalist theories.

To say that the king ruled by divine right meant primarily to say that he was answerable to no earthly authority. A divine-right theory of this weak sort could be employed to uphold the authority not only of a monarchy but even of a Venetian senate. Divine-right theorists of James's reign also argued that monarchy was a form of government particularly approved by God: it best embodied the principles of hierarchy and unity inherent in the idea of the Great Chain of Being. And central to the idea of monarchy, they claimed, was the idea of primogeniture: it was a divinely ordained principle that the king should be succeeded by his natural heir, and no Act of Parliament, no principle of the common law, no royal last will and testament could interfere with this principle.

Up to this point the theory of the divine right of kings was compatible with the notion of a monarchy restricted by law and custom, and up to this point, and only up to this point, most Englishmen accepted the theory. After all, even if the king could not be held to account should he break the law, his servants could be. But it was possible to argue – and it was argued, for example by Cowell, a civil lawyer, in 1608 and by Manwaring, a theologian, in 1627 – that no divine-right king could be bound by existing laws and customs, and that therefore, for example, the king was under no obligation to obtain consent for taxation, that everything the subject owned lay at the monarch's disposal. And it was also possible to argue, as the king did when Buckingham was impeached in 1626, that if the king could do no wrong neither could a faithful subject acting upon his orders. Such arguments were intensely unpopular because they made it impossible to distinguish absolute monarchy, with established laws and liberties, from 'Turk-like' despotism.

The arguments of Cowell, Manwaring and Charles himself had a certain plausibility to them. Less persuasive, but much more famous, are the arguments of Sir Robert Filmer. Filmer's best-known work, *Patriarcha*, was not published till 1680, long after his death. In this selection I have chosen a shorter work, a response to the Engagement crisis of 1650–52, to present the strengths and weaknesses of Filmer's position. The main strength of his position lay in the problems he was able to identify in any theory of representative government and his willingness, in common with Hobbes, to accept the analytical simplicity of despotic sovereignty. The main weakness lay in his positive theory that all power must be inherited from Adam, descending from eldest son to eldest son. The logical consequence of this theory was that Adam's true heir, could one identify him, was rightfully absolute ruler of the world.[8] Since Adam's heir could not be identified Filmer was obliged to accept that no authority was fully legitimate: hence his willingness, despite his uncompromising defence of royal authority, to recognize that established authorities could in practice, if not principle, be overthrown and replaced. Nevertheless, Filmer held that kings should be treated as if they were Adam's heirs, inheritors of Adam's fatherly right over Eve and their children.

Filmer's theory is often discussed on the presumption that his arguments gained in plausibility from the patriarchal authority of the father within seventeenth-century households. This, however, is scarcely the case. In seventeenth-century England children left home when they married and established themselves in essential independence. Every male saw himself as head or prospective head of his own household, with, once he was married, only a limited obligation to defer to his father or, on his father's death, his elder brother. Filmer's theory denied the independent authority of heads of households in order to uphold the authority of grandfathers and uncles. As such it ran contrary to contemporary patriarchal assumptions, making the lineage, not the household, the focus of authority.[9] Filmer's arguments were untypical of those of royalists in general, both in his own day and in the 1680s when they became a focus of controversy.[10] What was widely accepted was the quite different view that the authority of the king, far from being *identical* to the authority of the father, was *comparable* to it, in that the family was a little commonwealth, characterized by hierarchy and obedience. The commandment to honour one's father and mother was universally expounded as an injunction to obey the king. Conversely, for a wife to kill her husband was petty treason, punishable by hanging, drawing and quartering. (Perhaps it was this correspondence that made Sir John Davies's wife Eleanor prophesy with such pleasure the death of both her husband and her king.)

In contrast to Filmer and the exponents of an unchecked royal authority, most Englishmen held the view that the king was absolute only in some respects and limited in others, and believed as a consequence that he was limited by the law. This was the assumption of the lawyers, who turned to the common law to identify the fundamental laws of the kingdom and the privileges and ancient rights of the citizen.[11] Setting aside the problem of the succession (which Coke in his commentary on the case of the *post-nati*, which dealt with the right of Scotsmen to inherit land in England, treated as prior to, not subject to, the law), the lawyers argued that the common law provided the perfect foundation for government precisely because it was unwritten and customary. As such it had been tried by experience and tested by time, rendering it an 'artificial reason' superior to the judgement of any individual.

Coke tried to uphold this theory of the immemorial character of the common law by arguing that all the evidence suggested that it never really had changed. In doing so, though, he was deliberately flying in the face of the sort of evidence that had been used on the Continent to found a new science of the history of law, a science with which many English common lawyers were uneasily acquainted. It is worth contrasting Coke's account of the unchanging tradition of English law, reproduced below, with the opening words of the discourse *Of the Ancient Government of England* (1698), written by his contemporary Henry Spelman (1564–1641):

> To tell the government of England under the old Saxon laws seems an Utopia to us [at] present; strange and uncouth: yet can there be no period assigned, wherein either the frame of those laws was abolished, or this of ours entertained; but as day and night creep insensibly, one upon the other, so also has this alteration grown upon us insensibly, every age altering something, and no age seeing more than what themselves are actors in, nor thinking it to have been otherwise than as themselves discover it by the present. Like them in China, who, never travelling out of their own country, think the world to extend no further. As one therefore that has coasted a little further into former times, I will offer unto you a new map thereof, not like those of the exquisite cosmographers of our later ages, but like them of old, when as neither cross sails nor compass were yet known to navigators.

Spelman's view of the history of English liberties was genuinely historical, and he correctly identified many of them (the control of the House of Commons over taxation, for example) as being the consequence of the decay of feudalism. But Coke's vision corresponded to the lawyer's actual practice of relying upon precedent, and few were willing to directly question it. So long as legitimacy was associated with immemorial antiquity and uninterrupted practice, Spelman's approach could only benefit those royalists who were willing to argue that there were no fundamental English liberties. Many of the most important of Spelman's works were published posthumously, but even if they had been available earlier they would not necessarily have convinced the common lawyers that their approach was mistaken.

From Coke's point of view the common law represented the bastion of English liberties. Others, though, saw it as being exploited by the legal profession for their own benefit: the late sixteenth and early seventeenth centuries had seen the rapid rise of the lawyers as a profession. At many points the defence of the law provided by followers of Coke such as Sir John Davies corresponds to the issues which were to be raised by Civil War law reformers such as Warr and the Levellers. For the radicals the history of English law appeared not as a seamless web but as a torn fabric: the conquest of England by William the Conqueror had led to the establishment of the Norman yoke and the corruption of the law to serve the purposes of tyranny.

They had to be careful, however, not to attack the substance of the law, for they wanted at the same time to claim that imprisonment without trial and attempts to make defendants testify against themselves under oath were contrary to the law and to the inherited liberties of Englishmen. They argued, therefore, that not the substance of the law but the form of legal proceedings was corrupt.[12] Some of their criticisms implied the need for only mild reforms: they blamed the Normans, for example, for the establishment of law terms, which obliged people to await trial, and the practice of sending appeals to London, which involved defendants in time and expense. But their real argument was that professional lawyers should be abolished, that the law should be simplified and codified and written in English instead of law-French, and that the jury should be judge of matters of law as well as fact. The result would have been to change more than the forms of the law, making a local jury the final authority and abolishing all central control over their decisions. The national legal system would thus have been rendered more nearly comparable to a system of manor courts, where juries were indeed judges of law as well as fact. One may hazard a guess that under such circumstances decisions would have been made according to the jurors' conception of equity, a concept foreign to the English common law, and that the substance and not just the form of the law would have been transformed.

Both conservatives and radicals sought to find in the common law a secure foundation for the rights of Englishmen. The Five Knights' case of 1627, where the king established his right to imprison without cause shown five gentlemen who had refused to contribute to an illegal forced loan, rendered it evident that the law as it stood provided no constitutional protection against arbitrary government.[13] The consequence was an attempt to employ Parliament and statute law to remedy the defects of the law. Where Englishmen since 1603 had, with only an occasional exception (such as Sir James Whitelocke in a speech to Parliament in 1610), been willing to accept that they lived in an absolute monarchy, where arbitrary authority was tempered by the common law, now they increasingly turned to the old language of mixed monarchy and parliamentary government. Despite Hume's doubts, *absolute* had a different meaning in 1619, when Raleigh died, from the one it was to have in 1642. In 1619 an 'absolute' monarch was essentially a 'proper' monarch, not a mere Venetian doge. But it was agreed that absolute monarchs could exercise arbitrary authority only in certain spheres. Even Bodin, recognized as the greatest exponent of absolute monarchy, had denied that rulers had the right to levy taxes without the consent of their subjects. It may be presumed that limitations of this sort were taken for granted, not only by Raleigh but also by Cornwallis, whose purpose was to pay tribute to the absolute authority of the king in matters of foreign policy. Cornwallis, it may be noted, was later to have ample opportunity to ruminate on the nature of absolute power, for he spent a year confined in the Tower of London for conspiring with the parliamentary opposition.

After the Five Knights' case it no longer seemed possible to constrain absolutism within legal bounds. Sir Robert Phelips, a parliamentary leader, could say: 'We now little differ from the course in Turkey', while Pym, impeaching Manwaring, could define 'absolute monarchies' as those 'not regulated by laws or contracts between the king and his people'.[14] The Petition of Right was thus intended to end absolutism by introducing a new contract between king and people: it failed, as the Ship Money case of 1637 made clear, because it placed no constraint upon the extra-legal prerogative of the king and provided no definition of the circumstances under which he could have recourse to such a prerogative. In the Ship Money case the minority of judges who found with the defence had the better arguments. But judges served *durante bene placito*: the king could dismiss them if he did not like their judgements, and it is not surprising that Lilburne was later willing to accuse the judges in the Ship Money case of having bought justice wholesale and sold it retail (thus compounding corruption by engrossment).[15]

From 1627 constitutional change was inevitable.[16] The Petition of Right proved an inadequate instrument of such change, and it was long an open question whether change was to be carried out on the terms of king or Parliament: had the king been able to finance an army against the Scots in 1639 he would have been able successfully to transform England from a constitutional into an absolute (in Hume's meaning of the term) monarchy, and many would have accepted that the loss of liberty was a small price to pay for the guarantee of order. The king's prospects of success were smaller, however, than those, for example, of the kings of France. The religious policies of Laud threatened the religious convictions of the vast majority of the nation, while the gentry feared the implications of royal absolutism more acutely than their social counterparts on the Continent, since they were in principle liable to taxation (although justices of the peace were inclined to make evidently false returns on behalf of themselves and their friends) and since they had few prospects of benefiting financially from royal service. Faced with a war they could not approve they ceased to collect taxes and government rapidly collapsed.

Once royal government broke down Parliament was obliged to try to find some way of re-establishing mixed monarchy. The Nineteen Propositions of June 1642 were a logical attempt on Parliament's part to make absolute monarchy impossible: the king was to abandon control of the armed forces, to resign his right to choose his own counsellors and to dismiss judges who displeased him, to give up sole control of religion, foreign policy, and the education and marriage of the heir to the throne. Such terms were unacceptable to Charles. What he sought to offer in his reply was what Englishmen had taken to be the constitution prior to 1627, redescribed not as an absolute but as a limited monarchy, but still retaining absolute royal authority in key areas. The king, who had been the great innovator from 1629 to 1640, fought the Civil War under the banner of conservatism. Many of his supporters wished to retain the traditional language of absolute monarchy and sought to retreat from the terminology of the king's reply to the Nineteen Propositions (which had been drafted by a former parliamentarian, Falkland), while parliamentary supporters such as Hunton sought to exploit the king's linguistic concessions. But the key to the situation in 1642 was that it was Parliament, not the king, which now seemed to be undermining the ancient constitution, for otherwise the king, who had virtually no support when the Long Parliament assembled, would never have been able to rally a royalist party with which to fight the Civil War.

The division of the kingdom presented a basic difficulty: how was one to decide which side to support? To the royalists it was easy to argue that Parliament was trying to destroy the traditional prerogatives of the Crown, but their problem was that they could offer no clear guarantee that the king would abide within the recognized limits of the ancient constitution. Some Parliamentarians, like Henry Parker, were willing to argue that, in the event of conflict between king and Parliament, support must always go to Parliament, since Parliament was in the best position to judge what was in the true interest of the nation. But this doctrine of parliamentary infallibility left it unclear in what sense traditional monarchy was to be preserved, despite Parliament's claim to be fighting to defend the king against Charles Stuart.

Much the most acute analysis of the dilemma facing Englishmen was provided by Philip Hunton, who argued that, since there was no constitutional remedy to the crisis, each individual must decide for himself which side was most likely to restore the traditional functioning of the constitution. Hunton thus made the people the final judge of both king and Parliament, but he, like nearly everyone else publishing at the outbreak of the civil war, was convinced that the ancient constitution remained binding even in the circumstances of civil war. It was possible to dispute about what the provisions of that constitution were, but not about its legitimacy and ultimate authority. In this sense, no one was willing to contemplate a revolution, to lay claim to a new order. (Among Members of Parliament the only exception was Henry Marten, an avowed republican.)

We find it hard to imagine that people should take it for granted that a constitution must, strictly speaking, be unalterable. Our sympathies lie with Paine when he insisted that he could hardly be bound by the decisions of his ancestors. Men in the seventeenth century, however, were used to being bound by the decisions of their ancestors: the estates of most gentlemen, for example, were entailed, restricting (in theory, if not always in practice) the heir's freedom to mortgage or sell them. Moreover men and (more particularly) women were used to entering into irrevocable agreements, to accepting bonds which they might regret but could not untie. As Dudley Digges, a moderate royalist, expressed it in 1644:

> As in marriage, so in monarchy there are two parties in the contract; though without a mutual agreement there could be no covenant, yet after it is once made the dissent of the inferior party, let it be not upon fancied, but real discontents, cannot dissolve the compact. Consent therefore joined man and wife, king and people, but divine ordinance continues this union; marriages and governments both are ratified in heaven.[17]

The alternative, it was generally agreed, was to abandon all hope of order, hierarchy and unity. St John, a leader on the parliamentary side, expressed this fear during the trial of Strafford:

> Take the polity and government away, and England's but a piece of

earth, wherein so many men have their commorancy [i.e. residence] and abode, without ranks or distinction of men, without security in anything further than possession, without any law to punish the murdering or robbing one another.[18]

St John and his allies came to believe that they could preserve the polity and government while fighting a civil war. Events were to prove them wrong. It is not surprising that when, after the political and social upheaval of the Civil War, Charles II returned to the throne in 1660 as the divine-right ruler of a limited monarchy, committed (at least initially) to not imprisoning without cause shown, taxing without consent, or governing without Parliament, the traditional claim that the king must not be held accountable to his subjects was reasserted in the doctrine of non-resistance (a doctrine to which all members of corporations, clergymen, and teachers were required to declare their adherence in a solemn oath). But many royalists were willing to draw the obvious conclusion that the king, if he could not be resisted, was not limited but absolute. And in order to sustain the principle of non-resistance they found it necessary to mount a general assault upon the arguments which the Parliamentarians had employed during the Civil War. Thus when the University of Oxford drew up its catalogue of 'pernicious books and damnable doctrines' in 1683 it did so in defence not of the ancient constitution, but of a redefined, narrowly based royalism. We must now concern ourselves with the very first proposition they saw fit to condemn: 'All civil authority is derived originally from the people.'

Democracy: The People and the Multitude

For really I think that the poorest he that is in England has a life to live, as the greatest he; and therefore, truly sir, I think it's clear, that every man that is to live under a government ought first by his own consent to put himself under that government; and I do think that the poorest man in England is not at all bound in a strict sense to that government that he has not had a voice to put himself under; and I am confident that when I have heard the reasons against it, something will be said to answer those reasons, insomuch that I should doubt whether he was an Englishman or no, that should doubt of these things.

Colonel Rainsborough at the Putney Debates (1647)

We have seen that the citizens of seventeenth-century England did not expect to be accorded many of the rights that we take for granted. One of the last of the rights to which they thought to lay claim was the right to a vote for every adult male. All adult men did not have the vote in England until 1918, all women until 1928. Even in the late eighteenth century, the 'age of the democratic revolution', hardly anyone was willing to describe themselves as a 'democrat', a word which was generally accepted as pejorative.[19] Even when (as in the American Declaration of Independence, where governments are said to 'derive their just powers from the consent of the governed', or in the French Declaration of Rights of 1789, where all citizens are said to have the right to take part in the formation of laws) statements were made which seem to us to imply a commitment to democracy, or at least universal male suffrage, they were probably not intended to be understood – and were certainly not interpreted in practice – as implying more than that male taxpayers should have the vote. To look for democratic theories in the mid seventeenth century seems, therefore, to run the risk of anachronism and misunderstanding.

'Democracy', however, had different connotations in the seventeenth century. In the first place, a democracy was any government where power was distributed more broadly than in an aristocracy. For George Wither the Swiss cantons were democracies; for Henry Neville, Machiavelli was an advocate of democracy.[20] 'Democracy' thus often had a meaning close to that of 'republic' today. Mixed constitutions contained a democratic element: the House of Commons, the 'representative of the people', was therefore seen as a democratic authority, despite the fact that only a small part of the population was entitled to vote in elections.

James Harrington in *Oceana* (1656) was to seek to give 'democracy' a new and technical meaning. In his view a democracy was a political system in which all adult (over thirty) males other than servants (who lacked the independence required of citizens) had a right to vote. But Harrington insisted that the power to propose legislation should lie with senators who, although elected by the people as a whole, would be required to satisfy a strict property criterion. The people were to exercise their authority by balloting, not by de-liberating, for otherwise democracy would degenerate into anarchy. Harrington's limitations upon popular participation in politics make his conception of democracy significantly different from our own.[21] William Petty, however, following in his footsteps, was privately to defend democracy, and to specify that by it he meant that every adult male (over the age of eighteen) living as the head of a household should both have the vote and have the right to enter into political deliberations. Here something close to a modern conception of democracy clearly exists, except that it is not individuals but households that are given political representation.[22] The search for a seventeenth-century democratic theory is thus not entirely anachronistic, and I will suggest later that Petty's ideal political order was merely a restatement of the principles defended by the Levellers.

To pursue the issue of democracy in isolation, however, would certainly be to lose all sense of historical proportion. The key question in the minds of contemporaries was not so much the right to vote, as the right to revolt. It is from the claim that all citizens have the right to overthrow a tyrannical government and have a say in its replacement that modern democratic theory takes its origin.

When the University of Oxford drew the line at the claim that 'all civil authority is derived originally from the people' (see page 121), it was contradicting the weight of academic opinion since the establishment of universities. Filmer, in the opening words of *Patriarcha*, took pride in explaining how generally accepted were the views he was attacking:

> Since the time that school divinity began to flourish there has been a common opinion maintained, as well by divines as by divers other learned men, which affirms: 'Mankind is naturally endowed and born with freedom from all subjection, and at liberty to choose what form of government it please, and that the power which any one man has over others was at first bestowed according to the discretion of the multitude.' This tenet was first hatched in the schools, and has been fostered by all succeeding papists for good divinity. The divines, also, of the Reformed Churches have entertained it, and the common people everywhere tenderly embrace it as being most plausible to flesh and blood, for that it prodigally distributes a portion of liberty to the meanest of the multitude, who magnify liberty as if the height of human felicity were only to be found in it, never remembering that the desire of liberty was the first cause of the fall of Adam.

It was Filmer's intention to refute this generally held view, but his main motive for doing so was to block the road to another view, which was generally rejected: the view that the people, having once handed power to their rulers, could reclaim it if that power was abused. This second view, which Filmer attributes to the Jesuits and some Calvinists, was not a necessary corollary of the first. We have seen already that most seventeenth-century thinkers had no problem with the notion of an irrevocable transfer of rights. The minority opinion, upheld by a Jesuit such as Suarez, was that whenever a political authority is established implicit conditions are attached to the right to exercise that authority. The crucial question, then, was not whether power originated with the people, but whether and under what circumstances they or their representatives could reclaim it. It is the question, not of democracy, but of popular sovereignty.

On this subject there is now an impressive body of modern scholarship. Although this scholarship is divided on many issues, it is united in taking it as axiomatic that something like a modern theory of popular sovereignty is to be found in John Locke's *Second Treatise*. The question has thus in recent scholarship become: had a comparable theory been articulated before Locke, and if so how long before? Before tackling this question it is necessary to look more closely at Locke's theory of popular sovereignty.

It is sometimes suggested that Locke's views on political philosophy in general are sufficiently close to our own for him to constitute a useful benchmark for 'modernity' in political theory. In important respects though, Locke's argument is grounded on assumptions which we (along with his contemporaries) are likely to find questionable. To begin with, Locke's argument is based upon a presupposition which he himself knew that it was impossible to substantiate: the existence of a divinely ordained moral law. Locke was confident that one could demonstrate the existence of God, but not that one could prove the immortality of the soul, or, therefore, the system of rewards and punishments in the next life required to turn moral precepts into moral laws. Locke himself knew, as the passage from the *Reasonableness of Christianity* reproduced below shows, that reason could scarcely do what he needed it to: hence the necessity of Christian faith. The *Second Treatise* might thus more properly claim to be grounded in faith than, as it maintains, reason:

> The state of nature has a law of nature to govern it, which obliges every one: and reason, which is that law, teaches all mankind who will but consult it that, being all equal and independent, no one ought to harm another in his life, health, liberty, or possessions. For men, being all the workmanship of one omnipotent and infinitely wise maker, all the servants

of one sovereign master, sent into the world by his order and about his business, they are his property whose workmanship they are. . . .[23]

In treating divinely ordained moral obligations as the basis of human beings' relations with each other, Locke was, as we shall see, turning his back on Hobbes, Nicole and Bayle, who had tried to theorize social relations in terms of secular, rational self-interest, and he resolved instead to maintain that, as he insisted in the *Letter Concerning Toleration*, no atheist could be recognized as a citizen because no atheist could recognize his divinely ordained moral obligations. The first thing to be noted about Locke's political theory, then, is that, despite the fact that his argument does not rest upon Biblical quotations, it is grounded upon a religious faith in divine providence.

Secondly, Locke held what he himself characterized as the strange view that states have no rights other than those held in a state of nature by individuals. Locke's universe of rights is a closed one in which new rights and obligations cannot be created – rights and obligations can only, under certain circumstances, be transferred. It follows from this view that the power to punish, particularly the power to execute malefactors, belongs initially to each and every individual. Against this the orthodox view was that the authority to punish with death was a peculiar attribute of the state, derived directly from God as a part of the creation of political authority by divine ordinance after the Fall. Locke's view, which had been held before him only by Grotius and Sexby, was potentially anarchic in its implications, for, when combined with the view that political authorities receive the right to govern subject only to strict limitations, it gives each and every individual, and not merely political communities as a whole, the right, not only to defend themselves against, but also to punish, a tyrant who has broken the social contract.[24] By contrast most of us would probably believe that governments are different sorts of moral entities from individuals, with different rights and obligations, and that it is communities, not individuals, which have the right to stand in judgement on them. Governments and nations, we suppose, can declare war, but private individuals cannot.

Thirdly, Locke, like Rainsborough, held that nobody was a member of a political society who had not consented to join it. He seems to have been somewhat uncertain about how such consent was normally given, but he was clear that since men are born free (or rather with a title to freedom once they reach the age of reason), they cannot be made subject to political authority without their own consent. This view, which represents the political equivalent of Anabaptism, contrasts with the view, common among us today as among Locke's contemporaries, that nationality and the obligations of citizenship (such as the obligation to do military service) are acquired by birth, not by choice.

If these three peculiarities of Locke's argument have a common rationale, it lies in their insistence on the moral responsibility of the individual: individuals cannot shuffle off their responsibilities by appealing either to self-interest or to the authority of the state. This insistence on individual responsibility has direct consequences for Locke's theory of popular sovereignty, for it means that sovereignty is ultimately held not by the corporate community but by morally autonomous individuals who are all equal under the law of nature.

In order to understand Locke's theory of popular sovereignty it is necessary to identify the different types of consent that Locke discusses in analysing political obligations.[25] The first type, as we have seen, is the consent each and every individual must give to become a member of a political community. This consent is made necessary by mankind's prior agreement to recognize gold and silver as an expression of value: an agreement which makes possible social inequality and intensifies conflict between human beings. Second comes the agreement of the majority of the individuals belonging to a community to establish a particular form of government: a simple numerical majority is required here, since each individual is equally a member of the society and equally a moral agent under the law of God. The form of government established may or may not provide for a representative legislative assembly: Locke strongly recommends that it should. In any case the 'consent of the majority', based on a 'fair and equal' system of representation, is needed for taxation, for government was established to secure property (meaning our lives, our liberties and our possessions) and it would be contrary to its very purpose if people could be arbitrarily deprived of their properties. But despite Locke's use of the terms 'majority' and 'equal' he is not here thinking of a simple numerical majority, for Locke refers to two distinct criteria on the basis of which people should be represented: their numbers and their wealth. A city should be represented 'in proportion to the assistance which it affords to the public', and if rich communities deserve more influence than poor ones, so presumably do rich individuals: as taxpayers we are not equal. The resultant system of weighted representation enables government to obtain 'the consent of the people', or of the community. Finally, individuals tacitly consent to maintain an existing form of government while it serves the public interest: the alternative is revolution, which they may resort to whenever the government breaks its trust. If revolutionary conflict spreads, then 'the people become a confused multitude without order or connection', and they may choose for themselves any new order they please. They are not bound by the previous constitution, and are indeed culpable if they are overly respectful of 'old forms'.

Locke, I would maintain, employs the phrase the 'consent of the people' in two quite separate senses. The first is the consent of the people as a collection of individuals, a confused multitude: they give their consent as equals, through a numerical majority, when they establish a form of government. The second is the consent of the people as a 'body politic': the body politic gives its consent by a majority weighted to prevent the poor from outvoting the rich and depriving them of the property which they had entered into society to protect. The first type of consent of the people relates to Locke's conception of popular sovereignty, which we may term democratic. The second relates to his conception of representative government, which we may term oligarchic. We may conclude that although Locke does not believe in democratic government, or (for example) redistributive taxation, he does have what we may loosely call a modern or democratic conception of popular sovereignty.

Locke was not alone in employing both an individualist and a corporate conception of popular consent. Suarez, for example, writing at the beginning of the seventeenth century, had started from the assumption that 'in the nature of things all men are born free'. He concluded from this that the power to make laws rested initially in 'the multitude of mankind' when assembled in a community. However, 'infinite confusion and trouble would result if laws were established by the vote of every person; and therefore men straightway determine the said power by vesting it in one of the above-mentioned forms of government' (i.e. monarchy, aristocracy, etc.). Any agreement to set up a monarchy is understood to contain an exception against tyranny (or, for that matter, heresy: the condemned heretic is to be deposed as a tyrant). 'If, then, a lawful king is ruling in a tyrannical fashion, and if the state finds at hand no other means of self-defence then the expulsion and deposition of this king, the said state, acting as a whole, and in accordance with the public and general deliberations of its communities and leading men, may depose.'[26] The state which deposes a tyrant is thus not identical with the simple community of equals which originally established a form of government: it consists of a series of communities of unequals. It can act as a whole without counting everyone's vote as long as the established authorities act publicly.

The difference between Suarez and Locke lies in the fact that Locke's multitude of equals reacquire their right to power in face of tyranny; Suarez's view had been that power devolves merely to the corporate body of unequals (as it was to do in England in 1688, when the Whigs, impressed by 'old forms', tacitly agreed not to exercise what Locke would have taken to be their full rights and acquiesced in the preservation of the framework of the existing constitution).[27] In the event of a ruler being deposed, Suarez had simply taken it for granted that the next in line to the throne should succeed if the community is able to retain its political independence. He had not considered the possibility of a transformation of the constitution, a popular revolution, for in his view the state, the *res publica*, preserves its identity even in face of tyranny. Locke, on the other hand, came to hold that the state is dissolved by tyranny into the multitude of private individuals who constitute it, and that consequently private individuals may revolt against a tyrannical ruler, a right which Suarez had refused to private individuals (except by way of self-defence) when dealing with a legitimate ruler.

Suarez's unspoken assumption may be termed constitutionalist: the constitution always remains intact, despite the occasional actions of a tyrant, and there is thus no return to the equality and freedom of the first political society. This was the position of the Parliamentarians in 1642: indeed they went on to argue that it was a principle of the English constitution that the king could do no wrong, so that the people could not sit in judgement upon the person of the king, although they could convict his actions (arising from the bad advice of evil counsellors) of being tyrannical.

Not surprisingly, royalists were rendered impatient by Parliament's equivocations as it sought to prove that revolution could be constitutionally conservative. Henry Parker, Parliament's leading spokesman, had denied that power could ever revert to the 'moliminous [i.e. cumbersome] body' of the people once they had established a constitutional authority – Parliament – to represent their interests.[28] Nevertheless, Henry Ferne argued on behalf of the royalists that if Parliament, as representative of the people, could claim to reassume powers previously granted to the king, then the people as a whole could equally claim a right to rebel against Parliament, so that the arguments of the Parliamentarians made it impossible to locate any settled authority in the country.[29] Charles Herle justifiably replied in defence of Parker that it was false to claim that the Parliamentarians believed that

> in case the King and Parliament should neither discharge their trusts, the people might rise and make resistance against both, a position which no man I know maintains. He [Ferne] still pursues his own dream of the people's reassuming power, whereas we acknowledge no power can be employed but what is reserved, and the people have reserved no power in themselves from themselves in Parliament.[30]

John Spelman, the historian's son, attacked the parliamentary doctrine of representation from a different angle. He maintained that the notion that Parliament directly represented the people was a fiction, as only one tenth of the population could vote in elections. Far from the Lords and Commons being, as Parker had claimed, 'virtually the whole nation', they represented a tiny minority. Their authority derived only from the constitution, and from the fact that when that constitution had first been established *all* the people had agreed to submit themselves to it. Thus it was not the Lords and Commons who represented the nation, but the king within the constitution.[31] A similar view was taken by Dudley Digges, who argued that the Lords and the Commons 'are the people only to such purposes as the law nominates, *viz.* for consenting to laws or taxes upon the subject. To all other purposes (wherein regal power is not expressly limited) the king is the whole people, and what he does is legally their act.'[32] Unlike Spelman and Digges, Hobbes denied that any powers could have been reserved for Parliament: 'The people rule in all governments. . . . And in a monarchy . . . the king is the people.'[33]

Thus royalists and Parliamentarians disagreed about who could claim to be the representative of the people; but all seemed agreed that the people as a whole, acting outside constitutional authority, could have no right to represent themselves or act on their own behalf.[34] The royalists, however, maintained that the Parliamentarians were inconsistent because they treated representation as deriving not from an original act of submission, but from recent elections, thus making authority directly dependent upon the continuing consent of the electorate, and perhaps even of all the people whom they claimed to represent. In 1644 John Maxwell, in *Sacro-Sancta Regum Majestas*, reiterated the complaint that the Jesuits and Parliamentarians were mistaken in thinking that a popular right to resist tyranny could be confined within constitutionalist limits. If political authority depended upon continuing consent, then the parliamentarians ought to recognize the ultimate authority of all the people, allowing appeals from Parliament to the population at large, and acknowledging that the people, since their membership constantly changed, could not be bound by the constitutional arrangements of their ancestors. Maxwell thus argued that, to be consistent, the Parliamentarians ought to adopt what were later to be the arguments of Locke. His complaint was that none of them had done so. In fact he could find only one author who had come close to doing so, and that was Buchanan, who had written in defence of the deposition of Mary, Queen of Scots: he had maintained that laws passed by the Estates had no authority until the people had approved the actions of their repre sentatives. Buchanan alone had recognized that if the people were sovereign they could never transfer that sovereignty.

Maxwell's own view was the opposite of the one he thought the radicals should be willing to defend. He held that kings were as fathers to their people, that to depose a king was comparable to a wife divorcing her husband, that if kings *did* derive their authority from the people (which he did not accept) then the transfer of authority was irrevocable, and the king was not to be appointed only *durante bene placito*. His purpose was to persuade Parliamentarians that they must either maintain that the people as a multitude of equals had never alienated their ultimate authority, or accept that *populus* or *people* was a word to be used in a corporatist and inegalitarian sense. The first option led to democracy and anarchy. The second involved recognizing that the Commons and Lords were not the sole representatives of the people. Thus Maxwell claimed to reconcile the parliamentary principle that *salus populi suprema lex est* with his own claim that the people cannot hold their ruler to account by insisting that the word *populus* had been misinterpreted. It meant simply 'the public' and included all orders of society. *Salus populi* was consequently identical to *salus rei publicae*, a principle which required the safety of the king and his government, who were parts of the *populus* properly understood; thus any corporatist definition of *populus* must include the king himself. Consequently public authority could never stand against the person of the king.[35]

Like Spelman, Maxwell was trying to polarize the two senses in which the term 'the people' could be used, in order to leave no middle ground between democracy and royalism. In so doing, though, he knew that he was going against the traditional interpretation given to the concept of popular sovereignty, an interpretation which had regarded the Lords and Commons as the infallible representatives of the people. Where had this incoherent concept come from? he asked. Not from 'the sound Protestants of the Reformed Churches' but from the Catholics of the League, who had advocated tyrannicide during the French Wars of Religion, and, before them, from conciliarist opponents of papal power: Almain and the Sorbonnists, Gerson, Marsilius, and Ockham. Maxwell was no conciliarist – the conciliarists, after all, had failed to recognize that the only solution to papal claims of supremacy was the abolition of the papacy – and so he was not surprised that inconsistent and dangerous doctrines had been drawn from such 'polluted cisterns'.

Maxwell was right to claim that no one had sought to ground the argument upon a consistent theory of popular sovereignty in the sense in which we understand the term. His stress upon the contribution of conciliarism (albeit often indirect) to parliamentary theories has been confirmed in recent years by the work of two historians of conciliarist theory – Brian Tierney and Francis Oakley – who have documented the similarities between the arguments of Parliamentarians like Hunton, Parker, and Herle and medieval conciliarists.[36] No conciliarist, however, came close to defending a concept of popular sovereignty comparable to Locke's. For a Sorbonnist like Almain, for example, the authority of the church as the community of the faithful was directly embodied in the Council. And although radical conciliarists were willing to argue that, since the decision of a Council affected all Christians, all (even, *mirabile dictu*, women) had a right to be heard during its deliberations, they did not propose that all should have an equal voice, or a vote. They saw the Council as representing both the various churches of Christendom and the various orders of Christians, and took it for granted that bishops, clergy and laity should have unequal influence. John Major, for example, following in the tradition of Almain, insisted that decisions should not be made by a simple majority but by the *valentior pars*, the weightier part, appealing to a principle of quality as well as quantity. Applied to secular governments this principle led to a restrictive definition of 'the people'. As Major put it:

> It is from the people, and most of all from the chief men and nobility who act for the common people, that kings have their institution; it belongs, therefore, to the princes, prelates and nobles to decide [whether a king is a tyrant]; and their decision shall remain inviolable.[37]

Conciliarism thus led to a defence of the authority of the Estates (the secular analogue to a Church Council), not to a theory of the sovereignty of the people in general. It could also lead in the direction of federalism, for the General Council represented the various churches of Christendom. The Protestant Althusius, a contemporary of Suarez, is thus often upheld as a theorist of popular sovereignty, but Althusius was a federalist who believed that in the event of tyranny authority devolved to the communities and corporations out of which the state was constructed: and within these communities and corporations, of course, power was held, as in the churches of Catholic Christendom, by minoritarian elites.[38]

It is sometimes argued that, outside the narrowly conciliarist tradition, the Middle Ages saw the formulation of a genuine theory of popular sovereignty in the *Defensor Pacis* of Marsilius of Padua. But precisely the same restrictive definition of the people is to be found in Marsilius. For him final authority lies with the *valentior pars* of the people, and he states that the *valentior pars* refers not only to the quantity but also to the quality of the persons whose opinion should be adopted. Marsilius accepts without question Aristotle's view that citizens participate in the community according to rank, and that some lesser citizens will have no legislative role. Such citizens will, presumably, have virtually no claim to a say in determining the constitution of the state.[39]

The medieval tradition, continued into the seventeenth century, thus maintained that the people gave their consent not as equal individuals but as members of a hierarchical society. Maxwell was right to suspect that Buchanan (at least in some of his statements) came closest to stepping outside this tradition, but even he is careful not to uphold the final authority of a numerical majority when the people sit in judgement upon their king. In his dialogue *Of the Powers of the Crown in Scotland* he asks himself whether the majority may not be perverted in their judgement by fear or favour. Those so perverted, he replies, are no true citizens. 'Who then are to be accounted citizens? Those who obey the laws, who maintain human society, who would rather undergo every hardship and every peril for the well-being of their fellow-countrymen than, through cowardice, grow old in dishonourable ease.' Buchanan insists that citizens should be reckoned 'not by their number, but by their worth', although he seems to mean by 'worth' not rank but civic virtue.[40]

Replying to Maxwell, Samuel Rutherford, a Scottish Presbyterian, sought to marry the constitutionalist arguments of Suarez with the radicalism of Buchanan. Like Buchanan, he believed that a certain inalienable sovereignty remained originally and radically in the people. The people could refuse to obey a wicked Parliament that, for example, sought to impose popery upon them. They could spontaneously arm themselves against a tyrannical ruler, even a legitimately appointed one as opposed to a usurper, without awaiting parliamentary instructions. But Maxwell was wrong to argue, Rutherford maintained, that one was bound to conclude that they could reassume the power they had devolved to Parliament. In a constitutional monarchy the Estates had the legal right to depose a wicked ruler. Rutherford went so far as to argue that the constituencies could recall their representatives if they abused their trust. But he did not envisage the possibility of an appeal from the electorate to the people as a whole, or a revolutionary transformation of the constitution. By insisting that kings could be deposed and Parliaments could err, he adopted the most radical position which could be reconciled with the claim that the people as individuals could not reassume authority. He did not go beyond this point.[41]

Are we then to conclude that Locke was the first to enunciate a true theory of popular sovereignty? Scholars have tended to cite as Locke's precursors the authors we have discussed – Marsilius, Almain, Major, Althusius, Buchanan – none of whom held theories strictly comparable to Locke's.[42] Seeing the problem, Julian Franklin has argued that no theory comparable to Locke's was enunciated prior to George Lawson's *Politica* of 1657.[43] But the same problem occurs in Lawson as in Marsilius (indeed Lawson's arguments are in large part drawn from Marsilius) or in Buchanan. In Lawson's view only freeholders are properly members of the community, thus restricting 'the people' to the existing electorate, a tiny part of the nation. Even they are not truly sovereign: 'When I mention the people of England as the primary subject of power, and the heir of real majesty, I mean the rational, judicial party' (i.e. the *valentior pars*).[44]

Nevertheless, Locke was not without precursors. The Putney Debates provide us, through the imperfect transcript preserved in the Clarke manuscripts, with a unique opportunity to listen to radicals and constitutionalists arguing over the best form of government. With the king defeated on the battlefield but with Parliament and the City of London threatening to disband the army and make a conservative settlement with the king, representatives of the soldiers, known as 'agitators', and spokesmen for the Leveller party met at Putney with the army commanders, including Cromwell, to discuss whether the army was entitled to dictate terms to Parliament. The Leveller spokesmen, it is now generally agreed, came to the Putney Debates as defenders of manhood suffrage.[45] Behind them stood a rudimentary organization which entitles them to be considered the first modern political party. In an attempt to form an alliance with the army commanders they retreated from their democratic principles. Faced with the objection that master and servant should not be equal electors, Maximilian Petty, speaking for the Levellers, agreed that servants, apprentices and those that beg from door to door should be denied the vote. Assuming (as is surely the case) that by servants he meant living-in servants, not all wage-workers, and that by those who take alms he meant destitute vagrants, not all those benefiting from charity (including those on poor relief), the Levellers were left with what may be termed a householder franchise, of the sort later approved by William Petty (who was no relation of Maximilian): the head of every household would vote on behalf of his household, his servants being (as his wife and small children had always been assumed to be) 'included' in his vote. Keith Thomas has shown that in some urban constituencies what amounted to householder franchises were already in existence, so that the new Leveller programme was not without constitutional precedent.[46]

The Levellers, it would therefore seem, started out committed to adult male suffrage and retreated from this objective. But it should be noted that the status of servant or apprentice was for the vast majority only a temporary one, and one that was seen as comparable to an extended childhood. Adolescents always left home, so that a householder franchise would not have excluded adult sons from the vote unless they had indentured themselves as servants or apprentices. Marriage, in any case, always meant an end to apprenticeship and to living-in servanthood, so that all married men, a category including the vast majority of men over thirty, would have had the vote. The Levellers' retreat from the principle of manhood suffrage was not as great as might at first be thought.

Moreover, whatever compromise the Levellers may have been willing to strike on the question of the franchise, they showed no sign of compromising on the issue of popular sovereignty, which had been so clearly formulated by Rainsborough. The Agreement of the People itself is testimony to this: all (male) inhabitants were, without exception, invited to join in ratifying the Agreement, which was intended to be the first written constitution and the first to define and guarantee the inalienable rights of individuals. All were to benefit, if not from the right to vote, then from clauses such as that guaranteeing freedom of religious worship; consequently all should consent to the alienation of a part of their natural rights to the new political authority. The legitimacy of the new constitution was to be derived, apart from the inherent justice of its provisions, solely from the number of signatories the Agreement obtained. The Levellers may thus loosely be described as democrats, and may accurately be defined as proponents of popular sovereignty. Their ideas, we have seen, had no clear precedent in traditional political theory, although they may well have later influenced Locke, who was a friend of the former Leveller John Wildman.

If we are to look for the first blunt formulation of the modern theory of popular sovereignty we must turn, I believe, to the period between the publication of Maxwell's *Sacro-Sancta* in January 1644, when the royalists were still complaining that their opponents would not admit that their arguments pointed towards a doctrine of the sovereignty of all the people, and October 1647, when the Putney Debates began. It seems that the new theory made its first appearance, not as a bugbear with which to frighten constitutionalists, but as a serious account of political authority, in *England's Miserie and Remedie*, an anonymous tract of 1645, the year after Maxwell's *Sacro-Sancta Regum Majestas*.[47] Its author, by insisting on Lilburne's right, in view of the injustice of his imprisonment, to appeal from Parliament to the multitude, was at last presenting the argument that Ferne, Spelman and Maxwell had maintained consistent Parliamentarians should have the courage to put forward. It is not, I suppose, unlikely that he had read these royalist propagandists with silent approval, but it is the authority of Buchanan he appeals to, and in support of his views he quotes George Wither.

Wither, according to later (and possibly unreliable) authorities, had in 1642 or 3 joined with the sole republican in the House of Commons, Henry Marten, in mocking the coronation regalia of the king, in which Wither had dressed himself up to play the fool, while Marten declared that 'there should be no further use of those toys and trifles'. Marten and Wither make an odd (and possibly apocryphal) pair, for Marten was famous for unbelief and debauchery, and Wither for casting himself in the role of a prophet calling down God's anger on the sins of his people.[48] Certainly Wither in *Vox Pacifica* had called for the purging of a corrupt Parliament: for that reason Lilburne had already quoted him at length in *England's Birth-Right Justified*.

The author of *England's Miserie and Remedie* was thus not the first to believe that Wither and the emerging Leveller party shared common commitments, though it is far from certain that the 'greater thing Than an unrighteous Parliament or king' to which Wither appealed was the rude and inconsiderate multitude, and not, as it was later to be for Milton, a godly minority.[49] Neither Buchanan nor Wither had preceded the author of *England's Miserie and Remedie* in clearly formulating and advocating the principle of the sovereignty of the people as a multitude of equal individuals.[50]

Who was it who took this important step? The various proposals that have been put forward regarding the authorship of this tract seem to me to fall down on one simple point: its author was clearly capable of reading Latin. If we look for an associate of the Levellers who had the requisite learning one person in particular, I think, presents himself as a candidate: Edward Sexby. Sexby was to appear as the leading representative of the agitators at Putney. At the beginning of the first day's debate he explained:

The cause of our misery is upon two things. We sought to satisfy all men, and it was well; but in going about to do it we have dissatisfied all men. We have laboured to please a king, and, I think, except we go about to cut all our throats, we shall not please him; and we have gone to support an house which will prove rotten studs [i.e. timbers] – I mean the Parliament, which consists of a company of rotten members.[51]

The remedy was to sweep away king and Parliament, the policy first systematically upheld in *England's Miserie and Remedie*.

After the consolidation of Cromwell's power and the collapse of the Leveller movement, Sexby employed himself, while nominally acting as Cromwell's agent, in trying to persuade the people of Bordeaux, at that time in revolt, to adopt the Agreement of the People. Later, convinced that Cromwell's rule had become as tyrannical as Charles I's, he entered into collaboration with the royalists in attempting to arrange Cromwell's assassination: a delicate collaboration, since Sexby refused to agree to call for the restoration of the Stuarts. Clarendon was impressed by his eloquence and amazed at his use of words whose meaning, Clarendon was sure, he could not understand. *Killing Noe Murder* shows that Sexby was better educated than Clarendon had realized. It is indeed perhaps the finest of all tracts in favour of tyrannicide and is evidently the work of an accomplished author, but, like *England's Miserie and Remedie*, it seeks to conceal that author's true identity.

Whether *England's Miserie and Remedie* and *Killing Noe Murder* were the work of the same author or not, they are both striking for their dependence on classical and humanist sources. Blair Worden, in an essay on 'Classical Republicanism and the Puritan Revolution' has remarked: 'The relationship between puritan theology and puritan politics has been debated by many scholars. But who has investigated Thomas Hobbes's claim that the Civil War was largely caused by "the reading of the books of policy and histories of the ancient Greeks and Romans"?'[52] This is a particularly apposite comment when applied to the Levellers. Numerous efforts have been made to derive Leveller political theory from theological premises, but it is doubtful if such premises can have been the only or most important ones for a Walwyn, whose favourite reading was Montaigne and who was accused (not without grounds) of unbelief, for an Overton, whose *Man's Mortality* laid him open to similar charges, for a Sindercombe, against whom the same charges were made, for a Wildman, or for a Sexby.[53] *England's Miserie and Remedie*, as a pioneering presentation of the Leveller theory of popular sovereignty, invites a more secular interpretation of Leveller thinking, even though it is clear that the author saw himself as being in at least temporary alliance with Puritan radicals such as Wither.

The radical programme which took shape between 1644 and 1648 was based on the conviction that it was necessary to destroy the existing government in order to reconstruct it on a basis of equality. Parliamentary leaders such as St John or Ireton feared the collapse of government as much as did Hobbes, and all those who accepted the conventional view that government was a necessary restraint upon sin were bound to concur with Shakespeare's view:

> Take but degree away, untune that string,
> And hark, what discord follows! each thing meets
> In mere oppugnancy . . .

Locke, however, was to argue that tyranny was far worse than 'the state of nature, or pure anarchy; the inconveniences being all as great and as near, but the remedy farther off and more difficult'.[54] The same point had been made in 1649 by the pseudonymous author of *The Original and End of Civil Power* in defending popular sovereignty. He admitted

> that this opinion may introduce anarchy and confusion; yet it cannot be denied but the repressing of a rooted and reigning tyranny conduces to a greater good than a momentary anarchy can do hurt: if it should prove so that anarchy should be the consequent of restraining tyranny, which yet does not necessarily succeed it; yet anarchy cannot be so long a continuance as the other would have been, if born withal, because (as was said before) there is invayscerated into man a prompt inclination and a love to society and company, and this ushers in Government, which necessarily follows as the thread does the needle: and anarchy never was of any long continuance, but came as a sudden land-flood or murmuring torrent, that soon reduced and confined itself again within the banks of government.[55]

The radicals had to adopt one strategy or another to present a more favourable picture of the people who made up the multitude, 'the many-headed monster', to which they appealed.[56] The author of *The Original and End of Civil Power* appealed to Aristotle's account of man's natural sociability. Others, such as Wither and Milton, defended the Arminian doctrine of free will against the Calvinist orthodoxy of the day in order to assert man's capacity for goodness. Others, such as Walwyn and Roger Williams, were accused of antinomianism for arguing that God's grace was given freely to sinners, and that consequently all men should have equal rights in civil society, since any of them might be (in Williams's view), or all of them were (in Walwyn's view), loved by God. These different strategies all cast in doubt the established view that obedience to an established hierarchy was the best that could be hoped for of men in general.

Hobbes, of course, had no patience with ideas of natural sociability, free will or political equality. In 1642 he published *De Cive*, a work written in exile in France as mobs surrounded the Parliament in London calling for the abolition of episcopacy and as the House of Commons itself, with the Grand Remonstrance of December 1641, moved towards a policy of appealing directly for popular support.[57] Not surprisingly, Hobbes engaged in a violent denunciation of those who claimed to derive legitimacy from the support of the multitude. Legitimacy, Hobbes maintained, could derive only from the possession of sovereign authority: the wills of citizens are 'comprehended in' those of the sovereign. He could be confident that this argument would meet with widespread approval, for it was during this period that a royalist party was beginning to rally around a king who, in the early months of the Long Parliament, had had almost no support. Where Hobbes differed from other royalists, however, was, as we have seen, in denying the existence of any constitutional limitations upon royal authority.

Hobbes's account of sovereignty in *De Cive* is grounded on the claim that citizens renounce their rights to the sovereign. In *The Elements of Law* he may have assumed that even the right to self-defence could be renounced; in *De Cive* all rights except those which Hobbes's psychological theory render inalienable are given up.[58] In *Leviathan*, as David Gauthier has shown, a major alteration is made to the structure of Hobbes's argument. There Hobbes uses the concept of authorization to maintain that citizens do not straightforwardly renounce their rights to their rulers: rather the sovereign is at all times their representative, and his actions are authorized by their continuing grant of authority. Each citizen is the author of the sovereign's acts, and continues to be so because he has covenanted with his fellow citizens not to withdraw his authorization.

Gauthier argues that Hobbes's reference in *De Cive* to the will of the citizen being comprehended in that of the sovereign suggests that his thought was already developing in this direction in 1642.[59] But the view of representation that Hobbes held in 1642 was the same as that of other royalists: the king represented his subjects because they had in the past submitted themselves to him (just as a husband and wife were one person in law because of a marriage contract entered into in the past, not because of any continuing affection). There is no reason why Hobbes in 1642 should have found this view problematic: the royalist position was that it was much more coherent than any view of representation which opened the way to a theory of continuing consent. In 1651, however, the situation was quite different. The Levellers had denied that the people could be bound by past acts of submission, and insisted that government must be founded on the continuing consent of all citizens. They had denied that the people could be fully represented by any corporate body legally acting on their behalf, and insisted that they must give their consent as a multitude of individuals. It is this universal consent, this continuing sovereignty of the multitude, that Hobbes seeks to lay claim to through his theory of authorization. It is from this continuing consent that Leviathan derives his authority and power.

The title-page of *Leviathan* gives graphic illustration to this theory: Leviathan's body is made up from the bodies of the multitude of citizens. The same point was made even more strikingly by the title-page of the manuscript copy of Leviathan presented to Charles II. There Leviathan's body is made up of a multitude of heads – he is, quite literally, a many-headed monster.[60] Thus Hobbes sought to convey the idea that the acts of the sovereign are owned equally by each and every citizen, and to transform a view of the multitude as a threat to all order into a vision of its members as the substance of the state. Far from being an attempt to work out some inner logic already implicit in *De Cive*, Hobbes's theory of authorization is a radical departure, designed to meet the Levellers upon their own ground, and seeking to establish an unquestionable authority through a modified version of the radical theory of continuing popular sovereignty.

In one crucial respect, though, Hobbes agreed with the radicals. He accepted that the Stuarts had no continuing right to rule.[61] He disagreed with them, however, about why this was so: they maintained that the people had a right to overthrow a tyrannical ruler and an unsatisfactory form of government, while he maintained that the king's military defeat meant that he was no longer able to impose order, and thus no longer able to act as sovereign ruler. For Hobbes, portraying the sovereign as an artificial person, bearing not his own authority but other people's, made it easier to explain how his rights could revert to his subjects, and how they could be newly faced with the task of establishing security and legitimacy. At the same time though, he had to avoid suggesting that the dissolution of the government meant that authority once more lay with a democratic multitude. *Leviathan*, unlike Hobbes's previous works, avoids presenting democracy as historically the first form of government, from which all other types of government by institution derive. Hobbes believed that the correct solution to the problem of establishing authority after the execution of the king was to recognize as legitimate the most powerful existing political and military force. But to present this view effectively he had to break with a view of legitimacy as resulting not from present consent but previous submission, while at the same time avoiding a view which would require consent to be given by the counting of votes. It was this task which Hobbes's theory of authorization was designed to accomplish. It thus represents a brilliant response to the revolution in political argument which had been carried out by the Levellers. That revolution had helped push the army forward to demand the execution of the king. But the king's execution had rapidly been followed by efforts on Cromwell's part to defuse the threat from the radicals and to restore stability.[62] As we shall see, Hobbes in writing *Leviathan* was not only responding to the arguments of the Levellers, but also seeking to play his part in the defence of the new order. The first modern revolution had taken place, and Hobbes believed it would be wrong to seek to reverse it.[63] It had been made possible by a revolution in political debate: a revolution which Hobbes sought not to reverse, but to turn to his own advantage.

From Duty to Self-Interest

It is not from the benevolence of the butcher, the brewer, or the baker, that we expect our dinner, but from their regard to their own interest. We address ourselves, not to their humanity but to their self-love, and never talk to them of our own necessities but of their advantages.

Adam Smith, *The Wealth of Nations* (1776), book one, chapter two

Few people in seventeenth-century England accepted the Leveller theory of popular sovereignty. Until his death, John Locke went to great pains to conceal his authorship of the *Two Treatises*, in which his adherence to this dangerous theory was expressed. Judge Jeffreys had sent Algernon Sidney to the scaffold for defending the right to revolution in a private manuscript written at roughly the same time and for the same purposes as the *Two Treatises*, and even the revolution of 1688 had done little to render such arguments respectable. Democratic and republican ideas continued to be expounded in anonymous, pseudonymous and posthumous works, the ephemera of political debate which have been remembered only when it has suited the purposes of political propagandists of later generations.

Our quest for our own ancestors in the past can easily distract us from consideration of the principles which people in the past were generally agreed upon. First and foremost among these, as far as the seventeenth century is concerned, must stand the principle that (as Maxwell formulates it in *Sacro-Sancta*, translating a passage of Lactantius): 'Religion and the fear of God, and nothing else, preserves all societies amongst men.'[64] Without fear of God's judgement in the next world, men would have nothing to discourage them from lying, theft and murder, other than fear of the civil magistrate. Given the limitations of secular justice, all too many people would find themselves in situations where they could hope to escape justice in this world, and, if unchecked by fear of God's justice in the next, would act in a fashion which would tear asunder the bonds of society, creating a Hobbesian war of all against all. Only the god-fearing could therefore be accepted as members of society. Locke expressed this view in his *Essay Concerning Toleration* (1667): 'The belief of a deity is . . . the foundation of all morality and that which influences the whole life and actions of men, without which a man is to be considered no other than one of the most dangerous sorts of wild beasts, and so incapable of all society.'[65] This view was often stated, and often in similar terms. Thus, for example, Halifax wrote in *The Character of a Trimmer* (1684):

> Religion has such a superiority above all other things, and that indispensable influence upon all mankind, that it is as necessary to our being happy in this world as it is to our being saved in the next; without it man is an abandoned creature, one of the worst beasts nature has produced, and fit only for the society of wolves and bears.[66]

It was not only almost universally held, but of central importance to every institution in society. It was not until 1888, for instance, that the courts of England were to accept the testimony of unbelievers.

Few people in the seventeenth century questioned this conviction that only the god-fearing could be law-abiding members of society. Those who did so were for the most part enemies of the existing social order. In the view of a communist like Winstanley, fear of hell and hope of heaven were instilled by the church in order to secure obedience to authority and acceptance of inequality. In a communist society, however, such hopes and fears would be unnecessary: heaven would be built here upon earth, and hell would be recognized as a metaphor for social injustice and spiritual oppression.[67] William Walwyn came close to expressing similar views in *The Power of Love*, and it was perhaps in defence of the rights of radicals such as these that Wildman, a Leveller spokesman at the Whitehall debates of 1648, insisted that the state ought not to require any sort of religious belief – not even belief in heaven and hell – from its citizens.[68]

Winstanley and Walwyn are not, however, exceptions to the general rule. They accepted that society as then constituted depended on the fear of God for its preservation. Among those who sought political but not social revolution there was general agreement that atheists were incapable of making good citizens. Thus Roger Williams, who sought toleration for believers of all types, was persuaded that atheists were 'fit for the practice of any evil murders, adulteries, treasons, etc.'.[69] Even if one were to tolerate unbelief, one could not possibly tolerate the behaviour that must necessarily follow upon it. Seventeenth-century Englishmen consequently saw themselves as members of a society held together by the fear of God. Where we have a tendency to see citizens as united in society through their pursuit of their common interests in justice, security and prosperity, people in the seventeenth century were convinced that men's private interests must necessarily bring them into conflict with one another, unless their secular interests were overridden by their concern to avoid the pains of hell-fire. It was people's sense of a divinely ordained system of duties, not their worldly interests, which was, in a phrase employed by Maxwell and others, 'the cement of society'.

Recognition of this paradigm casts new light on the classic texts of seventeenth-century English political theory. It helps clarify, for example, the transformation that Hobbes sought to work upon existing assumptions. Hobbes's state of nature is a straightforward account of the behaviour to be expected of men who have no reason to fear either God or the civil magistrate: central to Hobbes's argument, therefore, is the presumption that natural reason does not demonstrate the existence of an afterlife and of divine justice. In Hobbes's view the truths of religion can be established only by political command, and so only after the creation of the state. As a consequence he believed it essential to identify a principle sufficiently powerful to override the conflicting interests even of citizens who do not believe in God. This principle is the fear of death, a fear instilled by the sovereign, who fulfils the role of an artificial or, as Hobbes calls him, 'mortal' God. Hobbes thus secularizes the notion of a god-fearing society, making God unnecessary for the establishment of order, at least among people who are capable of rationally calculating their own interests.[70]

Locke's approach is very different. He was well aware that the law of nature could be presented as a mere expression of men's selfish interests, but he refused to develop such a line of argument and conclude that faith was irrelevant to the creation of a just society.[71] We have seen that he held that only the god-fearing were capable of recognizing their true duties as citizens. Unfortunately Locke, like Hobbes, belonged to the small minority of intellectuals who held that, although natural reason was sufficient to establish the existence of a god, it was insufficient to demonstrate the immortality of the soul. As a consequence Locke was bound to hold that religious revelation was an essential prerequisite for the moralizing of man and the establishment of a legitimate political order. He did not state this conclusion in his political writings, which were directed at readers who took the truths of Christianity for granted, but it is clearly expressed in *The Reasonableness of Christianity*. There he presents the central truth of Christianity as being not Christ's death as a sacrifice for our sins, but his resurrection from the dead, for this is the proof of a life after death, and therefore the supreme motive to obey God's law. This type of argument was rightly regarded by Locke's contemporaries as being Socinian, although Locke refused to accept the Socinian conclusion that, since only true Christians can recognize the divine moral order, secular authority must be grounded in worldly, not spiritual, principles. In Locke's view the principles of

Christianity were essential preconditions for any adequate political order, and Hobbes had been profoundly mistaken to think he could find an alternative to the fear of God in worldly self-interest.

The paradigm of the god-fearing citizen presented particular problems for Hobbes and Locke because, just as neither was convinced that life after death was a rationally demonstrable fact, so too neither was persuaded that God's concern for mankind was apparent in daily events. Most of their contemporaries, however, were persuaded that they had good reason to fear God, not only as their judge in the hereafter, but also because his hand was to be seen at work in the world around them. For George Wither the London plague of 1625 was proof of God's anger against England's sins. For Oliver Cromwell victory in the Civil War was proof of God's support. Although trial by battle had been abandoned by the secular courts (Lilburne's father being one of the last to seek recourse to it), the assumption was widespread that God, as in the Old Testament, determined the outcome of battles. Had he not employed a 'Protestant wind' to defeat the Spanish armada? No individual and no nation, it was assumed, could hope to flourish without the assistance of divine providence, and only godly individuals and godly nations could hope for such assistance.[72]

The English were convinced that they were a nation chosen of God. Foxe's *Book of Martyrs* confirmed this conviction for all who read it, and authorized Milton to write of 'God's Englishmen'.[73] But godliness had to be preserved through vigilance: this was one of the chief arguments against the toleration of Roman Catholics, who threatened the welfare of a Protestant nation, not only by their attempts to spread heresy among believers, but also because the Catholic mass was, in the eyes of Protestants, idolatrous, and so liable to bring down the wrath of God upon any nation which tolerated it. On to these arguments, of course, were grafted the arguments that Catholics were agents in the service of a foreign power, the papacy (in Locke's view the only telling argument), and that Catholicism was inseparable from despotism and the persecution of true religion (the central argument of Halifax's *Letter to a Dissenter*). In the view of most people these arguments, invoked as of central importance by advocates of toleration for Dissenters but not Catholics, were of secondary importance. The consensus was that the teaching of true religion and the suppression of heresy were prerequisites for the secular and not merely the spiritual welfare of the nation. As Maxwell said in the opening words of *Sacro-Sancta*: 'Piety and policy, Church and State, prince and priest are so nearly and naturally conjoined in a mutual interest that, like to Hippocrates his twins, they rejoice and mourn, flourish and perish, live and die together.'

Piety and policy were not linked together merely because it was assumed that God would reward piety and punish heresy. Precisely because few Christians would tolerate what they took to be false religion, it was assumed that where there were differences of religion civil disorder must follow. Thus in Bacon's view innovation in religion was the first and foremost of the causes and motives of sedition, and unity of religion the best guarantor of civil peace.[74] Hobbes asked rhetorically, 'What civil war was there ever in the Christian world which did not either grow from or was nourished by this root?', that of religion.[75] Moreover, it was widely believed that the structure of authority in both church and state ought to be similar if one was to give support to the other. The state was therefore necessarily concerned with the affairs of the church, just as the church claimed the right to guide and direct the state. As James I succinctly said: 'No bishop, no king.'

The consequence of the conviction that it was necessary to establish a godly society was, inevitably, intolerance and persecution. Elizabeth might declare her opposition to 'making windows into men's souls', but this was primarily an argument against enforcing discriminatory laws too severely, not against having them at all. Prior to 1642 failure to attend the services of the Church of England made one liable to severe fines and other penalties. During the Civil War and interregnum parochial discipline broke down, and it could not be fully restored at the Restoration. But while non-attendance at church effectively ceased to be prosecuted, attendance at religious services other than those of the Church of England carried severe penalties under the Conventicles Acts of 1664 and 1670, while the Act of Uniformity of 1662 and the Corporations Act of 1664 excluded Catholics and Dissenters from all town corporations and from all teaching positions, public or private. Unlike atheists, Catholics and Dissenters were regarded as having civil rights, being allowed access to the courts, but they were not held to be full citizens, since church and nation were one.

This view of the unity of church and nation had found classic expression in Richard Hooker's polemics against the Puritans, and Hooker's influence was to grow, not diminish, as the century passed and as the Church of England became increasingly inclined to present itself as a *via media* between Protestantism and Catholicism, rather than as a Reformed church comparable to other Protestant churches. In Hooker's view most of the arguments of the Puritans were concerned with matters which were not essential to salvation – *adiaphora* – and people should be willing to put disagreements on such matters aside for the sake of unity within the national church. Hooker's argument involved a careful balancing of consent and authority; the legitimacy of laws, both in state and church, derived, he maintained, from consent. But that consent was expressed through the traditional practices of previous generations, and it was not a consent that could now be withdrawn. Past consent had established a legitimate authority – the King-in-Parliament – which could, so long as it remained within the framework of existing traditions, legitimately punish dissent in church and state.[76]

Hooker's view was faced, in the course of the century, by three main alternatives. The first was the claim that the identification of church and nation was unacceptable if the church was brought down to the level of the nation, and not the nation raised to the level of the church. For strict Puritans and for Presbyterians the key to the establishment of a godly nation was the enforcement of an effective church discipline. The ecclesiastical courts of the Church of England were, they maintained, unable to enforce moral discipline, for their sanctions were too easily evaded. For a Presbyterian like Baxter the defeat of Charles I opened the possibility of establishing a new church discipline, and of employing that discipline to create a godly nation. Baxter was thus determined to exclude the ungodly, not only from the church, but also from political life. The rights of full citizenship must be denied to those whose beliefs or whose behaviour (swearing, drunkenness, fornication) marked them out as reprobates. In developing this position Baxter was primarily concerned with opponents on two fronts. The first were those who believed that the millennium was at hand and that God would directly assist in the task of establishing godly rule and eliminating sin. In the face of such convictions Baxter insisted that questions of church organization and political authority must be separated from eschatological arguments for the imminence of the Second Coming.

The millenarians or Fifth Monarchists believed in the possibility of establishing a society of saints in short order.[77] But Baxter was also concerned to reject the arguments of those who denied the validity of any attempt to establish godly rule. Baxter himself, for all his Presbyterianism, was not a strict Calvinist when it came to the doctrines of the servitude of the will and of predestination. Stricter exponents of this aspect of Calvinist doctrine, such as Roger Williams, drew from it conclusions that would have horrified Calvin and which led the Presbyterian mainstream to label them antinomians or enemies of the moral law. Williams argued that it was impossible to identify the godly merely on the basis of outward professions of belief and public conduct. Nobody other than God could know who would be saved, nor could human beings alter God's decrees through their behaviour. If one thing was certain, however, it was that most ostensible Christians would be condemned at the day of judgement. The true church could only be the church of a minority, and to establish a national church must be to establish a church in which the reprobate predominated and therefore in which the devil ruled. In Williams's view faith must become a matter of private conviction, not public obligation, and individuals must be left free to pursue the promptings of their own consciences. This implied the abolition of the Church of England and of all national churches. Where Hooker and Baxter insisted that the state had spiritual as well as worldly purposes to fulfil, Williams argued that the state existed only to enable the pursuit of secular benefits. In place of the ideal of a godly nation he advocated a society of god-fearing individuals, pursuing in common, and on a basis of equality, the this-worldly benefits of peace, civic order and commercial prosperity. It was this argument, the argument of the separatists in the Civil War, which was to be taken up and adapted by John Locke in his *Letter Concerning Toleration*, a work in which verbal echoes of Williams's *Bloudy Tenent* are not difficult to find.

There was a fourth alternative to Hooker's comprehensive Anglicanism, Baxter's strict Presbyterian discipline and Williams's independent gathered churches, and that alternative found one of its earliest expressions in the works of William Walwyn, works such as *The Vanitie of the Present Churches* (1649), which was an attack not only on the existing churches but on any church that might be constructed.

Where Williams had argued that a national church was necessarily a corrupt church, Walwyn wrote as if all churches were necessarily suspect in that they made distinctions between clergy and laity, elders and congregation, and so attributed superior knowledge and godliness to a few. The worst offender in this respect, of course, was the Catholic Church, with its claim to papal infallibility, but the logic of Protestantism, of the priesthood of all believers, pointed, in Walwyn's view, to the abolition of all forms of clerical authority. Walwyn, like Williams, was opposed to a national church and to the compulsory taxation – the tithes – required to finance such a church. He was allied with the separatists, but was himself a member of no church in particular (and thus, almost by default, of his parish church). In matters of religious doctrine Walwyn was a sceptic: we have seen he can be commpared to Hobbes in this respect. But he found in the Christ of the Gospels a model of unselfish love for one's fellow men and women. Where Williams had sought rigorously to separate church and state so that the one could pursue spiritual and the other worldly purposes without mutual interference, Walwyn was primarily interested in the fact that churches appeared to have the defects of other worldly institutions and seemed to serve selfish ends. He argued that the clergy were simply monopolists, to be condemned on the same grounds as the numerous royal patentees attacked in the Parliaments of Elizabeth, James and Charles I. The illegality of monopolies (except those, Coke had argued, which were in the public interest, which he believed meant those which had been approved by Parliament) was a secular and egalitarian principle. From it Walwyn sought to derive the illegality of censorship of the press, of religious intolerance and of political inequality. This approach led him to treat the clergy as a selfish interest group, a corrupt profession, no different in kind from the lawyers or the Merchant-Adventurers. Walwyn's argument is thus similar, in its scepticism, its stress upon the need for freedom of debate and its attack upon doctrinal differences as merely a mask for secular interests, to that of the free-thinkers of the early eighteenth century: people like Collins, Toland, Tindal and Mandeville, who owed a great debt to Bayle, to Locke and, in the case of Toland at least, to Harringtonian republicanism. Walwyn did not have the same intellectual resources to draw upon – he was unable even to read Latin – and was writing hasty, polemical tracts to meet the urgent crises of the Civil War, but he produced arguments against the established religion and the social and political order of which it formed part which, if far from elegant or erudite, deservedly earned him a reputation as the most cunning and dangerous of all those spokesmen for religious toleration who were to join together in the Leveller party in order to campaign for political freedom. It is difficult to know whether he continued to have any influence after the Levellers were defeated, but his writings may have played a part in shaping the tradition of hostility to priestcraft in which even Locke's *Reasonableness* has a place.[78]

In the eyes of contemporaries the issue of toleration was the most important political issue of the seventeenth century, alongside, and inseparable from, that of the choice between constitutionalism and absolutism. The two issues were most hotly debated when they were conjoined, as they were in the early years of the Civil War and in the period between the conversion to Catholicism of James, Duke of York (the future James II), and the revolution of 1688. Just as we are inclined, from our twentieth-century vantage-point, to give insufficient weight to the debate over toleration, so we are inclined to give inadequate emphasis to other occasions on which religion played a central role in political debate. One of the most striking of these is the Engagement Debate of 1650–52. Following the execution of the king, Parliament required all those having dealings with the government, including clergymen and litigants, to take an oath acknowledging its legitimacy. This was no easy request. In the first place Parliament itself had, throughout the first Civil War, insisted on the sacrosanctity of the king's person. In the second place the king had been tried by an arbitrary, or 'prerogative', court, despite the fact that the Long Parliament had set out to abolish all such courts. In the third, Parliament itself could scarcely claim to be a legitimate representative of the people once Pride's Purge had given power to a minority within it, those willing to sanction the execution of the king. Worst of all though, in the eyes of most contemporaries, was the fact that the new Engagement Oath that Parliament required seemed directly at odds with previous oaths taken by Parliament's supporters, and above all with the Solemn League and Covenant of 1643, in which they had sworn not only to abolish episcopacy, but also 'to preserve and defend the King's Majesty's person and authority'.

We, of course, expect public policy to alter in the light of changing circumstances, and reserve the right to transfer our own allegiances from one party to another. But people in the seventeenth century did not only have to satisfy their consciences (as we do) before changing principles and commitments. They were often also obliged to ask themselves whether they were justified in going back upon a solemn oath. At the Putney Debates the Levellers and the army officers spent as much time debating whether the Agreement of the People was contrary to the army's existing engagements, or sworn undertakings, as they did in discussing what seems to us the substantive issue of the franchise. Later, after the revolution of 1688, the wording of the oath accepting the new government was similarly to prove a major issue of contention, provoking the non-juror movement. Oaths were, after all, as Locke said, 'the bonds of human society': to break them was to endanger the social order and to fly in the face of God's commands.[79]

Faced with the difficulty of justifying its actions, Parliament argued that the establishment of a Protestant Commonwealth would guarantee low taxes and prosperity, since monarchy and Catholicism were dependent upon extravagance and privilege, and raised a cry which was to echo through the eighteenth century: 'No popery, no wooden shoes.'[80] Parliament's stress upon the worldly benefits of republican government was taken up by its supporters, who came close to advocating a more secular approach to politics. In defence of the new regime Marchamont Nedham argued that all governments took their origin from acts of arbitrary violence, and that any authority, once established, was entitled to obedience, a view which has been termed *de factoism*. Anthony Ascham, in defence of the same view, argued that people are entitled to do almost anything to save their own skins (except, perhaps, swear false oaths), and that one should accept whatever government can best provide one with protection. (He was to go on to act contrary to the spirit of his advice by accepting the post of Commonwealth ambassador to Spain, in which exposed position he was quickly assassinated.)

It was as a contribution to the Engagement Debate that Hobbes wrote *Leviathan*. It is worth noting in this context that Hobbes devoted half of *Leviathan*, far more than in any of his previous works, to a discussion of religion.[81] Contemporaries, unlike recent commentators, were nearly unanimous in regarding that discussion as an attack upon any genuine Christian faith. Hobbes's ostensible purpose was to demonstrate that true Christianity was fundamentally different from the religion advocated by Catholics, Anglicans and Presbyterians (indeed Hobbes's materialism and mortalism led him to adopt theological positions which are more reminiscent of the views of radicals such as Winstanley than of the traditional teachings of the Church of England),[82] and in particular differed markedly from conventional Christianity in requiring an unquestioning outward obedience to secular authority, even in matters of faith. In this respect Hobbes's argument was a response not only to the role that Christian principles were playing in the Engagement Debate, but more broadly to the role that religion had played in legitimating the revolt against Charles I. It took the form it did, however, because for the first time he felt free to propose an appropriate theology to be adopted by the state. In the past his principles had obliged him to defend the established religion – in *The Elements of Law* (1640), for example, he had hardly dared go beyond declaring his acceptance of the Thirty-nine Articles – while now the establishment of a new state left him free to argue for the re-establishment of Christianity on new foundations.

In Hobbes's view the execution of the king was an irrelevance, for his military defeat had rendered him incapable of fulfilling the primary function of a ruler, that of providing protection by instilling fear. In the eyes of most people, by contrast, it was the execution of God's anointed, a view which was reinforced by the most successful work of political propaganda produced in the seventeenth century, the *Eikon Basilike*, the apocryphal political and religious testament of Charles I.[83] Many of those – one has only to think of Milton and Baxter – who supported the establishment of a Commonwealth were convinced that the arguments from religious principle did not tell in favour of a king who was suspected of collusion with Catholic rebels.[84] Nevertheless, the Engagement Debate invited a secular and cynical approach to questions of governmental legitimacy. Among Parliament's supporters the main beneficiaries of such a situation were bound to be the few genuine opponents of monarchy, for they could offer legitimacy to the new Commonwealth and their Machiavellian heritage placed them in an excellent position to exploit the new political realism which, for those uninfected by millenarian enthusiasm, seemed to offer the only hope of explaining a revolutionary upheaval which few had sought and which had resulted in an outcome which almost no one had intended. It is this desire to make sense of events which seems, for example, to have led James Harrington, who had been a close associate of the king in his last days, to explore the republican heritage with new eyes.

The term 'republican', however, is potentially a misleading one. The standard English translation of *res publica* was *commonwealth*, a term which had always been applied to England under royal rule. The term *republic* was new in the seventeenth century, while *republicanism* dates to 1689 and *republican*, in the sense of opponent of monarchy, is later. Indeed republicans or Commonwealthmen were not generally opposed to all forms of monarchy: they usually favoured a mixed constitution, and were thus often willing to accept a constitutional monarchy provided the king was answerable to the people.

There are three strains to seventeenth-century republicanism that may usefully be separated (and are on occasion to be found apart from each other). The first is the analysis of politics in terms of selfish interests and power blocks, an analysis often derived from Machiavelli and popularized in England by authors such as Raleigh and Bacon. The second is the idealization of civic virtue, the virtue of a Cato or a Brutus, usually presented in terms of the superiority of public benefit over private advantage and sometimes dramatized in the idealization of tyrannicide (as in Sexby's *Killing Noe Murder*). The third is the advocacy of a government accountable to the people, often modelled on ancient Rome or contemporary Venice. There was, however, no necessary harmony between these three elements. Machiavellian analysis of politics could be combined with the defence of monarchy (as in Clarendon);[85] the praise of civic virtue could be (indeed generally was) combined with an aristocratic contempt for the ill-discipline of the mob or the people at large; and the notion of government accountability could often be combined with admiration for the military conquests of republican Rome (as in Machiavelli and Sidney), and so with support for despotic rule over the Scots, the Irish and other foreigners.

At the heart of republican thinking lay a problem, that of reconciling an emphasis upon self-interest as the motor of politics, on the one hand, with an idealization of civic virtue as the source of political legitimacy, on the other. Many of Machiavelli's followers, often presenting themselves under the guise of admirers of Tacitus, treated self-interest as an iron law governing all political behaviour. If this was true it was hard to see what place could be found for civic virtue. For others selfishness was the consequence of the corruption induced by despotism; republican government required the corporate solidarity of virtuous citizens. But how could freedom be established if, as Milton maintained, none could love freedom but good men, and if despotism had inexorably corrupted antique virtue? For Milton there was no solution to this problem but the exclusion of the unruly multitude from power and the establishment of a virtuous senate whose members would hold power as long as they lived. For Sidney the solution lay in stressing economic self-interest alongside republican virtue: absolutism, as the Rump Parliament had declared, was infallibly associated with heavy taxation and poverty, republican government with low taxes and prosperity. But it was Harrington and his followers who identified a truly novel solution to the problem of harmonizing republican idealism with an emphasis on selfish interests.

In Harrington's view political power depended in the final analysis upon control of a supply of food to support soldiers and their horses. This meant that in most countries (the most important exception being Holland, where grain was in large part imported) political power must lie with those who owned most of the land. Different patterns of landownership thus led to different patterns of governmental authority, and Harrington argued that where, as in England, the bulk of land had come, as a consequence of the decline of the feudal aristocracy, to be held not by a few lords but by a large number of commoners, power must in the end lie with some form of representative institution.

Armed with this pioneering form of historical determinism, Harrington went on to present a complicated array of constitutional recommendations. In the first place, he maintained that if one could stabilize the pattern of landholding one could stabilize the distribution of power through society. In order to achieve this end he advocated an agrarian law governing the inheritance and acquisition of land. Secondly, since men were bound to pursue wealth and power, a stable popular government depended upon the harmonization of private interests with public benefits. Various measures, Harrington believed, could be taken to encourage this, in particular the rotation of offices to prevent a distinction between the interests of rulers and ruled, and the secret ballot to discourage intimidation and corruption. A virtuous commonwealth could, through such mechanisms, be constructed out of selfish individuals: what was needed, Harrington repeatedly insisted, was not good men but good laws, and his favourite example of the simplicity of the mechanisms required to harmonize selfishness with the common good was that of two country girls dividing a cake. One had only to say to the other, 'You cut and I'll choose', to make it in her friend's interest that the cake should be divided as equally as possible.[86] On the strength of this analogy Harrington advocated an elected senate of the wealthy and wise to propose legislation, or cut, and a popular assembly to vote upon such proposals, or choose.

Harrington could thus claim to have produced a republican theory which did not need to appeal to civic virtue; and in achieving this goal he had also produced a secular account of politics in which worldly interests acted as social cement. This new paradigm was expressed by Harrington's disciple John Trenchard in terms which could scarcely have been improved upon by Bentham or James Mill:

> There is nothing in which the generality of mankind are so much mistaken as when they talk of government. The different effects of it are obvious to everyone, but few can trace its causes. Most men having in- digested ideas of the nature of it, attribute all public miscarriages to the corruption of mankind. They think the whole mass is infected, that it's impossible to make any reformation, and so submit patiently to their country's calamities, or else share in the spoil: whereas complaints of this kind are as old as the world, and every age has thought their own the worst. We have not only our own experience, but the example of all times, to prove that men in the same circumstances will do the same things, call them by what names of distinction you please. A government is a mere piece of clockwork, and having such springs and wheels must act after such a manner: and therefore the art is to constitute it so that it must move to the public advantage. It is certain that every man will act for his own interest; and all wise governments are founded upon that principle: So that this whole mystery is only to make the interests of the governors and governed the same. In an absolute monarchy, where the whole power is in one man, his interest will be only regarded; in an aristocracy the interest of a few; and in a free government the interest of everyone.[87]

For Trenchard, writing *A Short History of Standing Armies in England* (1698), the central problem of contemporary politics was that Eng- land seemed once more to be in danger of succumbing to absolute monarchy (despite a distribution of landed wealth which favoured representative government) because the king had a standing army at his command and, more dangerously, because he was in a position to employ the revenues of taxation to corrupt the members of the

House of Commons with places and perquisites. In focusing on the problem of corruption Trenchard and his fellow neo-Harringtonians were not, however, appealing to a traditional republican conception of civic virtue, but to Harrington's theory of the regulation of private interests to bring them into harmony with the public welfare.[88] The neo-Harringtonians, however, were well aware that they faced difficulties of a new order because they were dealing not only with a rapidly commercializing society, but also with an expanding state.

Where in 1600 England had been economically backward and politically feeble, by 1700 a powerful state was beginning to take shape within the most advanced economy in the world. In the course of the seventeenth century London's population more than doubled, to over half a million. Between 1660 and 1700 exports increased by more than one half, while imports increased by only just over a third. In the same period the total tonnage of the merchant marine approximately doubled. By 1700 re-exports of colonial goods represented 30 per cent of the value of all exports: England was undergoing a commercial revolution as she became, in Charles Wilson's words, 'a world entrepôt, serving not only Europe but the extra-European world'.[89] This economic revolution was accompanied by a revolution in the financial resources of the state. When Charles II came to the throne in 1660 his income was set at £1·2 million a year; between 1688 and 1702 William III's income averaged almost £4 million a year; while by 1714 the government, which had been spending far beyond its income during successive European wars, was successfully carrying a debt of £36 million. All this was made possible by new taxes (on beer and windows), by new financial institutions (the Bank of England and the Stock Exchange), and by a new army of government servants (the customs, for example, ceased to be farmed out after 1671).

This transformation of the financial resources of government was soon to make possible the fifty-year rule of the Whig oligarchy, thanks to the monopoly of government patronage obtained by Walpole. Faced with such changes, political thinkers were bound to address themselves to new problems. To many of them the transformation of their society seemed evidence of advancing moral decay. In 1690 the first of the Societies for the Reformation of Manners was established in Tower Hamlets to encourage godliness and moral discipline. The movement's supporters were convinced that 'the public affairs of a nation must suffer certain detriment where wickedness runs loose and unrestrained', but they would have been shocked at the suggestion that the only secure foundation for national greatness was not virtue but a duly restrained vice.[90] This view, which stood in opposition to the lengthy tradition that had aspired to establish a godly society, had however already been expressed in *The Grounds of Sovereignty and Greatness* (1675), whose author had argued that as a result of the Fall people had become

> void of charity, yet still remained full of wants and necessities, and depending of one another in a great number of things. In order to the supplying these necessities, cupidity has taken the place of charity, and effects it after a manner which we cannot enough admire, and whereunto the ordinary charity could not arrive. For example, you see spread all over the country persons who are ready to assist you when you travel. They prepare your lodgings, and other accommodation. You command them what you please, and they not only obey, but acknowledge for a favour that you vouchsafe to accept their services. They excuse not themselves from any attendance you require. What could be more admirable than these persons, were they animated by charity? But it is cupidity which makes them act, and that with so good a grace and excess of duty that (I say) they look on it as a boon to have been employed in serving you.
>
> Where is that charity which is contented to build a house for you, replenish it with movables, adorn it with tapestry, and put the key thereof into your hands? Cupidity will do it, and cheerfully too. What charity will run to the Indies for medicines, stoop to the meanest employments, and not refuse the basest and most painful offices? Cupidity will perform all this without grudging.
>
> There is nothing, then, whereby greater services are done to men than by their cupidity itself. But that this cupidity may be fitly disposed to render them, it must be limited by something, since of itself it has neither bound nor measure, and, instead of being subservient to human society, would ruin and destroy it. There is no excess whereof it is not capable, being left alone and without check or tie; its natural inclination and bent tending towards injustice, rapine, murder and the greatest disorders.
>
> It was necessary, therefore, that some art should be found out for the regulating cupidity; and this art is the *politic order*, or *state-government*, which restrains cupidity by the fear of punishment, and applies it to the uses of civil society. This order gives us merchants, physicians, artists, and generally whatever conduces to the pleasures or satisfies the necessities of life. For which reason we have a great obligation to the preservers thereof, viz. such as hold that authority which regulates and maintains the state.
>
> People would admire a man that should tame lions, bears, tigers, and other savage beasts, and make them fit for service. This wonder is done by

state-government, since that men filled with cupidity are worse than tigers, bears, or lions; each one would devour the rest, but yet by means of the laws and policy they are tamed after such sort that services as useful are performed by them as could proceed from the purest charity.

State government is the most excellent invention found out by men, whereby each particular amongst them obtains more convenience than the greatest and richest king could do, were this order discomposed. How were it possible without this invention that any one man (whatever wealth he possessed, or how many servants soever attended him) should enjoy those advantages which now a citizen of London does with the rent of one thousand pounds per annum . . .? It may be said with truth that there are a million men who labour for him. He may reckon in the number of his servants all the artisans of England, and even those of neighbour countries. . . . These, who work for him, are not burdensome or incommodious to him in the least. He is neither obliged to provide for their necessities nor to make their fortunes. There is no need for superior officers to govern, or inferior to serve them; or if there be, he is not troubled therewith. Who is able to extol these advantages enough, which render the condition of private persons equal to that of kings, and, dispensing with the anxieties that attend great riches, afford them all sorts of convenience? [91]

I have quoted at length from *The Grounds of Sovereignty and Greatness* because it is perhaps the first elaborated account in English of a society, not just of wicked men restrained by good laws, nor merely of self-interest made to coincide with the public good, but of men united by the hidden hand of the market acting, within a regime of law and order enforced by government, as the primary regulator of selfish interests and transmuting private advantages into public benefits.[92] Its author may be said to have provided in embryo the key arguments of the opening chapters of Adam Smith's *Wealth of Nations*, dealing with the division of labour and the social benefits of the market. *The Grounds of Sovereignty and Greatness*, however, was not the work of an Englishman, but a translation of an essay by a French Catholic theologian, Pierre Nicole, an associate of Pascal.[93] By a strange paradox it is to the Jansenist Nicole that we owe the first clear formulation of the new philosophy of commercial society.

In France, Nicole's arguments were developed by Pierre Bayle in his *Pensées diverses sur la comète* of 1682, the first attempt in print to argue that atheists were as likely to be good citizens as other men. Far from being of necessity like savage beasts, they were greedy, jealous and proud just like other men, but equally capable of being domesticated by the fear of punishment and the hope of gain in this world. In Bayle's view the prospect of punishment and reward in the next life was largely irrelevant to the explanation of human behaviour. There were all too many examples of people who were both wicked and credulous. In fact most people responded to the prospect of immediate pleasures and pains, not long-term considerations of salvation and damnation.

Bayle's arguments were taken up in England by a Dutchman, Bernard de Mandeville, whose *Fable of the Bees* presented in systematic terms the paradox which lay at the heart of the work of Nicole and Bayle: that private vices are the only reliable source of public benefits. Mandeville's arguments shocked his contemporaries, who were not, I am afraid, above referring to him as 'Man Devil'. He outraged the Societies for the Reformation of Manners by propounding a scheme for the public management of prostitution, a scheme which he freely acknowledged aimed to preserve the virtue of women in general by sacrificing the virtue of a few: honest women would be relieved of the attentions of both the lovesick and the concupiscent by giving men ample opportunities to satisfy their natural drives in hygienic and well-managed surroundings.[94] Where the Societies for the Reformation of Manners wanted citizens to become god-fearing and church-attending, Mandeville proposed that the execution of criminals at Tyburn, currently an occasion for drunkenness and merriment, should be conducted in a more intimidating fashion, thus making the law a more effective deterrent.[95] Instead of praising modesty, frugality and industry in his *Fable of the Bees* (an insect traditionally appealed to as an exemplar of social virtue) Mandeville maintained that prosperity would be impossible without the stimulus the economy received from the vanity of fashion-conscious housewives, from the gluttony of drunken husbands and from the lazy self-indulgence of the unproductive and idle rich.

Mandeville's argument was that Christian virtue – which involved the abnegation of self-interest – was incompatible with prosperity and military might. This did not mean that people could be left, free of religious intimidation, to pursue their natural inclinations: he disagreed violently with Shaftesbury who had sought to argue that people were by nature sociable and benevolent. But in Mandeville's view people themselves had, as Nicole had maintained, to invent the means of regulating their naturally anti-social instincts. Virtue, in his view, was an artificial construct, one that must be grounded in natural

vice, and that derived its justification entirely from its socially ben-
eficent effects: effects which could never follow upon the adoption
of Christian values.

Like Harrington, Nicole and Bayle, all of whom owed a debt to
Hobbes, Mandeville saw political society as a means for the artificial
regulation and harmonization of competing interests. For Mandeville, as for Nicole, the key to this process lay in commercial
exchange. Once market relations had been established, the economy,
at least as far as the domestic market was concerned, could be allowed
to be self-regulating. Mandeville not only described the division of
labour as the key to increased productivity, as Petty had done before
him; he also argued that the market automatically distributed people
and resources to the employment in which they would be most
useful.[96] He was able to develop such a clear conception of the
market mechanism because nearly all his arguments were concerned
with the principle of unintended consequences. Just as the pursuit of
private profit could lead, through the workings of the market, to
public prosperity, so prostitution could lead, through public brothels,
to female chastity, and self-interested legislators could be made,
within a well-constructed constitution, to act as if they had the welfare
of the public at heart.

Mandeville's view of human nature leaves no scope for a genuine
concern for others. It was to be left to Hume to formulate a subtle
blend of the principles of Mandeville and those of Shaftesbury, whereby morality could be rooted in self-interest but could include a ben
evolent concern for others. His view of politics leaves no more
scope for appeals to rights or for the pursuit of social equality than
does that of Bentham. His arguments may not be convincing today,
when most philosophers are happy to rely on arguments that Bentham would have dismissed as 'nonsense upon stilts'. But he was
one of the pioneers who first conceived of a secular society, united
not by the fear of God but by the hope of prosperity, and was among
the first to approach the question of how citizens should behave in
terms not of theology and morality but of economics and sociology.
Seen from this point of view, Locke's *Two Treatises* and *The Reasonableness of Christianity* belong to an age of faith; Mandeville's *Fable
of the Bees* to a new age, an age of free-thinkers (the word dates
to 1708), or, in the terminology of the nineteenth century, of
Enlightenment.[97]

Notes

1. A somewhat optimistic view of who was represented in Parliament is provided by D. Hirst, *The Representative of the People?* (Cambridge, 1975).

2. J. P. Kenyon, *The Stuart Constitution, 1603–88* (Cambridge, 1966), pp. 25–6.

3. The Earl of Bristol summarized this traditional view in 1647 as follows: 'By free subjection, I understand when a people live under laws to which they have given a free consent, and not under the mere will of the prince: and that they retain such a property in that which is their own that without their assent or legal forfeiture it cannot be taken from them. And this is a true difference between a free subject and a slave or servant.' Quoted in J. Daly, *Sir Robert Filmer and English Political Thought* (Toronto, 1975), p. 54.

4. C. Russell, *The Crisis of Parliaments* (Oxford, 1971), p. 285.

5. id., 'The Theory of Treason in the Trial of Strafford', *English Historical Review*, LXXX (1965), pp. 30–50 (pp. 41–2).

6. F. Oakley, *Omnipotence, Covenant and Order* (Cornell, 1984).

7. See Peter Wentworth's attack (published in 1598) on those 'who stand so precisely for the absolute power and sovereignty of' Parliament, and as a consequence deny James's right to succeed (J. P. Cooper, 'A Revolution in Tudor History?', *Past and Present*, no. 26 (1963), 110–12 (p. 112)).

8. Filmer's theory of the origins of political power was similar to that previously propounded by Hadrian Saravia: J. P. Sommerville, 'Richard Hooker, Hadrian Saravia, and the Advent of the Divine Right of Kings', *History of Political Thought*, IV (1983), pp. 229–45. A similar view was also put forward by John Maxwell in *Sacro-Sancta Regum Majestas* (Oxford, 1644), pp. 84–6, prior to the publication of Filmer's views.

9. [S. Rutherford], *Lex, Rex* (Barnard Castle, 1644), pp. 111–15, attacking Maxwell.

10. M. Goldie has argued that Filmer's Bodinian absolutism had wide support among royalists in the 1680s ('John Locke and Anglican Royalism', *Political Studies*, XXXI (1983), pp. 61–85 (pp. 69–71)), but he does not claim that his version of patriarchalism was similarly influential.

11. Thus during the formulation of the Petition of Right, Coke, responding to a reference to Bodin, who had argued that the law was dependent upon the will of the sovereign, maintained that 'Magna Carta is such a fellow that will have no sovereign' (J. H. M. Salmon, *The French Religious Wars in English Political Thought* (Oxford, 1959), p. 62).

12. R. B. Seaberg, 'The Norman Conquest and the Common Law: the

Levellers and the Argument from Continuity', *Historical Journal*, XXIV (1981), pp. 791–806.

13. J. A. Guy, 'The Origins of the Petition of Right Reconsidered', *Historical Journal*, XXV (1982), pp. 289–312, throws new light on the constitutional crisis of 1628.

14. R. L. Greaves and R. Zaller (eds.), *Biographical Dictionary of British Radicals in the Seventeenth Century* (3 vols., Brighton, 1982–4), art. Phelips; Russell, 'The Theory of Treason', op. cit., p. 39.

15. [J. Lilburne], *England's Birth Right Justified* [1645], p. 36 (facsimile in W. Haller (ed.), *Tracts on Liberty in the Puritan Revolution*, 3 vols., New York, 1934).

16. Quite apart from the crisis provoked by the Five Knights' case and the Petition of Right, it might be thought that much of the political theory of the time was doomed by the new science's assault upon the Aristotelian conception of a Great Chain of Being. It was in 1611 that Donne described in *An Anatomy of the World* how 'new philosophy calls all in doubt', and went on from describing the revolution in science to express fears for the dissolution of social order: ' 'Tis all in pieces, all coherence gone; / All just supply and all relation. / Prince, subject, father, son are things forgot, / For every man alone thinks he hath got / To be a Phoenix, and that then can be / None of that kind of which he is but he.'
  But few were as quick to respond to Galileo's discoveries as Donne. Looking back, Aubrey believed that 'Till about the year 1649 [the year of the king's execution] . . . 'twas held a strange presumption for a man to attempt an innovation in learnings. . . . 'Twas held a sin to make a scrutiny into the ways of nature' (*Aubrey's Brief Lives*, ed. O. L. Dick (Harmondsworth, 1962), pp. 27–8). In the early seventeenth century natural and political philosophy were linked by an elaborate network of correspondences. To change one was therefore to change the other, and in the long run the scientific revolution was bound to encourage a revolution in political philosophy. In the short run, however, traditional ideas of hierarchy survived largely intact until 1642, and the Civil War probably did more to change most people's views of nature than the scientific revolution had done to change their view of society.

17. [D.Digges], *The Unlawfulnesse of Subjects Taking Up Armes against Their Soveraigne* (1643: January 1644), p. 113.

18. Russell, 'The Theory of Treason', op. cit., pp. 47–8.

19. R. R. Palmer, *The Age of the Democratic Revolution* (2 vols., Princeton, 1959–64), I, pp. 13–20.

20. *OED*, s.v. democracy; for Nevile's use of 'democracy' as roughly equivalent to a modern use of 'republic', see F. Raab, *The English Face of Machiavelli* (London, 1964), pp. 220–221.

21. Harrington's references to 'democracy' are indexed in *The Political Works of James Harrington*, ed. J. G. A. Pocock (Cambridge, 1977). See esp. pp. 212, 263, 479, 676, 858. Harrington is criticized as a proponent of 'democracy' (but meaning apparently republicanism) by the publisher of Nevile's *Plato Redivivus* (*Two English Republican Tracts*, ed. C. Robbins (Cambridge, 1969), p. 69).

22. F. Amati and T. Aspromourgos, 'Petty *contra* Hobbes', *Journal of the History of Ideas*, XLVI (1985), pp. 127–32, a translation of *The Petty Papers*, ed. Marquis of Lansdowne (2 vols., London, 1927), II, pp. 35–9.

23. J. Locke, *Two Treatises of Government* (1689), II, para. 6.

24. R. Tuck, *Natural Rights Theories: Their Origin and Development* (Cambridge, 1979). For Sexby, see below, page 373.

25. J. Dunn, 'Consent in the Political Theory of John Locke', in Dunn, *Political Obligation in Its Historical Context* (Cambridge, 1980), pp. 29–52; J. Richards, L. Mulligan and J. K. Graham, '"Property" and "People": Political Usages of Locke and Some Contemporaries', *Journal of the History of Ideas*, XLII (1981, pp. 29–51.

26. F. Suarez, *De Legibus ac Deo Legislatore* (1612), III, 4, 1; *Defensio Fidei Catholicae* (1613), VI, 4, 15: in *Selections from Three Works of Francisco Suarez*, trans. G. L. Williams *et al.* (Oxford, 1944), pp. 383, 718.

27. J. H. Franklin has shown that the Tories challenged the Whigs to argue that all the people should be represented in a constituent assembly after the revolution of 1688 (*John Locke and the Theory of Sovereignty*, (Cambridge, 1978), p. 103). Franklin assumes that the idea of the dissolution of government, so important to Locke, reaches him from Lawson. It is worth noting that Parliament had discussed whether the constitution was being dissolved (20 May 1642), that Hobbes writes of governments being dissolved, and that the dissolution of government is the subject of the Harringtonian *Humble Petition of Divers Well Affected Persons* (July 1659), prior to the publication of Lawson's *Politica Sacra et Civilis*. Wildman's *Letter to a Friend* is therefore not necessarily directly influenced by Lawson, although, as Mark Goldie has shown, Lawson was sometimes explicitly referred to by authors employing the idea of the dissolution of government ('The Roots of True Whiggism, 1688–94', *History of Political Thought*, I, pp. 195–236 (p. 215)). Locke's use of the idea of dissolution, even if it derives originally from Lawson, may well do so only indirectly.

28. H. Parker, *Observations Upon Some of His Majesties Late Answers and Expresses* (1642), in H. Erskine-Hill and G. Storey (eds.), *Revolutionary Prose of the English Civil War* (Cambridge, 1983), pp. 35–63 (pp. 46–7). See, in general, C. Hill, 'The Poor and the People in Seventeenth-Century England', in F. Krantz (ed.), *History From Below* (Montreal, 1985). pp. 75–93.

29. H. Fern[e], *The Resolving of Conscience* (Cambridge, 1642), p. 25.

30. C. Herle, *A Fuller Answer to a Treatise Written by Dr. Ferne* (1642), p. 25. Two radical parliamentarians were, however, soon to be tempted by Ferne's argument, despite their anxiety as to its implications: see *Plaine English* (1643) and J. Burroughs, 'A Briefe Answer to Dr. Ferne's Booke', in his *The Glorious Name of God* (1643).

31. J. Spelman, *A View of a Printed Book Intituled Observations* (Oxford, 1643): excerpts in A. Sharp (ed.), *Political Ideas of the English Civil Wars, 1641–49* (Harlow, 1983), pp. 111–12. Similar arguments recurred in the Exclusion crisis: R. Ashcraft, 'The *Two Treatises* and the Exclusion Crisis', in R. Ashcraft and J. G. A. Pocock, *John Locke* (Los Angeles, 1980), pp. 25–114 (pp. 68–72).

32. D. Digges, *The Unlawfulnesse of Subjects Taking Up Armes* (Oxford, 1644), p. 151.

33. T. Hobbes, *De Cive*, ch. 12, para. 8.

34. F. D. Dow, *Radicalism in the English Revolution, 1640–60* (Oxford, 1985), pp. 18–19.

35. J. Maxwell, *Sacro-Sancta Regum Majestas* (Oxford, 1644), esp. pp. 95–101, 146–9, 173–8.

36. B. Tierney, *Religion, Law, and the Growth of Constitutional Thought, 1150–1650* (Cambridge, 1982); F. Oakley, 'On the Road from Constance to 1688: The Political Thought of John Major and George Buchanan', *Journal of British Studies*, 11 (1962), pp. 1–31; id., 'Figgis, Constance and the Divines of Paris', *American Historical Review*, LXX (1965), pp. 673–90.

37. J. Major, *A History of Greater Britain*, trans. A. Constable, *Publications of the Scottish History Society*, x (Edinburgh, 1892), bk IV, ch. 17, p. 215.

38. An argument of this sort was employed by William Ball in *Tractatus de Iure Regnandi et Regni* (1645), pp. 13–15: discussed in Tuck, *Natural Rights Theories*, p. 148. Spelman and Rutherford had similarly seen the possibility of appealing from Parliament to the constituencies (see notes 31 and 41), and the idea was later taken up by Lawson (Franklin, *John Locke and the Theory of Sovereignty*, op. cit., pp. 74–5).

39. C. Condren, 'Democracy and the *Defensor Pacis*', *Il pensiero politico*, XIII (1980), pp. 301–16.

40. G. Buchanan, *De Iure Regni apud Scotos* (1579), trans. J. H. Burns in 'The Political Ideas of George Buchanan', *Scottish Historical Review*, XXX (1951), pp. 60–68, p. 64.

41. Rutherford, *Lex, Rex*, op. cit., esp. pp. 58–62, 152. The Elizabethan Presbyterian John Field had also recognized an inalienable right in the people as a whole when Parliament acted against the word of God: 'Seeing we cannot compass these things [i.e. church reform] by suit nor dispute, it is

the multitude and people that must bring the discipline to pass which we desire' (P. Collinson, 'John Field and Elizabethan Puritanism', in S. T. Bindoff, J. Hurstfield and C. H. Williams (eds.), *Elizabethan Government and Society* (London, 1961), pp. 127–62).

42.   See esp. Q. Skinner, *The Foundations of Modern Political Thought* (2 vols., Cambridge, 1978), and id., 'The Origins of the Calvinist Theory of Revolution', in B. Malament (ed.), *After the Reformation* (Philadelphia, 1980), pp. 309–30.

43.   Franklin, *John Locke and the Theory of Sovereignty*, op. cit., *passim*.

44.   G. Lawson, *Politica Sacra et Civilis* (1660), p. 383.

45.   C. Thompson, 'Maximilian Petty and the Putney Debate on the Franchise', *Past and Present*, no. 88 (1980), pp. 63–9.

46.   K. Thomas, 'The Levellers and the Franchise', in G. E. Aylmer (ed.), *The Interregnum* (London, 1972), pp. 57–78.

47.   It seems that it made its second appearance in R. Overton, *Appeale from the Degenerate Representative Body . . . to the Free People* (July 1647), and was taken up a few days later in J. Lilburne, *Jonah's Cry from the Whale's Belly* (July 1647): 'For if, as they have often said, *that tyranny be resistable*, then it is resistable in a Parliament as well as a king' (p. 4; see also pp. 13, 15).

48.   On this episode see P. B. Anderson, 'George Wither and the Regalia', *Philological Quarterly*, XIV (1935), pp. 366–8, and, with an expression of scepticism, A. Pritchard, 'George Wither and the Sale of the Estate of Charles I', *Modern Philology*, LXXVIII (1980), pp. 370–81. On Wither in general, see C. Hill, 'George Wither and John Milton', in *English Renaissance Studies Presented to Dame Helen Gardner* (Oxford, 1980), pp. 212–27.

49.   J. Milton, *The Readie and Easie Way to Establish a Free Commonwealth*, in Erskine-Hill and Storey (eds.), *Revolutionary Prose . . .*, op. cit., pp. 203–29 (pp. 218, 220).

50.   Apart from the royalists' propagandists, the most immediate precedents were provided by *Plaine English* and Burroughs's 'Briefe Answer'. Other precedents might be sought. Thus 'Euctatus Philodemius', in *The Original and End of Civil Power* (1649) (reprinted in Temple of Religion and Tower of Peace, *Pamphlets on Religion and Democracy, Sixteenth to Nineteenth Centuries* (San Francisco, 1940), pp. 181–219) appealed to Keckermann as having argued, 'If none of the governors of the Commonwealth will heed the welfare of his country, then the subjects, or people, may choose some one, or other, to be an avenger and restrainer of such a tyranny' (p. 214). However, he regards this position, which he adopts as his own, as being quite distinct from the arguments of those who speak 'as if the bulk of people, in their moliminous confused body, were the supreme and sovereign power' (p. 181). He differs from Keckermann, moreover, in that where he defends the House

of Commons' right, as representative of the people, to carry through a constitutional revolution, Keckermann had insisted that if a ruler was deposed the next in line to the throne should inherit, thus preserving the constitution intact (B. Keckermann, *Systema Disciplinae Politicae* (Hanover, 1608), bk 1, ch. 28, pp. 431–2).

It is possible that a genuine anticipation of the Leveller position is to be found in a passage where the Jesuit Cardinal R. Bellarmine talks of the right of the multitude to change the form of their government (*Disputationes de Controversiis Christianae Religionis* (1599), 11, iii, ch. 6; in R. Bellarmine, *Scritti Politici*, ed. C. Giacon (Bologna, 1950), p. 15). I doubt, however, whether Bellarmine meant to assert a Lockean conception of popular sovereignty. He probably assumed that in constitutional monarchies the Estates were the infallible representatives of the multitude.

51.   *Puritanism and Liberty*, ed. A. S. P. Woodhouse (London, 1928), p. 2.

52.   B. Worden, 'Classical Republicanism and the Puritan Revolution', in *History and Imagination*, ed. H. Lloyd-Jones *et al.* (London, 1981), pp. 182–200 (p. 182).

53.   On Walwyn and Overton, see in particular J. Frank, *The Levellers* (Cambridge, Mass., 1955). I hope to deal elsewhere with the difficult problem of Walwyn's attitude to Christianity.

54.   J. Locke, *Two Treatises of Government*, 11, para. 225.

55.   *The Original and End*, op. cit., pp. 211–12.

56.   C. Hill, 'The Many Headed Monster', in id., *Change and Continuity in Seventeenth Century England* (London, 1977), pp. 181–204.

57.   B. Manning, *The English People and the English Revolution* (London, 1976).

58.   Tuck, *Natural Rights Theories . . .*, op. cit., ch. 6.

59.   D. P. Gauthier, *The Logic of Leviathan* (Oxford, 1969), p. 112. On the differences between *De Cive* and *Leviathan* see also M. Forsyth, 'Thomas Hobbes and the Constituent Power of the People', *Political Studies*, xxix (1981), pp. 191–203, with a reply by J. Sanderson, ibid., xxx (1982), pp. 553–6.

60.   K. Brown, 'The Artist of the *Leviathan* Title-Page', *British Library Journal*, iv (1978), pp. 24–36.

61.   Readers of *De Cive* had not always realized the extent to which Hobbes's arguments differed from those of conventional royalists in leaving no scope for loyalty to a defeated ruler: see M. M. Goldsmith, 'Picturing Hobbes's Politics', *Journal of the Warburg and Courtauld Institutes*, xliv (1981), pp. 232–7.

62.   D. Underdown, *Pride's Purge: Politics in the Puritan Revolution* (Oxford, 1971).

63.   I have argued elsewhere that the English Civil War was the first true

revolution in modern Europe: D. Wootton, 'Continental Rebellions and the English Revolution', *Dalhousie Review*, LXIII (1983), pp. 349–57.

64. Maxwell, *Sacro-Sancta*, p. 2. On the history of this view, which was reinforced by both the Reformation and the Counter-Reformation, see D. Wootton, 'The Fear of God in Early Modern Political Theory', *Historical Papers 1983* (Canadian Historical Association), pp. 56–80.

65. J. Locke, 'Essay Concerning Toleration', in *Locke: Scritti editi e inediti sulla toleranza*, ed. C. A. Viano (Turin, 1961), p. 86.

66. *Halifax: Complete Works*, ed. J. P. Kenyon (Harmondsworth, 1969), p. 67. Halifax, who had a reputation as 'a bold and determined atheist' (ibid., p. 35), appears to have believed that human weakness required the invention of religion (p. 204). His views on religion (e.g. pp. 272–6) are reminiscent of those of Charron: see D. Wootton, 'Early Modern Unbelief', *History Workshop*, no. 20 (1985), pp. 82–100.

67. C. Hill, *The World Turned Upside Down* (London, 1972), ch. 8.

68. A. S. P. Woodhouse (ed.), *Puritanism and Liberty* (London, 1938), p. 161. See also W. Walwyn, *Toleration Justified and Persecution Condemned* (1646), in *Pamphlets on Religion and Democracy* (San Francisco, 1940), p. 169; R. Overton, *The Picture of the Counsel of State* (1649), in A. L. Morton (ed.), *Freedom in Arms* (London, 1975), pp. 221–3.

69. R. Williams, *The Bloody Tenent Yet More Bloody* (1652), in id., *Complete Writings* (7 vols., New York, 1963), III, p. 203.

70. A recent article by S. A. State ('Text and Context: Skinner, Hobbes and Theistic Natural Law', *Historical Journal*, XXVIII (1985), pp. 27–50) seeks to locate Hobbes within the tradition of theistic natural-law theorizing. Hobbes, of course, presents his view of natural law as theistic; but it is also evident that someone who denied the existence of divine providence would, if he accepted Hobbes's arguments, behave no differently from a theist. For Hobbes proof of immortality and knowledge of God's decrees are an inessential supplement to the calculation of rational self-interest, a supplement unavailable to rational men in a state of nature. It is this which places Hobbes outside the theistic tradition as understood by contemporaries (see Q. Skinner, 'Hobbes's *Leviathan*, *Historical Journal*, VII (1964), pp. 321–33). Harrington similarly appealed to theistic arguments, while simultaneously dismissing them as unnecessary: see below, page 408.

71. On the possibility of a non-theistic account of the law of nature, see *Essay Concerning Human Understanding*, bk. II, ch. 38, paras. 10–12, and below page 485. The contrast between Hobbes and Locke is well drawn by D. Gauthier, 'Why Ought One Obey God?', *Canadian Journal of Philosophy*, VII (1977), pp. 425–46.

72. On providence, see K. Thomas, *Religion and the Decline of Magic*

(London, 1971), pp. 78–112, and B. Worden, 'Providence and Politics in Cromwellian England', *Past and Present*, no. 109 (1985), pp. 55–99.

73. W. Haller, *Foxe's Book of Martyrs and the Elect Nation* (London, 1963).

74. Bacon, *Essays*: 'Of Seditions and Troubles' and 'Of Superstition'.

75. See below, page 476.

76. On the reception of Hooker, see R. Eccleshall, 'Richard Hooker and the Peculiarities of the English', *History of Political Thought*, 11 (1981), pp. 63–117. On Hooker's treatment of consent, see W. J. Cargill-Thompson, *Studies in the Reformation: Luther to Hooker* (London, 1980), pp. 131–91, and the criticism of J. P. Sommerville, 'Richard Hooker, Hadrian Saravia', op. cit.

77. B. S. Capp, *The Fifth Monarchy Men* (London, 1972).

78. The hostility to priestcraft of many republicans, combined with their insistence on the need for a state-approved religion, laid them open to charges of religious indifference and even unbelief. Thus Neville was accused of blasphemy and atheism in the Parliament of 1659 for saying that he preferred reading Cicero to the Bible. See W. Petty, *The Petty Papers* (2 vols., London, 1927), I, ch. 5; H. Neville, *Plato Redivivus*, and W. Moyle, *Essay upon the Constitution of the Roman Government*, in *Two English Republican Tracts*, ed. C. Robbins (Cambridge, 1969). Also M. Goldie, 'The Roots of True Whiggism', op. cit., p. 207, and id., 'John Locke and Anglican Royalism', *Political Studies*, xxxi (1983), pp. 61–85.

79. J. Locke, *The Second Treatise of Government and A Letter Concerning Toleration*, ed. J. W. Gough (Oxford, 1966), p. 158. For a sympathetic treatment of Locke's view, see J. Dunn, 'The Concept of Trust in the Politics of John Locke', in R. Rorty, J. B. Schneewind, Q. Skinner (eds.), *Philosophy in History* (Cambridge, 1984), pp. 279–301.

80. *A Declaration of the Parliament of England* (17 March 1649). As early as Parker's *Observations* poverty and absolutism were presented as inextricably linked together: see Erskine-Hill and Storey (eds.), *Revolutionary Prose*, op. cit., p. 37.

81. L. Strauss, *The Political Philosophy of Hobbes* (Chicago, 1952), pp. 71–8, discusses the changes in Hobbes's treatment of religion from *The Elements* to *Leviathan*.

82. J. G. A. Pocock, 'Time, History and Eschatology in the Thought of Thomas Hobbes', in id., *Politics, Language and Time* (New York, 1971), pp. 148–201.

83. H. R. Trevor-Roper, '*Eikon Basilike*: The Problem of the King's Book', in id., *Historical Essays* (London, 1957), pp. 211–20.

84. W. M. Lamont, *Richard Baxter and the Millennium* (London, 1979), ch. 2;

Milton, *Readie and Easie Way*, in Erskine-Hill and Storey (eds.), *Revolutionary Prose*, op. cit., p. 206.

85. B. H. G. Wormald, *Clarendon* (Cambridge, 1951), pp. 192–4.

86. *The Political Works of James Harrington*, ed. J. G. A. Pocock (Cambridge, 1977), p. 172.

87. J. Trenchard, *A Short History of Standing Armies in England*, in *A Collection of State Tracts Published During the Reign of King William* (3 vols., London, 1705–7), 11, p. 653. On this subject see L. G. Schwoerer, *No Standing Armies!* (Baltimore, 1974).

88. J. R. Goodale, 'J. G. A. Pocock's Neo-Harringtonians: A Reconsideration', *History of Political Thought*, 1 (1980), pp. 237–59; K. Toth, 'Interpretation in Political Theory: The Case of Harrington', *Review of Politics*, XXXVII (1975), pp. 317–39.

89. C. H. Wilson, *England's Apprenticeship, 1603–1763* (London, 1965), p. 161.

90. T. A. Horne, *The Social Thought of Bernard Mandeville* (London, 1978), p. 5.

91. (London, 1675), pp. 19–22.

92. This passage is an anticipation of Locke, *Second Treatise*, paras. 41–2, and of Mandeville, *Fable of the Bees*, p. 11, ll. 13–14 and Remark P, themselves anticipations of Adam Smith, *The Wealth of Nations*, bk. 1, ch. 1, para. 11.

93. This has escaped library cataloguers and J. A. W. Gunn, *Politics and the Public Interest*, (London, 1959), p. 213. There was a second edition of *The Grounds of Sovereignty and Greatness* in 1685, and a different translation of the same essay was also to be found in P. Nicole, *Essays* (3 vols., London, 1677–80).

94. [B. de Mandeville], *A Modest Defence of Public Stews* (1724).

95. B. de Mandeville, *An Enquiry into the Causes of the Present Executions at Tyburn* (London, 1725).

96. M. E. Scribano, *Natura umana e società competitiva* (Milan, 1980), pp. 184–208. Mandeville was conscious, however, of the fragility of the market mechanism. Thus he believed that free education would give the labouring classes false expectations. Under such circumstances the market could be trusted to distribute resources between enterprises, but not between classes. Philanthropy could thus endanger the social order.

97. J. Dunn, 'From Applied Theology to Social Analysis: The Break between John Locke and the Scottish Enlightenment', in I. Hont and M. Ignatieff (eds.), *Wealth and Virtue* (Cambridge, 1983), pp. 119–35.

A Technical Note

I have modernized the spelling and punctuation (including paragraphing) of the texts reprinted here. This practice is sufficiently common to require no comment, were it not for the fact that I have been somewhat more systematic in my modernization than is usual. A few general principles and particular examples are therefore worth noting.

I have departed from convention in uniformly altering third person-singular verb endings in -th to the modern -s (e.g. *giveth* to *gives*, *findeth* to *finds*). This not only makes the texts easier for us to read, but makes it easier to read them as contemporaries would have read them. Both the -th and -s forms were employed in seventeenth-century written English (with the -s form becoming increasingly common), but there is good evidence that it was the -s form which was for the most part used in speech. Thus Richard Hodges writes in 1649: 'Howsoever wee write them thus, leadeth it, maketh it, noteth it, we say lead's it, make's it, note's it.' This principle may not, however, have applied to *hath* and *doth*, so that the imposition of uniformity inevitably involves a measure of anachronism. (See O. Jesperson, *Growth and Structure of the English Language*, Leipzig, 1905, pp. 193–7; C. Barber, *Early Modern English*, London, 1976, pp. 237–41.) I have not, of course, altered the *thou* forms of verbs, as they represent a difference not only of written but of spoken usage. Nor, I might add, have I sought to mend grammatical 'errors', e.g. the combination of single subjects with plural verbs.

The modernization of spelling can involve difficulties where seventeenth-century writers gave the same spelling to what we think of as different words. *Than* was often written *then*, for example. A more difficult instance is the practice of spelling *case* as *cause* when referring to a legal case. The emergence of a new sense of the word *cause* to refer to an allegiance – as in 'the Good Old Cause', 'the common cause' – meant that phrases like 'the Parliamentary cause' took on a new ambiguity: 'the Parliamentary cause' could mean either the case presented by Parliament, or the common objectives of Parliamentarians. When I have felt confident that *cause* means *case*, and could so have been spelt by contemporaries (for both spellings were employed), I have adopted the modern spelling; when in doubt I have preserved *cause*.

It should be noted that I have adopted the modern spelling of names such as that of Machiavelli (often spelt Machiavel or Machiavell), and of all Biblical names, in order to facilitate recognition and, if necessary, recourse to works of reference. I have, however, retained words such as *Switzers* for Swiss.

In modernizing punctuation I have had to face the fact that the unavailability of quotation marks meant that seventeenth-century writers were often careless in distinguishing between a paraphrase and a direct quotation. I have introduced quotation marks where they make it easier to grasp the sense of the passage, rather than wherever I think direct speech may be implied.

The texts are reprinted entire except where dots are employed to indicate excisions. I have however silently suppressed footnotes and margin notes. Sexby and Sidney, for example, give references to their sources: scholars wishing to analyse their reading will want to turn, where possible, to modern standard editions, and failing that, to the original texts. Roger Williams employs margin notes to give a summary of his subject-matter: I have selected from among these suitable 'chapter titles' for the excerpts I have chosen. Letters and words in square brackets represent my own emendations and translations.

I have employed a calendar beginning the year on 1 January when referring to events such as births and deaths which can be precisely dated. Contemporaries, however, began the new year on 25 March, so that the dates recorded on title-pages do not correspond to this calendar. A case in point is King James's speech at Whitehall. Given on 21 March, it was dated 1609 by contemporaries. Since the date can be precisely established I have dated it 1610, but in other cases I have kept to the date given on the title-page, even when it seems likely that the actual date of publication was between 1 January and 24 March.

The key sources for the publishing history of the texts printed here are G. K. Fortescue (ed.), *Catalogue of the Pamphlets . . . Collected by George Thomason* (London, 1908), which gives the dates on which copies of Civil War pamphlets were purchased by Thomason, and, more generally, the short-title catalogues of Pollard and Redgrave (to 1640) and D. C. Wing (1641–1700). Within a few years all the works listed in those volumes – and consequently the first editions of almost all the works reprinted here – will be available in the Ann

Arbor microfilm series. The easy availability of photographic re-productions of first editions makes, I believe, the editorial practices I have adopted here justifiable where once they would have been properly regarded as reprehensible.

In the notes on the texts I have not given places of publication when they are either London or unknown.

CHAPTER ONE

THE DIVINE RIGHT
OF KINGS

1 *An Homily against Disobedience and Wylful Rebellion* (1570)

Homilies were issued by the government and required to be read in churches. They were the only exposition of Christian doctrine heard in those parishes where the minister was not licensed to preach. This particular homily was issued in response to the Northern Rebellion in support of Catholicism and Mary, Queen of Scots, of 1569. It provides a clear summary of the view of political authority which would have been most generally accepted when James I came to the throne, and reminds us that before the news-sheets and pamphlets of the Civil War most even of those who could read would have learnt about politics and political theory from the pulpit and from conversation, rather than from books.

2 James VI and I, *The Trew Law of Free Monarchies* (1598)

James (1566–1625) became king of Scotland in 1567 after his mother's flight to England. He was a notable scholar, partly thanks to the education he had received from his tutor, George Buchanan, one of the leading exponents of tyrannicide. In Scotland the king's power was under constant threat from the nobility and Presbyterian clergy, and it was in defence of an idealized conception of royal authority that James secretly published *The Trew Law of Free Monarchies*. Contemporaries would have accepted that it was appropriate to describe kings as fathers of their people and heads of the body politic, and many would have accepted the doctrine of non-resistance taught by James: in the years before 1570, indeed, very few Protestant theologians had been willing to condone rebellion under any circumstances, although their number had grown in company with the Calvinist revolts in Scotland, France and Holland.

3 James VI and I, *A Speech to the Lords and Commons of the Parliament at White-Hall* (1610)

James succeeded to the throne of England in 1603. In 1610 he had recently been in public controversy with the Jesuit Cardinal Bellarmine over the right of popes to depose kings, and in private conflict with Chief Justice Coke over the right of the common-law courts to act contrary to the king's wishes. Once again James relies upon a conventional set of comparisons between kings, God, fathers and the human body. But his argument is two-edged: on the one hand he maintains that kings in a 'settled kingdom' should abide by the existing laws; on the other he insists on their right to set aside all constitutional restrictions.

4 Robert Filmer, *Observations upon Aristotle's Politiques* (1652)

Sir Robert Filmer (d. 1653) was an obscure gentleman of Kent who was a consistent royalist during the Civil War and began publishing in defence of royal authority in 1648, when the royalist cause was already doomed. He did not acquire notoriety until *Patriarcha* was printed for the first time in 1680, provoking Locke's *Two Treatises*, Sidney's *Discourses Concerning Government,* and Tyrrell's *Patriarcha non Monarcha.* The *Observations* are, like all Filmer's writings, directed against the belief that power originates with, or can be exercised by, the people. The *Directions*, published with them and reprinted here in full, are, like Hobbes's *Leviathan*, a contribution to the Engagement Debate over whether the Commonwealth regime was entitled to obedience (see Chapter 6 below). Filmer's intention was to persuade royalists to accept the new regime, on the grounds (appealed to also by Hobbes and Ascham) that protection and subjection are reciprocal. However, he does not go the full distance in declaring loyalty to the government in power, arguing, for the first occasion in any of his works, that under certain circumstances subjects may have recourse to passive resistance.

5 *The Judgement and Decree of the University of Oxford ... against Certain Pernicious Books and Damnable Doctrines* (1683)

The University of Oxford's decree exemplifies the absolutist and divine-right principles espoused by the restored monarchy: principles that it was hoped to advance by the reprinting of Filmer's works, although they differed from Filmer's in not relying upon arguments from the authority of Adam and in opposing *de factoism*. This document provides a useful summary of the various directions from which divine-right monarchy had been assaulted over the previous eighty years, and a number of the texts it refers to – Baxter's *Holy Commonwealth*, Hunton's *Mixed Monarchy*, Hobbes's *De Cive* – are represented in the chapters which follow. Its immediate occasion was the Rye House Plot, a conspiracy by leading Whigs, who had failed to obtain the exclusion of the Catholic James, Duke of York, from succession to the throne by parliamentary means, to assassinate Charles II and his brother. It thus represents the opposite viewpoint from that presented in the writings of Sidney and Locke.

This decree, which required that the books it referred to be burnt, was itself burnt by order of the House of Lords in 1710 because it was felt that the views expressed in it were difficult, if not impossible, to reconcile with acceptance of the legitimacy of the revolution of 1688.

1 *An Homily against Disobedience and Wylful Rebellion* (1570)

As God the creator and lord of all things appointed his angels and heavenly creatures in all obedience to serve and to honour his majesty, so was it his will that man, his chief creature upon the earth, should live under the obedience of his creator and lord. And for that cause God, as soon as he had created man, gave unto him a certain precept and law, which he (being yet in the state of innocency, and remaining in paradise) should observe as a pledge and token of his due and bounden obedience, with denunciation of death if he did transgress and break the said law and commandment. And as God would have man to be his obedient subject, so did he make all earthly creatures subject unto man, who kept their due obedience unto man so long as man remained in his obedience unto God. In the which obedience if man had continued still, there had been no poverty, no diseases, no sickness, no death, nor other miseries wherewith mankind is now infinitely and most miserably afflicted and oppressed. So here appears the original kingdom of God over angels and man, and universally over all things, and of man over earthly creatures which God had made subject unto him, and withal the felicity and blessed state which angels, man and all creatures had remained in, had they continued in due obedience to God their king. For as long as in this first kingdom the subjects continued in due obedience to God their king, so long did God embrace all his subjects with his love, favour and grace, which to enjoy is perfect felicity.

Whereby it is evident that obedience is the principal virtue of all virtues, and indeed the very root of all virtues and the cause of all felicity. But as all felicity and blessedness should have continued with the continuance of obedience, so with the breach of obedience and breaking in of rebellion, all vices and miseries did withal break in, and overwhelm the world. The first author of which rebellion, the root of all vices and mother of all mischiefs, was Lucifer, first God's most excellent creature, and most bounden subject, who, by rebelling against the majesty of God, of the brightest and most glorious angel is become the blackest and most foulest fiend and devil, and from the height of heaven is fallen into the pit and bottom of hell.

Here you may see the first author and founder of rebellion, and the reward thereof. Here you may see the grand captain and father of all rebels, who, persuading the following of his rebellion against God their creator and lord, unto our first parents, Adam and Eve, brought them in high displeasure with God, wrought their exile and banishment out of Paradise, a place of all pleasure and goodness, into this wretched earth and vale of all misery, procured unto them sorrows of their minds, mischiefs, sickness, diseases, death of their bodies, and, which is far more horrible than all worldly and bodily mischiefs, he had wrought thereby their eternal and everlasting death and damnation, had not God by the obedience of his son, Jesus Christ, repaid that which man by disobedience and rebellion had destroyed, and so of his mercy had pardoned and forgiven him. Of which all and singular the premises the Holy Scriptures do bear record in sundry places.

Thus you do see that neither heaven nor paradise could suffer any rebellion in them, neither be places for any rebels to remain in. Thus became rebellion, as you see, both the first and greatest, and the very root of all other sins, and the first and principal cause both of all worldly and bodily miseries (sorrows, diseases, sicknesses and deaths), and, which is infinitely worse than all these, as is said, the very cause of death and damnation eternal also.

After this breach of obedience to God and rebellion against his majesty, all mischiefs and miseries breaking in therewith and over-flowing the world, lest all things should come into confusion and utter ruin, God forthwith, by laws given unto mankind, repaired again the rule and order of obedience thus by rebellion overthrown, and, besides the obedience due unto his Majesty, he not only ordained that in families and households the wife should be obedient unto her husband, the children unto their parents, the servants unto their masters, but also, when mankind increased and spread itself more largely over the world, he by his Holy Word did constitute and ordain in cities and countries several and special governors and rulers, unto whom the residue of his people should be obedient.

As in reading of the Holy Scriptures we shall find in very many and almost infinite places, as well of the Old Testament as of the New, that kings and princes, as well the evil as the good, do reign by God's ordinance, and that subjects are bound to obey them; that God does give princes wisdom, great power and authority; that God defends them against their enemies and destroys their enemies horribly; that the anger and displeasure of the prince is as the roaring of a lion, and the very messenger of death; and that the subject that provokes him to displeasure sins against his own soul; with many other things concerning both the authority of princes and the duty of subjects. But here let us rehearse two special places out of the New Testament, which may stand instead of all other.

The first out of St Paul's epistle to the Romans, the thirteenth chapter, where he writes thus unto all subjects: 'Let every soul be subject unto the higher powers, for there is no power but of God, and the powers that be are ordained of God. Whosoever therefore resists the power, resists the ordinance of God. And they that resist shall receive to themselves damnation. For princes are not to be feared for good works, but for evil. Wilt thou then be without fear of the power? Do well! So shalt thou have praise of the same. For he is the minister of God for thy wealth. But if thou do evil, fear. For he bears not the sword for nought, for he is the minister of God to take vengeance upon him that does evil. Wherefore you must be subject, not because of wrath only, but also for conscience' sake. For, for this cause you pay also tribute, for they are God's ministers, serving for the same purpose. Give to every man therefore his due: tribute, to whom tribute belongs; custom, to whom custom is due; fear, to whom fear belongs; honour, to whom you owe honour.' Thus far are St Paul's words. The second place is in St Peter's first epistle, at the second chapter, whose words are these: 'Submit yourselves unto all manner ordinance of man for the Lord's sake, whether it be unto the king as unto the chief head, either unto rulers as unto them that are sent of him for the punishment of evil doers, but for the cherishing of them that do well. For so is the will of God, that with well-doing you may stop the mouths of ignorant and foolish men: as free, and not as having the liberty for a cloak of malitiousness, but even as the servants of God. Honour all men, love brotherly fellowship, fear God, honour the king. Servants obey your masters with fear, not only if they be good and courteous, but also though they be froward.' Thus far out of St Peter.

By these two places of the Holy Scriptures, it is most evident that kings, queens and other princes (for he speaks of authority and power, be it in men or women) are ordained of God, are to be obeyed and honoured of their subjects; that such subjects as are disobedient or rebellious against their princes disobey God, and procure their own damnation; that the government of princes is a great blessing of God, given for the common weal, specially of the good and godly, for the comfort and cherishing of whom God gives and sets up princes; and on the contrary part, to the fear and for the punishment of the evil and wicked. Finally, that if servants ought to obey their masters, not only being gentle, but such as be froward, as well and much more ought subjects to be obedient, not only to their good and courteous, but also to their sharp and rigorous princes.

It comes therefore neither of chance and fortune (as they term it), nor of the ambition of mortal men and women climbing up of their own accord to dominion, that there be kings, queens and princes, and other governors over men being their subjects. But all kings, queens and other governors are specially appointed by the ordinance of God. And as God himself, being of an infinite majesty, power and wisdom, rules and governs all things in heaven and in earth, as the universal monarch and only king and emperor over all, as being only able to take and bear the charge of all, so has he constituted, ordained and set earthly princes over particular kingdoms and dominions in earth, both for the avoiding of all confusion, which else would be in the world if it should be without such governors, and for the great quiet and benefit of earthly men their subjects; and also that the princes themselves in authority, power, wisdom, providence and righteousness in government of people and countries committed to their charge, should resemble his heavenly governance, as the majesty of heavenly things may by the baseness of earthly things be shadowed and resembled. And for that similitude that is between the heavenly monarchy and earthly kingdoms well governed, our saviour Christ in sundry parables says that the kingdom of heaven is resembled unto a man, a king, and as the name of the king is very often attributed and given unto God in the Holy Scriptures, so does God himself in the same Scriptures sometimes vouchsafe to communicate his name with earthly princes, terming them Gods, doubtless for that similitude of government which they have or should have, not unlike unto God their king.

Unto the which similitude of heavenly government, the nearer and nearer that an earthly prince does come in his regiment, the greater blessing of God's mercy is he unto that country and people over whom he reigns. And the further and further that an earthly prince does swerve from the example of the heavenly government, the greater plague he is of God's wrath, and punishment by God's justice, unto that country and people over whom God for their sins has placed such a prince and governor. For it is indeed evident, both by the Scriptures and by daily experience, that the maintenance of all virtue and godliness, and consequently of the wealth and prosperity of a kingdom and people, does stand and rest more in a wise and good prince on the one part, than in great multitudes of other men, being subjects. And on the contrary part, the overthrow of all virtue and godliness, and consequently the decay and utter ruin of a realm and people, does grow and come more by an indiscreet and evil governor, than by many thousands of other men, being subjects. Thus say the Holy Scriptures: 'Well is thee, O thou land (says the preacher), whose king is come of nobles, and whose princes eat in due season, for necessity, and not for lust.' Again, 'a wise and righteous king makes his realm and people wealthy. And a good, merciful and gracious prince is as a shadow in heat, as a defence in storms, as dew, as sweet showers, as fresh water springs in great droughts.' Again the Scriptures of indiscreet and evil princes speak thus: 'Woe be to thee, O thou land, whose king is but a child, and whose princes are early at their banquets.' Again, 'When the wicked do reign, then men go to ruin.' And again, 'A foolish prince destroys the people, and a covetous king undoes his subjects.' Thus speak the Scriptures. Thus experience testifies of good and evil princes.

What shall subjects do then? Shall they obey valiant, stout, wise and good princes, and condemn, disobey and rebel against children being their princes, or against indiscreet and evil governors? God forbid. For first, what a perilous thing were it to commit unto the subjects the judgement which prince is wise and godly, and his government good, and which is otherwise. As though the foot must judge of the head: an enterprise very heinous, and must needs breed rebellion. For who else be they that are most inclined to rebellion but such haughty spirits? From whom springs such foul ruin of realms? Is not rebellion the greatest of all mischiefs? And who are most ready to the greatest mischiefs but the worst men? . . .

. . . .

2   James VI and I, *The Trew Law of Free Monarchies* (1598)

. . . . The king towards his people is rightly compared to a father of children, and to a head of a body composed of divers members, for as fathers the good princes and magistrates of the people of God acknowledged themselves to their subjects. And for all other well-ruled commonwealths, the style of *pater patriae* was ever, and is, commonly used to kings. And the proper office of a king towards his subjects agrees very well with the office of the head towards the body and all members thereof, for from the head, being the seat of judgement, proceeds the care and foresight of guiding, and preventing all evil that may come to the body or any part thereof. The head cares for the body: so does the king for his people. As the discourse and direction flows from the head, and the execution according thereunto belongs to the rest of the members, every one according to their office, so it is betwixt a wise prince and his people. As the judgement coming from the head may not only employ the members, every one in their own office, as long as they are able for it, but likewise, in case any of them be affected with any infirmity, must care and provide for their remedy, in case it be curable, and, if otherwise, gar cut them off for fear of infecting of the rest, even so is it betwixt the prince and his people. And as there is ever hope of curing any diseased member by the direction of the head, as long as it is whole; but by the contrary, if it be troubled all the members are partakers of that pain: so is it betwixt the prince and his people.

And now first for the father's part (whose natural love to his children I described in the first part of this my discourse, speaking of the duty that kings owe to their subjects) consider, I pray you, what duty his children owe to him, and whether, upon any pretext whatsoever, it will not be thought monstrous and unnatural to his sons to rise up against him, to control him at their appetite, and when they think good to slay him, or to cut him off and adopt to themselves any other they please in his room. Or can any pretence of wickedness or rigour on his part be a just excuse for his children to put hand into him? And although we see by the course of nature that love useth to descend more than to ascend, in case it were true that the father hated and wronged the children never so much, will any man endowed with the least spunk of reason think it lawful for them to meet him with the line? Yea, suppose the father were furiously following his sons with a drawn sword, is it lawful for them to turn and strike again, or make any resistance but by flight? I think, surely if there were no more but the example of brute beasts and un-- reasonable creatures, it may serve well enough to qualify and prove this my argument. We read often [of] the piety that the storks have to their old and decayed parents; and generally we know that there are many sorts of beasts and fowls that, with violence and many bloody strokes, will beat and banish their young ones from them, how soon they perceive them to be able to fend for themselves. But we never read or heard of any resistance on their part, except among the vipers: which proves such persons as ought to be reasonable creatures, and yet unnaturally follow this example, to be endued with their viperous nature.

And for the similitude of the head and the body, it may very well fall out that the head will be forced to gar cut off some rotten members (as I have already said) to keep the rest of the body in integrity. But what state the body can be in if the head, for any infirmity that can fall to it, be cut off, I leave it to the reader's judgement.

So as (to conclude this part) if the children may, upon any pretext that can be imagined, lawfully rise up against their father, cut him off, and choose any other whom they please in his room, and if the body for the weal of it may, for any infirmity that can be in the head, strike it off, then I cannot deny that the people may rebel, control, and displace or cut off their king at their own pleasure, and upon respects moving them. And whether these similitudes represent better the office of a king, or the offices of masters or deacons of crafts, or doctors in physic (which jolly comparisons are used by such writers as maintain the contrary proposition), I leave it also to the reader's discretion.

And in case any doubts might arise in any part of this treatise, I will (according to my promise) with the solution of four principal and most weighty doubts that the adversaries may object conclude this discourse. And first it is cast up by divers that employ their pens upon apologies for rebellions and treasons that every man is born to carry such a natural zeal and duty to his commonwealth as to his mother, that, seeing it so rent and deadly wounded as whiles it will be by wicked and tyrannous kings, good citizens will be forced, for the natural zeal and duty they owe to their own native country, to put their hand to work for freeing their commonwealth from such a pest.

Whereunto I give two answers. First, it is a sure axiom in theology that evil should not be done that good may come of it. The wickedness, therefore, of the king can never make them that are ordained to be judged by him to become his judges. And if it be not lawful to a private man to revenge his private injury upon his private adversary (since God has only given the sword to the magistrate) how much less is it lawful to the people, or any part of them (who all are but private men, the authority being always with the magistrate, as I have already proved), to take upon them the use of the sword, whom to it belongs not, against the public magistrate, whom to only it belongs.

Next, in place of relieving the commonwealth out of distress (which is their only excuse and colour) they shall heap double distress and desolation upon it, and so their rebellion shall procure the contrary effects that they pretend it for. For a king cannot be imagined to be so unruly and tyrannous, but the commonwealth will be kept in better order, notwithstanding thereof, by him than it can be by his way-taking. For first, all sudden mutations are perilous in commonwealths, hope being thereby given to all bare men to set up themselves, and fly with other men's feathers, the reins being loosed to all the insolencies that disordered people can commit by hope of impunity, because of the looseness of all things.

And next, it is certain that a king can never be so monstrously vicious, but he will generally favour justice and maintain some order, except in the particulars wherein his inordinate lusts and passions carry him away; where, by the contrary, no king being, nothing is unlawful to none. And so the old opinion of the philosophers proves true, that better it is to live in a commonwealth where nothing is lawful, than [one] where all things are lawful to all men: the commonwealth at that time resembling an undaunted young horse that has cast his rider. For, as the divine poet Du Bartas says, 'Better it were to suffer some disorder in the state, and some spots in the commonwealth, than in pretending to reform utterly to overthrow the republic.'

The second objection they ground upon the curse that hangs over the commonwealth where a wicked king reigns. And, say they, there cannot be a more acceptable deed in the sight of God, nor more dutiful to the commonweal, than to free the country of such a curse, and vindicate to them their liberty, which is natural to all creatures to crave.

Whereunto, for answer, I grant indeed that a wicked king is sent by God for a curse to his people, and a plague for their sins. But that it is lawful to them to shake off that curse at their own hand, which God has laid on them, that I deny, and may so do justly. Will any deny that the king of Babel was a curse to the people of God, as was plainly forespoken and threatened unto them in the prophecy of their captivity? And what was Nero to the Christian Church in his time? And yet Jeremiah and Paul (as ye have else heard) commanded them not only to obey them, but heartily to pray for their welfare.

It is certain then (as I have already by the law of God sufficiently proved) that patience, earnest prayers to God, and amendment of their lives, are the only lawful means to move God to relieve them of that heavy curse. As for vindicating to themselves their own liberty, what lawful power have they to revoke to themselves again those privileges which by their own consent before were so fully put out of their hands? For if a prince cannot justly bring back again to himself the privileges once bestowed by him or his predecessors upon any state or rank of his subjects, how much less may the subjects reave out of the prince's hand that superiority which he and his predecessors have so long brooked over them?

But the unhappy iniquity of the time, which has oft times given over good success to their treasonable attempts, furnishes them the ground of their third objection. For, say they, the fortunate success that God has so oft given to such enterprises proves plainly by the practice that God favoured the justness of their quarrel.

To the which I answer, that it is true indeed that all the success of battles, as well as other worldly things, lies only in God's hand. And therefore it is that in the Scripture he takes to himself the style of God of Hosts. But upon that general to conclude that he ever gives victory to the just quarrel would prove the Philistines and divers other neighbour enemies of the people of God to have oft times had the just quarrel against the people of God, in respect of the many victories they obtained against them. And by that same argument they had also just quarrel against the Ark of God, for they won it in the field, and kept it long prisoner in their country. As likewise by all good writers, as well theologians as other[s], the duels and singular combats are disallowed; which are only made upon pretence that God will kith thereby the justice of the quarrel. For we must consider that the innocent party is not innocent before God, and therefore God will make oft times them that have the wrong side revenge justly his quarrel, and, when he has done, cast his scourge in the fire, as he oft times did to his own people, stirring up and strengthening their enemies while they were humbled in his sight, and then delivered them in their hands. So God, as the great Judge, may justly punish his deputy, and for his rebellion against Him stir up his rebels to meet him with the like. And when it is done the part of the instrument is no better than the devil's part in tempting and torturing such as God commits to him as his hangman to do. Therefore, as I said in the beginning, it is oft times a very deceivable argument, to judge of the cause by the event.

And the last objection is grounded upon the mutual paction and adstipulation (as they call it) betwixt the king and his people at the time of his coronation. For there, say they, there is a mutual paction and contract bound up and sworn betwixt the king and the people. Whereupon it follows that if the one part of the contract or the indent be broken upon the king's side, the people are no longer bound to keep their part of it, but are thereby freed of their oath. For, say they, a contract betwixt two parties of all law frees the one party if the other break unto him.

As to this contract alleged made at the coronation of a king, although I deny any such contract to be made then, especially containing such a clause irritant as they allege, yet I confess that a king at his coronation, or at the entry to his kingdom, willingly promises to his people to discharge honourably and truly the office given him by God over them. But, presuming that thereafter he breaks his promise unto them never so inexcusably, the question is, who should be judge of the break, giving unto them [that] this contract were made unto them never so sicker, according to their allegiance. I think no man that has but the smallest entrance into the civil law will doubt that of all law, either civil or municipal of any nation, a contract cannot be thought broken by the one party, and so the other likewise to be freed therefrom, except that first a lawful trial and cognition be had by the ordinary judge of the breakers thereof. Or else every man may be both party and judge in his own case – which is absurd once to be thought. Now in this contract (I say) betwixt the king and his people, God is doubtless the only judge, both because to him only the king must make count of his administration (as is oft said before), as likewise, by the oath in the coronation, God is made judge and revenger of the breakers. For in his presence, as only judge of oaths, all oaths ought to be made. Then since God is the only judge betwixt the two parties contractors, the cognition and revenge must only appertain to him. It follows therefore of necessity that God must first give sentence upon the king that breaks, before the people can think themselves freed of their oath. What justice then is it that the party shall be both judge and party, usurping upon himself the office of God, may by this argument easily appear. And shall it lie in the hands of [the] headless multitude, when they please to weary of subjection, to cast off the yoke of government that God has laid upon them, to judge and punish him, whom-by they should be judged and punished, and in that case wherein by their violence they kythe themselves to be most passionate parties to use the office of an ungracious judge or arbiter? Nay, to speak truly of that case, as it stands betwixt the king and his people, none of them ought to judge of the other's break. For, considering rightly the two parties at the time of their mutual promise, the king is the one party and the whole people in one body are the other party. And therefore, since it is certain that a king, in case so it should fall out that his people in one body had rebelled against him, he should not in that case, as thinking himself free of his promise and oath, become an utter enemy and practise the wreck of his whole people and native country (although he ought justly to punish the principal authors and bellows of that universal rebellion), how much less then ought the people (that are always subject unto him and naked of all authority on their part) press to judge and overthrow him? Otherwise the people, as the one party contractors, shall no sooner challenge the king as breaker, but he as soon shall judge them as breakers; so as the victors making the tyners the traitors (as our proverb is) the party shall aye become both judge and party in his own particular, as I have already said.

And it is here likewise to be noted that the duty and allegiance which the people swears to their prince is not only bound to themselves, but likewise to their lawful heirs and posterity, the lineal succession of crowns being begun among the people of God and happily continued in divers Christian commonwealths. So as no objection either of heresy, or whatsoever private statute or law may free the people from their oath-giving to their king and his succession [as] established by the old fundamental laws of the kingdom. For, as he is their heritable overlord, and so by birth, not by any right in the coronation, comes to his crown, it is alike unlawful (the crown ever standing full) to displace him that succeeds thereto as to eject the former. For at the very moment of the expiring of the king reigning the nearest and lawful heir enters in his place. And so to refuse him, or intrude another, is not to hold out one coming in, but to expel and put out their righteous king. And I trust at this time whole France acknowledges the superstitious rebellion of the liguers, who, upon pretence of heresy, by force of arms held so long out, to the great desolation of their whole country, their native and righteous king from possessing of his own crown and natural kingdom.

Not that by all this former discourse of mine, and apology for kings, I mean that whatsoever errors and intolerable abominations a sovereign prince commit, he ought to escape all punishment, as if thereby the world were only ordained for kings, and they without controlment to turn it upside down at their pleasure. But by the contrary, by remitting them to God (who is their only ordinary judge) I remit them to the sorest and sharpest schoolmaster that can be devised for them, for the further a king is preferred by God above all other ranks and degrees of men, and the higher that his seat is above theirs, the greater is his obligation to his maker. And therefore in case he forget himself (his unthankfulness being in the same measure of height) the sadder and sharper will his correction be; and according to the greatness of the height he is in, the weight of his fall will recompense the same. For the further that any person is obliged to God, his offence becomes and grows so much the greater than it would be in any other. Jove's thunderclaps light oftener and sorer upon the high and stately oaks than on the low and supple willow trees, and the highest bench is slipperiest to sit upon. Neither is it ever heard that any king forgets himself towards God, or in his vocation, but God with the greatness of the plague revenges the greatness of his ingratitude. Neither think I by the force and argument of this my discourse so to persuade the people, that none will hereafter be raised up and rebel against wicked princes. But remitting to the justice and providence of God to stir up such scourges as pleases him for punishment of wicked kings (who made the very vermin and filthy dust of the earth to bridle the insolency of proud Pharaoh), my only purpose and intention in this treatise is to persuade, as far as lies in me, by these sure and infallible grounds, all such good Christian readers as bear not only the naked name of a Christian but kythe the fruits thereof in their daily form of life to keep their hearts and hands free from such monstrous and unnatural rebellions whensoever the wickedness of a prince shall procure the same at God's hands; that, when it shall please God to cast such scourges of princes and instruments of his fury in the fire, ye may stand up with clean hands and unspotted consciences, having proved yourselves in all your actions true Christians toward God, and dutiful subjects towards your king, having remitted the judgement and punishment of all his wrongs to Him, whom to only of right it appertains.

But craving at God, and hoping that God shall continue his blessing with us in not sending such fearful desolation, I heartily wish our king's behaviour so to be, and continue among us, as our God in earth and loving father, endued with such properties as I described a king in the first part of this treatise. And that ye (my dear countrymen and charitable readers) may press by all means to procure the prosperity and welfare of your king, that as he must on the one part think all his earthly felicity and happiness grounded upon your weal, caring more for himself for your sake than for his own, thinking himself only ordained for your weal, such holy and happy emulation may arise betwixt him and you as his care for your quietness and your care for his honour and preservation may in all your actions daily strive together, that the land may think themselves blessed with such a king, and the king may think himself most happy in ruling over so loving and obedient subjects.

3   James VI and I, *A Speech to the Lords and Commons of the Parliament at White-Hall* (1610)

... The state of monarchy is the supremest thing upon earth. For kings are not only God's lieutenants upon earth, and sit upon God's throne, but even by God himself they are called gods. There be three principal similitudes that illustrates the state of monarchy. One taken out of the word of God, and the two other out of the grounds of policy and philosophy. In the Scriptures kings are called gods, and so their power after a certain relation compared to the divine power. Kings are also compared to fathers of families, for a king is truly *parens patriae*, the politic father of his people. And lastly, kings are compared to the head of this microcosm of the body of man.

Kings are justly called gods for that they exercise a manner or resemblance of divine power upon earth. For if you will consider the attributes to God, you shall see how they agree in the person of a king. God has power to create, or destroy, make, or unmake at his pleasure, to give life, or send death, to judge all, and to be judged nor accountable to none; to raise low things, and to make high things low at his pleasure, and to God are both soul and body due. And the like power have kings: they make and unmake their subjects; they have power of raising and casting down, of life and of death; judges over all their subjects, and in all cases, and yet accountable to none but God only. They have power to exalt low things and abase high things, and make of their subjects like men at the chess: a pawn to take a bishop or a knight, and to cry up or down any of their subjects, as they do their money. And to the king is due both the affection of the soul and the service of the body of his subjects. . . .

As for the father of a family, they had of old under the law of nature *patriam potestatem*, which was *potestatem vitae et necis* [power of life and death], over their children or family. I mean such fathers of families as were the lineal heirs of those families whereof kings did originally come, for kings had their first original from them who planted and spread themselves in colonies through the world. Now a father may dispose of his inheritance to his children at his pleasure: yea, even disinherit the eldest upon just occasions, and prefer the youngest, according to his liking; make them beggars or rich at his pleasure; restrain, or banish out of his presence, as he finds them give cause of offence, or restore them in favour again with the penitent sinner. So may the king deal with his subjects.

And lastly, as for the head of the natural body, the head has the power of directing all the members of the body to that use which the judgement in the head thinks most convenient. It may apply sharp cures, or cut off corrupt members, let blood in what proportion it thinks fit, and as the body may spare, but yet is all this power ordained by God *ad aedificationem, non ad destructionem* [for constructive, not destructive use]. For though God have power as well of destruction as of creation or maintenance, yet will it not agree with the wisdom of God to exercise his power in the destruction of nature and overturning the whole frame of things, since his creatures were made that his glory might thereby be the better expressed. So were he a foolish father that would disinherit or destroy his children without a cause, or leave off the careful education of them. And it were an idle head that would in place of physic so poison or phlebotomize the body as might breed a dangerous distemper or destruction thereof.

But now in these our times we are to distinguish between the state of kings in their first original, and between the state of settled kings and monarchs that do at this time govern in civil kingdoms. For even as God, during the time of the Old Testament, spake by oracles and wrought by miracles, yet how soon it pleased him to settle a Church which was bought and redeemed by the blood of his only Son, Christ, then was there a cessation of both, he ever after governing his people and Church within the limits of his revealed will. So in the first original of kings, whereof some had their beginning by conquest, and some by election of the people, their wills at that time served for law. Yet how soon kingdoms began to be settled in civility and policy, then did kings set down their minds by laws, which are properly made by the king only, but at the rogation of the people, the king's grant being obtained thereunto. And so the king became to be *lex loquens* [a speaking law], after a sort, binding himself by a double oath to the observation of the fundamental laws of his kingdom: tacitly, as by being a king, and so bound to protect as well the people as the laws of his kingdom, and expressly, by his oath at his coronation. So as every just king in a settled kingdom is bound to observe that paction made to his people by his laws, in framing his government agreeable thereunto, according to that paction which God made with Noah after the deluge: 'Hereafter seed-time and harvest, cold and heat, summer and winter, and day and night shall not cease, so long as the earth remains.' And therefore a king governing in a settled kingdom leaves to be a king, and degenerates into a tyrant, as soon as he leaves off to rule according to his laws. In which case the king's conscience may speak unto him as the poor widow said to Philip of Macedon: 'Either govern according to your law, *aut ne rex sis* [or you are no king].' And though no Christian man ought to allow any rebellion of people against their prince, yet does God never leave kings unpunished when they transgress these limits. For in that same psalm where God says to kings *vos dii estis* [you are gods], he immediately thereafter concludes, 'But ye shall die like men.' The higher we are placed, the greater shall our fall be. *Ut casus sic dolor*: the taller the trees be, the more in danger of the wind; and the tempest beats sorest upon the highest mountains. Therefore all kings that are not tyrants, or perjured, will be glad to bound themselves within the limits of their laws; and they that persuade them the contrary are vipers and pests, both against them and the commonwealth. For it is a great difference between a king's government in a settled state and what kings in their original power might do in *individuo vago* [as unrestrained individuals]. As for my part, I thank God I have ever given good proof that I never had intention to the contrary. And I am sure to go to my grave with that reputation and comfort, that never king was in all his time more careful to have his laws duly observed, and himself to govern thereafter, than I.

I conclude then this point touching the power of kings with this axiom of divinity: that as to dispute what God may do is blasphemy, but *quid vult deus* [what God wishes], that divines may lawfully, and do ordinarily, dispute and discuss, for to dispute *a posse ad esse* [from potential to actual] is both against logic and divinity, so is it sedition in subjects to dispute what a king may do in the height of his power. But just kings will ever be willing to declare what they will do, if they will not incur the curse of God. I will not be content that my power be disputed upon. But I shall ever be willing to make the reason appear of all my doings, and rule my actions according to my laws.

. . . .

4   Robert Filmer, *Observations upon Aristotle's Politiques* (1652)

(From the Preface)

. . . .

It is not probable that any sure direction of the beginning of government can be found either in Plato, Aristotle, Cicero, Polybius, or in any other of the heathen authors, who were ignorant of the manner of the creation of the world: we must not neglect the scriptures and search in philosophers for the grounds of dominion and property, which are the main principles of government and justice. The first government in the world was monarchical, in the father of all flesh. Adam being commanded to multiply, and people the earth, and to subdue it, and having dominion given him over all creatures, was thereby the monarch of the whole world; none of his posterity had any right to possess anything, but by his grant or permission, or by succession from him. The earth (says the Psalmist) has he given to the children of men: which shows the title comes from the fatherhood. There never was any such thing as an independent multitude who at first had a natural right to a community. This is but a fiction or fancy of too many in these days, who please themselves in running after the opinions of philosophers and poets, to find out such an original of government as might promise them some title to liberty, to the great scandal of Christianity and bringing in of atheism, since a natural freedom of mankind cannot be supposed without the denial of the creation of Adam. And yet this conceit of original freedom is the only ground upon which not only the heathen philosophers, but also the authors of the principles of the civil law, and Grotius, Selden, Hobbes, Ascham and others, raise and build their doctrines of government, and of the several sorts or kinds, as they call them, of commonwealths.

Adam was the father, king and lord over his family: a son, a subject, and a servant or a slave were one and the same thing at first. The father had power to dispose or sell his children or servants; whence we find that, at the first reckoning up of goods in scripture, the manservant and the maidservant are numbered among the possessions and substance of the owner, as other goods were. As for the names of subject, slave and tyrant, they are not found in scripture, but what we now call a subject or a slave is there named no other than a servant. I cannot learn that either the Hebrew, Greek or Latin have any proper and original word for a tyrant or a slave: it seems these are names of later invention, and taken up in disgrace of monarchical government.

I cannot find any one place or text in the Bible where any power or commission is given to a people either to govern themselves, or to choose themselves governors, or to alter the manner of government at their pleasure. The power of government is settled and fixed by the commandment of 'honour thy father'; if there were a higher power than the fatherly, then this commandment could not stand and be observed. Whereas we read in scripture of some actions of the people in setting up of kings, further than to a naked declaration by a part of the people of their obedience, such actions could not amount, since we find no commission they have, to bestow any right. A true representation of the people to be made is as impossible as for the whole people to govern. The names of an aristocracy, a democracy, a commonwealth, a state, or any other of like signification are not to be met either in the law or gospel.

That there is a ground in nature for monarchy, Aristotle himself affirms, saying the first kings were fathers of families. As for any ground of any other form of government, there has been none yet alleged but a supposed natural freedom of mankind; the proof whereof I find none do undertake, but only beg it to be granted. We find the government of God's own people varied under the several titles of Patriarchs, Captains, Judges and Kings, but in all these the supreme power rested still in one person only. We nowhere find any supreme power given to the people, or to a multitude, in scripture, or ever exercised by them. The people were never the Lord's anointed, nor called gods, nor crowned, nor had the title of nursing fathers (Genesis xxxv, 11). The supreme power, being an indivisible beam of majesty, cannot be divided among, or settled upon, a multitude. God would have it fixed in one person, not sometimes in one part of the people, and sometimes in another; and sometimes, and that for the most part, nowhere, as when the assembly is dissolved it must rest in the air, or in the walls of the chamber where they were assembled.

If there were anything like a popular government among God's people, it was about the time of the Judges, when there was no king in Israel. For they had then some small show of government, such as it was, but it was so poor and beggarly that the scripture brands it with this note, that every man did what was right in his own eyes, because there was no king in Israel. It is not said, because there was no government, but because there was no king. It seems no government, but the government of a king, in the judgement of the scriptures, could restrain men from doing what they listed. Where every man does what he pleases, it may be truly said, there is no government; for the end of government is that every man should not do what he pleases, or be his own judge in his own case. For the scripture to say there was no king, is to say, there was no form of government in Israel.

. . . .

(From the Observations)

. . . .

Those that are willing to be persuaded that the power of government is originally in the people, finding how impossible it is for any people to exercise such power, do surmise that though the people cannot govern, yet they may choose representers or trustees, that may manage this power for the people, and such representers must be surmised to be the people. And since such representers cannot truly be chosen by the people, they are fain to divide the people into several parts, as of provinces, cities and borough-towns, and to allow to every one of those parts to choose one representer or more of their own. And such representers, though not any of them be chosen by the whole, or major part, of the people, yet still must be surmised to be the people; nay, though not one of them be chosen either by the people or the major part of the people of any province, city or borough for which they serve, but only a smaller part, still it must be said to be the people.

Now when such representers of the people do assemble or meet, it is never seen that all of them can at one time meet together; and so there never appears a true or full representation of the whole people of the nation, the representers of one part or other being absent, but still they must be imagined to be the people. And when such imperfect assemblies be met, though not half be present, they proceed; and though their number be never so small, yet it is so big that in the debate of any business of moment, they know not how to handle it, without referring it to a fewer number than themselves, though themselves are not so many as they should be. Thus those that are chosen to represent the people are necessitated to choose others to represent the representers themselves. A trustee of the north does delegate his power to a trustee of the south; and one of the east may substitute one of the west for his proxy. Hereby it comes to pass that public debates, which are imagined to be referred to a general assembly of a kingdom, are contracted into a particular or private assembly, than which nothing can be more destructive or contrary to the nature of public assemblies. Each company of such trustees has a prolocutor, or speaker; who, by the help of three or four of his fellows that are most active, may easily comply in gratifying one the other, so that each of them in their turn may sway the trustees, whilst one man, for himself or his friend, may rule in one business, and another man for himself or his friend prevail in another cause, till such a number of trustees be reduced to so many petty monarchs as there be men of it. So in all popularities, where a general council or great assembly of the people meet, they find it impossible to dispatch any great action either with expedition or secrecy if a public free debate be admitted; and therefore are constrained to epitomize and sub-epitomize themselves so long, till at last they crumble away into the atoms of monarchy, which is the next degree to anarchy; for anarchy is nothing else but a broken monarchy, where every man is his own monarch or governor.

. . . .

It is believed by many that, at the very first assembling of the people, it was unanimously agreed in the first place that the consent of the major part should bind the whole; and that though this first agreement cannot possibly be proved, either how or by whom it could be made, yet it must necessarily be believed or supposed, because otherwise there could be no lawful government at all. That there could be no lawful government, except a general consent of the whole people be first surmised, is no sound proposition; yet true it is that there could be no popular government without it. But if there were at first a government without being beholden to the people for their consent, as all men confess there was, I find no reason but that there may be so still, without asking leave of the multitude.

If it be true that men are by nature free-born, and not to be governed without their own consents, and that self-preservation is to be regarded in the first place, it is not lawful for any government but self-government to be in the world: it were sin in the people to desire, or attempt to consent to, any other government. If the fathers will promise for themselves to be slaves, yet for their children they cannot, who have always the same right to set themselves at liberty which their fathers had to enslave themselves.

To pretend that a major part, or the silent consent of any part, may be interpreted to bind the whole people is both unreasonable and unnatural; it is against all reason for men to bind others where it is against nature for men to bind themselves. Men that boast so much of natural freedom are not willing to consider how contradictory and destructive the power of a major part is to the natural liberty of the whole people; the two grand favourites of the subjects, liberty and property (for which most men pretend to strive), are as contrary as fire to water, and cannot stand together. Though by human laws in voluntary actions a major part may be tolerated to bind the whole multitude, yet in necessary actions, such as those of nature are, it cannot be so. Besides, if it were possible for the whole people to choose their representers, then either every [and] each one of these representers ought to be particularly chosen by the whole people, and not one representer by one part, and another representer by another part of the people, or else it is necessary that continually the entire number of the representers be present, because otherwise the whole people is never represented.

Again, it is impossible for the people, though they might and would choose a government, or governors, ever to be able to do it: for the people, to speak truly and properly, is a thing or body in continual alteration and change. It never continues one minute the same, being composed of a multitude of parts, whereof divers continually decay and perish, and others renew and succeed in their places. They which are the people this minute are not the people the next minute. If it be answered that it is impossible to stand so strictly, as to have the consent of the whole people, and therefore that which cannot be, must be supposed to be the act of the whole people, this is a strange answer: first to affirm a necessity of having the people's consent, then to confess an impossibility of having it. If but once that liberty, which is esteemed so sacred, be broken, or taken away but from one of the meanest or basest of all the people, a wide gap is thereby opened for any multitude whatsoever that is able to call themselves, or whomsoever they please, the people. . . .

Directions for Obedience to Government in Dangerous or Doubtful Times

All those who so eagerly strive for an original power to be in the people do with one consent acknowledge that originally the supreme power was in the fatherhood, and that the first kings were fathers of families. This is not only evident, and affirmed by Aristotle, but yielded unto by Grotius, Mr Selden, Mr Hobbes, Mr Ascham, and all others of that party, not one excepted, that I know of.

Now for those that confess an original subjection in children, to be governed by their parents, to dream of an original freedom in mankind is to contradict themselves. And to make subjects to be free and kings to be limited, to imagine such pactions and contracts between kings and people as cannot be proved ever to have been made, or can ever be described or fancied how it is possible for such contracts ever to have been, is a boldness to be wondered at.

Mr Selden confesses that Adam, by donation from God, was made the general lord of all things, not without such a private dominion to himself as (without his grant) did exclude his children. And by donation, or assignation, or some kind of concession (before he was dead, or left any heir to succeed him) his children had their distinct territories by right of private dominion. Abel had his flocks, and pastures for them; Cain had his fields for corn, and the land of Nod, where he built himself a city.

It is confessed that, in the infancy of the world, the paternal government was monarchical; but when the world was replenished with multitude of people, then the paternal government ceased, and was lost; and an elective government by the people was brought into the world. To this it may be answered that the paternal power cannot be lost. It may either be transferred or usurped; but never lost or ceases. God, who is the giver of power, may transfer it from the father to some other; he gave to Saul a fatherly power over his father Kish. God also has given to the father a right or liberty to alien[ate] his power over his children to any other, whence we find the sale and gift of children to have been much in use in the beginning of the world, when men had their servants for a possession and an inheritance as well as other goods: whereupon we find the power of castrating and making eunuchs much in use in old times. As the power of the father may be lawfully transferred or alien[at]ed, so it may be unjustly usurped. And in usurpation the title of a usurper is before, and better than, the title of any other than of him that had a former right: for he has a possession by the permissive will of God, which permission, how long it may endure, no man ordinarily knows. Every man is to preserve his own life for the service of God, and of his king or father, and is so far to obey a usurper as may tend not only to the preservation of his king and father, but sometimes even to the preservation of the usurper himself, when probably he may thereby be reserved to the correction, or mercy, of his true superior. Though by human laws a long prescription may take away right, yet divine right never dies, nor can be lost or taken away.

Every man that is born is so far from being free-born that by his very birth he becomes a subject to him that begets him. Under which subjection he is always to live, unless by immediate appointment from God, or by the grant or death of his father, he become possessed of that power to which he was subject.

The right of fatherly government was ordained by God for the preservation of mankind. If it be usurped the usurper may be so far obeyed as may tend to the preservation of the subjects, who may thereby be enabled to perform their duty to their true and right sovereign when time shall serve. In such cases, to obey a usurper is properly to obey the first and right governor, who must be presumed to desire the safety of his subjects. The command of a usurper is not to be obeyed in anything tending to the destruction of the person of the governor, whose being in the first place is to be looked after.

It has been said that there have been so many usurpations by conquest in all kingdoms that all kings are usurpers, or the heirs or successors of usurpers; and therefore any usurper, if he can but get the possession of a kingdom, has as good a title as any other.

Answer: The first usurper has the best title, being, as was said, in possession by the permission of God. And where a usurper has continued so long that the knowledge of the right heir be lost by all the subjects, in such a case a usurper in possession is to be taken and reputed by such subjects for the true heir, and is to be obeyed by them as their father, as no man has an infallible certitude, but only a moral knowledge, which is no other than a probable persuasion grounded upon a peaceable possession, which is a warrant for subjection to parents and governors. For we may not say, because children have no infallible or necessary certainty who are their true parents, that therefore they need not obey because they are uncertain. It is sufficient, and as much as human nature is capable of, for children to rely upon a credible persuasion, for otherwise the commandment of 'Honour thy father' would be a vain commandment, and not possible to be observed.

By human positive laws a possession time out of mind takes away, or bars, a former right to avoid a general mischief, of bringing all right into a disputation not decidable by proof, and consequently to the overthrow of all civil government in grants, gifts and contracts between man and man. But in grants and gifts that have their original from God or nature, as the power of the father has, no inferior power of man can limit, nor make any law of prescription against them: upon this ground is built that common maxim that *nullum tempus occurrit regi*, no time bars a king.

All power on earth is either derived or usurped from the fatherly power, there being no other original to be found of any power whatsoever. For if there should be granted two sorts of power without any subordination of one to the other, they would be in perpetual strife which should be the supreme, for two supremes cannot agree. If the fatherly power be supreme, then the power of the people must be subordinate and depend on it. If the power of the people be supreme, then the fatherly power must submit to it, and cannot be exercised without the licence of the people, which must quite destroy the frame and course of nature. Even the power which God himself exercises over mankind is by right of fatherhood: he is both the king and father of us all. As God has exalted the dignity of earthly kings, by communicating to them his own title, by saying they are gods, so on the other side he has been pleased as it were to humble himself by assuming the title of a king to express his power, and not the title of any popular government. We find it is a punishment to have no king (Hosea iii, 4); and promised as a blessing to Abraham (Genesis xvii, 6) that kings shall come out of thee.

Every man has a part or share in the preservation of mankind in general. He that usurps the power of a superior thereby puts upon himself a necessity of acting the duty of a superior in the preservation of them over whom he has usurped, unless he will aggravate one heinous crime by committing another more horrid. He that takes upon him the power of a superior sins sufficiently, and to the purpose; but he that proceeds to destroy both his superior and those under the superior's protection goes a strain higher by adding murder to robbery. If government be hindered, mankind perishes. A usurper, by hindering the government of another, brings a necessity upon himself to govern. His duty before usurpation was only to be ministerial or instrumental in the preservation of others by his obedience; but when he denies his own, and hinders the obedience of others, he does not only not help, but is the cause of the distraction. In hindering his superior to perform his duty he makes the duty his own. If a superior cannot protect, it is his part to desire to be able to do it, which he cannot do in the future if in the present they be destroyed for want of government. Therefore it is to be presumed that the superior desires the preservation of them that should be subject to him; and so likewise it may be presumed that a usurper in general does the will of his superior by preserving the people by government. And it is not improper to say that in obeying a usurper we may obey primarily the true superior, so long as our obedience aims at the preservation of those in subjection, and not at the destruction of the true governor. Not only the usurper, but those also over whom power is usurped may join in the preservation of themselves, yea, and in the preservation sometimes of the usurper himself.

Thus there may be a conditional duty or right in a usurper to govern; that is to say, supposing him to be so wicked as to usurp, and not willing to surrender or forgo his usurpation, he is then bound to protect by government, or else he increases and multiplies his sin.

Though a usurper can never gain a right from the true superior, yet from those that are subjects he may; for if they know no other that has a better title than the usurper, then as to them the usurper in possession has a true right. Such a qualified right is found at first in all usurpers as [it] is in thieves who have stolen goods, and during the time they are possessed of them have a title in law against all others but the true owners, and such usurpers to divers intents and purposes may be obeyed.

Neither is he only a usurper who obtains the government, but all they are partakers in the usurpation who have either failed to give assistance to their lawful sovereign, or have given aid either by their persons, estates or counsels for the destroying of that governor under whose protection they have been born and preserved. For although it should be granted that protection and subjection are reciprocal, so that where the first fails the latter ceases, yet it must be remembered that where a man has been born under the protection of a long and peaceable government, he owes an assistance for the preservation of that government that has protected him, and is the author of his own disobedience.

It is said by some that a usurped power may be obeyed in things that are lawful, but it may be obeyed not only in lawful things, but also in things indifferent. Obedience in things indifferent is necessary, not indifferent. For in things necessarily good God is immediately obeyed, superiors only by consequence. If men command things evil, obedience is due only by tolerating what they inflict, not by performing what they require. In the first place they declare what God commands to be done, in the latter what to be suffered. So it remains that things indifferent only are the proper object of human laws. Actions are to be considered simply and alone, and so are good as being motions depending on the first mover; or jointly with circumstances: and that in a double manner. (1) In regard of the ability or possibility, whilst they may be done. (2) In the act when they be performed. Before they be done they be indifferent; but once breaking out into act they become distinctly good or evil according to the circumstances which determine the same. Now an action commanded is supposed as not yet done (whereupon the Hebrews call the imperative mood the first future), and so remains many times indifferent.

Some may be of opinion that if obedience may be given to a usurper in things indifferent as well as to a lawful power, that then there is as much obedience due to a usurped power as to a lawful. But it is a mistake, for though it be granted that in things indifferent a usurper may be obeyed as well as a lawful governor, yet herein lies a main difference, that some things are indifferent for a lawful superior which are not indifferent but unlawful to a usurper to enjoin. Usurpation is the resisting and taking away the power from him who has such a former right to govern the usurper as cannot be lawfully taken away: so that it cannot be just for a usurper to take advantage of his own unlawful act, or create himself a title by continuation of his own injustice, which aggravates, and never extenuates, his crime. And if it never can be an act indifferent for the usurper himself to disobey his lawful sovereign, much less can it be indifferent for him to command another to do that to which he has no right himself. It is only, then, a matter indifferent for a usurper to command when the actions enjoined are such as the lawful superior is commanded by the law of God to provide for the benefit of his subjects by the same, or other like, restriction of indifferent things, and it is to be presumed, if he had not been hindered, would have commanded the same, or the like, laws.

5 The Judgment and Decree of the University of Oxford, Passed in Their Convocation, July 21, 1683, against Certain Pernicious Books and Damnable Doctrines, Destructive to the Sacred Persons of Princes, Their State and Government, and of All Humane Society

Although the barbarous assassination lately enterprised against the person of his sacred majesty and his royal brother engage all our thoughts to reflect with utmost detestation and abhorrence of that execrable villainy, hateful to God and man, and pay our due acknowledgements to the divine providence which, by extraordinary methods, brought it to pass that the breath of our nostrils, the anointed of the Lord, is not taken in the pit which was prepared for him, and that under his shadow we continue to live and enjoy the blessings of his government; yet, notwithstanding, we find it to be a necessary duty at this time to search into and lay open those impious doctrines which, having of late been studiously disseminated, gave rise and growth to these nefarious attempts, and pass upon them our solemn public censure and decree of condemnation.

Therefore, to the honour of the holy and undivided Trinity, the preservation of catholic truth in the church, and that the king's majesty may be secured from the attempts of open and bloody enemies and machinations of treacherous heretics and schismatics, we, the vice-chancellor, doctors, proctors and masters regent and not regent, met in convocation in the accustomed manner, time and place, on Saturday, the 21 of July, in the year 1683, concerning certain propositions contained in divers books and writings, published in English and also in the Latin tongue, repugnant to the Holy Scriptures, decrees of councils, writings of the fathers, the faith and profession of the primitive church, and also destructive of the kingly government, the safety of His Majesty's person, the public peace, the laws of nature and bonds of human society, by our unanimous assent and consent have decreed and determined in manner and form following:

The first proposition

All civil authority is derived originally from the people.

The second

There is a mutual compact, tacit or express, between a prince and his subjects, and that if he perform not his duty, they are discharged from theirs.

The third

That if lawful governors become tyrants, or govern otherwise than by the laws of God and man they ought to do, they forfeit the right they had unto their government.
Lex Rex; Buchanan, *de Iure Regni*; *Vindiciae contra Tyrannos*; Bellarmine, *de Conciliis, de Pontifice*; Milton; Goodwin; Baxter, *H.C.* [*Holy Commonwealth*].

*

The fourth

The sovereignty of England is in the three estates, viz. king, lords and commons. The king has but a coordinate power, and may be overruled by the other two.

Lex Rex; Hunton, *Of a Limited and Mixed Monarchy*; Baxter, *H.C.*; *Polit. Catechis.*

*

The fifth

Birthright and proximity of blood give no title to rule or government, and it is lawful to preclude the next heir from his right of succession to the crown.

Lex Rex; Hunt's *Postscript*; Doleman's *History of the Succession*; *Julian the Apostate*; *Mene Tekel*.

*

The sixth

It is lawful for subjects, without the consent and against the command of the supreme magistrate, to enter into leagues, covenants and associations for defence of themselves and their religion.

Solemn League and Covenant; *Late Association*.

*

The seventh

Self-preservation is the fundamental law of nature, and supersedes the obligation of all others whenever they stand in competition with it.

Hobbes, *de Cive*, *Leviathan*.

*

The eighth

The doctrine of the Gospel concerning patient suffering of injuries is not inconsistent with violent resisting of the higher powers in case of persecution for religion.

Lex Rex; *Julian Apostate*; *Apolog. Relat.*

*

The ninth

There lies no obligation upon Christians to passive obedience when the prince commands anything against the laws of our country; and the primitive Christians chose rather to die than to resist because Christianity was not yet settled by the laws of the empire.

Julian Apostate.

*

The tenth

Possession and strength give a right to govern, and success in a cause or enterprise proclaims it to be lawful and just; to pursue it is to comply with the will of God, because it is to follow the conduct of his providence.

Hobbes; Owen's sermon before the regicides, Jan. 31, 1648[/9]; Baxter; Jenkins' *Petition*, Oct. 1651.

*

The eleventh

In the state of nature there is no difference between good and evil, right and wrong; the state of nature is a state of war in which every man has a right to all things.

The twelfth

The foundation of civil authority is this natural right, which is not given but left [i.e. *lent*] to the supreme magistrate upon men's entering into societies; and not only a foreign invader but a domestic rebel puts himself again into a state of nature to be proceeded against, not as a subject, but an enemy, and consequently acquires by his rebellion the same right over the life of his prince as the prince for the most heinous crimes has over the life of his own subjects.

The thirteenth

Every man, after his entering into a society, retains a right of defending himself against force, and cannot transfer that right to the commonwealth when he consents to that union whereby a commonwealth is made; and in case a great many men together have already resisted the commonwealth, for which every one of them expects death, they have liberty then to join together to assist and defend one another. Their bearing of arms subsequent to the first breach of their duty, though it be to maintain what they have done, is no new unjust act, and if it be only to defend their persons is not unjust at all.

The fourteenth

An oath superadds no obligation to [a] pact, and a pact obliges no farther than it is credited; and consequently if a prince gives any indication that he does not believe the promises of fealty and allegi-

ance made by any of his subjects, they are thereby freed from their subjection; and, notwithstanding their pacts and oaths, may lawfully rebel against and destroy their sovereign.
Hobbes, *de Cive, Leviathan.*

*

The fifteenth

If a people that by oath and duty are obliged to a sovereign shall sinfully dispossess [him], and contrary to their covenants choose and covenant with another, they may be obliged by their later covenant, notwithstanding their former.
Baxter, *H.C.*

*

The sixteenth

All oaths are unlawful and contrary to the word of God.
Quakers.

*

The seventeenth

An oath obliges not in the sense of the imposer, but the takers.
Sheriff's case.

*

The eighteenth

Dominion is founded in grace.

The nineteenth

The powers of this world are usurpations upon the prerogative of Jesus Christ; and it is the duty of God's people to destroy them in order to the setting Christ upon his throne.
Fifth-Monarchy Men.

*

The twentieth

The presbyterian government is the sceptre of Christ's kingdom, to which kings as well as others are bound to submit; and the king's supremacy in ecclesiastical affairs, asserted by the church of England, is injurious to Christ, the sole king and head of his church.
Altare Damascenum; *Apolog. Relat.*; *Hist. Indulg.*; Cartwright; Travers.

*

The twenty-first

It is not lawful for superiors to impose anything in the worship of God that is not antecedently necessary.

The twenty-second

The duty of not offending a weak brother is inconsistent with all human authority of making laws concerning indifferent things.
Protestant Reconciler.

*

The twenty-third

Wicked kings and tyrants ought to be put to death; and if the judges and inferior magistrates will not do their office, the power of the sword devolves to the people. If the major part of the people refuse to exercise this power, then the ministers may excommunicate such a king; after which it is lawful for any of the subjects to kill him, as the people did Athaliah and Jehu Jezebel.
Buchanan; Knox; Goodman; Gilby; Jesuits.

*

The twenty-fourth

After the sealing of the scripture-canon, the people of God in all ages are to expect new revelations for a rule of their actions (a); and it is lawful for a private man, having an inward motion from God, to kill a tyrant (b).
(a) Quakers and other enthusiasts; (b) Goodman.

*

The twenty-fifth

The example of Phineas is to us instead of a command, for what God has commanded or approved in one age must needs oblige in all.
Goodman; Knox; Napthali.

*

The twenty-sixth

King Charles the first was lawfully put to death, and his murderers were the blessed instruments of God's glory in their generation.
Milton; Goodwin; Owen.

*

The twenty-seventh

King Charles the first made war upon his parliament; and in such a case the king may not only be resisted, but he ceases to be king.
Baxter.

*

We decree, judge and declare all and every of these propositions to be false, seditious and impious; and most of them to be also heretical and blasphemous, infamous to Christian religion, and destructive of all government in church and state.

We further decree that the books which contain the aforesaid propositions and impious doctrines are fitted to deprave good manners, corrupt the minds of unwary men, stir up seditions and tumults, overthrow states and kingdoms, and lead to rebellion, murder of princes, and atheism itself. And therefore we interdict all members of the university from the reading [of] the said books, under the penalties in the statutes expressed. We also order the before-recited books to be publicly burnt by the hand of our marshal in the court of our schools.

Likewise we order that, in perpetual memory hereof, these our decrees shall be entered into the registry of our convocation; and that copies of them being communicated to the several colleges and halls within this university, they be there publicly affixed in the libraries, refectories, or other fit places, where they may be seen and read of all.

Lastly, we command and strictly enjoin all and singular readers, tutors, catechists, and others to whom the care and trust of institution of youth is committed that they diligently instruct and ground their scholars in that most necessary doctrine which, in a manner, is the badge and character of the church of England, of submitting to every ordinance of man for the Lord's sake, whether it be to the king as supreme, or unto governors as unto them that are sent by him for the punishment of evil doers, and for the praise of them that do well; teaching that this submission and obedience is to be clear, absolute, and without exception of any state or order of men. Also that all supplications, prayers, intercessions and giving of thanks be made for all men, for the king, and all that are in authority, that we may lead a quiet and peaceable life in all godliness and honesty, for this is good and acceptable in the sight of God our Saviour. And in especial manner that they press and oblige them humbly to offer their most ardent and daily prayers at the throne of grace for the preservation of our sovereign lord King Charles from the attempts of open violence and secret machinations of perfidious traitors, that he, the Defender of the Faith, being safe under the defence of the Most High, may continue his reign on earth till he exchange it for that of a late and happy immortality.

NOTES ON THE TEXTS

1.   *Homily against Disobedience:* Written in the aftermath of the rebellion of 1569. Published separately in 1571(?), 1573(?) and also in the 1571 edition of the *Second Tome of Homilies*. Also in J. Griffiths (ed.), *The Two Books of Homilies* (1859).

2.   James VI and I, *Trew Law of Free Monarchies:* Published under pseudonym of C. Philopatris in Edinburgh (1598) and London (1603, two editions). Reprinted 1642. In the *Works* of 1616 and the *Opera* of 1619 and 1689. The standard edition is C. H. McIlwain (ed.), *The Political Works of James I* (Cambridge, Mass., 1918).

3.   James VI and I, Speech of 1610: Published in 1609 (i.e. 1610) and in the various editions of the works; also in *Parliamentary History*, vol. 1 (1806).

4.   Filmer, *Observations:* Published anonymously in 1652, and in all the collections of Filmer's works (1679, 1679/80, 1680, 1684, 1695, 1696). The standard edition is in P. Laslett (ed.), *Patriarcha and Other Political Works* (Oxford, 1949).

5.   *Judgment and Decree of the University of Oxford:* Latin edition and English translation, Oxford, 1683. In W.P., *Proteus Ecclesiasticus* (1691); *State Tracts* (1693); J. Somers, *Tracts* (1748 edition, vol. 3; 1809 edition, vol. 8); selections in J. P. Kenyon, *Stuart Constitution* (Cambridge, 1966).

FURTHER READING

The classic study of divine right of kings theory is J. N. Figgis, *The Divine Right of Kings* (1896; with introduction by G. R. Elton, New York, 1965). Since Figgis the ideas of order and harmony to which divine right of kings theorists made such frequent appeal have been systematically studied: particularly helpful are E. M. W. Tillyard, *The Elizabeth World Picture* (London, 1943) and J. W. Daly, 'Cosmic Harmony and Political Thinking in Early Stuart England', *Transactions of the American Philosophical Society*, LXIX (1979), pt. 7. On patriarchalism, which constitutes one aspect of this general theory of order, there is G. J. Schochet, *Patriarchalism in Political Thought* (Oxford, 1975) and R. W. K. Hinton, 'Husbands, Fathers and Conquerors', *Political Studies*, XV (1967), pp. 291–300, and XVI (1968), pp. 55–67. A major modification to previous accounts of the relationship between divine right of kings theory and ideas of order and harmony is F. Oakley, *Omnipotence, Covenant and Order* (Ithaca, 1984).

There has been a good deal of work on Filmer since Laslett's edition of his works. The standard authority is now J. W. Daly, *Sir Robert Filmer and English Political Thought* (Toronto, 1979), and Daly has reviewed some of the more recent literature in 'Some Problems in the Authorship of Sir

Robert Filmer's Works', *English Historical Review*, XCVIII (1983), pp. 737–62. J. P. Sommerville has offered an important reinterpretation of Filmer's relationship to his contemporaries in 'From Suarez to Filmer: a Reappraisal', *Historical Journal*, XXV (1982), pp. 525–40. The most recent discussion of the vexed question of the dating of *Patriarcha* is R. Tuck, 'A New Date for Filmer's *Patriarcha*', *Historical Journal*, XXIX (1986), pp. 183–6.

Scholars are divided on the question of whether early-seventeenth-century Englishmen generally believed they lived in an absolute monarchy. For a fine overview of their constitutional thinking see M. A. Judson, *The Crisis of the Constitution, 1603–45* (New Brunswick, 1949), and for a study of the changing meaning of the word 'absolute', see J. W. Daly, 'The Idea of Absolute Monarchy in Seventeenth Century England', *Historical Journal*, XXI (1978), pp. 227–50. Two contrasting studies on this subject are R. W. K. Hinton, 'English Constitutional Theories from Sir John Fortescue to Sir John Eliot', *English Historical Review*, LXXV (1969), pp. 410–25, and J. P. Cooper, 'Differences between English and Continental Governments in the Early Seventeenth Century', in J. S. Bromley and E. Kossman (eds.), *Britain and the Netherlands*, vol. I (1960). Valuable insight into constitutional assumptions is provided by C. Russell, 'The Theory of Treason in the Trial of Strafford', *English Historical Review*, LXXX (1965), pp. 30–50 (although Russell's account of the trial must be corrected in the light of J. H. Timmis, 'Evidence and I Eliz. I, Cap. 6', *Historical Journal*, XXI (1978), pp. 677–83).

On absolutist and divine-right thinking towards the end of the century there are M. Goldie, 'John Locke and Anglican Royalism', *Political Studies*, XXXI (1983), pp. 61–85, and G. Straka, 'The Final Phase of Divine Right Theory in England, 1688–1702', *English Historical Review*, LXXVII (1962), pp. 638–58.

CHAPTER TWO

THE COMMON LAW

1 Sir John Davies, *Le Primer Report des Cases et Matters en Ley Resolues et Adiudges en les Courts del Roy en Ireland* (1615)

Davies (1569–1626), a distinguished poet, was first Solicitor-General (1603–6) and then Attorney-General (1606–19) for Ireland, where he sought to replace Irish customary law by the English common law. He consistently upheld royal authority, supporting the legality of the forced loans which gave rise to the Five Knights' case and the Petition of Right, but died before he could take up the office of Chief Justice in England. The preface to the *Primer Report* (written in English although the rest of the work is mostly in law-French) is evidently influenced by Coke. It has come to be regarded as the classic exposition of the common lawyer's viewpoint.

2 Sir Edward Coke, *Le Tierce Part des Reportes* (1602)

Coke (1552–1634) holds a pre-eminent place among commentators on the common law. He was Attorney-General (1593–4), Chief Justice of the Common Pleas (1606), and Chief Justice of the King's Bench (1613). In 1616 he was suspended from this office, although he did not at first despair of returning to royal favour. In 1620 he led the parliamentary campaign against monopolies, and was briefly imprisoned after Parliament was dissolved. He played a prominent role in the formulation of the Petition of Right of 1628, and was the chief spokesman of the view that the law established limits upon the king's authority. The passage printed here is an example of his insistence on the immemorial character of the common law, despite the contrary evidence that might be adduced by historians.

3   John Lilburne, *The Just Defence of John Lilburn, against Such as Charge Him with Turbulency of Spirit* (1653)

John Lilburne (1615–57) was the central figure in the Leveller movement and the author of some eighty pamphlets in defence of the rights of citizens. He was cruelly punished by the Star Chamber in 1638 for his opposition to episcopacy, and was at first regarded as a hero by Puritan members of the Long Parliament such as Oliver Cromwell. He fought in the early stages of the Civil War, but resigned his commission rather than take the Solemn League and Covenant. He was imprisoned seven times between 1645 and his banishment for life in 1652 as a result of his campaigns against corruption and in favour of religious and political liberty. In 1653 he was tried for treason (for the third time in his life) after he had returned to England without permission, was acquitted, but was nevertheless returned to prison. Like several other defeated radicals, he died a Quaker.

The passage printed here is a summary of the principles he had struggled for during the Civil War. It was published a few days after his acquittal in 1653.

4   John Warr, *The Corruption and Deficiency of the Lawes of England Soberly Discovered: or Liberty Working up to Its Just Height* (1649)

Almost nothing is known about the life of John Warr (*fl.* 1642–86). He is remembered solely for three tracts he published in 1648–9, tracts which show him to have been the most systematic and radical of the Leveller advocates of law reform, and which, in their praise of an unrestrained liberty, make him appear a forerunner of anarchism. The complete text of one of his pamphlets is reprinted here.

1 Sir John Davies, *Le Primer Report des Cases et Matters en Ley Resolues et Adiudges en les Courts del Roy en Ireland* (1615)

. . . For indeed those reports are but comments or interpretations upon the text of the common law: which text was never originally written, but has ever been preserved in the memory of men, though no man's memory can reach to the original thereof.

For the common law of England is nothing else but the common custom of the realm; and a custom which has obtained the force of a law is always said to be *ius non scriptum* [unwritten law]: for it cannot be made or created, either by charter or by parliament, which are acts reduced to writing, and are always matter of record; but being only matter of fact, and consisting in use and practice, it can be recorded and registered nowhere but in the memory of the people.

For a custom takes beginning and grows to perfection in this manner: When a reasonable act once done is found to be good and beneficial to the people, and agreeable to their nature and disposition, they then do use it and practise it again and again, and so by often iteration and multiplication of the act it becomes a custom; and being continued without interruption time out of mind, it obtains the force of a law.

And this customary law is the most perfect and most excellent, and without comparison the best to make and preserve a commonwealth. For the written laws which are made either by the edicts of princes, or by councils of state, are imposed upon the subject before any trial or probation [is] made, whether the same be fit and agreeable to the nature and disposition of the people, or whether they will breed any inconvenience or not. But a custom does never become a law to bind the people until it has been tried and approved time out of mind, during all which time there did thereby arise no inconvenience: for if it had been found inconvenient at any time, it had been used no longer, but had been interrupted, and consequently it had lost the virtue and force of a law.

Therefore as the law of nature, which the Schoolmen call *ius commune*, and which is also *ius non scriptum*, being written only in the heart of man, is better than all the written laws in the world to make men honest and happy in this life, if they would observe the rules thereof: so the customary law of England, which we do likewise call *ius commune*, as coming nearest to the law of nature, which is the root and touchstone of all good laws, and which is also *ius non scriptum*, and written only in the memory of man (for every custom, though it took beginning beyond the memory of any living man, yet it is continued and preserved in the memory of men living), does far excel our written laws, namely our statutes or acts of parliament: which is manifest in this, that when our parliaments have altered or changed any fundamental points of the common law, those alterations have been found by experience to be so inconvenient for the commonwealth, as that the common law has in effect been restored again, in the same points, by other acts of parliament in succeeding ages.

And as our customary unwritten law does excel our parliament laws, which are written, so for the government of the commonwealth of England (which is as well instituted and established as any commonwealth in Christendom) our native common law is far more apt and agreeable than the civil [i.e. Roman] or canon law, or any other written law in the world besides: howsoever some of our own countrymen, who are *cives in aliena republica, et hospites in sua* [citizens of a foreign country, and strangers in their own], may perhaps affirm the contrary. But certain it is, that the great and wise men of England in the Parliament of Merton [1236] did not prefer a foreign law before their own when, motion being made by the clergy that children born before marriage might be judged legitimate, they all made answer with one voice: *Nolumus leges Angliae mutari* [We do not wish the laws of England to be changed]. And again in 11 R. 2 [1388–9], when a new course of proceeding in criminal cases, according to the form of the civil law, was propounded in that unruly parliament, answer was made by all the estates, 'That the realm of England neither had been in former times, nor hereafter should be ruled and governed by the civil law.'

And here I may observe for the honour of our nation, and of our ancestors who have founded this commonwealth wherein we live and enjoy so many felicities, that England, having had a good and happy genius from the beginning, has been inhabited always with a virtuous and wise people, who ever embraced honest and good customs, full of reason and convenience, which being confirmed by common use and practice, and continued time out of mind, became the common law of the land. And though this law be the peculiar invention of this nation, and delivered over from age to age by tradition (for the common law of England is a tradition, and learned by tradition as well as by books), yet may we truly say that no human law, written or unwritten, has more certainty in the rules and maxims, more coherence in the parts thereof, or more harmony of reason in it: nay, we may confidently aver, that it does excel all other laws in upholding a free monarchy, which is the most excellent form of government, exalting the prerogative royal, and being very tender and watchful to preserve it, and yet maintaining withal the ingenuous liberty of the subject.

Briefly, it is so framed and fitted to the nature and disposition of this people, as we may properly say it is connatural to the nation, so as it cannot possibly be ruled by any other law. This law therefore does demonstrate the strength of wit and reason and self-sufficiency which have been always in the people of this land, which have made their own laws out of their wisdom and experience, like a silk-worm that forms all her web out of herself only, not begging or borrowing a form of a commonwealth, either from Rome or from Greece, as all other nations of Europe have done, but, having sufficient provision of law and justice within the land, have no need *iustitiam et iudicium ab alienigenis emendicare* [to beg for justice from foreigners], as King John wrote most nobly to Pope Innocent the Third. . . . Neither could any one man ever vaunt that, like Minos, Solon or Lycurgus, he was the first law-giver to our nation: for neither did the king make his own prerogative, nor the judges make the rules or maxims of the law, nor the common subject prescribe and limit the liberties which he enjoys by the law. But, as it is said of every art or science which is brought to perfection, *per varios usus artem experientia fecit* [experience has engendered knowledge through trial and error], so may it properly be said of our law, *per varios usus legem experientia fecit*: long experience, and many trials of what was best for the common good, did make the common law.

But upon what reason then does Polydore Vergil [c. 1470–c. 1555] and other writers affirm that King William the Conqueror was our law-giver, and caused all our laws to be written in French? Assuredly the Norman Conqueror found the ancient laws of England so honourable and profitable both for the prince and people, as that he thought it not fit to make any alteration in the fundamental points or substance thereof. The change that was made was but *in formulis iuris*: he altered some legal forms of proceeding, and, to honour his own language and for a mark of conquest withal, he caused the pleading of divers actions to be made and entered in French, and set forth his public ordinances and acts of council in the same tongue. Which form of pleading in French continued till 36 Ed. 3 [1363] when, in regard that the French tongue began to grow out of use, which for many years after the Norman Conquest was as common as the English among the gentry of England, it was ordained by parliament that all pleas should be pleaded, debated and judged in the English tongue, and entered and enrolled in Latin. And as for our statutes or acts of parliament, the bills were for the most part exhibited in French, and passed and enrolled in the same language, even till the time of King Henry VII. And so are they printed in Rastell's first abridgement of statutes, published in the year 1559. But after the beginning of King Henry VII's reign we find all our Acts of Parliament recorded in English. Only our reports of the cases, resolutions and judgements in the law, whereof our books of the law do consist, have ever until this day been penned and published in that mixed kind of speech which we call the law-French; differing indeed not a little from the French tongue as it is now refined and spoken in France, as well by reason of the words of art and form, called the terms of the law, as for that we do still retain many other old words and phrases of speech which were used four hundred years since, and are now become obsolete and out of use among them, but are grown by long and continual use so apt, so natural, and so proper for the matter and subject of these reports, as no other language is significant enough to express the same, but only this law-French wherein they are written.

And this is the true and only cause why our reports and other books of the law for the most part are not set forth in English, Latin or the modern French, for that the proper and peculiar phrase of the common law cannot be so well expressed, nor any case in law be so succinctly, sensibly, and withal so fully reported, as in this speech, which is indeed mixed and compounded of all these three languages. Which reason has not been well understood by those who object it as a fault to the professors of our law that, forsooth, they write their reports and books of the law in a strange, unknown tongue, which none can understand but themselves, to the end that the people, being kept in ignorance of the law, may the more admire their skill and knowledge, and esteem and value it at a higher price . . .

And as this objection touching the speech or language wherein our reports are penned does arise out of ignorance of the cause thereof, as is before declared, so are there other vulgar imputations cast upon the law and lawyers, which may be as easily cleared, as having indeed no other ground but the mere misunderstanding of such as are strangers to the profession: namely,

(1)   That there is much uncertainty in the reasons and judgements of the law;

(2)   That there are extreme and unnecessary delays in the proceedings of the law;

(3)   That many bad and dishonest cases are wittingly defended by the professors of the law. But *sapientia justificatur a filiis suis* [wisdom is vindicated by her children].

(1)   Therefore, first, touching the uncertainty of the law: Certain it is that law is nothing but a rule of reason, and human reason is *lesbia regula*, pliable every way, or like a cup with two ears, as the French proverb is, which may be taken up on either side, as well with the left hand as with the right. So that not only the knowledge of the law but all other rational sciences that are subject to argument and discourse must needs be subject to uncertainty and to error. And therefore upon judgements given in our ordinary courts of justice the law does admit and allow writs of error to be brought, without any touch or dishonour to the judges, though their judgements be reversed for error in point of law.

Howbeit, there is no art or science that stands upon discourse of reason that has her rules and maxims so certain and infallible, and so little subject to diverse interpretation, as the common law of England; as it is observed by the Lord Chief Justice Coke, in his preface to the second part of his *Reports*, that in all his time there have not been moved in the courts of justice in England two questions touching the right of descents or escheats, or the like fundamental points of the common law, so certain, sure and without question are the principles and grounds thereof.

But whence then do so many debates and controversies arise? Whereupon do we plead and contend so much in the courts of justice, if there be so few doubts and uncertainties in law? Doubtless this question is soon resolved by one plain and common distinction.

In all the cases that are controverted there is either *quaestio iuris* or *quaestio facti*. But for one case wherein a question of law does arise that is indeed worth the debating there are a thousand cases at least wherein the fact is only in question, and wherein, if the truth of the fact were known, the law were clear and without question . . .

And therefore we may truly say for the honour of our law, notwithstanding that vulgar imputation of uncertainty, that the judgement and reason of it is more certain than of any other human law in the world: as well because the grounds of our common law have from the beginning been laid with such deep wisdom, policy and providence, as that they do provide for and meet with almost all cases that can possibly fall out in our commonwealth; as also because those grounds are so plain and so clear, as that the professors of our law have not thought it needful to make so many glosses and interpretations thereupon as other laws are perplexed and confounded withal. Which glosses, as one does well observe, 'do increase doubt and ignorance in all arts and sciences'. And therefore the civilians themselves confess that their law is a sea full of waves, the text whereof being digested into so many volumes, and so many doctors interpreting the text, and twice as many more commenting upon their interpretations, and so gloss upon gloss and book upon book, and every doctor's opinion being a good authority fit to be cited and vouched among them, must needs breed distraction of opinions and uncertainty in that law. The like may be said of the canon law, albeit the text thereof be scarce four hundred years old. But of the professors of our law, who ever yet has made any gloss or interpretation upon our master Littleton, though into that little book of his he has reduced the principal grounds of the common law, with exceeding great judgement and authority, and with singular method and order? And yet if he had been an author in the civil or canon law, I dare say there had been, by this time, so many comments and glosses made upon him as the books written upon this book only would have been more in number than all the volumes of our law at this day.

But the learned men in our law have ever thought that Littleton, being a learned and reverend judge, wrote with a purpose to be understood, and that therefore another man, especially if he were of less learning than he, could hardly express him better than he has expressed himself. And therefore his book has ever been read of our youngest students without any commentary or interpretation at all . . .

(2) But if the reason and judgement of our law be so little subject to uncertainty, how comes it to pass that the proceedings of our law are so much subject to delay? For this is another vulgar objection against our law and the professors thereof. But who are they that make this objection? Have they themselves been engaged in any suits of importance? Have they passed through the courts of justice either in course of law, or in course of equity? If they have not, they speak but by hearsay, and then their testimony in this behalf is of little credit. If they have had any long-depending suits of their own, then let them examine whether their own spleen and wilfulness, or the corruption of some needy solicitors (who pick their living out of the business they follow, and are loath to quench the fire that makes them warm), have not rather drawn their cases to an extraordinary length, than the ordinary process of law, or the advice of learned counsel. For such as are learned counsellors indeed are like good pilots, who, though their skill be best tried in a long and difficult voyage, do rather desire fair weather and a speedy arrival with their passengers in the haven.

But the truth is, it is the stomach or malice of such clients as will not stick to say that they will spend all they are worth to have their will of their adversaries, and therefore will not be satisfied with any judgement or decree, that does produce and prolong suits in law; who, when their learned counsel indeed do refuse to nourish that peccant humour in them, do seek out discarded impostors or idols, of whom there is an opinion among light and ignorant people of extraordinary cunning and sleight in carrying off business with advantage, and in curing of foiled and desperate causes. These men give them counsel according to their own heart because they soothe them in their litigious humour. Howbeit in the end, when they have wearied and wasted themselves, they find how weak those wiles and crafty courses are, and learn of Aesop, that the one only plain way which the cat had to escape from the dogs was better and safer than those hundred tricks of evasion whereof the fox did vaunt before he was taken. And they find withal the saying of Cicero true, *Ignoratio juris litigiosa est potius quam scientia* [He who is ignorant of the law is more litigious than he who is knowledgeable].

Besides this malignant and unquiet disposition of many clients, there is another cause why suits are not brought so soon to an end as perhaps they were in former ages: namely the multitude of cases now depending in every court of justice, every of which cases must have convenient time allowed, as well to prepare it and make it ripe to be heard or tried, as for the trial and hearing itself. And the true cause of the multitude of cases does proceed from this, that the commodities of the earth being more improved, there is more wealth, and consequently there are more contracts real and personal, than there were in former ages. Besides there is more luxury and excess in the world, which breeds unthrifts, bankrupts, and bad debtors; more covetousness and more malice, which begets force and fraud, oppression and extortion, breach of the peace and breach of trust. Out of these fountains innumerable suits do spring, which make the courts of justice so to swell. And hence it is that our statute laws since Henry VIII's time do make up so great a volume. And hence it is that the professors of the law are grown withal to so great a number, for where there is *magna messis* [a large harvest] there must be of necessity *operarii multi* [many labourers].

Indeed if we all lived according to the law of nature we should need few laws, and fewer lawyers. 'Do as thou wouldst be done unto' were a rule sufficient to rule us all, and every man's conscience would supply both the place of an advocate and a judge, and then we should suffer no costs of suit, nor delay of process.

And again, if we were a poor and naked people, as many nations in America be, we should easily agree to be judged by the next man we meet, and so make a short end of every controversy. When the people of Rome were little better than shepherds and herdsmen, all their laws were contained in ten or twelve ivory tables. But when they became lords of all the world what a world of books were there written of the Roman civil law! The like we see in every commonwealth. When it once begins to flourish, and to grow rich and mighty, the people grow proud withal, and their pride makes them contentious and litigious, so as there is need of many laws to bridle them, and many officers to execute those laws, and many lawyers to interpret those laws, and all little enough, as, when a body grows full and gross, it needs more physick than when it was lean.

And yet though our suits and cases be very many, and our courts of justice but a few, whereby it must needs come to pass that every particular business moving in his turn must have the slower motion, yet if we compare our legal proceedings with the process of other kingdoms and commonwealths (especially of France), we shall find that, according to the usual clause in divers writs, we have indeed *plenam et celerem iustitiam* [full and speedy justice] (though the briefest justice be not always best), and that our cases for the most part, being orderly pursued, may come to their period in a year, with the course of the sun; when there are many processes in foreign countries that seem to be governed by Saturn, which planet does scarce finish his course in the space of thirty years. As Bodin does testify of his own country, that there were more suits in law depending in France than in all Europe besides, and that many of those cases were an hundred year old: as that of the county of Rais, says he, which suit has been so well entertained in all the chambers of justice, as albeit the parties that began it are long since dead, yet the suit itself is still alive. Besides, we have not so many appeals, nor so many reviews of cases, as the civil and canon laws do admit, neither have we at this day so many delays by essoines, vicures, vouchers and protections, as were in use in former ages, when titles of land were tried only in actions real, which are now grown almost out of use, and a more speedy course of trial invented by mixed and personal actions.

Lastly, there is no nation in the world (I speak it for the honour of our nation and of our land) that has a course of justice so speedy, and withal so commodious and easy for the subject, as our trials by assise and *nisi prius* are. For what kingdom is there under the sun wherein every half year the public justice does make her progress into every part thereof, as it does in the kingdoms of England and Ireland? Whereby it comes to pass, that whereas the people of other countries do travel far to seek justice in their fixed and settled courts, as it were at fountains or cisterns, the streams of justice are derived unto our people and brought by conduit-pipes or quills even home, as it were, to their own doors. And thus much I thought fit to observe for the clearing of that unjust imputation of long and unnecessary delays in our legal proceedings.

(3) But there is yet another exception against the professors of our law, namely that wittingly and willingly they take upon them the defence of many bad cases, knowing the same to be unjust when they are first consulted with and retained. And this is objected by such as presume to censure our profession in this manner. In every case between party and party (say they), there is a right, and there is a

wrong; yet neither the one party nor the other did ever want a counsellor to maintain his case. This may be true for the most part, and yet in truth the learned counsel whose fortune it is to light on the wrong side may be free from imputation of any blame. For when does the right or wrong in every case appear? When is that distinguished and made manifest? Can it be discovered upon the first commencement of the suit, and before it be known what can be alleged and proved by either party? Assuredly it cannot. And therefore the counsellor, when he is first retained, cannot possibly judge of the case, whether it be just or unjust, because he hears only one part of the matter; and that also he receives by information from his client, who does ever put the case with the best advantage for himself. But when the parties have pleaded and are at issue, when they have examined witnesses in course of equity, or be descended to a trial in course of law, after publication and hearing in the one case, and full evidence delivered in the other, then the learned counsel of either side may perhaps discern the right from the wrong, and not before. But then are the cases come to their catastrophe, and the counsellors act their last part. And yet until then the true state of the case on both sides could not possibly be discovered.

If then the cases that are prosecuted do for the most part hang in a doubtful balance until the hearing or trial thereof (for if a case be undoubtedly and apparently nought on the one side, no man is so unwise as to follow it to the end, with the expense of money and hazard of his credit), how can it be justly said that the counsellor against whose client a decree or verdict does pass has wittingly defended an unjust cause, when he wist not how the balance would incline, until he had made his uttermost defence? Howbeit, if any of our counsellors do either in the prosecution of their clients' cases give sinister and crafty counsel, or upon the hearing or trial thereof make an over-bold defence of any dishonest action, our judges are so tender and jealous of the honour of our profession, as they lay a note of infamy upon such persons, so as they seldom or never after are permitted to rise to any higher degree in the law, or any office of trust in the commonwealth.

Whereby it comes to pass that no men, of any other calling or profession whatsoever, are more careful to preserve their good name and reputation, and stand more precisely upon their good behaviour, than the learned professors of the common law.

And as our judges do discountenance bad counsellors, so does our law abhor the defence and maintenance of bad causes, more than any other law in the world besides. For by what other law is unlawful maintenance, champerty, or buying of titles so severely punished? By what other law does the plaintiff *pro falso clamore*, or unjust vexation, or the defendant for pleading a false plea, pay an amerciament or fine to the public justice? And this is one cause, among others, why our law does not allow counsel unto such as are indicted of treason, murder, rape, or other capital crimes. So as never any professor of the law of England has been known to defend (for the matter of fact) any traitor, murderer, ravisher, or thief, being indicted and prosecuted at the suit of the king. *Turpe reos empta miseros defendere lingua* [it is a shameful thing to defend worthless prisoners for money], says the poet. And therefore it is an honour unto our law that it does not suffer the professors thereof to dishonour themselves (as the advocates and orators in other countries do) by defending such offenders. For example whereof, we have extant divers orations of Cicero, one *pro C. Rabirio perduellionis reo* [on behalf of a defendant in a case of treason]; another *pro Roscio Amerino*, who was accused of parricide; and another *pro Milone*, who was accused of murder.

But good lawyers have not with us that liberty which good physicians have: for a good physician may lawfully undertake the cure of a foul and desperate disease, but a good lawyer cannot honestly undertake the defence of a foul and desperate case. But if he fortune to be engaged in a case which, seeming honest in the beginning, does in the proceeding appear to be unjust, he follows the good counsel of the School-man, Thomas Aquinas: . . . ['If an advocate takes on a case believing it to be just, and discovers it to be unjust, he should not betray his client, to the benefit of his opponent, by revealing confidential information. Yet he can and should delay matters, or persuade his client either to give in or to reach an accommodation which is not disadvantageous to his opponent.']

And thus I conceive that the most common and colourable exceptions which are taken against our law and lawyers may be answered and cleared by the plain reasons and demonstrations before expressed: so as our profession may stand and be justified in all points against ignorance, envy, and ill-contented suitors, who, like choleric chess-players, when they have had a mate given them, could find in their hearts to cast both the chess-board and chess-men into the fire.

These vulgar errors being thus reversed, so as we may truly say that there is no such uncertainty in the rules of the law, no such delay in the proceedings, no such prevarication or corruption in the professors thereof as it is by some unjustly pretended, why may we not proceed further, and affirm confidently that the profession of the law is to be preferred before all other human professions and sciences, as being most noble for the matter and subject thereof, most necessary for the common and continual use thereof, and most meritorious for the good effects it does produce in the commonwealth?

For what is the matter and subject of our profession but justice, the lady and queen of all moral virtues? And what are our professors of the law but her councillors, her secretaries, her interpreters, her servants? Again, what is the king himself but the clear fountain of justice? And what are the professors of the law but conduit-pipes deriving and conveying the streams of his justice to all the subjects of his several kingdoms? So as if justice be rightly resembled to the sun in the firmament, in that she spreads her light and virtue unto all creatures, how can she but communicate part of her goodness and glory unto that science that is her handmaid, and waits upon her? And if kings be God's scholars (as Homer writes), and that the rules of justice be their principal lesson, and if God do honour kings with his own name, *Dixi quod dii estis* (as a more divine poet than Homer sings), especially for that they sit upon God's own seat when they minister justice unto the people, do not kings again highly honour those persons whose subordinate ministry and service they use in performing that principal part of their kingly office? Undoubtedly, touching the advancement of such persons, Solomon the king speaks, that 'they shall stand before kings', and 'God will set them', says David, 'with princes, even with the princes of his people.' . . .

And in very truth, as the commonwealth is much beholding to the profession of the law, so are the professors of the law not a little beholding to the commonwealth. For if they procure and preserve her peace and her plenty, does not she requite them again with riches and with honour? Does she not advance them to her chief benches and offices, and trust them with the livelihood and lives of all her people? Neither do our learned men of the law grow to good estates in the commonwealth by any illiberal means (as envy sometimes suggests), but in a most ingenuous and worthy manner. For the fees or rewards which they receive are not of the nature of wages or pay, or that which we call salary or hire, which are indeed duties certain, and grow due by contract for labour or service; but that which is given to a learned counsellor is called *honorarium* and not *merces*, being indeed a gift which gives honour as well to the taker as to the giver; neither is it certain or contracted for: for no price or rate can be set upon counsel, which is invaluable and inestimable, so as it is more or less according to circumstances, namely the ability of the client, the worthiness of the counsellor, the weightiness of the case, and the custom of the country. Briefly, it is a gift of such a nature, and given and taken upon such terms, as albeit the able client may not neglect to give it without note of ingratitude (for it is but a gratuity or token of thankfulness), yet the worthy counsellor may not demand it without doing wrong to his reputation, according to that moral rule: *Multa honeste accipi possunt; quae tamen honeste peti non possunt* [There are many things which can be honestly accepted which cannot be honestly requested].

Lastly, it is an infallible argument that the estates of such as rise by the law are builded upon the foundation of virtue, in that God's blessing is so manifestly upon them, not only in raising but in preserving their houses and posterities: whereof there are examples not a few, and those not obscure, in every shire of England, and of the English Pale in this kingdom of Ireland. . . .

2   Sir Edward Coke, *Le Tierce Part des Reportes* (1602)

Preface

.   .   .   .

And for that it is hard for a man to report any part or branch of any art or science justly and truly, which he professes not, and impossible to make a just and true relation of any thing that he understands not, I pray thee beware of chronicle law reported in our annals, for that will undoubtedly lead thee to error. For example, they say that William the Conqueror decreed that there should be sheriffs in every shire and justices of peace to keep the countries in quiet, and to see offenders punished; whereas the learned know that sheriffs were

great officers and ministers of justice, as now they are, long before
the Conquest, and justices of peace had not their being until almost
three hundred years after, viz. in the first year of Edward III. . . . But
if you will give any faith to them, let it be in those things they have
published concerning the antiquity and honour of the common laws.
First, they say that Brutus, the first king of this land, as soon as he
had settled himself in his kingdom, for the safe and peaceable
government of his people, wrote a book in the Greek tongue, calling
it the Laws of the Britons, and he collected the same out of the laws
of the Trojans. This king, say they, died after the creation of the
world 2860 years, and before the Incarnation of Christ 1103 years,
Samuel then being judge of Israel. I will not examine these things in
a *quo warranto*: the ground thereof I think was best known to the
authors and writers of them. But that the laws of the ancient Britons,
their contracts and other instruments, and the records and judicial
proceedings of their judges, were wrought and sentenced in the
Greek tongue, it is plain and evident by proofs luculent and uncontrollable. For proof whereof I shall be enforced only to point out
the heads of some few reasons, yet so as you may prosecute the same
from the fountains themselves at your good pleasure, and greater
leisure. And first, take a just testimony out of the Commentaries of
Julius Caesar, whose relations are as true as his style and phrase are
perfect. He, in his sixth book of the wars of France, says that in
ancient time the nobility of France were all of two sort, Druids or
Equites: the one for matters of government at home, the other for
martial employments abroad. To the Druids appertained the ordering
as well of matters ecclesiastical, as the administration of the laws and
government of the commonwealth. . . . Concerning the mysteries of
their religion, they neither did nor might commit them to writing;
but for the dispatching and deciding of cases, as well public as
private, says he, *Graecis literis utuntur*, they used to do it in the Greek
tongue, to the end that their disciplines might not be made common
among the vulgar. Now then, this being granted that the Druids
did customarily sentence cases, and order matters public and private, in the Greek language, it will easily follow, that the very same
was likewise used here in Britain; and the consequence is evident
and necessary, for that the whole society and all the discipline of
the Druids in France was nothing else but a very colony taken out
from our British Druids, as Caesar himself in the same place affirms

. . . . The very same witnesses Pliny. . . . Now for matters of religion, Strabo in his fourth book observes that the Britons worshipped Ceres and Proserpina, and sacrificed unto them according to the Greek form of superstition . . . hereby, as I think, it is sufficiently proved that the laws of England are of much greater antiquity than they are reported to be, and than any [of] the constitutions or laws imperial of Roman Emperors. Now, therefore, to return to our chronologers, they further say that 441 years before the Incarnation of Christ, Mulumucius, of some called Dunvallo Mulumucius, of some Dovebant, did write two books of the laws of the Britons, the one called *statuta municipalia*, and the other *leges judiciariae*, for so the same do signify in the British tongue wherein he wrote the same, which is as much to say as the statute law and the common law . . . and much more to like purpose shall you read in Gildas, Gervase of Tilbury, Geoffrey of Monmouth, William of Malmesbury, Hovenden, Matthew of Westminster, Polydore Vergil, Harding, Caxton, Fabian, Balaeus and others . . . and yet it were to be wished that they had kept themselves within their proper element, for peradventure with wise men some of them have reaped the reward of those that are not believed when they say the truth. To the grave and learned writers of histories my advice is that they meddle not with any point or secret of any art or science, especially with the laws of this realm, before they confer with some learned in that profession.

3   John Lilburne, *The Just Defence of John Lilburn, against Such as Charge Him with Turbulency of Spirit* (1653)

. . . yet a time will come when those that now are apt to censure me of rashness and turbulency of spirit will dearly repent that ever they admitted such a thought, confess they have done me wrong, and wish with all their hearts they had been all of my judgement and resolution. There being not one particular I have contended for, or for which I have suffered, but the right, freedom, safety and well-being of every particular man, woman and child in England has been so highly concerned therein, that their freedom or bondage has depended thereupon, insomuch that had they not been misled in their judgements, and corrupted in their understandings by such as sought their bondage, they would have seen themselves as much bound to have assisted me, as they judge themselves obliged to deliver their neighbour out of the hands of thieves and robbers. It being impossible for any man, woman or child in England to be free from the arbitrary and tyrannical wills of men, except those ancient laws and ancient rights of England, for which I have contended even unto blood, be preserved and maintained. The justness and goodness whereof I no sooner understood, and how great a check they were to tyranny and oppression, but my conscience enforced me to stand firm in their defence against all innovation and contrary practices in whomsoever.

For I bless God I have never been partial unto men, neither malicing any, nor having any man's person in admiration, nor bearing with that in one sort of men which I condemned in others. As for instance, the first fundamental right I contended for in the late King's and bishops' times, was for the freedom of men's persons against arbitrary and illegal imprisonments, it being a thing expressly contrary to the law of the land, which requires that no man be attached, imprisoned, etc. (as in Magna Carta, chapter 29), but by lawful judgement of a jury. A law so just and preservative as without which entirely observed every man's person is continually liable to be imprisoned at pleasure, and either to be kept there for months or years, or to be starved there, at the wills of those that in any time are in power, as has since been seen and felt abundantly, and had been more, had not some men strove against it. But it being my lot so to be imprisoned in those times, I conceive I did but my duty to manifest the injustice thereof, and claim and cry out for my right, and in so doing was serviceable to the liberties of my country, and no ways deserved to be accounted turbulent in so doing.

Another fundamental right I then contended for was that no man's conscience ought to be racked by oaths imposed, to answer to questions concerning himself in matters criminal, or pretended to be so. The ancient known right and law of England being that no man be put to his defence at law upon any man's bare saying, or upon his own oath, but by presentment of lawful men, and by faithful witnesses brought for the same face to face: a law and known right without which any that are in power may at pleasure rake into the breasts of every man for matter to destroy life, liberty or estate, when, according to true law and due proceedings, there is nought against them. Now it being my lot to be drawn out and required to take an oath, and to be required to answer to questions against myself and others whom I honoured, and whom I knew no evil by, though I might know such things by them as the oppressors and persecutors would have punished them for, in that I stood firm to our true English liberty, as resolvedly persisted therein, enduring a most cruel whipping, pillorying, gagging and barbarous imprisonment, rather than betray the rights and liberties of every man: did I deserve for so doing to be accounted turbulent? Certainly none will so judge, but such as are very weak, or very wicked, the first of which are inexcusable at this day, this ancient right having now for many years been known to all men, and the latter ought rather to be punished than to be countenanced, being still ready to do the like to me or any man.

I then contended also against close imprisonment as most illegal, being contrary to the known laws of the land, and by which tyrants and oppressors in all ages have broken the spirits of the English, and sometimes broken their very hearts: a cruelty few are sensible of, but such as have been sensible by suffering, but yet it concerns all men to oppose in whomsoever, for what is done to anyone may be done to everyone. Besides, being all members of one body, that is, of the English commonwealth, one man should not suffer wrongfully, but all should be sensible and endeavour his preservation, otherwise they give way to an inlet of the sea of will and power upon their laws and liberties, which are the boundaries to keep out tyranny and oppression. And who assists not in such cases betrays his own rights and is overrun, and of a free man made a slave when he thinks not of it, or regards it not, and so shunning the censure of turbulency, incurs the guilt of treachery to the present and future generations. Nor did I thrust myself upon these contests for my native rights, and the rights of every Englishman, but was forced thereupon in my own defence, which I urge not, but that I judge it lawful, praiseworthy, and expedient for every man continually to watch over the rights and liberties of his country, and to see that they are violated upon none, though the most vile and dissolute of men; or, if they be, speedily to endeavour redress. Otherwise such violations, breaches and encroachments will eat like a gangrene upon the common liberty, and become past remedy. But I urge it, that it may appear I was so far from what would in me have been interpreted turbulency, that I contended not till in my own particular I was assaulted and violated. . . .

4 John Warr, *The Corruption and Deficiency of the Lawes of England Soberly Discovered: or Liberty Working up to Its Just Height* (1649)

Wherein is set down:

(1) The standard or measure of all just laws, which is three-fold:
 (i) Their original and rise, viz. the free choice or election of the people;
 (ii) Their rule and square, viz. principles of justice, righteousness and truth;
 (iii) Their use and end, viz. the liberty/safety of the people.

(2) The laws of England weighed in this threefold balance and found too light:
 (i) in their original: force, power, conquest or constraint;
 (ii) in their rule: corrupt will, or principles of unrighteousness and wrong;
 (iii) in their end: the grievance, trouble and bondage of the people.

(3) The necessity of the reformation of the laws of England, together with the excellency (and yet difficulty) of this work.

(4) The corrupt interest of lawyers in this commonwealth.

Philip. Honor: . . . 'The laws of England are full of tricks, doubts and contrary to themselves; for they were invented and established by the Normans, which were of all nations the most quarrelsome, and most fallacious in contriving of controversies and suits.'

Chapter 1: Concerning the Just Measure of All Good Laws, in Their Original, Rule and End: Together with a Reflection (by Way of Antithesis) upon Unjust Laws

Those laws which do carry any thing of freedom in their bowels do owe their original to the people's choice, and have been wrested from the rulers and princes of the world by importunity of entreaty or by force of arms. For the great men of the world, being invested with the power thereof, cannot be imagined to eclipse themselves or their own pomp, unless by the violent interposition of the people's spirits, who are most sensible of their own burdens, and most forward in seeking relief. So that exorbitancy and injustice on the part of rulers was the rise of laws in behalf of the people, which consideration will afford us this general maxim, that the pure and genuine interest of laws was to bridle princes, not the people, and to keep rulers within the bounds of just and righteous government: from whence, as from a fountain, the rivulet of subjection and obedience on the people's part did reciprocally flow forth, partly to gratify, and partly to encourage good and virtuous governors. So that laws have but a secondary reflection on the people, glancing only at them, but looking with a full eye upon princes. Agreeable to this is that of Cicero (*de Officiis*, book 2), whose words are to this effect: . . . 'When the people did obtain redress of their wrongs from some just and good man, they were satisfied therewith; but when they failed thereof, they found out laws', etc.

From which assertion we may deduce a twofold corollary:

(1)   That at the foundation of governments, justice was in men before it came to be in laws, for the only rule of government to good princes was their own wills, and people were content to pay them their subjection upon the security of their bare words. So here in England, in the days of King Alfred, the administration of justice was immediately in the Crown, and required the personal attendance of the King.

(2)   But this course did soon bankrupt the world, and drive men to a necessity of taking bond from their princes and setting limits to their power. Hence it came to pass that justice was transmitted from men to laws, that both prince and people might read their duties, offences and punishments before them.

And yet such has been the interest of princes in the world, that the sting of the law has been plucked out as to them, and the weight of it fallen upon the people, which has been more grievous, because out of its place, the element of the law being beneficial, not cumbersome within its own sphere. Hence it is that laws, like swords, come to be used against those which made them, and, being put upon the rack of self- and worldly-interest, are forced to speak what they never meant, and to accuse their best friends, the people. Thus the law becomes anything or nothing, at the courtesy of great men, and is bended by them like a twig. Yea, how easy is it for such men to break those customs which will not bow, and erect traditions of a more complying temper to the wills of those whose end they serve. So that law comes to be lost in will and lust; yea, lust by the adoption of greatness is enacted law. Hence it comes to pass, that laws upon laws do bridle the people and run counter to their end; yea, the farther we go, the more out of the way. This is the original of unjust laws.

No marvel that freedom has no voice here, for an usurper reigns, and freedom is proscribed like an exile, living only in the understandings of some few men, and not daring to appear upon the theatre of the world. But yet the minds of men are the great wheels of things, thence come changes and alterations in the world. Teeming freedom exerts and puts forth itself; the unjust world would suppress its appearance, many fall in this conflict, but freedom will at last prevail, and give law to all things.

So that here is the proper fountain of good and righteous laws: a spirit of understanding big with freedom, and having a single respect to people's rights. Judgement goes before to create a capacity, and freedom follows after to fill it up. And thus law comes to be the bank of freedom, which is not said to straighten but to conduct the stream. A people thus watered are in a thriving posture, and the rather because the foundation is well laid, and the law reduced to its original state, which is the protection of the poor against the mighty.

If it were possible for a people to choose such laws as were prejudicial to themselves, this were to forsake their own interest: Here (you'll say) is free choice, but bring such laws to the rule, and there is a failure there. The rule of righteous laws are clean and righteous principles (according to the several appearances of truth within us), for reason is the measure of all just laws, though the size differ according to the various apprehensions of people, or tempers of commonwealths, so that choice, abstracted or considered in itself, is no undeniable badge of a just law, but as it is mixed with other ingredients; as on the contrary force and power are not therefore condemned, because they have hands to strike, but because they have no eyes to see, i.e. they are not usually balanced with understanding and right reason in making or executing of laws, the sword having commonly more of the beast in it than the man.

Otherwise, to be imposed upon by the art of truth is to be caught by a warrantable guile, and to be kept by force from injuring oneself or others has more of courtesy than severeness therein. And in this case reason will cast the scales and ascribe more to a seeing force than a blind choice. The righteousness or unrighteousness of things depends not upon the circumstances of our embracing or rejecting them, but upon the true nature of the things themselves. Let righteousness and truth be given out to the nation, we shall not much quarrel at the matter of conveyance, whether this way or that way, by the beast or by the man, by the vine or by the bramble.

There is a twofold rule of corrupt laws:

(1)   Principles of self and worldly greatness in the rulers of the world, who, standing upon the mountain of force and power, see nothing but their own land round about them, and make it their design to subdue laws as well as persons, and enforce both to do homage to their wills.

(2)   Obsequiousness, flattery or compliancy of spirit to the foresaid principles is the womb of all degenerous laws in inferior ministers. 'Tis hard indeed not to swim with the stream, and some men had rather give up their right than contend, especially upon apparent disadvantage. 'Tis true these things are temptations to men, and 'tis one thing to be destroyed, but to give up one's self to uncleanness is another. 'Tis better to be ravished of our freedoms (corrupt times have a force upon us), than to give them up as a free-will offering to the lusts of great men, especially if we ourselves have a share with them in the same design.

Easiness of spirit is a wanton frame, and so far from resisting that it courts an assault. Yea, such persons are prodigal of other men's stock, and give that away for the bare asking which will cost much labour to regain. Obsequious and servile spirits are the worst guardians of the people's rights. Upon the advantage of such spirits the interest of rulers has been heightened in the world and strictly guarded by severest laws. And truly, when the door of an interest flies open at a knock, no marvel that princes enter in.

And being once admitted into the bosom of the law, their first work is to secure themselves. And here, what servility and flattery are not able to effect, that force and power shall. And in order hereto a guard of laws is impressed to serve and defend prerogative power, and to secure it against the assaults of freedom, so that in this case freedom is not able to stir without a load of prejudice in the minds of men, and (as a ground thereof) a visible guilt as to the letter of the law.

But how can such laws be good which swerve from their end? The end of just laws is the safety and freedom of a people. As for safety, just laws are bucklers of defence. When the mouth of violence is muzzled by a law, the innocent feed and sleep securely. When the wolfish nature is destroyed there shall then be no need of law; as long as that is in being, the curb of the law keeps it in restraint, that the great may not oppress or injure the small. As for safety, laws are the manacles of princes, and the guards of private men. So far as laws advance the people's freedom, so far are they just, for as the power of the prince is the measure of unrighteous laws, so just laws are weighed in the balance of freedom. Where the first of these take place, the people are wholly slaves, where the second, they are wholly free. But most commonwealths are in a middle position, as having their laws grounded partly upon the interest of the prince, and partly upon the account of the people, yet so as that prerogative has the greatest influence, and is the chiefest ingredient in the mixture of the law, as in the laws of England will by and by appear.

Chapter 2: The Failures of Our English Laws in Their Origin, Rule and End

The influence of force and power in the sanction of our English laws appears by this, that several alterations have been made of our laws, either in whole or in part, upon every conquest. And if at any time the conqueror has continued any of the ancient laws, it has been only to please and ingratiate himself into the people, for so generous thieves give back part of their money to travellers to abate their zeal in pursuit.

Upon this ground I conceive it is, why Fortescue, and some others, do affirm, that notwithstanding the several conquests of this realm, yet the same laws have still continued. His words are these: . . . 'The kingdom of England was first inhabited by the Britons, afterwards 'twas governed by the Romans; and again by the Britons, and after that by the Saxons, who changed its name from Britain to England. In process of time the Danes ruled here, and again the Saxons, and last of all the Normans, whose posterity governs the kingdom at this day. And in all the times of these several nations, and of their kings, this realm was still ruled by the same customs that it is now governed withal.' Thus far Fortescue in the reign of Henry VI. Which opinion of his can be no otherwise explained, besides what we have already said, than that succeeding conquerors did still retain those parts of former laws which made for their own interest. Otherwise 'tis altogether inconsistent with reason, that the Saxons who banished the inhabitants, and changed the name, should yet retain the laws of this island. Conquerors seldom submit to the law of the conquered where conquests are complete, as the Saxons' was, but on the contrary, especially when they bear such a mortal feud to their persons. Which argument, if it were alone, were sufficient to demonstrate that the Britons and their laws were banished together, and to discover the weakness of the contrary opinion, unless you take the comment together with the text, and make that explanation of it which we have done.

And yet this is no honour at all to the laws of England, that they are such pure servants to corrupt interests that they can keep their places under contrary masters. Just and equal laws will rather endure perpetual imprisonment, or undergo the severest death, than take up arms on the other side: yea, princes cannot trust such laws. 'An hoary head (in a law) is no Crown, unless it be found in the way of righteousness.' Proverbs 16:31.

By this it appears that the notion of fundamental law is no such idol as men make it. For what, I pray you, is fundamental law, but such customs as are of the eldest date and longest continuance? Now freedom being the proper rule of custom, 'tis more fit that unjust customs should be reduced, that they may continue no longer, than that they should keep up their arms because they have continued so long. The more fundamental a law is, the more difficult, not the less necessary, to be reformed. But to return:

Upon every conquest our very laws have been found transgressors, and, without any judicial process, have undergone the penalty of abrogation. Not but that our laws needed to be reformed, but the only reason in the conqueror was his own will, without respect to the people's rights; and in this case the riders are changed, but the burdens continued, for mere force is a most partial thing, and ought never to pass in a jury upon the freedoms of the people. And yet thus it has been in our English nation, as by examining the original of it may appear. And in bringing down its pedigree to this present time we shall easily perceive that the British laws were altered by the Romans, the Roman law by the Saxons, the Saxon law by the Danes, the Danish law by King Edward the Confessor, King Edward's laws by William the Conqueror, which being somewhat moderated and altered by succeeding kings, is the present common law in force amongst us, as will by and by appear.

The history of this nation is transmitted down to us upon reasonable credit for 1700 years last past. But whence the Britons drew their original (who inhabited this island before the Roman Conquest) is as uncertainly related by historians, as what their laws and constitutions were. And truly, after so long a series of times, 'tis better to be silent, than to bear false witness. But certain it is that the Britons were under some kind of government, both martial and civil, when the Romans entered this island, as having perhaps borrowed some laws from the Greeks, the refiners of human spirits, and the ancientest inventors of laws. And this may seem more than conjectural, if the opinion of some may take place, that the Phoenicians or Greeks first sailed into Britain, and mingled customs and languages together: for it cannot be denied that the etymology of many British words seems to be Greekish, as (if it were material to this purpose) might be clearly shown.

But 'tis sufficient for us to know that whatever the laws of the Britons were upon the conquest of Caesar, they were reviewed and altered, and the Roman law substituted in its room, by Vespasian, Papinian and others who were in person here; yea divers of the British nobles were educated at Rome, on purpose to inure them to their laws. The civil law remaining in Scotland is said to have been planted there by the Romans, who conquered a part thereof. And this nation was likewise subject to the same law, till the subversion of this state by the Saxons, who made so barbarous a conquest of the nation, and so razed out the foundation of former laws, that there are less footsteps of the civil law in this, than in France, Spain, or any other province under the Roman power. So that while the Saxons ruled here they were governed by their own laws, which differed much from the British law. Some of these Saxon laws were afterwards digested into form, and are yet extant in their original tongue, and translated into Latin.

The next alteration of our English laws was by the Danes, who repealed and nulled the Saxon law, and established their own in its stead. Hence it is that the laws of England do bear great affinity with the customs of Denmark in descents of inheritance, trials of right, and several other ways. 'Tis probable that originally inheritances were divided in this kingdom amongst all the sons by gavelkind, which custom seems to have been instituted by Caesar, both amongst us and the Germans, and as yet remains in Kent, not wrested from them by the Conqueror. But the Danes, being ambitious to conform us to the pattern of their own country, did doubtless alter this custom, and allot the inheritance to the eldest son, for that was the course in Denmark, as Walsingham reports in his *Upodigma Neustriae*: . . . 'Fathers did expose and put forth all their sons, besides one whom they made heir of their estates.' So likewise in trials of rights by twelve men our customs agree with the Danish, and in many other particulars which were introduced by the Danes, disused at their expulsion, and revived again by William the Conqueror.

For after the massacre of the Danes in this island, King Edward the Confessor did again alter their laws, and though he extracted many particulars out of the Danish laws, yet he grafted them upon a new stock, and compiled a body of laws since known by his name, under the protection of which the people then lived: so that here was another alteration of our English laws. And as the Danish law was altered by King Edward, so were King Edward's laws disused by the Conqueror, and some of the Danish customs again revived. And, to clear this, we must consider that the Danes and Normans were both of a stock, and situated in Denmark, but called Normans from their northern situation, from whence they sailed into France, and settled their customs in that part of it which they called Normandy, by their own name, and from thence into Britain. And here comes in the great alteration of our English laws by William the Conqueror, who, selecting some passages out of the Saxon, and some out of the Danish law, and in both having great respect to his own interest, made by the rule of his government; but his own will was an exception to this rule as often as he pleased.

For the alterations which the Conqueror brought in were very great, as the clothing his laws with the Norman tongue, the appointing of terms at Westminster (whereas before the people had justice in their own countries, there being several courts in every county, and the supreme court in the county was called *generale placitum*, for the determining of those controversies which the parish or the hundred court could not decide), the ordaining of sheriffs and other court-officers in every county to keep people in subjection to the Crown, and upon any attempt for redress of injustice, life and land was forfeited to the king. Thus were the possessions of the inhabitants distributed amongst his followers, yet still upon their good behaviour, for they must hold it of the Crown, and in case of disobedience the property did revert: and in order hereto certain rents yearly were to be paid to the king. Thus, as the lords and rulers held of the king, so did inferior persons hold of the lords. Hence come landlord, tenant, holds, tenures, etc., which are slavish ties and badges upon men, grounded originally on conquest and power.

Yea, the laws of the Conqueror were so burdensome to the people that succeeding kings were forced to abate of their price and to give back some freedom to the people. Hence it came to pass that Henry I did mitigate the laws of his father the Conqueror, and restored those of King Edward; hence likewise came the confirmation of Magna Carta and Carta Forestae, by which latter the power of the king was abridged in enlarging of forests, whereas the Conqueror is said to have demolished a vast number of buildings to erect and enlarge New Forest by Salisbury, which must needs be a grievance to the people. These freedoms were granted to the people not out of any love to them, but extorted from princes by fury of war, or incessantness of address. And in this case princes, making a virtue of necessity, have given away that which was none of their own, and they could not well keep, in hope to regain it at other times, so that what of freedom we have by the law is the price of much hazard and blood. Grant that the people seem to have had a shadow of freedom in choosing of laws, as consenting to them by their representatives, or proxies, both before and since the Conquest (for even the Saxon kings held their conventions or parliaments), yet whosoever shall consider how arbitrary such meetings were, and how much at the devotion of the prince, both to summon and dissolve, and withal how the spirit of freedom was observed and kept under, and likewise how most of the members of such assemblies were lords, dukes, earls, pensioners to the prince and the royal interest, will easily conclude that there has been a failure in our English laws as to matter of election or free choice, there having been always a rod held over the choosers, and a negative voice, with a power of dissolution, having always nipped freedom in the bud.

The rule of our English laws is as faulty as the rise. The rule of our laws may be referred to a twofold interest:

(1)   The interest of the king, which was the great bias and rule of the law, and other interests but tributary to this. Hence it is all our laws run in the name of the king, and are carried on in an orb above the sphere of the people. Hence it is that saying of Philip Honor: . . . 'Since the laws of England were instituted by William the Conqueror, or tyrant, 'tis no wonder that they respect only the prerogative of the king, and neglect the freedom of the people.'

(2)   The interest of the people, which (like a worm) when trod upon did turn again and in smaller iotas and diminutive parcels wound in itself into the texture of law, yet so as that the royal interest was above it and did frequently suppress it at its pleasure. The freedom which we have by the law owns its original to this interest of the people, which, as it was formerly little known to the world, so was it misrepresented by princes, and laden with reproaches to make it odious: yea, liberty, the result thereof, was obtained but by parcels, so that we have rather a taste than a draught of freedom.

If then the rise and rule of our law be so much out of tune, no marvel that we have no good music in the end, but bondage instead of freedom, and instead of safety, danger. For the law of England is so full of uncertainty, nicety, ambiguity, and delay that the poor people are ensnared, not remedied, thereby. The formality of our English law is that to an oppressed man which school-divinity is to a wounded spirit, when the conscience of a sinner is pierced with remorse. 'Tis not the nicety of the casuist which is able to heal it, but the solid experience of the grounded Christian. 'Tis so with the law: when the poor and oppressed want right, they meet with law which, as 'tis managed, is their greatest wrong, so that law itself becomes a sin, and an experimented grievance in this nation. Who knows not that the web of the law entangles the small flies, and dismisses the great? So that a mite of equity is worth a whole bundle of law: yea, many times the very law is the badge of our oppression, its proper intent being to enslave the people, so that the inhabitants of this nation are lost in the law, such and so many are the references, orders and appeals that it were better for us to sit down by the loss than to seek for relief. For law is a chargeable physician, and he which has a great family to maintain may well take large fees.

For the officers or menial servants of the law are so numerous that the price of right is too high for a poor man. Yea, many of them procuring their places by sinister ways must make themselves savers by the vails of their office: yea, 'twere well if they rested her and did not raise the market of their fees, for they that buy at a great rate must needs sell dear. But the poor and the oppressed pay for all. Hence it is that such men grow rich upon the ruins of others, and whilst law and lawyer is advanced, equity and truth are under hatches, and the people subject to a legal tyranny, which of all bondages is one of the greatest.

Mere force is its own argument and has nothing to plead for it but itself, but when oppression comes under the notion of law 'tis most ensnaring, for sober-minded men will part with some right to keep the rest, and are willing to bear to the utmost. But perpetual burdens will break their backs (as the strongest jade tires at the last), especially when there is no hope of relief.

Chapter 3: Of the Necessity of the Reformation of the Laws of England, together with the Excellency (and yet Difficulty) of the Work

The more general a good is, the more divine and godlike. Grant that prerogative laws are good for princes, and advantageous to their interest, yet the shrubs are more in number than the cedars in the forest of the world, and laws of freedom in behalf of people are more useful because directed to a more general good. Communities are rather to be respected than the private interests of great men. Good patriots study the people as favourites do the prince, and it is altogether impossible that the people should be free without a reformation of the law, the source and root of freedom. An equal and speedy distribution of right ought to be the abstract and epitome of all laws, and if so:

Why are there so many delays, turnings and windings in the laws of England?

Why is our law a meander of intricacies, where a man must have contrary winds before he can arrive at his desired port?

Why are so many men destroyed for want of a formality and punctilio in law? And who would not blush to behold seemingly grave and learned sages to prefer a letter, syllable or word before the weight and merit of a case?

Why do the issue of most lawsuits depend upon precedents rather than the rule, especially the rule of reason?

Why are men's lives forfeited by the law upon light and trivial grounds?

Why do some laws exceed the offence? And, on the contrary, other offences are of greater demerit than the penalty of the law?

Why is the law still kept in an unknown tongue, and the nicety of it rather countenanced than corrected?

Why are not courts rejourned into every county, that the people may have right at their own doors, and such tedious journeyings may be prevented?

Why, under pretence of equity and a court of conscience, are our wrongs doubled and trebled upon us: the Court of Chancery being as extortionous (or more) than any other court? Yea, 'tis a considerable query, whether the Court of Chancery were not first erected merely to elude the letter of the law, which, though defective, yet had some certainty, and, under a pretence of conscience, to devolve all cases upon mere will, swayed by corrupt interest. If former ages have taken advantage to mix some wheat with the tares, and to insert some mites of freedom into our laws, why should we neglect (upon greater advantages) to double our files, and to produce the perfect image of freedom, which is therefore neglected, because not known?

How otherwise can we answer the call of God, or the cries of the people, who search for freedom as for an hid treasure? Yea, how can we be registered, even in the catalogue of heathens, who made less show but had more substance, and were excellent justiciaries as to the people's rights: so Solon, Lycurgus, etc.? Such moral appearances in the minds of men are of sufficient energy for the ordering of commonwealths, and it were to be wished that whole states which are called Christian were but as just as heathens in their laws, and such strict promoters of common right.

Pure religion is to visit the fatherless, and the most glorious fast [is] to abstain from strife and smiting with the fist of wickedness: in a word, to relieve the oppressed will be a just guerdon and reward for our pains and travail in the reformation of the law. And yet this work is very hard, there being so many concerned therein, and most being busier to advance and secure themselves than to benefit the public. Yea, our physicians being themselves parties, and engaged in those interests which freedom condemns, will hardly be brought to deny themselves, unless upon much conviction and assistance from above. And yet this we must hope for, that the reformation of the times may begin in the breasts of our reformers, for such men are likely to be the hopeful sire of freedom who have the image of it engrafted in their own minds.

Chapter 4: Of the Corrupt Interest of Lawyers in the Commonwealth of England

Of interests, some are grounded upon weakness, and some upon corruption. The most lawful interests are sown in weakness, and have their rise and growth there: apostle, prophet, evangelist were only for the perfecting of the saints; physicians are of the like interest to the body; a marriage is but a help and comfort in a dead state, for in the resurrection they neither marry, nor are given in marriage. Interest grounded upon weakness may be used, as long as our weakness does continue, and no longer, for the whole need not a physician, etc. Such interests are good, profitable, useful, and in their own nature self-denying, i.e. contented to sit down and give way to that strength and glory to which they serve.

But the interest of lawyers in this commonwealth seems to be grounded rather upon corruption than weakness, as by surveying its origin may appear. The rise and potency of lawyers in this kingdom may be ascribed to a twofold ground:

(1) The unknownness of the law, being in a strange tongue, whereas when the law was in a known language (as before the Conquest) a man might be his own advocate. But the hiddenness of the law, together with the fallacies and doubts thereof, render us in a posture unable to extricate ourselves, but we must have recourse to the shrine of the lawyer, whose oracle is in such request because it pretends to resolve doubts.

(2) The quarterly terms at Westminster, whereas when justice was administered in every county this interest could not possibly grow

to an height, but every man could mind and attend his own case without such journeying to and fro, and such chargeable attendance, as at Westminster Hall. For first, in the country the day was plain, and controversies decided by neighbours of the hundred, who could be soon informed in the state of the matter, and were very ready to administer justice, as making it their own case. But as for Common Lawyers, they carry only the idea of right and wrong in their heads, and are so far from being touched with the sense of those wrongs against which they seem to argue, that they go on merely in a formulary of words. I speak not this out of emulation or envy against any man's person, but singly in behalf of the people, against the corruption of the interest itself.

After the Conquest, when courts and terms were established at Westminster (for how could the darling of prerogative thrive, unless always under the King's eye?), men were not at leisure to take so much pains for their own, but sometimes they themselves, sometimes their friends in their behalf, came up in term time to London to plead their cases and to procure justice. As yet the interest of lawyers was a puny thing, for one friend would undertake to plead his case for another, and he which was more versed in the tricks of the law than his neighbour would undertake a journey to London, at the request of those who had business to do, perhaps his charges borne on the way and some small reward for his pains. There were then no stately mansions for lawyers, but such agents (whether parents, friends or neighbours to the parties) lodged like other travellers in inns, as country attorneys still do. Hence it came to pass that when the interest of lawyers came to be advanced in Edward III's time, their mansions or colleges were still called inns, but with an addition of honour, Inns of Court.

The proceed of lawyers' interest is as follows: when such agents as we have spoken of, who were employed by their neighbours at London, and by this means coming to be versed in the niceties of the law, found it sweeter than the plough, and, controversies beginning to increase, they took up their quarters here till such time as they were formed into an orderly body, and distinct interest, as they are now.

There is ground enough to conclude, even from the letter of the statute law (in 28 Edward I, cap. 11: 'But it may not be understood hereby that any persons shall be prohibited to have counsel of pleaders or of learned men in the law for his fee, or of his parents and next friends') that men's parents, friends or neighbours did plead for them, without the help of any other lawyer. After the lawyers were formed into a society, and had hired the temple of the Knights Templars for the place of their abode, their interest was not presently advanced, but by the contentions of the people, after a long series of time, so that the interest of lawyers (in the height which now it is) comes from the same root as pride and idleness, i.e. from fullness of bread or prosperity, the mother of strife. Not but that just and equal administrators of laws are very necessary in a commonwealth, but when once that which was at first but a title comes to be framed into an interest, then it sets up itself and grows great upon the ruins of others, and through the corruption of the people.

I take this to be a main difference between lawful and corrupt interests: just interests are the servants of all, and are of an humble spirit, as being content to have their light put out by the brightness of that glory which they are supplemental to. But corrupt interests fear a change, and use all wiles to establish themselves, that so their fall may be great, and their ruin as chargeable to the world as it can: for such interests care for none but themselves. The readiest way to inform such men is to do it within us, for most men have the common barrister within them, i.e. principles of contention and wrong. And thus the law becomes the engine of strife, the instrument of lust, the mother of debates, and lawyers are as make-hates between a man and his neighbour.

When Sir Walter Raleigh was upon his trial the lawyers that were of counsel for the king were very violent against him. Whereupon Sir Walter, turning to the jury, used these words: 'Gentlemen, I pray you consider that these men (meaning the lawyers) do usually defend very bad cases every day in the courts, against men of their own profession as able as themselves. What then will they not do against me?' Which speech of his may be too truly affirmed of many lawyers, who are anything or nothing for gain, and, measuring cases by their own interest, care not how long right be deferred and suits prolonged. There was a suit in Gloucestershire between two families which lasted since the reign of Edward IV, till of late composed, which certainly must be ascribed either to the ambiguity of the law, or the subtlety of the lawyers, neither of which are any great honour to the English nation.

How much better were it to spend the acuteness of the mind in the real and substantial ways of good and benefit to ourselves and others? And not to unbowel ourselves into a mere will, a frothy and contentious way of law, which the oppressed man stands in no more need of than the tender-hearted Christian of Thomas Aquinas to resolve him in his doubts.

If there be such a thing as right in the world, let us have it, *sine suco* [undiluted]. Why is it delayed, or denied, or varnished over with guily words? Why comes it not forth in its own dress? Why does it not put off law, and put on reason, the mother of all just laws? Why is it not ashamed of its long and mercenary train? Why can we not ask it and receive it ourselves, but must have it handed to us by others? In a word, why may not a man plead his own case? Or his friends and acquaintance (as formerly) plead for him? Memorable is that passage in King James, his speech in Star Chamber: 'In countries', says he, 'where the formality of law has no place, as in Denmark, all their state is governed only by a written law. There is no advocate or proctor admitted to plead. Only the parties themselves plead their own case, and then a man stands up and pleads the law, and there is an end. For the very law-book itself is their only judge. Happy were all kingdoms, if they could be so. But here curious wits, various conceits, different actions, and variety of examples breed questions in law.' Thus far he. And if this kingdom does resemble Denmark in so many other customs, why may it not be assimilated to it in this also? Especially considering that the world travails with freedom, and some real compensation is desired by the people for all their sufferings, losses, blood.

To clear the channel of the law is an honourable work for a senate, who should be preservers of the people's rights.

NOTES ON THE TEXTS

1. Davies, *Le Primer Report:* 1615 (Dublin); 1628 (London); 1674 (London and Dublin); English translation, 1762 (Dublin). Also in Davies's *Works* (three vols., 1859–76, Blackburn).

2. Coke, *Le Tierce Part des Reportes:* The first eleven parts of Coke's *Reports* appeared 1600–15 (St Omer) with English prefaces, French reports and Latin pleadings. They were reprinted 1609–15 and (with Latin trans-

lated into French) 1619–31, 1672, 1697 and 1762. They were published in English translation 1658–77, 1680, 1777 and 1826.

3. Lilburne, *Just Defence:* Published in 1653; reprinted in W. Haller and G. Davies (eds.), *The Leveller Tracts* (New York, 1944; Magnolia, 1964) and in A. L. Morton (ed.), *Freedom in Arms* (London, 1975).

4. Warr, *Corruption and Deficiency of the Lawes* (1649): Reprinted in successive editions of the *Harleian Miscellany* (1744–6, vol. III; 1808–11, vol. VI; 1808–13, vol. III).

FURTHER READING

The most influential book on seventeenth-century legal thought has been J. G. A. Pocock, *The Ancient Constitution and the Feudal Law* (Cambridge, 1957). Pocock's thesis that there was an insular, ahistorical, 'common-law mind', personified by Coke and Davies, has been supported by D. R. Kelley in 'History, English Law and the Renaissance', *Past and Present*, no. 65 (1974), pp. 24–51. Kelley's article was criticized by C. Brooks and K. Sharpe in *Past and Present*, no. 72 (1976), pp. 133–42 (with Kelley's reply, ibid., pp. 143–6). Pocock's view has also been criticized by H. S. Pawlisch in 'Sir John Davies, the Ancient Constitution and Civil Law', *Historical Journal*, XXIII (1980), pp. 689–702, and *Sir John Davies and the Conquest of Ireland* (Cambridge, 1985), and by M. A. Ziskind, 'John Selden: Criticism and Affirmation of the Common Law Tradition', *American Journal of Legal History*, XIX (1975), pp. 22–39.

On Coke, see in particular B. Malament, 'The "Economic Liberalism" of Sir Edward Coke', *Yale Law Journal*, LXXVI (1967), pp. 1321–58; D. Little, *Religion, Order and Law* (New York, 1969); and S. D. White, *Sir Edward Coke and the Grievances of the Commonwealth, 1621–28* (Chapel Hill, 1979).

On the Crown's relationship to the courts there are two useful studies by W. J. Jones: 'The Crown and the Courts', in A. G. R. Smith (ed.), *The Reign of James VI and I* (London, 1973); and *Politics and the Bench* (London, 1977).

Two useful introductions to the rights of seventeenth-century Englishmen are J. T. Langbein, *Torture and the Law of Proof* (Chicago, 1977) and L. W. Levy, *Origins of the Fifth Amendment* (New York, 1968). Levy discusses Lilburne's efforts to establish the principle that nobody should be required to incriminate himself. Lilburne's attempts to defend himself by appeal to the existing law of the land are analysed in D. Parkin-Speer, 'John Lilburne: A Revolutionary Interprets Statutes and Common Law Due Process', *Law and History Review*, I (1983), pp. 276–96.

On the Leveller theory of the common law as the consequence of the Norman Conquest, and so as a bastion of tyranny rather than a guarantor of the rights of citizens, the pathbreaking essay by Christopher Hill on 'The Norman Yoke' (in his *Puritanism and Revolution* (London, 1958)) should be supplemented by R. B. Seaberg's important essay: 'The Norman Conquest and the Common Law: The Levellers and the Argument from Continuity', *Historical Journal*, XXIV (1981), pp. 791–806. The relationship between theories of English history and politics is more generally surveyed by Q. Skinner in 'History and Ideology in the English Revolution', *Historical Journal*, VIII (1965), pp. 151–78.

There are two complementary books on efforts to reform the law in mid-century: S. E. Prall, *The Agitation for Law Reform during the Puritan Revolution* (The Hague, 1966) and D. Veall, *The Popular Movement for Law Reform, 1640–60* (Oxford, 1970). A longer time span is covered by B. Shapiro, 'Law Reform in Seventeenth Century England', *American Journal of Legal History*, XIX (1975), pp. 280–312. Warr is the subject of ch. 12 of C. Hill, *The World Turned Upside Down* (London, 1972). Other works on the Levellers are briefly mentioned in the notes to Chapter Five.

CHAPTER THREE

PARLIAMENTARY CONSTITUTIONALISM

1 *The Petition of Right* (1628)

The main grievances which gave rise to the Petition of Right resulted from the king's efforts to organize a military expedition in support of the Huguenots in France (an expedition which failed disastrously in 1627). To finance the expedition unparliamentary taxation was imposed in the form of forced loans; those who refused to pay were imprisoned; when the Five Knights brought a test case to court the legality of this imprisonment was upheld; at the same time compulsory billeting of the troops gathered for embarkation and the use of martial law created further grievances. Worst of all the king was believed to have attempted to tamper with the legal record of the Five Knights' case in order to entrench the case as a precedent in law. The key to the Petition of Right is that it represents an attempt to find a parliamentary solution to what were seen as inadequacies of the common law. Where a generation had believed that the law provided an adequate safeguard for the rights of free citizens within an absolute monarchy, this no longer seemed to be the case. The Petition of Right itself proved an inadequate remedy, as the courts' willingness to uphold the king's right to collect ship-money demonstrated.

2 Charles I, *His Majesties Answer to the Nineteen Propositions of Both Houses of Parliament* (1642)

Parliament's Nineteen Propositions called on the king to agree to give parliament control of the army which had to be raised to suppress the Irish revolt and requested him to agree to appoint councillors approved by parliament. The king's reply was written in June by Colepepper and Falkland. It represented a radical shift in the royalist position in that it denied that England was an absolute monarchy. This shift was designed to win moderate support away from Parliament as both sides prepared for Civil War. It went too far, however, not only for those willing to defend absolutism, but even for Hyde (later Clarendon), the leader of the constitutional royalists, who objected to the king being described as merely one of three estates. Traditionally the three estates were the clergy, peers and commons, represented in the two houses of parliament. Nevertheless the position adopted in the Answer to the Nineteen Propositions, although moderate and constitutionalist, was only likely to persuade those who were willing to trust to Charles I's good intentions should he find himself in command of a loyal army.

3   Philip Hunton, *A Treatise of Monarchy* (1643)

Hunton (*c.* 1604–82), a clergyman, had a successful career during the Interregnum, being appointed Master of Durham College in 1657, but was ejected from this office and from his livings at the Restoration. *A Treatise of Monarchy* was his most important publication and was one of several tracts which sought to take advantage of the terminology of His Majesty's Answer to the Nineteen Propositions. Hunton put forward a theory of corporate sovereignty where no one authority within the constitution could overrule the other. In doing so he was trying to find a middle way between the defence of absolute royal authority put forward by writers such as Hobbes and what amounted to a claim to parliamentary sovereignty put forward by writers such as Parker. His arguments were best designed to appeal to those who were genuinely undecided as to which side to support, but by making the conscience of each individual the final authority Hunton took an important step towards an idea of popular sovereignty.

1 *The Petition of Right* (1628)

The Petition exhibited to his Majesty by the Lords Spiritual and Temporal and Commons in this present Parliament assembled concerning divers rights and liberties of the subject

To the King's Most Excellent Majesty

I. Humbly show unto our Sovereign Lord the King, the Lords Spiritual and Temporal and Commons in Parliament assembled, that whereas it is declared and enacted by a statute made in the time of the reign of King Edward I commonly called *statutum de tallagio non concedendo*, that no tallage or aid should be laid or levied by the king or his heirs in this realm without the good will and assent of the archbishops, bishops, earls, barons, knights, burgesses and other the freemen of the commonalty of this realm; and by authority of parliament holden in the five and twentieth year of the reign of King Edward III it is declared and enacted that from henceforth no person should be compelled to make any loans to the king against his will because such loans were against reason and the franchise of the land, and by other laws of this realm it is provided that none should be charged by any charge or imposition called a benevolence nor by such like charge; by which the statutes before mentioned and other the good laws and statutes of this realm your subjects have inherited this freedom, that they should not be compelled to contribute to any tax, tallage, aid or other like charge not set by common consent in parliament.

II. Yet, nevertheless, of late divers commissions directed to sundry commissioners in several counties with instructions have issued, by means whereof your people have been in divers places assembled and required to lend certain sums of money unto your Majesty, and many of them upon their refusal so to do have had an oath administered unto them not warrantable by the laws or statutes of this realm, and have been constrained to become bound to make appearance and give attendance before your Privy Council and in other places; and others of them have been therefore imprisoned, confined, and sundry other ways molested and disquieted, and divers other charges have been laid and levied upon your people in several counties by Lord Lieutenants, Deputy Lieutenants, Commissioners for Musters, Justices of Peace and others by command or direction from your Majesty or your Privy Council against the laws and free customs of the realm.

III.   And where also by the statute called the Great Charter of the Liberties of England it is declared and enacted that no freeman may be taken or imprisoned or be disseised of his freehold or liberties or his free customs or be outlawed or exiled or in any manner destroyed, but by the lawful judgement of his peers or by the law of the land.

IV.   And in the eight and twentieth year of the reign of King Edward III it was declared and enacted by authority of Parliament that no man, of what estate or condition that he be, should be put out of his land or tenement, nor taken, nor imprisoned, nor disherited, nor put to death without being brought to answer by due process of law.

V.   Nevertheless, against the tenor of the said statutes and other the good laws and statutes of your realm to that end provided, divers of your subjects have of late been imprisoned without any cause shown; and when for their deliverance they were brought before your justices by your Majesty's writ of *habeas corpus*, there to undergo and receive as the court should order, and their keepers commanded to certify the causes of their detainer, no cause was certified, but that they were detained by your Majesty's special command signified by the Lords of your Privy Council, and yet were returned back to several prisons without being charged with anything to which they might make answer according to the law.

VI.   And whereas of late great companies of soldiers and mariners have been dispersed into divers counties of the realm, and the inhabitants against their will have been compelled to receive them into their houses, and there to suffer them to sojourn against the laws and customs of this realm and to the great grievance and vexation of the people.

VII.   And whereas also by authority of Parliament in the five and twentieth year of the reign of King Edward III it is declared and enacted that no man should be forejudged of life and limb against the form of the Great Charter and the law of the land; and by the said Great Charter, and other the laws and statutes of this your realm, no man ought to be adjudged to death but by the laws established in this your realm, either by the customs of the same realm or by act of parliament, and whereas no offender of what kind soever is exempted from the proceedings to be used and punishments to be inflicted by the laws and statutes of this your realm; nevertheless, of late time divers commissions under your Majesty's great seal have issued forth, by which certain persons have been assigned and appointed commissioners with power and authority to proceed within the land according to the justice of martial law against such soldiers or mariners or other dissolute persons joining with them as should commit any murder, robbery, felony, mutiny or other outrage or misdemeanour whatsoever, and by such summary course and order as is agreeable to martial law and as is used in armies in time of war to proceed to the trial and condemnation of such offenders, and them to cause to be executed and put to death according to the law martial.

By pretext whereof some of your Majesty's subjects have been by some of the said commissioners put to death, when and where, if by the laws and statutes of the land they had deserved death, by the same laws and statutes also they might and by no other ought to have been judged and executed.

And also sundry grievous offenders by colour thereof claiming an exemption have escaped the punishments due to them by the laws and statutes of this your realm, by reason that divers of your officers and ministers of justice have unjustly refused or forborne to proceed against such offenders according to the same laws and statutes upon pretence that the said offenders were punishable only by martial law and by authority of such commissions as aforesaid. Which commissions and all others of like nature are wholly and directly contrary to the said laws and statutes of this your realm.

VIII. They do therefore humbly pray your most excellent Majesty that no man hereafter be compelled to make or yield any gift, loan, benevolence, tax or such like charge without common consent by act of parliament, and that none be called to make answer or take such oath or to give attendance or be confined or otherwise molested or disquieted concerning the same or for refusal thereof. And that no freeman in any such manner as is before mentioned be imprisoned or detained. And that your Majesty would be pleased to remove the said soldiers and mariners, and that your people may not be so burdened in time to come. And that the aforesaid commissions for proceeding by martial law may be revoked and annulled. And that hereafter no commissions of like nature may issue forth to any person or persons whatsoever to be executed as aforesaid, lest by colour of them any of your Majesty's subjects be destroyed or put to death contrary to the laws and franchises of the land.

All which they most humbly pray of your most excellent Majesty as their rights and liberties according to the laws and statutes of this realm, and that your Majesty would also vouchsafe to declare that the awards, doings, and proceedings to the prejudice of your people in any of the premises shall not be drawn hereafter into consequence or example. And that your Majesty would be also graciously pleased for the further comfort and safety of your people to declare your royal will and pleasure, that in the thing aforesaid all your officers and ministers shall serve you according to the laws and statutes of this realm as they tender the honour of your Majesty and the prosperity of this kingdom.

2   Charles I, *His Majesties Answer to the Nineteen Propositions of Both Houses of Parliament* (1642)

... We call to God to witness that, as for our subjects' sake these rights are vested in us, so for their sakes, as well as for our own, we are resolved not to quit them, nor to subvert (though in a parliamentary way) the ancient, equal, happy, well-poised, and never enough commended Constitution of the Government of this Kingdom; nor to make ourself of a king of England, a duke of Venice; and this of a kingdom, a republic.

There being three kinds of government among men (absolute monarchy, aristocracy, and democracy), and all these having their particular conveniences and inconveniences, the experience and wisdom of your ancestors has so moulded this out of a mixture of these as to give to this kingdom (as far as human prudence can provide) the conveniences of all three, without the inconveniences of any one, as long as the balance hangs even between the three states, and they run jointly on in their proper channel (begetting verdure and fertility in the meadows on both sides), and the overflowing of either on either side raise no deluge or inundation. The ill of absolute monarchy is tyranny; the ill of aristocracy is faction and division; the ills of democracy are tumults, violence and licentiousness. The good of monarchy is the uniting a nation under one head to resist invasion from abroad and insurrection at home; the good of aristocracy is the conjunction of council in the ablest persons of a state for the public benefit; the good of democracy is liberty, and the courage and industry which liberty begets.

In this kingdom, the laws are jointly made by a king, by a house of peers, and by a house of commons chosen by the people, all having free votes and particular privileges. The government, according to these laws, is trusted to the king. Power of treaties, of war and peace; of making peers, of choosing officers and counsellors for state, judges for law, commanders for forts and castles; giving commissions for raising men to make war abroad, or to prevent or provide against invasions or insurrections at home; benefit of confiscations, power of pardoning, and some more of the like kind, are placed in the king. And this kind of regulated monarchy, having this power to preserve that authority, without which it would be disabled to preserve the laws in their force, and the subjects in their liberties and properties, is intended to draw to him such a respect and relation from the great ones as may hinder the ills of division and faction; and such a fear and reverence from the people as may hinder tumults, violence, and licentiousness.

Again, that the prince may not make use of this high and perpetual power to the hurt of those for whose good he has it, and make use of the name of *public necessity* for the gain of his private favourites and followers to the detriment of his people, the House of Commons (an excellent conserver of liberty, but never intended for any share in government, or the choosing of them that should govern) is solely entrusted with the first propositions concerning the levies of moneys (which is the sinews as well of peace as of war), and the impeaching of those who, for their own ends, though countenanced by any surreptitiously gotten command of the king, have violated that law which he is bound (when he knows it) to protect; and to the protection of which they were bound to advise him, at least not to serve him in the contrary. And the lords, being trusted with a judicatory power, are an excellent screen and bank between the prince and people, to assist each against any encroachments of the other, and by just judgements to preserve that law which ought to be the rule of every one of the three. For the better enabling them in this, beyond the examples of any of our ancestors, we were willingly contented to oblige our self both to call a parliament every three years, and not to dissolve it in fifty days, and for the present exigency, the better to raise money, and avoid the pressure (no less grievous to us than them) our people must have suffered by a longer continuance of so vast a charge as two great armies, and for their greater certainty of having sufficient time to remedy the inconveniences arisen during so long an absence of parliaments, and for the punishment of the causers and ministers of them, we yielded up our right of dissolving this parliament, expecting an extraordinary moderation from it, in gratitude for so unexampled a grace, and little looking that any malignant party should be encouraged or enabled to have persuaded them, first to countenance the injustices and indignities we have endured, and then, by a new way of satisfaction for what was taken from us, to demand of us at once to confirm what was so taken, and to give up almost all the rest.

Since, therefore, the power legally placed in both houses is more than sufficient to prevent and restrain the power of tyranny, and, without the power which is now asked from us, we shall not be able to discharge that trust which is the end of monarchy; since this would be a total subversion of the fundamental laws and that excellent constitution of this kingdom which has made this nation so many years both famous and happy to a great degree of envy; since to the power of punishing (which is already in your hands according to law) if the power of preferring be added, we shall have nothing left for us but to look on; since the encroaching of one of these states upon the power of the other is unhappy in the effects, both to them and all the rest; since this power of at most a joint government in us with our counsellors (or rather our guardians) will return us to the worst kind of minority, and make us despicable both at home and abroad, and beget eternal factions and dissensions (as destructive to public happiness as war) both in the chosen, and the houses that choose them, and the people who choose the choosers; since so new a power will undoubtedly intoxicate persons who were not born to it, and beget not only divisions among them as equals, but in them contempt of us, as become an equal to them, and insolence and injustice towards our people, as now so much their inferiors, which will be the more grievous unto them, as suffering from those who were so lately of a nearer degree to themselves, and being to have redress only from those that placed them, and fearing they may be inclined to preserve what they have made, both out of kindness and policy; since all great changes are extremely inconvenient, and almost infallibly beget yet greater changes, which beget yet greater inconveniences.

Since as great an one in the church must follow this of the kingdom, since the second estate would in all probability follow the fate of the first, and by some of the same turbulent spirits jealousies would be soon raised against them, and the like propositions for reconciliation of differences would be then sent to them as they now have joined to send to us, till (all power being vested in the House of Commons, and their number making them incapable of transacting affairs of state with the necessary secrecy and expedition, those being retrusted to some close committee) at last the common people (who in the mean time must be flattered, and to whom license must be given in all their wild humours, how contrary soever to established law, or their own real good) discover this *arcanum imperii*, that all this was done by them, but not for them, grow weary of journey-work, and set up for themselves, call parity and independence liberty, devour that estate which had devoured the rest; destroy all rights and properties, all distinctions of families and merit; and by this means this splendid and excellently distinguished form of government end in a dark equal chaos of confusion, and the long line of our many noble ancestors in a Jack Cade, or a Wat Tyler.

For all these reasons to all these demands our answer is *nolumus leges Angliae mutari*; but this we promise, that we will be as careful of preserving the laws in what is supposed to concern wholly our subjects, as in what most concerns our self. For, indeed, we profess to believe that the preservation of every law concerns us, those of obedience being not secure when those of protection are violated; and we being most of any injured in the least violation of that by which we enjoy the highest rights and greatest benefits, and are therefore obliged to defend no less by our interest than by our duty, and hope that no jealousies to the contrary shall be any longer nourished in any of our good people by the subtle insinuations and secret practices of men who, for private ends, are disaffected to our honour and safety, and the peace and prosperity of our people. . . .

3   Philip Hunton, *A Treatise of Monarchy, Containing Two Parts: I. Concerning Monarchy in General.   II. Concerning This Particular Monarchy. Wherein All the Maine Questions Occurrent in Both, are Stated, Disputed, and Determined. . . . Done by an Earnest Desirer of His Countries Peace* (1643)

Part I. Chapter I

Of political government, and its distinction into several kinds

Section I
Authority, how far from God, how far from men?

Government and subjection are relatives; so that what is said of the one, may in proportion be said of the other. Which being so, it will be needless to treat of both; because it will be easy to apply what is spoken of one to the other. Government is *potestatis exercitium*, the exercise of a moral power. One of these is the root and measure of the other; which, if it exceed, is exorbitant, is not government, but a transgression of it. This power and government is differenced with respect to the governed; to wit, a family, which is called economical; or a public society, which is called political, or magistracy. Concerning this magistracy we will treat: 1. In general. 2. Of the principal kind of it.

In general concerning magistracy, there are two things about which I find difficulty and difference, viz. the original, and the end.

First, for the original: there seem to be two extremes in opinion; while some amplify the divinity thereof, others speak so slightly of it, as if there were little else but human institution in it. I will briefly lay down my apprehensions of the evident truth in this point; and it may be, things being clearly and distinctly set down, there will be no real ground for contrariety in this matter. Three things herein must necessarily be distinguished, viz.: 1. The constitution or power of magistracy in general. 2. The limitation of it to this or that kind. 3. The determination of it to this or that individual person or line.

For the first of these: 1. It is God's express ordinance that, in the societies of mankind, there should be a magistracy or government. At first, when there were but two, God ordained it (Genesis 3: 16). St Paul affirms as much of the powers that be, none excepted (Romans 13: 1). 2. This power, wherever placed, ought to be respected as a participation of divine sovereignty (Psalm 82: 1, 6); and every soul ought to be subject to it for the Lord's sake (1 Peter 2: 13): that is, for conscience' sake of God's ordinance (Romans 13: 5), and under penalty of damnation (verse 2). These are truths, against which there is no colour of opposition. Indeed, this power may be claimed by them who have it not; and, where there is a limitation of this power, subjection may be claimed in cases which are without those limits, but to this ordinance of power, where it is, and when it requires subjection, it must be given, as before.

For the second: 1. In some particular communities the limitation of it to this or that kind is an immediate ordinance of God. So kingly power was appointed to the Jews, on their desire (1 Samuel viii: 9). Whether they had not a kind of monarchical government before, I will not stand on it; but it is evident that then, on their earnest desire, God himself condescended to an establishment of regality in that state. 2. But, for a general binding ordinance, God has given no word either to command or commend one kind above another. Men may, according to their relations, to the form they live under, to their affections and judgements in divers respects, prefer this or that form above the rest; but we have no divine limitation: and it were an absurdity to think so, for then we should uncharitably condemn all the communities which have not that form for violation of God's ordinance, and pronounce those other powers unlawful. 3. This then must have another and lower fountain to flow from, which can be no other than human. The higher power is God's ordinance. That it resides in one, or more, in such or such a way, is from human designment: for, when God leaves a matter indifferent, the restriction of this indifferency is left to secondary causes. And I conceive this is St Peter's meaning, when he calls magistracy ἀνθρωπίνη κτίσις, human creature. St Paul calls it God's ordinance, because the power is God's. St Peter calls it human ordinance, because the specification of it to this or that form is from the societies of mankind. I confess it may be called a human creature, in regard of its subject, which is a man, or men; or its end, which is to rule over men for the good of men; but the other seems more natural, and it induces no disparagement to authority, being so understood. But, however you take that place, yet the thing affirmed stands good: that God, by no word, binds any people to this or that form, till they, by their own act, bind themselves.

For the third: The same is to be said of it as of the second. Some particular men we find whom God was pleased, by his own immediate choice, to invest with this his ordinance of authority: Moses, Saul, David. Yea, God, by his immediate ordinance, determined the government of that people to David's posterity, and made it successive; so that that people (after his appointment and word was made known to them, and the room void by Saul's death) was as immediately bound by divine law to have David and his sons after him to be magistrates, as to magistracy itself. But God has not done so for every people: a *scriptum est* cannot be alleged for the endowing this or that person, or stock, with sovereignty over a community. They alone had the privilege of an extraordinary word. All others have the ordinary and mediate hand of God to enthrone them. They attain this determination of authority to their persons by the tacit and virtual, or else express and formal, consent of that society of men they govern, either in their own persons, or the root of their succession; as I doubt not in the sequel it will be made appear. But let no man think that it is any lessening or weakening of God's ordinance in them to teach that it is annexed to their persons by a human means: for though it be not so full a title to come to it by the simple providence of God as by the express precept of God, yet, when by the disposing hand of God's providence a right is conveyed to a person, or family, by the means of a public fundamental oath, contract and agreement of a state, it is equivalent then to a divine word; and, within the bounds of that public agreement, the conveyed power is as obligatory as if an immediate word had designed it. Thus it appears that they which say there is *divinum quiddam* in sovereigns, and that they have their power from God, speak, in some sense, truth; as also they which say that originally power is in the people may in a sound sense be understood. And in these things we have Dr Ferne's consent, in his late discourse upon this subject [*The Resolving of Conscience*, 1642] (Section III).

. . . . . .

Chapter II

Of the division of monarchy into absolute and limited

Section I
Whether absolute monarchy be a lawful government?

. . . Absolute monarchy is when the sovereignty is so fully in one that it has no limits or bounds under God, but his own will. It is when a people are absolutely resigned up, or resign up themselves, to be governed by the will of one man. Such were the ancient eastern monarchies, and that of the Persian and Turk at this day, as far as we know. This is a lawful government, and therefore where men put themselves into this utmost degree of subjection by oath and contract, or are born and brought unto it by God's providence, it binds them, and they must abide it because an oath to a lawful thing is obligatory. This, in Scripture, is very evident, as Ezekiel 17: 16, 18, 19, where judgement is denounced against the king of Judah, for breaking the oath made to the king of Babylon, and it is called God's oath: yet doubtless this was an oath of absolute subjection. And Romans xiii: the power, which then was, was absolute; yet the apostle, not excluding it, calls it 'God's ordinance', and commands subjection to it. So Christ commands tribute to be paid, and pays it himself: yet it was an arbitrary tax, the production of an absolute power. Also the sovereignty of masters over servants was absolute, and the same in economy as absolute monarchy is in policy: yet the apostle enjoins not masters called to Christianity to renounce that title as too great and rigid to be kept, but exhorts them to moderation in the exercise of it; and servants to remain contented in the condition of their servitude. More might be said to legitimate this kind of government, but it needs not in so plain a case.

Section II
Three degrees of absoluteness

This absolute monarchy has three degrees, yet all within the state of absoluteness. The first: when the monarch, whose will is the people's law, does set himself no stated rule or law to rule by, but by immediate edicts and commands of his own will governs them, as in his own council's judgement he thinks fit. Secondly: when he sets down a rule and law by which he will ordinarily govern, reserving to himself liberty to vary from it, wherein and as often as in his discretion he judges fit. And in this the sovereign is as free as the former, only the people are at a more certainty what he expects from them in ordinary. Thirdly: when he not only sets down an express rule and law to govern by, but also promises and engages himself, in many cases, not to alter that rule. But this engagement is an after condescent and act of grace, not dissolving the absolute oath of subjection, which went before it; nor is intended to be the rule of his power, but of the exercise of it. This ruler is not so absolute as the former in the use of his power, for he has put a bond on that, which he cannot break without breach of promise; that is, without sin. But he is as absolute in his power, if he will sinfully put it forth into act. It has no political bounds, for the people still owe him absolute subjection, that not being dissolved or lessened by an act of grace coming afterwards.

Section III
Whether resistance be lawful in absolute monarchy?

Now, in governments of this nature, how far obedience is due, and whether any resistance be lawful, is a question which here must be decided; for the due effecting whereof we must premise some needful distinctions to avoid confusion. Obedience is twofold. First, positive and active, when in conscience of an authority we do the thing commanded. Secondly, negative and passive, when, though we answer not authority by doing, yet we do it by contented undergoing the penalty imposed. Proportionably, resistance is twofold. First, positive, by an opposing force. Secondly, negative, when only so much is done as may defend ourselves from force, without return of force against the assailant. Now, this negative resistance is also twofold. First, in inferior and sufferable cases. Secondly, or in the supreme case and last necessity of life and death. And then, too, it is first either of a particular person or persons; secondly, or of the whole community. And if of particular persons, then either under plea and pretence of equity assaulted; or else without any plea at all, merely for will and pleasure's sake; for to that degree of rage and cruelty some times the heart of man is given over. All these are very distinguishable cases, and will be of use either in this or the ensuing disputes.

To the question, I say: first, positive obedience is absolutely due to the will and pleasure of an absolute monarch in all lawful and indifferent things; because in such a state the will of the prince is the supreme law, so that it binds to obedience in everything not prohibited by a superior, that is divine, law: for it is in such case the higher power, and is God's ordinance.

Secondly, when the will of an absolute monarch commands a thing forbidden to be done by God's law, then it binds not to active obedience; then is the apostle's rule undoubtedly true, 'It is better to obey God than men', for the law of the inferior gives place to the superior. In things defined by God, it should be all one with us for the magistrate to command us to transgress that, as to command us an impossibility; and impossibilities fall under no law. But on this ground no man must quarrel with authority, or reject its commands as unlawful, unless there be an open unlawfulness in the face of the act commanded. For, if the unlawfulness be hidden in the ground or reason of the action, inferiors must not be curious to inquire into the grounds or reasons of the commands of superiors; for such license of inquiry would often frustrate great undertakings, which must depend on speed and secrecy of execution. I speak all this of absolute government, where the will and reason of the monarch is made the higher power, and its expression the supreme law of a state.

Thirdly, suppose an absolute monarch should so degenerate into monstrous, unnatural tyranny as apparently to seek the destruction of the whole community, subject to him in the lowest degree of vassalage; then such a community may negatively resist such subversion. Yea, and if constrained to it by the last necessity, positively resist; and defend themselves by force against any instruments whatsoever employed for the effecting thereof. 1. David did so in his particular case, when pursued by Saul. He made negative resistance by flight; and, doubtless, he intended positive resistance against any instrument, if the negative would not have served the turn: else why did he so strengthen himself by forces? Sure not to make positive resistance, and lay violent hands upon the person of the Lord's anointed, as it appeared. Yet for some reason he did it, doubtless; which could be none other, but by that force of arms to defend himself against the violence of any misemployed inferior hands. If then he might do it for his particular safety, much rather may it be done for the public. 2. Such an act is without the compass of any of the most absolute potentates; and therefore to resist, in it, can be to resist no power, nor the violation of any due of subjection. For, first, the most submiss subjection ever intended by any community, when they put themselves under another's power, was the command of a reasonable will and power: but to will and command the destruction of the whole body over which a power is placed were an act of will most unreasonable and self-destructive; and so not the act of such a will to which subjection was intended by any reasonable creatures. Secondly, the public good and being is aimed at in the utmost bond of subjection: for, in the constitution of unlimited sovereignty, though every particular man's good and being is subjected to the will of one supreme, yet certainly the conservation of the whole public was intended by it; which being invaded, the intent of the constitution is overthrown, and an act is done which can be supposed to be within the compass of no political power. So that did Nero, as it was reported of him, in his inhumanity, thirst for the destruction of whole Rome; and if he were truly what the senate pronounced him to be, *humani generis hostis*, then it might justify a negative resistance of his person; and a positive of any agent should be set on so inhuman a service. And the United Provinces are allowed in resisting Philip II, though he had been their absolute monarch, if he resolved the extirpation of the whole people, and the planting the country with Spaniards, as it is reported he did. And that assertion of some, that all resistance is against the apostle's prohibition – resistance by power of arms is utterly unlawful – cannot be justified in such a latitude. But of this more will be spoken in the current of this discourse.

Fourthly, suppose by such a power any particular person or person's life be invaded without any plea of reason or cause for it, I suppose it hard to deny him liberty of negative resistance of power; yea, and positive, of any agents, in such assault of murder. For, though the case be not so clear as the former, yet it seems to me justified by the fact of David, and the rescuing of Jonathan from the causeless cruel intent of his father's putting him to death: as also such an act of will, carrying no colour of reason with it, cannot be esteemed the act of a rational will, and so no will intended to be the law of sovereignty. Not that I think a monarch of such absoluteness is bound to yield a reason why he commands any man to be put to death before his command be obeyed; but I conceive the person so commanded to death may be justified before God and men for protecting himself by escape, or otherwise; unless some reason or cause be made known to him of such command.

Fifthly, persons subject to an unlimited dominion must, without resistance, subject their estates, liberties, persons to the will and pleasure of their lord, so it carry any plea or show of reason and equity. First, it seems to be evident, 1 Peter 2: 18, 19, 20: if well-doing be mistaken by the reason and judgement of the power for ill-doing, and we be punished for it, yet, the magistrate going according to his misguided reason, it is the command of a reasonable will, and so to be submitted to, because such a one suffers by law in a state where the lord's will is the law. Secondly, in commands of the power, where is the plea of reason and equity on the part of the commander? Whether it be such indeed, some power must judge; but the constitution of absolute monarchy resolves all judgement into the will of the monarch, as the supreme law. So that, if his will judicially censure it just, it must be yielded to; as if it were just without repeal of redressment by any created power. And let none complain of this as a hard condition when they or their ancestors have subjected themselves to such a power by oath or political contract. If it be God's ordinance to such, it must be subjected to, and its exorbitances borne (as he says in Tacitus) as men bear famine, pestilence, and other effects of God's displeasure.

Sixthly, in absolute monarchy the person of the monarch is above the reach of just force and positive resistance: for such a full resignation of men's selves to his will and power by the irrevocable oath and bond of political contract does make the person as sacred as the unction of Saul or David. In such a state all lawful power is below him; so that he is incapable of any penal hand, which must be from a superior, or it is unjust.

I have been the longer on this absolute monarchy because, though it does not concern us, yet it will give light to the stating of doubts in governments of a more restrained nature; for what is true here, in the full extent of power, is there also as true within the compass of their power.

Section IV
What makes a monarchy limited

In moderate or limited monarchy, it is an inquiry of some weight to know, what it is which constitutes it in the state of a limited monarchy?

First, a monarchy may be stinted in the exercise of its power and yet be an absolute monarchy (as appeared before, in our distinction of absolute monarchy) if that bounds be a subsequent act, and proceeding from free will and grace in the monarch. For it is not the exercise, but the nature and measure of power, wherewith he is radically invested, which denominates him a free, or conditionate monarch.

Secondly, I take it that a limited monarch must have his bounds of power *ab externo*, not from the free determination of his own will. And now kings have not divine words and binding laws to constitute them in their sovereignty, but derive it from ordinary providence; the sole means hereof is the consent and fundamental contract of a nation or men, which consent puts them in their power, which can be no more nor other than is conveyed to them by such contract of subjection. This is the root of all sovereignty individuated and existent in this or that person or family. Till this come and lift him up he is a private man, not differing in state from the rest of his brethren; but then he becomes another man, his person is sacred by that sovereignty conveyed to it, which is God's ordinance and image. The truth hereof will be more fully discovered when we come to speak of elective and successive monarchy.

Thirdly, he is then a limited monarch who has a law, beside his own will, for the measure of his power. First, the supreme power of the state must be in him, so that his power must not be limited by any power above his; for then he were not a monarch, but a subordinate magistrate. Secondly, this supreme power must be restrained by some law according to which this power was given, and by direction of which this power must act; else he were not a limited monarch, that is, a liege sovereign, or legal king. Now a sovereignty comes thus to be legal, or defined to a rule of law, either by original constitution, or by after condescent. By original constitution when the society public confers on one man a power by limited contract, resigning themselves to his government by such a law, reserving to themselves such immunities: in this case, they, which at first had power over themselves, had power to set their own terms of subjection; and he which has no title of power over them but by their act can, *de jure*, have no greater than what is put over to him by that act. By after condescent, viz. when a lord who, by conquest or other right, has an absolute arbitrary power, but, not liking to hold by such a right, does either formally or virtually desert it and take a new legal right, as judging it more safe for him to hold by, and desirable of the people to be governed by. This is equivalent to that by original constitution; yea, is all one with it. For this is, in that respect, a secondary original constitution. But if it be objected that this, being a voluntary condescent, is an act of grace, and so does not derogate from his former absoluteness, as was said before of an absolute monarch who confines himself to govern by one rule: I answer this differs essentially from that; for there a free lord of grace yields to rule by such a law, reserving the fullness of power, and still requiring of the people a bond and oath of utmost indefinite subjection; so that it amounts not to a limitation of radical power; whereas here is a change of title, and a resolution to be subjected to in no other way than according to such a frame of government. And, accordingly, no other bond or oath of allegiance is required or taken, than according to such a law: – this amounts to a limitation of radical power. And therefore they speak too generally who affirm of all acts of grace proceeding from princes to people as if they did not limit absoluteness. It is true of acts of grace of that first kind; but yet you see an act of grace may be such a one as may amount to a resignation of that absoluteness into a more mild and moderate power, unless we should hold it out of the power of an absolute lord to be other; or that, by free condescent and act of grace, a man cannot as well part with, or exchange, his right and title to a thing as define himself in the use and exercise, which I think none will affirm.

Section V
How far subjection is due in a limited monarchy?

In all governments of this allay and legal constitution, there are three questions of special moment to be considered:

First, how far subjection is due? As far as they are God's ordinance, as far as they are a power; and they are a power as far as the contract fundamental, from which, under God, their authority is derived, does extend. As absolute lords must be obeyed as far as their will enjoins, because their will is the measure of their power, and their subjects' law; so these, in the utmost extent of the law of the land, which is the measure of their power, and their subjects' duty of obedience. I say so far, but I do not say no further; for I believe, though on our former grounds it clearly follows that such authority transcends its bounds if it command beyond the law, and the subject legally is not bound to subjection in such case; yet, in conscience, a subject is bound to yield to the magistrate even when he cannot, *de jure*, challenge obedience, to prevent scandal, or any occasion of slighting the power, which may sometimes grow even upon a just refusal. I say, for these cases, a subject ought not to use his liberty, but *morem gerere*, if it be in a thing in which he can possibly without subversion, and in which his act may not be made a leading case, and so bring on a prescription against public liberty.

Section VI
How far it is lawful to resist

Secondly, how far is it lawful to resist the exorbitant illegal commands of such a monarch? 1. As before, in lighter cases, in which it may be done, for the reasons alleged and for the sake of public peace, we ought to submit and make no resistance at all, but *de jure recedere*.

2. In cases of a higher nature, passive resistance, viz. by appeal to law, by concealment, by flight, is lawful to be made; because such a command is politically powerless. It proceeds not from God's ordinance in him, and so we sin not against God's ordinance in such non-submission, or negative resistance.

3. For instruments or agents in such commands, if the strait be such, and a man be surprised, that no place is left for an appeal, nor evasion by negative resistance, I conceive against such positive resistance may be made; because, authority failing or [of?] this act in the supreme power, the agent or instrument can have none derived to him, and so is but in the nature of a private person, and his act as an offer of private violence, and so comes under the same rules for opposition.

4. For the person of the sovereign, I conceive it as well above any positive resistance as the person of an absolute monarch; yea, though by the whole community, except there be an express reservation of power in the body of the state, or any deputed persons, or court, to use (in case of intolerable exorbitance) positive resistance. Which, if there be, then such a governor is no monarch; for that fundamental

reservation destroys its being a monarchy, inasmuch as the supreme power is not in one. For wherever there is a sovereign politic power constituted, the person or persons who are invested with it are sacred, and out of the reach of positive resistance or violence; which, as I said, if just, must be from no inferior or subordinate hand.

But it will be objected that since every monarch has his power from the consent of the whole body, that consent of the whole body has a power above the power of the monarch, and so the resistance which is done by it is not by an inferior power; and to this purpose is brought that axiom: *quicquid efficit tale est magis tale*. I answer: that rule, even in natural causes, is liable to abundance of restrictions, and in the particular in hand, it holds not. Where the cause does bereave himself of that perfection by which it works, in the very act of causing, and convey it to that effect, it does not remain more such than the effect, but much less, and below it. As, if I convey an estate of land to another, it does not hold that after such conveyance I have a better estate remaining in me than that other, but rather the contrary; because what was in one is passed to the other. The servant who, at the year of jubilee, would not go free, but have his ear bored, and giving his master a full lordship over him; can we argue, that he had afterward more power over himself than his master, because he gave his master that power over him by that act of economical contract?

Thus the community, whose consent establishes a power over them, cannot be said universally to have an eminency of power above that which they constitute: sometimes they have, sometimes they have not; and to judge when they have, when not, respect must be had to the original contract and fundamental constitution of that state. If they have constituted a monarchy (that is, invested one man with a sovereignty of power, and subjected all the rest to him), then it were unreasonable to say they yet have it in themselves, or have a power of recalling that supremacy which, by oath and contract, they themselves transferred on another; unless we make this oath and contract less binding than private ones, dissoluble at pleasure, and so all monarchs tenants at will from their people. But if they, in such constitution, reserve a power in the body to oppose and displace the magistrate for exorbitances, and reserve to themselves a tribunal to try him in, that man is not a monarch, but the officer and substitute of him, or them, to whom such power over him is referred or conferred. The issue is this: if he be a monarch, he hath the *apex*, or *culmen potestatis*; and all his subjects, *divisim* and *conjunctim*, are below him; they have divested themselves of all superiority, and no power left for a positive opposition of the person of him whom they have invested.

Section VII
Who shall be the judge of the excesses of the monarch?

Thirdly, who shall be the judge of the excesses of the sovereign lord in monarchies of this composure? I answer: a frame of government cannot be imagined of that perfection, but that some inconveniences there will be possible for which there can be provided no remedy: many miseries to which a people under an absolute monarchy are liable are prevented by this legal allay and definement of power. But this is exposed to one defect, from which that is free; that is, an impossibility of constituting a judge to determine this last controversy, viz. the sovereign's transgressing his fundamental limits. This judge must be either some foreigner, and then we lose the freedom of the state by subjecting it to an external power in the greatest case, or else within the body. If so, then, 1. either the monarch himself, and then you destroy the frame of the state, and make it absolute: for to define a power to a law, and then to make him judge of his deviations from that law, is to absolve him from all law. Or else, 2. the community and their deputies must have this power; and then, as before, you put the *apex potestatis*, the prime ἀρχεί in the whole body, or a part of it, and destroy the being of monarchy; the ruler not being God's immediate minister, but of that power (be it where it will) to which he is accountable for his actions. So that, I conceive, in a limited legal monarchy there can be no stated internal judge of the monarch's actions if there grow a fundamental variance betwixt him and the community. But you will say, it is all one way to absoluteness to assign him no judge, as to make him his own judge.

Answer. I say not simply in this case, there is no judge, but that there can be no judge legal and constituted within that frame of government. But it is a transcendent case beyond the provision of that government, and must have an extraordinary judge and way of decision.

In this great and difficult case, I will deliver my apprehensions freely and clearly, submitting them to the censure of better judgements. Suppose the controversy to happen in a government fundamentally legal, and the people no further subjected than to government by such a law:

1. If the act in which the exorbitance and transgression is supposed to be, be of lesser moment, and not striking at the very being of that government, it ought to be borne by public patience, rather than to endanger the being of the state by a contention betwixt the head and body politic.

2. If it be mortal, and such as, suffered, dissolves the frame and life of the government and public liberty, then the illegality and destructive nature is to be set open, and redressment sought by petition; which, if failing, prevention by resistance ought to be. But first, that it is such must be made apparent; and if it be apparent, and an appeal made *ad conscientiam generis humani*, especially of those of that community, then the fundamental laws of that monarchy must judge and pronounce the sentence in every man's conscience, and every man (as far as concerns him) must follow the evidence of truth in his own soul, to oppose, or not oppose, according as he can in conscience acquit or condemn the act of [or] carriage of the governor. For, I conceive, in a case which transcends the frame and provision of the government they are bound to, people are unbound, and in state as if they had no government; and the superior law of reason and conscience must be judge, wherein every one must proceed with the utmost advice and impartiality. For if he err in judgement, he either resists God's ordinance, or puts his hand to the subversion of the state and policy he lives in.

And this power of judging argues not a superiority in those who judge over him who is judged; for it is not authoritative and civil, but moral, residing in reasonable creatures and lawful for them to execute, because never divested and put off by any act in the constitution of a legal government, but rather the reservation of it intended. For when they define the superior to a law, and constitute no power to judge of his excesses from that law, it is evident they reserve to themselves, not a formal authoritative power, but a moral power, such as they had originally before the constitution of the government; which must needs remain, being not conveyed away in the constitution.

Chapter III

Of the division of monarchy into elective and successive

. . . .

Section II
All monarchy whether originally from consent?

I do conceive that in the first original all monarchy, yea, any individual frame of government whatsoever, is elective: that is, is constituted, and draws its force and right from the consent and choice of that community over which it sways. And that triple distinction of monarchy into that which is gotten by conquest, prescription, or choice is not of distinct parts, unless by choice be meant full and formal choice. My reason is, because man, being a voluntary agent, and subjection being a moral act, it does essentially depend on consent; so that a man may by force and extremity be brought under the power of another, as unreasonable creatures are, to be disposed of, and trampled on, whether they will or no: but a bond of subjection cannot be put on him, nor a right to claim obedience and service acquired, unless a man become bound by some act of his own will. For suppose another, from whom I am originally free, be stronger than I, and so bring me under his mercy. Do I therefore sin, if I do not what he commands me? Or can that act of violence pass into a moral title without a moral principle?

. . . .

Section V
Monarchy by conquest. Whether conquest gives a just title?

But the main question is concerning monarchy achieved by conquest; where, at first sight, the right seems gotten by the sword, without the consent and choice of the people: yea, against it. Conquest is either, first, total, where a full conquest is made by a total subduing a people to the will of the victor. Or, secondly, partial, where an entrance is made by the sword. But the people, either because of the right claimed by the invader, or their unwillingness to suffer the miseries of war, or their apparent inability to stand out in a way of resistance, or some other consideration, submit to a composition and contract of subjection to the invader. In this latter it is evident the sovereign's power is from the people's consent; and the government is such as the contract and fundamental agreement makes it to be, if it be the first agreement and the pretender has no former title which remains in force: for then this latter is invalid if it include not, and amount to, a relinquishing and disannulling of the old. But the difficulty is concerning a full and mere conquest, and of this I will speak my mind clearly. Such a war and invasion of a people which ends in a conquest: first, it is either upon the pretence or claim of a title of sovereignty over the people invaded. And then if the pretender prevail it is properly no conquest, but the vindication of a title by force of arms, and the government not original, but such as the title is by which he claims it. Secondly, or it is by one who has no challenge of right descending to him to justify his claim and invasion of a people. Then, if he subdue, he may properly be said to come to his government by conquest.

And there be who wholly condemn this title of conquest as unlawful, and take it for nothing else but a national and public robbery. So one of the answerers to Dr Ferne says in his p. 10. 'Conquest may give such a right as plunderers use, to take in houses they can master – It is inhuman to talk of right of conquest in a civil, in a Christian state.' But I cannot allow of so indefinite a censure: rather, I think, the right of conquest is such as the precedent war was. If that were lawful, so is the conquest, for a prince may be invaded, or so far injured by a neighbouring people, or they may be set on such a pernicious enmity against him and his people, that the safety of himself and people may compel to such a war. Which war, if it end in conquest, who can judge such title unlawful? Suppose then conquest may be a lawful way of acquisition, yet an immediate cause of right of sovereignty, that is, of a civil power of government to which obedience is due, it cannot be. I say, an immediate cause; for a remote impulsive cause it often is, but not an immediate formal cause, for that must ever be the consent of the people, whereby they accept of and resign up themselves to a government, and then their persons are morally bound, and not before. Thus far the force of conquest may go: it may give a man title over and power to possess and dispose of the country and goods of the conquered; yea, the bodies and lives of the conquered are at the will and pleasure of the conqueror. But it still is at the people's choice to come into a moral condition of subjection, or not. When they are thus at the mercy of the victor, if, to save life, they consent to a condition of servitude or subjection, then that consent, oath or covenant, which they in that extremity make, being *in re licita*, binds them, and they owe moral duty. But if they would rather suffer the utmost violence of the conqueror, and will consent to no terms of subjection (as Numantia in Spain, and many other people have resolved), they die, or remain, a free people. Be they captived or possessed at pleasure, they owe no duty, neither do they sin in not obeying. Nor do they resist God's ordinance if at any time of advantage they use force to free themselves from such a violent possession: yea, perhaps, if before by contract they were bound to another, they should sin if, to avoid death or bondage, they should swear and covenant fealty to a conqueror; and it were more noble and laudable to die in the service and for the faith to their natural sovereign. Thus, I am persuaded, it will appear an uncontrollable truth in policy that the consent of the people, either by themselves or their ancestors, is the only mean in ordinary providence by which sovereignty is conferred on any person or family; neither can God's ordinance be conveyed, and people engaged in conscience, by any other means.

.   .   .   .

Chapter IV

Of the division of monarchy into simple and mixed

Section I
Simple and mixed monarchy, what?

The third division is into simple and mixed. Simple is when the government, absolute or limited, is so entrusted in the hands of one that all the rest is by deputation from him, so that there is no authority in the whole body but his, or derived from him. And that one is either individually one person, and then it is a simple monarchy; or one associate body, chosen either out of the nobility, whence the government is called a simple aristocracy, or out of the community without respect of birth or estate, which is termed a simple democracy. The supreme authority, residing exclusively in one of these three, denominates the government simple, which ever it be.

Now experience teaching people that several inconveniences are in each of these which is avoided by the other: as aptness to tyranny in simple monarchy, aptness to destructive factions in an aristocracy, and aptness to confusion and tumult in a democracy; as, on the contrary, each of them has some good which the others want: viz. unity and strength in a monarchy, counsel and wisdom in an aristocracy, liberty and respect of common good in a democracy. Hence the wisdom of men deeply seen in state matters guided them to frame a mixture of all three, uniting them into one form; that so the good of all might be enjoyed, and the evil of them avoided. And this mixture is either equal, when the highest command in a state, by the first constitution of it, is equally seated in all three; and then (if firm union can be in a mixture of equality) it can be called by the name of neither of them but by the general style of 'a mixed state'. Or, if there be priority of order in one of the three (as I think there must be, or else there can be no unity), it may take the name of that which has the precedency. But the firmer union is where one of the three is predominant, and in that regard gives the denomination to the whole: so we call it 'a mixed monarchy' where the primity of share in the supreme power is in one.

Section II
What it is which constitutes a mixed monarchy

Now I conceive to the constituting of mixed monarchy (and so proportionately it may be said of the other):

1. The sovereign power must be originally in all three, viz. if the composition be of all three, so that one must not hold his power from the other, but all equally from the fundamental constitution; for, if the power of one be original, and the other derivative, it is no mixture, for such a derivation of power to others is the most simple monarchy. Again, the end of mixture could not be obtained, for why is this mixture framed but that they might confine each other from exorbitance, which cannot be done by a derivative power? It being unnatural that a derivative power should turn back and set bounds to its own beginning.

2. A full equality must not be in the three estates, though they are all sharers in the supreme power; for, if it were so, it could not have any ground in it to denominate it a monarchy more than an aristocracy or democracy.

3. A power then must be sought, wherewith the monarch must be invested, which is not so great as to destroy the mixture, nor so titular as to destroy the monarchy; which I conceive may be in these particulars:

(a) If he be the head and fountain of the power which governs and executes the established laws, so that both the other estates, as well *conjunctim* as *divisim*, be his sworn subjects, and owe obedience to his commands, which are according to the established laws.

(b) If he has a sole or chief power in capacitating and putting those persons or societies in such estates and conditions, as whereunto such supreme power by the foundations of the government does belong and is annexed. So that though the aristocratical and democratical power which is conjoined to his be not from him, yet the definement and determination of it to such persons is from him by a necessary consecution.

(c) If the power of convocating, or causing to be put in existence, and dissolving such a court of meeting of the two other estates as is authoritative be in him.

(d) If his authority be the last and greatest, though not the sole, which must establish and add a consummation to every act.

I say, these, or any of these, put into one person, make that state monarchical, because the other, though they depend not on him *quoad essentiam et actus formales*, but on the prime constitution of the government, yet, *quoad existentiam et determinationem ad subjecta*, they do.

The supreme power being either the legislative or the gubernative, in a mixed monarchy sometimes the mixture is the seat of the legislative power, which is the chief of the two, the power of constituting officers for government by those laws being left to the monarch, or else the primacy of both these powers is jointly in all three. For if the legislative be in one, then the monarchy is not mixed but simple, for that is the superior; if that be in one, all else must needs be so too. By legislative, I mean the power of making new laws, if any new be needful to be added to the foundation, and the authentic power of interpreting the old, for I take it this is a branch of the legislative, and is as great and in effect the same power.

. . . .

Section IV
How far the prince's power extends in a mixed monarchy

Now concerning the extent of the prince's power and the subject's duty in a mixed monarchy, almost the same is to be said which was before in a limited. For it is a general rule in this matter: such as the constitution of government is, such is the ordinance of God; such as the ordinance is, such must our duty of subjection be. No power can challenge an obedience beyond its own measure; for if it might, we should destroy all rules and differences of government, and make all absolute and at pleasure. In every mixed principality:

First, look what power is solely entrusted and committed to the prince by the fundamental constitution of the state. In the due execution thereof all owe full subjection to him, even the other estates, being but societies of his subjects bound to him by oath of allegiance, as to their liege lord.

Secondly, those acts belonging to the power which is stated in a mixed principle, if either part of that principle, or two of the three, undertake to do them, it is invalid; it is no binding act. For in this case all three have a free negative voice; and take away the privilege of a negative voice so that, in case of refusal, the rest have power to do it without the third, then you destroy that third, and make him but a looker-on: so that in every mixed government, I take it, there must be a necessity of concurrence of all three estates in the production of acts belonging to that power which is committed in common to them. Else, suppose those acts valid which are done by any major part (that is, any two of the three), then you put it in the power of any two, by a confederacy at pleasure, to disannul the third, or suspend all its acts, and make it a bare cipher in government.

Thirdly, in such a composed state, if the monarch invade the power of the other two, or run in any course tending to the dissolving of the constituted frame, they ought to employ their power in this case to preserve the state from ruin; yea, that is the very end and fundamental aim in constituting all mixed policies: not that they, by crossing and jarring, should hinder the public good; but that, if one exorbitate, the power of restraint and providing for the public safety should be in the rest. And the power is put into divers hands that one should counterpoise and keep even the other: so that, for such other estates, it is not only lawful to deny obedience and submission to illegal proceedings (as private men may), but it is their duty; and by the foundation of the government they are bound to prevent the dissolution of the established frame.

Fourthly, the person of the monarch, even in these mixed forms (as I said before in the limited) ought to be above the reach of violence in his utmost exorbitances. For, when a people have sworn allegiance, and invested a person or line with supremacy, they have made it sacred; and no abuse can divest him of that power, irrevocably communicated. And, while he has power in a mixed monarchy, he is the universal sovereign, even of the other limiting estates: so that, being above them, he is *de jure* exempt from any penal hand.

Fifthly, that one inconvenience must necessarily be in all mixed governments, which I showed to be in limited governments: there can be no constituted, legal, authoritative judge of the fundamental controversies arising betwixt the three estates. If such do arise, it is the fatal disease of these governments, for which no *salvo* can be prescribed. For the established being of such authority would, *ipso facto*, overthrow the frame, and turn it into absoluteness. So that, if one of these, or two, say their power is invaded, and the government assaulted by the other, the accused denying it, it does become a controversy. Of this question there is no legal judge: it is a case beyond the possible provision of such a government. The accusing side must make it evident to every man's conscience. In this case, which is beyond the government, the appeal must be to the community, as if there were no government; and as, by evidence, men's consciences are convinced, they are bound to give their utmost assistance. For the intention of the frame, in such states, justifies the exercise of any power conducing to the safety of the universality and government established.

Part II

Of this particular Monarchy

Chapter I
Whether the power wherewith our kings are invested be an absolute, or limited and moderated power?

Section I

Having thus far proceeded in general, before we can bring home this to a stating of the great controversy which, now, our sins, God's displeasure, and evil turbulent men have raised up in our lately most flourishing but now most unhappy kingdom, we must first look into the frame and composure of our monarchy. For till we fully are resolved of that, we cannot apply the former general truths, nor on them ground the resolution of this ruining contention.

Concerning the essential composure of this government, that it is monarchical, is by none to be questioned: but the inquiry must be about the frame of it. And so there are seven great questions to be prosecuted.

First, whether it be a limited monarchy, or absolute? Here the question is not concerning power in the exercise, but the root and being of it. For none will deny but that the way of government used, and to be used, in this realm is a defined way. Only some speak as if this definement was an act of grace from the monarchs themselves, being pleased, at the suit and for the good of the people, to let their power run into act through such a course and current of law. Whereas, if they at any time should think fit, on great causes, to vary from that way and use the full extent of their power, none ought to contradict or refuse to obey. Neither is it the question whether they sin against God if they abuse their power, and run out into acts of injury at pleasure, and violate those laws which they have, by public faith and oath, promised to observe. For none will deny this to be true, even in the most absolute monarch in the world. But the point controverted is punctually this, whether the authority which is inherent in our kings be boundless and absolute, or limited and determined; so that the acts which they do, or command to be done, without that compass and bounds, be not only sinful in themselves, but invalid and non-authoritative to others.

Section II

Now, for the determining hereof, I conceive . . . had we no other proof, yet that of prescription were sufficient. In all ages, beyond record, the laws and customs of the kingdom have been the rule of government. Liberties have been stood upon, and grants thereof, with limitations of royal power, made and acknowledged by *Magna*

Carta and other public and solemn acts; and no obedience acknowledged to be due, but that which is according to law; nor claimed, but under some pretext or title of law. . . .

Section III

Having set down those reasons on which my judgement is settled on this side, I will consider the main reasons whereby some have endeavoured to prove this government to be of an absolute nature, and will show their invalidity. Many divines (perhaps inconsiderately, perhaps wittingly for self ends) have been, of late years, strong pleaders for absoluteness of monarchical power in this land, and pressed obedience on the consciences of people in the utmost extremity which can be due in the most absolute monarchy in the world. But I seldom, or never, heard or read them make any difference of powers, but usually bring their proofs from those Scriptures, where subjection is commanded to the higher powers, and all resistance of them forbidden, and from examples taken out of the manner of the government of Israel and Judah; as if any were so impious to contradict those truths, and they were not as well obeyed in limited government as in absolute. Or as if examples taken out of one government do always hold in another, unless their aim was to deny all distinction of governments, and to hold all absolute who have anywhere the supreme power conveyed to them. . . .

But let us come to the arguments. First, say they, our kings came to their right by conquest . . . it is an assertion most untrue in itself, and pernicious to the state. Our princes profess no other way of coming to the crown but by right of succession to rule free subjects in a legal monarchy. All the little show of proof these assertors have is from the root of succession: so William, commonly called 'The Conqueror'. For that of the Saxons was an expulsion, not a conquest; for, as our histories record, they, coming into the kingdom, drove out the Britons, and by degrees planted themselves under their commanders, and no doubt continued the freedom they had in Germany. Unless we should think that by conquering they lost their own liberties to the kings for whom they conquered and expelled the Britons into Wales. Rather, I conceive, the original of the subject's liberty was by those our forefathers brought out of Germany: where (as Tacitus reports) *nec regibus infinita aut libera potestas* (their kings had no absolute, but limited power) and all weighty matters were dispatched by general meetings of all the estates. Who sees not here the antiquity of our liberties, and frame of government? So they were governed in Germany, and so here to this day. For by transplanting themselves they changed their soil, not their manners and government. Then that of the Danes was indeed a violent conquest; and, as all violent rules, it lasted not long. When the English expelled them, they recovered their countries and liberties together. Thus, it is clear, the English liberty remained to them till the Norman invasion, notwithstanding that Danish interruption.

Now for Duke William, I know nothing they have in him, but the bare style of conqueror, which seems to make for them. The very truth is (and every intelligent reader of the history of those times will attest it) that Duke William pretended the grant and gift of King Edward, who died without children; and he came with forces into this kingdom, not to conquer, but make good his title against his enemies. His end of entering the land was not to gain a new absolute title, but to vindicate the old limited one, whereby the English-Saxon kings, his predecessors, held this kingdom. Though his title was not so good as it should be, yet it was better than Harold's, who was the only son of Godwyn, steward of King Edward's house, whereas William was cousin to Emma, mother to the said King Edward, by whom he was adopted, and by solemn promise of King Edward was to succeed him. Of which promise Harold himself became surety, and bound by oath to see it performed. Here was a fair title; especially Edgar Atheling, the right heir, being of tender age, and disaffected by the people. Neither did he proceed to a full conquest, but after Harold, who usurped the crown, was slain in battle, and none to succeed him, the throne being void, the people chose rather to submit to William and his title than endure the hazard of ruining war, by opposing him, to set up a new king. It is not to be imagined that such a realm as England could be conquered by so few, in such a space, if the people's voluntary acceptance of him and his claim had not facilitated and shortened his undertaking.

Thus we have it related in Mr Camden that before Harold usurped the crown most men thought it the wisest policy to set the crown on William's head, that by performing the oath and promise a war might be prevented. And that Harold, by assuming the crown, provoked the whole clergy and ecclesiastical estate against him; and we know how potent in those days the clergy were in state affairs. Also that, after one battle fought wherein Harold was slain, he went to London, was received by the Londoners, and solemnly inaugurated king; as unto whom, by his own saying, the kingdom was by God's providence appointed, and by virtue of a gift from his lord and cousin King Edward the Glorious granted. So that, after the battle, the remainder of the war was dispatched by English forces and leaders.

But suppose he did come in a conqueror; yet he did not establish the kingdom on these terms, but on the old laws, which he retained and authorized for himself and his successors to govern by. Indeed, after his settlement in the kingdom, some Norman customs he brought in, and (to gratify his soldiers) dispossessed many English of their estates, dealing in it too much like a conqueror. But the trial by twelve men, and other fundamentals of government, wherein the English freedom consists, he left untouched, which have remained till this day. On the same title he claimed and was inaugurated, was he king, which was a title of rightful succession to Edward. Therefore he was indeed king, not as conqueror, but as Edward's successor; and on the same right as he and his predecessors held the crown. As also, by the grant of the former laws and form of government, he did equivalently put himself and successors into the state of legal monarchs, and in that tenure have all the kings of this land held the crown till this day; when these men would rake up and put a title of conquest upon them, which never was claimed or made use of by him who is the first root of their succession.

. . . .

Chapter II
Supposing it to be in the platform limited, wherein, and how far forth it is limited and defined

I conceive it fundamentally limited in five particulars:

First, in the whole latitude of the nomothetical power; so that their power extends not to establish any act which has the being and state of a law of the land, nor give an authentic sense to any law of a doubtful and controverted meaning, solely and by themselves, but together with the concurrent authority of the two other estates in parliament.

Secondly, in the governing power there is a confinement to the fundamental common laws, and to the superstructive statute laws by the former concurrence of powers enacted, as to the rule of all their acts and executions.

Thirdly, in the power of constituting officers and means of governing: not in the choice of persons (for that is entrusted to his judgement, for aught I know), but in the constitution of courts of judicature. For, as he cannot judge by himself, or officers, but in courts of justice, so those courts of justice must have a constitution by a concurrence of the three estates; they must have the same power to constitute them as the laws which are dispensed in them.

Fourthly, in the very succession. For, though succession has been brought as a medium to prove the absoluteness of this government, yet, if it be more thoroughly considered, it is rather a proof of the contrary; and every one who is a successive monarch is so far limited in his power that he cannot leave it to whom he pleases, but to whom the fundamental law concerning that succession has designed it. And herein, though our monarchy be not so limited as that of France is said to be, where the king cannot leave it to his daughter, but to his heir male, yet restrained it is: so that should he affect another more, or judge another fitter to succeed, yet he cannot please himself in this, but is limited to the next heir born, not adopted, nor denominated; which was the case betwixt Queen Mary and the Lady Jane.

Lastly, in point of revenue; wherein their power extends not to their subjects' estates, by taxes and impositions to make their own what they please, as has been acknowledged by Magna Carta, and lately by the Petition of Right, the case of ship-money, conduct-money, etc., nor, as I conceive, to make an alienation of any lands or other revenues annexed by law to the crown. I meddle not with personal limitations (whereby kings, as well as private men, may limit themselves by promise and covenant), which, being particular, bind only themselves; but with those which are radical, and have continued during the whole current of succession, from unknown times. Other limitations, it is likely, may be produced by those who are skilful in the laws. But I believe they will be such as are reducible to some of these, which I take to be the principal and most apparent limitations of this monarchy, and are a most convincing induction to prove my assertion in the former chapter, 'That this monarchy, in the very mould and frame of it, is of a limited constitution.'

Chapter III

Whether it be of a simple or mixed constitution?

Section I

When the government is simple, when mixed; also where the mixture must be, which denominates a mixed government, is explained [in] Part I, Chapter III. Now I conceive it a clear and undoubted truth that the authority of this land is of a compounded and mixed nature, in the very root and constitution thereof; and my judgement is established on these grounds:

First, it is acknowledged to be a monarchy mixed with aristocracy in the house of peers, and democracy in the house of commons. Now (as before was made appear, in the first part) it is no mixture which is not in the root and supremacy of power; for, though it have a subordination of inferior officers, and though the powers inferior be seated in a mixed subject, yet that makes it not a mixed government, for it is compatible to the simplest in the world to have subordinate mixtures.

Secondly, that monarchy, where the legislative power is in all three, is, in the very root and essence of it, compounded and mixed of those three; for that is the height of power to which the other parts are subsequent and subservient. So that, where this resides in a mixed subject (that is, in three distinct concurrent estates), the consent and concourse of all most free, and none depending on the will of the other, that monarchy is, in the most proper sense, and in the very model of it, of a mixed constitution. But such is the state of this monarchy, as appears in the former question, and is self-apparent.

Thirdly, that monarchy in which three estates are constituted to the end that the power of one should moderate and restrain from excess the power of the other is mixed in the root and essence of it. But such is this, as is confessed in the answer to the said propositions. The truth of the major will appear if we consider how many ways provision may be made, in a political frame, to remedy and restrain the excesses of monarchy. I can imgine but three ways: first, by constituting a legal power above it, that it may be regulated thereby, as by an overruling power. Thus we must not conceive of our two houses of parliament as if they could remedy the exorbitances of the prince by an authority superior to his; for this were to subordinate him to the two houses, to set a superior above the sovereign; that is, to destroy the being of his monarchical power. Secondly, by an original conveyance to him of a limited and legal power, so that beyond it he can do no potestative act; yet constituting no formal legal power to refrain or redress his possible exorbitances. Here is limitation without mixture of another constituted power. As the former of these overthrows the power of the sovereign, so this makes no provision for the indemnity of the people. Thirdly, now, the never-enough-to-be-admired wisdom of the architects and contrivers of the frame of government in this realm (whoever they were) have found a third way, by which they have conserved the sovereignty of the prince, and also make an excellent provision for the people's freedom, by constituting two estates of men, who are for their condition subjects, and yet have that interest in the government that they can both moderate and redress the excesses and illegalities of the royal power. Which (I say) cannot be done but by a mixture, that is, by putting into their hands a power to meddle in acts of the highest function of government; a power not depending on his will, but radically their own, and so sufficient to moderate the sovereign's power.

. . . .

Chapter V
How far forth the two estates may oppose and resist the will of the monarch

Section I

This question is, in the general, already handled in the first part; so that it will be easy to draw those answers there to this particular here. Therefore, conformably to what I then affirmed, I will answer this question by divers positions.

First, the monarch working according to his power, not exceeding the authority which God and the laws have conferred on him, is no way to be opposed either by any or all his subjects, but in conscience to God's ordinance obeyed. This is granted on all sides.

Secondly, if the will and command of the monarch exceed the limits of the law, it ought for the avoidance of scandal and offence to be submitted to, so it be not contrary to God's law, nor bring with it such an evil to ourselves, or the public, that we cannot be accessory to it by obeying. This also will find no opposition. Disobedience in light cases, in which we are not bound, makes an appearance of slighting the power, and is a disrespect to the person of the magistrate. Therefore Christ, to avoid such offence, would pay tribute, though he tells Peter, he was free, and need not have done it.

Thirdly, if he command a thing which the law gives him no authority to command, and if it be such as would be inconvenient to obey, in this case obedience may lawfully be denied. This also finds allowance from them which stand most for royal power. Dr Ferne, in his preface, acknowledges obedience to be limited and circumscribed by the established laws of the land, and accordingly to be yielded or denied. In section i, says he, 'We may and ought to deny obedience to such commands of the prince as are unlawful by the law of God; yea, by the established laws of the land.' Here he says more than we say, yea more than should be said, as appears in the second position: it is not universally true that we ought.

Fourthly, if he exceed the limits of the law, and proceed in courses illegal, means there are which it is agreed upon the subjects may use to reduce him to legal government; so much Dr Ferne allows, section iv: Cries to God, petition to the prince, denial of obedience, denial of subsidy, etc.

Fifthly, but the point in controversy is about positive and forcible resistance; the lawfulness of which some do utterly deny, and others do as confidently maintain. But yet this point might be brought to a narrower state than, in the confused handling of it, it usually is: by distinguishing betwixt forcible resistance used against the king's own person, or against inferior officers and instruments, advising to or executing the illegal commands.

Section II

For the first, as I have before expressed myself, force ought not to be used against the person of the sovereign on any pretence whatever, by any or all his subjects, even in limited and mixed monarchies. For if they be truly monarchs, they are irrevocably invested with sovereignty, which sets their persons above all lawful power and force. . . .

Section III
Whether resistance of instruments of will be lawful?

Now concerning this case of forcible resistance of inferior persons misemployed to serve the illegal, destructive commands of the prince, I will do two things. 1. I will maintain my assertion by convincing arguments. 2. I will show the invalidity of what is said against it.

This, then, is my assertion. The two estates in parliament may lawfully, by force of arms, resist any persons, or number of persons, advising or assisting the king in the performance of a command illegal and destructive to themselves or the public.

First, because that force is lawful to be used for the public conservation which is no resistance of the ordinance of God, for that is the reason condemning the resistance of the powers. Now, this is no resistance of God's ordinance; for, by it, neither the person of the sovereign is resisted nor his power. Not his person, for we speak of agents employed, not of his own person. Nor his power, for the measure of that, in our government, is acknowledged to be the law. And therefore he cannot confer authority beyond law; so that those agents, deriving no authority from him, are mere instruments of his will, unauthorized persons, in their assaults robbers, and (as Dr Ferne calls them) cut-throats. If the case be put, 'What if the sovereign himself, in person, be present with such assailants, joining his personal assistance in the execution of his commands?' It is much to be lamented that the will of the prince should be so impetuous in any subverting act as to hazard his own person in the prosecution of it: yet, supposing such a case, all counsels and courses must be taken that no violence be offered to his person, and profession of none intended. But no reason the presence of his person should privilege ruining instruments from suppression, and give them an impunity to spoil and destroy subjects better than themselves. His person being secured from wrong, his power cannot be violated in such an act, in which none of it can be conferred on the agents. And sure David, though he avoided laying hands, or using any violence against the person of Saul, and on no extremity would have done it; yet, for the cut-throats about him, if no other means would have secured him, he would have rescued himself by force from their outrage, though Saul was in their company; else what intended he by all the force of soldiers, and his inquiry of God at Keilah? By which it is plain, he had an intent to have kept the place by force, if the people would have stuck to him. . . .

Secondly, because, without such power of resistance in the hands of subjects, all distinction and limitation of government is vain, and all forms resolve into absolute and arbitrary. For that is so which is unlimited, and that is unlimited not only which has no limits set, but also which has no sufficient limits; for to be restrained from doing what I will by a power which can restrain me no longer, nor otherwise, than I will, is all one as if I were left at my own will. I take this to be clear. Now it is as clear that, unless this forcible resistance of instruments of usurped power be lawful, no sufficient limits can be to the prince's will, and all laws bounding him are to no purpose. This appears by enumerating the other means: prayer to God, petition to the prince, denial of obedience, denial of subsidy, a moderate use of the power of denying, as Dr Ferne calls it. These are all. But what are these to hinder, if a prince be minded to overthrow all and bring the whole government to his own will? For prayer and petition, these are put in to fill up the number: they are no limitations; they may be used in the most absolute monarchy. For denial of obedience, that may keep me from being an instrument of public servitude. But princes' wills never want them which will yield obedience, if I deny it: yea, enough to destroy all the rest if nothing be left them but to suffer. Then, for denial of subsidy, if he may, by thousands of instruments, take all, or what he or they please, and I must not resist, what need he care whether the people deny or grant, if a prince be taught that he may do it? Cases and reasons will soon be brought to persuade him that in them he may lawfully do it, as late experiences have given us too much testimony. Thus it is apparent that the denial of this power of resistance of instruments overthrows and makes invalid all government but that which is absolute, and reduces the whole world *de jure* to an absolute subjection, that is, servitude. For the end of all constitution of moderated forms is not that the supreme power might not lawfully exorbitate, but that it might have no power to exorbitate. . . .

Thirdly, because such power is due to a public state for its preservation as is due to a particular person. But every particular person may lawfully, by force, resist illegal destructive ministers, though sent by the command of a legal sovereign, provided no other means of self-preservation be enough. This assumption the doctor seems to grant: he denies it to be lawful against the person of the prince, but, in effect, yields it against subordinate persons. But the main is against the proposition; and the doctor is so heavy a friend to the state that he thinks it not fit to allow it that liberty he gives every private man. But whose judgement will concur with his herein I cannot imagine; for sure the reason is greater: the public safety being far more precious and able to satisfy the damages of a public resistance than one particular man's is of a private. . . .

Chapter VI
In what cases the other estates may, without or against the king's personal consent, assume the arms of the kingdom?

Section I
Whether it be lawful to take up arms against the magistrate, perverting his power to a wrong end?

Whoever were the authors of that book lately published, styled *Scripture and Reason Pleaded for Defensive Arms*, have laid new and over-large grounds for resistance. Two assertions they endeavour to maintain: first, 'Those governors (whether supreme, or others) who, under pretence of authority from God's ordinance, disturb the quiet and peaceable life in godliness and honesty, are far from being God's ordinance, in so doing' (section iii). Secondly, 'This tyranny not being God's ordinance, they which resist it even with arms, resist not the ordinance of God' (hereon, section iv). They free Christians, even in the apostle's time, and so under the Roman emperors, or any other government, from a necessity of passive subjection in case of persecution, affirming that the Christians, in those first persecutions, had they been strong enough, might have used arms for defence against the tyranny of their emperors . . . I approve the received doctrine of the saints in ancient and modern times . . . and do concur with master Burroughs, professing against resistance of authority, though abused: 'If those (says he, in his answer to Dr Ferne, section ii) who have power to make laws, make sinful laws, and so give authority to any to force obedience; we say, here there must be either flying, or passive obedience.' And again: 'We acknowledge, we must not resist for religion, if the laws of the land be against it.' But what do they say against this? In making such laws against religion, the magistrates are not God's ordinance; and therefore to resist is not to resist God's ordinance. As an inferior magistrate who has a commission of power for such ends is resistible if he exceed his commission and abuse his power for other ends, so princes, being God's ministers, and having a deputed commission from him to such ends (viz. the promotion of godliness, peace and justice), if they pervert their power to contrary ends, may be resisted without violation of God's ordinance. That I may give a satisfactory answer to this, which is the sum of their long discourse, I must lay it down in several assertions:

First, I acknowledge, God's ordinance is not only power, but power for such ends, scil. the good of the people.

Secondly, it is also God's ordinance that there should be in men by public consent called thereto, and invested therein, a power to choose the means, the laws and rules of government conducing to that end; and a judging, in relation to those laws, who be the well-doers which ought to be praised, and who the evil-doers who ought to be punished. This is as fully God's ordinance as the former; for, without this, the other cannot be performed.

Thirdly, when they who have this final civil judicature shall censure good men as evil-doers, or establish iniquity by a law, to the encouragement of evil-doers; in this case, if it be a subordinate magistrate that does it, appeal must be made (as St Paul did) to the supreme. If it be the supreme, which through mistake, or corruption, does miscensure, from whom there lies no civil appeal, then, without resistance of that judgement, we must passively submit. And he who, in his own knowledge of innocency or goodness of his cause, shall by force resist, that man erects a tribunal in his own heart against the magistrate's tribunal, clears himself by a private judgement against a public, and executes his own sentence by force against the magistrate's sentence, which he has repealed and made void in his own heart. In unjust censures by the highest magistrate, from whom there is no appeal but to God, the sentence cannot be opposed till God reverse it, to whom we have appealed. In the meantime we must suffer, as Christ did, notwithstanding his appeal (1 Peter 2: 23), and so must we, notwithstanding our appeal (1 Peter 4: 19), for he did so for our example. If an appeal to God, or a censure in the judgement of the condemned, might give him power of resistance, none would be guilty, or submit to the magistrate's censure any further than they please. . . .

Section II

1. When arms ought not to be assumed

2. When they may be assumed

Now to the proposed question I answer, first, negatively: scil. First, it ought not to be done against all illegal proceedings, but such which are subversive and insufferable. Secondly, not public resistance, but in excesses inducing public evils. For to repel private injuries of the highest nature with public hazard and disturbance will not quit cost, unless in a private case the common liberty be struck at. Thirdly, not when the government is actually subverted and a new form (though never so injuriously) set up, and the people already engaged in an oath of absolute subjection. For the remedy comes too late, and the establishment of the new makes the former irrevocable by any justifiable power, within the compass of that oath of God. This was the case of the senate of Rome in St Paul's time. Secondly, affirmatively: I conceive three cases when the other estates may lawfully assume the force of the kingdom, the king not joining, or dissenting, though the same be by law committed to him. First, when there is invasion actually made, or imminently feared, by a foreign power. Secondly, when by an intestine faction the laws and frame of government are secretly undermined or openly assaulted. In both these cases, the being of the government being endangered, their trust binds, as to assist the king in securing, so to secure it by themselves, the king refusing. In extreme necessities the liberty of voices cannot take place, neither ought a negative voice to hinder in this exigence, there being no freedom of deliberation and choice when the question is about the last end. Their assuming the sword, in these cases, is for the king, whose being (as king) depends on the being of the kingdom; and, being interpretatively his act, is no disparagement of his prerogative. Thirdly, in case the fundamental rights of either of the three estates be invaded by one or both the rest, the wronged may lawfully assume force for its own defence; because else it were not free, but dependent on the pleasure of the other. Also the suppression of either of them, or the diminishing of their fundamental rights, carries with it the dissolution of the government: and therefore those grounds, which justify force to preserve its being, allow this case, which is a direct innovation of its being and frame.

Chapter VII

Where the legal power of final judging in these cases does reside, in case the three estates differ about the same?

Section I

The question stated. Determination of the question

In this question (for our more distinct proceeding) some things are necessarily to be observed: first, that we meddle not here with the judicature of questions of an inferior nature, viz. such as are betwixt subject and subject, or the king and a subject, in a matter of particular right, which may be decided another way without detriment of the public frame, or diminution of the privileges of either of the three estates. Secondly, difference is to be made even in the questions of utmost danger. 1. For it may be alleged to be either from without, by invasion of foreign enemies, or by a confederacy of intestine subverters, in which neither of the three estates are alleged to be interested, and so the case may be judged without relation to either of them, or detriment to their privileges. Here I conceive a greater latitude of power may be given to some to judge without the other, for it infers not a subordinating of any of the three to the other. 2. Or else it may be alleged by one or two of the estates against the other that, not contenting itself with the powers allowed to it by the laws of the government, it seeks to swallow up or entrench on the privileges of the other, either by immediate endeavours, or else by protecting and interesting itself in the subversive plots of other men. 3. In this case we must also distinguish betwixt, i. authority of raising forces for defence against such subversion, being known and evident; ii. and authority of judging and final determining that the accused estate is guilty of such design and endeavour of subversion, when it is denied and protested against. This last is the particular in this question to be considered. Not whether the people are bound to obey the authority of two or one of the legislative estates, in resisting the subversive essays of the other, being apparent and self-evident, which I take in this treatise to be clear. But, when such plea of subversion is more obscure and questionable, which of the three estates has the power of ultimate and supreme judicature, by vote or sentence to determine it against the other, so that the people are bound to rest in that determination, and accordingly to give their assistance, *eo nomine*, because it is by such power so noted and declared?

For my part, in so great a case, if my earnest desire of public good and peace may justify me to deliver my mind, I will prescribe to the very question, for it includes a solecism. In government of a mixed temperature, to demand which estate may challenge this power of final determination of fundamental controversies arising betwixt them is to demand which of them shall be absolute. For I conceive that, in the first part hereof, I have made it good that this final utmost controversy, arising betwixt the three legislative estates, can have no legal constituted judge in a mixed government. For, in such difference, he who affirms that the people are bound to follow the judgement of the king against that of the parliament destroys the mixture into absoluteness. And he who affirms that they are bound to cleave to the judgement of the two houses against that of the king resolves the monarchy into an aristocracy or democracy, according as he places this final judgement. Whereas I take it to be an evident truth that, in a mixed government, no power is to be attributed to either estate which, directly or by necessary consequence, destroys the liberty of the other.

Section II
Dissolution of the arguments placing it in the king; and of the arguments placing it in the two houses

Yet it is strange to see how, in this epidemical division of the kingdom, the abettors of both parts claim this unconcessible judgement. . . .

Section III
What is to be done in such a contention?

If it be demanded, then, how this case can be decided and which way must the people turn in such a contention, I answer: if the non-decision be tolerable, it must remain undecided whilst the principle of legal decision is thus divided, and by that division each suspends the other's power. If it be such as is destructive, and necessitates a determination, this must be evident; and then every person must aid that part which, in his best reason and judgement, stands for public good against the destructive. And the laws and government which he stands for, and is sworn to, justify and hear him out in it; yea, bind him to it.

If any wonder I should justify a power in the two houses to resist and command aid against any agents of destructive commands of the king, and yet not allow them power of judging when those agents or commands are destructive, I answer, I do not simply deny them a power of judging and declaring this; but I deny them to be a legal court ordained to judge of this case authoritatively, so as to bind all people to receive and rest in their judgement for conscience of its authority, and because they have voted it. It is the evidence, not the power of their votes, must bind our reason and practice in this case. We ought to conceive their votes the discoveries made by the best eyes of the kingdom, and which in likelihood should see most: but, when they vote a thing against the proceedings of the third and supreme estate, our consciences must have evidence of truth to guide them, and not the sole authority of votes; and that for the reason so often alleged.

NOTES ON THE TEXTS

1. *The Petition of Right:* There are seventeenth-century editions in 1628 (despite royal opposition), 1642, 1659 and 1660, as well as in collections of the Statutes of the Realm. It is frequently reproduced in collections of constitutional documents: e.g. J. P. Kenyon, *The Stuart Constitution, 1603– 88* (Cambridge, 1966).

2. *His Majesties Answer to the Nineteen Propositions:* D. Wing's *Short-Title Catalogue, 1641–1700* lists five separate editions of this text in 1642. It is reproduced in the various editions of J. Rushworth, *Historical Collections*, vol. v (1659–1701, 1703–8, 1718, 1721–2). Selections from it are frequently reprinted, e.g. Kenyon, *The Stuart Constitution*, op. cit.

3. Hunton, *Treatise of Monarchy:* Published anonymously in 1643, with further editions in 1680 and 1689 (two editions). Reprinted in the various editions of the *Harleian Miscellany* (1744–6; 1753; 1808–11; 1808–13, vol. vi). There has been no modern edition of this text.

FURTHER READING

The political and institutional context within which the Petition of Right should be viewed is a matter of heated controversy. The traditional view, expressed in W. Notestein, *The Winning of the Initiative by the House of Commons* (London, 1924), that it is part of a pattern of growing self-assertiveness on the part of the Commons, has been questioned by a number of recent scholars, most notably C. Russell, whose *Parliaments and English Politics, 1621–29* (Oxford, 1979) represents a new orthodoxy. The recent literature is reviewed by J. H. Hexter in 'The Early Stuarts and Parliament', *Parliamentary History*, I (1982), pp. 181–215. On the immediate background to the Petition of Right itself there is a valuable article by J. A. Guy: 'The Origins of the Petition of Right Reconsidered', *Historical Journal*, XXV (1982), pp. 289–312 (which should be read in conjunction with the comment by M. B. Young, *Historical Journal*, XXVII (1984), pp. 449–52). It is interesting to compare the Petition of Right to the Declaration of Rights of 1689, on which see L. G. Schwoerer, 'The Contributions of the Declaration of Rights to Anglo-American Radicalism', in M. Jacob and J. Jacob (eds.), *The Origins of Anglo-American Radicalism* (London, 1984).

The constitutional debate of the opening phase of the Civil War is discussed both in M. A. Judson, *Crisis of the Constitution* (New Brunswick, 1949) and in J. W. Allen, *English Political Thought, 1603–44* (London, 1938). There is a useful selection of texts in A. Sharp, *Political Ideas of the English Civil Wars, 1641–49* (London, 1983).

The 'mixed monarchy' theory adopted by the king in 1642 has been the subject of a number of studies by C. C. Weston, of which the first was 'The Theory of Mixed Monarchy under Charles I and After', *English Historical Review*, LXXV (1960), pp. 426–43, and the most recent is 'Co-ordination: a Radicalising Principle in Stuart Politics', in M. Jacob and J. Jacob (eds.), *The Origins of Anglo-American Radicalism* (London, 1984).

The two leading parliamentary publicists who sought to respond to the royalist propagandists were Henry Parker and Philip Hunton. There is a facsimile reprint of Parker's *Observations* in W. Haller (ed.), *Tracts on Liberty in the Puritan Revolution* (three vols., New York, 1934, 1965), and a substantial selection in H. Erskine-Hill and G. Storey (eds.), *Revolutionary Prose of the English Civil War* (Cambridge, 1983). On Parker see M. A. Judson, 'Henry Parker and the Theory of Parliamentary Sovereignty', in *Essays in Honor of C. H. McIlwain* (Cambridge, Mass., 1936), and W. K. Jordan, *Men of Substance: Henry Parker and Henry Robinson* (Chicago, 1942). On Hunton see the articles by C. H. McIlwain, in his *Constitutionalism and the Changing World* (Cambridge, 1939), and T. Sanderson: 'Philip Hunton's "Appeasement": Moderation and Extremism in the English Civil War', *History of Political Thought*, III (1982), pp. 447–61. Hunton's importance is stressed by J. H. Franklin in *John Locke and the Theory of Sovereignty* (Cambridge, 1978). It is useful to compare his position with that of a moderate royalist, for which purpose there is J. W. Daly, 'John Bramhall and the Theoretical Problems of Royalist Moderation', *Journal of British Studies*, XI (1971), pp. 26–44.

CHAPTER FOUR

GODLY RULE AND TOLERATION

1   Richard Hooker, *Of the Lawes of Ecclesiasticall Politie; The Sixth and Eighth Books* (1648)

Hooker (1554?–1600) was appointed Master of the Temple in 1585, a position which brought him into conflict with spokesmen for a Puritan reformation of the theology, liturgy and hierarchy of the Church of England. In 1591 he retired to a country living to write a defence of the Church of England as by law established. Prior to his death in 1600 five of eight promised books of *The Lawes of Ecclesiasticall Politie* were published. The authenticity of the last three books, published long after his death, has been a matter of continuing debate. Anglicans in the Restoration period were particularly unhappy that these books contained no defence of divine-right episcopacy. Recent scholars, however, have been satisfied that they are Hooker's.

Hooker was opposed to the Puritan insistence on arguing from the Scriptures alone. His preferred starting-points were natural reason and natural law, which he interpreted in scholastic fashion, and it was upon the foundation these provided that he sought to build a Christian philosophy which took account of Scriptural revelation. Hooker's defence of tradition and authority made him attractive to later generations of Anglicans, but the role he assigned to consent meant that radicals like Locke could also seek to appeal to his authority. The passage selected here is a helpful guide, not only to Anglican ideals of a national church, but also to constitutional assumptions prior to the accession of James I.

2   Richard Baxter, *A Holy Commonwealth, or Political Aphorisms, Opening the True Principles of Government* (1659)

Baxter (1615–91) was ordained a clergyman in the Church of England in 1638, but he had had a Puritan upbringing and was soon critical of the lack of discipline within the church. By 1640 he had become convinced the existing structure of episcopal authority was indefensible. In 1642 he supported Parliament and as a consequence was forced to abandon his position as lecturer at Kidderminster. He served as an army chaplain, but disagreed with orthodox Presbyterians and with the Independents. He was opposed to the execution of the King and to the Engagement oath. In 1660 he supported the Restoration, but refused a bishopric, and became in many respects the conscience and spokesperson of the Dissenters, being several times imprisoned. He wrote over one hundred and fifty books and his autobiography, *Reliquiae Baxterianae*, has always been regarded as one of the most compelling portraits of the Puritan mind. His *Holy Commonwealth* gives a clear indication of the sort of government he would have liked to have seen emerge from the Civil War.

3   Roger Williams, *The Bloudy Tenent of Persecution, for Cause of Conscience, Discussed* (1644)

Williams (*c.* 1603–83) fled religious persecution in England in 1630, emigrating to Massachusetts where he sought to evangelize the Indians. His strict separatist principles led him into conflict with the government, and in 1636 he was expelled and helped to establish the settlement of Providence, Rhode Island. In 1643 he went to England to seek a charter for the new colony, and there he entered into the debate on toleration, writing the *Bloudy Tenent of Persecution*, which was burnt by order of Parliament in August of 1644. He returned to England in 1652–4 and once more wrote in favour of toleration (*The Bloody Tenent Yet More Bloody*). Williams has long been regarded as one of the first exponents of what were to become central principles of the American constitution: the sovereignty of the people and the separation of church and state.

4   William Walwyn, *The Compassionate Samaritane* (1644)

Walwyn (1600–1680) was a member of the Merchant-Adventurers and by consequence a member of the business establishment. Nevertheless, his radical beliefs seem to have been formed before the Civil War began: as early as 1641 he was writing anonymous tracts in favour of a general toleration, and by 1643 he was advocating a moral and social revolution that could scarcely have been confined within constitutional limits. He supported his egalitarian and democratic arguments by attacking the belief that Christ had died for a few and maintaining that all would equally be saved. In 1645 he joined forces with Lilburne, although criticizing his appeals to Magna Carta: Walwyn wanted not to restore traditional liberties but to establish for the first time principles that could be approved by reason. Working quietly and behind the scenes, often publishing anonymously, he seems to have been a central figure in the political organization of the Levellers, a key link between them and the sects, and an architect of the Agreement of the People. In March 1649, when Cromwell destroyed the Leveller party, he was arrested and imprisoned for a time, and for some time he had to fight off accusations of atheism as well as communism. His last publication on a political subject was *Juries Justified* of 1651. He spent his last years practising as a physician or apothecary. *The Compassionate Samaritane* (the second edition of which is presented here complete, with the omission of the preface) is perhaps the most systematic of his defences of toleration.

1   Richard Hooker, *Of the Lawes of Ecclesiasticall Politie; The Sixth and Eighth Books* (1648)

. . . .

The eighth book: their seventh assertion, that unto no civil prince or governor there may be given such power of ecclesiastical dominion as by the laws of this land belongs unto the supreme regent thereof.

1. An admonition concerning men's judgements about the question of regal power

We come now to the last thing whereof there is controversy moved, namely the power of supreme jurisdiction, which for distinction sake we call the power of ecclesiastical dominion.

It was not thought fit in the Jews' commonwealth that the exercise of supremacy ecclesiastical should be denied unto him to whom the exercise of chiefty civil did appertain, and therefore their kings were invested with both. This power they gave unto Simon when they consented that he should be their prince, not only to set men over the works and over the country, and over the weapons and over the fortresses, but also to provide for the holy things, and that he should be obeyed of every man, and that all the writings in the country should be made in his name, and that it should not be lawful for any of the people or priests to withstand his words or to call any congregation in the country without him. And if it be haply surmised that thus much was given until Simon as being both prince and high priest, which otherwise (being only their civil governor) he could not lawfully have enjoyed, we must note that all this is no more than the ancient kings of that people had, being kings and not priests. By this power David, Asa, Jehoshaphat, Ezekias, Josias and the rest made those laws and orders which the sacred history speaks of concerning matter of mere religion, the affairs of the temple and service of God. Finally, had it not been by the virtue of this power, how should it possibly have come to pass that the piety or impiety of the king did always accordingly change the public face of religion, which thing the priests by themselves never did, neither could at any time hinder from being done? Had the priests alone been possessed with all power in spiritual affairs how should any law concerning matter of religion have been made, but only by them? In them it had been, and not in the king, to change the face of religion at any time. The altering of religion, the making of ecclesiastical laws, with other the like actions belonging unto the power of dominion, are still termed the deeds of the king, to show that in him was placed supremacy of power even in this kind over all, and that unto their high priests the same was never committed, saving only at such times as their priests were also kings or princes over them.

According to the pattern of which example, the like power in cases ecclesiastical is by the laws of this realm annexed unto the Crown. And there are which imagine that kings, being mere lay persons, do by this means exceed the lawful bounds of their calling. Which thing to the end that they may persuade, they first make a necessary separation perpetual and personal between the church and commonwealth. Secondly, they so tie all kind of power ecclesiastical unto the church as if it were in every degree their only right which are by proper spiritual function termed church-governors, and might not to Christian princes any wise appertain. To lurk under shifting ambiguities and equivocations of words in matters of principal weight is childish. A church and a commonwealth we grant are things in nature the one distinguished from the other: a commonwealth is one way, and a church another way defined. In their opinion the Church and the commonwealth are corporations not distinguished only in nature and definition, but in subsistence perpetually severed, so that they that are of the one can neither appoint nor execute, in whole nor in part, the duties which belong unto them which are of the other, without open breach of the law of God, which has divided them and does require that being so divided they should distinctly and severally work, as depending both upon God, and not hanging one upon the other's approbation for that which either has to do.

We say that the care of religion being common unto all societies politic, such societies as do embrace the true religion have the name of the church given unto every of them for distinction from the rest. So that every body politic has some religion, but the church that religion which is only true. Truth of religion is that proper difference whereby a church is distinguished from other politic societies of men. We here mean true religion in gross, and not according to every particular. For they which in some particular points of religion do swerve from the truth may nevertheless most truly, if we compare them to men of an heathenish religion, be said to hold and profess that religion which is true. For which cause, there being of old so many politic societies established throughout the world, only the commonwealth of Israel, which had the truth of religion, was in that respect the church of God. And the church of Jesus Christ is every such politic society of men as does in religion hold that truth which is proper to Christianity. As a politic society it does maintain religion; as a church that religion which God has revealed by Jesus Christ. With us therefore the name of a church imports only a society of men, first united into some public form of regiment and, secondly, distinguished from other societies by the exercise of Christian religion. With them, on the other side, the name of the church in this present question imports not only a multitude of men, so united and so distinguished, but also further the same divided necessarily and perpetually from the body of the commonwealth. So that even in such a politic society as consists of none but Christians, yet the church of Christ and the commonwealth are two corporations independently, each subsisting by itself. We hold that seeing there is not any man of the Church of England, but the same man is also a member of the commonwealth, nor any man a member of the commonwealth which is not also of the Church of England, therefore, as in a figure triangular the base does differ from the sides thereof, and yet one and the selfsame line is both a base and also a side – a side simply, a base if it chance to be the bottom and underlie the rest – so, albeit properties and actions of one kind do cause the name of a commonwealth, qualities and functions of another sort the name of a church to be given unto a multitude, yet one and the selfsame multitude may in such sort be both; and is so with us, that no person appertaining to the one can be denied to be also of the other. Contrariwise (unless they against us should hold that the church and the commonwealth are two both distinct and separate societies, of which two the one comprehends always persons not belonging to the other) that which they do, they could not conclude out of the difference between the church and the commonwealth; namely that bishops may not meddle with the affairs of the commonwealth because they are governors of another corporation, which is the church, nor kings with making laws for the church, because they have government not of this corporation but of another divided from it, the commonwealth, and the walls of separation between these two must for ever be upheld. They hold the necessity of personal separation, which clean excludes the power of one man's dealing in both; we of natural, which does not hinder but that one and the same person may in both bear a principal sway.

The causes of common received error in this point seem to have been especially two: One, that they who embrace true religion living in such commonwealths as are opposite thereunto, and in other public affairs retaining civil communion with such, are constrained for the exercise of their religion to have a several communion with those who are of the same religion with them. This was the state of the Jewish church both in Egypt and Babylon, the state of Christian churches a long time after Christ. And in this case, because the proper affairs and actions of the church, as it is the church, have no dependency upon the laws or upon the governors of the civil state, an opinion has thereby grown that even so it should be always. This was it which deceived Allen in his writing of his *Apology*. 'The apostles', says he, 'did govern the church in Rome when Nero did bear rule, even as at this day in all the Turk's dominions the church has a spiritual regiment without dependence, and so ought she to have, live she amongst heathens, or with Christians.'

Another occasion of which misconceit is that things appertaining unto religion are both distinguished from other affairs, and have always had in the church special persons chosen to be exercised about them. By which distinction of spiritual affairs, and persons therein employed, from temporal, the error of personal separation always necessary between the church and the commonwealth has strengthened itself; for, of every politic society that being true which Aristotle has, namely 'that the scope thereof is not simply to live, nor the duty so much to provide for life as for means of living well', and that even as the soul is the worthier part of man, so human societies are much more to care for that which tends properly unto the soul's estate than for such temporal things as this life does stand in need of. Other proof there needs none to show that, as by all men 'the kingdom of God is first to be sought for', so in all commonwealths things spiritual ought above temporal to be provided for. And of things spiritual the chiefest is religion. For this cause persons and things employed peculiarly about the affairs of religion are by an excellency termed *spiritual*. The heathen themselves had their spiritual laws, cases and offices always severed from the temporal. Neither did this make two independent states amongst them. God, by revealing true religion, does make them that receive it his church. Unto the Jews he so revealed the truth of religion that he gave them in special consideration laws, not only for the administration of things spiritual, but also temporal. The Lord himself appointing both the one and the other in that commonwealth did not thereby distract it into several independent communities, but instituted several functions of one and the same community. Some reason therefore must be alleged, why it should be otherwise in the church of Christ. . . .

2. What Their Power of Dominion is

Without order there is no living in public society, because the want thereof is the mother of confusion, whereupon division of necessity follows, and out of division inevitable destruction. The apostle therefore, giving instruction to public societies, requires that all things be orderly done. Order can have no place in things unless it be settled amongst the persons that shall by office be conversant about them. And if things or persons be ordered, this does imply that they are distinguished by degrees. For order is a gradual disposition. The whole world, consisting of parts so many, so different, is by this only thing upheld: he which framed them has set them in order. Yea, the very deity itself both keeps and requires for ever this to be kept as a law, that wheresoever there is a coagmentation of many, the lowest be knit to the highest by that which, being interjacent, may cause each to cleave unto other and so all to continue one. This order of things and persons in public societies is the work of polity, and the proper instrument thereof in every degree is power: power being that ability which we have of ourselves or receive from others for performance of any action. If the action which we are to perform be conversant about matter of mere religion the power of performing it is then spiritual. And if that power is such as has not any other to overrule it, we term it dominion or power supreme, so far as the bonds thereof do extend. When, therefore, Christian kings are said to have spiritual dominion or supreme power in ecclesiastical affairs and cases, the meaning is that within their own precincts and territories they have authority and power to command even in matters of Christian religion, and that there is no higher, nor greater, that can in those cases over-command them, where they are placed to reign as kings.

But withal we must likewise note that their power is termed supremacy as being the highest not simply, without exception of anything. For what man is there so brainsick as not to except in such speeches God himself, the king of all the kings of the earth? Besides, where the law does give dominion, who doubts but that the king who receives it must hold it of and under the law, according to that old axiom, *attribuat rex legi quod lex attribuit ei potestatem et dominium.* And again, *rex non debet esse sub homine, sed sub deo et lege.* Thirdly, whereas it is not altogether without reason that kings are judged to have, by virtue of their dominion, although greater power than any, yet not than all the estates of those societies conjoined wherein such sovereign rule is given them, there is not hereunto anything contrary by us affirmed, no not when we grant supreme authority unto kings, because supremacy is no otherwise intended or meant than to exclude partly foreign powers, and partly the power which belongs in several unto others contained as parts within that politic body over which those kings have supremacy. Where the king has power of dominion or supreme power, there no foreign state or potentate, no estate or potentate domestical, whether it consist of one or of many, can possibly have in the same affairs and cases authority higher than the king. Power of spiritual dominion, therefore, is in cases ecclesiastical that ruling authority which neither any foreign state, nor yet any part of that politic body at home wherein the same is established, can lawfully overrule.

3. By What Right, after What Sort, in What Measure, with What Conveniency, and According to What Example Christian Kings May Have It. In a Word, Their Manner of Holding Dominion

By what right: namely such as though men do give, God does ratify. Unto which supreme power in kings two kinds of adversaries there are that have opposed themselves: one sort defending that supreme power in cases ecclesiastical throughout the world appertains of divine right to the bishop of Rome, another sort that the said power belongs in every national church unto the clergy thereof assembled. We, which defend as well against the one as the other that kings within their own precincts may have it, must show by what right it may come unto them.

First, unto me it seems almost out of doubt and controversy

that every independent multitude, before any certain form of regiment established, has under God's supreme authority full dominion over itself, even as a man not tied with the bond of subjection as yet unto any other has over himself the like power. God creating mankind did endue it naturally with full power to guide itself in what kinds of societies soever it should choose to live. A man which is born Lord of himself may be made another's servant, and that power which naturally whole societies have may be derived into many few or one, under whom the rest shall then live in subjection. Some multitudes are brought in subjection by force, as they who, being subdued, are fain to submit their necks unto what yoke it pleases their conquerors to lay upon them. Which conquerors by just and lawful wars do hold their power over such multitudes as a thing descending unto them, divine providence itself so disposing. For it is God who gives victory in the day of war, and unto whom dominion in this sort is derived, the same they enjoy according unto that law of nations, which law authorizes conquerors to reign as absolute lords over them whom they vanquish. Sometimes it pleases God himself by special appointment to choose out and nominate such as to whom dominion shall be given, which thing he did often in the commonwealth of Israel. They who in this sort receive power have it immediately from God by mere divine right; they by human on whom the same is bestowed according unto men's discretion when they are left free by God to make choice of their own governor. By which of these means soever it happen that kings or governors be advanced unto their seats, we must acknowledge both their lawful choice to be approved of God, and themselves for God's lieutenants, and confess their power his.

As for supreme power in ecclesiastical affairs, the Word of God does nowhere appoint that all kings should have it, neither that any should not have it. For which cause it seems to stand altogether by human right that unto Christian kings there is such dominion given. Again, on whom the same is bestowed, even at men's discretion, they likewise do hold it by divine right if God in his own revealed word have appointed such power to be, although himself extraordinarily bestow it not, but leave the appointment of the persons unto men. Yea, albeit God do neither appoint the thing, nor assign the person, nevertheless, when men have established both, who does doubt but that sundry duties and offices depending thereupon are prescribed in the Word of God, and consequently by that very right to be exacted?

For example's sake, the power which the Roman emperors had over foreign provinces was not a thing which the law of God did ever institute, neither was Tiberius Caesar by special commission from heaven therewith invested. And yet the payment of tribute unto Caesar, being made emperor, is the plain law of Jesus Christ. Unto kings by human right, honour by very divine right is due. Man's ordinances are many times presupposed as grounds in the statutes of God. And therefore of what kind soever the means be whereby governors are lawfully advanced unto their seats, as we by the law of God stand bound meekly to acknowledge them for God's lieutenants, and to confess their power his, so they by the same law are both authorized and required to use that power as far as it may be in any sort available to his honour. The law appoints no man to be an husband, but if a man have betaken himself into that condition, it gives him then authority over his own wife. That the Christian world should be ordered by kingly regiment the law of God does not anywhere command. And yet the law of God does give them right which once are' exalted to that estate to exact at the hands of their subjects general obedience in whatsoever affairs their power may serve to command. So God does ratify the works of that sovereign authority which kings have received by men.

. . . .

In What Measure

In power of dominion all kings have not an equal latitude. Kings by conquest make their own charter, so that how large their power, either civil or spiritual, is we cannot with any certainty define further, than only to set them in general the law of God and nature for bounds. Kings by God's own special appointment have also that largeness of power which he does assign, or permit with approbation. Touching kings which were first instituted by agreement and composition made with them over whom they reign, how far their power may lawfully extend the articles of compact between them must show: not the articles only of compact at the first beginning, which for the most part are either clean worn out of knowledge, or else known unto very few, but whatsoever has been after in free and voluntary manner condescended unto, whether by express consent, whereof positive laws are witnesses, or else by silent allowance famously notified through custom reaching beyond the memory of man. By which means of after agreement it comes many times to pass in kingdoms that they whose ancient predecessors were by violence and force made subject do grow even by little and little into that most sweet form of kingly government which philosophers define to be regency, willingly sustained and endued with chiefty of power in the greatest things. Many of the ancients in their writings do speak of kings with such high and ample terms, as if universality of power even in regard of things and not of persons only did appertain to the very being of a king. The reason is because their speech concerning kings they frame according to the state of those monarchs to whom unlimited authority was given. Which some not observing, imagine that all kings, even in that they are kings, ought to have whatsoever power they find any sovereign ruler lawfully to have enjoyed. But that most judicious philosopher, whose eye scarce anything did escape which was to be found in the bosom of nature, he, considering how far the power of one sovereign ruler may be different from another's regal authority, notes in Spartan kings that, of all others lawfully reigning, they had the most restrained power. A king which has not supreme power in the greatest things is rather entitled a king than invested with real sovereignty. We cannot properly term him a king of whom it may not be said, at the least wise as touching certain the very chiefest affairs of state . . . , his right in them is to have rule not subject to any other predominant.

I am not of opinion that simply always in kings the most, but the best limited power is best, both for them and for the people; the most limited is that which may deal in fewest things, the best that which in dealing is tied unto the soundest, perfectest and most indifferent rule; which rule is the law. I mean not only the law of nature and of God, but very national or municipal law consonant thereunto. Happier that people whose law is their king in the greatest things than that whose king is himself their law. Where the king does guide the state and the law the king, that commonwealth is like a harp or melodious instrument, the strings whereof are tuned and handled all by one hand, following as laws the rules and canons of musical science. Most divinely therefore Archytas makes unto public felicity these four steps, every latter whereof does spring from the former as from a mother cause: . . . 'The king ruling by law, the magistrate following, the subject free, and the whole society happy', adding on the contrary side, that where this order is not, it comes by transgression thereof to pass that the king grows a tyrant, he that rules under him abhors to be guided and commanded by him, the people subject unto both have freedom under neither, and the whole commmunity is wretched. In which respect I cannot choose but commend highly their wisdom by whom the foundations of this commonwealth have been laid, wherein, though no manner person or case be unsubject to the king's power, yet so is the power of the king over all and in all limited, that unto all his proceedings the law itself is a rule. The axioms of our regal government are these: *lex facit regem* [the law makes the king]. The king's grant of any favour made contrary to law is void. *Rex nihil potest, nisi quod iure potest* [the king can do nothing he cannot do by law]. Our kings therefore, when they take possession of the room they are called into, have it pointed out before their eyes, even by the very solemnities and rites of their inauguration, to what affairs by the said law their supreme authority and power reaches. Crowned we see they are, and enthroned and anointed: the crown a sign of military, the throne of sedentary or judicial, the oil of religious or sacred power. It is not on any side denied that kings may have such authority in secular affairs. The question then is what power they lawfully may have and exercise in cases of God. . . .

. . . .

It has been declared already in general how the best established dominion is where the law does most rule the king, the true effect whereof particularly is found as well in ecclesiastical as in civil affairs. In these the king, through his supreme power, may do sundry great things himself, both appertaining unto peace and war, both at home by commandment and by commerce with states abroad, because so much the law does permit. Some things on the other side the king alone has no power to do without consent of the lords and commons assembled in parliament. The king of himself cannot change the nature of pleas nor courts, no not so much as restore blood, because the law is a bar unto him: not any law divine or natural, for against neither it were, though kings of themselves might do both; but the positive laws of the realm have abridged therein and restrained the king's power. Which positive laws, whether by custom or otherwise established, without repugnancy unto the law of God and nature, ought no less to be of force even in the spiritual affairs of the Church. Wherefore in regard of ecclesiastical laws we willingly embrace that of Ambrose: *imperator bonus intra ecclesiam, non supra ecclesiam est*: kings have dominion to exercise in ecclesiastical cases, but according to the laws of the Church. Whether it be therefore the nature of courts, or the form of pleas, or the kind of governors, or the order of proceedings in whatsoever spiritual businesses, for the received laws and liberties of the Church the king has supreme authority and power, but against them none. What such positive laws have appointed to be done by others than the king, or by others with the king, and in what form they have appointed the doing of it, the same of necessity must be kept, neither is the king's sole authority to alter it.

Yea, even as it were a thing unreasonable if in civil affairs the king (albeit the whole universal body did join with him) should do anything by their absolute supreme power for the ordering of their state at home in prejudice of any of those ancient laws of nations which are of force throughout the world because the necessary commerce of kingdoms depends on them, so, in principal matters belonging to Christian religion, a thing very scandalous and offensive it must needs be thought if either kings or laws should dispose of the affairs of God without any respect had to that which of old has been reverently thought of throughout the world, and wherein there is no law of God which forces us to swerve from the way wherein so many and so holy ages have gone. Wherefore, not without good consideration, the very law itself has provided that judges ecclesiastical appointed under the king's commission shall not adjudge for heresy anything but that which heretofore has been so adjudged by the authority of the canonical scriptures, or by the first four general councils, or by some other general council wherein the same has been declared heresy by the express words of the said canonical scriptures, or such as hereafter shall be termed heresy by the High Court of Parliament of this realm, with the assent of the clergy in the convocation. By which words of the law, who does not plainly see how, in that one branch of proceeding by virtue of the king's supreme authority, the credit which those four general councils has throughout all churches evermore had, was judged by the makers of the foresaid act a just cause wherefore they should be mentioned in that case as a requisite part of the rule wherewith dominion was to be limited. But of this we shall further consider when we come unto that which sovereign power may do in making ecclesiastical laws.

. . . .

According unto What Example or Pattern

The service which we do unto the true God, who made heaven and earth, is far different from that which heathens have done unto their supposed gods, though nothing else were respected but only the odds between their hope and ours. The offices of piety or true religion sincerely performed have the promises both of this life and of the life to come, the practices of superstition have neither. If, notwithstanding, the heathens, reckoning upon no other reward for all which they did but only protection and favour in the temporal estate and condition of this present life, and perceiving how great good did hereby publicly grow as long as fear to displease (they knew not what) divine power was some kind of bridle unto them, did therefore provide that the highest degree of care for their religion should be the principal charge of such as, having otherwise also the greatest and chiefest power, were by so much the more fit to have custody thereof, shall the like kind of provision be in us thought blameworthy?

A gross error it is to think that regal power ought to serve for the good of the body and not of the soul, for men's temporal peace and not their eternal safety; as if God had ordained kings for no other end and purpose but only to fat up men like hogs, and to see that they have their mash? . . .

2 Richard Baxter, *A Holy Commonwealth, or Political Aphorisms, Opening the True Principles of Government: For the Healing of the Mistakes, and Resolving the Doubts, that Most Endanger and Trouble England at This Time (If Yet There May be Hope) and Directing the Desires of Sober Christians that Long to See the Kingdoms of This World Become the Kingdoms of the Lord, and of His Christ* (1659)

. . . .

Thesis 190: The happiest commonwealth is that which most attains the ends of government and society, which are the public good, especially in matters of everlasting concernment, and the pleasing of God, the absolute Lord and King of all.

The ultimate end is the chief good. This denominates all the means to be more or less good; and all things to be indifferent, as to amiableness, that are neither for it nor against it; and all things to be evil that are against it. That which is neither our end, nor a means to our end, is not good or amiable to us.

Food and raiment and our outward wealth are to furnish our own and others' bodies with such requisites as fit them for the serving of our souls, that both may serve God and enjoy and please him. He that takes down this end (the pleasing and enjoying of God in glory) takes down all the world as a means to it, and destroys the very use and relative nature of all things under the sun, and makes another thing of himself and all things. As his fleshly brutish end is below the high and glorious end that God appointed all ends for, so does he accordingly brutify and debase them all. For the means receive their excellency from their end, and their aptitude thereto. An atheistical, infidel politician, that makes not these heavenly glorious things the ends of his policy, does set kings, and commonwealths, and laws as far below a Christian king, commonwealth, and law as earth is below heaven, and almost as a dog is below a man; and commit the highest treason almost that men are capable of committing, destroying (doctrinally) God's kingdom and men's, and setting up a malkin in the place; and indeed are intolerable in a Christian commonwealth.

Thesis 191: That commonwealth is likely to be most happy which in the constitution and administration is fullest suited to this heavenly end; and therefore that is the best form of government.

This needs no proof to any that do believe that to be the ultimate end.

Thesis 192: The more theocratical or truly divine any government is, the better it is.

None can deny this that denies not God. If he have more authority than man, and be wiser and better, and more powerful to defend his subjects, and repress his enemies, and do justice in the execution of his laws, then, as no man should dare to compare with God, so no government with his.

Thesis 193: A government may be theocratical (or divine): (1) In the constitution; (2) And the administration. (1) In the constitution: (a) as to the subjects; (b) the relations and their foundations; (c) and the ends. (2) In the administration: (a) as to the officers; (b) laws; (c) judgement and execution.

It is the first part only that, in order, I should here treat of because I am not come to the administration of commonwealths; but, preferring the method that suits my ends, I shall touch briefly of somewhat of this here in the way. I take it for granted that every man, except the atheist (alias the fool, or brute), does consent that we should desire the best, that is the most divine, commonwealth that we are able to procure.

Thesis 194: (1) In a divine commonwealth, God the universal King is the sovereign; and none that rule pretend to a power that is not from him and subservient to him, nor do any else claim the honour of being the original of power.

The *majestas* or *pars imperans* is essential to the commonwealth: and that God be king is essential to a theocracy. If any infidel say that God will not condescend to be our king, and that therefore this supposition deludes us, and lifts us up too high, I answer that he contradicts not only the stream of Scripture that calls God our king, but the clearest light of nature, which from his creation and sole capacity shows that, by necessary resultancy, he must rule (as I have showed).

Thesis 195: (2) In a divine commonwealth it is supposed that the subjects are all God's subjects, not only by obligation (as every man is), but also by consent.

Others may possibly be permitted as *incolae*, on the terms as catechumens in or among the church. But only the voluntary subjects of God should be the proper *cives* or free subjects of a divine commonwealth; and only Christians of a Christian commonwealth.

Thesis 196: (3) In a divine commonwealth a covenant between God and the people is the foundation or necessary condition; and all the free subjects are engaged first to God.

As I showed in the beginning, as they are *obligati ad obedientiam*, the law of nature is the *fundamentum* or cause. As they have right to the benefits of the commonwealth and are free of it, God's promise or covenant, as on his part, is the *fundamentum* and the cause; and their consent or covenant, on their part, is the *sine qua non* or condition: as they are self-obliged, or bound by their own consent, it is the efficient or foundation of that secondary obligation.

Thesis 197: (4) In a divine commonwealth the prince or other human sovereign does hold his power as from God, and under him, and the people consent and subject themselves to him principally as God's officer.

Though God choose not his officers now in the same manner as in Moses' and the following judges' days (as to the extraordinary call), yet are they now as truly his officers as then. And therefore the people are first to be engaged in covenant with God, and then with the prince as God's officer: and on these terms are princes to hold their power.

Thesis 198: (5) In a divine commonwealth the honour and pleasing of God and the salvation of the people are the principal ends, and their corporal welfare but subordinate to these.

For it is much denominated *a termino vel fine:* that which is but for earthly ends is but an earthly society. The body that is not for the soul and subject to it is not the body of a man but of a brute. And the kingdom that subjects not corporal felicity to spiritual, and temporal to eternal, and looks not to that, is but a brutish, sensual kingdom. For though rational men are the subjects of it, yet while that reason is subjected to the flesh and appetite they are *a fine* to be denominated brutish. For that is a man's predominant faculty, which is next that which he makes his chiefest end. And therefore if he have a brutish end, his brutish appetite is predominant, though reason serve it. And the man, and so also the society and government, is denominated from that which is predominant; and therefore from this end and brutish ruling faculty it must be called brutish.

Thesis 199: (6) Where the gospel is published, Jesus Christ, our Lord and King by the title of redemption, is also to be acknowledged by prince and people, and taken in as the beginning and end of the commonwealth.

The Kingdom of Christ is proved before. If any man will but read the Scripture, he need no other confutation of Hobbes, that from Scripture would prove that the Kingdom of Christ is only at his second coming, and not at present.

Thesis 200: In the administration of a divine commonwealth the officers should be such as God will own; that is, men fearing God and working righteousness; men sober, righteous, and godly, that by faith and love are subjected themselves to God, their Creator and Redeemer.

If the inferior magistrates be infidels, or ungodly men, they are false to their highest King. And how can they be fit to govern for him, and promote his interest?

Thesis 201: In the administration of a divine commonwealth, God must be allowed all that causality in the choice of individual magistrates which he condescends to; that is: (1) All the descriptions and precepts of his law must be observed; (2) Those that by his gifts and providence do answer his law must be elected; (3) And to that end, those that he has made capable only, should be electors; (4) And that which cannot by these gifts be well discerned, if it be of moment, should be referred to a lot.

Of these I shall anon speak somewhat more fully in order to practice.

Thesis 202: In a divine commonwealth the laws of God, in nature and Scripture, must be taken for the principal laws, which no ruler can dispense with; and all their laws must be as by-laws, subordinate to them for the promoting of their execution.

Though the law of Moses as such obliges us not, yet the matter of it under another form may oblige; that is, the moral law still binds us, both as the law of nature, and of the Redeemer. And the reasons of the laws commonly called political (though indeed the moral was political) do still bind, so far as, our case agreeing with theirs, we can perceive in those laws how God would have such a case determined. If God's laws keep not the pre-eminency, his government is rejected. He rules by laws; and to reject them is to reject his rule. All the world have the law of nature; Christians also have the law of grace, and the law of nature in the most legible characters. These are to be the principal statutes for the government of the commonwealth; and man's laws should subserve them.

Thesis 203: In a divine commonwealth the sins against God must be accounted the most heinous crimes. The denying or blaspheming God, or his essential attributes or sovereignty, is to be judged the highest treason; and the drawing men to other gods, and seeking the ruin of the commonwealth in spirituals, is to be accounted the chiefest enmity to it.

The offence against the highest authority must needs be the greatest offence (*caeteris paribus*). And though the chief punishment be reserved for the life to come, yet that will not excuse the magistrate from the due punishing of it here. For magistrates' executions are for the public good of that particular commonwealth; which will not frustrate God's executions for the glory of his justice, and other ends that are to man unknown. The chief punishment for murder, theft and other injuries to man are reserved for the life to come: and yet we will not let them here go unpunished, lest present impunity encourage them to invade men's lives and estates. No more should notorious impiety go unpunished here, lest impunity encourage men to destroy their own and others' souls, and by their examples and temptations to undo men everlastingly, and bring down God's temporal judgements on the place.

Thesis 204: In a divine commonwealth holiness must have the principal honour and encouragement, and a great difference be made between the precious and the vile.

King David says (Psalm 16: 2, 3) that 'his good extended to the saints that are in the earth, and to the excellent, in whom was all his delight'. Psalm 101: 6: He professes that 'his eyes shall be upon the faithful of the land, that they may dwell with him; he that walks in a perfect way, he shall serve him'. But – verse 8 – a froward heart shall depart from him, and he will not know a wicked person, and that he 'will early destroy all the wicked of the land, that he may cut off all wicked doers from the city of the Lord'. This is a theocracy, when princes govern from God, by God and for God in all things.

Thesis 205: By this it appears that in a true theocracy, or divine commonwealth, the matter of the church and commonwealth should be altogether or almost the same, though the form of them and administrations are different.

(1) That the materials or subjects should be the same appears from what is said: They must all be such as enter the covenant with God, which in a Christian commonwealth can be no other than the baptismal covenant which enters them into the church: circumcision entered them by the holy covenant into church and commonwealth, which among the Jews were materially the same. He that is by this covenant given up to God in Christ is a member of God's universal church and kingdom.

Yea, indeed, the universal church and the universal kingdom, in the strict sense, are both materially and formally all one, though the particulars are not so. There are three senses of God's universal kingdom: (1) As the word signifies all that are obliged as subjects to obey him: and so all men, even rebels, are members of this kingdom; (2) As it signifies those that obey him *secundum quid*, or analogically, but not simply or acceptably (nor profess so much): and so Turks and many infidels that worship God, but not by Christ, are in his kingdom; (3) As it comprehends only faithful accepted subjects, and those that by profession seem to be such: and thus his kingdom and his church universal are all one formally.

(2) But the reason why particular churches and commonwealths are not formally the same, but distinct polities, is because though the universal, being united in one undivided Head, is but one, as being denominated from that Head, yet from unity proceeds multiplicity. God does not communicate all that power in kind which is eminently and transcendently in himself to any one man or sort of officers, but

distributes to each their part – civil power to civil rulers, and ecclesiastical to church rulers. When we are once come down below God the fountain in our observation, we find a present division of that communicable power into many hands, which flows from the incommunicable power that is in God alone. For man has not God's sufficiency to be all. The pope's flatterers may extol him as an universal vice-God or vice-Christ, but as Scripture tells us that he wants the form, that is the authority, so nature tells us that he wants the aptitude and capacity of matter. And therefore, though the universal kingdom (in the strict sense) and the universal church are one, in one God, yet particular kingdoms and churches are diversified *in specie*, as shall anon be showed.

When I say that the matter, ordinarily, should be the same, I mean not to tie the governors of church or state to a necessary conformity of their administrations as to the matter, in taking in or casting out of members (save only in point of advantage and conveniency, to be mentioned in the next chapter). For each sort of governors have the charge of their own distinct administrations. It is not only possible, but too common, that one sort is much more careless and unfaithful to God and men than the other. If a good magistrate has bad pastors over the same people, and the pastors will not difference between the precious and the vile, but will keep the impious and filthy in the church, the magistrate is not therefore bound to keep such as freemen in the commonwealth, but must make it (as containing freemen) narrower than the church. And if faithful pastors live under a careless prince that takes the filthiest and most impious as *cives* [citizens], the pastors must not do so in the church, for they must be accountable to God for the discharge of their own trust.

But that which I mean is that the same qualification makes a man capable of being a member both of a Christian church and commonwealth, which is his covenant with God in Christ, or his membership of the universal church, supposing the other circumstantials or accidental capacities, which are indeed distinct.

Lastly, note that I exclude not some just exceptions of ordinary or extraordinary cases in which the members of one sort of society may be excluded from the other. Persons that are through scruples (innocent or sinful) kept from joining with a particular church for a time, being yet capable of their communion, may yet be members of the commonwealth. Want of riches may do more also to keep men out of a freedom in the commonwealth than out of the church. And yet I think that in a theocracy care should be taken to keep some members from swelling to excess, and others from extremity of want, as among the Israelites there was; yet so as no man's industry be discouraged, nor property invaded, nor idleness in any cherished. And riches and poverty should not make altogether so great a difference as they do in profane societies. If men's poverty be not so great as to make them the servants of others, and deprive them of ingenuous freedom, it should not deprive them of civil freedom: especially where criminal and civil cases have different judges, they may have more freedom about criminals than civils. Where wealth is concerned men of wealth should have the power; but where virtue or vice, honesty or dishonesty is the matter of debate, the honest though poor should have more power than the impious that are rich.

I conclude therefore that though variety of outward states, and the neglects of either magistrate or pastors, may be an exception to the rule, yet as to inward qualifications, ordinarily the same persons are fit to be members of church and commonwealth.

But as the church has only the members within, and yet the *competentes* and catechumens, and in a more distant sort the excommunicate, and the neighbour infidels, under her care, as owing them some help, so a Christian commonwealth, though it own none as *cives* (or free subjects, commonly called burgesses, or enfranchised persons) but such as are fit to be church members, yet has it many that are mere subjects, and are to have the protection of the laws for their lives and possessions, that are of a lower form.

(3) And yet that church and commonwealth are not formally (nor *de facto* always, nor usually materially in a great part) the same societies appears: (1) From the difference of governors. Magistrates rule the commonwealth, and the church as in the commonwealth, but not the church with that peculiar government proper to it as a church. And ministers may teach in the commonwealth, but as pastors they govern only the church as such. (2) From the manner of government and administrations. The magistrate rules imperiously, and by force, having power upon men's estates and persons. But the pastors have none such, but govern only by the Word of God explained and applied to the conscience. (3) From the nearest foundation. The commonwealth is constituted by a (virtual or actual) contract between the civil sovereign and the people. But the church (particular) is

constituted by a consent between the pastors and the flock. (4) From the extent. The commonwealth contains all the people in a whole nation or more, as united in one sovereign. But particular churches (distinct from the universal, united in Christ) have no general ecclesiastical officers in whom a nation must unite as one church, but [are] as corporations in one kingdom, or as so many schools, that have a peculiar form and government, but such only as is under the magistrates' government in its kind, or as several colleges in one university. (5) From the accidental incapacities of men to be members of each. A servant or beggar is to be a free member of the church, that is to be limited much more in his freedom in the commonwealth. And a man that lives as a carrier or messenger, in constant travel from place to place (especially if he have no home), is scarce capable of being a member of a particular church, who yet may be a member of the commonwealth. (6) From the nearest end. Civil order is the nearest end of civil policy. But church order, for holy communion in God's worship, is the nearest end of church policy. So that formally they are diverse, though materially, if princes and pastors would do their duties in reformation and righteous government, they would be, if not altogether, yet for the most part the same, as consisting of the same persons.

Thesis 206: It is this theocratical policy or divine commonwealth which is the unquestionable reign of Christ on earth, which all Christians are agreed may be justly sought, and that temporal dignity of saints which undoubtedly would much bless the world.

Whether there be any other reign of Christ on earth to be expected, that is, by his visible, personal abode (which I perceive some papists of late very busy, under their several masks, to indigitate, partly in order to persuade men that the church is a body that has a universal visible head, which must be Christ's vicar, but in the interspace betwixt his first and second coming), this controversy I do not now determine. For my own part, I reverence the ancients that were of that mind, and many later that have followed them. I am myself as merely neutral in it as in almost any point of so great moment so often propounded to my consideration. I oppose them not in the least, nor am I for them: not from a carelessness or unwillingness to know the truth, but the difficulty of the case, and the weakness of my understanding. I live in hope of the coming and appearance of our

Lord Jesus Christ, and pray that he may come quickly. But that he will after his coming reign visibly on earth, and if so in what manner, are things that I have read much of, but am uncertain after all, and scarce can perceive which way my judgement most inclines.

But in the meantime, why should we not all conspire in our longings after that reign of Christ, and dignity of the saints, and reformation of the world which is undoubtedly our duty, and which all agree about that have the fear of God?

. . . .

3 Roger Williams, *The Bloudy Tenent of Persecution, for Cause of Conscience, Discussed, in a Conference betweene Truth and Peace* (1644)

Syllabus:

First: That the blood of so many hundred thousand souls of protestants and papists, spilt in the wars of present and former ages for their respective consciences, is not required nor accepted by Jesus Christ, the Prince of Peace.

Secondly: Pregnant scriptures and arguments are throughout the work proposed against the doctrine of persecution for cause of conscience.

Thirdly: Satisfactory answers are given to scriptures and objections produced by Mr Calvin, Beza, Mr Cotton, and the ministers of the New England churches, and others former and later, tending to prove the doctrine of persecution for cause of conscience.

Fourthly: The doctrine of persecution for cause of conscience is proved guilty of all the blood of the souls crying for vengeance under the altar.

Fifthly: All civil states, with their officers of justice, in their respective constitutions and administrations, are proved essentially civil, and therefore not judges, governors, or defenders of the spiritual, or Christian, state and worship.

Sixthly: It is the will and command of God that, since the coming of his Son, the Lord Jesus, a permission of the most paganish, Jewish,

Turkish, or anti-Christian consciences and worships be granted to all men in all nations and countries; and they are only to be fought against with that sword which is only, in soul matters, able to conquer: to wit, the sword of God's Spirit, the word of God.

Seventhly: The state of the land of Israel, the kings and people thereof, in peace and war, is proved figurative and ceremonial, and no pattern nor precedent for any kingdom or civil state in the world to follow.

Eighthly: God requires not an uniformity of religion to be enacted and enforced in any civil state; which enforced uniformity, sooner or later, is the greatest occasion of civil war, ravishing of conscience, persecution of Christ Jesus in his servants, and of the hypocrisy and destruction of millions of souls.

Ninthly: In holding an enforced uniformity of religion in a civil state, we must necessarily disclaim our desires and hopes of the Jews' conversion to Christ.

Tenthly: An enforced uniformity of religion throughout a nation or civil state confounds the civil and religious, denies the principles of Christianity and civility, and that Jesus Christ is come in the flesh.

Eleventhly: The permission of other consciences and worships than a state professes only can, according to God, procure a firm and lasting peace; good assurance being taken, according to the wisdom of the civil state, for uniformity of civil obedience from all sorts.

Twelfthly: Lastly, true civility and Christianity may both flourish in a state or kingdom, notwithstanding the permission of divers and contrary consciences, either of Jew or Gentile.

.   .   .   .

Chapter VI: What Civil Peace is

.   .   .   .

Truth: . . . First, for civil peace, what is it but *pax civitatis*, the peace of the city, whether an English city, Scotch, or Irish city, or further abroad, French, Spanish, Turkish city, etc. Thus it pleased the Father of Lights to define it (Jeremiah, 29: 7), 'Pray for the peace of the city.' Which peace of the city, or citizens so compacted in a civil way of union, may be entire, unbroken, safe, etc., notwithstanding so many thousands of God's people, the Jews, were there in bondage, and would neither be constrained to the worship of the city Babel, nor restrained from so much of the worship of the true God as they then could practise, as is plain in the practice of the three worthies, Shadrach, Meshach, and Abednego, as also of Daniel (Daniel iii and vi) – the peace of the city or kingdom being a far different peace from the peace of the religion, or spiritual worship, maintained and professed of the citizens. This peace of their worship (which worship also in some cities being various) being a false peace, God's people were and ought to be nonconformitants, not daring either to be restrained from the true, or constrained to false worship; and yet without breach of the civil or city peace, properly so called.

Peace: Hence it is that so many glorious and flourishing cities of the world maintain their civil peace; yea, the very Americans and wildest pagans keep the peace of their towns or cities, though neither in one nor the other can any man prove a true church of God in those places, and consequently no spiritual and heavenly peace. The peace spiritual, whether true or false, being of a higher and far different nature from the peace of the place or people, being merely and essentially civil and human.

Truth: Oh! how lost are the sons of men in this point! To illustrate this: – the church, or company of worshippers, whether true or false, is like unto a body or college of physicians in a city – like unto a corporation, society, or company of East India or Turkey merchants, or any other society or company in London. Which companies may hold their courts, keep their records, hold disputations, and in matters concerning their society may dissent, divide, break into schisms and factions, sue and implead each other at the law, yea, wholly break up and dissolve into pieces and nothing, and yet the peace of the city not be in the least measure impaired or disturbed because the essence or being of the city, and so the well-being and peace thereof, is essentially distinct from those particular societies, the city courts, city laws, city punishments distinct from theirs. The city was before them, and stands absolute and entire when such a corporation or society is taken down. For instance further, the city or civil state of Ephesus was essentially distinct from the worship of Diana in the city, or of the whole city. Again, the church of Christ in Ephesus, which were God's people, converted and called out from the worship of that city unto Christianity, or worship of God in Christ, was distinct from both.

Now suppose that God remove the candlestick from Ephesus,

yea, though the whole worship of the city of Ephesus should be altered: yet, if men be true and honestly ingenuous to city covenants, combinations, and principles, all this might be without the least impeachment or infringement of the peace of the city of Ephesus. Thus in the city of Smyrna was the city itself, or civil estate, one thing; the spiritual or religious state of Smyrna another; the church of Christ in Smyrna distinct from them both; and the synagogue of the Jews, whether literally Jews, as some think, or mystically false Christians, as others, called the synagogue of Satan (Revelation ii), distinct from all these. And notwithstanding these spiritual oppositions in point of worship and religion, yet hear we not the least noise — nor need we, if men keep but the bond of civility — of any civil breach, or breach of civil peace amongst them; and to persecute God's people there for religion, that only was a breach of civility itself.

. . . .

Chapter LXI: The Princes of the World Seldom Take Part with Christ

. . . .

Truth: . . . for mine own part, I would not use an argument from the number of princes witnessing in profession of practice against persecution for cause of conscience; for the truth and faith of the Lord Jesus must not be received with respect of faces, be they never so high, princely and glorious. Precious pearls and jewels, and far more precious truth, are found in muddy shells and places. The rich mines of golden truth lie hid under barren hills, and in obscure holes and corners.

The most high and glorious God has chosen the poor of the world, and the witnesses of truth (Revelation xi) are clothed in sackcloth, not in silk or satin, cloth of gold or tissue. And, therefore, I acknowledge, if the number of princes professing persecution be considered, it is rare to find a king, prince, or governor like Christ Jesus, the King of kings, and Prince of the princes of the earth, and who tread not in the steps of Herod the fox, or Nero the lion, openly or secretly persecuting the name of the Lord Jesus: such were Saul, Jeroboam, Ahab, though under a mask or pretence of the name of the God of Israel.

To that purpose was it a noble speech of Buchanan, who, lying on his death-bed, sent this item to King James: 'Remember my humble service to his majesty, and tell him that Buchanan is going to a place where few kings come.'

. . . .

Chapter XCI: Few Magistrates, Few Men Spiritually and Christianly Good; Yet Divers Sorts of Goodness: Natural, Artificial, Civil, etc.

Peace: Dear Truth, it seems not to be unreasonable to close up this passage with a short descant upon the assertion, viz., 'A subject without godliness will not be *bonus vir*, a good man, and a magistrate, except he see godliness preserved, will not be *bonus magistratus*.'

Truth: I confess that without godliness, or a true worshipping of God with an upright heart, according to God's ordinances, neither subjects nor magistrates can please God in Christ Jesus, and so be spiritually or Christianly good. Which few magistrates and few men either come to, or are ordained unto, God having chosen a little flock out of the world, and those generally poor and mean (1 Corinthians 1: 26; James 2: 5), yet this I must remember you of, that when the most high God created all things of nothing, he saw and acknowledged divers sorts of goodness, which must still be acknowledged in their distinct kinds: a good air, a good ground, a good tree, a good sheep, etc.

I say the same in artificials: a good garment, a good house, a good sword, a good ship. I also add: a good city, a good company or corporation, a good husband, father, master. Hence also we say: a good physician, a good lawyer, a good seaman, a good merchant, a good pilot for such and such a shore or harbour; that is, morally, civilly good in their several civil respects and employments.

Hence (Psalm 122) the church, or city of God, is compared to a city compact within itself; which compactness may be found in many towns and cities of the world where yet has not shined any spiritual or supernatural goodness. Hence the Lord Jesus (Matthew 12) describes an ill state of a house or kingdom, viz., to be divided against itself, which cannot stand.

These I observe to prove that a subject, a magistrate, may be a good subject, a good magistrate, in respect of civil or moral goodness, which thousands want; and where it is, it is commendable and beautiful, though godliness, which is infinitely more beautiful, be wanting, and which is only proper to the Christian state, the commonwealth of Israel, the true church, the holy nation (Ephesians 2; 1 Peter 2).

Lastly, however, the authors deny that there can be *bonus magistratus*, a good magistrate, except he see all godliness preserved; yet themselves confess that civil honesty is sufficient to make a good subject in these words, viz., 'He must see that honesty be preserved within his jurisdiction, else the subject will not be *bonus civis*, a good citizen'; and doubtless, if the law of relations hold true, that civil honesty which makes a good citizen must also, together with qualifications fit for a commander, make also a good magistrate.

Chapter XCII: Civil Power Originally and Fundamentally in the People

. . . .

Truth: . . . First, whereas they say that the civil power may erect and establish what form of civil government may seem in wisdom most meet: I acknowledge the proposition to be most true, both in itself, and also considered with the end of it, that a civil government is an ordinance of God, to conserve the civil peace of people so far as concerns their bodies and goods, as formerly has been said. But from this grant I infer, as before has been touched, that the sovereign, original and foundation of civil power lies in the people – whom they must needs mean by the civil power [as] distinct from the government set up; and if so, that a people may erect and establish what form of government seems to them most meet for their civil condition. It is evident that such governments as are by them erected and established have no more power, nor for no longer time, than the civil power, or people consenting and agreeing, shall betrust them with. This is clear not only in reason, but in the experience of all commonwealths where the people are not deprived of their natural freedom by the power of tyrants.

And if so – that the magistrates receive their power of governing the church from the people – undeniably it follows that a people, as a people, naturally considered, of what nature or nation soever in Europe, Asia, Africa, or America, have fundamentally and originally, as men, a power to govern the church, to see her do her duty, to correct her, to redress, reform, establish, etc. And if this be not to pull God, and Christ, and Spirit out of heaven and subject them unto natural, sinful, inconstant men, and so consequently to Satan himself, by whom all peoples naturally are guided, let heaven and earth be judge. . . .

. . . .

Chapter CXX: Civil Compulsion was Proper in the National Church of the Jews, but Most Improper in the Christian, Which is Not National

. . . .

Truth: . . . But to your last proposition, whether the kings of Israel and Judah were not types of civil magistrates? Now I suppose, by what has been already spoken, these things will be evident:

First, that those former types of the land, of the people, of their worships were types and figures of a spiritual land, spiritual people, and spiritual worship under Christ. Therefore, consequently, their saviours, redeemers, deliverers, judges, kings must also have their spiritual anti-types, and so consequently not civil but spiritual governors and rulers, lest the very essential nature of types, figures, and shadows be overthrown.

Secondly, although the magistrate by a civil sword might well compel that national church to the external exercise of their national worship, yet it is not possible, according to the rule of the New Testament, to compel whole nations to true repentance and regeneration, without which (so far as may be discerned true) the worship and holy name of God is profaned and blasphemed. An arm of flesh and sword of steel cannot reach to cut the darkness of the mind, the hardness and unbelief of the heart, and kindly operate upon the soul's affections to forsake a long-continued father's worship and to embrace a new, though the best and truest. This work performs alone that sword out of the mouth of Christ, with two edges (Revelation 1 and 3).

Thirdly, we have not one tittle in the New Testament of Christ Jesus concerning such a parallel, neither from himself, nor from his ministers, with whom he conversed forty days after his resurrection, instructing them in the matters of his kingdom (Acts i: 3). Neither find we any such commission or direction given to the civil magistrate to this purpose, nor to the saints for their submission in matters spiritual, but the contrary (Acts 4 and 5; 1 Corinthians 7: 23; Colossians 2: 18).

Fourthly, we have formerly viewed the very matter and essence of a civil magistrate, and find it the same in all parts of the world, wherever people live upon the face of the earth, agreeing together in towns, cities, provinces, kingdoms: – I say the same essentially civil, both from (1) the rise and fountain whence it springs, to wit the people's choice and free consent; (2) the object of it, viz. the common weal or safety of such a people in their bodies and goods, as the authors of this model have themselves confessed. This civil nature of the magistrate we have proved to receive no addition of power from the magistrate being a Christian, no more than it receives diminution from his not being a Christian, even as the commonwealth is a true commonwealth although it have not heard of Christianity; and Christianity professed in it, as in Pergamon, Ephesus, etc., makes it never no more a commonwealth; and Christianity taken away and the candlestick removed makes it nevertheless a commonwealth. . . .

Chapter CXXI: The Rewards or Punishments of the Laws of Israel Not to be Paralleled

. . . .

Truth: . . . consider we the punishments and rewards annexed to the breach or observation of these laws. First, those which were of a temporal and present consideration of this life – blessings and curses of all sorts opened at large (Leviticus 26 and Deuteronomy 28) – which cannot possibly be made good in any state, country, or kingdom, but in a spiritual sense in the church and kingdom of Christ. The reason is this: such a temporal prosperity of outward peace and plenty of all things – of increase of children, of cattle, of honour, of health, of success, of victory – suits not temporally with the afflicted and persecuted state of God's people now: and therefore spiritual and soul-blessedness must be the anti-type, viz. in the midst of revilings and all manner of evil speeches for Christ's sake, soul-blessedness; in the midst of afflictions and persecutions, soul-blessedness (Matthew 5 and Luke 6). And yet herein the Israel of God should enjoy their spiritual peace (Galatians 6: 16).

Out of that blessed temporal state to be cast, or carried captive, was their excommunication or casting out of God's sight (2 Kings 17: 23). Therefore was the blasphemer, the false prophet, the idolater to be cast out or cut off from this holy land: which punishment cannot be paralleled by the punishment of any state or kingdom in the world, but only by the excommunicating or outcasting of person or church from the fellowship of the saints and churches of Christ Jesus in the gospel. And therefore, as before I have noted, the putting away of the false prophet by stoning him to death (Deuteronomy xiii) is fitly answered, and that in the very same words, in the anti-type: when, by the general consent (or stoning) of the whole assembly, any wicked person is put away from amongst them, that is, spiritually cut off out of the land of the spiritually living, the people or church of God (1 Corinthians 5; Galatians 5).

Lastly, the great and high reward or punishment of the keeping or breach of these laws to Israel was such as cannot suit with any state or kingdom in the world beside. The reward of the observation was life, eternal life. The breach of any of these laws was death, eternal death, or damnation from the presence of the Lord (so Romans 10; James 2). Such a covenant God made not before nor since with any state or people in the world. For 'Christ is the end of the law for righteousness to every one that believes' (Romans 10: 4). And 'he that believes in that Son of God has eternal life; he that believes not has not life, but is condemned already' (John 3 and 1 John 5).

Chapter CXXXII: The Magistrate Like a Pilot in the Ship of the Commonwealth

Peace: Oh! that thy light and brightness, dear Truth, might shine to the dark world in this particular! Let it not therefore be grievous if I request a little further illustration of it.

Truth: In his season, God will glorify himself in all his truths. But to gratify thy desire, thus: A pagan or anti-Christian pilot may be as skilful to carry the ship to its desired port as any Christian mariner or pilot in the world, and may perform that work with as much safety and speed; yet have they not command over the souls and consciences of their passengers, or mariners under them, although they may justly see to the labour of the one, and the civil behaviour of all in the ship. A Christian pilot, he performs the same work, as likewise does the metaphorical pilot in the ship of the commonwealth, from a principle of knowledge and experience; but more than this, he acts from a root of the fear of God and love to mankind in his whole course. Secondly, his aim is more to glorify God than to gain his pay or make his voyage. Thirdly, he walks heavenly with men and God, in a constant observation of God's hand in storms, calms, etc. So that the thread of navigation being equally spun by a believing or unbelieving pilot, yet is it drawn over with the gold of godliness and Christianity by a Christian pilot, while he is holy in all manner of Christianity (1 Peter 1: 15). But lastly, the Christian pilot's power over the souls and consciences of his sailors and passengers is not greater than that of the anti-Christian, otherwise than he can subdue the souls of any by the two-edged sword of the Spirit, the word of God, and by his holy demeanour in his place, etc.

. . . .

4 William Walwyn, *The Compassionate Samaritane: Liberty of Conscience Asserted and the Separatist Vindicated* (1644)

Having heretofore met with an apologetical narration of Thomas Goodwin, Philip Nye, Sydrach Sympson, Jeremy Burroughs, William Bridge, I did with gladness of heart undertake the reading thereof, expecting therein to find such general reasons for justification of themselves to the world as would have justified all the Separation, and so have removed by one discourse those prejudices and misapprehensions which even good men have of that harmless and well-meaning sort of people. But finding, contrary to that expectation, that their apology therein for themselves and their toleration was grounded rather upon a remonstrance of the nearness between them and the Presbyterian, being one in doctrine with them, and very little differing from them in discipline; how they had been tolerated by other Presbyter churches, and indulged with greater privileges than the separatist; how they differed from the separatist, and had cautiously avoided those rocks and shelves against which the separatist had split themselves: – confirming by these words the people's disesteem of separatists, suggesting by that phrase of theirs, as if there were amongst the separatists some dangerous paths or opinions, which they warily shunned, though no mention be made what they are, which is the worst sort of calumny.

Finding to my heart's grief the separatist thus left in the lurch, and likely to be exposed to greater dangers than ever by the endeavours of these men, my heart abounded with grief, knowing the innocency of their intentions and honesty of their lives; that they are necessarily enforced to be of the mind they are; upon long examination of their own tenets that they desire nothing more than that they should be publicly and impartially reasoned; knowing likewise their affection to the commonwealth, their forwardness of assistance in purse and person; knowing their meetings to be so innocent, so far from confederacy or counter-plots (though they are very sensible of the sad and perplexed condition that they are in) that they have not yet so much as spoken aught in their own defence, but trusting to the goodness of God, the equity of the Parliament, the simplicity and integrity of their own ways, do quietly enjoy themselves and their worship, let what will be brewing against them, being resolved like Hester to do their duties, and if in doing thereof they perish, they perish: – Methinks every man is bound in conscience to speak and do what he can in the behalf of such a harmless people as these. What, though you are no separatist (as I myself am none) the love of God appears most in doing good for others: that love which aims only at itself, those endeavours which would procure liberty only to themselves can at best be called but self-love and self-respects. 'Tis common freedom every man ought to aim at, which is every man's peculiar right so far as 'tis not prejudicial to the common.

Now because little can be done in their behalf, unless liberty of conscience be allowed for every man, or sort of men, to worship God in that way, and perform Christ's ordinances in that manner as shall appear to them most agreeable to God's Word, and no man be punished or discountenanced by authority for his opinion, unless it be dangerous to the state, I have endeavoured in this discourse to make appear by the best reason I have that every man ought to have liberty of conscience, of what opinion soever, with the caution above

named. In doing whereof I have upon occasion removed all prejudices that the people have concerning the separatist, and vindicated
them from those false aspersions that are usually cast upon them to
make them odious. Wherein my end, I make account, will evidently
appear to be the peace and union of all, and to beget this judgement
in the people and Parliament, that 'tis the principal interest of the
commonwealth that authority should have equal respect, and afford
protection to all peaceable good men alike, notwithstanding their
difference of opinion, that all men may be encouraged to be alike
serviceable thereunto.

Liberty of conscience is to be allowed every man for the following
reasons:

First reason: Because of what judgement soever a man is, he cannot
choose but be of that judgement. That is so evident in itself, that I
suppose it will be granted by all. Whatsoever a man's reason does
conclude to be true or false, to be agreeable or disagreeable to God's
Word, that same to that man is his opinion or judgement, and so man
is by his own reason necessitated to be of that mind he is. Now
where there is a necessity there ought to be no punishment, for
punishment is the recompense of voluntary actions. Therefore no
man ought to be punished for his judgement.

Objection: But it will be objected that the separatists are a rash,
heady people, and not so much concluded by their reason as their
fancy. That they have their enthusiasms and revelations, which
nobody knows what to make of, and that if they were a people that
examined things rationally, the argument would hold good for them.

Answer: That I suppose this to be the argument not of the present,
but of the loose-witted times before the Parliament, where some
politic bishop, or Dr Ignorant University Man, or knave poet would
endeavour by such a suggestion to the people to misguide their
credulous hearts into hatred of those good men, who they knew to
be the constant enemies to their delusions. But let all men now have
other thoughts, and assure themselves that the Brownist and Anabaptist are rational examiners of those things they hold for truth,
mild discoursers, and able to give an account of what they believe.
They who are unsatisfied in that particular may, if they please to visit
their private congregations, which are open to all-comers, have further
satisfaction. Perhaps here and there amongst them may be a man
that, out of his zeal and earnestness for that which he esteems truth,

may outrun his understanding and show many weaknesses in his discourse. I would the like frailty and inabilities were not to be found in many of us. But if the slips and wanderings of a few, and those the weakest, be an argument sufficient to discountenance the Separation, and work them out of the world's favour, I pray God the same argument may never be made use of against us, amongst whom many, and they not esteemed the weakest neither, would give great advantages that way. In the meantime I wish with all my heart we could all put on the spirit of meekness, and rather endeavour to rectify by argument and persuasion one another's infirmities, than upbraid the owners of them with a visible rejoicing that such things are slipped from them to their disadvantage.

One custom they have amongst them which does make even the generality of them able arguers in defence of their way, and that is either a use of objecting against anything delivered amongst them, or proposing any doubt, whereof any desires to be resolved, which is done in a very orderly manner. By which means the weakest becomes in a short time much improved, and every one able to give an account of their tenets (not relying upon their pastors, as most men in our congregations do). Which may serve to remove the objection and put us to consider whether the like custom be not wanting amongst us.

Second reason: The uncertainty of knowledge in this life. No man, nor no sort of men, can presume of an unerring spirit. 'Tis known that the Fathers, General Councils, National Assemblies, Synods and Parliaments in their times have been most grossly mistaken. And though the present times be wiser than the former, being much freed from superstition, and taking a larger liberty to themselves of examining all things, yet since there remains a possibility of error, notwithstanding never so great presumptions of the contrary, one sort of men are not to compel another, since this hazard is run thereby, that he who is in an error may be the constrainer of him who is in the truth.

Objection: But unity and uniformity in religion is to be aimed at, and confusion above all things to be avoided. By toleration new opinions will every day break forth, and, to the scandal of the nation, we shall become a very monster in matters of religion, one part being Presbyter, another Anabaptist, Brownist another, and a fourth an Independent, and so divers according to the diversity of opinions that are already, or may be broached hereafter.

Answer: I answer that in truth this objection appears specious at the first gloss, and therefore is very moving upon the people. Which the bishops well knew, whose it was, and taken up as the fairest pretence for the suppression of those who, it is to be feared, will prove the suppressors. For answer whereunto I aver that a compulsion is of all ways the most unlikely to beget unity of mind and uniformity in practice, which experience will make evident. For the fines, imprisonments, pillories, etc. used by the bishops as means to unite rather confirmed men in their judgements, and begot the abomination and odium which these times have cast upon the hierarchy, being in the worst kind tyrannical, as endeavouring by the punishment of the person the bowing and subjecting of the conscience. And if it be instanced that some there were that turned with the wind, and were terrified by fear of punishment into a compliance, I answer that such men are so far from being examples to be followed, that they may more justly be condemned for weather-cocks (fit to be set up for men to know which way blows the wind) of favour, delicacy, ease and preferment.

Secondly, the conscience, being subject only to reason (either that which is indeed, or seems to him which hears it to be so), can only be convinced or persuaded thereby. Force makes it run back and struggle. It is the nature of every man to be of any judgement rather than his that forces. 'Tis to be presumed that 'tis upon some good grounds of reason that a man is of that judgement whereof he is. Wouldst thou have him be of thine? Show him thy grounds, and let them both work, and see which will get the victory in his understanding. Thus, possibly, he may change his mind, and be of one judgement with thee. But if you will use Club Law, instead of convincing and uniting, you arm men with prejudice against you to conclude that you have no assurance of truth in you, for then you would make use of that, and presume of the efficacy thereof, and not fight with weapons which you do (or at least should) know not to be the weapons of truth.

But I fear there is something more in it. I cannot think that the bishops in their times used so many stratagems of vexation and cruelty against good people to gain them to be of their mind. They could not be ignorant that they set the Nonconformists of all sorts thereby at an irreconcilable hatred against them. No, their end rather was this: They had consulted who were opposed to their designs, and finding the Puritan and Sectary so to be, their interest was by all possible means to suppress them, that so they might without opposition trample upon the people. And therefore in these times men should consider what they do. For if they who have the public countenance do bear themselves after the same manner towards the Anabaptists and Brownists, or whatsoever other sect there is, or may be, that cannot comply with them in judgement or practice (as by their beginnings we fear they will), what can we judge of them but that their ends and intentions are the same with the bishops? For by their fruits (says our Saviour) ye shall know them. We may be deceived by words: their turnings and contextures are so infinite that they may be framed so as to make the worst seem good. The actions of men are the best rules for others to judge them by.

Now upon view of the actions of the divines that are now in favour, men do speak very strangely. Some say the tyranny over conscience that was exercised by the bishops is like to be continued by the Presbyters: that the oppressors are only changed, but the oppression not likely to be removed. Others say that the Anabaptist and Brownist are like to find harder masters, for that the bishops made the punishment of them a matter of sport and profit to themselves, and reserved their punishments to be diversions of the people's minds from taking too much notice of their entrenchments upon the laws and common liberty, suffering their societies notwithstanding to remain, though so low and dejected that they were past fear of them. But the Presbyters, as it is conceived, will be more violent, as slaves usually are when they become masters: and thus talk not only the Anabaptist and Brownist and Antinomian (being chiefly in danger), but other the most moderate and ingenious men that are not swayed by the divines' interest.

They say too, that as it is not just, so neither is it politic, that in the beginnings and first rise, when the divines are but laying the foundation of their greatness, wealth and sway over the people's consciences, and twisting their interest insensibly with the Parliament's: – that in the infancy of their tyranny they should carry themselves so high and presumptuous as they do over other men, shows that their wisdom here comes somewhat short of the serpent's, or else that they are so impatient at the not compliance of other men that they break out even against their own interest. Nay, some say further that they did well indeed in being so zealous against the bishops, those drones and caterpillars of the commonwealth, in making deservedly odious to the people their oppressive courts, fines, censures and imprisonments. But they begin to fear that some bad ends of their own were aimed at herein, and not so much the liberty of the people, as that they might get up into the chair and become to them instead of a lord bishop a ruling presbytery, which they fear will bring in more rigidness and austerity, no less ambition and domination than the former.

And the reason they have to fear is because our divines have not dealt clearly with us in many particulars, but continue certain interests of the bishops, which they find advantageous to advance their honour and esteem with the people, and have entered already into many of their steps, which in them at first they did seem so much to abominate. That the interest only of the bishop in particular and of that sort of prelates is exploded, but the general interests of the clergy, whereby another prelacy may be erected, and the mystery of the divines maintained in credit amongst the people, is still with all art and industry preserved. I will take the pains both to tell you what those general interests are, and what in reason may be said against them.

1. Their first interest is to preserve amongst the people the distinction concerning government of ecclesiastical and civil, though upon consideration it will be found that two governments in one commonwealth has ever been, and will ever prove, inconsistent with the people's safety. The end of government being to promote virtue, restrain vice, and to maintain to each particular his own, one sort of government, which we call the civil, either is sufficient, or by the wisdom of the Parliament may be made sufficient, for these ends. At the beginning of this Parliament it was confessed that it was both too burdensome for the divines, and too hazardous for the state, that they should be trusted with anything of government: their preaching and instructing the people being, if well discharged, sufficient to take up the whole man. But the times change, and the men with them. The design is feasible, and it must now again be thought necessary that the divines should have a stroke in the government. And therefore that distinction is again maintained, which being taken up at first by proud churchmen for ambitious ends, is still continued for ends, though not in everything the same, yet differing (I fear me) rather in the degrees than nature of them. We cannot tell what else to think of it, but that finding our divines aiming at authority and

jurisdiction, have judged it most politic to gain a preeminence, less stately and pompous, but altogether as imperious and awful over men as the former. Which, because it is not so garish outwardly as the bishops', they may presume will therefore be the easier admitted, and prove of longer continuance.

2. The second interest of the divine is to preserve amongst the people the distinction of clergy and laity, though not now in those terms, because they have been unhappily discovered, the Scriptures so evidently making the people God's clergy by way of distinction from the ministers (1 Peter 5: 3), but never the ministers by way of distinction from the people. And then for laity, a people (as the word signifies): I hope the ministers are such as well as any others. Well, the distinction by words is not so material as a real distinction which their interest is to preserve. They would not have us to think that a minister comes to be so, as another man comes to be a merchant, book-seller, tailor, etc., either by disposal of him by his friends in his education, or by his own making choice to be of such a trade. No, there must be something spiritual in the business, a *iure divino* [divine law] must be brought in, and a succession from the apostles. And even, as some would have us think kings to be anointed of God because the Israelitish kings were by his command, so we are made to believe that because the apostles were ordained by God to be teachers of the people, and endowed with gifts for that end, that therefore there is a like divine, though secret, ordination from God in making of our ministers, and spiritual gifts and qualifications thereunto.

Because otherwise, if the people did not believe so, they would examine all that was said, and not take things upon trust from the ministers, as if whatsoever they spake, God spake in them. They would then try all things, and what they found to be truth they would embrace as from God, for God is the author of truth. What they found to be otherwise they would reject, and then for the most part they might spare their notings and repetitions too, unless the more to discover the groundlessness of the doctrine and the giddiness of the divinity which they generally hear. They would then handle their ministers familiarly, as they do one another, shaking off that timorousness and awe which they have of the divines, with which they are ignorantly brought up. He that bade us try all things, and hold fast that which was good, did suppose that men have faculties and abilities wherewithal to try all things, or else the counsel had been given in vain.

And therefore however the minister may, by reason of his continual exercise in preaching, and discoursing, by his daily study and reading, by his skill in arts and languages, by the conceit of the esteem he has with a great part of admiring people (in whom is truly fulfilled the prophecy of St Paul, 2 Timothy 4: 3–4), presume it easy to possess us, that they are more divine than other men (as they style themselves); yet if the people would but take boldness to themselves, and not distrust their own understandings, they would soon find that use and experience is the only difference, and that all necessary knowledge is easy to be had, and by themselves acquirable: and that it is the ministers' interest, their living depending thereupon, to frame long methods and bodies of divinity, full of doubts and disputes, which indeed are made of purpose difficult to attain unto, that their hearers may be always learning, and never come to the knowledge of the truth, begetting disquiet and unsettledness of mind, continual controversies, sadness, and many times desperation. All which makes for them, for that upon all occasions men have recourse to them for comfort and satisfaction, which, how weak and short soever it be in itself, must be current, because from them. The keys of the Church (a prerogative which our Saviour gave to his apostles) they arrogate to themselves. A new authority they make mention of in their sermons, which they call ministerial (though no such thing belongs to them, nor is yet settled upon them, nor I hope ever will be). Thus their interest is to make of themselves a peculiar tribe, of a nearer relation to God than other men: His more immediate servants, the labourers in his vineyard, the co-workers with him, and all other titles they claim, given in Scripture to the apostles, though neither for their abilities, much less for their virtues or conversations, or in any other respect can be due unto them.

3. The third interest is to persuade the people that the Scriptures, though we have them in our own tongue, are not yet to be understood by us without their help and interpretation, so that in effect we are in the same condition with those we have so long pitied, that are forbidden to have the Scriptures in their own tongue. For 'tis all one not to have them in our own tongue and to be made believe that we cannot understand them, though we have them in our own. Is the cabinet open to us, and do we yet want a key? Has so much labour

been spent, so many translations extant, and we are yet to seek? Let us argue a little with them: Either the Scriptures are not rightly translated or they are. If they are not, why have we not been told so all this while? Why have we been cheated into errors? If they are rightly translated, why should not Englishmen understand them? The idioms and properties of the Hebrew and Greek languages, which some say cannot word for word be expressed in English, might all this while have been translated into as many English words as will carry the sense thereof. There is nothing in the Hebrew or Greek but may be expressed in English, though not just in so many words (which is not material). So that it must be confessed, that either we have not been fairly dealt withal hitherto in the conveyance of the Scripture (a thing which few dare suspect), or else the Scriptures are as well to be understood by us as by any linguist whatsoever.

Well, notwithstanding all this, how evident soever it be: a great part of us people do believe just as they would have us, and therefore, silly men as we are, in case of doubt to them we go to be resolved. And hereby is maintained the necessity and excellency of learning, and the languages, and so of universities, and a supposal that the arts likewise are of necessity to a divine. Seven years at least are allotted to the attaining thereof, to fit and dispose men for the study of divinity, the arts being, as they say, handmaids and preparations to theology. But I hear wise men suspect all this, and say: that the divines, of what sort soever, have other ends in urging all these things to be of necessity.

First, they have hereby made it a difficult thing to be a minister, and so have engrossed the trade to themselves, and left all other men by reason of their other professions in an incapacity of being such in their sense.

And therefore, secondly, if any do take upon them their profession without university breeding and skill in the arts and languages (how knowing a man soever he be otherwise) they have fastened such an odium in the hearts of most of the people against him that a thief or murderer cannot be more out of their favour than he. Thirdly, they, being furnished with these arts and languages, have a mighty advantage over all such as have them not and are admirers thereof (as most men are), so that hereby they become masters of all discourses, and can presently stop the people's mouths, that put them too hard to it, by telling them that it is not for laymen to be too confident, being no scholars, and ignorant of the original; that the original has it otherwise than our translations. And thus they keep all in a mystery, that they only may be the oracles to dispense what and how they please, so that this third interest is of much concernment to them.

I know what the scruple of most men will be in reading of this last particular: almost all will be the divines' advocate for learning, and have him in great hate and derision that is an enemy thereto. For as Diana was, so is learning those craftsmen's living and the people's goddess. However I will make no apology for myself, but desire that every man would give his reason scope, boldly to examine what it is; what good the world receives from it; whether the most learned or unlearned men have been the troublers of the world; how presumptuous and confident the learned scribes, priests, and doctors of the law were, that they best understood the Scriptures; how the poor and unlearned fishermen and tent-makers were made choice of for Christ's disciples and apostles, before any of them; how in process of time they that took upon them to be ministers, when they had acquired to themselves the mystery of arts and learning, and confounded thereby the clear streams of the Scripture, and perverted the true Gospel of Jesus Christ, and by politic glosses and comments introduced another Gospel, suitable to the covetous, ambitious and persecuting spirit of the clergy (which their esteem with the people made authentic), they then began to scorn the simplicity and meanness of the apostles; to call that the infancy of the church, and to engross great livings, lordships, territories and dominions; to embroil states in wars; to supplant one another and divert the people from the prosecution of their own interest (which is their safety and liberty); to maintain their quarrels, and erect that government the then rising part of them could agree upon.

So that the priests and ministers of Christendom (though others have the name) yet they are indeed the lords and leaders thereof, as at present by England's sad experience may evidently appear. For I would have all wise men consider whether the party who are now in arms to make us slaves consists not chiefly of such as have had esteem for the most learned arts men in the kingdom, or of others who, if not learned themselves, are admirers of such as are. Yea, to examine whence most of the wars of Christendom have sprung, and whether these artificial clergy men have not been the chief causers, and still are the grand incendiaries of our present miseries which threaten our utter ruin. And although the episcopal clergy pretend to strive for the regal prerogative on the one side, and the Presbyterian prelacy for reformation and the liberty of the subject on the other side, yet both of these mainly intend their own respective profits and advancements. So that which should soever prevail (if such may have their wills), both aiming at their own greatness and dominion over the consciences of their brethren, extremest misery and barest kind of slavery will unavoidably follow; whilst each of them by all sly insinuations and cunning contrivances seek to obtain authority to compel the whole nation to be subject to their doubtful, yea groundless, determinations, which of all other is the greatest and worst sort of oppression and tyranny.

The people may, if they please, dote upon that which ever has been and will be their destruction. It would be more safe for them (I am sure) to distinguish of knowledge and to reject what is useless (as most of that which has hitherto borne the name of learning will upon impartial examination prove to be), and esteem that only which is evidently useful to the people; to account better of them that, having no by-ends or respects, have studied the Scriptures for their own and others' information and do impart the same to the people out of a desire of their good, for nothing (as the Anabaptists do to their congregations), than of such men as use all means to augment their tithes and profits, who, being rich and abundantly provided for, yet exact them from poor people, even such whose very bellies can hardly spare it; whose necessities ought to be relieved by them, and not the fruit of their labours so unreasonably wrested from them, as oft it is, and the same so superfluously spent, or so covetously hoarded up, as for the most part is known to be. When they commend learning it is not for learning's sake but their own. Her esteem gets them their livings and preferments, and therefore she is to be kept up or their trade will go down. 'Have a care therefore, O ye clergy, as you esteem your honour and preferment, your profit and observance, that you keep this Diana of yours high in the people's esteem. Rouse up yourselves, and imagine some new ways to quicken the admiration of this your goddess; for I can assure you, men's eyes begin to open, they find that she is not so beautiful as she once seemed to be; that her lustre is not natural but painted and artificial. Bestir yourselves or your Diana will down.' But why should I excite you, who I know are too industrious in the preservation of your own interests?

Divers other interests they have plied, as to make themselves the only public speakers, by which means whom and what they please they openly condemn, cry up or cry down what makes for or against themselves. There they brand men with the name of heretics, and fasten what errors they think are most hateful to the people upon those men they purpose to make odious. There they confute all opinions, and boldly they may do it, for as much as no liberty of reply or vindication in public is allowed to any, though never so much scandalized by them. And that men may not vindicate themselves by writing, their next interest is to be masters of the press, of which they are lately become by an ordinance for licensing of books; which, being intended by the Parliament for a good and necessary end, namely the prohibition of all books dangerous or scandalous to the state, is become by means of the licensers, who are divines and intend their own interest, most serviceable to themselves (scandalous books being still dispersed) in the stopping of honest men's writings, that nothing may come to the world's view but what they please – unless men will run the hazard of imprisonment, as I now do. So that in public they may speak what they will, write what they will, they may abuse whom they will, and nothing can be said against them. Well may they presume of making themselves masters of the people, having these foundations laid, and the people generally willing to believe they are good.

I might proceed to show what usage wise men expect from their government, being once established, how rigid and austere some think they will prove, countenancing no recreations but what themselves are addicted to; how covetous others deem them, observing that they have more regard to the benefice than the people, and do usually change and shift upon proffer of a better parsonage. Some say that they are a people sick of the Pharisees' disease: they love to sit uppermost at feasts, and to be reverenced in public places; that their respects towards men are as they are rich and beneficial to them, and that a poor man can hardly obtain a visit, though at the time when the world conceives there is greatest necessity of it; that they hover about dying men for their fee and hope of legacy; and many other things are commonly talked of them which, because I suspect to be true, I will set myself hereafter more narrowly to observe.

The objection whereupon all this, I hope necessary, digression is built, was that men may be compelled, though against conscience, to what the synod or present ministry shall conclude to be good and agreeable to God's Word, because unity and uniformity in the church is to be endeavoured. To which I further:

Answer: answer, that to force men, against their mind and judgement, to believe what other men conclude to be true would prove such tyranny as the wicked Procrustes (mentioned by Plutarch) practised, who would fit all men to one bed by stretching them out that were too short, and by cutting them shorter that were too long. If we believe as the synod would have us, what is this but to be brought into their miserable condition, that must believe as the church believes, and so become (as said an honest man) not the disciples of Christ, but of the synod.

Third reason: The third reason for liberty of conscience is grounded upon these foundations, that whatsoever is not of faith is sin, and that every man ought to be fully persuaded of the trueness of that way wherein he serves the Lord. Upon which grounds I thus argue: To compel me against my conscience is to compel me against what I believe to be true, and so against my faith. Now whatsoever is not of faith is sin. To compel me therefore against my conscience is to compel me to do that which is sinful: for though the thing be in itself good, yet if it do not appear to be so to my conscience, the practice thereof in me is sinful, which therefore I ought not to be compelled unto. Again, I am counselled by the apostle to be persuaded in my own mind of the truth of that way wherein I serve the Lord. I am not, therefore, to be compelled to worship God in such a way, of the justness whereof I am not yet persuaded, much less in such a way as is against my mind.

Objection: Nothing is more dangerous to a state, especially in these times, than division and disturbance by several ways of brethren, which have encreased our miseries. And therefore to avoid division, they who will not of their own accords comply are, for the quiet of the state, to be compelled and punished.

Answer: I answer that it is verily thought that the harshness only of this proposition hinders that it is not yet put in execution, till time and cunning have fitted it for the people; for we are told in the last *Consideration tending to dissuade from further gathering of churches* that suffering is like to be the portion of such as shall judge the right rule not to be delivered to them. A man would think that those people that so lately were the sufferers, the noise of whose exclamations against such courses is scarce yet out of the people's ears, that they should not so soon think of being the tyrants. But to the objection I answer, that the diversity of men's judgements is not the occasion of division, because the word division has reference to a falling off from the common cause. Now, though the provocations and incitements against the Brownists and Anabaptists, and some of the Independents, have been many, yet their affections to the public weal are so hearty in them, and grounded upon such sound principles of reason, that no assay of the synod can make them cease to love and assist their country. And it is more than evident by the prosperity of our neighbours in Holland that the several ways of our brethren in matters of religion hinder not, but that they may live peaceably one amongst another, and the Spaniard will witness for them that they unite sufficiently in the defence of their common liberties and opposition of their common enemies. Besides, it's very material to consider that it has ever been the practice of those that are countenanced by authority to endeavour the suppression of those that are not. Who is therefore in the fault? The quiet separatist who, being persuaded in his conscience of the truth of that way he desires to serve the Lord in, peaceably goes on to do his duty as he thinks himself bound to do? Or they who out of a lordly disposition care not what injury they do to others, though to the hazard of the Commonwealth? To advance themselves and their government they defame the Separation in their writings and sermons, bid their proselytes beware of them, as of a dangerous and factious people, stop their mouths, keep the press from them, provoke them by all ways possible, and then like the crafty politician cry out upon them as the causers of division.

I hear some men say, that it concerns the minister so to do because his living (depending upon his tithes and gifts) is the greater the more rich and numerous his audience is. And therefore the separatists are not to be suffered, who they find by experience draw many people after them, and though not the devout honourable women, nor the chief men of the City, yet many whose number might much increase the yearly revenue of the minister. And therefore you must think it has concerned them to meet together and to say amongst themselves: 'Sirs, you know that by this our craft we have our wealth; moreover ye see and hear, that not alone at London, but in most parts of the kingdom, these separatists have persuaded and turned away much people, saying that our ministry is no true ministry, our church no true church, our doctrine in many things erroneous, that our succession from the apostles is but a pretended thing, and, as we ourselves do derive it, descended for many hundred years through the detestable papacy and Romish ministry; so that, if these men be suffered, our gain, and the magnificence of the ministry, which not England only but all Christendom does highly magnify and reverence, would quickly down.'

For what other reason than this can be imagined why the Separation should be the eyesore of our ministers? It cannot be instanced in one particular whereby the commonwealth receives prejudice from them. And then for the charge of separating, for their making a schism, which is endeavoured to be cast so heavily upon them:

I answer that, by reason of the Church of Rome's corruptions, the Church of England did long since make a schism from the Church of Rome, for which cause likewise many of the present ministers in leave of the anti-Christian domineering bishops thought it no robbery to make schism from England; and even this idolizing synod, which, though not yet upon her throne, sticks not to let her clients see 'she says in her heart, "Behold I sat a queen, I am no widow, and shall see no sorrow" ' (Revelation 18: 7). May I not say this, Reverend Synod: if to be proceeded against by such carnal, sandy principles, such human ordinances, by which the separatists stand prejudiced, be legally found to have made the greatest and most transcendent schism which England ever knew or heard of, since the Papistry was discarded; if then the Separation have gone a little further, and not only with the bishops separated from Rome, with the ministers from the bishops, but, by reason of some corruptions still remaining among the ministers, are by their consciences necessitated to separate from them likewise: in all these separations there was difference in judgement. The bishops differ in some things from Rome, our ministers from the bishops, and amongst themselves too, which differences by the Scriptures they cannot determine, as appears both by their writings and preachings, wherein with much vehemency they urge the same against others. Of little force then will the major vote of a synod be for the determining thereof, having so lately most notoriously discovered themselves to be men-pleasers and temporizers by crying down the things which but yesterday they so highly magnified in their pulpits, and also practised with much devotion (at least seemingly), and having withal their own interests so much concerned therein (as is before in part declared). And further, knowing that the same persons themselves, and their tenets (as well as the opinions of Independents, Brownists and Anabaptists, whom they oppose) do stand condemned not by the major vote of divers synods only, but by many General Councils also (who are accounted to represent the whole church upon earth), no whit inferior to them either in arts or learning, or any other qualification: let it be then no wonder, nor so much as seem blameable hereafter, that the separatists should differ in some opinions from this present synod, since the ministers therein no little differ amongst themselves, much more than yet appears, and will do so while sun and moon endures, until we have courage and strength enough to abandon all private interests and advantages.

All times have produced men of several ways, and I believe no man thinks there will be an agreement of judgement as long as this world lasts. If ever there be, in all probability it must proceed from the power and efficacy of truth, not from constraint.

Objection: An assembly of divines, men that have employed all their time in the study of religion, are more likely to find out the truth than other men that have not so spent their time; who, being now consulting what doctrines and what discipline is most agreeable to the Word of God, it is but meet that all men should wait their leisure, till it be manifest what they shall produce.

Answer: To this objection I say first, that they being now in consultation, not for themselves, but, as they say, for the whole people, it is but reasonable that they should publish to the world whatsoever is in debate amongst them, and invite every man to give them their best light and information, that so they may hear all voices, and not conclude aught against men's judgements before it be heard what they can say for themselves. This might peradventure be a means to find out all truth, and settle things so as that every man might be satisfied. You will say that they consider of all objections amongst themselves. I reply that is not sufficient, for 'tis a known case men are generally partial to themselves and their own judgements, urging the weakest objections, and that but slightly: and it can give no satisfaction to men to have their cases pleaded by their adversaries.

Secondly, how palpable soever it appear that an assembly of divines are more likely to find out truth than other men; yet it is to be considered that it will puzzle any man to instance when they did so. Besides, grant it be more probable, yet it may be otherwise, and 'tis well known has proved so. The liturgy was by universal consent approved, and by the Parliament's authority authorized, particular men being these many years averse to it, and separating from the public congregations because of it: it now appears who were in the right. How confident soever therefore the divines (as they style themselves) are that they shall find out the right rule; yet since it may be, and hitherto has been, otherwise, it is but meet that they should decree only for themselves and such as are of their own mind, and allow Christian liberty to all their brethren to follow that way which shall seem to them most agreeable to truth.

Objection: But we are told in the divines' *Considerations* that all men must wait, otherwise the Parliament are like to be provoked.

Answer: Aye, marry sir, this is a good strong argument, and speaks home to us. I cannot blame the separatists now for crying out: they fear your club more than your reason. I see what they might expect if the sword and authority were in your hand: your nine *Considerations* informs me, wherein are these two suppositions. First, 'that the right rule may not be delivered us', and secondly, 'that then men may be called to suffer'. It is a wonder to observe the wretched condition of man and his foul ingratitude. Is it so long since the yokes were broken off these men's necks, that they forget the burden and injustice of them, or that assistance they had from their separatist brethren in breaking those yokes, that now so soon as they are got into reputation, they should suppose a time of suffering for their brethren for doing what to them appears to be their duty! 'Regard, O God, since man is become thus forgetful. Take thy distressed servants the separatists into thine own protection. Thou, O Lord, thou art the judge of all the earth. Put into the hearts of the Parliament to do right in this case, and to suffer those afflicted people no longer to endure reproach or molestation for doing of their duties.'

Objection: But some may say I beat the air all this while. There is no purpose in the divines to force the conscience. They are sufficiently informed that the conscience cannot be forced, being in no wise subject to compulsion. Only it concerns them, they say, to prevent the growth and increase of errors; which cannot otherwise be done but by punishing those that are the authors and maintainers of them, that so truth only may flourish, and the Gospel with the ordinances according to the true institution of them be maintained and practised by all the people of the nation.

Answer: I answer that though it were certain that what they esteem truth were so indeed, and that the true Gospel and ordinances were, in every part and circumstance of them, that which they judge them to be: however, though they are earnestly to endeavour by argument and persuasion to reduce all men to the same belief and practice with themselves, yet those that cannot be thereunto persuaded, they ought not by any means to punish, for the first and third reasons afore given. But then for the assurance of the divines that their conclusions and articles are certainly true, if it be built upon certain foundations, they need not avoid the combat with any sort of men of what opinion soever. Truth was not used to fear, or to seek shifts or stratagems for its advancement! I should rather think that they who are assured of her should desire that all men's mouths should be open, that so error may discover its foulness, and truth become more glorious by a victorious conquest after a fight in open field: they shun the battle that doubt their strength. Wise men are at a stand to see, that whilst the press was open no man undertook the Anabaptists, and that now their adversaries have bound their hands they begin to buffet them. What can they do else but necessarily suspect that our divines have not the truth, nor by any evidence thereof are able to make good their own standings or practices?

To stop men's mouths, or punish men for speaking their minds, was profitable indeed, and necessary for the bishops, who had proposed to themselves such ends as could endure no discourse upon them, and framed such constitutions, ceremonies and doctrines as must be received without scanning, or else must appear empty and groundless. But that the reforming clergy, that pretend to have truth in its simplicity, and the gospel in its purity, and seem to abominate all by-ends or respects, should yet take the same course of prohibitions with the bishops, lock up the press, and then vent themselves in a furious and evidently scandalizing way, as in their late preachings and pamphlets against the Anabaptists, will make, I believe, all wise men suspect that either they doubt their own tenets, or know some gross errors amongst themselves, which yet their interests and professions engage them to maintain.

To say they go not about to compel the conscience, which is

incapable of compulsion, but will only punish the person, is as if they were sportful in their cruelty, and shows as if it proceeded from men settled and long practised in tyranny. I could wish for Christianity's sake they had more wisdom than to play with men's afflictions. I profess unto you, did I still dote upon the persons and seeming holiness of our ministers (as I have done) such carriage as this I think would open mine eyes, and make me see they are not the men they seem to be, that in so short a time can grow so wanton with their own estate and preeminence as to gibe and scoff at their brethren's miseries.

Is it not a shame to our profession, and scandal to our cause, that well-affected men, real and irreconcilable enemies to tyranny and our common adversaries, should be necessitated to leave their native country because they can hope nothing from you, our divines, but to be imprisoned or punished for exercising their consciences, though by their help you should be settled in your liberties? I cannot tell what else to make of this for my part, but that you had rather be slaves to the king, and hazard the freedom of the whole nation, than that these men should have freedom with you. You may flatter yourselves that you are rich in spiritual graces, and presume that you are in the right, and have found out the truth of the Gospel and ordinances, but so long as you want the main evidences hereof – love and lowliness of mind – so long as you propose dominion and the sway over your brethren, which our Saviour said his followers should not do (Matthew 20: 25–6; Mark 10: 42), you must give men that are unwilling to be deceived leave to think that you have yet but the form and show of religion, but want the inward sweetness and most excellent fruits and effects thereof.

I could wish I had no occasion for speaking thus much, but when sores begin to fester they must not be nourished and swathed, but lanced and corracived. 'Tis no time to hide and excuse men's imperfections when they strive to take root for perpetuity. Were it in mine own cause, I could not speak so much; but in behalf of such a harmless people as I have found those of the Separation to be, after much inquiry and examination of their tenets and practice, I think myself bound in conscience to break silence and become their advocate.

Objection: There is one objection more against the Anabaptists in particular, and that is that they allow not of civil government, and therefore [are] not to be tolerated because they hold an opinion directly destructive to the Commonwealth.

Answer: Who says they hold this opinion? Why, the divines commonly in their pulpits. And what ground have they for their so saying? They find it in books that they who have written of them affirm that they maintain this position. But how, if the societies of Anabaptists in this kingdom are most zealous and rational defenders of our government? As to my knowledge they are, and that experience can testify for them that no men have more forwardly and constantly than they assisted the Parliament against those that would dissolve our free government and bring in tyranny. How is it true then that the Anabaptists hold such an opinion? O, then they tell us that our Anabaptists are no Anabaptists. To what purpose then do they exclaim against Anabaptists that have been of that opinion (as they say, though for my part I believe neither them, nor the books that tells them so), when they cannot but know, if they know anything, that the Anabaptists which now are be not of that opinion? Why, for this end and purpose: they resolve to make the Anabaptists odious to the people, and nothing, they think, will sooner do it than by making the people believe that they are the harbourers of such an opinion as would dissolve all society, and bring into confusion the state. Now this they speak of the Anabaptists in general, knowing that the people will apply it to the Anabaptists in England. Concerning whom, how true it is you may judge by that which follows:

The Anabaptists' opinion concerning government is that the world being grown so vicious and corrupt as it is, there can possibly be no living for honest men without government; that the end of making governments is the people's quiet and safety, and that whatsoever does not conduce thereto is tyranny or oppression and not government; that the government of England is of all others that they know the most excellent, the people by their chosen men being the makers and reformers thereof; that therein the parliament is the supreme power, and that the king is accountable to them for the not performance of his office, as all other officers of the commonwealth are; that the parliament only are the makers and alterers of laws for the regulation and ordering of the people; that of right they are to be called by those laws they have made in that behalf, and to dissolve when they themselves see good; that it is not at the king's will or pleasure to sign or refuse those bills the parliament shall pass, but that he is of duty to sign them; that all great officers and magistrates of the kingdom are to be chosen by them; that the king is to have his personal abode near the parliament, that they may have free conference with him at pleasure touching the former discharge of his office, or the present state of the commonwealth; that to parliaments alone belong the disposal of shipping, forts, magazines, and all other the kingdom's strengths, both by sea and land, the making of peace and war, the pressing of soldiers, the raising of money for the preserving or regaining the safety or freedom of the people, which for any other person to do is treasonable. The grounds and principles of our government they, knowing, could not but see the exorbitancies of the king, and whereto all his lawless courses and designs tended, and therefore have not ignorantly (as perhaps others), but upon these grounds assisted the Parliament, and will do till the last. Judge by this, then, whether these men hold an opinion against government, or at what wretchless pass those men are that would make the people believe they do.

I might insist here upon a book called *The Confutation of Anabaptists*, lately set forth, which says, 'They are absolute and professed enemies to the essential being of civil government.' But I find people so little regard the book, it being so full of nonsense, and in this particular so evidently contrary to truth and the experience of every man that looks abroad and knows anything of the Anabaptists, that it will be but loss of time to take notice of it. Only it were worth observation to see how easily it obtained an imprimatur, and how open the press is to anything, true or false, sense or nonsense, that tends to the Anabaptists' scandal or disgrace.

In the beginning of the Parliament a book was published, called *The History of the Anabaptists in High and Low Germany*, the aim whereof was by fastening odious errors and feigned mutinies upon the Anabaptists to deter this present Parliament in their reformation of bishops, for fear, as the book says, lest they who now cry out for Christ's rule strike not so much at the misrule of episcopacy, as quarrel at all rules. So that what course was taken by the bishops and their friends to hinder the reformation of that hierarchy, namely the affrighting the reformers by airy and imaginary consequences, the same are used by our divines to prevent a thorough reformation of many errors and mistakes in our clergy, which they exceedingly fear, and therefore they have and do continue early and late to render the

Anabaptists as odious to the people as their wits and inventions can make them. But as the bishops then failed of their ends by the wisdom of the Parliament, so I trust the present endeavours of our divines in striving to raise themselves upon their brethren's disgrace and ruin will, by the continued courage and prudence of the Parliament, prove vain and fruitless.

They who echo the King's words and take the bishops' course, I will not say have the King's ends, but, so far, do the King's work. The King, I confess, has reason to cry out upon the Anabaptists, because he knows them to be enemies not of government, but oppression in government. And all those who intend to oppress in any manner ought, if they will be true to themselves, to do so too, for the Anabaptists are oppression's enemies, whoever be the oppressors.

And whereas they say they find in books that the Anabaptists are enemies to all government, it were well if they would consider who wrote those books. It may be that they were written either by mistake, or for the same end that they repeat them. We can show you books, too, that say the Parliament are Brownists and Anabaptists. And past all question, if the King should thrive in this unnatural war, this Parliament should, in their court histories, not only be called Anabaptists, but branded also to all posterity with that opinion, falsely and maliciously fathered upon the Anabaptists, that they were enemies to government, and went about to bring all into confusion. Little credit therefore is to [be] given to books in matter of obloquy and scandal, but the men and their judgements in the times they live are to be considered. And then I am confident it will appear that the Anabaptists be of well-affected minds, and peaceable dispositions, meriting a fair respect from the state, and may well challenge amongst others the quiet enjoyment of themselves as they are men, and the ordinances of Christ as they are Christians.

I will add one thing more to the Brownists' and Anabaptists' glory: that in the times of the bishops domineering, when many of the Presbyterians complied, some to the very top of Wren's conformity, and preached for those things they now pretend chiefly to reform, and the Independents fled to places where they might live at ease and enjoy their hundred pounds a year without danger, the Brownists and Anabaptists endured the heat and brunt of persecution, and, notwithstanding the several ways of vexing them, continued doing their duties, counting it the glory of a Christian to endure tribulation for the name of Christ. And the times altering, the Presbyterian soon comes about, and the Independent comes over, to be leaders in the reformation, when, forgetting the constancy and integrity of those who bore the heat and burden of the day, they hold the same heavy hand over them that their fathers the bishops did. And as the Brownists' and Anabaptists' affection to the common good of all was then firm, and was able to endure the trial of persecution, so has it in these present searching times continued constant and unshaken, notwithstanding the many almost insufferable injuries and provocations of the divines on the one side, and the fair promises and frequent invitations of the King on the other. So that had any ends of their own been aimed at, they could not have continued such resolved and immovable enemies of tyranny and friends to their country. I believe if we would suppose other men to be in their condition, we could hardly expect the like even and upright carriage from them, amidst so many storms and temptations surrounding them.

I hope all good men will take all that has been said into consideration, especially the Parliament, who I presume are most ingenuous and impartial of all others, and whom it chiefly concerns, they being called and trusted to vindicate and preserve the people's liberties in general, and not to enthral the consciences, persons or estates of any of them unto a pragmatical, pretended clergy, whether episcopal, Presbyterian, or any other whatsoever. The greatest glory of authority is to protect the distressed, and for those that are judges in other men's causes to bear themselves as if the afflicted men's cases were their own, observing that divine rule of our Saviour, 'Whatsoever you would that men should do unto you, even so do you to them.' And if to the Parliament it shall appear for the reasons given, or other better reasons they can suggest to themselves, that it is most unjust, and much more unChristian, that any man should be compelled against his conscience to a way he approves not of, I doubt not but they will be pleased for God's glory, and union sake; and likewise for these good men's sake, which for the present it principally concerns; at least for their own sakes (for who knows how soon this may be his own case), speedily to stop all proceedings that tends thereunto; and for the future provide that as well particular or private congregations as public may have public protection, so that upon a penalty no injury or offence be offered, either to them from others, or by them to others; that all statutes against the separatists be reviewed and repealed, especially that of the 35 of Elizabeth; that the press may be free for any man that writes nothing scandalous or dangerous to the state. That so this Parliament may prove themselves loving fathers to all sorts of good men, bearing equal respect to all, according to the trust reposed in them, and so inviting an equal affection and assistance from all; that after ages may report of them, they did all these things, not because of the importunity of the people, or to please a party, but from the reason and justness of them, which did more sway with them than a petition subscribed with twenty thousand hands could have done.

NOTES ON THE TEXTS

1. Hooker, *Ecclesiasticall Politie*, books VI and VIII: 1648 (three editions), 1651, 1666. Reprinted in editions of Hooker's *Works*, 1662, 1666, 1676, 1682. The later editions of the *Ecclesiasticall Politie* are too numerous to list: the standard edition of Hooker's works is now that published in four volumes: Cambridge, Mass., 1977-82.

2. Baxter, *Holy Commonwealth*: 1659 (two editions). The Restoration barred republication of this work, which was condemned by the University of Oxford in 1683. Selections from it, along with other political works by Baxter, appear in R. Schlatter (ed.), *Richard Baxter and Puritan Politics* (New Brunswick, 1957).

3. Williams, *Bloudy Tenent*: 1644 (two editions), 1848; in *Works* (Providence, 1867; reprinted New York, 1963). Selections in A. S. P. Woodhouse, *Puritanism and Liberty* (London, 1938, 1974).

4. (Walwyn), *Compassionate Samaritane*: 1644 (two editions). Facsimile reprint in W. Haller (ed.), *Tracts on Liberty* (three vols., New York, 1934, 1965).

FURTHER READING

For a brief overview of the history of toleration there is H. Kamen, *The Rise of Toleration* (London, 1967). For more detailed studies, see J. Lecler, *Toleration and the Reformation* (two vols., New York, 1969), and W. K. Jordan, *The Development of Religious Toleration in England* (four vols., Cambridge, Mass., 1932–40).
Three works which help bring out the logic of intolerance are C.

Russell, 'Arguments for Religious Unity in England, 1530–1650', *Journal of Ecclesiastical History*, XVIII (1967), pp. 201–26, W. M. Lamont, *Godly Rule: Politics and Religion, 1603–60* (London, 1969), and L. W. Levy, *Treason Against God: A History of the Offence of Blasphemy* (New York, 1981). The question of tolerance and intolerance in seventeenth-century England is inextricably intertwined with that of anti-Catholicism, on which there are a number of helpful studies: C. Z. Weiner, 'The Beleaguered Isle', *Past and Present*, no. 51 (1971), pp. 27–62; R. Clifton, 'The Popular Fear of Catholics during the English Revolution', *Past and Present*, no. 52 (1971), pp. 23–55; the same author's 'Fear of Popery', in C. Russell (ed.), *The Origins of the English Civil War* (London, 1973); and J. Miller, *Popery and Politics in England, 1660 88* (Cambridge, 1973).

Two indispensable studies of the toleration debate during the Civil War are W. Haller, *Liberty and Reformation during the Puritan Revolution* (New York, 1955) and R. Sirluck's introduction to volume two of D. M. Wolfe (ed.), *The Complete Prose Works of John Milton* (New Haven, 1953–82), which establishes the context in which *Areopagitica* should be read. Two theological developments were important to the toleration debate: the emergence of a new Arminianism in authors such as Baxter, Milton and Goodwin, and the appearance of various types of 'antinomianism' or arguments for 'free grace'. A good overview of these developments has perhaps yet to be written, but A. L. Morton, *The World of the Ranters* (London, 1970), R. T. Kendall, *Calvin and English Calvinism to 1649* (Oxford, 1979), and E. Moore, 'John Goodwin and the Origins of the New Arminianism', *Journal of British Studies*, XXII (1982), pp. 50–70, give some indication of the issues.

There is a rapidly growing literature on Hooker. I have found the essay by W. D. J. Cargill-Thompson in his *Studies in the Reformation: Luther to Hooker* (London, 1980) and J. P. Sommerville's 'Richard Hooker, Hadrian Saravia, and the Advent of the Divine Right of Kings', *History of Political Thought*, IV (1983), pp. 229–45, particularly interesting. The best studies of Baxter are G. F. Nuttal, *Richard Baxter* (London, 1965), and W. M. Lamont, *Richard Baxter and the Millennium* (London, 1979). On Williams, P. G. E. Miller, *Roger Williams* (Indianapolis, 1953; New York, 1962) is much superior to its predecessors. A helpful introduction to Walwyn is provided by J. Frank, *The Levellers* (Cambridge, Mass., 1965). It should now be supplemented by L. Mulligan, 'The Religious Roots of William Walwyn's Radicalism', *Journal of Religious History*, XII (1982), pp. 162–79, although I remain to be convinced that Walwyn was not a sceptical disciple of Montaigne and no Christian.

CHAPTER FIVE

DEMOCRACY AND COMMUNISM

1 *England's Miserie and Remedie* (1645)

This anonymous work of 1645 was attributed by Thomason, the
contemporary book-dealer, to Lilburne. Its use of Latin and its style
of argument are, however, quite untypical of Lilburne. P. Gregg has
suggested that Walwyn might have assisted Lilburne in writing it,
but the same objections apply to this proposal. D. Wolfe has attributed it to Overton, and J. Frank has proposed Wildman as its author.
This last is the most plausible of all the suggestions made so far, but
in my view the style of this tract, the argument, and the sources it
draws upon (Livy, Machiavelli, Buchanan) all suggest that Sexby is
the author.

It is one of several tracts written in defence of Lilburne in 1645
when the Leveller movement was first taking shape. More important,
it is, I believe, the first work to argue for the ultimate sovereignty of
the people and to mean by the people 'the multitude', a word which
had almost a technical meaning when used to refer to all those,
without distinction of rank, who had originally gathered together to
form a body politic. The author of *England's Miserie and Remedie* is
thus seeking to defend the rights of the people not as a corporate
body but as a group of equal individuals.

2 *An Agreement of the People* (1647)

Published in October or November of 1647, this proposal claimed to
come from the representatives (the 'agents' or 'agitators') of five
cavalry regiments in the New Model Army, but it was almost certainly
drawn up in close consultation with the Leveller leaders. Both representatives of the regiments and of the Levellers were present at
the Putney Debates to decide whether it should be adopted by the

army. It is a historic document because it is the first occasion on which a written constitution was proposed, establishing a democratic government (or something close to one), and protecting certain inalienable rights.

3   *The Putney Debates* (1647)

The Putney Debates took place in the context of a conflict between Parliament and its creation, the new Model Army. The army had defeated and captured the king, but the majority in Parliament wanted to disband it, opening the way to a conservative and Presbyterian settlement based on negotiation with Charles. Parliament was unwilling to offer guarantees for the payment of the extensive arrears owed the soldiers in back pay, or to offer them an indemnity for illegal acts committed during the war (the confiscation of horses, for example). The soldiers therefore elected representatives to press for their rights and established links with the Levellers. The issue at Putney was whether the programme of these allied radicals should be imposed upon the Parliament by the army. But events moved too quickly for the outcome of the debate to be clear: on 11 November the king escaped from custody, and with the prospect of renewed civil war looming, it was easy for the officers to restore discipline amongst their troops (suppressing the Ware mutiny on 15 November) and to put aside their dispute with Parliament until after the second Civil War.

The Putney Debates are unique because they provide us with a more or less faithful record of an actual verbal argument over political principles. Moreover, from individuals like Rainsborough we hear, almost for the first time in history, the case for a truly representative government being made. The selection here covers the entire discussion centring on the first clause of the Agreement of the People and the issue of the franchise.

4   Gerrard Winstanley, *A New-Yeers Gift for the Parliament and Armie* (1650)

Winstanley (*c*. 1609–1676?) worked in the cloth trade until 1643 when his business failed and he became a farm labourer. Between 1648 and 1652 he published some twenty tracts and broadsheets, the first five of them expressing a radical religious mysticism. Near the end of 1648 he reached the conclusion that a communist society would make possible the triumph of the Spirit over the Flesh, and the establishment of the kingdom of God (or, as Winstanley preferred to say, Reason). In April 1649 a communist (or Digger) community was established on common land at St George's Hill in Surrey, but its members were harried by local landlords and their crops destroyed. *A New-Yeers Gift* was written partly in protest against this harassment. It shows clearly how the religious convictions of Winstanley's first writings had been adapted to present the case for communism. Winstanley's final publication, *The Law of Freedom* (1652), written after the collapse of the Digger movement he had organized, provides the fullest account of his political philosophy. Thereafter he disappears from political life, although there is evidence to suggest he died a Quaker.

1 England's Miserie and Remedie in a Judicious Letter from an Utter-Barrister to His Speciall Friend, Concerning Leiutenant Col. Lilburn's Imprisonment in Newgate, Sept. 14 1645

Kind Sir,

Out of the firm confidence and certain knowledge which you seem to have of the integrity and honesty of Lieutenant Colonel Lilburne, and that his letter of the 25th of July contains nothing but the truth, I send you here my sense and opinion concerning his imprisonment.

And for the clearer explanation of what you demand, and our better understanding of one another, I conceive it necessary that we be at a point upon these two things: first, what the House of Commons is; next, for what end and purpose they are convened and called together.

I believe you agree with me that the House of Commons is nothing less than the representative body of the people, elected and sent up by the several shires and boroughs respectively (and, joined with the two other estates), of capacity to make, alter, abrogate laws, as occasion shall require; to hear and relieve the grievances of the people, and to reform what is amiss in the commonwealth. Here is the character and description of the House of Commons (which themselves, I think, will allow of), and here is the end and purpose for which they serve. In this description you may plainly see two bodies of the people – the representative and the represented – which together make up the body of the commonwealth; and of this latter Lieutenant Colonel Lilburne is an eminent member.

Now for any man to imagine that the shadow or representative is more worthy than the substance, or that the House of Commons is more valuable and considerable than the body for whom they serve, is all one as if they should affirm that an agent or ambassador from a prince has the same or more authority than the prince himself; which, in matters of proxy for marriage, I believe no prince will allow of.

I will not undertake to define the limits of power or extent of parliaments, having found the practice in my reading more or less lengthened or shortened (like a pair of stirrups) according to circumstances and current of times, or the weakness or power of the prince under whom they serve, who has for the most part subjected them to his will and made them act his designs. Neither will I go about to cast the apple of division betwixt the people and their agents, who should be linked together by common interest and mutual respects of common preservation; yet this much I cannot forbear to intimate, that the one is but the servant of the other (the House of Commons, I mean, of the people), elected by them to provide for their welfare and freedoms against all in-bred tyranny or foreign invasion, which, by reason of their numbers, they cannot conveniently do in their own persons without hazard both of confusion and desolation.

But to come to our business: Mr Lilburne complains that three times since the first of May last he has been imprisoned by authority from the House of Commons before he knew his accuser or accusation, or was suffered to speak one word in his own defence. Certainly thieves and murderers, taken *in flagrante delicto*, in the very act of a heinous crime, are not thus hardly dealt withal. This calls to my mind the very words of a member of the House, Mr Edward Stephens by name, uttered with passion openly in Westminster Hall in a case of the like injustice: viz.: 'That we have not withdrawn ourselves from our obedience to the king to yield ourselves slaves and vassals to the tyranny of our fellow subjects.'

But some will say, 'How shall we mend ourselves? We have given ourselves, lives, liberties and all, into the Parliament's power.'

To this I answer that this free and abandoned confidence of ours, where they are entrusted with all that is dear and precious unto us, ought the rather to oblige them to a tender and conscientious care of the dispensation of that power. Besides, this sovereign or legislative power (which they make use of) is not lent them for the ruin and destruction of our laws and liberties (no more than the king's prerogative), but for the edification and strengthening of the same, in particular as well as general. The abuse and overflowing of this power is odious to God and man. For princes, or what estate soever, when they arrogate to themselves an unlimited jurisdiction do degenerate into tyrants, and become *hostes humani generis*, enemies of mankind. And the angels (which would be like to the Most High) were by his just judgement changed into the most wretched of all creatures. It belongs to God, and to God alone, to rule by the law of his blessed will.

As for princes and states, when they break out into exorbitancy, and will be imitators of the power of God, in governing by an uncircumscribed authority, they run themselves into inevitable mischiefs, and the people (whom they serve) into unavoidable inconveniencies. And this comes to pass of necessity, for every state governed by fantastical and arbitrary power must needs be floating, inconstant, and subject to change; besides, man is naturally ambitious and apt to encroach and usurp upon the liberty of his inferiors. Hence is derived that excellent maxim, *melius sub iniquissima lege, quam sub equissimo arbitro vivere*: it is better to live under a rigorous and unjust law, than an arbitrary government, though just. The reason is, because by the first he is at certainty and knows what he must trust to; the last leaves him uncertain and so in danger.

But to return to Lieutenant Colonel Lilburne, who stands imprisoned by a vote of the House of Commons for refusing to answer to the Committee's interrogatories before cause shown of his former imprisonment: I am informed by some members that this vote was obtained by Bastwick surreptitiously, when the House was thin and empty. And therefore I conceive he may appeal from the House thin and empty to the House full and complete. If this will not be accepted of, why should he not appeal to the people?

For Buchanan, an author without reproach, in his book *De jure regni apud Scotos* (*Concerning the Scottish Laws*) does boldly and positively affirm, *supremam potestatem esse in populo*, the supreme power to be in the people. And before Buchanan, the commonwealth of Rome (which remains a pattern and example to all ages both for civil and military government), I say this commonwealth in its best perfection did allow of this last refuge of appeal to the people. To this purpose Titus Livius, an unreprovable author, speaks in these terms (Decade 5 of his *History*): 'C. Flaminius was the first (or one of the first) that, understanding the majesty of Rome to be indeed wholly in the people, and no otherwise in the senate than by way of delegacy or grand commission, did not stand highly upon his birth and degree, but made his address to the multitude, and taught them to know and use their power over himself and his fellow senators in reforming their disorders. For this the commons highly esteemed him, and the senators as deeply hated him.' Etc.

But I hope the wisdom and providence of the Parliament will prevent these extremities. Yet I cannot but put them in remembrance that small sparks do oftentimes occasion great fires. And that the English nation is sensible of nothing more than the breach of their liberties and of violence offered to the freedom of their persons: witness the Magna Carta, thirty times confirmed by the princes of this island; and witness the cheerful readiness of the people to serve the public in this present great quarrel. And let no man dream that the Parliament may trench boldly thereon without check: a silly conceit and aggravating the offence, for a dog that devours his own kind we account more unnatural than a lion or a bear of another kind; besides the heart-burning which is easily kindled when our own fellows domineer over us. There are but two things [*sic*, i.e. ways] of ruling a people: either by fear or love. The first may be more agreeable to Master Corbitt, as suitable to his gallant and imperious nature, or to Sir Robert Pye's canine humour, but is brittle, and will last no longer than the foam which supports it. The second, of love, is safe and durable. Camillus the Roman speaks of it in two words: *firmissimum imperium quo obedientes gaudent*, the most stable lasting government [is one] under which the people rejoice and live cheerfully.

But Lilburne's case is singular – that a member of the body represented, a free-born subject, in life and conversation without exception, considerable both in his actions and sufferings in this great cause – that such a subject, contrary to the tenor of Magna Carta, contrary to the late Covenant and Petition of Right, yea, and the direct rule alleged in Scripture, should be three times imprisoned without showing cause by a Parliament professing reformation and defence of our laws and liberties, and without any urgent or apparent necessity of state enforcing it: this, I profess, is to me a riddle beyond all that this monstrous age has brought forth. I need not say how much the public liberty is wounded in the injury doubled and trebled upon their fellow member, nor the consequences thereof, which if drawn into a precedent, who can count himself free? Nor the consequences of a wicked sentence, which (as Chancellor Bacon says) is infinitely worse than a wicked fact, as being held a precedent or pattern, whereby oppression beginning upon one is extended as warrantable upon all. And this conclusion he draws out of this place of Scripture: *Fons turbatus pede et vena corrupta est justus cadens coram impio*, a just man falling into the hands of the wicked is like a fountain troubled with the foot, or the urines corrupted in the body.

The horror of this sentence has stricken the generality of the people with amazement, to behold the kid seething in the milk of the dam, that is to say, the chamber of justice ordained for our comfort, preservation and safety, unkindly wrested to enslave, ruin and destroy us. Surely after ages, when they shall ponder these proceedings in cold and sober blood, will be ashamed to own the actors for their parents or predecessors. And it is to be feared that the stones from the pavement will rise in judgement one day against the abusers of the trust committed unto them.

And let no man deceive himself, to think with senseless and frivolous distinctions to award the dishonour and danger which may arise to the Parliament hence: as to say that the Great Charter is but suspended as to Lilburne, but not abrogated; and that the duty of the Parliament is to provide for generalities, but is not at leisure to attend particular grievances. These answers satisfy none but idiots, or those that seek profit under their command.

I mentioned before the danger and dishonour arising to the Parliament hereby, which of necessity must ensue, for seeing that *omne imperium in consensu et assensu parentium fondatur* (Pliny, *Paneg.*) – all lawful empire or sovereign command has its basis or firm foundation in the consent, approbation and good liking of the people – a rule without exception, what consent or good liking can be expected from those who daily see themselves abused in their liberties, and ruined in their estates? Nay, what hope of redress, when as our petitions will not be accepted without great friends in the House? To be short, it is not credible that either people or person, in any outward condition under which they mourn, sigh, or groan, will continue any longer therein than they have occasion of good terms to be delivered, according to the saying of Livy, book 8: *Non credibile est illum populum, vel hominem denique, in ea conditione cujus eum poeniteat diutius quam necesse sit mansurum*. Hence it must necessarily follow that the multitude, touched to the quick in their liberties and means of living, will be easily persuaded to shake off all bonds of obedience, so necessary to the magistrate, and to cast the blame of their sufferings upon the authors, either as false to their trust, or uncapable of the great weight of authority committed unto them. For who but a madman will yield obedience unto those who are regardless of their laws and liberties, or negligent of the means of their subsistence, livelihood, and safety – the main and only ends for which they are convened and called together, and not to provide offices for themselves, or to solicit the cases of their particular friends, sometimes the greatest enemies of the state?

I beseech you, pass not lightly by these considerations as idle and vain fears. For who shall hinder the multitude if, stung with a lively sense of their lost freedoms and means of subsisting, they shall endeavour the regaining thereof by some sudden attempt; seeing that (if the worst happen) they cannot be in much worse condition than they now are. As to the Committee for Examinations (mentioned in Mr Lilburne's letter), which ought to be the touchstone whereby to discern gold from counterfeit, and, in equity and reason, ought to be free, equal and open as well to the plaintiff as defendant, especially in criminal cases – but in cases of treason, or which concern the public safety, ought rather to lend an attentive ear to the delators or accusers, than any way to discourage them: for if these necessary evils shall be disheartened, who will watch over the safety of the state? Besides, it is more safe and tolerable in the condition wherein we now are that a mischief should happen to one man, than a ruin to the whole kingdom. As to this Committee, I wish from my soul that Lieutenant Colonel Lilburne were the only complainant against them. Let Westminster Hall, the Exchange, and other places of public meeting inform you: what making of sides, browbeating of witnesses, baffling of evidences, facing and out-facing of the truth! What impertinent distinguishing and abusing the formalities of the law is there complained of! And all this noise and turmoil to keep a knave out of the briars.

It were more for the honour of their justice, and the satisfaction of the people, if the usual forms of proceeding in cases of charge of treason were observed: that is, that the person accused were secured; and the accusers heard with all equanimity, patience and attention. Whereas on the contrary, the accused is permitted to sit down covered, as peer and companion with the commissioners, and to arraign his accusers. O wretched times! O miserable England! which does labour with all the symptoms, marks and tokens of a declining and dying state! Injustice avowed; treason countenanced; oppression become familiar, almost legal; oaths, protestations and covenants, solemnly made in the presence of God and man, slighted and set at nought; then, to fill up the measure of our sorrows, a civil war within our own bowels, nay, almost in every family; and last of all a general corruption of manners, which assures us the malady will be lasting, if not incurable. What will be the end and issue of all this? Seek to that oracle which cannot lie: *Propter injustitiam, et injurias, et contumelias et diversos dolos, regnum a gente in gentem transfertur* (Ecclesiasticus 10: 8): 'Because of unrighteous dealings, injuries and riches got by deceit, the kingdom is translated from one people to another.'

To the Reader:

Christian reader, having a vacant place for some few lines, I have made bold to use some of Major George Wither, his verses out of *Vox Pacifica*, page 199:

> Let not your King and Parliament in one,
> Much less apart, mistake themselves for that
> Which is most worthy to be thought upon:
> Or think they are, essentially, the state;
> Let them not fancy that th'authority
> And privileges upon them bestown,
> Conferred, to set up a majesty,
> A power, or a glory, of their own.
> But let them know t'was for another thing,
> Which they but *represent*; and which, ere long,
> Them to a strict account will, doubtless, bring,
> If any way they do it wilful wrong:
> For that, indeed, is really the face,
> Whereof they are the shadow in the glass.
> Moreover, thus inform them, that, if either
> They, still divided, grow from bad to worse,
> Or without penitence unite together,
> And, by their sin, provoke him to that course;
> GOD, out of their confusions, can, and will
> Create a cure; and raise a lawful power,
> His promise to his people to fulfil,
> And his and their opposers to devour.
> Yea, bid both King and Parliament make haste,
> In penitence, united to appear:
> Lest into those confusions they be cast,
> Which will affright them both; and make them fear,
> And know there is, on earth, a greater thing,
> Than an unrighteous Parliament, or King.

2 *An Agreement of the People for a Firm and Present Peace, upon Grounds of Common-Right and Freedom; as It was Proposed by the Agents of the Five Regiments of Horse; and Since by the General Approbation of the Army, Offered to the Joint Concurrence of All Free COMMONS of ENGLAND (1647)*

. . . .

Having by our late labours and hazards made it appear to the world at how high a rate we value our just freedom, and God having so far owned our cause as to deliver the enemies thereof into our hands, we do now hold ourselves bound in mutual duty to each other to take the best care we can for the future, to avoid both the danger of returning into a slavish condition, and the chargeable remedy of another war. For as it cannot be imagined that so many of our countrymen would have opposed us in this quarrel if they had understood their own good; so may we safely promise to ourselves that when our common rights and liberties shall be cleared, their endeavours will be disappointed that seek to make themselves our masters. Since, therefore, our former oppressions and scarce yet ended troubles have been occasioned, either by want of frequent national meetings in council, or by rendering those meetings ineffectual, we are fully agreed and resolved to provide that hereafter our representatives be neither left to an uncertainty for the time, nor made useless to the ends for which they are intended. In order whereunto we declare,

I

That the people of England, being at this day very unequally distributed by counties, cities, and boroughs for the election of their deputies in parliament, ought to be more indifferently proportioned, according to the number of inhabitants: the circumstances whereof, for number, place, and manner, are to be set down before the end of this present Parliament.

II

That to prevent the many inconveniences apparently arising from the long continuance of the same persons in authority, this present Parliament be dissolved upon the last day of September, which shall be in the year of our Lord, 1648.

III

That the people do, of course, choose themselves a parliament once in two years, viz., upon the first Thursday in every second March, after the manner as shall be prescribed before the end of this Parliament, to begin to sit upon the first Thursday in April following at Westminster, or such other place as shall be appointed from time to time by the preceding representatives; and to continue till the last day of September, then next ensuing, and no longer.

That the power of this and all future representatives of this nation is inferior only to theirs who choose them, and does extend, without the consent or concurrence of any other person or persons, to the enacting, altering, and repealing of laws; to the erecting and abolishing of offices and courts; to the appointing, removing, and calling to account magistrates, and officers of all degrees; to the making war and peace; to the treating with foreign states; and, generally, to whatsoever is not expressly or implicitly reserved by the represented to themselves.

Which are as follows

1. That matters of religion, and the ways of God's worship, are not at all entrusted by us to any human power, because therein we cannot remit or exceed a tittle of what our consciences dictate to be the mind of God, without wilful sin: nevertheless, the public way of instructing the nation (so it be not compulsive) is referred to their discretion.

2. That the matter of impressing and constraining any of us to serve in the wars is against our freedom; and therefore we do not allow it in our representatives; the rather, because money (the sinews of war) being always at their disposal, they can never want numbers of men apt enough to engage in any just cause.

3. That after the dissolution of this present Parliament no person be at any time questioned for anything said or done in reference to the late public differences, otherwise than in execution of the judgements of the present representatives, or House of Commons.

4.   That in all laws made, or to be made, every person may be bound alike, and that no tenure, estate, charter, degree, birth, or place do confer any exception from the ordinary course of legal proceedings whereunto others are subjected.

5.   That as the laws ought to be equal, so they must be good, and not evidently destructive to the safety and well-being of the people.

These things we declare to be our native rights, and therefore are agreed and resolved to maintain them with our utmost possibilities, against all opposition whatsoever, being compelled thereunto, not only by the examples of our ancestors, whose blood was often spent in vain for the recovery of their freedoms, suffering themselves, through fraudulent accommodations, to be still deluded of the fruit of their victories, but also by our own woeful experience, who, having long expected, and dearly earned, the establishment of these certain rules of government, are yet made to depend for the settlement of our peace and freedom upon him that intended our bondage, and brought a cruel war upon us.

3   *The Putney Debates: The Debate on the Franchise* (1647)

[From the second day's debate in the General Council of the Army, Putney Church, 29 October 1647.]

The Paper called the Agreement read.
Afterwards the first Article read by itself

Commissary [*General*] *Ireton:* The exception that lies in it is this: it is said, they are to be distributed according to the number of the inhabitants, 'The people of England', etc. And this does make me think, that the meaning is that every man that is an inhabitant is to be equally considered, and to have an equal voice in the election of those representers, the persons that are for the general representative, and if that be the meaning then I have something to say against it, but if it be only that those people that by the civil constitution of this kingdom, which is original and fundamental, and beyond which I am sure no memory of record does go.
[*Interjection*] Not before the Conquest.

But before the Conquest it was so. If it be intended, that those that by that constitution that was before the Conquest, that has been beyond memory, such persons that have been under that constitution should be the electors, I have no more to say against it.

Colonel Rainsborough: Moved, that others might have given their hands to it.

Captain Denne: Denied, that those that were set of their regiment, that they were their hands.

Ireton: Whether those men whose hands are to it, or those that brought it do know so much of the matter as that they mean that all that had a former right of election, or those that had no right before are to come in?

Commissary [General] Cowling: In the time before the Conquest, and since the Conquest, the greatest part of the kingdom was in vassalage.

Mr Pettus [Maximilian Petty]: We judge that all inhabitants that have not lost their birthright should have an equal voice in elections.

Rainsborough: I desired that those that had engaged in it, for really I think that the poorest he that is in England has a life to live as the greatest he; and therefore truly, sir, I think it's clear, that every man that is to live under a government ought first by his own consent to put himself under that government; and I do think that the poorest man in England is not at all bound in a strict sense to that government that he has not had a voice to put himself under; and I am confident that, when I have heard the reasons against it, that something will be said to answer those reasons, insomuch that I should doubt whether I was an Englishman or no, that should doubt of these things.

Ireton: That's this:

Give me leave to tell you, that if you make this the rule, I think you must fly for refuge to an absolute natural right, and you must deny all civil right; and I am sure it will come to that in the consequence. This, I perceive, is pressed as that which is so essential and due, the right of the people of this kingdom, and as they are the people of this kingdom, distinct and divided from other people, as that we must for this right lay aside all other considerations. This is so just; this is so due; this is so right to them; and those that they must thus choose, and that those that they do thus choose, must have such a power of binding all, and loosing all, according to those limitations. This is pressed as so due, and so just, as is argued that it is an engagement paramount all others, and you must for it lay aside all others; if you have engaged any others, you must break it; so look upon these as thus held out to us; so it was held out by the gentlemen that brought it yesterday.

For my part, I think it is no right at all. I think that no person has a right to an interest or share in the disposing of the affairs of the kingdom, and in determining or choosing those that shall determine what laws we shall be ruled by here, no person has a right to this that has not a permanent fixed interest in this kingdom, and those persons together are properly the represented of this kingdom who, taken together, and consequently are to make up the representers of this kingdom; are the representers who, taken together, do comprehend whatsoever is of real or permanent interest in the kingdom, and I am sure there is otherwise (I cannot tell what), otherwise any man can say why a foreigner coming in amongst us, or as many as will coming in amongst us, or by force or otherwise settling themselves here, or at least by our permission having a being here, why they should not as well lay claim to it as any other.

We talk of birthright. Truly, birthright there is thus much claim: men may justly have by birthright, by their very being born in England, that we should not seclude them out of England. That we should not refuse to give them air and place and ground, and the freedom of the highways and other things, to live amongst us, not any man that is born here, though he in birth or by his birth there come nothing at all that is part of the permanent interest of this kingdom to him. That I think is due to a man by birth. But that by a man's being born here he shall have a share in that power that shall dispose of the lands here, and of all things here, I do not think it a sufficient ground.

But I am sure if we look upon that which is the utmost, within man's view, of what was originally the constitution of this kingdom, upon that which is most radical and fundamental, and which if you take away, there is no man has any land, any goods, you take away any civil interest, and that is this: that those that choose the representers for the making of laws by which this state and kingdom are to be governed are the persons who, taken together, do comprehend the local interest of this kingdom; that is, the persons in whom all land lies, and those in corporations in whom all trading lies. This is the most fundamental constitution of this kingdom, and which if you do not allow, you allow none at all. This constitution has limited and determined it, that only those shall have voices in elections.

It is true, as was said by a gentleman near me. 'The meanest man in England ought to have.' I say this: that those that have the meanest local interest, that man that has but forty shillings a year, he has as great [a] voice in the election of a knight for the shire as he that has ten thousand a year or more, if he had never so much, and therefore there is that regard had to it. But this still the constitution of this government has had an eye to, and what other government has not an eye to this. It does not relate to the interest of the kingdom if it do not lay the foundation of the power that's given to the representers in those who have a permanent and a local interest in the kingdom, and who, taken altogether, do comprehend the whole, and if we shall go to take away this, we shall plainly go to take away all property and interest that any man has, either in land by inheritance, or in estate by possession, or anything else, if you take away this fundamental part of the civil constitution.

There is all the reason and justice that can be: if I will come to live in a kingdom, being a foreigner to it, or live in a kingdom, having no permanent interest in it, if I will desire as a stranger, or claim as one freeborn here, the air, the free passage of highways, the protection of laws, and all such things, and if I will either desire them or claim them, I (if I have no permanent interest in that kingdom) must submit to those laws and those rules, who taken together do comprehend the whole interest of the kingdom.

Rainsborough: Truly, sir, I am of the same opinion I was, and am resolved to keep it till I know reason why I should not. I confess my memory is bad, and therefore I am fain to make use of my pen. I remember that in a former speech this gentleman brought before this, he was saying that in some cases he should not value 'whether a king or no king, whether lords or no lords, whether a property or no property'. For my part I differ in that. I do very much care whether a king or no king, lords or no lords, property or no property; and I think, if we do not all take care, we shall all have none of these very shortly.

But as to this present business, I do hear nothing at all that can convince me why any man that is born in England ought not to have his voice in election of burgesses. It is said that if a man have not a permanent interest, he can have no claim; and we must be no freer than the laws will let us to be, and that there is no chronicle will let us be freer than that we enjoy. Something was said to this yesterday, and I do think that the main cause why Almighty God gave men reason, it was that they should make use of that reason, and that they should improve it for that end and purpose that God gave it them, and truly I think that half a loaf is better than none if a man be an-hungry, yet I think there is nothing that God has given a man that any else can take from him, and therefore I say, that either it must be the law of God or the law of man that must prohibit the meanest man in the kingdom to have this benefit as well as the greatest. I do not find anything in the law of God, that a lord shall choose twenty burgesses, and a gentleman but two, or a poor man shall choose none: I find no such thing in the law of nature, nor in the law of nations. But I do find that all Englishmen must be subject to English laws, and I do verily believe that there is no man but will say that the foundation of all law lies in the people. And if in the people, I am to seek for this exemption and truly I have thought something: in what a miserable distressed condition would many a man that has fought for the Parliament in this quarrel be? I will be bound to say that many a man whose zeal and affection to God and this kingdom has carried him forth in this cause, has so spent his estate that, in the way the state, the army are going this way, he shall not hold up his head, and when his estate is lost, and not worth forty shillings a year, a man shall not have any interest. And there are many other ways by which men have estates [which] (if that be the rule which God in his providence does use) do fall to decay; a man, when he has an estate, he has an interest in making laws; when he has none, he has no power in it. So that a man cannot lose that which he has for the maintenance of his family, but he must [also] lose that which God and nature have given him. And therefore I do, and am still of the same opinion, that every man born in England cannot, ought not, neither by the law of God nor the law of nature, to be exempted from the choice of those who are to make laws and for him to live under, and for him (for aught I know) to lose his life under, and therefore I think there can be no great stick in this.

Truly, I think that there is not this day reigning in England a greater fruit or effect of tyranny than this very thing would produce, for, sir, what is it? The king he grants a patent under the Broad-Seal of England to such a corporation to send burgesses. He grants to a city to send burgesses. Truly I know nothing free but only the knight of the shire, nor do I know anything in a parliamentary way that is clear from the height and fullness of tyranny. But as for this of corporations, it is as contrary to freedom as may be when a poor base corporation from the king shall send two burgesses, when five hundred men of estate shall not send one, when those that are to make their laws are called by the king, or cannot act by [i.e. without] such a call, truly I think that the people of England have little freedom.

Ireton: I think there was nothing that I said to give you occasion to think that I did contend for this, that such a corporation should have the electing of a man to the parliament. I think I agreed to this matter, that all should be equally distributed, but the question is whether it should be distributed to all persons, or whether the same persons that are the electors should be the electors still, and it equally distributed amongst them. I do not see anybody else that makes this objection; and if nobody else be sensible of it I shall soon have done. Only I shall a little crave your leave to represent the consequences of it, and clear myself from one misrepresentation of the thing that was misrepresented by the gentleman that sat next me. I think, if the gentleman remember himself, he cannot but remember that what I said was to this effect: that if I saw the hand of God leading so far as to destroy king, and destroy lords, and destroy property, and no such thing at all amongst us, I should acquiesce in it; and so I did not care, if no king, no lords, or no property, how in comparison of the tender care that I have of the honour of God, and of the people of God, whose name is so much concerned in this army. This I did deliver, and not absolutely.

All the main thing that I speak for, is because I would have an eye to property. I hope we do not come to contend for victory, but let every man consider with himself that he do not go that way to take away all property; for here is the case of the most fundamental part of the constitution of the kingdom, which if you take away, you take away all by that. Here are men of this and this quality are determined to be the electors of men to the parliament, and they are all those who have any permanent interest in the kingdom, and who, taken together, do comprehend the whole interest of the kingdom. I mean by permanent, local, that is not anywhere else. As for instance, he that has a freehold, and that freehold cannot be removed out of the kingdom. And so there's a corporation, a place which has the privilege of a market and trading, which if you should allow to all places equally, I do not see how you could preserve any peace in the kingdom, and that is the reason why in the constitution we have but some few market towns. Now those people by the former constitution were looked upon to comprehend the permanent interest of the kingdom, and those are the freemen of corporations; for he that has his livelihood by his trade, and by his freedom of trading in such a corporation, which he cannot exercise in another, he is tied to that place, his livelihood depends upon it; and secondly, that man has an interest, has a permanent interest there, upon which he may live, and live a freeman without dependence. These constitutions this kingdom has looked at.

Now I wish we may all consider of what right you will challenge, that all the people should have right to elections. Is it by the right of nature? If you will hold forth that as your ground, then I think you must deny all property too, and this is my reason. For thus: by that same right of nature, whatever it be that you pretend, by which you can say a man has an equal right with another to the choosing of him that shall govern him, by the same right of nature he has the same right in any goods he sees: meat, drink, clothes, to take and use them for his sustenance; he has a freedom to the land, the ground, to exercise it, till it. He has the freedom to anything that anyone does account himself to have any property in. Why now I say, then, if you will, against the most fundamental part of civil constitution (which I have now declared), will plead the law of nature, that a man should, paramount this, and contrary to this, have a power of choosing those men that shall determine what shall be law in the state, though he himself have no permanent interest in the state, whatever interest he has he may carry about with him, if this be allowed, we are free, we are equal, one man must have as much voice as another. Then show me what step or difference, why, by the same right of necessity to sustain nature, it is for my better being. And possibly not for it neither: possibly I may not have so real a regard to the peace of the kingdom as that man who has a permanent interest in it; but he that has no permanent interest, that is here today and gone tomorrow, I do not see that he has such a permanent interest. Since you cannot plead to it by anything but the law of nature, but for the end of better being, and that better being is not certain, and more destructive to another; upon these grounds, if you do, paramount all constitutions, hold up this law of nature, I would fain have any man show me their bounds, where you will end, and take away all property?

Rainsborough: I shall now be a little more free and open with you than I was before. I wish we were all true-hearted, and that we did all carry ourselves with integrity; if I did mistrust you, I would use such asseverations. I think it does go on mistrust, and things are thought too matters of reflection that were never intended for my part; as I think you forgot something that was in my speech. You forgot something in my speech, and you do not only yourselves believe that men are inclining to anarchy, but you would make all men believe that; and, sir, to say because a man pleads that every man has a voice, that therefore it destroys the same that there's a property. The law of God says it, else why God made that law, thou shalt not steal? I am a poor man, therefore I must be pressed; if I have no interest in the kingdom, I must suffer by all their laws, be they right or wrong. Nay thus, a gentleman lives in a county and has three or four lordships as some men have, God knows how they got them, and when a parliament is called, he must be a parliament-man; and it may be he sees some poor men they live near, this man he can crush them. I have known an evasion to make sure he has turned the poor man out of doors, and I would fain know whether the potency of men do not this, and so keep them under the greatest tyranny that was thought of in the world; and therefore I think that to that it is fully answered. God has set down that thing as to property with this law of his, thou shalt not steal. And for my part I am against any such thought, and I wish you would not make the world believe that we are for anarchy, as for yourselves.

Lieutenant-General [*Cromwell*]: I know nothing but this, that they that are the most yielding have the greatest wisdom; but really, Sir, this is not right as it should be. No man says that you have a mind to anarchy, but the consequence of this rule tends to anarchy, must end in anarchy; for where is there any bound or limit set, if you take away this, that men that have no interest but the interest of breathing [should have no voice]. Therefore I am confident on't, we should not be so hot one with another.

Rainsborough: I know that some particular men we debate with [claim we] are for anarchy.

Ireton: I have, with as much plainness and clearness of reason as I could, showed you how I did conceive the doing of this takes away that which is the most original, the most fundamental civil constitution of this kingdom, and which is, above all, that constitution by which I have any property. And if you will take away that and set up whatever a man may claim as a thing paramount that by the law of nature, though it be not a thing of necessity to him for the sustenance of nature, if you do make this your rule, I desire clearly to understand where then remains property.

Now then, that which (I would misrepresent nothing) the great and main answer which had anything of matter in it, that seemed to be the answer upon which that which has been said against this rests, I profess I must clear myself as to that point; I desire, I would not, I cannot allow myself to lay the least scandal upon any body. And truly, for that gentleman that did take so much offence, I do not know why he should take it so: we speak to the paper, not to persons, and to the matter of the paper, and I hope that no man is so much engaged to the matter of the paper. I hope our persons, and our hearts, and judgements are not pinned to papers, but that we are ready to hear what good or ill consequence will flow from it.

Now then, as I say to that which is to the main answer: that it will not make the breach of property, then that there is a law, thou shalt not steal. The same law says, honour thy father, and mother: and that law does likewise hold out that it does extend to all that, in that place where we are in, are our governors, so that by that there is a forbidding of breaking a civil law when we may live quietly under it, and a divine law; and again it is said, indeed before, that there is no law, no divine law, that tells us that such a corporation must have the election of burgesses, of such a shire or the like. Divine law extends not to particular things; and so on the other side, if a man were to demonstrate his property by divine law, it would be very remote, but our property descends from other things, as well as our right of sending burgesses; that divine law does not determine particulars but generals, in relation to man and man, and to property, and all things else. And we should be as far to seek if we should go to prove a property in divine law as to prove that I have an interest in choosing burgesses of the parliament by divine law; and truly under favour I refer it to all whether these be anything of solution to that objection that I made, if it be understood. I submit it to any man's judgement.

Rainsborough: To the thing itself – property – I would fain know how it comes to be the property: as for estates, and those kind of things and other things that belong to men, it will be granted that it is property, but I deny that that is a property, to a lord, to a gentleman, to any man more than another in the kingdom of England. If it be a property, it is a property by a law; neither do I think that there is very little property in this thing by the law of the land, because I think that the law of the land in that thing is the most tyrannical law under heaven, and I would fain know what we have fought for; and this is the old law of England and that which enslaves the people of England, that they should be bound by laws in which they have no voice at all. So the great dispute is who is a right father and a right mother. I am bound to know who is my father and mother, and I take it in the same sense you do. I would have a distinction, a character whereby God commands me to honour. And for my part, I look upon the people of England so, that wherein they have not voices in the choosing of their fathers and mothers, they are not bound to that commandment.

Petty: I desire to add one word, concerning the word property.

It is for something that anarchy is so much talked of. For my own part I cannot believe in the least, that it can be clearly derived from that paper. 'Tis true, that somewhat may be derived in the paper against the king, the power of the king, and somewhat against the power of the lords; and the truth is when I shall see God going about to throw down king and lords and property, then I shall be contented; but I hope that they may live to see the power of the king and the lords thrown down, that yet may live to see property preserved. And for this of changing the representative of the nation, of changing those that choose the representative, making of them more full, taking more into the number than formerly, I had verily thought we had all agreed in it, that more should have chosen, all that had desired a more equal representation than now we have. For now those only choose who have forty shillings freehold. A man may have a lease for one hundred pounds a year, a man may have a lease for three lives; but for this, that it destroys all right that every Englishman that is an inhabitant of England should choose and have a voice in the representatives. I suppose it is the only means to preserve all property. For I judge every man is naturally free; and I judge the reason why the men when they are in so great numbers that every man could not give his voice, was that they who were chosen might preserve property; and therefore men agreed to come into some form of government that they might preserve property, and I would fain know, if we were to begin a government: 'you have not forty shillings a year, therefore you shall not have a voice.' Whereas, before there was a government every man had such a choice, and afterwards, and for this very cause, they did choose representatives, and put themselves into forms of government that they may preserve property, and therefore it is not to destroy it.

Ireton: I think we shall not be so apt to come to a right understanding in this business if one man, and another man, and another man do speak their several thoughts and conceptions to the same purpose, as if we do consider what the objection is, and where the answer lies to which it is made; and therefore I desire we may do so too. That which this gentleman spoke last, the main thing that he seemed to answer was this, that he would make it appear that the going about to establish this government, such a government, is not a destruction of property, nor does not tend to the destruction of property, because the people's falling into a government is for the preservation of property. What weight there [is] lies in this: since there is a falling into a government, and government is to preserve property, therefore this cannot be against property. The objection does not lie in that, the making of it more equal, but the introducing of men into an equality of interest in this government who have no property in this kingdom, or who have no local permanent interest in it. For if I had said that I would not wish at all that we should have any enlargement of the bounds of those that are to be the electors, then you might have excepted against it, but that I would not go to enlarge it beyond all bounds, so that upon the same ground you may admit of so many men from foreign states as would outvote you: the objection lies still in this, that I do not mean that I would have it restrained to that proportion, but to restrain it still to men who have a local, a permanent interest in the kingdom, who have such an interest that they may live upon it as free men, and who have such an interest as is fixed upon a place, and is not the same equally everywhere. If a man be an inhabitant upon a rack rent for a year, for two years, or twenty years, you cannot think that man has any fixed permanent interest; that man, if he pay the rent that his land is worth, and he has no advantage but what he has by his land, that man is as good a man, may have as much interest, in another kingdom. But here I do not speak of an enlarging this at all, but of keeping this to the most fundamental constitution in this kingdom. That is, that no person that has not a local and permanent interest in the kingdom should have an equal dependence in election; but if you go beyond this law, if you admit any man that has a breath and being, I did show you how this will destroy property. It may come to destroy property thus: you may have a major part, you may have such men chosen, or at least the major part of them, why those men may not vote against all property. You may admit strangers by this rule, if you admit them once to inhabit, and those that have interest in the land may be voted out of their land; it may destroy property that way. But here is the rule that you go by: for that by which you infer this to be the right of the people, of every inhabitant, and that because this man has such a right in nature, though it be not of necessity for the preserving of his being; therefore you are to overthrow the most fundamental constitution for this. By the same rule, show me why you will not, by the same right of nature, make use of anything that any man has for the necessary sustenance of me. Show me what you will stop at, wherein you will fence any man in a property by this rule.

Rainsborough: I desire to know how this comes to be a property in some men, and not in others.

Colonel Rich: I confess that objection that the Commissary-General last insisted upon; for you have five to one in this kingdom that have no permanent interest. Some men [have] ten, some twenty servants, some more, some less; if the master and servant shall be equal electors, then clearly those that have no interest in the kingdom will make it their interest to choose those that have no interest. It may happen, that the majority may by law, not in a confusion, you may destroy property. There may be a law enacted, that there shall be an equality of goods and estate[s]. I think that either of the extremes may be urged to inconveniency; that is, men that have no interest as to estate should have no interest as to election. But there may be a more equal division and distribution than that he that has nothing should have an equal voice; and certainly there may be some other way thought of, that there may be a representative of the poor as well as the rich, and not to exclude all. I remember there were many workings and revolutions, as we have heard, in the Roman senate; and there was never a confusion that did appear, and that indeed was come to, till the state came to know this kind of distribution of election: that is how the people's voices were bought and sold, and that by the poor; and thence it came that he that was the richest man, and of some considerable power among the soldiers, made himself a perpetual dictator and one they resolved on. And if we strain too far to avoid monarchy in kings, [beware] that we do not call for emperors to deliver us from more than one tyrant.

Rainsborough: I should not have spoken again. I think it is a fine gilded pill, but there is much danger, and it may seem to some that there is some kind of remedy. I think that we are better as we are, that the poor shall choose many; still the people be in the same case, be over-voted still. And therefore truly, sir, I should desire to go close to the business; and the thing that I am unsatisfied in is how it comes about that there is such a property in some freeborn Englishmen, and not others.

Cowling: Whether the younger son have not as much right to the inheritance as the eldest?

Ireton: Will you decide it by the light of nature?

Cowling: Why election was only forty shillings a year, which was more than forty pounds a year now, the reason was: that the commons of England were overpowered by the lords, who had abundance of vassals. But that still they might make their laws good against encroaching prerogatives; therefore they did exclude all slaves. Now the case is not so; all slaves have bought their freedoms. They are more free that in the commonwealth are more beneficial. There are men in the country in Staines: there is a tanner in Staines worth three thousand pounds, and another in Reading worth three horseskins.

Ireton: In the beginning of your speech you seem to acknowledge by law, by civil constitution, the property of having voices in election was fixed in certain persons. So then your exception of your argument does not prove that by civil constitution they have no such property, but your argument does acknowledge by civil property. You argue against this law, that this law is not good.

Mr Wildman: Unless I be very much mistaken we are very much deviated from the first question. And instead of following the first proposition to inquire what is just, I conceive we look to prophecies, and look to what may be the event, and judge of the justness of a thing by the consequence. I desire we may recall whether it be right or no. I conceive all that has been said against it will be reduced to this, that it is against a fundamental law; and another reason that every person ought to have a permanent interest: because it is not fit that those should choose parliaments that have no lands to be disposed of by parliament.

Ireton: If you will take it by the way, it is not fit that the representees should choose the representers, or the persons who shall make the law in the kingdom, who have not a permanent fixed interest in the kingdom.

Wildman: Sir, I do so take it; and I conceive that that is brought in for the same reason, that foreigners might come as well to have a notice in our elections as well as the native inhabitants.

Ireton: That is upon supposition, that these should be all inhabitants.

Wildman: I shall begin with the last first. The case is different from the native inhabitant and foreigner. If a foreigner shall be admitted to be an inhabitant in the nation, he may, so he will submit to that form of government as the natives do; he has the same right as the natives but in this particular. Our case is to be considered thus: that we have been under slavery, that's acknowledged by all. Our very laws were made by our conquerors; and whereas it's spoken much of chronicles, I conceive there is no credit to be given to any of them; and the reason is because those that were our lords, and make us their vassals, would suffer nothing else to be chronicled. We are now engaged for our freedom; that's the end of parliaments, not to constitute what is already, according to the just rules of government. Every person in England has as clear a right to elect his representative as the greatest person in England. I conceive that's the undeniable maxim of government: that all government is in the free consent of the people. If then upon that account, there is no person that is under a just government, or has justly his own, unless he by his own free consent be put under that government. This he cannot be unless he be consenting to it, and therefore, according to this maxim, there is never a person in England; if, as that gentleman says be true, there are no laws that, in this strictness and rigour of justice, that are not made by those who he does consent to. And therefore I should humbly move, that if the question be stated, which would soonest bring things to an issue, it might rather be this: whether any person can justly be bound by law not by his own consent, who does not give his consent that such persons shall make laws for him.

Ireton: Let the question be so: whether a man can be bound to any law that he does not consent to? And I shall tell you, that he may and ought to be, [despite the fact] that he does not give a consent to, nor does not choose any; and I will make it clear. If a foreigner come within this kingdom, if that stranger will have liberty who has no local interest here: he is a man, it's true, has air, that, by nature, we must not expel our coasts, give him no being amongst us, nor kill him because he comes upon our land, comes up our stream, arrives at our shore. It is a piece of hospitality, of humanity, to receive that man amongst us. But if that man be received to a being amongst us, I think that man may very well be content to submit himself to the law of the land; that is, the law that is made by those people that have a property, a fixed property in the land. I think, if any man will receive protection from this people, though he nor his ancestors, not any between him and Adam, did ever give concurrence to this constitution, I think this man ought to be subject to those laws, and to be bound by those laws, so long as he continues amongst them; that is my opinion. A man ought to be subject to a law, that did not give his consent. But with this reservation, that if this man do think himself unsatisfied to be subject to this law, he may go into another kingdom; and so the same reason does extend in my understanding, that a man that has no permanent interest in the kingdom, if he has money, his money is as good in another place as here; he has nothing that does locally fix him to this kingdom. If that man will live in this kingdom, or trade amongst us, that man ought to subject himself to the law made by the people who have the interest of this kingdom in us. And yet I do acknowledge that which you take to be so general a maxim, that in every kingdom, within every land, the original of power, of making laws, of determining what shall be law in the land, does lie in the people that are possessed in the permanent interest in the land. But whoever is extraneous to this, that is, as good a man in another land, that man ought to give such a respect to the property of men that live in the land. They do not determine, why should I [i.e. they] have any interest of determining, what shall be the law of this land.

Major [William] Rainsborough: I think if it can be made to appear that it is a just and reasonable thing, and that it is for the preservation of all the freeborn men, I think it ought to be made good unto them; and the reason is, that the chief end of this government is to preserve persons as well as estates, and if any law shall take hold of my person, it is more dear than my estate.

Colonel Rainsborough: I do very well remember that the gentleman in the window [said] that if it were so, there were no property to be had, because a fifth [five?] part[s] of the poor people are now excluded and would then come in. So I say one on the other side said, if otherwise, then rich men shall be chosen; then, I say, the one part shall make hewers of wood and drawers of water of the other five, and so the greatest part of the nation be enslaved. And truly I think we are where we were still; and I do not hear any argument given but only that it is the present law of the kingdom. I say what shall become still of those many that have laid out themselves for the Parliament of England in this present war, that have ruined themselves by fighting, by hazarding all they had. They are Englishmen. They have now nothing to say for themselves.

Rich: I should be very sorry to speak anything here that should give offence, or that may occasion personal reflection that we spoke against just now. I did not urge any thing so far as was represented, and I did not at all urge them that there should be a consideration, and that man that is, shall be, without consideration, he deserves to be made poor and not to live at all. But all that I urged was this: that I think it worthy consideration, whether they should have an equality in their interest. But however, I think we have been a great while upon this point, and if we be as long upon all the rest, it were well if there were no greater difference than this.

Mr Peters [*Hugh Peter*]: I think that this may be easily agreed on, that is, there may be a way thought of; but I would fain know whether that will answer the work of your meeting. I think you should do well to sit up all night, but I think that three or four might be thought of in this company. You will be forced to put characters upon electors or elected. Therefore I do suppose that if there be any here that can make up a representative to your mind, the thing is gained. But the question is, whether you can state any one question for the present danger of the kingdom, if any one question or no will dispatch the work.

Sir, I desire, that some question may be stated to finish the present work, to cement us wherein lies the distance; and if the thought's of the commonwealth, the people's freedom, I think that's soon cured. But I desire that all manner of plainness may be used, that we may not go on with the lapwing and carry one another off the nest. There is something else in that, must cement us where the awkwardness of our spirits lies.

Rainsborough: For my part, I think we cannot engage one way or other in the army if we do not think of the people's liberties; if we can agree where the liberty and freedom of the people lies, that will do all.

Ireton: I cannot consent so far before. As I said before, when I see the hand of God destroying king, and lords, and commons too, any foundation of human constitution, when I see God has done it, I shall, I hope, comfortably acquiesce in it; but first, I cannot give my consent to it, because it is not good, and secondly, as I desire that this army should have regard to engagements, wherever they are lawful, so would I have them have regard to this: that they should not bring that scandal upon the name of God, that those that call themselves by that name, those whom God has owned and appeared with, that we should not represent ourselves to the world as men so far from being of that peaceable spirit which is suitable to the Gospel, as we would have bought peace of the world upon such terms. We would not have peace in the world but upon such terms as should destroy all property, if the principle upon which you move this alteration, or the ground upon which you press that we should make this alteration, do destroy all kind of property or whatsoever a man has by human constitution. The law of God does not give me property, nor the law of nature, but property is of human constitution. I have a property and this I shall enjoy. Constitution founds property. If either the thing itself that you press or the consequence that you press [abolishes property], though I shall acquiesce in having no property, yet I cannot give my heart or hand to it; because it is a thing evil in itself, and scandalous to the world, and I desire this army may be free from both.

Mr Sexby: I see that though it [liberty?] were our end, there is a degeneration from it. We have engaged in this kingdom and ventured our lives, and it was all for this: to recover our birthrights and privileges as Englishmen; and by the arguments urged there is none. There are many thousands of us soldiers that have ventured our lives; we have had little property in the kingdom as to our estates, yet we have had a birthright; but it seems now, except a man has a fixed estate in this kingdom, he has no right in this kingdom. I wonder we were so much deceived. If we had not a right to the kingdom, we were mere mercenary soldiers. There are many in my condition, that have as good a condition; it may be little estate they have at present, and yet they have as much a right as those too who are their lawgivers, as any in this place. I shall tell you in a word my resolution. I am resolved to give my birthright to none, whatsoever may come in the way; and be thought that I will give it to none, if this thing that with so much pressing after. There was one thing spoken to this effect: 'that if the poor and those in low condition [. . .]'. I think this was but a distrust of providence. I do think the poor and meaner of this kingdom, I speak as in that relation in which we are, have been the means of the preservation of this kingdom. I say, in their stations, and really I think that to their utmost possibility; and their lives have not been dear for purchasing the good of the kingdom. Those that act to this end are as free from anarchy or confusion as those that oppose it, and they have the law of God and the law of their conscience. But truly, I shall only sum up this in all: I desire that we may not spend so much time upon these things. We must be plain. When men come to understand these things, they will not lose that which they have contended for. That which I shall beseech you is to come to a determination of this question.

Ireton: I am very sorry we are come to this point, that from reasoning one to another we should come to express our resolutions. I profess for my part what I see is good for the kingdom, and becoming a Christian to contend for. I hope through God I shall have strength and resolution to do my part towards it, and yet I will profess direct contrary in some kind to what that gentleman said. For my part, rather than I will make a disturbance to a good constitution of a kingdom wherein I may live in godliness and honesty, and peace and quietness, I will part with a great deal of my birthright. I will part with my own property rather than I will be the man that shall make a disturbance in the kingdom for my property; and therefore if all the people in this kingdom, or representative[s] of them all together, should meet and should give away my property, I would submit to it, I would give it away. But that gentleman, and I think every Christian spirit, ought to bear that, to carry that in him, that he will not make a public disturbance upon a private prejudice.

Now let us consider where our difference lies. We all agree that you should have a representative to govern, but this representative to be as equal as you can; but the question is, whether this distribution can be made to all persons equally, or whether amongst those equals that have the interest of England in them? That which I have declared my opinion, I think we ought to keep to; that, both because it is a civil constitution, it is the most fundamental constitution that we have, and there is so much justice and reason and prudence, as I dare confidently undertake to demonstrate, as that there are many more evils that will follow in case you do alter than there can in the standing of it. But I say but this in the general, that I do wish that they that talk of birthrights, we any of us when we talk of birthrights, would consider what really our birthright is. If a man me[a]n by birthright whatsoever he can challenge by the law of nature, suppose there were no constitution at all, supposing no civil law and civil constitution, that that I am to contend for against constitution, [then] you leave no property, nor no foundation for any man to enjoy anything. But if you call that your birthrights which is the most fundamental part of your constitution, then let him perish that goes about to hinder you or any man of the least part of your birthright, or will do it. But if you will lay aside the most fundamental constitution, and I will give you consequence for consequence, of [i.e. as] good upon constitution as you for your birthright, which is as good for aught you can discern as anything you can propose. At least it is a constitution; and if you were merely upon pretence of a birthright, of the right of nature, which is only true as for your better being, if you will upon that ground pretend that this constitution, the most fundamental constitution, the thing that has reason and equity in it, shall not stand in your way, is the same principle to me (say I), but for your better satisfaction you shall take hold of anything that a man calls his own.

Rainsborough: Sir, I see that it is impossible to have liberty but all property must be taken away. If it be laid down for a rule, and if you will say it, it must be so, but I would fain know what the soldiers have fought for all this while; he has fought to enslave himself, to give power to men of riches, men of estates, to make him a perpetual slave. We do find in all presses that go forth none must be pressed that are freehold men. When these gentlemen fall out among themselves, they shall press the poor shrubs to come and kill them.

Ireton: I must confess I see so much right in the business that I am not easily satisfied with flourishes. If you will lay the stress of the business upon the consideration of reason, or right relating to anything of human constitution, or anything of that nature, but will put it upon consequences, I will show you greater ill consequences; I see enough to say that, to my apprehensions, I can show you greater ill consequences to follow upon that alteration which you would have, by extending to all that have a being in this kingdom, than that by this a great deal. This is a particular ill consequence. This is a general ill consequence, and that is as great as this or any else, though I think you will see that the validity of that argument must lie, that for one ill lies upon that which now is, and I can show you a thousand upon this.

Give me leave but this one word. I tell you what the soldier of the kingdom has fought for. First, the danger that we stood in was that one man's will must be a law. The people of the kingdom must have this right at least, that they should not [*sic*] be concluded by the representative of those that had the interest of the kingdom. So men fought in this because they were immediately concerned and engaged in it; other men who had no other interest in the kingdom but this, that they should have the benefit of those laws made by the representative, yet that they should have the benefit of this representative. They thought it was better to be concluded by the common consent of those that were fixed men, and settled men, that had the interest of this kingdom, and from that way I shall know a law and have a certainty. And every man that was born in it, that has a freedom, is a denizen; he was capable of trading to get money, and to get estates by; and therefore this man, I think, had a great deal of reason to build up such a foundation of interest to himself; that is, that the will of one man should not be a law, but that the law of this kingdom should be by a choice of persons to represent, and that choice to be made by the generality of the kingdom. Here was a right that induced men to fight, and those men that had not this interest, and though this be not the utmost interest that other men have, yet they had some interest.

Now why we should go to plead whatsoever we can challenge by the right of nature against whatsoever any man can challenge by constitution; I do not see where that man will stop, as to point of property, that he shall not use that right he has by the law of nature against that constitution. I desire any man to show me where there is a difference. I have been answered: 'Now we see liberty cannot stand without property.' Liberty may be had and property not be destroyed; first, the liberty of all those that have the permanent interest in the kingdom, that is provided for. And [i.e. but] in a general sense liberty cannot be provided for if property be preserved. For, if property be preserved, that I am not to meddle with such a man's estate, his meat, his drink, his apparel, or other goods, then the right of nature destroys liberty. By the right of nature I am to have sustenance rather than perish; yet property destroys it for a man to have by the light of nature, suppose there be no human constitution.

Peter: I will mind you of one thing, that 'upon the will of one man abusing us', and so forth. So that I profess to you, for my part I hope it is not denied by any man, that any wise, discreet man that has preserved England or the government of it [should have the vote]. I do say still under favour there is a way to cure all this debate. I think they will desire no more liberty if there were time to dispute it. I think he will be satisfied and all will be satisfied, and if the safety of the army be in danger, for my part I am clear it should be amended, the point of election should be mended.

Cromwell: I confess I was most dissatisfied with that I heard Mr Sexby speak of any man here, because it did savour so much of will. But I desire that all of us may decline that, and if we meet here really to agree to that which is for the safety of the kingdom, let us not spend so much time in such debates as these are, but let us apply ourselves to such things as are conclusive, and that shall be this: everybody here would be willing that the representative might be mended, that is, it might be better than it is. Perhaps it may be offered in that paper too lamely, if the thing be insisted upon too limited; why perhaps there are a very considerable part of copy-holders by inheritance that ought to have a voice; and there may be somewhat too reflects upon the generality of the people. I know our debates are endless if we think to bring it to an issue this way. If we may but resolve upon a committee. If I cannot be satisfied to go so far as these gentlemen that bring this paper, I say it again, I profess it, I shall freely and willingly withdraw myself, and I hope to do it in such a manner that the army shall see that I shall by my withdrawing satisfying [satisfy] the interest of the army, the public interest of the kingdom, and those ends these men aim at. And I think if you do bring this to a result it were well.

Rainsborough: If these men must be advanced, and other men set under foot, I am not satisfied; if their rules must be observed, and other men, that are in authority, do not know how this can stand together, I wonder how that should be thought wilfulness in one man that is reason in another; for I confess I have not heard anything that does satisfy me, and though I have not so much wisdom or notions in my head, but I have so many that I could tell an hundred to the ruin of my people. I am not at all against a committee's meeting; and as you say, and I think every Christian ought to do the same, for my part I shall be ready, if I see the way that I am going, and the thing that I would insist on, will destroy the kingdom, I shall withdraw it as soon as any. And therefore, till I see that, I shall use all the means, and I think it is no [*sic*] fault in any man to sell that which is his birthright.

Sexby: I desire to speak a few words. I am sorry that my zeal to what I apprehend is good should be so ill resented. I am not sorry to see that which I apprehend is truth, but I am sorry the Lord has darkened some so much as not to see it, and that is in short. Do you think it were a sad and miserable condition, that we have fought all this time for nothing? All here, both great and small, do think that we fought for something. I confess, many of us fought for those ends which, we since saw, was not that which caused us to go through difficulties and straits to venture all in the ship with you; it had been good in you to have advertised us of it, and I believe you would have fewer under your command to have commanded. But if this be the business, that an estate does make men capable, it is no matter which way they get it, they are capable, to choose those that shall represent them; but I think there are many that have not estates that in honesty have as much right in the freedom, their choice as free, as any that have great estates. Truly, sir, your putting off this question and coming to some other, I dare say, and I dare appeal to all of them, that they cannot settle upon any other until this be done; it was the ground that we took up arms, and it is the ground which we shall maintain. Concerning my making rents and divisions in this way, as to a particular, if I were but so, I could lie down and be trodden there. Truly I am sent by a regiment; if I should not speak, guilt shall lie upon me, and I think I were a covenant-breaker. And I do not know how we have answered in our arguments, and I conceive we shall not accomplish them to the kingdom when we deny them to ourselves. For my part, I shall be loath to make a rent and division, but for my own part unless I see this put to a question, I despair of an issue.

Captain Clarke: The first thing that I shall desire was, and is, this: that there might be a temperature and moderation of spirit within us; that we should speak with moderation, not with such reflection as was boulted [sifted, i.e. polarized] one from another, but so speak and so hear as that which may be the droppings of love from one another to another's hearts.

Another word I have to say is: the grand question of all is, whether or no it be the property of every individual person in the kingdom to have a vote in election? And the ground is the law of nature, which, for my part, I think to be that law which is the ground of all constitutions. Yet really properties are the foundation of constitutions; for if so be there were no property, that the law of nature does give a principle to have a property of what he has, or may have, which is not another man's: this property is the ground of *meum* and *tuum*. Now there may be inconveniences on both hands, but not so great freedom. The greater freedom, as I conceive, that all may have whatsoever. And if it come to pass that there be a difference, and that the one does oppose the other, then nothing can decide it but the sword, which is the wrath of God.

Captain Audley: I see you have a long dispute, that you do intend to dispute here till the tenth of March. You have brought us into a fair pass, and the kingdom into a fair pass, for if your reasons are not satisfied, and we do not fetch all our waters from your wells, you threaten to withdraw yourselves. I could wish, according to our several protestations, we might sit down quietly, and there throw down ourselves where we see reason. I could wish we might all rise, and go to our duties, and see our work in hand. I see both at a stand, and if we dispute here both are lost.

Cromwell: Really, for my own part I must needs say, while we say we would not make reflections, we do make reflections; and if I had not come hither with a free heart, to do that that I was persuaded in my conscience is my duty, I should a thousand times rather have kept myself away; for I do think I had brought upon myself the greatest sin that I was guilty of, if I should have come to have stood before God in that former duty which is before you, and if that my saying [that] which I did say, and shall persevere to say, that I should not, I cannot against my conscience do anything. They that have stood so much for liberty of conscience, if they will not grant that liberty to every man but say it is a deserting I know no what. If that be denied me, I think there is not that equality that I professed to be amongst us. I said this, and I say no more, that make your businesses as well as you can, we might bring things to an understanding; it was to be brought to a fair composure. And when you have said: if you should put this paper to the question without any qualification, I doubt whether it would pass so freely; if we would have no difference, we ought to put it. And let me speak clearly and freely; I have heard other gentlemen do the like. I have not heard the Commissary-General answered, not in a part to my knowledge, not in a tittle; if therefore, when I see there is an extremity of difference between you, to the end it may be brought nearer to a general satisfaction; and if this be thought a deserting of that interest, if there can be anything more sharply said, I will not give it an ill word. Though we should be satisfied in our consciences in what we do, we are told we purpose to leave the army, or to leave our commands, as if we took upon us to do it in matter of will. I did hear some gentlemen speak more of will than anything that was spoken for this way, for more was spoken by way of will than of satisfaction; and if there be not a more equality in our minds, I can but grieve for it. I must do no more.

Ireton: I should not speak, but reflections do necessitate, do call upon us to vindicate ourselves, as if we who have led men into engagements and services, that we had divided because we did not concur with them. I will ask that gentleman whom I love in my heart that spoke, whether when they drew out to serve the Parliament in the beginning, whether when they engaged with the army at Newmarket, whether then they thought of any more interest or right in the kingdom than this, whether they did think that they should have as great interest in parliament-men as freeholders had, or whether from the beginning we did not engage for the liberty of parliaments, and that we should be concluded by the laws that such did make. Unless somebody did make you believe before now that you should have an equal interest in the kingdom; unless somebody do make that to be believed, there is no reason to blame men for leading so far as they have done; and if any man was far enough from such an apprehension, that man has not been deceived.

And truly I shall say but this word more for myself in this business, because the whole objection seems to be pressed to me and maintained by me. I will not arrogate that I was the first man that put the army upon the thought either of successive parliaments or more equal parliaments. Yet there are some here that know who they were put us upon that foundation of liberty, of putting a period to this Parliament, that we might have successive parliaments, and that there might be a more equal distribution of elections. [T]Here are many here that know who were the first movers of that business in the army. I shall not arrogate that but I can argue this with a clear conscience: that no man has prosecuted that with more earnestness, and that will stand to that interest more than I do, of having parliaments successive and not perpetual, and the distributions of it; but, notwithstanding, my opinion stands good, that it ought to be a distribution amongst the fixed and settled people of this nation; it's more prudent and safe, and more upon this ground of right for it. Now it is the fundamental constitution of this kingdom; and that which you take away for matter of wilfulness, notwithstanding this universal conclusion, that 'all inhabitants' as it stands. Though I must declare that I cannot yet be satisfied, yet for my part I shall acquiesce; I will not make a distraction in this army, though I have a property in being one of those that should be an elector; though I have an interest in the birthright, yet I will rather lose that birthright, and that interest, than I will make it my business, if I see but the generality of those whom I have reason to think honest men, and conscientious men, and godly men, to carry them another way. I will not oppose, though I be not satisfied to join with them, and I desire. I am agreed with you, if you insist upon a more equal distribution of elections; I will agree with you, not only to dispute for it, but to fight for it, and contend for it. Thus far I shall agree with you. On the other hand, those who differ their terms, I will not agree with you except you go further. Thus far I can go with you; I will go with you as far as I can. If you will appoint a committee to consider of some of that, so as you preserve the equitable part of that constitution, who are like to be freemen, and men not given up to the wills of others, keeping to the latitude which is the equity of constitutions, I will go with you as far as I can. I will sit down. I will not make any disturbance among you.

Rainsborough: If I do not speak my soul and conscience, I do think that there is not an objection made, but that it has been answered; but the speeches are so long. I am sorry for some passion and some reflections, and I could wish where it is most taken the cause had not been given. It is a fundamental constitution of the kingdom; there I would fain know, whether the choice of burgesses in corporations should not be altered.

The end wherefore I speak is only this: you think we shall be worse than we are, if we come to a conclusion by a vote. If it be put to the question, we shall all know one another's mind; if it be determined, and the resolutions known, we shall take such a course as to put it in execution. This gentleman says, if he cannot go he will sit still. He thinks he has a full liberty; we think we have not. There is a great deal of difference between us two. If a man has all he does desire, but I think I have nothing at all of what I fought for, I do not think the argument holds that I must desist as well as he.

Petty: The rich would very unwillingly be concluded by the poor. And there is as much reason, and indeed no reason, that the rich should conclude the poor as the poor the rich; but there should be an equal share in both. I understood your engagement was that you would use all your endeavours for the liberties of the people, that they should be secured. If there is a constitution, that the people are not free, that should be annulled. That constitution which is now set up is a constitution of forty shillings a year, but this constitution does not make people free.

Cromwell: Here's the mistake: whether that's the better constitution in that paper, or that which is. But if you will go upon such a ground as that is, although a better constitution was offered for the removing of the worse, yet some gentlemen are resolved to stick to the worse. There might be a great deal of prejudice upon such an apprehension. I think you are by this time satisfied, that it is a clear mistake; for it is a dispute whether or not this be better, nay, whether it be not destructive to the kingdom.

Petty: I desire to speak one word to this business, because I do not know whether my occasions will suffer me to attend it any longer. The great reason that I have heard is the constitution of the kingdom, the utmost constitution of it; and if we destroy this constitution, there is no property. I suppose that if constitutions should tie up all men in this nature, it were very dangerous.

Ireton: First, the thing itself were dangerous, if it were settled to destroy property. But I say the principle that leads to this is destructive to property; for by the same reason that you will alter this constitution, merely that there's a greater constitution by nature, by the same reason, by the law of nature, there is a greater liberty to the use of other men's goods, which that property bars you of. And I would fain have any man show me why I should destroy that liberty which the freeholders and burghers in corporations have in choosing burgesses, that which if you take away, you leave no constitution; and this because there is a greater freedom due to me from some men by the law of nature. More than that, I should take another man's goods because the law of nature does allow me.

Rainsborough: I would grant something that the Commissary-General says. But whether this be a just property, the property says that forty shillings a year enables a man to elect; if it were stated to that, nothing would conduce so much whether some men do agree or no.

Captain Rolfe: I conceive that, as we are met here, there are one or two things mainly to be prosecuted by us; that is especially unity, preservation of unity in the army, and so likewise to put ourselves into a capacity thereby to do good to the kingdom. And therefore I shall desire that there may be a tender consideration had of that which is so much urged, in that of an equal, as well as of a free representative. I shall desire that a medium, or some thoughts of a composure in relation to servants, or to foreigners, or such others such as shall be agreed upon. I say then, I conceive, excepting those, there may be a very equitable sense [p]resented to us from that offer in our own declarations wherein we do offer the common good of all, unless they have made any shipwreck or loss of it.

[*Lieutenant*] *Chillenden:* In the beginning of this discourse there were overtures made of imminent danger. This way we have taken this afternoon is not the way to prevent it. I should humbly move that we should put a speedy end to this business, and that not only to this main question of the paper, but also according to the Lieutenant-General's motion, that a committee may be chosen seriously to consider the things in that paper, and compare them with divers things in our declarations and engagements. That so as we have all professed, to lay down ourselves before God, if we take this course of debating upon one question a whole afternoon, if the danger be so near as it is supposed, it were the ready way to bring us into it. That things may be put into a speedy dispatch.

Clarke: I presume that the great stick here is this: that if every one shall have his property, it does bereave the kingdom of its principal fundamental constitution, that it has. I presume that all people and all nations whatsoever have a liberty and power to alter and change their constitutions, if they find them to be weak and infirm. Now if the people of England shall find this weakness in their constitution, they may change it if they please. Another thing is this: if the light of nature be only in this, it may destroy the property which every man can call his own. The reason is this, because this principle and light of nature does give all men their own: as for example the clothes upon my back because they are not another man's. If every man has this property of election to choose those whom you fear may beget inconveniencies, I do not conceive that anything may be so nicely and precisely done, but that it may admit of inconveniency. If it be in that wherein it is now, there may those inconveniences rise from them. For my part I know nothing but the want of love in it, and the sword must decide it. I shall desire before the question be stated, it may be moderated as for foreigners.

Sir Hardress Waller: This was that I was saying: I confess I have not spoken yet, and I was willing to be silent, having heard so many speak, that I might learn to. But it is not easy for us to say when this dispute will have an end; but I think it is easy to say when the kingdom will have an end. But if we do not breathe out ourselves, we shall be kicked and spurned of all the world. I would fain know how far the question will decide it; for certainly we must not expect, while we have tabernacles here, to be all of one mind. If it be to be decided by a question, and that all parties are satisfied in that, I think the sooner you hasten to it the better. If otherwise, we shall needlessly discover our dividing opinion, which as long as it may be avoided I desire it may. Therefore I desire to have a period.

Audley: I chanced to speak a word or two. Truly there was more offence taken at it. For my part I spoke against every man living, not only against yourself and the Commissary, but every man that would dispute till we have our throats cut. I profess, if so be there were none but you and the Commissary-General alone to maintain that argument, I would die in any place in England, in asserting that it is the right of every free-born man to elect, according to the rule, *quod omnibus spectat, ab omnibus tractari debet,* that which concerns all ought to be debated by all. He knew no reason why that law should oblige when he himself had no finger in appointing the lawgiver, and therefore I desire I may not lie in any prejudice before your persons.

Captain Bishop: You have met here this day to see if God would show you any way wherein you might jointly preserve the kingdom from its destruction, which you all apprehend to be at the door. God is pleased not to come in to you. There is a gentleman, Mr Saltmarsh, did desire what he has wrote may be read to the General Council. If God do manifest anything by him, I think it ought to be heard.

Ireton: That you will alter that constitution from a better to a worse, from a just to a thing that is less just in [is] my apprehension; and I will not repeat the reasons of that, but refer to what I have declared before. To me, if there were nothing but this, that there is a constitution, and that constitution which is the very last constitution, which if you take away you leave nothing of constitution, and consequently nothing of right or property. I would not go to alter that, though a man could propound that which in some respects might be better, unless it could be demonstrated to me that this were unlawful, or that this were destructive. Truly, therefore, I say for my part, to go on a sudden to make such a limitation as that in general, if you do extend the latitude that any man shall have a voice in election who has not that interest in this kingdom that is permanent and fixed, who has not that interest upon which he may have his freedom in this kingdom without dependence, you will put it into the hands of men to choose, of men to preserve their liberty who will give it away.

I have a thing put into my heart which I cannot but speak. I profess I am afraid, that if we from such apprehensions as these are, of an imaginable right of nature, opposite to constitution, if we will contend and hazard the breaking of peace upon this enlargement of that business, I am confident our discontent and dissatisfaction, in that if ever they do well they do in this, if there be anything at all that is a foundation of liberty, it is this: that those who shall choose the lawmakers shall be men freed from dependence upon others. I think if we, from imaginations and conceits, will go about to hazard the peace of the kingdom, to alter the constitution in such a point, I am afraid we shall find the hand of God will follow it; we shall see that that liberty, which we so much talk of and contended for, shall be nothing at all by this our contending for it, by putting it into the hands of those men that will give it away when they have it.

Cromwell: If we should go about to alter these things, I do not think that we are bound to fight for every particular proposition. Servants, while servants, are not included. Then you agree that he that receives alms is to be excluded.

Lieutenant-Colonel Reade: I suppose it's concluded by all, that the choosing of representatives is a privilege; now I see no reason why any man that is a native ought to be excluded that privilege, unless from voluntary servitude.

Petty: I conceive the reason why we would exclude apprentices, or servants, or those that take alms, it is because they depend upon the will of other men and should be afraid to displease. For servants and apprentices, they are included in their masters, and so for those that receive alms from door to door; but if there be any general way taken for those that are not bound, it would do well.

[*Mr*] *Everard:* I being sent from the agents of five regiments with an answer unto a writing, the committee was very desirous to inquire into the depth of our intentions. Those things that they had there manifested in the paper, I declared it was the Lieutenant-General's desire for an understanding with us, and what I did understand as a particular person, I did declare, and were presuming those things I did declare did tend to unity. And if so, you will let it appear by coming unto us. We have gone thus far: we have had two or three meetings to declare and hold forth what it is we stand upon, the principles of unity and freedom. We have declared in what we conceive these principles do lie: I shall not name them all because they are known unto you. Now in the progress of these disputes and debates we find that the time spends, and no question but our adversaries are harder at work than we are. I heard that there were meetings (but I had no such testimony as I could take hold of), that there are meetings daily and contrivances against us. Now for our parts I hope you will not say all is yours, but we have nakedly and freely unbosomed ourselves unto you. Though these things have startled many at the first view, yet we find there is good hopes; we have fixed our resolutions, and we are determined, and we want nothing but that only God will direct us to what is just and right. But I understand that all these debates, if we shall agree upon any one thing: this is our freedom; this is our liberty; this liberty and freedom we are debarred of, and we are bereaved of all those comforts. In case we should find half a hundred of these, yet the main business is how we should find them, and how we should come by them. Is there any liberty that we find ourselves deprived of? If we have grievances let us see who are the hindrances, and when we have pitched upon that way. I conceive I speak humbly in this one thing as a particular person, that I conceive myself, that these delays, these disputes, will prove little encouragement. As it was told me by these gentlemen, that he had great jealousies that we would not come to the trial of our spirits and that perhaps there might happen another design in hand. I said to his Honour again, if they would not come to the light, I would judge they had the works of darkness in hand. Now as they told me again on the other hand, when it was questioned by Colonel Hewson, they told me: 'These gentlemen, not naming any particular persons, they will hold you in hand, and keep you in debate and dispute till you and we come all to ruin.' Now I stood as a moderator between these things. When I heard the Lieutenant-General speak I was marvellously taken up with the plainness of the carriage. I said, I will bring them to you. You shall see if their hearts be so; for my part I see nothing but plainness and uprightness of heart made manifest unto you. I will not judge, nor draw any long discourses upon our disputes this day. We may differ in one thing, that you conceive this debating and disputation will do the work; we must put ourselves into the former privileges which we want.

Waller: I think this gentleman has dealt very ingenuously and plainly with us. I pray God we may do so too, and for one I will do it. I think our disputings will not do the thing. I think if we do make it our resolution that we do hold it forth to all powers, Parliament or King, or whoever they are, to let them know that these are our rights, and if we have them not we must get them the best way we can.

Cromwell: I think you say very well; and my friend at my back, he tells me that [there] are great fears abroad; and they talk of some things such as are not only specious to take a great many people with, but real and substantial, and such as are comprehensive of that that has the good of the kingdom in it. And truly if there be never so much desire of carrying on these things, never so much desire of conjunction, yet if there be not liberty of speech to come to a right understanding of things, I think it shall be all one as if there were no desire at all to meet. And I may say it with truth, that I verily believe there is as much reality and heartiness amongst us, to come to a right understanding, and to accord with that that has the settlement of the kingdom in it, though when it comes to particulars we may differ in the way. Yet I know nothing but that every honest man will go as far as his conscience will let him; and he that will go farther, I think he will fall back. And I think, when that principle is written in the hearts of us, and when there is not hypocrisy in our dealings, we must all of us resolve upon this, that 'tis God that persuades the heart. If there be a doubt of sincerity, it's the devil that created that effect; and 'tis God that gives uprightness. And I hope with such an heart that we have all met withal; if we have not, God find him out that came without it; for my part I do it.

Ireton: When you have done this according to the number of inhabitants, do you think it is not very variable? I would have us fall to something that is practicable, with as little pains and dissatisfaction as may be. I remember that in the proposals that went out in the name of the army, it is propounded as a rule to be distributed according to the rates that the counties bear in the kingdom. And remember then you have a rule, and though this be not a rule of exactness, for the number will change every day; yet there was something of equality in it, and it was a certain rule, where all are agreed; and therefore we should come to some settling. Now I do not understand wherein the advantage does lie from a sudden danger upon a thing that will continue so long, and will continue so uncertain as this is.

Waller: 'Tis thought there's imminent danger; I hope to God we shall be so ready to agree for the future that we shall all agree for the present to rise as one man if the danger be such, for it is an impossibility to have a remedy in this. The paper says that this Parliament is to continue a year, but will the great burden of the people be ever satisfied with papers? You eat and feed upon them. I shall be glad that there be not any present danger; if not that you will think of some way to ease the burden, that we may take a course, and [deal with this] when we have satisfied the people that we do really intend the good of the kingdom. Otherwise, if the four Evangelists were here, and lay free quarter upon them, they will not believe you.

Colonel Rainsborough: Moved, that the army might be called to a rendezvous, and things settled. . . .

4 Gerrard Winstanley, *A New-Yeers Gift for the Parliament and Armie* (1650)

. . . .

The Curse and Blessing that is in Mankind

In the beginning of time, the spirit of universal love appeared to be the father of all things. The creation of fire, water, earth, and air came out of him, and is his clothing. Love is the Word. The creation is the house or garden in which this one spirit has taken up his seat, and in which he manifests himself. For if ever love be seen or known, he appears either in the inward feeling within your hearts, loving all with tender love; or else appears towards you from outward objects, as from other men, or other creatures.

There are two earths in which the spirit of love declares himself. First, the living earth, called mankind: this is the creation or the living soul. And when this spirit of universal love rules king therein, this earth is then in peace, and is grown up to the perfection of a man anointed. But when self or particular love rules, which is called the sin covetousness, then this earth is brought into bondage, and sorrow fills all places. This is the dark side of the cloud, in which there is no true peace.

Secondly, in the great body of earth in which all creatures subsist the spirit of universal love appears to preserve his creation in peace: for universal love unites not only mankind into an oneness, but unites all other creatures into a sweet harmony of willingness to preserve mankind. And this spirit of love spread abroad is the same spirit of love that is supreme in man: and this is the righteous man.

But when covetousness or particular love began to work, then not only mankind was divided amongst themselves, but all creatures were divided, and enmity rose up amongst them, setting one against another; and this power is the wicked man. Mark him where you see him, which is the murderer, and must be cast out.

Well, in the beginning universal love appeared to be the father of all things (though self-love in our experience rules in man first), and as he made mankind to be the lord of the earth, so he made the earth to be a common treasury of livelihood to whole mankind without respect of persons; and for all other creatures likewise that were to proceed from the earth.

Mankind is the chief creature, and the spirit of universal love in his branches is the lord of all the earth; and this spirit in man unfolds himself in light and darkness. His face is called the universal power of love. His back parts is called the selfish power. Or thus: the one is called the son of bondage, which causes shame, the other is called the son of freedom, which brings peace and honour. These two strive in the womb of the earth, which shall come forth first, and which shall rule. The fleshy man has got the start; but the other will prove the stronger and cast him out with honour.

While this spirit of lordship, in the last daytime of mankind, was universal love and righteousness, leading every single branch of mankind to do to another as he would be done unto, then everything was in peace, and there was a sweet communion of love in the creation. And as the spirit was a common treasury of unity and peace within, so the earth was a common treasury of delight for the preservation of their bodies without, so that there was nothing but peace upon the face of the whole earth.

This was man's estate before the Fall, or the day-time of mankind; for since the time that our Bibles speak of Adam to this day is about six thousand years: and this time has been the night-time of mankind. And Esau's time was about midnight when in one of his words he cries, 'Watchman, what of the night? Watchman, what of the night?' The seventh thousand year, which is now dawning, will be the rising of the son of universal love again, and of the dispersing of the night or darkness; for as the night and day, sun and moon, has their exchanges, so has these two powers, called sons of God, in mankind. And in this age wherein we now live is the expiring of the selfish power, and the rising up of the blessing which has been spoke of in all ages, but now appearing like lightning from east to west, casting out the mystery of iniquity, or self-power, by the word of his mouth, and by the brightness of his coming, and so bringing peace.

So that, as there is the power of light, which is universal love, called the blessing, which brings peace; so there is the power of darkness, which is particular or self-love, and this is called the curse, for it brings sorrow. And while this rules king in the earth, as it does at this day visibly through the whole earth, few are saved, that is, few enter into rest and peace; for this power has filled all places with his stinking self-seeking government, and troubles everybody.

As there is light and darkness, day and night, clouds and clearness moving upon the face of the great earth; and as there is earth and waters in the great world which runs round, so mankind is called sometimes earth, sometimes waters; and as the sun in the skies moves upon the great earth and makes that fruitful which seemed dead while the sun is under the dark, cloudy winter quarter: even so the son of universal love, who is the spirit and power of universal freedom, he moves upon the living waters – mankind – and makes him, who all the dark time past was a chaos of confusion, lying under types, shadows, ceremonies, forms, customs, ordinances, and heaps of waste words, under which the spirit of truth lay buried, now to enlighten, to worship in spirit and truth, and to bring forth fruit of righteousness in action.

In our present experience the darkness, or self-love, goes before, and light, or universal love, follows after; the flesh runs hasty and quick, and loses himself in unrational excessive action; the true spirit comes slowly after, and takes the crown. Darkness and bondage does oppress liberty and light; and the power of universal love appears most sweet and full of glory when the power of self-love or covetousness has tortured the creation (mankind) with bitter tyranny: for this is the dragon or murderer that must be cast out before the creation (man) can sing Hallelujah in peace.

So, then, you may see that the innocency, light, and purity of mankind is this, when the spirit of universal love lives in him, and he lives in love, enjoying the sweet union and communion of spirit, each with other. When they enjoy the sweet delight of the unity of one spirit, and the free content of the fruits and crops of this outward earth, upon which their bodies stand: this was called the man's innocency, or pleasure in the Garden before his Fall, or the daytime of mankind; and day is more glorious than night; and greater honour to be a child of the day than of the night.

The fall of mankind, or his darkness, is this: When that son of universal love, which was the seed out of which the creation sprang forth, did begin to go behind the cloud of flesh, and to let self-seeking flesh, which would needs be a god, stand alone by his imaginary light: as we see, while the sun is in the skies a man sees and knows his footsteps, but when the sun is set under the cloud of the dark night, then he imagines his way, and oft-times stumbles and falls. Even so, when universal love shines in his glory in mankind, he stumbles not, he walks in the light, because the light is in him; but when the light within withdraws and lets flesh stand alone, flesh, that is, the selfish power, will not wait in peace, and acknowledge himself in a loss and in darkness, till the sun rise again, but will fain be a God, and calls his weakness strength. And though there appears nothing but deformity, yet he would have it called beauty; and because his inward power is not suitable to his outward profession, he is tormented. He is a saint without, but a devil within. But if thou wouldst have peace, act as thou art, show thyself abroad in action what thou art secretly; but when thou beginst to imagine a content and happiness to thyself, by thy hypocritical self-invention, then thou art tormented, or shalt be.

And by this imagination mankind tears himself in pieces; as one of your colonels of the army said to me, that the Diggers did work upon George Hill for no other end but to draw a company of people into arms; and says our knavery is found out, because it takes not that effect.

Truly, thou Colonel, I tell thee, thy knavish imagination is thereby discovered, which hinders the effecting of that freedom which by oath and covenant thou hast engaged to maintain: for my part, and the rest, we had no such thought. We abhor fighting for freedom: it is acting of the curse and lifting him up higher; and do thou uphold it by the sword, we will not. We will conquer by love and patience, or else we count it no freedom. Freedom gotten by the sword is an established bondage to some part or other of the creation, and this we have declared publicly enough. Therefore thy imagination told thee a lie, and will deceive thee in a greater matter, if love does not kill him. Victory that is gotten by the sword is a victory that slaves get one over another; and hereby men of the basest spirit (says Daniel) are set to rule. But victory obtained by love is a victory for a king.

But by this you may see what a liar imagination is, and how he makes hate, and tears the creation in pieces; for after that self-love has subdued others under him, then imagination studies how to keep himself up and keep others down.

This is your very inward principle, O ye present powers of England. You do not study how to advance universal love. If you did, it would appear in action. But imagination and self-love mightily disquiets your mind, and makes you call up all the powers of darkness to come forth and help to set the crown upon the head of self, which is that kingly power you have oathed and vowed against, and yet uphold it in your hands.

Imagination begets covetousness after pleasure, honour, and riches. Covetousness begets fear lest others should cross them in their design, or else begets a fear of want, and this makes a man to draw the creatures to him by hook or crook, and to please the strongest side, looking what others do, not minding what himself does. Like some of your great officers, that told me that we Diggers took away other men's property from them by digging upon the common; yet they have taken mine and other men's property of money (got by honest labour) in taxes and free-quarter to advance themselves, and not allow us that they promised us; for it [is] this beam in their own eyes they cannot see.

This fear begets hypocrisy, subtlety, envy and hardness of heart, which makes a man to break all promises and engagements, and to seek to save himself in others' ruin, and to suppress and oppress everyone that does not say as he says and do as he does. And this hardness of heart begets pride and security, and this begets luxury and lust of the flesh, and this runs into all excess with greediness, and being in discontent against any that crosses his pleasure, till his heart become fully like the heart of a beast, as it is apparent in some at this day.

And thus by the power of self-love being advanced by the covetous sword against universal love, that power of darkness rises up to perfection in mankind, and so he makes one branch to tear and devour another by divisions, evil surmisings, envious fightings, and killing, and by oppressing the meek in spirit, by unrighteous laws, or by his self-will managing good laws unrighteously, as corrupt judges know how to do it, and think none sees them, whereby part of mankind has freedom, and another part is cast out, and thrown under bondage.

And all this falling out or quarrelling among mankind is about the earth, who shall and who shall not enjoy it, when indeed it is the portion of everyone and ought not to be striven for, nor bought, nor sold, whereby some are hedged in, and other hedged out. For better not to have had a body, than to be debarred the fruit of the earth to feed and clothe it. And if everyone did but quietly enjoy the earth for food and raiment, there would be no wars, prisons, nor gallows, and this action which man calls theft would be no sin, for universal love never made it a sin, but the power of covetousness made that a sin, and made laws to punish it, though he himself live in that sin in a higher manner than he [whom he] hangs or punishes. Those very men that punish others for theft do thieve and rob, as judges and lawyers that take bribes, or that takes their clients' money, and through neglect lose their case. Parliament and army lives in theft, when as they take the commoners' money and free-quarter and tell them what they do is to make England a free commonwealth, and yet all they do is to make the gentry free, and leaves the commoners under bondage still; or else why do you send your soldiers to beat a few naked spademen off from digging the commons for a livelihood, why do you not let the oppressed go free? Have they not bought it of you by their moneys and blood as well as the gentry, and will not you make good your contract? Well, he that made the earth for us as well as for you will set us free, though you will not. When will the veil of darkness be drawn off your faces? Will you not be wise, O ye rulers?

Well, this power of darkness is man's fall, or the night-time of mankind. But universal love has declared that he will rise again, and he himself who is the seed will bruise that serpent's head and reconcile mankind to himself again, and restore him to that innocency and peace which he is fallen from. When this son arises in more strength, and appears to be the saviour indeed, he will then make mankind to be all of one heart and one mind, and make the earth to be a common treasury, though for the present in outward view there is nothing but darkness and confusion upon the face of the earth, mankind.

When self-love began to arise in the earth, then man began to fall; this is Adam or the power of darkness that stops up the waters and well-springs of life, or the clouds that hide the son of righteousness from man. This Adam, or dark power, was small at the first, but he is risen to great strength, and the whole earth is now filled with him, as Isaiah says, 'Darkness has covered the earth', mankind. For let any that has eyes look either to them above or them below, and they see darkness or the devil rule, and this curse destroys the earth. The creation sits like Rachel, sighing, mourning, and groaning under his oppressing power, and will not be comforted because they see no saviour to appear for their deliverance.

Indeed there are many saviours in word, but none in deed, and these great false Christs and false prophets does destroy the creation under the colour of saving it, and the people sees them not, but looks upon them as saviours, calling others false Christs and false prophets that speak against them.

The first false Christ that promises to save the creation is covetous kingly power, resting in the hand of one man, or in the hand of many, but this power saves but part, and holds another part of the creation in bondage, and any government that rules by swordly power does so throughout all lands; therefore he is a false Christ, and no true saviour.

The preaching clergy, or universative power, promises to save the creation declaratively, but he is a false Christ; he says and does not, Pharisee-like, but will force people to maintain him from the earth by their labours for his sayings, by the laws of the kingly power. He says some are elected to salvation and others are reprobated; he puts some into heaven, thrusts others into hell never to come out, and so he is not a universal saviour. That is no salvation to the creation, mankind, while any part groans for the true saviour. When he comes he will wipe away all tears. He comes not to destroy any but to save all.

Then the power of the lawyers: he says he will save the creation, and this false Christ proves the greatest devourer and tearer of the creation of any other, for while he carries burdened men from one court to another promising to save them, he at last saves himself and destroys others, and laughs at others' loss, and throws men further from peace than he found them before he meddled with them. Well, from the bailiff to the judge, these are the creations of this Egyptian taskmaster, and no burden of cheating like to it, for he promises justice, but behold nothing but oppression is in his hands.

Then, next, the art of buying and selling promises to save the creation and bring it into peace, but this is a hypocritical, false, cheating Christ too, for hereby covetous self-love with his flattering tongue cheats honest-hearted ones, and casts them under tyranny, and gets the fullness of the earth into his hands, and locks it up in chests and barns from others, and says this is righteous, and God gave it him. But, thou cheater, thou liest. God, the king of righteousness, gave it thee not. He bids thee sell all that thou hast and give to the poor; he does not bid thee lock it up from the poor. Therefore, thou trading art, thou art no true saviour neither, but a devil. Thou savest part, and destroyest another part; yea, and afterwards destroyest that part which at first thou seemedst to save.

Now all these saviours are linked together: if one truly fall all must fall. They all promise to save the creation, but destruction is in their hands and actions. They all seek to set up self and particular power, and so to save but part of the creation, for every one are destroyers of universal love. They that sit in these seats would be called men of public spirits, but truly you are all selfish, you are afraid to own public-spirited men; nay, you are ashamed, some of you, to be seen walking or talking with true public-spirited men, called Levellers.

But well, yet there is a promise of restoration and salvation to the whole creation, and this must be wrought by a power contrary to darkness, for all those former saviours lie under darkness, nay are branches of the power of darkness itself, and darkness can never kill darkness; but now the true saviour must be a power quite opposite to darkness. And this is the power of universal love, light and righteousness. And if ever the creation be wholly saved, this power must be the saviour, for this is the blessing, and he will declare himself the true saviour indeed. The other is but the curse; this is the true restorer, the true seed with us. As he arises and spreads, he will bruise the serpent's head in everyone, and bring peace to all, and wipe away all tears from the creation, and make a thorough salvation of it through the whole earth; and leave none under bondage.

This is the sun of righteousness. When he arises, he disperses darkness, and will make all ashamed that had hands in promoting of the other false saviours' power. But I must leave this and speak a little more of the present condition mankind lies under, and this is darkness or the fall, and in this estate ignorant enslaved flesh would ever run round in it, and never come out, but counts it freedom. But they that know the burden of this estate hunger after freedom.

This darkness is twofold. First inward, and that is the power of darkness in his branches, as covetousness, envy, pride, hypocrisy, self-love. This is the curse in man, and this darkness has, and yet does cover the earth. This power would be as God, and makes one to rule over another, and he is so proud that he will hasten to rule though he kill others for honour. And this is he that stirs up wars and dissension, and thereby he destroys himself.

Secondly, this inward power sets one against another, and so fills the earth with dark actions, and causes some part of mankind to tread others under foot and puts them into bondage. And they that act this power calls it the power and ordinance of God. Which is true: It is God indeed, but it is the god of the world, the prince of darkness, not the king of righteousness. It is the power of the beast, who is limited to rule for a time, times, and dividing of time. And England is under that dividing of time; therefore, I hope, England shall be the tenth part of the city confusion that shall fall from the beast first. And this dark power or imaginary covetousness has raised a platform of oppression in the creation, under which the creation groans, and waits to be delivered. And it is raised thus:

First this dark power within makes everyone to love himself with others' loss, just like beasts of the field; and this made mankind to begin to loathe or envy each other's freedom and peace, and hereby the union and communion of love within is broken, and mankind is fallen from it. Then this inward covetousness makes mankind to fight one against another for the earth, and breaks communion in that, and falls from content therein likewise, and everyone seeks to save himself, to take the earth to himself, but none or few seeks the things of Christ, or of universal love.

Nay, covetousness is such a god that where he rules he would have all the earth to himself, and he would have all to be his servants. And his heart swells most against community, calling community a thief that takes other men's rights and property from them. But community will force nothing from anyone, but take what is given in love of that which others have wrought for. But no man yet has bestowed any labour upon the commons that lies waste; therefore the Diggers does take no man's proper goods from them in so doing. But those that by force spoils their labours takes their proper goods from them, which is the fruit of their own labours.

Well, you see how covetousness would have all the earth to himself, though he let it lie waste. He stirs up divisions among men, and makes parties fight against parties, and all is but for this: who shall enjoy the earth, and live in honour and ease and rule over others. And the stronger party always rules over the weaker party. And hence came in kingly power to rule outwardly, dividing between members of that one body, mankind, giving the earth to that party called gentry, who are the successors of some late conquests, and denying the earth to the poor commoners, who are the successors of some that were last conquered.

So that by kingly power the earth is divided as it is now at this day: but as the Scriptures say, kings were given for a plague to the people, not a blessing. And I believe the nations have found this very true, to their great sorrow. And the way to cast out kingly power again is not to cast them out by the sword, for this does but set him in more power, and removes him from a weaker to a stronger hand: but the only way to cast him out is for the people to leave him to himself, to forsake fighting and all oppression, and to live in love one towards another. This power of love is the true saviour.

The party that is called a king was but the head of an army, and he and his army having conquered, shuts the conquered out of the earth, and will not suffer them to enjoy it, but as a servant and slave to him; and by this power the creation is divided, and part are cast into bondage. So that the best you can say of kingly power that rules by the sword is this: he is a murderer and a thief. And by this power the earth is thus divided: the several nations of the earth where kings rule are the several situation of such grand thieves and murderers, that will rule over others by the sword, upholding a forced property, which is the curse, and persecuting the community of love, which is Christ the blessing.

And under them they have their chief favourites or nearest soldiers in office to himself, and to these he allows the greatest portion of the earth, every one his part, called a lordship. And next to them the inferior officers or soldiers are appointed out lesser parcels of the earth, called freeholders, paying no slavish rent or homage to any, but only acknowledgement that the king is their general or head still.

And these lords of manors and freeholders, having thus seated themselves in the earth by taking other men's proper labours from them by the sword, are appointed by the king as watchmen, that if any of the conquered slaves seek to plant the common waste earth without their leave, they may be known and beaten off. So that the god from whom they claim title to the land as proper to them, shutting out others, was covetousness, the murderer, the swordly power, that great red dragon who is called the god of the world.

But the king of righteousness, who is universal love, who is the Lord God Almighty, bidding every one do as they would be done by, made the earth for all, without respect of person, and shuts out none from enjoying a peaceable livelihood that has a body; therefore they that build upon the power of the sword, upholding covetous property, are enemies to the law of righteousness, which is, Love your enemies, do as you would be done by.

But one of your officers told me: 'What', says he, 'if we grant to every one to have the land of England in common, we do not only destroy property, but we do that which is not practised in any nation in the world.'

I answered: It was true. Property came in, you see, by the sword, therefore the curse; for the murderer brought it in, and upholds him by his power, and it makes a division in the creation, casting many under bondage; therefore it is not the blessing, or the promised seed.

And what other lands do, England is not to take [as a] pattern; for England (as well as other lands) has lain under the power of that beast, kingly property. But now England is the first of nations that is upon the point of reforming; and if England must be the tenth part of the city, Babylon, that falls off from the beast first, and would have that honour, he must cheerfully (and dally no longer) cast out kingly covetous property, and set the crown upon Christ's head, who is the universal love or free community, and so be the leader of that happy restoration to all the nations of the world. And if England refuse, some other nation may be chosen before him, and England then shall lose his crown, for if ever the creation be restored, this is the way, which lies in this twofold power:

First, community of mankind, which is comprised in the unity of [the] spirit of love, which is called Christ in you, or the law written in the heart, leading mankind into all truth, and to be of one heart and one mind.

Second is community of the earth, for the quiet livelihood in food and raiment without using force, or restraining one another. These two communities, or rather one in two branches, is that true levelling which Christ will work at his more glorious appearance; for Jesus Christ, the saviour of all men, is the greatest, first, and truest Leveller that ever was spoke of in the world.

Therefore, you rulers of England, be not ashamed nor afraid of Levellers. Hate them not. Christ comes to you riding upon these clouds. Look not upon other lands to be your pattern. All lands in the world lie under darkness. So does England yet, though the nearest to light and freedom of any other; therefore let no other land take your crown. You have set Christ upon his throne in England by your promises, engagements, oaths, and two acts of parliament: the one to cast out kingly power, the other to make England a free commonwealth. Put all these into sincere action, and you shall see the work is done, and you with others shall sing Hallelujah to him that sits upon the throne, and to the Lamb for evermore.

But if you do not, the Lamb shall show himself a lion, and tear you in pieces for your most abominable, dissembling hypocrisy, and give your land to a people who better deserves it.

I have varied a little, therefore I will return to what I was speaking. I told you that the murdering and thieving sword has found out a platform of tyrannical government, called kingly power. First, here is the king, the head of the murdering power, or great red dragon. Then there are lords of manors, who have the greatest circuit of land, because the next in power to the head. Then there are freeholders, that took the particular enclosures which they found in a land when they conquered it, and had turned out those that had bestowed labour upon it by force of the sword, in the field, or else by sequestering afterwards. These several parcels of land are called freehold land because the enjoyers or their ancestors were soldiers, and helped the king to conquer; and if any of latter years came to buy these freeholds with money got by trading, it does not alter the title of the conquest, for evidences are made in the king's name, to remove the freeholds so bought from one man's hand to another.

But now copyhold lands are parcels hedged in, and taken out of the common waste land, since the conquest, acknowledging homage, fines, and heriots to the lord of that manor or circuit in which that enclosure by his leave is made: this homage still confirms the power of the conquests.

The lords of manors acknowledged homage to the king in that court of wards which you have taken away to ease yourselves. But the copyholders you will have to acknowledge homage to lords of manors still; and is not this partiality? O you rulers, make the poor as free to the earth as yourselves, and honour righteousness.

Now for the drawing in of the people to yield obedience to this platform of kingly tyrannical power, to which people are made subject through fear: The kingly power sets up a preaching clergy to draw the people by insinuating words to conform hereunto, and for their pains kingly power gives them the tithes. And when the kingly power has any design to lift up himself higher, then the clergy is to preach up that design, as of late in our wars the preachers most commonly in their sermons meddled with little but state matters. And then if people seem to deny tithes, then the kingly power by his laws does force the people to pay them. So that there is a confederacy between the clergy and the great red dragon: the sheep of Christ shall never fare well so long as the wolf or red dragon pays the shepherd their wages.

Then, next after this, the kingly power sets up a law and rule of government to walk by: and here justice is pretended, but the full strength of the law is to uphold the conquering sword, and to preserve his son, property. Therefore if anyone steal, this law will hang them; and this they say is of God. And so this kingly power has power over the lives and labours of men at his pleasure; for though they say the law does punish, yet, indeed, that law is but the strength, life, and marrow of the kingly power, upholding the conquest still, hedging some into the earth, hedging out others; giving the earth to some, and denying the earth to others, which is contrary to the law of righteousness, who made the earth at first as free for one as for another.

Yea, that kingly power in the laws appointed the conquered poor to work for them that possess the land, for three pence and four pence a day, and if any refused, they were to be imprisoned; and if any walked abegging and had no dwelling, he was to be whipped; and all was to force the slaves to work for them that had taken their property of their labours from them by the sword, as the laws of England are yet extant, and truly most laws are but to enslave the poor to the rich, and so they uphold the conquest, and are laws of the great red dragon.

And at this very day poor people are forced to work in some places for four, five, and six pence a day; in other places for eight, ten, and twelve pence a day; for such small prizes, now corn being dear, that their earnings cannot find them bread for their family; and yet if they steal for maintenance the murdering law will hang them; when as lawyers, judges, and court officers can take bribes by wholesale to remove one man's property by that law into another man's hands: and is not this worse thievery than the poor man's that steals for want? Well, this shows that if this be law, it is not the law of righteousness; it is a murderer, it is the law of covetousness and self-love. And this law that frights people and forces people to obey it by prisons, whips and gallows is the very kingdom of the devil, and darkness, which the creation groans under at this day.

And if any poor enslaved man that dares not steal begins to mourn under that bondage and says, 'We that work most have least comfort in the earth, and they that work not at all, enjoy all'; contrary to the scripture, which says, 'The poor and the meek shall inherit the earth', presently the tithing priest stops his mouth with a slam, and tells him that is meant of the inward satisfaction of mind which the poor shall have, though they enjoy nothing at all. And so, poor creatures, it is true, they have some ease thereby, and made to wait with patience, while the kingly power swims in fullness, and laughs at the others' misery; as a poor Cavalier gentlewoman presented a paper to the general in my sight, who looked upon the woman with a tender countenance; but a brisk little man and two or three more colonels pulled back the paper, not suffering the general to receive it, and laughed at the woman, who answered them again: 'I thought', said she, 'you had not sat in the seat of the scornful.' This was done in Whitehall, upon the 12 of December, 1649.

Well, all that I shall say to these men that will enjoy the earth in reality, and tell others they must enjoy it in conceit, surely your judgement from the Most High sleeps not; the law of retaliation, like for like, laughing for laughing, may be your portion. For my part, I was always against the Cavaliers' cause; yet their persons are part of the creation as well as you, and many of them may enter into peace before some of you scoffing Ishmaelites. I am sure you act contrary to the Scripture, which bids you, 'Love your enemies, and do as you would be done by', and this Scripture you say you own. Why then do you not practise it? And do to the Cavaliers as the prophet Elijah bid the king of Israel do to his enemies whom he had taken prisoners: 'Set bread and water', says he, 'before them, and send them to their master in peace?'

Come, make peace with the Cavaliers your enemies, and let the oppressed go free, and let them have a livelihood, and love your enemies, and do to them as you would have had them do unto you if they had conquered you. Well, let them go in peace, and let love wear the crown.

For I tell you and your preachers, that Scripture which says 'the poor shall inherit the earth' is really and materially to be fulfilled, for the earth is to be restored from the bondage of sword property, and it is to become a common treasury in reality to whole mankind, for this is the work of the true saviour to do, who is the true and faithful Leveller, even the spirit and power of universal love, that is now rising to spread himself in the whole creation, who is the blessing, and will spread as far as the curse had spread to take it off, and cast him out, and who will set the creation in peace.

This powerful saviour will not set up his kingdom nor rule his creation with sword and fighting, as some think and fear, for he has declared to you long since that they that take the sword to save themselves shall perish with the sword.

But this shall be the way of his conquest, even as in the days of the beast the whole world wondered after him, set him up, and was subject to him, and did persecute universal love, and made war against him and his saints, and overcame them for a time. Even so the spirit of love and blessing shall arise and spread in mankind like the sun, from east to west, and by his inward power of love, light and righteousness, shall let mankind see the abomination of the swordly, kingly power, and shall [c]lothe themselves in dust and ashes, in that they have owned and upheld him so long, and shall fall off from him, loathe him and leave him.

And this shall be your misery, O you covetous oppressing tyrants of the earth, not only you great self-seeking powers of England, but you powers of all the world. The people shall all fall off from you, and you shall fall on a sudden like a great tree that is undermined at the root. And you powers of England, you cannot say another day, but you had warning, this falling off is begun already, divisions shall tear and torture you, till you submit to community. O come in, come in to righteousness, that you may find peace.

You, or some of you, hate the name Leveller, and the chiefest of you are afraid and ashamed to own a Leveller, and you laugh and jeer at them. Well, laugh out, poor blind souls, the people and common soldiers both lets you alone, but they laugh in their hearts at you, and yet desire that you did know the things that concern your peace.

The time is very near that the people generally shall loathe and be ashamed of your kingly power, in your preaching, in your laws, in your councils, as now you are ashamed of the Levellers. I tell you, Jesus Christ, who is that powerful spirit of love, is the head Leveller, and 'as he is lifted up, he will draw all men after him', and leave you naked and bare, and make you ashamed in yourselves. His appearance will be with power; therefore kiss the Son, O ye rulers of the earth, lest his anger fall upon you. The wounds of conscience within you from him shall be sharper than the wounds made by your sword. He shook heaven and earth when Moses' law was cast out, but he will shake heaven and earth now to purpose much more, and nothing shall stand but what is lovely. Be wise, scorn not the counsel of the poor, lest you be whipped with your own rod.

This great Leveller, Christ our King of righteousness in us, shall cause men to beat their swords into ploughshares, and spears into pruning hooks, and nations shall learn war no more, and everyone shall delight to let each other enjoy the pleasures of the earth, and shall hold each other no more in bondage. Then what will become of your power? Truly he must be cast out for a murderer; and I pity you for the torment your spirit must go through, if you be not fore-armed, as you are abundantly forewarned from all places; but I look upon you as part of the creation who must be restored, and the spirit may give you wisdom to foresee a danger, as he has admonished divers of your rank already to leave those high places, and to lie quiet and wait for the breakings forth of the powerful day of the Lord. Farewell once more. Let Israel go free!

NOTES ON THE TEXTS

1. *England's Miserie and Remedie* (1645): This is the first time this text has been reprinted.

2. *An Agreement of the People:* Published in 1648 and reprinted in the various editions of J. Rushworth, *Historical Collections* (1659–1701, 1703–8, 1718, 1721–2). It has frequently been reprinted in twentieth-century collections of Civil War and Leveller documents. The standard edition of the Leveller party-political programmes is D. M. Wolfe (ed.), *Leveller Manifestoes of the Puritan Revolution* (New York, 1949, 1967).

3. *The Putney Debates:* The debates were first published, from the papers of William Clarke, secretary to the Army Council, by C. Firth in 1891. They were re-edited by A. S. P. Woodhouse in *Puritanism and Liberty* (1938). Selections have appeared elsewhere: e.g. C. Blitzer (ed.), *The Commonwealth of England, 1641–60* (New York, 1963). An extensive section, including the passage reprinted here, was printed by G. E. Aylmer in *The Levellers in the English Revolution* (London, 1975). Aylmer's edition is based on a re-examination of the manuscript, and I have used it as the basis of my own text, while making modifications to the punctuation and adding conjectural emendations in square brackets.

4. Winstanley, *A New-Yeers Gift:* Published in 1650, and reprinted both in G. H. Sabine (ed.), *The Works of Gerrard Winstanley* (Ithaca, 1941; New York, 1965) and C. Hill (ed.), *The Law of Freedom and Other Writings of Gerrard Winstanley* (Harmondsworth, 1973; Cambridge, 1983). The section of the pamphlet not reprinted here is to be found in H. Erskine-Hill and G. Storey (eds.), *Revolutionary Prose of the English Civil War* (Cambridge, 1983).

FURTHER READING

There has been a great deal published on the Levellers in the last few decades. The best overall surveys are H. N. Brailsford, *The Levellers* (London, 1961); J. Frank, *The Levellers* (Cambridge, Mass., 1955; New York, 1966); and G. E. Aylmer, *The Levellers in the English Revolution* (London, 1975).

An important debate on whether the Levellers were or were not democrats was sparked off by C. B. Macpherson, *The Political Theory of Possessive Individualism* (Oxford, 1962). For effective criticism of Macpherson's view, see J. C. Davis, 'The Levellers and Democracy', in C. Webster (ed.), *The Intellectual Revolution of the Seventeenth Century* (London, 1974); K. Thomas, 'The Levellers and the Franchise', in G. E. Aylmer (ed.), *The Interregnum* (London, 1972); A. L. Morton, 'Leveller Democracy: Fact or Myth?', in his collection of essays, *The World of the Ranters* (London, 1970); I. Hampsher-Monk, 'The Political Theory of the Levellers', *Political Studies*, XXIV (1976), pp. 397–422; and C. Thompson, 'Maximillian Petty and the Putney Debate on the Franchise', *Past and Present*, no. 88 (1980), pp. 63–9. Macpherson has defended his view in *Democratic Theory* (Oxford, 1972).

In a number of studies M. A. Kishlansky has sought to minimize the radicalism of the army in 1647 and the organizational coherence of the Levellers: 'The Army and the Levellers: The Roads to Putney', *Historical Journal*, XXII (1979), pp. 795–824; 'Consensus Politics and the Structure of Debate at Putney', *Journal of British Studies*, XX (1981), pp. 50–69; 'What Happened at Ware?', *Historical Journal*, XXV (1982), pp. 827–39. The view that there was a Leveller organization is defended by N. Carlin, 'Leveller Organisation in London', *Historical Journal*, XXVII (1984), pp. 955–60. On the nature of support for the Levellers, M. Tolmie, *The Triumph of the Saints* (Cambridge, 1977), and B. S. Manning, *The English People and the English Revolution* (London, 1976), are particularly helpful.

The intellectual origins of the Levellers' views constitute a third vexed question. J. C. Davis has argued that their political views derive from their religious beliefs in 'The Levellers and Christianity', in B. S. Manning (ed.), *Religion, Politics and the English Civil War* (London, 1973). They are placed in a context of natural-rights theories by R. Tuck in *Natural Rights Theories* (Cambridge, 1979). But they were evidently a political movement uniting individuals with different intellectual backgrounds. It is arguable that a crucial radicalizing influence came from Walwyn and Sexby, whose intellectual debts were in large part humanist.

Winstanley has also been the subject of much debate. The best starting-point is C. Hill's introduction to his edition of *The Law of Freedom* (Harmondsworth, 1973). The view expressed by Hill there, and earlier in *The World Turned Upside Down* (London, 1972), that Winstanley's communism involved a rejection rather than an expression of Christianity, was attacked by a number of scholars: J. C. Davis, 'Gerrard Winstanley and the Restoration of True Magistracy', *Past and Present*, no. 70 (1976), pp.

76–93; G. Juretic, 'Digger No Millenarian', *Journal of the History of Ideas*, XXXVI (1975), pp. 263–80; L. Mulligan, J. K. Graham and A. Richards, 'Winstanley: A Case for the Man as He Said He was', *The Journal of Ecclesiastical History*, XXVIII (1977), pp. 57–75. Hill replied to his critics in a fine study of 'The Religion of Gerrard Winstanley', *Past and Present*, Supplement no. 5 (1978), and the debate with Mulligan, Graham and Richards continued in *Past and Present*, no. 89 (1980), pp. 144–51. Two other recent discussions of Winstanley are T. W. Hayes, *Winstanley the Digger: A Literary Analysis* (Cambridge, Mass., 1979), and J. C. Davis, *Utopia and the Ideal Society* (Cambridge, 1981). The most recent biographical information is in J. D. Alsop, 'Gerrard Winstanley: Religion and Respectability', *Historical Journal*, XXVIII (1985), pp. 705–9.

CHAPTER SIX

USURPATION AND TYRANNICIDE

1 Anthony Ascham, *Of the Confusions and Revolutions of Goverments* (1649)

Ascham (*c.* 1618–50), of a distinguished gentry family, sided with Parliament on the outbreak of the Civil War. In 1647 he was made tutor to the captive James, Duke of York (later James II). He is reputed to have played a part in drawing up charges against the king in 1649. He then became the Commonwealth's agent in Hamburg, and in 1650 was sent to Spain to serve there as the Commonwealth's ambassador. He was assassinated in Madrid before he had time to present his credentials.

During the period 1648–50 he published two versions *Of the Confusions and Revolutions of Goverments* and a defence of that work, along with at least two anonymous tracts, all of them in defence of the new regime. By linking acceptance of the new government directly to a recognition of self-interest, Ascham attacked established notions of legitimacy as deriving from tradition and divine sanction. His secular approach to politics is comparable to that of Hobbes, who published *Leviathan* in defence of the government in whose service Ascham died. Hobbes took easily to *de factoism* as he was naturally and self-consciously timorous; it may be wondered whether Ascham, who was fully aware of the dangers of his assignment in Spain, was as sceptical and cynical as he chose to appear in his writings.

2 Robert Sanderson, *A Resolution of Conscience* (1649)

Sanderson (1587–1663) had been appointed chaplain to Charles I, on Laud's recommendation, in 1631. Charles I was said to have declared: 'I carry my ears to hear other preachers, but I carry my conscience to hear Dr Sanderson.' He was appointed Regius Professor of Divinity at Oxford in 1642, was ousted by Parliament in 1648, and reinstated in 1660. In that year he was also made bishop of Lincoln.

His 1646 lectures on the nature and obligation of oaths were published in 1647, and translated into English at the king's command in 1655. His 1647 lectures on the obligation of conscience were published posthumously in 1678. Sanderson's professional interest in moral philosophy and theology, his academic standing and his close ties with the king made it natural that in 1650 he should be regarded as an authoritative judge of how far royalists could make their accommodation with the new regime.

3   *An Act for the Abolishing the Kingly Office* (17 March 1649)

On 16 November 1648 the officers of the New Model Army called for the trial of the king, 'the capital and grand author of our troubles', whom they held responsible for the unnecessary bloodshed of the second Civil War. When Parliament failed to act it was 'purged' by the army in December 1648 in order to create a majority for the king's trial, which took place in January, and led inevitably to the king's execution on 30 January 1649. Parliament claimed to have brought the king before a court of law, but to do so it had had to set aside the king himself and the House of Lords, and to establish a court which had no legal precedent. Such actions led naturally to the establishment of a republic, an end result that hardly any member of the Rump Parliament would have desired when first elected, and that none would have predicted. There is, therefore, some difficulty in accepting at face value their sudden avowal of republican principles. By and large republicanism was adopted out of expediency not conviction, and Charles I was executed, not because monarchy itself was unpopular, but because he personally was distrusted.

Charles himself believed he was the victim of the novel doctrine that the people should govern themselves. On the scaffold he said: 'For the people, and truly I desire their liberty and freedom as much as anybody whatsoever; but I must tell you that their liberty and freedom consists in having of government those laws by which their life and their goods may be most their own. It is not having share in government, sirs; that is nothing pertaining to them.'

4   *An Act for Subscribing the Engagement* (2 January 1650)

Parliament had conducted the Civil War on the claim that it represented the people. But a majority even of those members of Parliament who had stayed in London (those who sided with the king having joined him in Oxford before the first Civil War) had opposed the execution of the king, an execution which was unpopular with the people at large. The Rump Parliament therefore had to take rigorous measures to ensure acceptance of its authority. Only those who engaged to be loyal to it were to be allowed to hold offices under government control or to do business in the courts of law.

Since 1648 the legitimacy of the new regime had been the subject of urgent debate. That debate was given new urgency by the test of conscience which the Engagement represented for all those who felt ties of loyalty to the old order.

5   *Some Scruples of Conscience Which a Godly Minister in Lancashire Did Entertain* (1650)

The identity of the godly minister is unknown, and we know about his scruples only because one of the supporters of the Engagement Oath selected his letter as a pithy statement of the opposition case he had taken it upon himself to refute. And indeed this letter brings out clearly just how difficult it was to find arguments in defence of the new regime, other than the arguments from self-interest and *force majeure* relied on by Ascham.

6   William Allen (i.e. Edward Sexby), *Killing Noe Murder* (1657)

Sexby (*c.* 1616–58) emerged from obscurity in 1647 as an army agitator and Leveller spokesperson. In 1648 he acted as an intermediary between Cromwell and the Levellers, and, having been a private in 1647, he was governor of Portland, Dorset, with the rank of captain, in 1649. In 1650 he was ordered to Scotland, and was court-martialled there the next year. It seems likely that the charges against him were trumped up and, although he was cashiered, he rapidly reappears as an agent of the Council of State sent to La Rochelle and Bordeaux to assist the Frondeurs. Sexby was never one to act merely as the tool of others, and in France he translated and published the final version of the Agreement of the People. By 1653 his alienation from the

Cromwellian regime was complete and he was engaged in subversive plotting, making contact with the royalists in 1655. In September 1656 and January 1657 several attempts to assassinate Cromwell were made by Miles Sindercombe, acting on Sexby's instructions. When Sindercombe was captured Sexby returned to England, both to try his own hand at assassination, and to distribute copies of *Killing Noe Murder*, which he had written, possibly with the assistance of Silius Titus, a royalist. He was captured in July 1657, and died in the Tower, January 1658.

1 Anthony Ascham, *Of the Confusions and Revolutions of Goverments* (1649)

The First Part

. . . .

Chapter VII: Concerning the Parties (Just or Unjust) Which, by the Variety of Success in Civil War, Command Us and Our Subsistence, and Reduce Us to These Extreme Necessities: Whether for a Justifiable Obedience to Them It be Necessary for Us to Assure Ourselves that Those Parties Have a Justifiable Cause of War, or Right to Command Us?

(1) Wherefore difficult for us to assure our consciences in the points of right?
(2) Whether prescription make a right?
(3) A cause of war depending on a matter of fact, not a certain way of confirming us that we lawfully obey.
(4) War for dominion and for possession.

These things being thus stated concerning our own persons, the lawfulness and transcendent right which we have both by God and nature in ourselves and that which is ours, yea, and in case of extreme misery in other things also, above all those rights, privileges and obligations which others may pretend upon us; I may the easilier descend now into the bottom of the question, and speak to the many parties, whether just or unjust, who, by the variety of success, may one after another command us and our estates, and in both reduce us to the forementioned extreme necessity. In which condition or confusion, the question is : What is lawful for us to do?

I find that most here seek to satisfy their scruples in searching, first, whether those parties have lawful power over us or no. That, so finding the lawfulness of their right, they may be easier assured of the lawfulness of their own obedience. Secondly, in examining the cause of their wars, whether it be justifiable or no. They supposing that if the cause be bad, all effects which have any dependence on it must needs be so too. I conceive that these two considerations serve only to add to the perplexity of a man's conscience, and are not necessary at all for us to be informed of.

(1) As for the point of right, it is a thing always doubtful, and would ever be disputable in all kingdoms if those governors who are

in possession should freely permit all men to examine their titles *ab origine*, and those large pretended rights which they exercise over the people. And though this party's title may be as good or as [a] little better than that party's, yet a man in conscience may still doubt whether he have *limpidum titulum*, a just title or clear right, especially in those things which are constituted by so various and equivocal a principle as the will of man is.

Besides, most governors on purpose take away from us the means of discovering how they come by their rights, insomuch that though they may really have that right to which they pretend, yet through the ignorance we are in of what may be omitted in their history, either through fear, flattery, negligence, or ignorance, it is dangerous for us, upon probable human grounds only, to swear their infallible right, as is shown in the following treatise of oaths. Upon this ground Tacitus says well, *Tiberii Caiique et Claudii ac Neronis res, florentibus ipsis, ob metum falsae, postquam occiderant recentibus odiis compositae sunt*. And if the party's rights be but one as good as another's, then his is the best who has possession, which generally is the strongest title that princes have. A whole kingdom may be laid waste before it can be infallibly informed concerning the party's true rights, which they require men to die for, and to avow by oath.

(2) As for prescription of long time, every man's conscience is not satisfied that that, added to possession, makes a true right. This we know, that it conduces much to public quiet; but the Canonists maintain it against the Civilians, that prescription upon an unjust beginning *et ex titulo inhabili* does by its continuance of time increase and not diminish the injustice and faultiness of the act. For the lapse of time cannot change the morality of an act. It is no plea in divinity to argue the prescription which sin has on us as an excuse. A lie is almost as old as truth, but there is no prescription against God and truth. This concerning the point of right.

(3) As for the point of fact on which we would ground matter of right, or a justifiable case, viz. that such or such things have been done, or plotted, or advised, therefore the other party may lawfully do this or that, that we know is without end, and ever is perplexed and difficult to have perfect intelligence of, especially such as a man may safely venture his own life, or take away another's, upon it. Wherefore, if we may reasonably doubt of the point of right (which yet is a more clear and uniform thing), then we may be more reasonably perplexed in the story of fact, which

depends on so many accidents, so various circumstances, both in its principle (the will), in its existence, and in evidence for the infallible knowledge of it.

From hence, therefore, I conclude that we may in this great case ease ourselves of this vast perplexity in examining whether or no the invading party have a just title or case, or no. Or whether he have a juster than he whom he opposes. But here I desire to be rightly understood, for I affirm this, not as if the knowledge of all this were not very convenient, and much to be desired, but that (as it is almost impossible for us to have, so) it is not necessary for us to search after; except in one case, which comes not out of the historical occasion of this discourse: viz. in assisting to the beginning of a war. These negatives show only what we need not ground our consciences on, in order to a lawful obedience; but it must be a positive and a clear principle which we must ground on, if we would be warranted of a just submission to the orders of one who commands us perhaps unjustly. For it is a matter which concerns the misery of others who never did us wrong.

(4) There is a war for dominion, and a war for possession. If it be for dominion, we may contribute our money, arms and oaths to the expelling perhaps of an innocent family. If it be for possession (which is the worst), then it is for the slavery of thousands of innocent families. And before either can be compassed, we may assure ourselves that thousands may be as innocently killed by the means of them who contribute to the strengthening of an unjust party. But because I state this question in a war already formed, and actually introduced upon the people, therefore in answer to this positive demand, I as positively say, *that for a justifiable obedience, it is best, and enough, for us to consider whether the invading party have us and the means of our subsistence in his possession, or no.*

. . . .

The Second Part

Chapter I: Whether a Man May Lawfully and with a Good Conscience Pay Taxes to an Unjust Party during the War?

(1) What was meant by paying tribute to Caesar.
(2) In what case a man at the beginning of a war may contribute to it, though he finds not its cause good.
(3) The manner of a levy.

(4) We cannot properly scruple at that which is out of our power.

(5) Of the condition of those who live upon frontiers.

(6) What liberty have we, when the right governor declares that he will not have us pay anything to the invading party? Likewise, whether any law but that which derives immediately from God does indispensably oblige the conscience?

In the first part the ground for all the particular questions in this is laid and treated generally; but here we come to closer and more particular proofs: and, first, of tribute and taxes.

There are many who, not finding this liberty in their consciences, unnecessarily choose rather to give their bodies up to restraint, and to abandon their whole means of subsistence in this world, both for themselves and their children, which ought not fondly to be done, unless we would be worse than infidels, as St Paul says.

Objection: They object that they know not whether the moneys they give may not furnish to the destruction of many innocents, and perhaps of the just magistrate himself; that though a man may give away his own as he pleases, yet not in this case, when it is to the prejudice of another, etc.

They who thus scruple are in conscience obliged thus to suffer, because they have not faith to do otherwise. But the question now to be examined is whether these be necessary scruples in themselves, and such as admit of no exception or liberty? Perhaps upon examination we may find these scruples to be like scandals, whereof some are rather taken than given. And therefore, to state the question aright, I shall paraphrase a little upon another question which was propounded to our Saviour. It may possibly appear to be the same with this, though propounded with more subtlety and malice.

The Scribes and Pharisees sought two ways to entrap our Saviour. One was, as if he had blasphemously taught a new religion, and a new God, viz. himself. They hoped the people would be provoked to stone him for this, according to the 13 of Deuteronomy. The other was to bring his actions into the compass of treason, as if he could not lead great multitudes after him without traitorous designs. But this gin failed too, because the multitude which followed him was always ready to defend him. However, when he was at Jerusalem, where the Roman troops and praetor were, they thought they had him sure by propounding this subtlety to him:

(1) 'Is it lawful for us to pay tribute to Caesar?' Which was as

much as to say: 'We who are descended from Abraham, and are the peculiar people to whom God has given the large privileges of the earth, at home to bathe ourselves in rivers of milk and honey, to have full barns and many children, yea, that God himself will be adored in no other place of the world, but at this our Jerusalem, and that abroad we should triumph over the barbarous and uncircumcised world by virtue of that militia which he never ordered for any but ourselves: how are we then in duty or conscience to submit now to the ordinances of the uncircumcised Roman? Or what right can he have to exercise supreme jurisdiction over us, the privileged seed of Abraham, by levying taxes on our estates and land, which God himself laid out for us? By which means he holds this very temple in slavery, and insults over our consciences and religion by defiling our very sacrifices with the mixture of impure blood; which, as they are the price of our souls, and a tribute far above Caesar's, payable in no other place but this temple, which God himself built, so our blood ought not to seem too dear to be sacrificed for the liberty of these altars. And though the Roman state could pretend right, yet what can this Caesar pretend? Every man's conscience knows that it was but the other day he usurped over the senate, in which resides the true jurisdiction of Rome. And if that were otherwise, yet how can he pretend to a title, unless poison be a pedigree, or violent usurpation a just election, by which he who is but the greatest thief in the world would pass now for the most sovereign and legislative prince? How then are we in conscience obliged to pay tribute to this Caesar?'

Though these lawyers thought in their consciences that they were not truly obliged to pay it, and that our Saviour likewise, as a Jew, thought so too, yet they supposed he durst not say so much in the crowd, nor yet deny it by shifting it off in silence, lest the Roman officers should apprehend him. But when our Saviour showed them Caesar's face upon the coin, and bade them render to Caesar that which was Caesar's, and to God that which was God's, his answer ran quite otherwise. Not, as some would have it, that by a subtlety he answered nothing to the point proposed, for then the sense of the whole text would sound very ill in such terms, viz. that if there be anything due to Caesar, pay him it, and if anything be due from you to God, then pay it likewise. This had been a weakening of God's right for Caesar's, and to have left a desperate doubting in a necessary truth. 'Tis beyond all cavil that our Saviour's opinion was positive for paying of tribute to that very Caesar, because *de facto* he did pay it. And the plain reason of it appears evident in this his answer: Caesar's face was upon the coin; that is to say, Caesar, by conquest, was in possession of that coin by possessing the place where he obliged them to take it: coining of money being one prerogative of sovereign power.

And now to answer more particularly to the forementioned objections at the beginning of the chapter:

(a) In the first place, I distinguish between *perferre et inferre bellum*: the one is active, and properly at the beginning of a war, and in a place where yet no war is, and where its cause only and not its effects can be considered. In this case everything ought to be very clear for warrant of a man's conscience, because of the calamities which he helps to introduce, and is in some manner author of. The other is passive, and there where war or the power of war is actually formed, which is the cause of this discourse.

(b) Secondly, I distinguish betwixt that which cannot be had, nor the value of it, unless I actually give it; and that which may be taken whether I contribute it or no. In the force of this second distinction lies the reason wherefore I have so much examined the nature of possession in the former part. To apply all this to the objections, I say that if a man scruple, he may not *inferre bellum* by any act which may be properly his own; I say, *properly his own*.

(2) Because, though war be not yet actually formed in a place, yet a scrupling conscience which likes not the cause may be excused in contributing to it in this one case, viz. if some number of men able to take what they ask demand (with an armed power) the payment of a certain sum to be employed in war, then in such a case the man of whom we speak may pay it as a ransom for his life, or give it as a man does his purse when he is surprised in the highway. The reason is, because to this man it is as much as if the whole country were possessed by an armed power.

(3) The manner of the levy is here principally to be considered. For if the person taxed be not for the time in the full possession of him whose cause he scruples at, and that he have not a probable fear of extreme danger, nor as probable assurance that, without his help, the thing demanded, nor its value, can be taken from him, then there's little excuse remains for the act, because the said act (which his conscience dislikes) participates more of action than of passion.

But in the case of this discourse, where a man is fully possessed by an unjust invading power (from whom whole countries cannot possibly fly, nor make away all their goods and estates), there, I say, a man's paying of taxes is no gift, which if proved takes away the master scruple. Let us judge of this by that case which we all grant: if a man fall into the hands of many desperate thieves who assault him for his money, though with his own hand he put his purse into their hands, yet the law calls not that a gift, nor excuses the thief from taking it, but all contrary.

(4) By this it's apparent what a groundless scruple it is for a man thus taxed to say, 'He knows not to what evil they may employ the money so put into their desperate hands.' For this supposes a gift, and a man's proper voluntary act: of which indeed he is always to be scrupulous, because it proceeds from that principle which is totally in his own power, whereas other men's actions are as far out of our power as winds and tempests are; to which two, as we contribute nothing, so we cannot properly be scrupulous in our consciences concerning their bad effects.

For further proof I might aptly reflect on those arguments which were discussed at the beginning of the first part, concerning the transcendent right which we naturally have in the preservation of ourselves, and of those things without which we cannot be preserved. As also on the high privilege of extreme necessity, nature itself being more intent to the preservation of particular than of public bodies, which are made out of particulars, and, as much as may be, for the particular ends and preservation of each singular, no man obliging himself to any particular society of this or that country without the consideration of self-preservation, according to the right of the more general society of mankind.

(5) Thus much concerning those who are fully possessed by the unjust invading power. Now I shall speak to the condition of those who live upon frontiers; whose condition is more ticklish and deplorable because they are not fully possessed nor taken into the line of either party. These live, as it were, in the suburbs of a kingdom, and enjoy not the security or privileges of others. Though they can owe true allegiance but to one party, yet they may lawfully contribute to both. For though they be but partly possessed by one and by the other, in respect of their sudden abandoning them, yet both parties have the power of destroying them wholly. Wherefore those former

reasons which justify those fully possessed do also acquit the payments of these, for their condition here is more calamitous, seeing they are really but tenants at will, exposed to a perpetual alarm, and that both parties wound one the other only through their sides.

(6)   The last consideration in this scruple is of the wills of them whom we acknowledge our lawful governors, viz.

Objection: When they declare to us that they will not permit us to pay anything to their enemies.

Answer: To this I answer that the declared wills of governors cannot make all those our acts sins when we obey that power which, against our wills (as much as against theirs, and it may be with more of our misery), has divested them of the power of their rights, and deprived us of the comfort of their governments.

Question: I would not here willingly dispute whether any law but that which derives immediately from God does indispensably oblige the conscience. For there is but one lawgiver who can save and destroy the soul for the observation or violation of laws, and this is God, who therefore has the sole power of obliging consciences to laws as the lord of them, through his creating, governing, and moving them. Ephesians 33: 22; James 4: 12: 'There is one lawgiver who is able to save and destroy: who art thou that judgest another?' Princes cannot by their commands change the nature of [the] human condition, which is subject naturally to those forementioned changes: this were to pretend to a power of obliging us to moral impossibilities and repugnancies in the reason of government. And though those political commands were as laws, yet they ought not to be made, nor to be obliging, but according to the legislative rule, which is *cum sensu humanae imbecillitatis*. This is that which usually is called the presumptive will of a governor, or the mind of a law. For in extreme necessity it is to be presumed that both their wills recede from the rigour of what they have declared, rather than, by holding to that which is their supposed right, introduce certain misery and confusion, without receiving any benefit thereby themselves.

Neither are such commands without their sense and profit, though they be not positively obeyed. For thereby governors show to all the world that they renounce no part of their right, no though it be there where they cannot exercise any part of their just power. Secondly, they may thereby help to retard their subjects from being forward in giving admittance to their enemies, or in being actively assisting to them, but rather to themselves. Besides which sense there can be no sense; for if they mean by those commands that they would not have their enemies strengthened or advantaged by them, and withal mean that they would not that their subjects should submit themselves at all to those usurpers, though it were then when they and all their subsistence are absolutely possessed by them, I say then that these are commands which dash against themselves, and the one countermands the other. For if they refuse to submit in such a case, then they do that which advantages their enemies, because at that time they will take all, whereas in case of submission they ask but a part. In all wars there are always some by whose disaffections enemies gain more than by their compliance, just as physicians do by distempers. Though after variety of successes the just governors should recover that place which so submitted to the power of their enemies, and for that reason should punish those who were pliable to extreme necessity, yet it follows not upon that, that they who so conformed sinned, or did that which was absolutely unlawful. For we know reason of state oft calls for sacrifices where there is no fault to expiate. Ostracism and jealousy make away those who are known to deserve most: *in republica idem est nimium et nihil mereri.* But in right (which is the term of this question) the just governor ought to look upon them as more unfortunate than faulty. And perhaps in equity he ought to consider that the original fault of all might possibly be on his part, God sometimes punishing the people for the prince, and sometimes the prince for the people. But of this more shall be said in the following treatises of new allegiance and of opposite oaths.

Chapter II: Whether We May Lawfully Serve an Unjust Party in Our Persons or No?

The answer to this question is very present, and negative, for here action is required to an end which our consciences allow not. Our estates are separate from us, and therefore may be had without us, or without our wills. But our persons are ourselves, and cannot be had nor act without us, and therefore a man has not the same liberty in the one as in the other.

But yet there are two cases wherein a man may lawfully serve an unjust party in his person.

First, when it is in order to a just and necessary action which concerns not the opposing of the just party at all, but only our own necessary preservation. In which case we consider the unjust governor abstractively, not as a governor but as a man. Suppose the case were such that if the lawful governor himself were with us, he would probably command us the same thing; and though perhaps he would not command it, yet we might lawfully put ourselves into that action against his will, as if the Turk, or any other common enemy, should invade those provinces which the unjust party has divested the just of. For such an enemy would deprive one as well as the other. Wherefore, betwixt two unjust parties, it's better to follow him who is in possession, especially if his government be probably better for the society and religion of mankind. And as for the just government, he must consider that such actions are not so much *contra* as *praeter suam voluntatem*.

The second case relates in some manner to the opposing of our lawful magistrate, but not by a direct intention. For example, when we see much cruelty exercised upon the continuance of a war, and probable ruin of those places where the armies seek one another, then if the said armies fall into our quarters, and we be summoned to assist the unlawful party, we may then arm ourselves, not for him, but for ourselves, not in any regard of the cause of the war, but of its effects, which are destruction of life, or of livelihood. In this case nature helps us to put on our arms, and shows us the way to the place where we may redeem our lives, and find a remedy, though it be in our very disease.

Objection: But is not this to do evil to advance our own good, to cut the throats of those whose innocency our own consciences absolves? Can our extravagant fears warrant us to take away other men's real rights? *Cato habet potius qua exeat* (Seneca): brave men would rather die. How then can any of this be lawful?

Answer: Here I confess lies the knot of the scruple, but yet by the third treatise of *The Lawfulness of Some Wars*, chapter 2, it is clearly evinced, 'How innocents may be innocently killed', and this objection goes no further, nay, not so far as that which is there cleared. For children and babes could never threaten us with the sad effects of war, yet we see how they may be innocently destroyed by the course of war. For nature commends me to myself for my own protection and preservation, and that not as if I had not that right of defending myself unless they were first faulty who threaten me the danger. For

though they fight *bona fide* on their side, and ignorantly take me
to be another kind of person than I really am, just as men pas-
sionately distracted (and in dreams) use to do, yet I am not for
this reason obliged to desert myself, nor to suffer all which they
prepare, probably, to inflict upon me: no more than I am when
another man's irrational beast or dog falls upon me with fury or
mistake. Governors of men are like keepers of beasts; every man,
as he is an animal, participating half with the brute: *alterum nobis
cum diis, alterum cum bestiis commune est*, says Sallust. When an irregular passion breaks out in a state, an irrational beast has broke
out of his grate or cave, and puts the keeper to a great deal of
trouble, and those whom he meets with in the way in a great deal
of danger. If he invade anyone he may be killed, whether the
keeper please or no, although whilst he kept his cave quietly he
might not be stirred without his permission. It is a known case
that if a man unjustly assault another, and be slain in the act by
the other, this other shall not suffer for it.

But in this case we must be certain of two things: first, that we
have tried all other means of saving ourselves and our livelihood.
Secondly, that we enter not the army with an offensive mind, but *cum
moderamine inculpatae tutelae*: not with a direct design to kill, but rather
to frighten, weaken, and to drive away the cruel enemy. Before we
may strike, we must see our danger imminent, and *in ipso pene puncto*.
Then it is that we may *occupare facinus*, prevent our own deaths by
the invaders' deaths. For when lives are to be lost, then the possession
which we have of our own is to be preferred by us before our
enemies' lives.

The rule of defence is very difficult because on every hand it is
full of circumstances: yet a point in moral actions, even as in mech-
anical ([though] not in Euclidean geometry), is not without some
breadth. Hence the law says *potentia proxima actui, pro ipso actu
habetur*. The reason wherefore the law, which justly is so favourable
to life, takes that for killing which immediately goes before the blow
is because if it should not be favourable to us before the blow, or act,
it would not be favourable to us at all. A man's life is that which can
be lost but once, and, after that, nothing can make it good to us again,
wherefore we are obliged to a perpetual guard of it, if not for our
own sakes, yet at least for theirs whose life it may be as well as ours.

. . . .

Chapter VIII: Concerning Subjects' Oaths to Their Princes

.   .   .   .

(9) . . . All that which has been cleared above serves mainly to help us in this difficulty, and to lead us to a true harmony of oaths; which some stretch wildly to find even in the very terms of opposite oaths, at least by a secret sense which they say the swearer has liberty to put on them for himself, *quasi propositio mixta ex mentali et vocali esset legitima*; which opinion is in some manner perhaps refuted above.

(10) I conceive but two ways of taking such opposite oaths.

[11] First, when it is in a thing wherein a man may justly presume that the right party for a time releases him of his former oath or duty to him. This is meant during the war only, at which time usurpers never declare their full intentions, because they are not as yet certain whether they shall finally possess the power whereby they may be enabled to make good what they pretend; neither can they foresee what their after-necessities may be.

(11) [i.e. 12] Secondly, a man cannot by oath, or any other way, be obliged further to any power than to do his utmost in the behalf

thereof. And though the oath for the right magistrate be taken in the strictest terms of undergoing death and danger, yet it is to be understood always conditionally, as most promises are, viz. if the action or passion may be for that power's or prince's advantage.

Let us take the case as we see it practised. In an army each man is or may be obliged by oath to lose his life for the prince whose army it is, rather than turn back or avoid any danger. Such an oath is called *sacramentum militare*. This army, after having done its utmost, is beaten, and now the soldiers can do no more for their prince than die, which indeed is to do nothing at all, but to cease from ever doing anything, either for him or for themselves. In these straits, therefore, it is not repugnant to their oath to ask quarter or a new life; and, having taken it, they are bound in a new and a just obligation of fidelity to those whom they were bound to kill [a] few hours before, neither can the prince expect that by virtue of their former oath to him they should kill any in the place where their quarter was given them. They who live under the full power of the unjust party may be said to take quarter, and to be in the same condition with the former, and to have the liberty to oblige themselves to that which the prince may now expect from them, viz. to swear to those under whose power they live that they will not attempt anything against them.

All that this amounts to is that it is *praeter non contra prius iuramentum*; and as the condition which was the ground of this promissory oath is such that it is impossible for a man in it to advance his party's cause, so is it impossible for him to be bound to an impossibility.

(13) *Question:* But what if the usurping power should exact an oath in terms more repugnant to a man's conscience? As that he shall now swear not only not to do anything against him, but to do all he can for him, and besides will have him swear that the very right of the case belongs to him, and not to the other party, as in Edward IV and Richard III's cases, etc.? In answer to this I first say:

Answer: That probably the man called to swear here formerly obliged himself to the other party by oath, but not as if that party positively had a clear right, but that he knew none who had a clearer, and therefore upon the same ground he may neither swear action nor positive right to this party. Though my hand trembles to write further of this case, perhaps as much as his would who should come to swear it *tactis Evangeliis*, yet I find great doctors who have taught us that which favours oaths in such terms: [that they should be understood] not as if they had a positive or grammatical sense in them, but that they require only that we should do nothing contrary to the terms of the oaths, or of their sense, which is as much as to say that though we know not wherein that party's rights positively consist, yet we take our oaths that we will not do anything to weaken his pretensions. Though this sense satisfy not the terms of the oath in their rigour, yet those doctors say it may satisfy the scope of it, beyond which a man is not obliged unless he will himself. For instance, no man could formerly be admitted to the ministry in our Church unless he subscribed first to the articles, liturgy, canons, and jurisdiction of our Church. And though there were a great contradiction betwixt the Arminian, Episcopal and Calvinists' opinions in the matter to be subscribed, yet they all concurred in this, that they might subscribe in this sense: First, that they meant not to disturb the peace of the Church for anything contained either in the articles, canons or episcopal government, whatever their positive opinions about them might be. Secondly, that they thought these in a savable condition who conformed to the strict sense of them. And this they conceived was all that was meant by subscription: witness Master Chillingworth, who [not] only writes so much, but the doctors and divinity professors at Oxford licensed the printing of it, and the Archbishop presented it to his Majesty, so that it passed an avowed sense both in Church and State.

(14)   Were it not, but that usurping princes have so much of the Caesar in them that, being once by their usurpations engaged, they cannot stop till they have acquired all they aimed at (as he did who because Rubicon was passed, *et quia iacta erat alea*, could not rest until he had supped in the Capitol), they would find it a greater security to put a penalty upon those who should question their rights, than to force their subjects to acknowledge their pretensions by this oath. For such an oath may be broken in the very taking of it; and he who scruples not to forfeit his oath for fear or interest will disavow any pretended rights whensoever he shall *stare in lubrice*.

. . . .

2 Robert Sanderson, *A Resolution of Conscience* (1649)

Upon perusal of Mr Ascham's book you left with me, I find not myself in my understanding thereby convinced of the necessity or lawfulness of conforming unto, or complying with, an unjust prevailing power further than I was before persuaded it might be lawful or necessary so to do: viz. as paying taxes and submitting to some other things, in themselves not unlawful, by them imposed or required, such as I had a lawful liberty to have done in the same manner though they had not been so commanded, and seem to me in the conjuncture of present circumstances prudentially necessary to preserve myself or my neighbour from the injuries of those that would be willing to make use of my non-submission, to mine or his ruin, so as it be done with these cautions:

(1) Without violation either of duty to God or any other just obligation that lies upon me by oath, law, or otherwise.

(2) Only in the case of necessity otherwise not to be avoided.

(3) Without any explicit or implicit acknowledgement of the justice and legality of their power. I may submit . . . to the force, but not acknowledge . . . the authority, or by any voluntary act give strength, assistance or countenance thereunto.

(4) Without any prejudice unto the claim of the oppressed party that has a right title, or casting myself into an incapacity of lending him my due and bounden assistance if, in time to come, it may be useful to him towards the recovery of his right.

(5) Where I may reasonably and *bona fide* presume the oppressed power (to whom my obedience is justly due), if he perfectly knew the present condition I am in, together with the exigence and necessity of the present case, and of all circumstances thereof, would give his willing consent to such my conformity and compliance.

So that, upon the whole matter and in short, I conceive I may so far submit unto the impositions, or comply with the persons, of a prevailing usurped power, unjustly commanding things not in themselves unlawful, or make use of their power to protect one from other's injuries, as I may submit unto, comply with, or make use of an highway thief, or robber, when I am fallen into his hands and lie at his mercy.

As for Mr Ascham's *Discourse*, though it be handsomely framed, yet all the strength of it, to my seeming, if he would speak out, would be in plain English these:

(1) That self-preservation is the first and chiefest obligation in the world, to which all other bonds and relations (at least between man and man) must give place.

(2) That no oath, at least no imposed oath, at what terms soever expressed, binds the taker further than he intended to bind himself thereby, and it is presumed that no man intended to bind himself to the prejudice of his own safety.

Two dangerous and desperate principles, which evidently tend:

(1) To the taking away of all Christian fortitude and suffering in a righteous cause.

(2) To the encouraging of daring and ambitious spirits to attempt continued innovations, with this confidence, that if they can by any means (how unjust soever) possess themselves of the supreme power, they ought to be submitted unto.

(3) To the obstructing unto the oppressed party all possible ways and means, without a miracle, of ever recovering that just right of which he shall have been unjustly dispossessed.

And (to omit further instancing): (4) To the bringing in of atheism, with the contempt of God and all religion, whilst every man, by making his own preservation the measure of all his duties and actions, makes himself thereby his own idol.

3 *An Act for the Abolishing the Kingly Office in England and Ireland, and the Dominions thereunto Belonging* (17 March 1649)

Whereas Charles Stuart, late King of England ...[etc.], has by authority derived from Parliament been and is hereby declared to be justly condemned, adjudged to die, and put to death, for many treasons, murders and other heinous offences committed by him, by which judgement he stood and is hereby declared to be attainted of high treason, whereby his issue and posterity, and all others pretending

title under him, are become incapable of the said crowns, or of being
king or queen of the said kingdom or dominions, or either or any of
them; be it therefore enacted and ordained . . . by this present Parliament and by authority thereof, that all the people of England
and Ireland . . ., of what degree or condition soever, are discharged
of all fealty, homage and allegiance which is or shall be pretended to
be due unto any of the issue and posterity of the said late King, or
any claiming under him; and that Charles Stuart, eldest son, and
James called Duke of York, second son, and all other the issue and
posterity of him the said late King, and all and every person and
persons pretending title from, by or under him, are and be disabled
to hold or enjoy the said Crown of England and Ireland. . . .

And whereas it is and has been found by experience that the
office of a king in this nation and Ireland, and to have the power
thereof in any single person, is unnecessary, burdensome and dangerous to the liberty, safety and public interest of the people, and
that for the most part use has been made of the regal power and
prerogative to oppress and impoverish and enslave the subject, and
that usually and naturally any one person in such power makes it his
interest to encroach upon the just freedom and liberty of the people,
and to promote the setting up of their own will and power above the
laws, that so they might enslave these kingdoms to their own lust, be
it therefore enacted and ordained by this present Parliament . . . that
the office of a king in this nation shall not henceforth reside in or be
exercised by any one single person, and that no one person whatsoever shall or may have or hold the office, style, dignity, power or
authority of king of the said kingdoms and dominions, or any of
them, or of the Prince of Wales, any law . . . notwithstanding.

And whereas by the abolition of the kingly office provided for in
this Act a most happy way is made for this nation (if God see it
good) to return to its just and ancient right of being governed by its
own Representatives or National Meetings in Council, from time to
time chosen and entrusted for that purpose by the people; it is
therefore resolved and declared by the Commons assembled in Parliament that they will put a period to the sitting of this present
Parliament, and dissolve the same, so soon as may possibly stand
with the safety of the people that has betrusted them, and with what
is absolutely necessary for the preserving and upholding the
government now settled in the way of a Commonwealth, and that

they will carefully provide for the certain choosing, meeting and sitting of the next and future Representatives with such other circumstances of freedom in choice and equality in distribution of Members to be elected thereunto as shall most conduce to the lasting freedom and good of this Commonwealth.

And it is hereby further enacted and declared, notwithstanding anything contained in this Act, [that] no person or persons of what condition and quality soever, within the Commonwealth of England and Ireland, Dominion of Wales, the Islands of Guernsey and Jersey, and [the] town of Berwick upon Tweed, shall be discharged from the obedience and subjection which he and they owe to the government of this nation, as it is now declared, but all and every of them shall in all things render and perform the same, as of right is due unto the Supreme Authority hereby declared to reside in this and the successive Representatives of the people of this nation, and in them only.

4 *An Act for Subscribing the Engagement* (2 January 1650)

Whereas divers disaffected persons do by sundry ways and means oppose and endeavour to undermine the peace of the nation under this present government, so that unless special care be taken a new war is likely to break forth, for the preventing whereof, and also for the better uniting of this nation, as well against all invasions from abroad as the common enemy at home, and to the end that those which receive benefit and protection from this present government may give assurance of their living quietly and peaceably under the same, and that they will neither directly nor indirectly contrive or practise anything to the disturbance thereof, the Parliament now assembled do enact and ordain . . . that all men whatsoever within the Commonwealth of England, of the age of eighteen years and upwards, shall as is hereafter in this present Act directed take and subscribe this Engagement following, viz., *I do declare and promise that I will be true and faithful to the Commonwealth of England as it is now established, without a king or House of Lords.*

And for the due taking and subscribing thereof, be it further enacted . . . that all and every person and persons that now has, or hereafter shall have, hold or enjoy any place or office of trust or profit, or any place or employment of public trust whatsoever within the said Commonwealth ... that has not formerly taken the said Engagement, by virtue of any order or direction of Parliament, shall take and subscribe the said Engagement at or before the twentieth day of February....

. . . .

And it is further enacted and declared, that all and every person or persons that expects benefit from the courts of justice of this Commonwealth, and that either now are or hereafter shall be plaintiff or plaintiffs, demandant or demandants, in any suit, plaint, bill, action, information, writ, demand, execution, or any other process whatsoever, in any of the courts ... [of justice] within the Commonwealth of England ... shall take and subscribe, and are hereby required to take and subscribe the aforesaid Engagement.... And that it shall and may be lawful for all and every person or persons that are or shall be defendant or defendants, or that are or shall be sued, impleaded, attached, arrested, molested or complained against in any such courts ... from and after the twentieth of April ... to plead, aver, or to move in arrest of judgement ... that the plaintiff or plaintiffs ... have not taken and subscribed the said Engagement....

. . . .

5 Some Scruples of Conscience Which a Godly Minister in Lancashire Did Entertain Against the Taking of the Engagement (1650)

Worthy Sir,

I have delayed writing for a time, in that I have been uncertain whether I should come to London or no. But now at the last resolving to wait a while before I come, do make bold to present my humble thankfulness for your former kindness shown to me. I have been much perplexed in mind concerning the Engagement and still am; by which means my maintenance is, and has for a season been, withheld.

Those scruples which I stick at, I shall make bold to acquaint you with, and they are these:

(1) The late government voted down was in itself lawful, wholesome and good, and no evil ever yet did appear to me in the power, but only in the persons who did exercise that power, which was no sufficient ground of change, and it is not safe to meddle in it.

(2) To that said government I am bound by many solemn and sacred ties, to maintain it in my place, not only in the substance and main parts of it, but also in the form and circumstance thereof. And those said obligations are not merely civil and human, but sacred and divine, and above the absolution of any earthly power.

(3) I conceive it unlawful to engage against the undoubted rights of any man. I suppose there may be found such lawful heirs of the Crown as have not anyways forfeited their rights, and also great interests and privileges which many innocent peers of this land may fairly challenge, which they have not lost by their miscarriage, treason or rebellion.

(4) I cannot be satisfied, but that the liberty of the free-born English is by that means much infringed in this late settlement and constitution: (i) in that many of the innocent and faithful members, the representatives of the people, were at the voting of this new establishment thrust out and debarred the House, which makes it seem rather a combination or confederacy, than a lawful constitution; for if a people have liberty in anything, certainly it is to choose their governors and government; (ii) the subscription is forced upon us, under the penalties of outlawing and fining, so that this power are our absolute lords, which is that heavy yoke that we have feared and fought against.

(5) I consider if men at their inition and instalment will walk so arbitrarily, and domineer with so high a hand, what will they do (may we expect) when they come to a full settlement, by the consent of all the people of the nation?

(6) The grieving and troubling the hearts and consciences, not of loose, perverse and seditious, but of grave, sober, pious and peaceable men is made nothing of; but they are trampled upon, and wholly neglected, whilst many atheists, Cavaliers, and base wretches that will take the Engagement, are embraced, privileged and respected.

These and such, dear Sir, are the troubles of my heart, which I make bold to express thus plainly, not doubting of your favour in construing my harsh and too-high phrases and over-bold expressions; only I follow this as the safest way to satisfaction and resolution, hoping that the Lord will of his goodness stir you up and direct you to satisfy me, or candidly to think of and bear with me.

Sir, your loving invitation and encouragement has made me thus bold to trouble you; and, as for those other businesses I formerly mentioned, I conceive little can be done, etc.

Dated 9 May, 1650

6 William Allen (i.e. Edward Sexby), *Killing Noe Murder. Briefly Discourst in Three Quaestions* (1657)

And all the people of the land rejoiced: and the city was quiet, after that they had slain Athaliah with the sword. 2 Chr. 23: 21
Now after the time that Amaziah did turn away from following the Lord, they made a conspiracy against him in Jerusalem, and he fled to Lachish; but they sent to Lachish after him, and slew him there. 2 Chr. 25: 27

To His Highness
Oliver Cromwell:

May it please your Highness,

How I have spent some hours of the leisure your Highness has been pleased to give me, this following paper will give your Highness an account. How you will please to interpret it I cannot tell; but I can with confidence say my intention in it is to procure your Highness that justice nobody yet does you, and to let the people see the longer they defer it, the greater injury they do both themselves and you. To your Highness justly belongs the honour of dying for the people; and it cannot choose but be unspeakable consolation to you in the last moments of your life to consider with how much benefit to the world you are like to leave it. 'Tis then only, my Lord, the titles you now usurp will be truly yours. You will then be indeed the deliverer of your country, and free it from a bondage little inferior to that from which Moses delivered his. You will then be that true reformer which you would be thought. Religion shall be then restored, liberty asserted, and parliaments have those privileges they have fought for.

We shall then hope that other laws will have place besides those of the sword, and that justice shall be otherwise defined than the will and pleasure of the strongest. And we shall then hope men will keep oaths again, and not have the necessity of being false and perfidious to preserve themselves, and be like their rulers. All this we hope from your Highness's happy expiration, who are the true father of your country: for while you live we can call nothing ours, and it is from your death that we hope for our inheritances. Let this consideration arm and fortify your Highness's mind against the fears of death and the terrors of your evil conscience, that the good you will do by your death will something balance the evils of your life. And if in the black catalogue of high malefactors few can be found that have lived more to the affliction and disturbance of mankind than your Highness has done, yet your greatest enemies will not deny but there are likewise as few that have expired more to the universal benefit of mankind than your Highness is like to do. To hasten this great good is the chief end of my writing this paper; and if it have the effects I hope it will, your Highness will quickly be out of the reach of men's malice and your enemies will only be able to wound you in your memory, which strokes you will not feel. That your Highness may be speedily in this security is the universal wishes of your grateful country. This is the desires and prayers of the good and of the bad, and it may be as the only thing wherein all sects and factions do agree in their devotions, and is our only common prayer. But amongst all that put in their requests and supplications for your Highness's speedy deliverances from all earthly troubles, none is more assiduous, nor more fervent, than he who, with the rest of the nation, has the honour to be

May it please your Highness,
Your Highness's present slave and vassal,
W.A.

To all officers and soldiers of the army that remember their engagements and dare be honest:

I heartily wish for England's sake that your number may be far greater than I fear it is; and that his Highness his frequent purgations may have left any amongst you that by these characters are concerned in this dedication. That I and all men have reason to make this a doubt, your own actions, as well as your tame sufferings, do but too plainly manifest. For you that were the champions of our liberty, and to that purpose were raised, are not you become the instruments of our slavery? And your hands that the people employed to take off the yoke from off our necks, are not those very hands they that now put it on? Do you remember that you were raised to defend the privileges of Parliament, and have sworn to do it; and will you be employed to force elections and dissolve Parliaments because they will not establish the tyrant's iniquity, and our slavery, by a law? I beseech you think upon what you have promised and what you do, and give not posterity as well as your own generation the occasion to mention you with infamy, and to curse that unfortunate valour and success of yours that only has gained victories (as you use them) against the common weal. Could ever England have thought to have seen that army, that was never mentioned without the titles of religious, zealous, faithful, courageous, the fence of her liberty at home, the terror of her enemies abroad, become her gaolers? Not her guard, but her oppressors? Not her soldiers, but a tyrant's executioners, drawing to blocks and gibbets all that dare be honester than themselves? This you do; and this you are; nor can you ever redeem your own honour, the trust and love of your country, the estimation of brave men, or the prayers of good, if you let not speedily the world see you have been deceived; which they will only then believe when they see your vengeance upon his faithless head that did it. This if you defer too long to do, you will find too late to attempt, and your repentance will neither vindicate you, nor help us. To let you see you may do this as a lawful action, and to persuade you to it as a glorious one, is the principal intent of this following paper, which, whatever effects it has upon you, I shall not absolutely fail of my ends, for if it excites not your virtue and courage, it will yet exprobrate your cowardice and baseness.

This is from one that was once one amongst you: and will be so again when you dare be so as you were.

Killing No Murder

It is not any ambition to be in print when so few spare paper and the press; nor any instigations of private revenge or malice (though few that dare be honest now want their causes) that have prevailed with me to make myself the author of a pamphlet, and to disturb that quiet which at present I enjoy by his Highness' great favour and injustice. Nor am I ignorant to how little purpose I shall employ that time and pains which I shall bestow upon this paper. For to think that any reasons or persuasions of mine, or conviction of their own, shall draw men from anything wherein they see profit or security, or to anything wherein they fear loss, or see danger, is to have a better opinion both of myself and them than either of us both deserve.

Besides, the subject itself is of that nature that I am not only to expect danger from ill men, but censure and disallowance from many that are good; for these opinions only looked upon, not looked into (which all have not eyes for), will appear bloody and cruel; and these compellations I must expect from those that have a zeal, but not according to knowledge. If, therefore, I had considered myself, I had spared whatever this is of pains, and not distasted so many, to please so few as are, in mankind, the honest and the wise. But at such a time as this, when God is not only exercising us with a usual and common calamity of letting us fall into slavery that used our liberty so ill, but is pleased so far to blind our understandings and to debase our spirits as to suffer us to court our bondage, and to place it among the requests we put to him, indignation makes a man break that silence that prudence would persuade him to use, if not to work upon other men's minds, yet to ease his own.

A late pamphlet tells us of a great design discovered against the person of his Highness, and of the Parliament's coming (for so does that Junto profane that name) to congratulate with his Highness his happy delivery from that wicked and bloody attempt. Besides this, that they have ordered that God Almighty shall be mocked with a day of thanksgiving (as I think the world is with the plot), and that the people shall give public thanks for the public calamity that God is yet pleased to continue his judgements upon them, and to frustrate all means that are used for their deliverance. Certainly none will now deny that the English are a very thankful people. But I think if we had read in Scripture that the Israelites had cried unto the Lord not for their own deliverance, but the preservation of their task-masters, and that they had thanked God with solemnity that Pharaoh was yet living, and that there was still great hopes of the daily increase of the number of their bricks, though that people did so many things not only impiously and profanely, but ridiculously and absurdly, yet certainly they did nothing we should more have wondered at, than to have found them ceremoniously thankful to God for plagues that were commonly so brutishly unthankful for mercies; and we should have thought that Moses had done them a great deal of wrong if he had not suffered them to enjoy their slavery, and left them to their tasks and garlic.

I can with justice say my principal intention in this paper is not to declaim against my Lord Protector or his accomplices, for were it not more to justify others than to accuse them, I should think their own actions did that work sufficiently, and I should not take pains to tell the world what they knew before. My design is to examine whether, if there has been such a plot as we hear of, and that it was contrived by Mr Sindercombe against my Lord Protector, and not by my Lord Protector against Mr Sindercombe (which is doubtful), whether it deserves those epithets Mr Speaker is pleased to give it, of bloody, wicked, and proceeding from the Prince of Darkness. I know very well how incapable the vulgar are of considering what is extraordinary and singular in every case, and that they judge of things and name them by their exterior appearances, without penetrating at all into their causes or natures. And without doubt when they hear the Protector was to be killed they straight conclude a man was to be murdered, not a malefactor punished, for they think the formalities do always make the things themselves, and that 'tis the judge and the crier that makes the justice, and the gaol the criminal. And therefore when they read in the pamphlet Mr Speaker's speech, they certainly think he gives these plotters their right titles; and, as readily as a High Court of Justice, they condemn them, without ever examining whether they would have killed a magistrate or destroyed a tyrant, over whom every man is naturally a judge and an executioner, and whom the laws of God, of nature, and of nations expose, like beasts of prey, to be destroyed as they are met.

That I may be as plain as I can, I shall first make it a question (which indeed is none), whether my Lord Protector be a tyrant or not? Secondly, if he be, whether it is lawful to do justice to upon him without solemnity, that is, to kill him. Thirdly, if it be lawful, whether it is like to prove profitable or noxious to the commonwealth?

The civil law makes tyrants of two sorts: *tyrannus sine titulo,* and *tyrannus exercitio.* The one is called a tyrant because he has no right to govern; the other because he governs tyrannically. We will very briefly discourse of them both, and see whether the Protector may not with great justice put in his claim to both titles.

We shall sufficiently demonstrate who they are that have not a right to govern if we show who they are that have, and what it is that makes the power just which those that rule have over the natural liberty of other men. To fathers within their private families nature has given a supreme power. Every man, says Aristotle, of right governs his wife and children, and this power was necessarily exercised everywhere whilst families lived dispersed, before the constitutions of commonwealths; and in many places it continued after, as appears by the laws of Solon, and the most ancient of those of Rome. And indeed, as by the laws of God and nature the care, defence, and support of the family lies upon every man whose it is, so by the same law there is due unto every man from his family a subjection and obedience, in compensation of that support. But several families uniting themselves together to make up one body of a commonwealth, and being independent one of another, without any natural superiority or obligation, nothing can introduce amongst them a disparity of rule and subjection but some power that is over them; which power none can pretend to have but God and themselves. Wherefore all power which is lawfully exercised over such a society of men (which from the end of its institution we call a commonwealth) must necessarily be derived either from the appointment of God Almighty, who is supreme lord of all and every part, or from the consent of the society itself, who have the next power to his of disposing of their own liberty as they shall think fit for their own good. This power God has given to societies of men, as well as he gave it to particular persons; and, when he interposes not his own authority and appoints not himself who shall be his vicegerents and rule under him, he leaves it to none but the people themselves to make the election, whose benefit is the end of all government. Nay, when he himself has been pleased to appoint rulers for that people which he was pleased peculiarly to own, he many times made the choice but left the confirmation and ratification of that choice to the people themselves. So Saul was chosen by God, and anointed king by his prophet, but made king by all the people at Gilgal. David was anointed king by the same prophet, but was afterwards, after Saul's death, confirmed by the people of Judah, and seven years after by the Elders of Israel, the people's deputies, at Hebron. And it is observable that though they knew that David was appointed king by God and anointed by his prophet, yet they likewise knew that God allowed to themselves not only his confirmation, but likewise the limitation of his power, for before his inauguration they made a league with him: that is, obliged him by compact to the performance of such conditions as they thought necessary for the securing [of] their liberty. Nor is it less remarkable that when God gives directions to his people concerning their government he plainly leaves the form to themselves, for he says not 'When thou shalt have come into the land which the Lord thy God gives thee, *statues super te regem*', but '*si dixeris statuam*'. God says not 'thou shalt appoint a king over thee', but 'if thou shalt say, I will appoint', leaving it to their choice whether they would say so or no. And it is plain in that place that God gives the people the choice of their king, for he there instructs them whom they shall choose: *e medio fratrum tuorum*, one out of the midst of thy brethren. Much more might we say, if it were less manifest truth that all just power of government is founded upon those two bases of God's immediate command or the people's consent. And therefore whosoever arrogates to himself that power, or any part of it, that cannot produce one of those two titles, is not a ruler but an invader, and those that are subject to that power are not governed, but oppressed.

This being considered, have not the people of England much reason to ask the Protector this question: *Quis constituit te virum Principem et judicem super nos?* Who made thee a prince and a judge over us? If God made thee, make it manifest to us. If the people, where did we meet to do it? Who took our subscriptions? To whom deputed we our authority? And when and where did those deputies make the choice? Sure these interrogations are very natural, and I believe would much trouble his Highness, his Council and his Junto to answer. In a word, that I may not tire my reader (who will not want proofs for what I say, if he wants not memory), if to change the government without the people's consent; if to dissolve their representatives by force and disannul their acts; if to give the name of the people's representatives to confederates of his own, that he may establish iniquity by a law; if to take away men's lives out of all course of law, by certain murderers of his own appointment, whom he names a High Court of Justice; if to decimate men's estates, and by his own power to impose upon the people what taxes he pleases;

and to maintain all by force of arms: if, I say, all this does make a tyrant, his own impudence cannot deny, but he is as complete a one as ever has been since there have been societies of men. He that has done and does all this is the person for whose preservation the people of England must pray; but certainly if they do, 'tis for the same reason that the old woman of Syracuse prayed for the long life of the tyrant Dionysius, lest the devil should come next.

Now if, instead of God's command, or the people's consent, his Highness has no other title but force and fraud, which is to want all title; and if to violate all laws, and propose none to rule by, but those of his own will, be to exercise that tyranny he has usurped, and to make his administration conformable to his claim, then the first question we proposed is a question no longer.

But before we come to the second, being things are more easily perceived and found by the description of their exterior accidents, and qualities, than the defining their essences, it will not be amiss to see whether his Highness has not as well the outward marks and characters by which tyrants are known, as he has their nature and essential properties: whether he has not the skin of the lion and tail of the fox, as well as he has the violence of the one and deceit of the other. Now in this delineation which I intend to make of a tyrant, all the lineaments, all the colours, will be found so naturally to correspond with the life, that it cannot but be doubted whether his Highness be the original, or the copy. Whether I have in drawing the tyrant represented him? Or in representing him expressed a tyrant? And therefore lest I should be suspected to deal un-sincerely with his Highness, and not to have applied these following characters, but made them, I shall not give you any of my own stamping, but such as I find in Plato, Aristotle, Tacitus, and his Highness' own Evangelist, Machiavelli.

The Marks of a Tyrant

1. Almost all tyrants have been first captains and generals for the people, under pretences of vindicating, or defending, their liberties. *Ut imperium evertant, libertatem praeferunt; cum perverterunt, ipsam aggrediuntur*, says Tacitus; to subvert the present government, they pretend liberty for the people; when the government is down, they then invade that liberty themselves: this needs no application.

2. Tyrants accomplish their ends much more by fraud than force. Neither virtue nor force, says Machiavelli, are so necessary to that purpose as *una astutia fortunata,* a lucky craft, which, says he, without force has been often found sufficient, but never force without that. And in another place he tells us their way is *aggirare li cervelli de gli huomini con astutia,* etc.: with cunning plausible pretences to impose upon men's understandings, and in the end they master those that had so little wit as to rely upon their faith and integrity. 'Tis but unnecessary to say that had not his Highness had a faculty to be fluent in his tears and eloquent in his execrations, had he not had spongy eyes and a supple conscience, and, besides, to do with a people of great faith but little wit, his courage and the rest of his moral virtues, with the help of his Janizaries, had never been able so far to advance him out of the reach of justice that we should have need to call for any other hand to remove him but that of the hangman.

3. They abase all excellent persons, and rid out of the way all that have noble minds, *et terrae filios extollunt*: and advance sons of the earth. To put Aristotle into other words, they purge both parliament and army, till they leave few or none there that have either honour or conscience, either wit, interest, or courage to oppose their designs. And in these purgations (says Plato) tyrants do quite contrary to physicians, for they purge us of our humours, but tyrants of our spirits.

4. They dare suffer no assemblies, not so much as horse races.

5. In all places they have their spies and delators, that is, they have their Fleetwoods, their Broughalls, their St Johns (besides innumerable small spies) to appear discontented and not to side with them; that under that disguise they may get trust, and make discoveries. They likewise have their emissaries to send with forged letters. If any doubt this, let him send to Major General Brown, and he will satisfy him.

6. They stir not without a guard, nor his Highness without his life-guard.

7. They impoverish the people, that they may want the power, if they have the will, to attempt anything against them. His Highness' way is by taxes, excise, decimations, etc.

8. They make war to divert and busy the people; and, besides, to have a pretence to raise moneys, and to make new levies, if they

either distrust their old forces, or think them not sufficient. The war with Spain serves his Highness to this purpose, and upon no other justice was it begun at first, or is still continued.

9. They will seem to honour and provide for good men: that is, if the ministers will be orthodox and flatter, if they will wrest and torture the Scripture to prove his government lawful, and furnish him with the title, his Highness will likewise be then content to understand Scripture in their favour, and furnish them with tithes.

10. Things that are odious and distasteful they make others executioners of; and when the people are discontented they appease them with sacrificing those ministers they employ: I leave it to his Highness his Major-Generals to ruminate a little upon this point.

11. In all things they pretend to be wonderful careful of the public: to give general accounts of the money they receive, which they pretend to be levied for the maintenance of the state, and the prosecuting of the war. His Highness made an excellent comment upon this place of Aristotle in his speech to this Parliament.

12. All things set aside for religious uses they set to sale, that while those things last they exact the less of the people. The Cavaliers would interpret this of the Dean and Chapter's lands.

13. They pretend inspirations from God, and responses from oracles to authorize what they do. His Highness has been ever an enthusiast; and as Hugh Capet, in taking the Crown, pretended to be admonished to it in a dream by St Valéry and St Richard, so I believe will his Highness do the same at the instigation of St Henry and St Richard, his two sons.

14. Lastly, above all things they pretend a love to God and religion. This Aristotle calls *artium tyrannicarum potissimam*: the surest and best of all the arts of tyrants, and we all know his Highness has found it so by experience. He has found indeed that in godliness there is great gain, and that preaching and praying, well managed, will obtain other kingdoms as well as that of heaven. His indeed have been pious arms, for he has conquered most by those of the Church: by prayers and tears. But the truth is, were it not for our honour to be governed by one that can manage both the spiritual and temporal sword, and, Roman like, to have our emperor our High Priest, we might have had preaching at a much cheaper rate, and it would have cost us but our tithes, which now costs us all.

Other marks and rules there are mentioned by Aristotle to know tyrants by: but they being unsuitable to his Highness' actions, and impracticable by his temper, I insist not on them. As among other things, Aristotle would not have a tyrant insolent in his behaviour, nor strike people. But his Highness is naturally choleric, and must call men rogues, and go to cuffs. At last he concludes he should so fashion his manners, as neither to be really good, nor absolutely bad, but half one, half t'other. Now this half good is too great a proportion for his Highness, and much more than his temper will bear.

But to speak truths more seriously, and to conclude this first question: certainly whatever these characters make any man, it cannot be denied but his Highness is; and then if he be not a tyrant, we must confess we have no definition nor description of a tyrant left us; and may well imagine there is no such thing in nature, and that 'tis only a notion and a name. But if there be such a beast, and we do at all believe what we see and feel, let us now inquire, according to the method we proposed, whether this be a beast of game that we are to give law to, or a beast of prey to destroy with all means are allowable and fair?

Whether It be Lawful to Kill a Tyrant?

In deciding this question authors very much differ as far as it concerns supreme magistrates who degenerate into tyrants. Some think they are to be borne with as bad parents; and place them in the number of those mischiefs that have no other cure but our patience. Others think they may be questioned by that supreme law of the people's safety; and that they are answerable to the people's representatives for the breach of their trust. But none of sober sense makes private persons judges of their actions: which were, indeed, to subvert all government. But, on the other side, I find none (that have not been frighted or corrupted out of their reason) that have been so great enemies to common justice and the liberty of mankind as to give any kind of indemnity to a usurper who can pretend no title but that of being stronger, nor challenge the people's obedience upon any other obligation but that of their necessity and fear. Such a person, as one out of all bonds of human protection, all men make the Ishmael, against whom is every man's hand, as his is against every man. To him they give no more security than Cain, his fellow murderer and oppressor, promised to himself, to be destroyed by him that found him first.

The reason why a tyrant's case is particular, and why in that every man has that vengeance given him which in other cases is reserved to God and the magistrate, cannot be obscure if we rightly consider what a tyrant is, what his crimes are, and in what state he stands with the commonwealth, and with every member of it. And certainly if we find him an enemy to all human society, and a subverter of all laws, and one that by the greatness of his villainies secures himself against all ordinary course of justice, we shall not at all think it strange if then he have no benefit from human society, no protection from the law, and if, in his case, justice dispenses with her forms.

We are therefore to consider that the end for which men enter into society is not barely to live, which they may do dispersed, as other animals, but to live happily, and a life answerable to the dignity and excellency of their kind. Out of society this happiness is not to be had, for singly we are impotent and defective, unable to procure those things that are either of necessity or ornament for our lives, and as unable to defend and keep them when they are acquired. To remedy these defects we associate together, that what we can neither joy nor keep singly, by mutual benefits and assistance one of another we may be able to do both. We cannot possibly accomplish these ends if we submit not our passions and appetites to the laws of reason and justice, for the depravity of man's will makes him as unfit to live in society as his necessity makes him unable to live out of it. And if that perverseness be not regulated by laws, men's appetites to the same things, their avarice, their lust, their ambition would quickly make society as unsafe, or more, than solitude itself, and we should associate only to be nearer our misery and our ruin.

That, therefore, by which we accomplish the ends of a sociable life is our subjection and submission to laws: these are the nerves and sinews of every society or commonwealth, without which they must necessarily dissolve and fall asunder. And indeed (as Augustine says) those societies where law and justice is not are not commonwealths or kingdoms, but *magna latrocinia*, great confederacies of thieves and robbers. Those therefore that submit to no law are not to be reputed in the society of mankind, which cannot consist without a law. Therefore, Aristotle says, tyranny is against the law of nature, that is, the law of human society, in which human nature is preserved. For this reason they deny a tyrant to be *partem civitatis*, for every part is subject to the whole, and a citizen (says the same author) is he who is as well obliged to the duty of obeying as he is capable of the power of commanding. And, indeed, he does obey whilst he does command, that is, he obeys the laws, which, says Tully, *magistratibus praesunt, ut magistratus praesunt populo*, are above the magistrates as the magistrates are above the people.

And therefore a tyrant that submits to no law, but his will and lust are the law by which he governs himself and others, is no magistrate, no citizen or member of any society, but an ulcer and a disease that destroys it; and, if it be rightly considered, a commonwealth, by falling into a tyranny, absolutely loses that name, and is actually another thing: *non est civitas quae unius est viri* (says Sophocles), that which is one man's is no city. For there is no longer king and people, or parliament and people, but those names are changed (at least their natures) into masters and servants, lords and slaves. And *servorum non civitas erit sed magna familia* (says Grotius): where all are slaves, 'tis not a city but a great family. And the truth is, we are all members of Whitehall, and when our master pleases he may send for us thither, and there bore through our ears at the door-posts. But to conclude, a tyrant, as we have said, being no part of the commonwealth, nor submitting to the laws of it, but making himself above all law, there is no reason he should have the protection that is due to a member of a commonwealth, nor any defence from laws, that does acknowledge none. He is therefore in all reason to be reckoned in the number of those savage beasts that fall not with others into any herd, that have no other defence but their own strength, making a prey of all that's weaker, and, by the same justice, being a prey to all that's stronger than themselves.

In the next place, let it be considered that a tyrant, making himself above all law, and defending his injustice by a strength which no power of magistrates is able to oppose, he becomes above all punishment, above all other justice than that he receives from the stroke of some generous hand. And, certainly, the safety of mankind were but ill provided for, if there were no kind of justice to reach great villainies, but tyrants should be *immanitate scelerum tuti*, secured by the greatness of their crimes. Our laws would be then but cobwebs indeed, made only to catch flies, but not to hold wasps or hornets; and it might be then said of all commonwealths what was said of

Athens, that there only small thieves were hanged, but the great ones were free, and condemned the rest. But he that will secure himself of all hands must know he secures himself from none. He that flies justice in the court must expect to find it in the street, and he that goes armed against every man arms every man against himself. *Bellum est in eos qui judiciis coerceri non possunt* (says Cicero), we have war with those against whom we can have no law. The same author: *cum duo sint decertandi genera*, etc.: there being two ways of deciding differences, the one by judgement and arbitration, the other by force, the one proper to men, the other to beasts, we must have recourse to the latter when the former cannot be obtained. And certainly, by the law of nature, *ubi cessat judicium*, when no justice can be had, every man must be his own magistrate, and do justice for himself. For the law (says Grotius) that forbids me to pursue my right but by a course of law certainly supposes *ubi copia est judicii*, [that one is] where law and justice is to be had: otherwise that law were a defence for injuries, not one against them, and, quite contrary to the nature of all laws, would become the protection of the guilty against the innocent, not of the innocent against the guilty.

Now, as it is contrary to the laws of God and nature that men, who are partial to themselves, and therefore unjust to others, should be their own judges where others are to be had, so it is contrary to the law of nature and the common safety of mankind, that when the law can have no place men should be forbidden to repel force by force, and so to be left without all defence and remedy against injuries. God himself left not the slave without remedy against the cruel master: and what analogy can it hold with reason, that the slave, that is but his master's money and but part of his household-stuff, should find redress against the injuries and insolencies of an imperious master, and a free people, who have no superior but their God, should have none at all against the injustice and oppression of a barbarous tyrant? And were not the incongruity fully as great, that the law of God permitting every man to kill a thief if he took him breaking open his house in the night, because then it might be supposed he could not bring him to justice, but a tyrant, that is the common robber of mankind, and whom no law can take hold on, his person should be *sacrosancta, cui nihil sacrum aut sanctum*, to whom nothing is sacred, nothing inviolable?

But the vulgar judge ridiculously, like themselves. The glister of things dazzles their eyes, and they judge of them by their appearances and the colours that are put on them. For what can be more absurd in nature, and contrary to all common sense, than to call him thief and kill him that comes alone or with a few to rob me, and to call him Lord Protector and obey him that robs me with regiments and troops? As if to rove with two or three ships were to be a pirate, but with fifty an admiral? But if it be the number of adherents only, not the cause, that makes the difference between a robber and a Protector, I wish that number were defined, that we might know where the thief ends and the prince begins, and be able to distinguish between a robbery and a tax.

But sure, no Englishman can be ignorant that it is his birthright to be master of his own estate, and that none can command any part of it but by his own grant and consent, either made expressly by himself, or virtually by a parliament. All other ways are mere robberies in other names: *auferre, trucidare, rapere, falsis nominibus imperium atque, ubi solitudinem faciunt, pacem apellant*, to rob, to extort, to murder tyrants falsely called to govern, and to make desolation they call to settle peace. In every assessment we are robbed: the excise is robbery, the custom's robbery, and, without doubt, whenever 'tis prudent, 'tis always lawful to kill the thieves whom we can bring to no other justice. And not only lawful, and to do ourselves right, but glorious, and to deserve [praise] of mankind, to free the world of that common robber, that universal pirate, under whom, and for whom, these lesser beasts prey. This firebrand I would have any way extinguished. This ulcer I would have any hand to lance. And I cannot doubt but God will suddenly sanctify some hand to do it, and bring down that bloody and deceitful man, who lives not only to the misery, but the infamy of our nation.

I should have reason to be much less confident of the justice of this opinion if it were new and only grounded upon collections and interpretations of my own. But herein, if I am deceived, I shall however have the excuse to have been drawn into that error by the examples that are left us by the greatest and most virtuous, and the opinions of the wisest and gravest men that have left their memories to posterity. Out of the great plenty of confirmations I could bring for this opinion from examples and authorities I shall select a very few: for manifest truths have not need of those supports, and I have as little mind to tire myself as my reader.

First, therefore, a usurper that by only force possesses himself of government, and by force only keeps it, is yet in the state of war with every man, says the learned Grotius; and therefore everything is lawful against him that is lawful against an open enemy, whom every private man has a right to kill. *Hostis hostem occidere volui*, says Scaevola to Porsena, when he was taken after he had failed in his attempt to kill him: I am an enemy, and an enemy I would have killed, which every man has a right to do.

Contra publicos hostes et majestatis reos, omnis homo miles est, says Tertullian: against common enemies and those that are traitors to the commonwealth, every man is a soldier. This opinion the most celebrated nations have approved, both by their laws and practices. The Grecians (as Xenophon tells us), who suffered not murderers to come into their temples, in those very temples they erected statues to those that killed tyrants, thinking it fit to place their deliverers amongst their gods. Cicero was an eyewitness of the honours that were done such men: *Graeci homines*, etc. – 'the Greeks', says he, 'attribute the honours of the gods to those that killed tyrants. What have I seen in Athens and other cities of Greece! What religion paid to such men! What songs! What elegies! By which they are consecrated to immortality and almost deified!' In Athens, by Solon's law, death was not only decreed for the tyrant that oppressed the state, but for all those that took any charge, or did bear any office while the tyranny remained. And Plato tells us the ordinary course they took with tyrants in Greece. If, says he, the tyrant cannot be expulsed by accusing him to the citizens, then by secret practices they dispatch him.

Amongst the Romans the Valerian law was *si quis injussu populi* etc.: whosoever took magistracy upon him without the command of the people, it was lawful for any man to kill him. Plutarch makes this law more severe, *ut injudicatum occidere eum liceret qui dominatum concupisceret*: that it was lawful by that law, before any judgement passed, to kill him that but aspired to tyranny. Likewise the consular law which was made after the suppression of the tyranny of the decemvirate made it lawful to kill any man that went about to create magistrates, *sine provocatione,* etc.: without reference and appeal to the people. By these laws and innumerable testimonies of authors, it appears that the Romans, with the rest of their philosophy, had learned from the Grecians what was the natural remedy against a tyrant. Nor did they honour those less that durst apply it. Who, as Polybius says, speaking of conspiracies against tyrants, were not *deterrimi civium, sed generosissimi quique, et maximi animi*: not the worst and meanest of the citizens, but the most generous, and those of greatest virtue. So were most of those that conspired against Julius Caesar. He himself thought Brutus worthy to succeed him in the empire of the world; and Cicero, who had the title of *pater patriae*, if he were not conscious of the design, yet he at least affected the honour of being thought so. *Quae enim res unquam*, etc.: 'what act,' says he, 'O Jupiter, more glorious, more worthy of eternal memory, has been done, not only in this city but in the whole world! In this design, as the Trojan horse, I willingly suffer myself to be included with the princes.' In the same place he tells us what all virtuous Romans thought of the fact as well as he: *Omnes boni, quantum in ipsis fuit, Caesarem occiderunt; aliis consilium, aliis animus, aliis occasio defuit, voluntas nemini* – all good men, says he, as much as in them lay, killed Caesar. Some wanted capacity, some courage, others opportunity, but none the will to do it.

But yet we have not declared the extent of their severity against a tyrant. They exposed him to fraud as well as force, and left him no security in oaths and compacts, that neither law nor religion might defend him that violated both. *Cum tyranno Romanis nulla fides, nulla juris jurandi religio*, says Brutus in Appian: with a tyrant the Romans think no faith to be kept, observe no religion of an oath. Seneca gives the reason: *quia quicquid erat, quo mihi cohaereret,* etc.: for whatever there was of mutual obligation betwixt us, his destroying the laws of human society has dissolved. So these that thought that there was *in hostem nefas*, that a villainy might be committed against an enemy, these that professed *non minus juste quam fortiter arma gerere*, to manage their arms with justice as well as courage, these that thought faith was to be kept even with the perfidious, yet they thought a tyrant could receive no injustice but to be let live, and that the most lawful way to destroy him was the readiest. No matter whether by force or fraud, for against beasts of prey men use the toil and the net, as well as the spear and the lance. But so great was their detestation of a tyrant that it made some take their opinions from their passions, and vent things which they could but ill justify to their morality. They thought a tyrant had so absolutely forfeited all title to humanity and all kind of protection they could give him or his that they left his wife without any other guard for her chastity but age and deformity, and thought it not adultery what was committed with her. Many more testimonies might I bring, for 'tis harder to make choice than to find plenty, but I shall conclude with authorities that are much more authentic, and examples which we may much more safely imitate.

The law of God itself decreed certain death to that man that would do presumptuously and submit to no decision of justice. Who can read this and think a tyrant ought to live? But certainly neither that, nor any other law, were to any effect, if there were no way to put it in execution. But in a tyrant's case process and citation have no place; and if we will only have formal remedies against him, we are sure to have none. There's small hope of justice where the malefactor has a power to condemn the judge.

All remedy, therefore, against a tyrant is Ehud's dagger, without which all our laws were fruitless and we helpless. This is that High Court of Justice where Moses brought the Egyptian; whither Ehud brought Eglon; Samson, the Philistines; Samuel, Agag; and Jehoiada, the she-tyrant Athaliah.

Let us a little consider in particular these several examples, and see whether they may be proportioned to our purpose.

First, as to the case of Moses and the Egyptian: certainly every Englishman has as much call as Moses, and more cause than he, to slay this Egyptian that is always laying on burdens, and always smiting both our brethren and ourselves. For as to his call, he had no other that we read of, but the necessity his brother stood in of his help. He looked on his brethren's burdens, and seeing an Egyptian smiting an Hebrew, knowing he was out of the reach of all other kind of justice, he slew him.

Certainly this was and is as lawful for any man to do as it was for Moses, who was then but a private man, and had no authority for what he did but what the law of nature gives every man: to oppose force to force and to make justice where he finds none. As to the cause of that action, we have much more to say than Moses had. He saw one Hebrew smitten, we many English men murdered; he saw his brethren's burdens and their blows, we our brethren's burdens, imprisonments, and deaths. Now sure, if it were lawful for Moses to kill that Egyptian that oppressed one man, being there was no way to procure an ordinary course of justice against him, it cannot be but absurd to think it unlawful to kill him that oppresses a whole nation, and one that justice as little reaches as it defends.

The remedy of Ehud shows us the natural and almost the only

remedy against a tyrant, and the way to free an oppressed people from the slavery of an insulting Moabite: 'tis done by prayers and tears, with the help of a dagger, by crying to the Lord, and the left hand of an Ehud. Devotion and action go well together, for believe it, a tyrant is not of that kind of devil that is to be cast out by only fasting and prayer. And here the Scripture shows us what the Lord thought a fit message to send a tyrant from himself: a dagger of a cubit in his belly. And every worthy man that desires to be an Ehud, a deliverer of his country, will strive to be the messenger.

We may here likewise observe in this and many places of Judges that when the Israelites fell to idolatry, which of all sins certainly is one of the greatest, God Almighty, to proportion the punishment and the offence, still delivered them into the hands of tyrants, which sure is one of the greatest of all plagues.

In the story of Samson, 'tis manifest that the denying him his wife, and after the burning her and her father, which, though they were great, yet were but private injuries, he took for sufficient grounds to make war upon the Philistines, being himself but a private man, and not only not assisted but opposed by his servile countrymen. He knew what the law of nature allowed him where other laws have no place, and thought it a sufficient justification for smiting the Philistines hip and thigh to answer for himself that, as they did unto him, so had he done unto them.

Now that which was lawful for Samson to do against many oppressors, why is it unlawful for us to do against one? Are our injuries less? Our friends and relations are daily murdered before our faces. Have we other ways for reparation? Let them be named and I am silenced. But if we have none, the firebrands or the jaw-bone, the first weapons our just fury can lay hold on, may certainly be lawfully employed against that circumcised Philistine that oppresses us. We have too the opposition and discouragements that Samson had, and therefore have the more need of his courage and resolution. As he had the men of Judah, so we have the men of Levi crying to us out of the pulpit, as from the top of the rock Etam, 'Know you not that the Philistine is a ruler over you?' The truth is, they would fain make him so, and bind us with Samson in new cords; but we hope they will become as flax, and that they will either loose from our hands, or we shall have the courage to cut them.

Upon the same grounds of retaliation did Samuel do justice with his own hand upon the tyrant Agag. As thy sword, says the prophet, has made women childless, so shall thy mother be childless amongst women: nor is there any law more natural and more just.

How many mothers has our Agag, for his own ambition, made childless? How many children fatherless? How many have this reason to hew this Amalekite in pieces before the Lord? And let his own relations, and all theirs that are confederates with him, beware, lest men come at last to revenge their own relations in them. They make many a woman husbandless, many a father childless. Their wives may come at last to know what 'tis to want a husband, and themselves to lose their children. Let them remember what their great apostle Machiavelli tells them, that in contestations for the preserving their liberty, people many times use moderation; but when they come to vindicate it, their rigour exceeds all mean, like beasts that have been kept up and are afterwards let loose, they always are more fierce and cruel.

To conclude with the example Jehoiada has left us: six years he hid the right heir of the crown in the house of the Lord, and, without all doubt, amongst the rest of God's services there he was all that time contriving the destruction of the tyrant that had aspired to the crown by the destruction of those that had the right to it. Jehoiada had no pretence to authorize this action but the equity and justice of the act itself. He pretended no immediate command from God for what he did, nor any authority from the Sanhedrin, and therefore any man might have done what Jehoiada did as lawfully, and could have done it as effectually. Now what citation was given to Athaliah, what appearance was she called to before any court of justice? Her fact was her trial. She was without any expostulation taken forth of the ranges, and only let live till she got out of the Temple that that holy place might not be defiled by the blood of a tyrant, which was fitter to be shed on a dung-hill; and so they slew her at the Horse-gate. And by the King's house, the very Whitehall, where she had caused the blood royal to be spilt, and which herself had so long unjustly possessed, there by Providence did she receive her punishment, where she had acted so great a part of her crimes. How the people approved of this glorious action of destroying a tyrant, this chapter tells us at the last verse: 'And all the people of the land rejoiced, and the city was quiet, after they had slain Athaliah with the sword.' And that it may appear they no less honoured the authors of such actions than other nations did, as in his lifetime they obeyed Jehoiada as a king, so after his death, for the good he had done in Israel (says the Scripture), they buried him amongst the kings.

I must not conclude this story without observing that Jehoiada commanded that whosoever followed Athaliah should be put to death, letting us see what they deserve that are confederates with tyrants and will side with them, and but appear to defend them or allow them. His Highness his council, his junto, and the agas of his janizaries may, if they please, take notice of this, and repent, lest they likewise perish. And likewise his Highness his chaplains, and triers, who are to admit none into the ministry that will preach liberty with the gospel, may, if they think fit, observe that with the tyrant fell Mattan, the priest of Baal. And indeed none but Baal's priests will preach for tyrants. And certainly those priests that sacrifice to our Baal, our idol of a magistrate, deserves as well to be hanged before their pulpits as ever Mattan did to fall before his altars.

I should think now I had said much more than enough to the second question, and should come to the third and last I proposed in my method, but I meet with two objections lying in my way. The first is:

Objection One
That these examples out of Scripture are of men that were inspired of God, and that therefore they had that call and authority for their actions, which we cannot pretend to, so that it would be unsafe for us to draw their actions into examples, except we had likewise their justification to allege.

Objection Two
The other objection is that there being now no opposition made to the government of his Highness, that the people following their callings and traffic, at home and abroad, making use of the laws, and appealing to his Highness's courts of justice, that all this argues the people's tacit consent to the government, and that therefore now 'tis to be reputed lawful, and the people's obedience voluntary.

Solution One
To the first I answer with learned Milton, that if God commanded these things, 'tis a sign they were lawful and are commendable. But secondly, as I observed in the relations of the examples themselves, neither Samson nor Samuel alleged any other cause or reason for what they did but retaliation and the apparent justice of the actions

themselves. Nor had God appeared to Moses in the bush when he slew the Egyptian; nor did Jehoiada allege any prophetical authority or other call to do what he did, but that common call which all men have, to do all actions of justice that are within their power, when the ordinary course of justice ceases.

Solution Two

To the second my answer is that if commerce and pleadings were enough to argue the people's consent, and give tyranny the name of government, there was never yet any tyranny of many weeks' standing in this world. Certainly we then extremely wrong Caligula and Nero in calling them tyrants, and they were rebels that conspired against them; except we will believe that all the while they reigned in Rome they kept their shops shut, and opened not their temples, or their courts. We are likewise with no less absurdity to imagine that the whole eighteen years' time which Israel served Eglon, and six years that Athaliah reigned, that the Israelites quite desisted from traffic, pleadings and all public acts: otherwise Ehud and Jehoiada were both traitors, the one for killing his king, the other his queen.

Third Question

Having showed what a tyrant is, his marks and practices, I can scarce persuade myself to say anything to that I made my third question, whether the removing him is like to prove of advantage to the commonwealth or not? For methinks 'tis to inquire whether 'tis better the man die, or the imposthume be lanced, or the gangrened limb be cut off? But yet there be some whose cowardice and avarice furnish them with some arguments to the contrary, and they would fain make the world believe that to be base and degenerate is to be cautious and prudent, and what is in truth a servile fear they falsely call a Christian patience. It will not be therefore amiss to make appear that there is indeed that necessity which we think there is, of saving the vineyard of the commonwealth, if possible, by destroying the wild boar that is broke into it. We have already showed that it is lawful, and now we shall see whether it is expedient.

First, I have already told you that to be under a tyrant is not to be a commonwealth, but a great family, consisting of master and slaves. *Vir bone* [sic] *servorum nulla est usquam civitas,* says an old poet: a number of slaves makes not a city. So that whilst this monster lives we are not members of a commonwealth, but only his living tools and instruments, which he may employ to what use he pleases. *Servi tua est fortuna, ratio ad te nihil*, says another: thy condition is a slave's; thou art not to inquire a reason. Nor must we think we can continue long in the condition of slaves and not degenerate into the habits and temper that is natural to that condition: our minds will grow low with our fortune, and by being accustomed to live like slaves we shall become unfit to be anything else. *Etiam fera animalia si clausa teneas virtutis obliviscuntur*, says Tacitus: the fiercest creatures by long constraint lose their courage. And, says Sir Francis Bacon, the blessing of Issachar and that of Judah falls not upon one people, to be asses crouching under burdens, and to have the spirit of lions. And with their courage, 'tis no wonder if they lose their fortune, as the effect with the cause, and act as ignominiously abroad as they suffer at home. 'Tis Machiavelli's observation that the Roman armies that were always victorious under consuls, all the while they were under the slavery of the decemviri never prospered. And certainly people have reason to fight but faintly where they are to gain the victory against themselves, when every success shall be a confirmation of their slavery, and a new link to their chain.

But we shall not only lose our courage, which is a useless and an unsafe virtue under a tyrant, but by degrees we shall, after the example of our master, all turn perfidious, deceitful, irreligious, flatterers, and what ever else is villainous and infamous in mankind. See but to what a degree we are come to already. Can there any oath be found so fortified by all religious ties which we easily find not a distinction to break, when either profit or danger persuades us to it? Do we remember any engagements? Or, if we do, have we any shame to break them? Can any man think with patience upon what we have professed when he sees what we vilely do and tamely suffer? What have we of nobility amongst us but the name, the luxury and vices of it? Poor wretches, these that now carry that title are so far from having any of the virtues that should grace, and indeed give them, their titles that they have not so much as the generous vices that attend greatness: they have lost all ambition and indignation. As for our ministers, what have they, or indeed desire they, of their calling, but the tithes? How do these horrid prevaricators search for distinctions to piece [peace?] contrary oaths? How do they rake Scriptures for flatteries and impudently apply them to his monstrous Highness? What is the city but a great tame beast that eats and carries, and cares not who rides it? What's the thing called a Parliament but a mock? Composed of a people that are only suffered to sit there because they are known to have no virtue, after the exclusion of all others that were but suspected to have any? What are they but pimps of tyranny, who are only employed to draw in the people to prostitute their liberty? What will not the army fight for? What will they not fight against? What are they but janizaries, slaves themselves, and making all others so? What are the people in general but knaves, fools and cowards, principled for ease, vice and slavery? This our temper, his tyranny had brought us to already; and if it continues the little virtue that is yet left to stock the nation must totally extinguish, and then his Highness had completed his work to reformation. And the truth is, till then his Highness cannot be secure. He must not endure virtue, for that will not endure him. He that will maintain tyranny must kill Brutus, says Machiavelli. A tyrant, says Plato, must dispatch all virtuous persons, or he cannot be safe; so that he is brought to that unhappy necessity, either to live among base and wicked persons, or not to live at all.

Nor must we expect any cure from our patience. *Inganno si gli huomini*, says Machiavelli, *credendo con la humilità vincere la superbia*. Men deceive themselves, that think to mollify arrogancy with humility. A tyrant's never modest but when he's weak. 'Tis in the winter of his fortune when this serpent bites not: we must not therefore suffer ourselves to be cozened with hopes of his amendment. For *nemo unquam imperium flagitio quaesitum, bonis artibus exercuit* [Tacitus]: never did any man manage that government with justice, that got it by villainy. The longer the tyrant lives, the more the tyrannical humour increases in him, says Plato, like those beasts that grow more cursed as they grow old. New occasions daily happen that necessitate them to new mischiefs, and he must defend one villainy with another.

But suppose the contrary of all this, and that his Highness were *vi dominationis convulsus, et mutatus*, changed to the better by great fortune (of which yet he gives no symptoms). What, notwithstanding, could be more miserable than to have no other security for our liberty, no other law for our safety, than the will of a man, though the most just living? We have all our beast within us, and whosoever (says Aristotle) is governed by a man without a law is governed by a man and by a beast. *Etiam si non sit molestus dominus, tamen est miserrimum posse si velit*, says Tully: though a master does not tyrannize, yet 'tis a most miserable thing that 'tis in his power to do so if he will. If he be good, so was Nero for five years, and how shall we be secure that he will not change? Besides, the power that is allowed to a good man, we may be sure will be claimed and taken by an ill. And therefore it has been the custom of good princes to abridge their own power, it may be distrusting themselves, but certainly fearing their successors, to the chance of whose being virtuous, they would not hazard the welfare of their people. An unlimited power therefore is to be trusted to none; which, if it does not find a tyrant, commonly makes one; or, if one uses it modestly, 'tis no argument that others will; and therefore Augustus Caesar must have no greater power given him than you would have Tiberius take. And Cicero's moderation is to be trusted with a consideration, that there are others be consuls, as well as he.

But before I press this business further, if it needs be any further pressed, that we should endeavour to rescue the honour, the virtue and liberty of our nation, I shall answer to some few objections that have occurred to me. This I shall do very briefly.

Some I find of a strange opinion, that it were a generous and a noble action to kill his Highness in the field, but to do it privately they think it unlawful, but know not why. As if it were not generous to apprehend a thief till his sword were drawn, and he in a posture to defend himself and kill me. But these people do not consider that whosoever is possessed of power any time will be sure to engage so many either in guilt, or profit, or both, that to go about to throw him out by open force will very much hazard the total ruin of the Commonwealth. A tyrant is a devil that tears the body in the exorcizing; and they are all of Caligula's temper, that if they could, they would have the whole frame of nature fall with them. 'Tis an opinion that deserves no other refutation than the manifest absurdity of itself, that it should be lawful for me to destroy a tyrant with hazard, blood, and confusion, but not without.

Another objection, and more common, is the fear of what may succeed if his Highness were removed. One would think the world were bewitched. I am fallen into a ditch, where I shall certainly perish if I lie, but I refuse to be helped out for fear of falling into another. I suffer a certain misery for fear of a contingent one, and let the disease kill me, because there is hazard in the cure. Is not this that ridiculous policy, *ne moriare, mori*: to die for fear of dying. Sure, 'tis frenzy not to desire a change when we are sure we cannot be worse; *et non incurrere in pericula, ubi quiescenti paria metuuntur*: and not then to hazard, when the danger and the mischiefs are the same in lying still.

Hitherto I have spoken in general to all Englishmen. Now I address my discourse particularly to those that certainly best deserve that name: ourselves, that have fought, however unfortunately, for our liberties under this tyrant; and in the end, cozened by his oaths and tears, have purchased nothing but our slavery with the price of our blood. To us particularly it belongs to bring this monster to justice, whom he has made the instruments of his villainy, and sharers in the curse and detestation that is due to himself from all good men. Others only have their liberty to vindicate; we, our liberty and our honour. We engaged to the people with him, and to the people for him, and from our hands they may justly expect a satisfaction of punishment, being they cannot have that of performance. What the people at present endure, and posterity shall suffer, will be all laid at our doors: for only we under God have the power to pull down this Dagon which we have set up. And if we do it not all mankind will repute us approvers of all the villainies he has done, and authors of all to come. Shall we that would not endure a king attempting tyranny, shall we suffer a professed tyrant? We that resisted the lion assailing us, shall we submit to the wolf tearing us? If there be no remedy to be found, we have great reason to exclaim *utinam te potius* (Carole) *retinuissemus quam hunc habuissemus, non quod ulla sit optanda servitus, sed quod ex dignitate domini minus turpis est conditio servi* [Cicero]: we wish we had rather endured thee (*O Charles*) than have been condemned to this mean tyrant; not that we desire any kind of slavery, but that the quality of the master something graces the condition of the slave.

But if we consider it rightly, what our duty, our engagements, and our honour exact from us, both our safety and our interest oblige us to, and 'tis as unanswerable, in us, to discretion as 'tis to virtue to let this viper live. For, first, he knows very well 'tis only we that have the power to hurt him, and therefore of us he will take any course to secure himself: he is conscious to himself how falsely and perfidiously he has dealt with us, and therefore he will always fear that from our revenge which he knows he has so well deserved.

Lastly, he knows our principles, how directly contrary they are to that arbitrary power he must govern by, and therefore he may reasonably suspect that we that have already ventured our lives against tyranny will always have the will, when we have the opportunity, to do the same again.

These considerations will easily persuade him to secure himself of us, if we prevent him not, and secure ourselves of him. He reads in his practice of piety [i.e. Machiavelli] *chi diviene patron*, etc.: he that makes himself master of a city that has been accustomed to liberty, if he destroys it not, he must expect to be destroyed by it. And we may read too in the same author, and believe him, that those that are the occasion that one becomes powerful, [one] always ruins them, if they want the wit and courage to secure themselves.

Now as to our interest: we must never expect that he will ever trust those that he has provoked and seared. He will be sure to keep us down, lest we should pluck down him. 'Tis the rule that tyrants observe, when they are in power, never to make much use of those that helped them to it, and indeed 'tis their interest and security not to do it: for those that have been the authors of their greatness, being conscious of their own merit, they are bold with the tyrant, and less industrious to please him. They think all he can do for them is their due, and still they expect more: and when they fail in their expectations (as 'tis impossible to satisfy them) their disappointment makes them discontented, and their discontents dangerous. Therefore all tyrants follow the example of Dionysius, who was said to use his friends as he did his bottles: when he had use for them, he kept them by him; when he had none, that they would not trouble him and lie in his way, he hung them up.

But to conclude this already over-long paper, let every man to whom God has given the spirit of wisdom and courage be persuaded by his honour, his safety, his own good and his country's, and indeed the duty he owes to his generation, and to mankind, to endeavour by all rational means to free the world of this pest. Let not other nations have the occasion to think so meanly of us, as if we resolved to sit still and have our ears bored, or that any discouragement or disappointments can ever make us desist from attempting our liberty, till we have purchased it, either by this monster's death, or by our own. Our nation is not yet so barren of virtue that we want noble examples to follow amongst ourselves. The brave Sindercombe has showed as great a mind as any old Rome could boast of; and had he lived there his name had been registered with Brutus and Cato, and he had had his statues as well as they.

But I will not have so sinister an opinion of ourselves (as little generosity as slavery has left us) as to think so great a virtue can want its monuments, even amongst us. Certainly in every virtuous mind there are statues reared to Sindercombe. Whenever we read the elegies of those that have died for their country, when we admire those great examples of magnanimity that have tired tyrants' cruelties, when we extol their constancy whom neither bribes nor terrors could make betray their friends, 'tis then we erect Sindercombe statues, and grave him monument. Where all that can be said of a great and noble mind [is said], we justly make an epitaph for him. And though the tyrant caused him to be smothered, lest the people should hinder an open murder, yet he will never be able either to smother his memory, or his own villainy. His poison was but a poor and common device to impose only on those that understood not tyrant's practices, and are unacquainted (if any be) with his cruelties and falsehoods. He may therefore, if he please, take away the stake from Sindercombe's grave; and, if he have a mind it should be known how he died, let him send thither the pillows and feather-beds with which Barkstead and his hangman smothered him.

But, to conclude, let not this monster think himself the more secure, that he has suppressed one great spirit: he may be confident that *longus post illum sequitur ordo idem petentium decus*: there's a great roll behind, even of those that are in his own muster-rolls, that are ambitious of the name of the deliverers of their country, and they know what the action is that will purchase it. His bed, his table is not secure; and he stands in need of other guards to defend him against his own. Death and destruction pursues him wheresoever he goes: they follow him everywhere like his fellow-travellers, and at last they will come upon him like armed men. Darkness is hid in his secret places. A fire not blown shall consume him; it shall go ill with him that is left in his tabernacle. He shall flee from the iron weapon, and a bow of steel shall strike him through. Because he has oppressed and forsaken the poor, because he has violently taken away a house which he builded not, we may be confident – and so may he – that ere long all this will be accomplished. For the triumphing of the wicked is but short, and the joy of the hypocrite but for a moment. Though his Excellency mount up to the Heavens, and his head reaches unto the clouds, yet he shall perish for ever, like his own dung. They that have seen him shall say: Where is he?

. . . Courteous Reader,

Expect another sheet or two of paper of this subject if I escape the tyrant's hands, although he gets (in the interim) the crown upon his head, which he has (underhand) put his confederates on to petition his acceptance thereof.

NOTES ON THE TEXTS

1. Ascham, *Of the Confusions and Revolutions of Goverments* (1649): First edition, *A Discourse: Wherein is Examined, What is Particularly Lawfull during the Confusions and Revolutions of Government* (1648 (2 edns.), 1689); revised edition, *Of the Confusions* . . . 1649; facsimile reprint of this edition, Delmar, N.Y., 1975.

2. Sanderson, *A Resolution of Conscience* (1649): Reprinted in [A. Ascham], *A Reply to a Paper of Dr. Sanderson's* (1650); in G. D'Oyly, *Life of W. Sancroft* (two vols., Oxford, 1821, 1840) and in Sanderson's *Works* (six vols., Oxford, 1854).

3, 4. *Act for the Abolishing the Kingly Office* (1649) and *Act for Subscribing the Engagement* (1650): The standard edition is C. H. Firth and R. S. Rait (eds.), *Acts and Ordinances of the Interregnum, 1642–60* (three vols., London, 1911). I have also consulted the text given in J. P. Kenyon (ed.), *The Stuart Constitution* (Cambridge, 1966).

5. *Some Scruples of Conscience* (1650): Printed in J. Dury, *Objections Against the Taking of the Engagement Answered* (1650), and reprinted here for the first time.

6. Allen [Sexby], *Killing Noe Murder*: 1657 (printed in the Low Countries); 1658 (French translation; Brussels?); 1659 (Brussels?), with appendix by S. Titus; 1689 (two editions, each surviving in two states; one of the two editions attributed to S. Titus). Apart from these seventeenth-century editions, O. Lutaud, *Des révolutions d'Angleterre à la Révolution française* (The Hague, 1973), lists a further seventeen English editions and five French editions, plus five editions of the epistle dedicatory to Cromwell, prior to his own re-edition of the first English and French editions.

FURTHER READING

The political events which led to the trial and execution of the king and the establishment of the Commonwealth are brilliantly analysed in D. Underdown, *Pride's Purge* (Oxford, 1971). The best modern account of the trial is C. V. Wedgwood, *The Trial of Charles I* (London, 1964).

The most famous of the spokesmen for the Commonwealth was, of course, John Milton. Two accounts of Milton in relationship to the Civil War are C. Hill, *Milton and the English Revolution* (London, 1977), and A. Milner, *John Milton and the English Revolution* (London, 1981). Milton's defences of tyrannicide are in M. Y. Hughes (ed.), *The Complete Prose Works of John Milton*, vol. III (New Haven, 1962).

The literature of the Engagement controversy has been detailed by J. M. Wallace, 'The Engagement Controversy, 1649–52', *Bulletin of the New York Public Library*, LXVIII (1964), pp. 384–405. Accounts of the controversy are to be found in the same author's *Destiny His Choice: The Loyalism of Andrew Marvell* (Cambridge, 1968), and M. A. Judson, *From Tradition to Political Reality, 1649–53* (Hamden, Conn., 1980). Two tracts defending the Engagement which have been reprinted are M. Nedham, *The Case of the Commonwealth of England, Stated*, ed. P. A. Knachel (Charlottesville, 1969) and J. Dury, *Considerations Concerning the Present Engagement* (Exeter, 1979).

Current interest in the Engagement controversy derives in large part from the fact that Quentin Skinner has argued in a number of overlapping studies that Hobbes's *Leviathan* should be read in the light of it: 'The Ideological Context of Hobbes's Political Thought', *Historical Journal*, IX (1966), pp. 286–317; 'Conquest and Consent: Thomas Hobbes and the Engagement Controversy', in G. E. Aylmer (ed.), *The Interregnum* (London, 1972); 'The Context of Hobbes's Theory of Political Obligation', in R. S. Peters and M. Cranston (eds.), *Hobbes and Rousseau* (New York, 1972). Skinner's account both of Hobbes and the controversy is criticized by S. A. State in 'Text and Context: Skinner, Hobbes and Theistic Natural Law', *Historical Journal*, XXVIII (1985), pp. 27–50.

There is a seventeenth-century biography of Sanderson by Izaak Walton and a modern study by K. Kelly (*Conscience: Dictator or Guide?* (London, 1967)). On *Killing Noe Murder* there is O. Lutaud, *Des révolutions d'Angleterre à la Révolution française* (The Hague, 1973).

CHAPTER SEVEN

THE SCIENCE OF LIBERTY

1   Francis Bacon, *The Essayes or Counsels, Civill and Morall* (1625)

Bacon (1561–1626) was the younger son of a prominent Elizabethan politician. In 1597 he published the first of his *Essays*, and in 1605 his *Advancement of Learning*. After repeatedly serving in Parliament he became Solicitor-General in 1607 and Attorney-General in 1613. In this post he faithfully supported James in his conflicts with Coke and in 1617 he inherited Coke's position as Lord Keeper. In 1618 he became Lord Chancellor and Baron Verulam, and in 1621 Viscount St Albans. In that same year Parliament accused him of accepting bribes, a charge which he did not deny, although he claimed not to have been influenced by them, and he lost all his offices. In 1620 he had published *Novum Organum* and in 1625 he published the third and final edition of his *Essays*. He died in 1626, supposedly a victim of the new science he had advocated. He is said to have caught a chill after stuffing a chicken with snow in order to see if the cold would delay putrefaction.

His *Essays* exhibit many of the features which were later to characterize republican writings: a preoccupation with self-interest, a love of Machiavelli and a respect for republican governments. But they also serve as a warning that these features do not always imply a commitment to republicanism, or a distaste for unchecked authority, in practice.

2   James Harrington, *The Art of Lawgiving in Three Books* (1659)

Harrington (1611–77) came from a distinguished family, but little is known of his life before 1646, beyond the fact that he travelled in Italy and the Netherlands. In that year he briefly appears as a Gentleman of the Bedchamber to the captive Charles I, but then disappears from view again until he emerges in 1656 as the author of *Oceana*, the most original of seventeenth-century republican tracts, and a key work in the development of the idea of a science of politics. *Oceana* is sometimes described as a Utopia, but (as with many works to which that term is applied) Harrington's intention was to give a practical analysis of the problems and possibilities of his own society. *The Art of Lawgiving* was Harrington's second major work, and by 1659 a group of members of Parliament, led by Henry Neville, were employing Harringtonian arguments in order to urge the construction of a new type of republican regime. During 1659–60 Harrington published ten further pamphlets arguing for a republic and against the restoration of the monarchy and attacking those (such as Milton and Baxter) who wished to confine political power to the godly. He was arrested in 1661 and during his brief imprisonment lapsed into an insanity which never entirely left him thereafter.

3 Algernon Sidney, *Discourses Concerning Government* (1698)

Sidney (1622–83) was a younger son of the second Earl of Leicester and was raised at Penshurst. He served in the parliamentary armies during the first Civil War, being wounded at Marston Moor (1644), after which he became governor of Chester. He was elected to the Long Parliament in 1646, and was made Lieutenant of Dover in 1648. He opposed the execution of the king and refused to serve on the court which tried him. In 1651 he resigned his post as Lieutenant of Dover under threat of court-martial, but he was elected to the Council of State in 1652. He boycotted the Protectorate, but returned to Parliament in 1659 and was once more elected to the Council of State. He was abroad in Denmark as ambassador of the Commonwealth at the time of the Restoration and opted to stay in exile rather than make his terms with the new government. As a consequence he was pursued by assassins. In 1677 he finally returned to England to collect his legacy, and, after the failure of the Whigs' efforts to obtain the exclusion of James from succession to the throne by parliamentary means, he became actively involved in conspiracies against the government. He was arrested in 1683 and tried for treason in front of Judge Jeffreys. The main evidence against him was the manuscript of the *Discourses*. The prosecution maintained that 'the whole book is an argument for the people to rise and vindicate their

wrongs', and that 'compassing and imagining the death of the king is
the act of the mind, and is treason while it remains in the heart'. Thus
Sidney was condemned not for his deeds but his thoughts, although
not entirely without justification, since his *Discourses*, like Locke's
Two Treatises, were probably written not merely to undermine Fil-
merian absolutism, but to give legitimacy to the violent revolution
intended by those involved in the Rye House Plot. Sidney's brave
death, and the publication of the *Discourses* by Toland in 1698, made
him a hero of eighteenth-century radicals and revolutionaries.

1 Francis Bacon, *The Essayes or Counsels, Civill and Morall* (1625)

XIV: Of Nobility

We will speak of nobility, first as a portion of an estate, then as a condition of particular persons. A monarchy where there is no nobility at all is ever a pure and absolute tyranny, as that of the Turks. For nobility attempers sovereignty, and draws the eyes of the people somewhat aside from the line royal. But for democracies they need it not; and they are commonly more quiet, and less subject to sedition than where there are stirps of nobles. For men's eyes are upon the business and not upon the persons; or, if upon the persons, it is for the business' sake, as fittest, and not for flags and pedigree. We see the Switzers last well, notwithstanding their diversity of religion and of cantons; for utility is their bond and not respects. The United Provinces of the Low Countries in their government excel; for where there is an equality, the consultations are more indifferent, and the payments and tributes more cheerful. A great and potent nobility adds majesty to a monarch, but diminishes power, and puts life and spirit into the people, but presses their fortune. It is well when nobles are not too great for sovereignty, nor for justice, and yet maintained in that height, as the insolency of inferiors may be broken upon them, before it come on too fast upon the majesty of kings. A numerous nobility causes poverty and inconvenience in a state; for it is a surcharge of expense; and besides, it being a necessity that many of the nobility fall in time to be weak in fortune, it makes a kind of disproportion between honour and means.

As for nobility in particular persons, it is a reverend thing to see an ancient castle or building not in decay; or to see a fair timber tree sound and perfect. How much more to behold an ancient noble family which has stood against the waves and weathers of time. For new nobility is but the act of power; but ancient nobility is the act of time. Those that are first raised to nobility are commonly more virtuous but less innocent than their descendants; for there is rarely any rising but by a co-mixture of good and evil arts. But it is reason the memory of their virtues remain to their posterity, and their faults die with themselves. Nobility of birth commonly abates industry;

and he that is not industrious envies him that is. Besides, noble persons cannot go much higher; and he that stands at a stay, when others rise, can hardly avoid motions of envy. On the other side, nobility extinguishes the passive envy from others towards them, because they are in possession of honour. Certainly, kings that have able men of their nobility shall find ease in employing them, and a better slide into their business; for people naturally bend to them as born in some sort to command.

XXI: Of Delays

Fortune is like the market, where many times, if you can stay a little, the price will fall. And, again, it is sometimes like Sibylla's offer, which at first offers the commodity at full, then consumes part and part, and still holds up the price; for occasion, as it is in the common verse, 'turns a bald noddle after she has presented her locks in front, and no hold taken'; or, at least, turns the handle of the bottle first to be received, and after the belly, which is hard to clasp. There is surely no greater wisdom than well to time the beginnings and onsets of things. Dangers are no more light if they once seem light, and more dangers have deceived men than forced them; nay, it were better to meet some dangers half-way, though they come nothing near, than to keep too long a watch upon their approaches; for if a man watch too long, it is odds he will fall asleep. On the other side, to be deceived with too long shadows, as some have been when the moon was low and shone on their enemy's back, and so to shoot off before the time, or to teach dangers to come on, by over early buckling towards them, is another extreme. The ripeness, or unripeness, of the occasion, as we said, must ever be well weighed, and generally it is good to commit the beginnings of all great actions to Argos with his hundred eyes, and the ends to Briareus with his hundred hands, first to watch and then to speed; for the helmet of Pluto, which makes the politic man go invisible, is secrecy in the counsel, and celerity in the execution. For when things are once come to the execution there is no secrecy comparable to celerity, like the motion of a bullet in the air, which flies so swift as it outruns the eye.

2 James Harrington, *The Art of Lawgiving in Three Books* (1659)

The First Book: Showing the Foundations and Superstructures of All the Kinds of Government

If the foundations be destroyed, what can the righteous do? (Or, when foundations are destroyed, what have the righteous done?)

Psalms 11: 3

The Preface: Considering the Principles or Nature of Family Government

Divines and like studious assertors of monarchy have taken their rise (not so fairly while they have concealed one part) from the right of paternity or from the government of families; which may be of two kinds, whereof they have taken notice but of one. For family government may be as necessarily popular in some cases as monarchical in others.

To show the nature of the monarchical family: put the case a man have one thousand pounds a year or so; he marries a wife, has children, has servants depending upon him at his good will, in the distribution of his estate for their livelihood. Suppose then that this estate come to be spent or lost, where is the monarchy of this family? But if the master were no otherwise monarchical than by virtue of his estate, then the foundation or balance of his empire was in the thousand pounds a year.

That from these principles there may also be a popular family is apparent: for suppose six or ten, having each three hundred pounds a year or so, shall agree to dwell together as one family; can any one of these pretend to be lord and master of the same, or to dispose of the estates of all the rest? Or do they not agree together upon such orders unto which they consent equally to submit? But if so, then certainly must the government of this family be a government of laws or orders, and not a government of a man, or of some three or four of these men.

Not but that, the one man in the monarchical family giving laws, and the many in the popular family doing no more, it may in this sense be indifferently said that all laws are made by men; but that where the law is made by one man, there it may be unmade by one man, so that the man is not governed by the law, but the law by the man; which amounts unto the government of the man, and not of the law; whereas, the law being not to be made but by the many, no man is governed by another man, but by that only which is the common interest, by which means this amounts unto a government of laws, and not of men.

That the politics may not be thought an unnecessary or difficult art, if these principles be less than obvious and undeniable, even unto any woman that knows what belongs to housekeeping, I confess that I have no more to say. But in case what has been said be unto all sorts and all capacities undeniable, it is most humbly submitted unto princes and parliaments whether, without violence or moving of property, they can make a popular family of the monarchical, or a monarchical family of the popular; or whether that be practicable or possible in a nation upon like balance or foundation in property, which is not in a family; a family being but a smaller society or nation, and a nation but a greater society or family.

That which is usually answered at this point is that the six or ten, thus agreeing to make one family, must have some steward; and to make such a steward in a nation is to make a king. But this is to resolve that the steward of a family is not answerable unto the masters of it, or to them upon whose estates, and not upon his own, he defrays the whole charge; for otherwise this stewardship cannot amount unto dominion, but must come only unto the true nature of magistracy, and indeed of annual magistracy in a commonwealth; forasmuch as such accounts, in the year's end at the farthest, use to be cast up, and the steward, body and estate, to be answerable for the same unto the proprietors or masters, who also have the undoubted right of constituting such other steward or stewards as to them shall seem good, or of prolonging the office of the same.

Now where a nation is cast by the unseen ways of providence into disorder of government, the duty of such especially as are elected by the people is not so much to regard what has been as to provide for the supreme law, or for the safety of the people, which consists in the true art of lawgiving.

The art of lawgiving is of two kinds: the one (as I may say) untrue, the other true. The untrue consists in the reduction of the balance unto arbitrary superstructures, which requires violence, as being contrary unto nature. The other in the erecting necessary superstructures, that is such as are conformable unto the balance or foundation; which, being purely natural, requires that all interposition of force be removed.

Chapter 1: Considering the Principles or Balance of National Governments, with the Different Kinds of the Same

'The heaven', says David, 'even the heavens are the Lord's; but the earth has he given unto the children of men'; yet, says God unto the father of these children, 'In the sweat of thy face shalt thou eat thy bread.' *Dii laborantibus sua munera vendunt.* The donation of the earth by God unto man comes unto a kind of selling it for industry, a treasure which seems to purchase of God. From the different kinds and successes of this industry, whether in arms or in other exercise of the mind or body, derives the natural equity of dominion or property; and from the legal establishment or distribution of this property (be it more or less approaching towards the natural equity of the same) derives all government.

The distribution of property, so far forth as it regards the nature or procreation of government, lies in the over-balance of the same; after the manner that a man who has two thousand pounds a year may have a retinue, and so a strength, that is three times greater than his who has but five hundred pounds a year. Not to speak at this time of money, which in small territories may be of like effect, but to insist upon the main, which is property in land, the over-balance of this, as it was at first constituted or comes insensibly to be changed in a nation, may be especially of three kinds: that is, in one, in the few, or in the many.

The over-balance of land, three to one or thereabouts, in one man against the whole people, creates absolute monarchy, as when Joseph had purchased all the lands of the Egyptians for Pharaoh. The constitution of a people in which, and like cases, is capable of entire servitude: 'Buy us and our land for bread, and we and our land will be servants unto Pharaoh.'

The over-balance of land, unto the like proportion, in the few against the whole people creates aristocracy, or regulated monarchy, as of late in England; and hereupon says Samuel unto the people of

Israel when they would have a king: 'He will take your fields, even the best of them, and give them unto his servants.' The constitution of a people in this and in like cases is neither capable of entire liberty, nor of entire servitude.

The over-balance of land unto the like proportion in the people, or where neither one nor the few over-balance the whole people, creates popular government; as in the division of the land of Canaan unto the whole people of Israel by lot. The constitution of a people in which, and like cases, is capable of entire freedom, nay, not capable of any other settlement; it being certain that if a monarch or single person in such a state, through the taint or improvidence of counsels, should carry it, yet, through the irresistible force of nature, or the reason alleged by Moses ('I am not able to bear all this people alone, because it is too heavy for me') he could not carry it, but out of the deep waters would cry unto them whose feet he had stuck in the mire.

Wherever the balance of a government be, there naturally is the militia of the same; and against him or them where the militia is naturally, there can be no negative vote.

If a prince hold the over-balance, as in Turkey, in him is the militia, as the janissaries and timariots. If a nobility hold the over-balance, the militia is in them, as among us was seen in the Barons' Wars, and those of York and Lancaster; and in France is seen when, any considerable part of that nobility flying out, they are not to be reduced but by the major part of their order remaining unto the king.

If a people have the over-balance, as in Israel, the militia is in them, as in the four hundred first decreeing and then waging war against Benjamin; where it may be inquired what power there was on earth having a negative voice unto this assembly.

This where there is settlement, or where a government is natural. Where there is no settlement, or where the government is unnatural, it arises from one of two causes: either imperfection in the balance, or such corruption in the lawgivers whereby a government is instituted contrary unto the balance. Imperfections of the balance, that is where it is not good or downweight, cause imperfect governments, as those of the Roman and of the Florentine people, and those of the Hebrew kings and Roman emperors, being each exceedingly bloody, or at the least stormy.

Government against the balance, in one, is tyranny, as that of the Athenian Peisistratus; in the few, is oligarchy, as that of the Roman decemvirs; in the many, is anarchy, as that under the Neapolitan Masaniello.

Where, through causes unforeseen by human providence, the balance comes to be entirely changed, it is the more immediately to be attributed unto divine providence; and whereas God cannot will the necessary cause, but he must also will the necessary effect or consequence, what government soever is in the necessary direction of the balance, the same is of divine right; whereof, though of the Israelites God says, 'They have set up kings, and not by me; they have made princes, and I knew it not,' yet to the small countries adjoining unto the Assyrian empire, he says, 'Now have I given all these lands into the hand of the king of Babylon my servant . . . Serve the king of Babylon, and live.'

Chapter 2: Showing the Variation of the English Balance

The lands in the hold of the nobility and clergy of England, till Henry VII, cannot be esteemed to have over-balanced those in the hold of the people less than four to one. Whereas in our days, the clergy being destroyed, the lands in hold of the people over-balance those in the hold of the nobility, at the least nine in ten. In showing how this change came about, some would have it that I assume unto myself more than my share; albeit they find not me delivering that which must rely upon authority and not vouching my authors. But Henry VII, being conscious of infirmity in his title, yet finding with what strength and vigour he was brought in by the nobility, conceived jealousies of like power in case of decay or change of affections. *Nondum orbis adoraverat Romam:* the lords yet led country lives; their houses were open to retainers, men experienced in military affairs, and capable of leading; their hospitality was the delight of their tenants, by their tenures or dependence obliged to follow their lords in arms. So that this being the militia of the nation, a few noblemen discontented could at any time levy a great army; the effect whereof, both in the Barons' Wars and those of York and Lancaster, had been well known unto divers kings. This state of affairs was that at which Henry VII made advantage of troubled times, and frequent unruliness of retainers, to take his aim; while, under pretence of curbing riots, he obtained the passing of such laws as cut off retainers, in which the nobility lost their officers. Then, whereas the dependence of the people upon their lords was of a strict tie or nature, he found means to loosen this also, by laws which he obtained upon as fair a pretence, even that of population. Thus:

> Farms were so brought unto a standard that, the houses being kept up, each of them did of necessity enforce a dweller; and the proportion of land laid unto each house did of necessity enforce that dweller not to be a beggar or cottager, but a man able to keep servants, and set the plough on going. By which means a great part of the lands of this nation came in effect to be amortized unto the hold of the yeomanry or middle people.

whereof consisted the main body of the militia, hereby incredibly advanced, and which henceforth, like cleaner underwood less choked by their staddles, began to grow exceedingly. But the nobility, who by the former laws had lost their officers, by this lost their soldiery. Yet remained unto them their estates till, the same prince introducing the statutes for alienations, these also became loose; and the lords, less taken (for the reasons shown) with their country lives, where their trains were clipped, by degrees became courtiers – where greater pomp and expense, by the statutes of alienations, began to plume them of their estates. The court was yet at Bridewell, nor reached London any farther than Temple Bar. The later growth of this city, and in that the declining of the balance unto popularity, derives from the decay of the nobility and of the clergy. In the reign of the succeeding king were abbeys (than which nothing more dwarfs a people) demolished.

I did not, I do not attribute the effects of these things thus far unto my own particular observation, but always did and do attribute a sense thereof unto the reign of Queen Elizabeth, and the wisdom of her council. There is yet living testimony that the ruin of the English monarchy, through the causes mentioned, was frequently attributed unto Henry VII by Sir Henry Wotton; which tradition is not unlike to have descended upon from the Queen's council. But there is difference between having a sense of a thing, and making a right use of that sense. Let a man read Plutarch in the lives of Agis and of the Gracchi: there can be no plainer demonstration of the Lacedaemonian or Roman balance. Yet read his discourse of government in his *Morals*, and he has forgotten it: he makes no use, no mention at all of any such thing. Who could have been plainer upon this point than Sir Walter Raleigh where, to prove that the kings of Egypt were not elective but hereditary, he alleges that if the kings of Egypt had been elective, 'the children of Pharaoh must have been more mighty than the king, as landlords of all Egypt and the king himself their tenant'? Yet when he comes to speak of government he has no regard unto, no remembrance of, any such principle. In Mr Selden's *Titles of Honour*, he has demonstrated the English balance of the peerage, without making any application of it, or indeed perceiving it, there or in times when the defect of the same came to give so full a sense of it. The like might be made apparent in Aristotle, in Machiavelli, in my Lord Verulam, in all, in any politician; there is not one of them in whom may not be found as right a sense of this principle as in this present narrative, or in whom may be found a righter use of it than was made by any of the parties thus far concerned in this story, or by Queen Elizabeth and her council.

> If a prince (says a great author [Machiavelli]), to reform a government, were obliged to depose himself, he might, in neglecting of it, be capable of some excuse; but, reformation of government being that with which a principality may stand, he deserves no excuse at all.

It is indeed not observed by this author that where, through declination of the balance unto popularity, the state requires reformation in the superstructures, there the prince cannot rightly reform unless from sovereign power he descend unto a principality in a commonwealth; nevertheless, upon like occasions this fails not to be found so in nature and experience. The growth of the people of England, since the ruins mentioned of the nobility and the clergy, came in the reign of Queen Elizabeth to more than stood with the interest, or indeed the nature of well-founded or durable monarchy; as was prudently perceived, but withal temporized, by her council, who (if the truth of her government be rightly weighed) seem rather to have put her upon the exercise of principality in a commonwealth, than of sovereign power in a monarchy. Certain it is that she courted not her nobility, nor gave her mind, as monarchs seated upon the like order, to balance her great men, or reflect upon their power now inconsiderable, but ruled wholly (with an art she had unto high perfection) by humouring and blessing her people. For this but shadow of a commonwealth is she yet famous, and shall ever be. Though had she introduced the full perfection of the orders requisite unto popular government, first, it had established such principality unto her successors as they might have held. Secondly, this principality (the commonwealth, as Rome of Romulus, being born of such a parent) might have retained the royal dignity and revenue to the full, improved and discharged of all envy. Thirdly, it had saved all the blood and confusion which, through this neglect in her and her successors, has ensued. Fourthly, it had bequeathed unto the people a light not so naturally by them to be discovered, which is [a] pity:

> For even as the many, through the difference of opinions that must needs abound among them, are not apt to introduce a government, as not understanding the good of it, so the many, having by trial or experience once attained unto this understanding, agree not to quit such a government. [Machiavelli]

And lastly, it had estated this nation in that full felicity which, so far as concerns mere prudence, is in the capacity of human nature. To this queen succeeded King James, who likewise regardless of this point (in which nevertheless he was so seen, as not seldom to prophesy sad things unto his successors), neither his new peerage (which in abundance he created) nor the old availed him against that dread wherein, more freely than prudently, he discovered himself to stand of parliaments, as now mere popular councils, and running unto popularity of government like a bowl down the hill; not so much (I may say) of malice prepensed, as of natural instinct, whereof the Petition of Right, well heeded, is sufficient testimony. All persuasion of court eloquence, all patience for such as but looked that way, was now lost. There remained nothing unto the destruction of a monarchy retaining but the name, more than a prince who by striving should make the people to feel those advantages which they could not see.

And this happened in the next king, who, too secure in that undoubted right whereby he was advanced unto a throne which had no foundation, dared to put this unto unseasonable trial; on whom therefore fell the tower in Siloam. Nor may we think that they upon whom this tower fell were sinners above all men; but that we, unless we repent and look better unto foundations, must likewise perish. We have had later princes, later parliaments; in what have they excelled, or where are they? The balance not heeded, no effectual work can be made as to settlement; and heeded, as it now stands in England, requires unto settlement no less than the superstructures natural unto popular government; and the superstructures natural unto popular government require no less than the highest skill or art that is in political architecture. The sum of which particulars amounts unto this: that the safety of the people of England is now plainly cast upon skill or sufficiency in political architecture. It is not enough that there are honest men addicted unto all the good ends of a commonwealth, unless there be skill also in the formation of those proper means whereby such ends may be attained unto. Which is as sad as a true account; this being in all experience, and in the judgement of all politicians, that whereof the many are incapable. And though the meanest citizen, not informing the commonwealth of what he knows or conceives to concern her safety, commit[s] an heinous crime against God and his country, such is the temper of later [i.e. recent] times that a man, having offered any aid at this loss, has escaped well if he be scorned and not ruined.

But to proceed: if the balance or state of property in a nation be the efficient cause of government, and, the balance being fixed, the government (as by the present narrative is evinced) must remain inconstant or floating, then the process in formation of a government must be first by fixation of the balance, and next by erecting such superstructures as to the nature thereof are necessary.

Chapter 3: Of Fixation of the Balance, or of Agrarian Laws

Fixation of the balance of property is not to be provided for but by laws; and the laws whereby such provision is made are commonly called agrarian laws. Now as governments through the diverse balance of property are of diverse or contrary natures, that is monarchical or popular, so are such laws. Monarchy requires of the standard of property that it be vast or great, and of agrarian laws that they bar recess or diminution, at least insomuch as is thereby entailed upon the honour. But popular government requires that her standard be moderate, and that her agrarian bar accumulation. In a territory not exceeding England in revenue, if the balance be in more hands than three hundred, it is upon swaying from monarchy; and if it be in fewer than five thousand hands, it is swaying from a commonwealth; which as to this point may suffice at present.

Chapter 4: Showing the Superstructures of Governments

That the policy or superstructures of all absolute monarchs, more particularly of the eastern empires, are not only contained but meliorated in the Turkish government, requires no further proof than to compare them; but because such a work would not lie in a small compass, it shall suffice for this time to say that such superstructures of government as are natural unto an absolute prince, or sole landlord of a large territory, require for the first storey that, what demesnes he shall think fit to reserve being set apart, the rest divided into horse quarters, or military farms, for life or at will, and not otherwise. And that every tenant, for every hundred pounds a year so holden, be by condition of his tenure obliged to attend his sovereign lord in person, in arms, and at his proper cost and charges, with one horse, so often and so long as he shall be commanded upon service. These among the Turks are called timariots.

The second storey of this building requires that these horse quarters or military farms be divided by convenient precincts or proportions into distinct provinces; and that each province have one governor or commander in chief of the same, at the will and pleasure of his grand signor, or for three years and no longer. Such among the Turks (unless by additional honours they be called bashaws or viziers) are the *beglerbegs*.

For the third storey, there must of necessity be a mercenary army, consisting both of horse and foot, for the guard of the prince's person and for the guard of his empire, by keeping the governors of provinces so divided that they be not suffered to lay their arms or heads together, or to hold correspondence or intelligence with each other. Which mercenary army ought not to be constituted of such as have already contracted some other interest, but to consist of men so educated from their very childhood as not to know that they have any other parent or native country than the prince and his empire. Such among the Turks are the foot, called janizaries, and the horse, called spahis.

The prince, accommodated with a privy council consisting of such as have been governors of provinces, is the top stone. This council among the Turks is called the divan, and this prince the grand signor.

The superstructures proper unto regulated monarchy, or unto the government of a prince some three or four hundred of whose nobility, or of whose nobility and clergy, hold three parts in four of the territory, must either be by his personal influence upon the balance, or by virtue of orders.

If a prince, by easing his nobility of taxes and feeding them with such as are extorted from the people, can so accommodate their ambition and avarice with great offices and commands that, a party flying out, he can over-balance and reduce them by a greater part of their own order, he may have greater power and less security, as at present in France.

The safer way of this government is by orders; and the orders proper hereunto consist especially of an hereditary senate of the nobility, admitting also of the clergy, and of a representative of the people made up of their menial servants, or such as by tenure and for livelihood have immediate dependence upon them, as formerly in England.

An aristocracy or state of nobility, to exclude the people, must govern by a king; or to exclude a king, must govern by the people. Nor is there, without a senate or mixture of aristocracy, any popular government. Whence, though for discourse sake politicians speak of pure aristocracy and pure democracy, there is no such thing as either in nature, art or example.

Where the people are not over-balanced by one man or by the few, they are not capable of any other superstructures of government, or of any other just and quiet settlement whatsoever, than of such as consists of a senate as their counsellors, or themselves or their representatives as sovereign lords, and of a magistracy answerable unto the people as distributors and executioners of the laws made by the people; and thus much is of absolute necessity unto any or every government that is or can properly be called a commonwealth, whether it be well- or ill-ordered. But the necessary definition of a commonwealth anything well-ordered is that it is a government consisting of the senate proposing, the people resolving and the magistracy executing. (Magistracy is a style proper unto the executive part; yet because in discourse of this kind it is hardly avoidable but such as are of the proposing or resolving assemblies will be sometimes comprised under this name or style, it shall be enough for excuse to say that magistracy may be esteemed of two kinds: the one proper or executive, the other improper or legislative.)

A senate may consist of an hereditary order, elective for life by itself [i.e. by co-optation], or by some magistrate or magistrates of the same; as the senate of Rome consisted of the patrician order, thereinto eligible first by the consuls and then by the censors. A senate may consist of senators elected by the people for life, as that of Lacedaemon. It may consist of senators eligible by the people for terms, without vacation or interval, as the senate of Venice; or with interval, as the senate of Athens, which also, for another difference, was elected by lot.

A popular assembly may consist of the whole people, as the great council of Venice (for the Venetians, though called in respect of their subjects nobility, are all that free people which is comprised in that commonwealth) or of a representative, as in Israel. Again, a representative of the people may be for life, as in the particular cities and sovereignties of Holland, improperly called senates; or it may be upon rotation, that is to say by changes or courses, as that of Israel and the present representative in England; it may also be by lot, as the Roman tribes called the prerogative and the *jure vocatae*.

To speak of magistrates in a commonwealth, and all their kinds, were to begin an endless discourse; the present I shall therefore confine to such only as may be called supreme magistrates. The supreme magistracy of a commonwealth may be in one or more; and it may be for life, or for terms and vacations. In one elective by the people for life, as in the duke of Venice, whose function is civil and not military. In two hereditarily, as in the two kings of Lacedaemon, whose function was rather military than civil. In nine annually elective by the people, as in the nine princes or *archontes* of Athens. In two annually elected by the people, as the Roman consuls, whose power was both military and civil. In fine, it may be, whether in one or more, for life or for terms and vacations, as shall best suit with the occasion.

Some commonwealths consist of distinct sovereignties, as Switz[erland] and Holland; others are collected into one and the same sovereignty, as most of the rest. Again, some commonwealths have been upon rotation or courses in the representative only, as Israel; others in the magistracy only, as Rome; some in the senate and in the magistracy, as Athens and Venice; others in some part of the magistracy, and in others not, as Lacedaemon, in the *ephori* and not in the kings, and Venice, not in the duke nor in the *procuratori*, but in all the rest. Holland, except in the election of states provincial (which is emergent), admits not of any rotation or courses. There may be a commonwealth admitting of rotation throughout, in the senate, in the representative and in the magistracy, as that proposed in *Oceana*.

Rotation, if it be perfect, is equal election by, and succession of, the whole people unto magistracy by terms and vacations. Equal election may be by lot, as that of the senate of Athens; by suffrage, as that of Lacedaemon; or by ballot, as that of Venice, which of all other is the most equal. The ballot as it is used in Venice consists of a lot, whence derives the right of proposing, and of an unseen way of suffrage or of resolving [i.e. a nominating committee is selected by lot, and its recommendations are then voted on by secret ballot].

From the wonderful variety of parts and difference of mixture, hitherto scarce touched, result those admirable differences that are in the constitution and genius of popular governments; some being for defence, some for increase [i.e. conquest]; some more equal, others unequal; some turbulent and seditious, others like soft streams in perpetual tranquillity.

That which causes innate sedition in a commonwealth is inequality, as in Rome, where the senate oppressed the people. But if a commonwealth be perfectly equal, she is void of sedition, and has attained unto perfection, as being void of all internal causes of dissolution. An equal commonwealth is a government founded upon a balance which is perfectly popular, and well fixed by a suitable agrarian; and which, from the balance through the free suffrage of the people given by the ballot, amounts in the superstructures unto a senate debating and proposing, a representative of the people resolving, and a magistracy executing; each of these three orders being upon courses or rotation, that is, elected for certain terms, enjoining like intervals.

Such constitutions in a government as regard the frame or model of it are called orders; and such things as are enacted by [i.e. according to] the legislative orders are called laws. To undertake the binding of a prince from invading liberty, and yet not to introduce the whole orders necessary unto popular government, is to undertake a flat contradiction, or plain impossibility.

A people or assembly, not discerning of true principles, give least credit unto the best orders, and so come to cast themselves upon men;

for where orders are not credited, there men must be trusted; and where men are trusted they find themselves so well that they are either for bringing in a commonwealth by degrees or not at all. The desire of bringing in a commonwealth by degrees arises from want of consideration that the whole of a commonwealth, as to charge or trouble, is less than the half. He who has a journey to go does not choose to have but half a bridle, or but one boot or stirrup, though these be fewer things, and come but unto half the charge; because this would but necessitate unto more things, and more chargeable or dangerous things.

> *Optimus ille animi vindex, laedentia pectus*
> *Vincula qui rupit, dedoluitque semel.*
> [He best wins freedom for himself who has broken the chains that hurt his soul, and once and for all overcome the pain]
>
> Ovid, *Remedium Amoris*, ll. 293–4

The Conclusion: Observing that the Principles of Human Prudence, being Good without Proof out of Scripture, are Nevertheless Such as are Provable out of Scripture

Who imagines that the Romans governed by proof out of Scripture? Yet says Peter, 'Submit yourselves unto' human prudence or 'every ordinance of man', which relates more particularly unto the government of the Romans. The most frequent comparison of a commonwealth is to a ship; but who imagines that a ship ought not to be built according to the art of the shipwright, or governed according unto the compass, unless these be proved out of Scripture? Nevertheless, as hitherto I have proved the principles of human prudence in the parts out of Holy Scripture, so I undertake to vindicate them in the whole, as to the entire frame of popular government, in the ensuing book, by the same authority and undeniable evidence. [There follows the Second Book, *Showing the Frames of the Commonwealths of Israel and of the Jews*, omitted here.]

. . . .

The Third Book: Containing a Model of Popular Government Practicably Proposed According to the Foregoing Art, Confirmed by the Scripture, and According to the Present Balance or State of Property in England

Thy youth is renewed like the eagle's. Psalm 103: 5

The Preface: Containing a Model of Popular Government Proposed Notionally

There is, between the discourses of such as are commonly called natural philosophers and those of anatomists, large difference; the former are facile, the latter difficult. Philosophers discoursing of elements – for example, that the body of man consists of fire, air, earth and water – are easily both understood and credited, in that by common experience we see the body of man returns unto the earth from whence it was taken. Like entertainment may befall the elements of government, as in the first of these books they are stated. But the fearful and wonderful making, the admirable structure and great variety of the parts of man's body, in which the discourses of anatomists are altogether conversant, are understood by so few that I may say they are not understood by any. Certain it is that the delivery of a model of government (which either must be of none effect, or embrace all those muscles, nerves, arteries and bones which are necessary unto any function of a well-ordered commmonwealth) is no less than political anatomy. If you come short of this, your discourse is altogether ineffectual; if you come home, you are not understood. You may, perhaps, be called a learned author; but you are obscure and your doctrine is impracticable.

Now had I suffered in this, and not the people, I should long since have left them unto their humour, but seeing it is they that suffer by it, and not myself, I will be yet more a fool, or they shall be yet wiser. It comes into my head that I saw long since, upon an Italian stage, while the spectators wanted hoops for their sides: a country fellow came with an apple in his hand, unto which, in strange variety of faces, his teeth were undoubtedly threatened, when entered a young anatomist brimful of his last lesson, who, staying in good time the hand of this same country fellow, would by no means suffer him to go on with so great an enterprise, till he had first named and described unto him all the bones, nerves and muscles which are naturally necessary unto that motion; at which the good man being with admiration plainly chap-fallen, comes me in a third, who, snatching away the apple, devoured it in the presence of them both. If the people, in this case whereof I am speaking, were naturally so well furnished, I had here learned enough to have kept silence; but their eating in the political way of absolute necessity requires the aid of some political anatomist, without which they may have appetites, but will be chap-fallen. Examples whereof they have had but too many; one I think may be insisted upon without envy.

This is that which was called *The [Second] Agreement of the People*, consisting in sum of these propositions:

> That there be a representative of the nation consisting of four hundred persons, or not above.

Which proposition puts the bar on the quite contrary side; this being the first example of a commonwealth wherein it was conceived that five hundred thousand men or more might be represented by four hundred. The representation of the people in one man causes monarchy, and in a few causes oligarchy; the many can be no otherwise represented in a state of liberty than by so many, and so qualified, as may within the compass of that number and nature embrace the interest of the whole people. Government should be established upon a rock, not set upon a precipice; a representative consisting but of four hundred, though in the nature thereof it be popular, is not in itself a weapon that is fixed, but has something of the broken bow, as still apt to start aside unto monarchy.

But the paucity of number is tempered with the shortness of term, it being further provided:

> That this representative be biennial, and sit not above eight months.

But seeing a supreme council in a commonwealth is neither assembled nor dissolved but by stated orders, directing upwards an irresistible strength from the root, and as one tooth or one nail is driven out by another, how is it provided that this biennial council shall not be a perpetual council? Whereas there is nothing more dangerous in a commonwealth than entire removes of councils, how is it provided that these shall be men sufficiently experienced for the management of affairs? And last of all, whereas dissolution unto sovereign power is death, unto whom are these after eight months to bequeath the commonwealth? .

In this case it is provided:

> That there be a council of state elected by each new representative, within twenty days after their first meeting, to continue till ten days after the meeting of the next representative.

In which the faults observed in the former order are so much worse as this council consists of fewer.

Thus far this commonwealth is oligarchy; but it is provided:

That these representatives have sovereign power, save that in some things the people may resist them by arms.

Which first is a flat contradiction, and next is downright anarchy. Where the sovereign power is not as entire and absolute as in monarchy itself, there can be no government at all. It is not the limitation of sovereign power that is the cause of a commonwealth, but *such a libration or poise of orders, that there can be in the same no number of men, having the interest, that can have the power, nor any number of men, having the power, that can have the interest, to invade or disturb the government.* As the orders of commonwealths are more approaching to or remote from this maxim (of which this of the Levellers has nothing), so are they more quiet or turbulent.

In the religious part only – proposing a national religion and liberty of conscience – though without troubling themselves much with the means, they are right in the end. And for the military party they provide:

That no man (even in case of invasion) be compellable to go out of the country [i.e. county] where he lives if he procure another to serve in his room.

Which plainly entails upon this commonwealth a fit guard for such liberty, even a mercenary army; for what one does of this kind may and (where there is no bar) will be done by all; so every citizen, by money procuring his man, procures his master.

Now if this be work of that kind which the people in like cases (as those also of Rome, when they instituted their tribunes) do usually make, then have I good reason, not only to think but to speak it audibly, that to soothe up the people with an opinion of their own sufficiency in these things is not to befriend them, but to feed up all hopes of liberty unto the slaughter. Yet *The Leveller*, a late pamphlet, having gathered out of *Oceana* the principles by him otherwise well insinuated, attributes it unto the agitators, or that assembly which framed this wooden agreement of the people: 'That then some of that council asserted these principles, and the reason of them.'

But, raillery apart, we are not to think it has been for nothing that the wisest nations have, in the formation of government, as much relied upon the invention of some one man as upon themselves. For whereas it cannot be too often inculcated that reason consists of two parts, the one invention, the other judgement, a people or an assembly are not more eminent in the matter of judgement than void of invention. Nor is there in this anything at all against the sufficiency of a people in the management of a proper form, being once introduced, though they should never come to a perfect understanding of it. For were the bodies of the people such as they could commonly understand, they would be (as I may say) wooden bodies, or such as they could not use; whereas their bodies, being such as they understand not, are such in the use whereof they are perfect.

There are in models of government things of so facile use, and yet of so difficult understanding, that we must not think them even in Venice, who use their commonwealth with the greatest prudence and facility, to be all, or any considerable number of them, such as do perfectly understand the true reason or anatomy of that government; less is not to be presumed, in that not any of those Venetians who have written hitherto of their own form have brought the truth of it unto any perfect light. The like perhaps (and yet with due acknowledgement unto Livy) might be said of the Romans. The Lacedaemonians had not the right understanding of their model till, about the time of Aristotle, it was first written by Dicaearchus, one of his scholars. How egregiously our ancestors, till those foundations were broken which at length have brought us round, did manage the English sway is sufficiently known. Yet by one of the wisest of our writers (even my Lord Verulam) is Henry VII paralleled with the legislators of ancient and heroic times for the institution of those very laws which have now brought the monarchy unto utter ruin. The commonwealths upon which Machiavelli in his *Discourses* is incomparable, are not by him any one of them sufficiently explained or understood. Much less is it to be expected from a people that they should overcome like difficulties, through which the wisest nations, finding themselves in necessity of a change or of a new government, have usually done – by such offers as promised fair, or against which they could find no exceptions – as men do by new clothes: that is put them on, as such which, if they be not exactly fit at first, will either fit themselves unto the body in wearing, or thereby more plainly show wherein they may be mended, even by such as would otherwise prove but bad workmen. Nor has any like offer been thought to have more presumption, much less treason, in it, than if one conscious of skill in architecture should make offer of himself unto the prince or state to build a more convenient parliament-house.

England is now in such a condition that he who may be truly said to give her law shall never govern her; and he who will govern her shall never give her law. Yet some will have it that to assert popular power is to sow the seed of civil war, and object against a commonwealth, as not to be introduced but by arms, which, by the undeniable testimony of later experience, is of all other objections the most extravagant; for if the good old cause, against the maw even of the army, and of all men well affected to their country, could be trodden under foot without blood, what more certain demonstration can there be that, let the deliberations upon or changes of government be of what kind soever shall please a parliament, there is no appearance that they can occasion any civil war? Streams that are stopped may urge their banks; but the course of England into a commonwealth is both certain and natural.

The ways of nature require peace. The ways of peace require obedience unto laws. Laws in England cannot be made but by parliaments. Parliaments in England are come to be mere popular assemblies. The laws made by popular assemblies, though for a time they may be awed or deceived, in the end must be popular laws; and the sum of popular laws must amount unto a commonwealth.

The whole doubt or hazard of this sequel remains upon this one question: whether a single council – consisting but of four hundred; indued both with debate and result; the keys of whose doors are in the hands of ambitious men; in the crowd and confusion of whose election the people are as careless as tumultuous, and easy, through the want of good orders, to be deluded; while the clergy (declared and inveterate enemies of popular power) are there, laying about and sweating in the throng, as if it were in the vineyard; upon whose benches lawyers, being feathered and aimed like sharp and sudden arrows, with a private interest point-blank against the public, may and frequently do swarm – can indeed be called a popular council. This, I confess, may set the whole state of liberty upon the cast of a die; yet questionless is it more than odds for a commonwealth in often or long throwing: not through any certain run of genius or nature that can be in such a council, but through the impotence of such conclusions as can go awry, and the external force or state of property now fully introduced. Whence such a council may wander, but never find any rest or settlement, save only in that natural and proper form of government which is to be erected upon a mere popular foundation. All other ways of proceeding must be void, as inevitably guilty of contradiction in the superstructures unto the foundation. They have amounted and may amount unto discouragement of honest men, but with no other success than to embroil or retard business; England being not capable of any other permanent form than that only of a commonwealth, though her supreme council be so constituted that it may be monarchically inclined.

From this contradiction in the frame is the frequent rise of contradictory expostulations and questions. How, say they, should we have a commonwealth? Which way is it possible that it should come in? And how, say I, can we fail of a commonwealth? What possibility is there that we should miss of it? If a man answer, he answers thus: no army ever set up a commonwealth. To the contrary, I instance in the army of Israel under Moses; in that of Athens about the time of Alcibiades; in that of Rome upon the expulsion of the Tarquins; in those of Switz[erland] and of Holland. But, say they, other armies have not set up commonwealths.

True indeed, divers other armies have not set up commonwealths; yet is not that any argument why our armies should not. For in all armies that have not set up commonwealths, either the officers have had no fortunes or estates at all, but [have been] immediately dependent upon the mere will of the prince, as the Turkish armies and all those of the Eastern countries; or the officers have been a nobility commanding their own tenants. Certain it is that either of these armies can set up nothing but monarchy. But our officers have not [the] estates of noblemen, able upon their own lands to levy regiments, in which case they would take home their people to plough or make hay; nor are yet so put to it for their livelihood as to depend wholly upon a prince, in which case they would fall on robbing the people; but have good honest popular estates to them and their heirs for ever. Now an army where the estates of the officers were of this kind, in no reason can, in no experience ever did, set up monarchy. Aye but, say they, for all that, their pay unto them is more considerable than their estates. But so much more must they be for a commonwealth, because the parliament must pay; and they have found by experience that the pay of a parliament is by far better than that of a prince. But the four hundred, being monarchically inclined, or running upon the interest of those irreconcilable enemies of popular power, divines and lawyers, will rather pay an army for commanding or for supporting of a prince, than for obeying. Which may be true, as was acknowledged before, in the way; but in the end, or at the long run, for the reasons mentioned, must be of none effect.

These arguments are from the cause; now for an argument to sense, and from the effect: if our armies would raise money of themselves, or, which is all one, would make a king, why have they not made a king in so many years? Why did they not make one yesterday? Why do they not today? Nay, why have they ever been, why do they still continue to be, of all others in this point the most adverse and refractory?

But if so it be with us that nature runs wholly unto a commonwealth, and we have no such force as can withstand nature; why may we not as well have golden dreams of what this commonwealth may be as of the Indies, of Flanders, or the Sound? The frame of a commonwealth may be dreamed on, or proposed, two ways: the one notionally, in which it is of facile understanding but of difficult practice; the other practicably, in which it is of difficult understanding but of facile use. One of these ways is a shoeing-horn, and the other the shoe: for which cause I shall propose in both, as first notionally, thus:

1. That the native territory of the commonwealth be divided, so equally as with any convenience it may, into fifty tribes or precincts.
2. That the people in each tribe be distinguished, first, by their age, and next, by the valuation of their estates: all such as are above eighteen and under thirty being accounted youth, and all such as are thirty or upwards being accounted elders; all such as have under one hundred pounds a year in lands, goods or moneys being accounted of the foot, and all such as have so much or upwards being accounted of the horse.
3. That each tribe elect annually, out of the horse of their number, two elders to be knights, [plus] three elders of the same, and four elders more out of the foot of their number, to be deputies or burgesses. That the term of each knight and burgess or deputy

so elected be triennial; and that whoever has served his triennial term in any one of these capacities may not be re-elected into any one of the same, till a triennial vacation be expired.

4. That, in the first year of the commonwealth, there be a senate so constituted of three hundred knights that the term of one hundred may expire annually; and that the hundred knights annually elected by two in each tribe take the places in the senate of them whose term comes thus to be thus annually expired.

5. That in the first year of the commonwealth there be a representative of the people consisting of one thousand and fifty deputies; four hundred and fifty of them being horse, and the rest foot. That this representative be so constituted that the term of two hundred of the foot, and one hundred and fifty of the horse, expire annually; and that the two hundred foot and one hundred and fifty horse elected annually, by four of the foot and three of the horse in each tribe, take the places in this representative of them whose term comes thus annually to be expired.

6. That the senate have the whole authority of debate; that the representative have the whole power of result, in such manner that whatever, having been debated by the senate, shall by their authority be promulgated – that is printed and published for the space of six weeks – and afterwards, being proposed by them unto the representative, shall be resolved by the people of the same in the affirmative, be the law of the land.

Thus much may suffice to give implicitly a notional account of the whole frame. But a model of government is nothing as to use, unless it be given practicably; and the giving of a model practicably is so much more difficult that men not versed in the way say of it (as they would of the anatomy of their own bodies) that it is impracticable. Here lies the whole difficulty; such things as, try them never so often, they cannot make hang together, they will yet have to be practicable; and if you would bring them from this kind of shifts, or of tying and untying all kind of knots, unto the natural nerves and ligaments of government, it is impracticable. But to render that which is practicable facile, or to do my last endeavour of this kind, of which if I miss this once more I must hereafter despair, I shall do two things: first, omit the ballot, and then make some alteration in my former method.

They who have interwoven the ballot with the description of a commonwealth have thereby rendered the same by far the more complete in itself, but in the understanding of their readers as much defective; wherefore, presuming the use of the ballot throughout the orders of this model, I shall refer it unto practice, in which it will be a matter of as much facility as it would have been of difficulty in writing. And for the method I have chosen, it is the most natural and facile, being no more than to propose the whole practicably: first in the civil, secondly in the religious, then in the military, and, last of all, in the provincial part of the model.

[The rest of the book is given over to a detailed account of Harrington's model commonwealth.]

3 Algernon Sidney, *Discourses Concerning Government* (1698)

Chapter 1

Section One: Introduction

Having lately seen a book entitled *Patriarcha*, written by Sir Robert Filmer, concerning the universal and undistinguished right of all kings, I thought a time of leisure might be well employed in examining his doctrine and the questions arising from it, which seem so far to concern all mankind that, besides the influence upon our future life, they may be said to comprehend all that in this world deserves to be cared for. If he say true, there is but one government in the world that can have anything of justice in it, and those who have hitherto been esteemed the best and wisest of men, for having constituted commonwealths or kingdoms, and taken much pains so to proportion the powers of several magistracies that they might all concur in procuring the public good, or so to divide the powers between the magistrates and people that a well-regulated harmony might be preserved in the whole, were the most unjust and foolish of all men. They were not builders but overthrowers of governments. Their business was to set up aristocratic, democratic, or mixed governments in opposition to that monarchy which, by the immutable laws of God and nature, is imposed upon mankind, or presumptuously to put shackles upon the monarch who, by the same laws, is to be absolute and uncontrolled. They were rebellious and disobedient sons, who rose up against their father, and not only refused to hearken to his voice, but made him bend to their will. In their opinion such only deserved to be called good men who endeavoured to be good to mankind, or to that country to which they were more particularly related. And, inasmuch as that good consists in a felicity of estate and perfection of person, they highly valued such as had endeavoured to make men better, wiser and happier. This they understood to be the end for which men entered into societies, and, though Cicero says that commonwealths were instituted for the obtaining of justice, he contradicts them not, but comprehends all in that word, because 'tis just that whosoever receives a power should employ it wholly for the accomplishment of the ends for which it was given. This work could be performed only by such as excelled in virtue; but, lest they should deflect from it, no government was thought to be well constituted unless the laws prevailed above the commands of men, and they were accounted as the worst of beasts who did not prefer such a condition before a subjection to the fluctuating and irregular will of a man.

If we believe Sir Robert, all this is mistaken. Nothing of this kind was ever left to the choice of men. They are not to inquire what conduces to their own good: God and nature have put us into a way from which we are not to swerve. We are not to live to him, nor to ourselves, but to the master that he has set over us. One government is established over all, and no limits can be set to the power of the person that manages it. This is the prerogative, or, as another author of the same stamp calls it, 'the royal charter' granted to kings by God. They all have an equal right to it: women and children are patriarchs, and the next in blood, without any regard to age, sex, or other qualities of the mind or body, are fathers of as many nations as fall under their power. We are not to examine whether he or she be young or old, virtuous or vicious, sober-minded or stark-mad; the right and power is the same in all. Whether virtue be exalted or suppressed, whether he that bears the sword be a praise to those that do well, and a terror to those that do evil, or a praise to those that do evil, and a terror to such as do well, it concerns us not; for the king must not lose his right, nor have his power diminished on any account.

I have been sometimes apt to wonder how things of this

nature could enter into the head of any man: or, if no wickedness and folly be so great but some may fall into it, I could not well conceive why they should publish it to the world. But these thoughts ceased when I considered that a people from all ages in love with liberty, and desirous to maintain their own privileges, could never be brought to resign them unless they were made to believe that in conscience they ought to do it: which could not be, unless they were also persuaded to believe that there was a law set to all mankind, which none might transgress, and which put the examination of all those matters out of their power. This is our author's work. By this it will appear whose throne he seeks to advance, and whose servant he is, whilst he pretends to serve the king. And that it may be evident he has made use of means suitable to the ends proposed for the service of his great master, I hope to show that he has not used one argument that is not false, nor cited one author whom he has not perverted and abused. Whilst my work is so to lay open these snares that the most simple may not be taken in by them, I shall not examine how Sir Robert came to think himself a man fit to undertake so great a work as to destroy the principles which from the beginning seem to have been common to all mankind; but, only weighing the positions and arguments that he alleges, will, if there be either truth or strength in them, confess the discovery comes from him that gave us least reason to expect it; and that, in spite of the ancients, there is not in the world a piece of wood, out of which a Mercury may not be made.

. . . .

Section Three: Implicit Faith Belongs to Fools; and Truth is Comprehended by Examining Principles

Whilst Filmer's business is to overthrow liberty and truth, he, in his passage, modestly professes 'not to meddle with mysteries of state', or *arcana imperii*. He renounces those inquiries through an implicit faith, which never entered into the head of any but fools, and such as, through a carelessness of the point in question, acted as if they were so. This is the foundation of the papal power; and it can stand no longer than those that compose the Roman church can be persuaded to submit their consciences to the word of the priests, and esteem themselves discharged from the necessity of searching the scriptures in order to know whether the things that are told them are true or false. This may show whether our author or those of Geneva do best agree with the Roman doctrine: but his instance is yet more sottish than his profession. 'An implicit faith', says he, 'is given to the meanest artificer.' I wonder by whom! Who will wear a shoe that hurts him because the shoemaker tells him it is well made? Or who will live in a house that yields no defence against the extremities of weather because the mason or carpenter assures him it is a very good house? Such as have reason, understanding or common sense will and ought to make use of it in those things that concern themselves and their posterity, and suspect the words of such as are interested in deceiving or persuading them not to see with their own eyes, that they may be more easily deceived. This rule obliges us so far to search into matters of state as to examine the original principles of government in general, and of our own in particular. We cannot distinguish truth from falsehood, right from wrong, or know what obedience we owe to the magistrate, or what we may justly expect from him, unless we know what he is, why he is, and by whom he is made to be what he is. These perhaps may be called 'mysteries of state', and some would persuade us they are to be esteemed *arcana*; but whosoever confesses himself to be ignorant of them must acknowledge that he is uncapable of giving any judgement upon things relating to the superstructure; and in so doing evidently shows to others that they ought not at all to hearken to what he says.

His argument to prove this is more admirable: 'If an implicit faith', says he, 'is given to the meanest artificer in his craft, much more to a prince in the profound secrets of government.' But where is the consequence? If I trust to the judgement of an artificer, or one of a more ingenuous profession, it is not because he is of it, but because I am persuaded he does well understand it, and that he will be faithful to me in things relating to his art. I do not send for Lower or Micklethwait when I am sick, nor ask the advice of Mainard or Jones in a suit of law, because the first are physicians and the other lawyers; but because I think them wise, learned, diligent and faithful, there being a multitude of others who go under the same name, whose opinion I would never ask. Therefore if any conclusion can be drawn from thence in favour of princes, it must be of such as have all the qualities of ability and integrity that should create this confidence in me; or it must be proved that all princes, inasmuch as they are princes, have such qualities. No general conclusion can be drawn from the first case, because it must depend upon the circumstances, which ought to be particularly proved: and if the other be asserted, I desire to know whether Caligula, Claudius, Nero, Vitellius, Domitian, Commodus, Heliogabalus, and others not unlike to them, had those admirable endowments upon which an implicit faith ought to have been grounded; how they came by them; and whether we have any promise from God that all princes should for ever excel in those virtues, or whether we by experience find that they do so. If they are or have been wanting in any, the whole falls to the ground; for no man enjoys as a prince that which is not common to all princes: and if every prince have not wisdom to understand these profound secrets, integrity to direct him according to what he knows to be good, and a sufficient measure of industry and valour to protect me, he is not the artificer to whom the implicit faith is due. His eyes are as subject to dazzle as my own. But it is a shame to insist on such a point as this. We see princes of all sorts; they are born as other men. The vilest flatterer dares not deny that they are wise or foolish, good or bad, valiant or cowardly, like other men. And the crown does neither bestow extraordinary qualities, ripen such as are found in princes sooner than in the meanest, nor preserve them from the decays of age, sickness, or other accidents, to which all men are subject: and if the greatest king in the world fall into them, he is as uncapable of that mysterious knowledge, and his judgement is as little to be relied on, as that of the poorest peasant.

This matter is not mended by sending us to seek those virtues in the ministers which are wanting in the prince. The ill effects of Rehoboam's folly could not be corrected by the wisdom of Solomon's counsellors: he rejected them; and such as are like to him will always do the same thing. Nero advised with none but musicians, players, chariot-drivers, or the abominable ministers of his pleasures and cruelties. Arcadius's senate was chiefly composed of buffoons and cooks, influenced by an old rascally eunuch. And it is an eternal truth that a weak or wicked prince can never have a wise council, nor receive any benefit by one that is imposed upon him, unless they have a power of acting without him; which would render the government in effect aristocratical, and would probably displease our author as much as if it were so in name also. Good and wise counsellors do not grow up like mushrooms: great judgement is required in choosing and preparing them. If a weak or vicious prince should be so happy to find them chosen to his hand, they would avail him nothing. There will ever be variety of opinions amongst them; and he that is of a perverted judgement will always choose the worst of those that are proposed, and favour the worst men, as most like to himself. Therefore, if this implicit faith be grounded upon a supposition of profound wisdom in the prince, the foundation is overthrown, and cannot stand; for to repose confidence in the judgement and integrity of one that has none is the most brutish of all follies. So that if a prince may have or want the qualities upon which my faith in him can be rationally grounded, I cannot yield the obedience he requires unless I search into the secrets relating to his person and commands, which he forbids. I cannot know how to obey unless I know in what, and to whom; nor in what unless I know what ought to be commanded; nor what ought to be commanded unless I understand the original right of the commander, which is the great arcanum.

Our author, finding himself involved in many difficulties, proposes an expedient as ridiculous as anything that had gone before, being nothing more than an absurd begging the main question, and determining it without any shadow of proof. He enjoins an active or passive obedience before he shows what should oblige or persuade us to it. This indeed were a compendious way of obviating that which he calls popular sedition, and of exposing all nations that fall under the power of tyrants to be destroyed utterly by them. Nero or Domitian would have desired no more than that those who would not execute their wicked commands should patiently have suffered their throats to be cut by such as were less scrupulous: and the world that had suffered those monsters for some years must have continued under their fury till all that was good and virtuous had been abolished. But, in those ages and parts of the world where there has been anything of virtue and goodness, we may observe a third sort of men, who would neither do villainies, nor suffer more than the laws did permit, or the consideration of the public peace did require. Whilst tyrants, with their slaves and the instruments of their cruelties, were accounted the dregs of mankind, and made the objects of detestation and scorn, these men, who delivered their countries from such plagues, were thought to have something of divine in them, and have been famous above all the rest of mankind to this day. Of this sort were Pelopidas, Epaminondas, Thrasybulus, Harmodius, Aristogiton, Philopoemen, Lucius Brutus, Publius Valerius, Marcus Brutus, C. Cassius, M. Cato, with a multitude of others amongst the ancient heathens. Such as were the instruments of the like deliverances amongst the Hebrews, as Moses, Othniel, Ehud, Barak, Gideon, Samson, Jephthah, Samuel, David, Jehu, the Maccabees, and others, have from the Scriptures a certain testimony of the righteousness of their proceedings when they neither would act what was evil, nor suffer more than was reasonable. But lest we should learn by their examples, and the praises given to them, our author confines the subject's choice to acting or suffering, that is, doing what is commanded, or lying down to have his throat cut, or to see his family and country made desolate. This he calls giving to Caesar that which is Caesar's; whereas he ought to have considered that the question is not whether that which is Caesar's should be rendered to him, for that is to be done to all men; but who is Caesar, and what does of right belong to him, which he no way indicates to us: so that the question remains entire, as if he had never mentioned it, unless we do in a compendious way take his word for the whole.

Chapter 2

Section Eleven: Liberty Produces Virtue, Order, and Stability; Slavery is Accompanied with Vice, Weakness and Misery

Our author's judgement, as well as inclinations to virtue, are manifested in the preference he gives to the manners of the Assyrians, and other eastern nations, before the Grecians and Romans: whereas the first were never remarkable for anything but pride, lewdness, treachery, cruelty, cowardice, madness, and hatred of all that is good, whilst the others excelled in wisdom, valour, and all the virtues that deserve imitation. This was so well observed by St Augustine that he brings no stronger argument to prove that God leaves nothing that is good in man unrewarded than that he gave the dominion of the best part of the world to the Romans, who in moral virtues excelled all other nations. And I think no example can be alleged of a free people that has ever been conquered by an absolute monarch, unless he did incomparably surpass them in riches and strength; whereas many great kings have been overthrown by small republics: and the success being constantly the same, it cannot be attributed to fortune, but must necessarily be the product of virtue and good order. Machiavelli, discoursing of these matters, finds virtue to be so essentially necessary to the establishment and preservation of liberty that he thinks it impossible for a corrupted people to set up a good government, or for a tyranny to be introduced if they be virtuous; and makes this conclusion: 'That where the matter (that is the body of the people) is not corrupted, tumults and disorders do no hurt; and where it is corrupted, good laws do no good.' Which, being confirmed by reason and experience, I think no wise man has ever contradicted him.

But I do not more wonder that Filmer should look upon absolute monarchy to be the nurse of virtue, though we see they did never subsist together, than that he should attribute order and stability to it; whereas order does principally consist in appointing to everyone his right place, office or work; and this lays the whole weight of the government upon one person, who very often does neither deserve, nor is able to bear, the least part of it. Plato, Aristotle, Hooker, and (I may say, in short) all wise men have held that order required that the wisest, best and most valiant men should be placed in the offices where wisdom, virtue and valour are requisite. If common sense did not teach us this, we might learn it from the scripture. When God gave the conduct of his people to Moses, Joshua, Samuel and others, he endowed them with all the virtues and graces that were required for the right performance of their duty. When the Israelites were oppressed by the Midianites, Philistines, and Ammonites, they expected help from the most wise and valiant. When Hannibal was at the gates of Rome, and had filled Italy with fire and blood, or when the Gauls overwhelmed that country with their multitudes and fury, the senate and people of Rome put themselves under the conduct of Camillus, Manlius, Fabius, Scipio, and the like; and when they failed to choose such as were fit for the work to be done they received such defeats as convinced them of their error. But if our author say true, order did require that the power of defending the country should have been annexed as an inheritance to one family, or left to him that could get it, and the exercise of all authority committed to the next in blood, though the weakest of women, or the basest of men.

The like may be said of judging, or doing of justice; and it is absurd to pretend that either is expected from the power, not the person, of the monarch; for experience does too well show how much all things halt in relation to justice or defence when there is a defect in him that ought to judge us and to fight our battles. But of all things this ought least to be alleged by the advocates for absolute monarchy, who deny that the authority can be separated from the person, and lay it as a fundamental principle that whosoever has it may do what he pleases, and be accountable to no man.

Our author's next work is to show that stability is the effect of this good order. But he ought to have known that stability is then only worthy of praise when it is in that which is good. No man delights in sickness or pain because it is long or incurable; nor in slavery and misery because it is perpetual: much less will any man in his senses commend a permanency in vice and wickedness. He must therefore prove that the stability he boasts of is in things that are good, or all that he says of it signifies nothing.

I might leave him here with as little fear that any man who shall espouse his quarrel will ever be able to remove this obstacle, as that he himself should rise out of his grave and do it: but I hope to prove that of all things under the sun, there is none more mutable or unstable than absolute monarchy; which is all that I dispute against, professing much veneration for that which is mixed, regulated by law, and directed to the public good.

This might be proved by many arguments, but I shall confine myself to two: the one drawn from reason, the other from matter of fact.

Nothing can be called stable that is not so in principle and practice: in which respect human nature is not well capable of stability. But the utmost deviation from it that can be imagined is when such an error is laid for a foundation as can never be corrected. All will confess that if there be any stability in man it must be in wisdom and virtue, and in those actions that are thereby directed; for in weakness, folly and madness there can be none. The stability therefore that we seek, in relation to the exercise of civil and military powers, can never be found, unless care be taken that such as shall exercise those powers be endowed with the qualities that should make them stable. This is utterly repugnant to our author's doctrine: he lays for a foundation that the succession goes to the next in blood, without distinction of age, sex, or personal qualities; whereas even he himself would not have the impudence to say that children and women (where they are admitted), or fools, madmen, and such as are full of all wickedness, do not come to be the heirs of reigning families, as well as of the meanest. The stability therefore that can be expected from such a government either depends upon those who have none in themselves, or is referred wholly to chance, which is directly opposite to stability.

This would be the case, though it were (as we say) an even wager, whether the person would be fit or unfit, and that there were as many men in the world able as unable to perform the duty of a king. But experience showing that, among many millions of men, there is hardly one that possess the qualities required in a king, it is so many to one that he upon whom the lot shall fall will not be the man we seek, in whose person and government there can be such a stability as is asserted. And this failing, all must necessarily fail; for there can be no stability in his will, laws, or actions, who has none in his person. . . .

. . . .

Section Sixteen: The Best Governments of the World Have been Composed of Monarchy, Aristocracy, and Democracy

Our author's cavils concerning I know not what vulgar opinions that democracies were introduced to curb tyranny deserve no answer; for our question is, whether one form of government be prescribed to us by God and nature, or we are left according to our own understanding to constitute such as seem best to ourselves. As for democracy, he may say what pleases him of it; and I believe it can suit only with the convenience of a small town, accompanied with such circumstances as are seldom found. But this no way obliges men to run into the other extreme, inasmuch as the variety of forms between mere democracy and absolute monarchy is almost infinite: and if I should undertake to say there never was a good government in the world that did not consist of the three simple species of monarchy, aristocracy and democracy, I think I might make it good. This at the least is certain, that the government of the Hebrews, instituted by God, had a judge, the great Sanhedrin, and general assemblies of the people. Sparta had two kings, a senate of twenty-eight chosen men, and the like assemblies. All the Dorian cities had a chief magistrate, a senate, and occasional assemblies. The Ionian (Athens and others) had an archon, the areopagi, and all judgements concerning matters of the greatest importance, as well as the election of magistrates, were referred to the people. Rome in the beginning had a king and a senate, whilst the election of kings, and judgements upon appeals, remained in the people; afterwards consuls representing kings, and vested with equal power, a more numerous senate, and more frequent meetings of the people. Venice has at this day a duke, a senate of the *pregadi*, and the great assembly of the nobility, which is the whole city, the rest of the inhabitants being only *incolae*, not *cives*; and those of the other cities or countries are their subjects, and do not participate of the government. Genoa is governed in like manner; Lucca not unlike to them. Germany is at this day governed by an emperor, the princes or great lords in their several precincts, the cities by their own magistrates, and by general diets, in which the whole power of the nation resides, and where the emperor, princes, nobility and cities have their places in person, or by their deputies. All the northern nations, which, upon the dissolution of the Roman empire, possessed the best provinces that had composed it, were under that form which is usually called the Gothic polity: they had king, lords, commons, diets, assemblies of estates, cortez, and parliaments, in which the sovereign powers of those nations did reside, and by which they were exercised. The like was practised in Hungary, Bohemia, Sweden, Denmark, Poland; and if things are changed in some of these places within few years, they must give better proofs of having gained by the change than are yet seen in the world, before I think myself obliged to change my opinion.

Some nations, not liking the name of king, have given such a power as kings enjoyed in other places to one or more magistrates, either limited to a certain time, or left to be perpetual, as best pleased themselves. Others, approving the name, made the dignity purely elective. Some have in their elections principally regarded one family as long as it lasted. Others considered nothing but the fitness of the person, and reserved to themselves a liberty of taking where they pleased. Some have permitted the crown to be hereditary, as to its ordinary course, but restrained the power, and instituted officers to inspect the proceedings of kings, and to take care that the laws were not violated: of this sort were the *ephori* of Sparta; the *maires du palais*, and afterwards the constable of France; the *justicia* in Aragon; *rijckshofmeister* in Denmark; the high-steward in England; and in all places such assemblies as are before mentioned under several names, who had the power of the whole nation. Some have continued long, and it may be always in the same form; other have changed it. Some, being incensed against their kings, as the Romans exasperated by the villainies of Tarquin, and the Tuscans by the cruelties of Mezentius, abolished the name of king. Others, as Athens, Sicyon, Argos, Corinth, Thebes, and the Latins, did not stay for such extremities, but set up other governments when they thought it best for themselves, and by this conduct prevented the evils that usually fall upon nations when their kings degenerate into tyrants, and a nation is brought to enter into a war by which all may be lost, and nothing can be gained which was not their own before. The Romans took not this salutary course; the mischief was grown up before they perceived, or set themselves against it; and when the effects of pride, avarice, cruelty and lust were grown to such a height that they could no longer be endured, they could not free themselves without a war. And whereas upon other occasions their victories had brought them increase of strength, territory and glory, the only reward of their virtue in this was to be delivered from a plague they had unadvisedly suffered to grow up among them. I confess this was most of all to be esteemed; for if they had been overthrown, their condition under Tarquin would have been more intolerable than if they had fallen under the power of Pyrrhus or Hannibal; and all their following prosperity was the fruit of their recovered liberty. But it had been much better to have reformed the state after the death of one of their good kings, than to be brought to fight for their lives against that abominable tyrant.

Our author, in pursuance of his aversion to all that is good, disapproves this, and, wanting reasons to justify his dislike, according to the custom of impostors and cheats, has recourse to the ugly terms of a 'back-door sedition' and 'faction': as if it were not as just for a people to lay aside their kings when they receive nothing but evil, and can rationally hope for no benefit by them, as for others to set them up in expectation of good from them. But, if the truth be examined, nothing will be found more orderly than the changes of government, or of the persons and races of those that governed, which have been made by many nations. When Pharamond's grandson seemed not to deserve the crown he had worn, the French gave it to Meroveus, who more resembled him in virtue; in process of time, when this race also degenerated, they were rejected, and Pepin advanced to the throne; and the most remote in blood of his descendants having often been preferred before the nearest, and bastards before the legitimate issue, they were at last all laid aside, and the crown remains to this day in the family of Hugh Capet, on whom it was bestowed upon the rejection of Charles of Lorraine. In like manner the Castilians took Don Sancho surnamed the Brave, second son to Alphonso the Wise, before Alphonso el Desheredado, son of the elder brother Ferdinand. The states of Aragon preferred Martin, brother to John the first, before Mary his daughter, married to the count de Foix, though females were not excluded from the succession; and the house of Austria now enjoys that crown from Joan, daughter to Ferdinand. In that and many other kingdoms bastards have been advanced before their legitimate brothers. Henry, count of Trastamara, bastard to Alphonso XI, king of Castile, received the crown as a reward of the good service he had done to his country against his brother Peter the Cruel, without any regard had to the house of La Cerda, descended from Alphonso el Desheredado, which to this day never enjoyed any greater honour than that of duke de Medina Celi. Not long after, the Portuguese, conceiving a dislike of their king Ferdinand and his daughter, married to John king of Castile, rejected her and her uncle by her father's side, and gave the crown to John, a knight of Calatrava and bastard to an uncle of Ferdinand their king. About the beginning of this age the Swedes deposed their king Sigismund for being a papist, and made Charles, his uncle, king. Divers examples of the like nature in England have been already mentioned. All these transportations of crowns were acts performed by assemblies of the three estates in the several kingdoms; and these crowns are to this day enjoyed under titles derived from such as were thus brought in by the deposition or rejection of those who, according to descent of blood, had better titles than the present possessors. The acts therefore were lawful and good, or they can have no title at all; and they who made them had a just power so to do.

If our author can draw any advantage from the resemblance of regality that he finds in the Roman consuls and Athenian archons, I shall without envy leave him the enjoyment of it; but I am much mistaken if that do not prove my assertion that those governments 'were composed of the three simple species'. For if the monarchical part was in them, it cannot be denied that the aristocratical was in the senate or areopagi, and the democratical in the people. But he ought to have remembered that if there was something of monarchical in those governments when they are said to have been popular, there was something of aristocratical and democratical in those that were called regal; which justifies my proposition on both sides, and shows that the denomination was taken from the part that prevailed; and if this were not so the governments of France, Spain and Germany might be called democracies, and those of Rome and Athens monarchies, because the people have a part in the one, and an image of monarchy was preserved in the other.

If our author will not allow the cases to be altogether equal, I think he will find no other difference than that the consuls and archons were regularly made by the votes of the consenting people, and orderly resigned their power when the time was expired for which it was given; whereas Tarquin, Dionysius, Agathocles, Nabis, Phalaris, Caesar, and almost all his successors, whom he takes for complete monarchs, came in by violence, fraud and corruption, by the help of the worst men, by the slaughter of the best, and most commonly (when the method was once established) by that of his predecessor, who, if our author say true, was the father of his country, and his also. This was the root and foundation of the only government that deserves praise: this is that which stamped the divine character upon Agathocles, Dionysius and Caesar, and that had bestowed the same upon Manlius, Marius or Catiline, if they had gained the monarchies they affected. But I suppose that such as God has blessed with better judgement, and a due regard to justice and truth, will say that all those who have attained to such greatness as destroys all manner of good in the places where they have set up themselves by the most detestable villainies came in by a 'back-door'; and that such magistrates as were orderly chosen by a willing people were the true shepherds who came in by the gate of the sheepfold, and might justly be called the ministers of God, so long as they performed their duty in providing for the good of the nations committed to their charge.

. . . .

Section Twenty-Three: That is the Best Government Which Best Provides for War

Our author, having huddled up all popular and mixed governments into one, has, in some measure, forced me to explain the various constitutions and principles upon which they are grounded: but as the wisdom of a father is seen, not only in providing bread for his family, or increasing his patrimonial estate, but in making all possible provision for the security of it; so that government is evidently the best which, not relying upon what it does at first enjoy, seeks to increase the number, strength and riches of the people; and by the best discipline to bring the power so improved into such order as may be of most use to the public. This comprehends all things conducing to the administration of justice, the preservation of domestic peace, and the increase of commerce, that the people, being pleased with their present condition, may be filled with love to their country, encouraged to fight boldly for the public cause, which is their own; and as men do willingly join with that which prospers, that strangers may be invited to fix their habitations in such a city, and to espouse the principles that reign in it. This is necessary for several reasons; but I shall principally insist upon one, which is that all things in their beginning are weak: the whelp of a lion newly born has neither strength nor fierceness. He that builds a city and does not intend it should increase commits as great an absurdity as if he should desire his child might ever continue under the same weakness in which he is born. If it do not grow, it must pine and perish; for in this world nothing is permanent; that which does not grow better will grow worse. This increase also is useless, or perhaps hurtful, if it be not in strength, as well as in riches or number: for everyone is apt seize upon ill guarded treasures; and the terror that the city of London was possessed with when a few Dutch ships came to Chatham shows that no numbers of men, though naturally valiant, are able to defend themselves unless they be well armed, disciplined, and conducted. Their multitude brings confusion; their wealth, when it is like to be made a prey, increases the fears of the owners; and they who, if they were brought into good order, might conquer a great part of the world, being destitute of it, durst not think of defending themselves.

If it be said that the wise father mentioned by me endeavours to secure his patrimony by law, not by force, I answer that all defence terminates in force; and if a private man does not prepare to defend his estate with his own force, it is because he lives under the protection of the law, and expects the force of the magistrate should be a security to him. But kingdoms and commonwealths, acknowledging no superior, except God alone, can reasonably hope to be protected by him only; and by him if with industry and courage they make use of the means he has given them for their own defence. God helps those who help themselves; and men are by several reasons (suppose to prevent the increase of a suspected power) induced to succour an industrious and brave people; but such as neglect the means of their own preservation are ever left to perish with shame. Men cannot rely upon any league: the state that is defended by one potentate against another becomes a slave to their protector; mercenary soldiers always want fidelity or courage, and most commonly both. If they are not corrupted or beaten by the invader, they make a prey of their masters. These are the followers of camps, who have neither faith nor piety, but prefer gain before right. They who expose their blood to sale look where they can make the best bargain, and never fail of pretences for following their interests.

Moreover, private families may by several arts increase their wealth, as they increase in number; but when a people multiplies (as they will always do in a good climate under a good government) such an enlargement of territory as is necessary for their subsistence can be acquired only by war. This was known to the northern nations that invaded the Roman empire; but, for want of such constitutions as might best improve their strength and valour, the numbers they sent out when they were overburdened provided well for themselves, but were of no use to the countries they left; and whilst those Goths, Vandals, Franks and Normans enjoyed the most opulent and delicious provinces of the world, their fathers languished obscurely in their frozen climates. For the like reasons, or through the same defect, the Switzers are obliged to serve other princes; and often to employ that valour in advancing the power of their neighbours which might be used to increase their own. Genoa, Lucca, Geneva and other small commonwealths, having no wars, are not able to nourish the men they breed; but, sending many of their children to seek their fortunes abroad, scarce a third part of those that are born among them die in those cities; and, if they did not take this course, they would have no better than the nations inhabiting near the river Niger, who sell their children as the increase of their flocks.

This does not less concern monarchies than commonwealths; nor the absolute less than the mixed: all of them have been prosperous or miserable, glorious or contemptible, as they were better or worse armed, disciplined or conducted. The Assyrian valour was irresistable under Nebuchadnezzar; but was brought to nothing under his base and luxurious grandson Belshazzar. The Persians, who under Cyrus conquered Asia, were like swine exposed to slaughter when their discipline failed and they were commanded by his proud, cruel and cowardly successors. The Macedonian army overthrown by Paullus Emilius was not less in number than that with which Alexander gained the empire of the east; and perhaps had not been inferior in valour if it had been as well commanded. Many poor and almost unknown nations have been carried to such a height of glory by the bravery of their princes that I might incline to think their government as fit as any other for disciplining a people to war, if their virtues continued in their families, or could be transmitted to their successors. The impossibility of this is a breach never to be repaired; and no account is to be made of the good that is always [un]certain, and seldom enjoyed. This disease is not only in absolute monarchies, but in those also where any regard is had to succession of blood, though under the strictest limitations. . . .

. . . .

We have already said enough to obviate the objections that may be drawn from the prosperity of the French monarchy. The beauty of it is false and painted. There is a rich and haughty king who is blessed with such neighbours as are not likely to disturb him, and has nothing to fear from his miserable subjects; but the whole body of that state is full of boils, and wounds, and putrid sores: there is no real strength in it. The people is so unwilling to serve him that he is said to have put to death above four score thousand of his own soldiers within the space of fifteen years for flying from their colours; and if he were vigorously attacked little help could be expected from a discontented nobility, or a starving and despairing people. If, to diminish the force of these arguments and examples, it be said that in two or three thousand years all things are changed, the ancient virtue of mankind is extinguished, and the love that everyone had to his country is turned into a care of his private interests, I answer that time changes nothing, and the changes produced in this time proceed only from the change of governments. The nations which have been governed arbitrarily have always suffered the same plagues, and been infected with the same vices; which is as natural as for animals ever to generate according to their kinds, and fruits to be of the same nature with the roots and seeds from which they come. The same order that made men valiant and industrious in the service of their country during the first ages would have the same effect if it were now in being. Men would have the same love to the public as the Spartans and Romans had if there was the same reason for it. We need no other proof of this than what we have seen in our own country, where, in a few years, good discipline, and a just encouragement given to those who did well, produced more examples of pure, complete, incorruptible, and invincible virtue than Rome or Greece could ever boast; or, if more be wanting, they may easily be found among the Switzers, Hollanders, and others: but it is not necessary to light a candle to the sun.

. . . .

Section Twenty-Six: Civil Tumults and Wars are Not the Greatest Evils that Befall Nations

'But skin for skin,' says our author, 'and all that a man has, will he give for his life.' And since it was necessary to grace his book with some scripture phrases, none could be fitter for that purpose than those that were spoken by the devil: but they will be of little use to him; for though I should so far recede from truth as to avow those words to be true, I might safely deny the conclusions he draws from them, 'That those are the worst governments under which most men are slain; or that more are slain in popular governments than in absolute monarchies.' For, having proved that all the wars and tumults that have happened in commonwealths have never produced such slaughters as were brought upon the empires of Macedon and Rome, or the kingdoms of Israel, Judah, France, Spain, Scotland or England, by contests between several competitors for those crowns, if tumult, war and slaughter be the point in question, those are the worst of all governments where they have been most frequent and cruel. But though these are terrible scourges, I deny that government to be simply the worst that has most of them. It is ill that men should kill one another in seditions, tumults and wars; but it is worse to bring nations to such misery, weakness and baseness as to have neither strength nor courage to contend for anything; to have left nothing worth defending; and to give the name of peace to desolation. I take Greece to have been happy and glorious when it was full of populous cities, flourishing in all the arts that deserve praise among men; when they were courted and feared by the greatest kings, and never assaulted by any but to his own loss and confusion; when

Babylon and Susa trembled at the motion of their arms; and their valour, exercised in those wars and tumults which our author looks upon as the greatest evils, was raised to such a power that nothing upon earth was found able to resist them. And I think it now miserable, when peace reigns within their empty walls, and the poor remains of those exhausted nations, sheltering themselves under the ruins of the desolated cities, have neither anything that deserves to be disputed amongst them, nor spirit or force to repel the injuries they daily suffer from a proud and insupportable master.

The like may be said of Italy: whilst it was inhabited by nations governing themselves by their own will they fell sometimes into domestic seditions, and had frequent wars with their neighbours. When they were free they loved their country, and were always ready to fight in its defence. Such as succeeded well increased in vigour and power; and even those that were the most unfortunate in one age found means to repair their greatest losses, if their government continued. Whilst they had a property in their goods they would not suffer the country to be invaded, since they knew they could have none if it were lost. This gave occasion to wars and tumults; but it sharpened their courage, kept up a good discipline, and the nations that were most exercised by them always increased in power and number; so that no country seems ever to have been of greater strength than Italy was when Hannibal invaded it, and after his defeat the rest of the world was not able to resist their valour and power. They sometimes killed one another; but their enemies never got anything but burying places within their territories.

All things are now brought into a very different method by the blessed governments they are under. The fatherly care of the king of Spain, the pope, and other princes has established peace amongst them. We have not in many ages heard of any sedition among the Latins, Sabines, Volsci, Equi, Samnites, or others. The thin half-starved inhabitants of walls supported by ivy fear neither popular tumults, nor foreign alarms; and their sleep is only interrupted by hunger, the cries of their children, or the howling of wolves. Instead of many turbulent, contentious cities, they have a few scattered, silent cottages; and the fierceness of those nations is so tempered that every rascally collector of taxes extorts without fear from every man that which should be the nourishment of his family. And if any of those countries are free from that pernicious vermin, it is through the extremity of their poverty. Even in Rome a man may be circumvented by the fraud of a priest, or poisoned by one who would have his estate, wife, whore, or child; but nothing is done that looks like tumult or violence. The governors do as little fear Gracchus as Hannibal; and, instead of wearying their subjects in wars, they only seek, by perverted laws, corrupt judges, false witnesses, and vexatious suits, to cheat them of their money and inheritance. This is the best part of their condition. Where these arts are used, there are men, and they have something to lose; but for the most part the lands lie waste, and they who were formerly troubled with the disorders incident to populous cities, now enjoy the quiet and peaceable estate of a wilderness.

Again, there is a way of killing worse than that of the sword: for, as Tertullian says upon a different occasion, *Prohibere nasci est occidere:* those governments are in the highest degree guilty of blood which, by taking from men the means of living, bring some to perish through want, drive others out of the country, and generally dissuade men from marriage by taking from them all ways of subsisting their families. Notwithstanding all the seditions of Florence, and other cities of Tuscany, the horrid factions of Guelphs and Ghibellines, Neri and Bianchi, nobles and commons, they continued populous, strong, and exceeding rich. But in the space of less than a hundred and fifty years the peaceable reign of the Medici is thought to have destroyed nine parts in ten of the people of that province. Amongst other things, it is remarkable that when Philip II of Spain gave Sienna to the duke of Florence, his ambassador then at Rome sent him word that he had given away more than 650,000 subjects; and it is not believed there are now 20,000 souls inhabiting that city and territory. Pisa, Pistoia, Arezzo, Cortona, and other towns that were then good and populous, are in the like proportion diminished, and Florence more than any. When that city had been long troubled with seditions, tumults and wars, for the most part unprosperous, they still retained such strength that when Charles VIII of France, being admitted as a friend with his whole army, which soon after conquered the kingdom of Naples, thought to master them, the people, taking arms, struck such a terror into him that he was glad to depart upon such conditions as they thought fit to impose. Machiavelli reports that in that time Florence alone, with the Val d'Arno, a small territory belonging to that city, could in a few hours, by the sound of a bell, bring together 135,000 well-armed men; whereas now that city, with all the others in that province, are brought to such despicable weakness, emptiness, poverty and baseness, that they can neither resist the oppressions of their own prince, nor defend him or themselves if they were assaulted by a foreign army. The people are dispersed or destroyed, and the best families sent to seek habitations in Venice, Genoa, Rome, Naples and Lucca.

This is not the effect of war or pestilence; they enjoy a perfect peace, and suffer no other plague than the government they are under. But he who has thus cured them of disorders and tumults does, in my opinion, deserve no greater praise than a physician who should boast that there was not a sick person in a house committed to his care, when he had poisoned all that were in it. The Spaniards have established the like peace in the kingdoms of Naples and Sicily, the West Indies, and other places. The Turks by the same means prevent tumults in their dominions. And they are of such efficacy in all places that Mario Chigi, brother to pope Alexander VII, by one sordid cheat upon the sale of corn, is said within eight years to have destroyed above a third part of the people in the ecclesiastical state; and that country which was the strength of the Romans in the time of the Carthaginian wars suffered more by the covetousness and fraud of that villain than by all the defeats received from Hannibal.

It were an endless work to mention all the places where this peaceable solitude has been introduced by absolute monarchy; but popular and regular governments have always applied themselves to increase the number, strength, power, riches and courage of their people by providing comfortable ways of subsistence for their own citizens, inviting strangers, and filling them all with such a love to their country that every man might look upon the public cause as his own, and be always ready to defend it. This may sometimes give occasion to tumults and wars, as the most vigorous bodies may fall into distempers. When everyone is solicitous for the public, there may be difference of opinion, and some, by mistaking the way, may bring prejudice when they intend profit. But, unless a tyrant do arise and destroy the government which is the root of their felicity, or they be overwhelmed by the irresistible power of a virtue or fortune greater than their own, they soon recover, and, for the most part, rise up in greater glory and prosperity than before. This was seen in the commonwealths of Greece and Italy, which for this reason were justly called nurseries of virtue, and their magistrates preservers of men; whereas our author's peace-making monarchs can deserve no better title than that of enemies and destroyers of mankind.

I cannot think him in earnest when he exaggerates Sulla's cruelties as a proof that the mischiefs suffered under free states are more universal than under kings and tyrants: for there never was a tyrant in the world if he was not one, though through weariness, infirmity of body, fear, or perhaps the horror of his own wickedness, he at length resigned his power. But the evil had taken root so deep that it could not be removed; there was nothing of liberty remaining in Rome; the laws were overthrown by the violence of the sword; the remaining contest was, who should be lord; and there is no reason to believe that if Pompey had gained the battle of Pharsalia he would have made a more modest use of his victory than Caesar did; or that Rome would have been more happy under him than under the other. His cause was more plausible because the senate followed him, and Caesar was the invader; but he was no better in his person, and his designs seem to have been the same. He had been long before *suarum legum auctor et eversor*. He gave the beginning to the first triumvirate; and it were folly to think that he who had been insolent when he was not come to the highest pitch of fortune would have proved moderate if success had put all into his hands. The proceedings of Marius, Cinna, Catiline Octavius, and Antonius were all of the same nature. No laws were observed, no public good intended; the ambition of private persons reigned, and whatsoever was done by them, or for their interests, can no more be applied to popular, aristocratical, or mixed governments than the furies of Caligula and Nero.

. . . .

Chapter 3

. . . .

Section Thirty-Six: The General Revolt of a Nation Cannot be Called a Rebellion

As impostors seldom make lies to pass in the world without putting false names upon things, such as our author endeavour to persuade the people they ought not to defend their liberties by giving the name of rebellion to the most just and honourable actions that have been performed for the preservation of them, and, to aggravate the matter, fear not to tell us that rebellion is like the sin of witchcraft. But those who seek after truth will easily find that there can be no such thing in the world as the rebellion of a nation against its own magistrates, and that rebellion is not always evil. That this may appear, it will not be amiss to consider the word, as well as the thing understood by it, as it is used in an evil sense.

The word is taken from the Latin *rebellare*, which signifies no more than to renew a war. When a town or province had been subdued by the Romans, and brought under their dominion, if they violated their faith after the settlement of peace, and invaded their masters who had spared them, they were said to rebel. But it had been more absurd to apply that word to the people that rose against the *decemviri*, kings, or other magistrates, than to the Parthians, or any of those nations who had no dependence upon them; for all the circumstances that should make a rebellion were wanting, the word implying a superiority in them against whom it is, as well as the breach of an established peace. But though every private man, singly taken, be subject to the commands of the magistrate, the whole body of the people is not so; for he is by and for the people, and the people is neither by nor for him. The obedience due to him from private men is grounded upon, and measured by, the general law; and that law, regarding the welfare of the people, cannot set up the interest of one or a few men against the public. The whole body, therefore, of a nation cannot be tied to any other obedience than is consistent with the common good, according to their own judgement; and, having never been subdued, or brought to terms of peace with their magistrates, they cannot be said to revolt or rebel against them to whom they owe no more than seems good to themselves, and who are nothing, of or by themselves, more than other men.

Again, the thing signified by rebellion is not always evil: for, though every subdued nation must acknowledge a superiority in those who have subdued them, and rebellion do imply a breach of the peace, yet that superiority is not infinite; the peace may be broken upon just grounds, and it may be neither a crime nor infamy to do it. The Privernates had been more than once subdued by the Romans, and had as often rebelled. Their city was at last taken by Plautius the consul, after their leader Vitruvius, and great numbers of their senate and people, had been killed. Being reduced to a low condition, they sent ambassadors to Rome to desire peace; where, when a senator asked them what punishment they deserved, one of them answered, 'The same which they deserve who think themselves worthy of liberty.' The consul then demanded what kind of peace might be expected from them, if the punishment should be remitted. The ambassador answered, 'If the terms you give be good, the peace will be observed by us faithfully and perpetually; if bad, it will soon be broken.' And though some were offended with the ferocity of the answer, yet the best part of the senate approved it, as 'worthy of a man and a freeman'; and, confessing that no man or nation would continue under an uneasy condition longer than they were compelled by force, said, 'They only were fit to be made Romans who thought nothing valuable but liberty.' Upon which they were all made citizens of Rome, and obtained whatsoever they had desired.

I know not how this matter can be carried to a greater height; for if it were possible that a people resisting oppression and vindicating their own liberty could commit a crime and incur either guilt or infamy, the Privernates did, who had been often subdued, and often pardoned; but, even in the judgement of their conquerors, whom they had offended, the resolution they professed of standing to no agreement imposed upon them by necessity was accounted the highest testimony of such a virtue as rendered them worthy to be admitted into a society and equality with themselves, who were the most brave and virtuous people of the world.

But if the patience of a conquered people may have limits, and they who will not bear oppression from those who had spared their lives may deserve praise and reward from their conquerors, it would be madness to think that any nation can be obliged to bear whatsoever their own magistrates think fit to do against them. This may seem strange to those who talk so much of conquests made by kings; immunities, liberties, and privileges granted to nations; oaths of allegiance taken; and wonderful benefits conferred upon them. But having already said as much as is needful concerning conquests, and that the magistrate, who has nothing except what is given to him, can only dispense out of the public stock such franchises and privileges as he has received for the reward of services done to the country, and encouragement of virtue, I shall at present keep myself to the two last points.

Allegiance signifies no more (as the words *ad legem* declare) than such an obedience as the law requires. But as the law can require nothing from the whole people, who are masters of it, allegiance can only relate to particulars, and not to the whole. No oath can bind any other than those who take it, and that only in the true sense and meaning of it. But single men only take this oath, and therefore single men are only obliged to keep it. The body of a people neither does nor can perform any such act. Agreements and contracts have been made, as the tribe of Judah, and the rest of Israel afterward, made a covenant with David, upon which they made him king, but no wise man can think that the nation did thereby make themselves the creature of their own creature.

The sense also of an oath ought to be considered. No man can by any oath be obliged to anything beyond, or contrary to, the true meaning of it: private men, who swear obedience *ad legem*, swear no obedience *extra* or *contra legem*. Whatsoever they promise or swear can detract nothing from the public liberty, which the law principally intends to preserve. Though many of them may be obliged, in their several stations and capacities, to render peculiar services to a prince, the whole people continue as free as the internal thoughts of a man, and cannot but have a right to preserve their liberty, or avenge the violation.

If matters are well examined, perhaps not many magistrates can pretend to much upon the title of merit, most especially if they or their progenitors have continued long in office. The conveniences annexed to the exercise of the sovereign power may be thought sufficient to pay such scores as they grow due, even to the best; and as things of that nature are handled, I think it will hardly be found that all princes can pretend to an irresistible power upon the account of beneficence to their people. When the family of Medici came to be masters of Tuscany that country was without dispute, in men, money and arms, one of the most flourishing provinces in the world, as appears by Machiavelli's account, and the relation of what happened between Charles VIII and the magistrates of Florence, which I have mentioned already from Guicciardini. Now, whoever shall consider the strength of that country in those days, together with what it might have been in the space of a 140 years, in which they have had no war, nor any other plague than the extortion, fraud, rapine and cruelty of their princes, and compare it with their present desolate, wretched and contemptible condition, may, if he please, think that much veneration is due to the princes that govern them; but will never make any man believe that their title can be grounded upon beneficence. The like may be said of the Duke of Savoy, who, pretending (upon I know not what account) that every peasant in the duchy ought to pay him two crowns every half year, did in 1662 subtly find out that in every year there were thirteen halves; so that a poor man, who had nothing but what he gained by hard labour, was, through his fatherly care and beneficence, forced to pay six-and-twenty crowns to his royal highness, to be employed in his discreet and virtuous pleasures at Turin.

The condition of the seventeen provinces of the Netherlands (and even of Spain itself) when they fell to the house of Austria was of the same nature: and I will confess as much as can be required, if any other marks of their government do remain, than such as are manifest evidences of their pride, avarice, luxury and cruelty.

France, in outward appearance, makes a better show; but nothing in this world is more miserable than that people under the fatherly care of their triumphant monarch. The best of their condition is, like asses and mastiff-dogs, to work and fight, to be oppressed and killed for him; and those among them who have any understanding well know that their industry, courage and good success is not only unprofitable, but destructive to them; and that, by increasing the power of their master, they add weight to their own chains. And if any prince, or succession of princes, have made a more modest use of their power, or more faithfully discharged the trust reposed in them, it must be imputed peculiarly to them, as a testimony of their personal virtue, and can have no effect upon others.

The rights, therefore, of kings are not grounded upon conquest; the liberties of nations do not arise from the grants of their princes; the oath of allegiance binds no private man to more than the law directs, and has no influence upon the whole body of every nation; many princes are known to their subjects only by the injuries, losses and mischiefs brought upon them; such as are good and just ought to be rewarded for their personal virtue, but can confer no right upon those who no-way resemble them; and whoever pretends to that merit must prove it by his actions; rebellion, being nothing but a renewed war, can never be against a government that was not established by war, and of itself is neither good nor evil, [no] more than any other war, but is just or unjust according to the cause or manner of it. Besides, that rebellion which by Samuel is compared to witchcraft is not of private men, or a people, against the prince, but of the prince against God: the Israelites are often said to have rebelled against the law, word or command of God; but though they frequently opposed their kings, I do not find rebellion imputed to them on that account, nor any ill character put upon such actions. We are told also of some kings who had been subdued, and afterwards rebelled against Chedorlaomer and other kings; but their cause is not blamed, and we have some reason to believe it good, because Abraham took part with those who had rebelled. However, it can be of no prejudice to the cause I defend: for though it were true that those subdued kings could not justly rise against the person who had subdued them, or that generally no king, being once vanquished, could have a right of rebellion against his conqueror, it could have no relation to the actions of a people vindicating their own laws and liberties against a prince who violates them; for that war which never was, can never be renewed. And if it be true in any case that hands and swords are given to men that they only may be slaves who have no courage, it must be [true] when liberty is overthrown by those who of all men ought with the utmost industry and vigour to have defended it.

That this should be known is not only necessary for the safety of nations, but advantageous to such kings as are wise and good. They who know the frailty of human nature will always distrust their own; and, desiring only to do what they ought, will be glad to be restrained from that which they ought not to do. Being taught by reason and experience that nations delight in the peace and justice of a good government, they will never fear a general insurrection whilst they take care it be rightly administered; and finding themselves by this means to be safe, will never be unwilling that their children or successors should be obliged to tread in the same steps.

If it be said that this may sometimes cause disorders, I acknowledge it; but no human condition being perfect, such a one is to be chosen which carries with it the most tolerable inconveniences. And it being much better that the irregularities and excesses of a prince should be restrained or suppressed, than that whole nations should perish by them, those constitutions that make the best provision against the greatest evils are most to be commended. If governments were instituted to gratify the lusts of one man, those could not be good that set limits to them; but all reasonable men confessing that they are instituted for the good of nations, they only can deserve praise who above all things endeavour to procure it, and appoint means proportioned to that end. The great variety of governments which we see in the world is nothing but the effect of this care; and all nations have been and are more or less happy as they or their ancestors have had vigour of spirit, integrity of manners, and wisdom to invent and establish such orders as have better or worse provided for this common good which was sought by all. But as no rule can be so exact to make provision against all contestations, and all disputes about right do naturally end in force when justice is denied (ill men never willingly submitting to any decision that is contrary to their passions and interests), the best constitutions are of no value if there be not a power to support them. This power first exerts itself in the execution of justice by the ordinary officers: but no nation having been so happy as not sometimes to produce such princes as Edward and Richard the Seconds, and such ministers as Gaveston, Spencer, and Tresilian, the ordinary officers of justice often want the will, and always the power, to restrain them. So that the rights and liberties of a nation must be utterly subverted and abolished if the power of the whole may not be employed to assert them, or punish the violation of them. But as it is the fundamental right of every nation to be governed by such laws, in such manner, and by such persons as they think most conducing to their own good, they cannot be accountable to any but themselves for what they do in that most important affair.

. . . .

NOTES ON THE TEXTS

1. Bacon, *Essayes* (1625). The first of Bacon's *Essayes* were published in 1597 (with further editions in 1598, 1606 and 1612). In 1612 an enlarged collection of *Essayes* appeared, containing 'Of Nobility' for the first time. There were further editions of this collection in 1612, 1613 (three editions) 1614 and 1624, and both an Italian translation (1617, 1618) and a French translation (1619) were published in England. In 1625 a new collection appeared, in which essays which had previously appeared were revised, and new ones (including 'Of Delays') added. There were further seventeenth-century editions of this collection in 1629, 1632, 1639, 1642, 1663, 1664, 1668/9, 1673, 1680, 1688, 1691 (four editions), 1696 (three editions). The standard edition is now that edited by M. Kiernan (Oxford, 1985).

2. Harrington, *Art of Lawgiving* (1659). Reprinted in *Works*, 1700, 1737 (editions in London and Dublin), 1758 (Dublin), 1771. French translation, 1795. The standard edition is now J. G. A. Pocock (ed.), *The Political Works of James Harrington* (Cambridge, 1977).

3. Sidney, *Discourses Concerning Government:* 1698, 1702 (French translation), 1704, 1750, 1751, 1763, 1794 (French translation). Extracts published in 1795 and 1797. Printed in Sidney's *Works*, 1772. There is a facsimile edition of the edition of 1751 (Farnborough, 1968).

FURTHER READING

Three valuable works dealing with English seventeenth- and early-eighteenth-century republicanism are: Z. S. Fink, *The Classical Republicans* (Evanston, 1945, 1962); F. Raab, *The English Face of Machiavelli* (London, 1964); C. Robbins, *The Eighteenth Century Commonwealthsman* (Cambridge, Mass., 1959). There is a lucid general survey of republicanism up to the Restoration in B. Worden, 'Classical Republicanism and the Puritan Revolution', in *History and Imagination: Essays in Honour of H. R. Trevor-Roper* (London, 1981). Two important tracts, by Neville and Moyle, are edited by C. Robbins as *Two English Republican Tracts* (Cambridge, 1969).

For a general account of Bacon as a philosopher there is A. Quinton, *Francis Bacon* (Oxford, 1981). The political philosophy of the *Essays* is discussed in I. Box, 'Bacon's *Essays:* From Political Science to Political Prudence', *History of Political Thought*, III (1982), pp. 31–49.

Modern discussions of Harrington start with R. H. Tawney's British Academy Lecture of 1941 (reprinted in L. S. Sutherland (ed.), *Studies in History* (Oxford, 1966)). The chapter devoted to Harrington by C. B. Macpherson in his *Possessive Individualism* (Oxford, 1962) provoked a debate with J. F. H. New in the pages of *Past and Present* on how broadly power and wealth were to be distributed in Harrington's *Oceana*: this can now be found in C. Webster (ed.), *The Intellectual Revolution of the Seventeenth Century* (London, 1974). The most challenging recent interpreter of Harrington and neo-Harringtonianism has been J. G. A. Pocock. The interpretation put forward in 'Machiavelli, Harrington and English Political Ideologies in the Eighteenth Century' (reprinted in his *Politics, Language and Time* (New York, 1971)), developed in *The Machiavellian Moment* (Princeton, 1975), and deepened in his lengthy introduction to *The Political Works of James Harrington* (Cambridge, 1977), has been forcefully criticized by J. C. Davis in 'Pocock's Harrington', *Historical Journal*, XXIV (1981), pp. 683–97, and by J. R. Goodale in 'J. G. A. Pocock's Neo-Harringtonians', *History of Political Thought*, I (1980), pp. 237–59. Davis's own interpretation of Harrington is to be found in his *Utopia and the Ideal Society* (Cambridge, 1980).

The key account of Sidney's life and thought is now B. Worden, 'The Commonwealth Kidney of Algernon Sidney', *Journal of British Studies*, XXIV (1985), pp. 1–40. The political context in which *The Discourses* and Locke's *Two Treatises* were written is illuminated by J. R. Jones, *The First Whigs* (Oxford, 1961), and R. Ashcraft, 'Revolutionary Politics and Locke's *Two Treatises*', *Political Theory*, VIII (1980), pp. 429–86.

CHAPTER EIGHT

THE DOMESTICATION
OF MAN

1   John Selden, *Table Talk* (1689)

Selden (1584–1654) was the son of a yeoman. He was called to the
bar in 1613. Between 1606 and 1629 he wrote ten books, including
the Erastian *History of Tithes* (1618), and established himself as one of
the leading legal historians of his day. He served in the Parliaments
of 1624, 1626 and 1628–9. In 1627–8 he was Hampden's counsel in
the Five Knights' case, and he played a prominent role in the debate
leading to the Petition of Right. Following the dissolution of Parliament in 1629 he was briefly imprisoned. In 1635 he published *Mare
Clausum*, a rebuttal of Grotius's argument for the freedom of the
seas, and in 1640 *De Iure Naturali et Gentium Juxta Disciplinam
Ebraeorum*, his major study of natural law. He sat in the Long
Parliament, and, although he opposed the attainder of Strafford,
supported the parliamentary side until Pride's Purge. He was, as a
member of the parliamentary delegation to the Westminster
Assembly of Divines, the most prominent of the spokesmen for the
rights of the laity against the clergy. It is to this period that his *Table
Talk*, which remained unpublished until after the revolution of 1688,
dates. In 1647 he published *Dissertatio ad Fletam*, a study of the
history of Roman law in medieval Europe and England.

The view of natural law expressed in the passage reproduced here
was typical of the day in its insistence that the law of nature must be
something other than a mere precept of good behaviour: it must be a
command, carrying with it penalties for disobedience. The vexed
question was whether natural reason was sufficient to establish the
existence of such a command, and Selden appears to imply that only
revelation, the direct word of God, could give us knowledge of the
existence of a law of nature. The view that without such a law there
could be no consistent morality was generally held.

2   Thomas Hobbes, *Philosophicall Rudiments Concerning Government and Society* (1651)

Hobbes (1588–1679) was the son of a clergyman. He was tutor and then secretary to William, second Earl of Cavendish, from 1608 to 1628. From 1629 to 1631 he was tutor to the son of Sir George Clifton. He was then tutor to William Cavendish, third Earl of Devonshire. He travelled on the continent with each of his pupils and became a friend of Galileo and of Mersenne. In England he was an associate of Bacon, of Selden and of Clarendon. In 1640 he wrote *The Elements of Law*, a work which circulated in manuscript prior to its publication in 1650. He fled to Paris after the impeachment of Strafford, apparently afraid that Parliament might accuse him of seeking to subvert the constitution. In 1642 he published *De Cive*, of which this text is an English translation. In 1646 he was engaged to teach mathematics to the Prince of Wales, but in 1651, after the publication of *Leviathan*, he returned to England. There he was widely attacked as an atheist. *Behemoth*, a history of the Civil War, probably finished in 1668, was published in 1679.

By maintaining that one could have no knowledge of the law of nature as the command of God, carrying with it supernatural rewards and punishments, in the state of nature, Hobbes reduced the law of nature to a set of precepts which acquired binding force only when authorized by the sovereign. Hobbes's argument thus made divine law secondary to human law, and placed the burden of controlling men's passions upon the sovereign, whose duty it was to control men by instilling fear. In Hobbes's view mankind, although not naturally fit for society, could domesticate itself by establishing an unchecked power over itself.

3   John Locke, *The Reasonableness of Christianity* (1695)

Locke (1632–1704) was the son of a country attorney. In 1652 he was elected a fellow of Christ Church, Oxford, and he then commenced a career in the university which led him to the posts of reader in rhetoric and censor of moral philosophy. He also pursued studies in medicine, and in 1674 he acquired a licence to practise. In 1665–6 he was secretary to a diplomatic mission to the Elector of Brandenburg. Locke at this time seems to have been an opponent of toleration and an advocate of non-resistance. However in 1666 he met Anthony

Ashley Cooper, later Earl of Shaftesbury, and the next year entered his service, acting as medical adviser, tutor to his son, and political secretary. In 1673 he returned briefly to Oxford, and from 1675 to 1680 he was in France for reasons of ill-health. On his return to England he re-entered Shaftesbury's service and was active as a political adviser during the Exclusion crisis. In 1683, suspected of complicity in the Rye House Plot (in support of which he had probably written the *Two Treatises*), he fled abroad to Holland. He returned to England shortly after the Glorious Revolution. In 1689 he published, anonymously, the first *Letter on Toleration* and in 1690 there followed both *An Essay Concerning Human Understanding* and (anonymously) *Two Treatises of Government*. There followed *Some Thoughts Concerning Education* in 1693 and *The Reasonableness of Christianity* in 1695. He was a commissioner of trade from 1696 to 1700.

The Reasonableness of Christianity, like the *Essay*, was regarded by its opponents as a threat to orthodox religion, and was much admired by the first free-thinkers. Locke's own commitment to Christianity appears to have been entirely sincere, but his theology appears to have been close to Socinianism, especially in his insistence that the immortality of the soul could be known only through revelation and constituted the central promise of Christianity. It followed from this that Locke agreed with Hobbes in thinking that there could be no adequate knowledge of natural law without revelation. While he felt that the state should require belief in such a law, he also felt that most societies in history had been deprived of a knowledge that could only be obtained through Christianity. In this respect his views are comparable to those expressed by the Renaissance humanist Lorenzo Valla in *On Pleasure*.

4   Bernard Mandeville, *The Fable of the Bees; or, Private Vices, Publick Benefits* (1714)

Mandeville (1670?–1733) was born in Dort, in Holland. He graduated as a doctor of medicine from the University of Leyden in 1691 and came to practise in London. Almost nothing is known about him beyond the books he wrote, in particular *The Fable of the Bees*, which appeared in an enlarged edition in 1723, when it was presented as a public nuisance by the grand jury of Middlesex; *Free Thoughts on Religion* (1720); *An Enquiry into the Origin of Honour and the Usefulness of Christianity in War* (1732); and *A Modest Defence of Publick Stews* (1740).

Mandeville's importance lies in his belief that mankind, far from needing to be made virtuous by hope of heaven or fear of secular punishment, could be made fit for society through the channelling of vice into acceptable channels. Pride and greed, in particular, could provide the foundations for national power and prosperity. Mandeville thus marks a key stage in the secularization of political and social theory as a consequence of the emergence of market relations as the paradigmatic form of social relationship.

1 John Selden, *Table Talk* (1689)

Law of Nature

I cannot fancy to myself what the law of nature means, but the law of God. How should I know I ought not to steal, I ought not to commit adultery, unless somebody had told me, or why are these things against nature? Surely, 'tis because I have been told so. 'Tis not because I think I ought not to do them, nor whether you think I ought not. If so, our minds might change. Whence then comes the restraint? From a higher power. Nothing else can bind. I cannot bind myself, for I may untie myself again; nor an equal cannot bind me: we may untie one another. It must be a superior, even God Almighty. If two of us make a bargain, why should either of us stand to it? What need you care what you say, or what need I care what I say? Certainly because there is something above me, tells me *fides est servanda* [contracts are to be kept]. And if we after alter our minds and make a new bargain, there's *fides servanda* there too.

2 Thomas Hobbes, *Philosophicall Rudiments Concerning Government and Society* (1651)

Part One: Liberty

Chapter 1: Of the State of Men without Civil Society

1. The introduction.   2. That the beginning of civil society is from mutual fear.   3. That men by nature are all equal.   4. Whence the will of mischieving each other arises.   5. The discord arising from comparison of wits.   6. From the appetite many have to the same thing.   7. The definition of *right*.   8. A right to the end gives a right to the means necessary to that end.   9. By the right of nature every man is judge of the means which tend to his own preservation.   10. By nature all men have equal right to all things.   11. This right which all men have to all things is unprofitable.   12. The state of men without civil society is a mere state of war: the definitions of *peace* and *war*.   13. War is an adversary to man's preservation.   14. It is lawful for any man, by natural right, to compel another whom he has gotten in his power to give caution of his future obedience.   15. Nature dictates the seeking after peace.

1.   The faculties of human nature may be reduced unto four kinds:

bodily strength, experience, reason, passion. Taking the beginning of this following doctrine from these, we will declare, in the first place, what manner of inclinations men who are endued with these faculties bear towards each other, and whether, and by what faculty, they are born apt for society, and so preserve themselves against mutual violence. Then, proceeding, we will show what advice was necessary to be taken for this business, and what are the conditions of society, or of human peace; that is to say, changing the words only, what are the fundamental *laws of nature*.

2.   The greatest part of those men who have written aught concerning commonwealths either suppose, or require us, or beg us to believe that man is a creature born fit for society.[1] The Greeks call him ζῶον πολιτικον [a political animal]; and on this foundation they so build up the doctrine of civil society, as if for the preservation of peace, and the government of mankind, there was nothing else necessary than that men should agree to make certain covenants and conditions together, which themselves should then call laws. Which axiom, though received by most, is yet certainly false, and an error proceeding from our too slight contemplation of human nature. For they who shall more narrowly look into the causes for which men come together and delight in each other's company shall easily find that this happens, not because naturally it could happen no otherwise, but by accident. For if by nature one man should love another, that is, as man, there could no reason be returned why every man should not equally love every man, as being equally man; or why he should rather frequent those whose society affords him honour or profit.

We do not therefore by nature seek society for its own sake, but that we may receive some honour or profit from it: these we desire primarily, that [i.e. society] secondarily. How, by what advice, men do meet will be best known by observing those things which they do when they are met. For if they meet for traffic, it's plain every man regards not his fellow, but his business; if to discharge some office, a certain market-friendship is begotten, which has more of jealousy in it than true love, and whence factions sometimes may arise, but good will never; if for pleasure and recreation of mind, every man is wont to please himself most with those things which stir up laughter, whence he may, according to the nature of that which is ridiculous, by comparison of another man's defects and infirmities, pass the more current in his own opinion. And although this be sometimes innocent and without offence, yet it is manifest they are not so much delighted with the society, as their own vain glory. But, for the most part, in these kinds of meetings we wound the absent; their whole life, sayings, actions are examined, judged, condemned. Nay, it is very rare but some present receive a fling before they part, so as his reason was not ill who was wont always at parting to go out last. And these are indeed the true delights of society, unto which we are carried by nature, i.e. by those passions which are incident to all creatures, until either by sad experience or good precepts it so fall out, which in many never happens, that the appetite of present matters be dulled with the memory of things past: without which the discourse of most quick and nimble men on this subject is but cold and hungry.

But if it so happen that, being met, they pass their time in relating some stories, and one of them begins to tell one which concerns himself, instantly every one of the rest most greedily desires to speak of himself too; if one relate some wonder, the rest will tell you miracles if they have them; if not they'll feign them. Lastly, that I may say somewhat of them who pretend to be wiser than others: if they meet to talk of philosophy, look, how many men, so many would be esteemed masters, or else they not only love not their fellows, but even persecute them with hatred. So clear is it by experience to all men who a little more narrowly consider human affairs that all free congress arises either from mutual poverty, or from vain glory, whence the parties met endeavour to carry with them either some benefit, or to leave behind them that same ἐνδοκιμεῖν, some esteem and honour with those with whom they have been conversant.

The same is also collected by reason out of the definitions themselves of *will*, *good*, *honour*, *profitable*. For when we voluntarily contract society, in all manner of society we look after the object of the will, i.e. that which every one of those who gather together propounds to himself for good. Now whatsoever seems good is pleasant, and relates either to the senses or the mind. But all the mind's pleasure is either glory (or to have a good opinion of one's self), or refers to glory in the end; the rest are sensual, or conducing to sensuality, which may be all comprehended under the word *conveniences*. All society, therefore, is either for gain or for glory: i.e. not so much for love of our fellows, as for love of ourselves. But no society can be great or lasting which begins from vain glory, because that glory is like honour: if all men have it no man has it, for they consist in comparison and precellence [pre-eminence]. Neither does the society of others advance any whit the cause of my glorying in myself, for every man must account himself such as he can make himself without the help of others. But though the benefits of this life may be much furthered by mutual help, since yet those may be better attained to by dominion than by the society of others, I hope nobody will doubt but that men would much more greedily be carried by nature, if all fear were removed, to obtain dominion than to gain society. We must therefore resolve that the original of all great and lasting societies consisted not in the mutual good will men had towards each other, but in the mutual fear they had of each other.[2]

3.   The cause of mutual fear consists partly in the natural equality of men, partly in their mutual will of hurting: whence it comes to pass that we can neither expect from others, nor promise to ourselves, the least security. For if we look on men full-grown, and consider how brittle the frame of our human body is, which perishing, all its strength, vigour and wisdom itself perishes with it, and how easy a matter it is, even for the weakest man to kill the strongest, there is no reason why any man, trusting to his own strength, should conceive himself made by nature above others. They are equals who can do equal things one against the other; but they who can do the greatest things, namely kill, can do equal things. All men therefore among themselves are by nature equal; the inequality we now discern has its spring from the civil law.

4.   All men in the state of nature have a desire and will to hurt, but not proceeding from the same cause, neither equally to be condemned. For one man, according to that natural equality which is among us, permits as much to others as he assumes to himself – which is an argument of a temperate man, and one that rightly values his power. Another, supposing himself above others, will have a license to do what he lists, and challenges respect and honour, as due to him before others – which is an argument of a fiery spirit. This man's will to hurt arises from vain glory, and the false esteem he has of his own strength; the other's from the necessity of defending himself, his liberty, and his goods against this man's violence.

5.   Furthermore, since the combat of wits is the fiercest, the

greatest discords which are must necessarily arise from this contention. For in this case it is not only odious to contend against, but also not to consent. For not to approve of what a man says is no less than tacitly to accuse him of an error in that thing which he speaks; as in very many things to dissent is as much as if you accounted him a fool whom you dissent from. Which may appear hence, that there are no wars so sharply waged as between sects of the same religion, and factions of the same commonwealth, where the contestation is either concerning doctrines or politic prudence. And since all the pleasure and jollity of the mind consists in this, even to get some, with whom comparing, it may find somewhat wherein to triumph and vaunt itself, it's impossible but men must declare sometimes some mutual scorn and contempt, either by laughter, or by words, or by gesture, or some sign or other, than which there is no greater vexation of mind, and than from which there cannot possibly arise a greater desire to do hurt.

6. But the most frequent reason why men desire to hurt each other arises hence, that many men at the same time have an appetite to the same thing, which yet very often they can neither enjoy in common, nor yet divide it. Whence it follows that the strongest must have it, and who is strongest must be decided by the sword.

7. Among so many dangers, therefore, as the natural lusts of men do daily threaten each other withal, to have a care of one's self is not a matter so scornfully to be looked upon as if so be there had not been a power and will left in one to have done otherwise. For every man is desirous of what is good for him, and shuns what is evil, but chiefly the chiefest of natural evils, which is death; and this he does by a certain impulsion of nature, no less than that whereby a stone moves downward. It is therefore neither absurd nor reprehensible, neither against the dictates of true reason, for a man to use all his endeavours to preserve and defend his body and the members thereof from death and sorrows. But that which is not contrary to right reason, that all men account to be done justly and with right. Neither by the word *right* is anything else signified than that liberty which every man has to make use of his natural faculties according to right reason. Therefore the first foundation of natural right is this, that *every man, as much as in him lies, endeavour to protect his life and members.*

8. But because it is in vain for a man to have a right to the end if the right to the necessary means be denied him, it follows that since

every man has a right to preserve himself, he must also be allowed a right *to use all the means, and do all the actions, without which he cannot preserve himself.*

9.   Now whether the means which he is about to use, and the action he is performing, be necessary to the preservation of his life and members, or not, he himself, by the right [of] nature, must be judge. For say another man judge that it is contrary to right reason that I should judge of mine own peril: why now, because he judges of what concerns me, by the same reason, because we are equal by nature, will I judge also of things which do belong to him. Therefore it agrees with right reason, that is, it is the right of nature, that I judge of his opinion, i.e. whether it conduce to my preservation or not.

10.   Nature has given *to everyone a right to all*; that is, it was lawful for every man, in the bare state of nature, or before such time as men had engaged themselves by any covenants or bonds, to do what he would, and against whom he thought fit, and to possess, use and enjoy all what he would or could get.[3] Now because whatsoever a man would, it therefore seems good to him because he wills it, and either it really does, or at least seems to him to contribute towards his preservation (but we have already allowed him to be judge, in the foregoing article, whether it does or not, insomuch as we are to hold all for necessary whatsoever he shall esteem so), and by the seventh article it appears that by the right of nature those things may be done, and must be had, which necessarily conduce to the protection of life and members, it follows that in the state of nature to have all and do all is lawful for all. And this is that which is meant by that common saying *nature has given all to all.* From whence we understand likewise that in the state of nature profit is the measure of right.

11   But it was the least benefit for men thus to have a common right to all things. For the effects of this right are the same, almost, as if there had been no right at all. For although any man might say of everything, 'this is mine', yet could he not enjoy it by reason of his neighbour, who, having equal right and equal power, would pretend the same thing to be his.

12.   If now to this natural proclivity of men to hurt each other, which they derive from their passions, but chiefly from a vain esteem of themselves, you add the right of all to all, wherewith one by right invades, the other by right resists, and whence arise perpetual jealousies and suspicions on all hands, and how hard a thing it is to

provide against an enemy invading us with an intention to oppress and ruin, though he come with a small number and no great provision, it cannot be denied but that the natural state of men, before they entered into society, was a mere war, and that not simply, but a war of all men against all men. For what is *war* but that same time in which the will of contesting by force is fully declared, either by words or deeds? The time remaining is termed *peace*.

13. But it is easily judged how disagreeable a thing to the preservation either of mankind, or of each single man, a perpetual war is. But it is perpetual in its own nature, because, in regard of the equality of those that strive, it cannot be ended by victory. For in this state the conqueror is subject to so much danger, as it were to be accounted a miracle if any, even the most strong, should close up his life with many years and old age. They of America are examples hereof, even in this present age. Other nations have been in former ages, which now indeed are become civil and flourishing, but were then few, fierce, short-lived, poor, nasty, and destroyed of all that pleasure and beauty of life which peace and society are wont to bring with them. Whosoever therefore holds that it had been best to have continued in that state in which all things were lawful for all men, he contradicts himself. For every man by natural necessity desires that which is good for him, nor is there any that esteems a war of all against all (which necessarily adheres to such a state) to be good for him. And so it happens that, through fear of each other, we think it fit to rid ourselves of this condition and to get some fellows, that if there needs must be war, it may not yet be against all men, nor without some helps.

14. Fellows are gotten either by constraint, or by consent. By constraint when after fight the conqueror makes the conquered serve him, either through fear of death or by laying fetters on him; by consent when men enter into society to help each other, both parties consenting without any constraint. But the conqueror may by right compel the conquered, or the strongest the weaker (as a man in health may one that is sick, or he that is of riper years a child), unless he will choose to die, to give caution of his future obedience. For since the right of protecting ourselves according to our own wills proceeded from our danger, and our danger from our equality, it's more consonant to reason, and more certain for our conservation, using the present advantage to secure ourselves by taking caution,

than, when they shall be full grown and strong, and got out of our power, to endeavour to recover that power again by doubtful fight. And, on the other side, nothing can be thought more absurd than by discharging whom you already have weak in your power to make him at once both an enemy and a strong one. From whence we may understand likewise as a corollary in the natural state of men, that a *sure and irresistible power confers the right of dominion and ruling over those who cannot resist*; insomuch as the right of all things that can be done adheres essentially and immediately unto this omnipotence hence arising.

15. Yet cannot men expect any lasting preservation, continuing thus in the state of nature, i.e. of war, by reason of that equality of power and other human faculties they are endued withal. Wherefore to seek peace where there is any hopes of obtaining it, and where there is none to inquire out for auxiliaries of war, is the dictate of right reason, that is, the law of nature; as shall be showed in the next chapter.

Notes to Chapter 1

1. Since we now see actually a constituted society among men, and none living out of it, since we discern all desirous of congress and mutual correspondence, it may seem a wonderful kind of stupidity to lay in the very threshold of this doctrine such a stumbling block before the reader, as to deny *man to be born fit for society*. Therefore I must more plainly say that it is true indeed that to man by nature, or as man, that is, as soon as he is born, solitude is an enemy; for infants have need of others to help them to live, and those of riper years to help them to live well. Wherefore I deny not that men (even nature compelling) desire to come together.

But civil societies are not mere meetings, but bonds, to the making whereof faith and compacts are necessary; the virtue whereof to children and fools, and the profit whereof to those who have not yet tasted the miseries which accompany its defects, is altogether unknown; whence it happens that those, because they know not what society is, cannot enter into it; these, because ignorant of the benefit it brings, care not for it. Manifest therefore it is, that all men, because they are born in infancy, are born unapt for society. Many also, perhaps most men, either through defect of mind or want of education, remain unfit during the whole course of their lives; yet have they, infants as well as those of riper years, a human nature. Wherefore man is made fit for society not by nature but by education. Furthermore, although man were born in such a condition as to desire it, it follows not that he therefore were born fit to enter into it. For it is one thing to desire, another to be in capacity fit for what we desire. For even they who, through their pride, will not stoop to equal conditions, without which there can be no society, do yet desire it.

2.   [The original of all lasting societies consists not in mutual good will but in mutual fear.] It is objected: it's so improbable that men should grow into civil societies out of fear that, if they had been afraid, they would not have endured each other's looks. They presume, I believe, that to fear is nothing else than to be affrighted. I comprehend in this word *fear* a certain foresight of future evil; neither do I conceive flight the sole property of fear, but to distrust, suspect, take heed, provide so that they may not fear, is also incident to the fearful. They who go to sleep shut their doors; they who travel carry their swords with them because they fear thieves. Kingdoms guard their coasts and frontiers with forts and castles; cities are compassed with walls; and all for fear of neighbouring kingdoms and towns. Even the strongest armies, and most accomplished for fight, yet sometimes parley for peace, as fearing each other's power, and lest they might be overcome. It is through fear that men secure themselves by flight indeed, and in corners, if they think they cannot escape otherwise; but, for the most part, by arms and defensive weapons, whence it happens that, daring to come forth, they know each other's spirits. But then if they fight, civil society arises from the victory; if they agree, from their agreement.

3.   [It was lawful for every man, in the bare state of nature, to do what he would.] This is thus to be understood: what any man does in the bare state of nature is injurious to no man; not that in such a state he cannot offend God, or break the laws of nature; for injustice against men presupposes human laws, such as in the state of nature there are none. Now the truth of this proposition thus conceived is sufficiently demonstrated to the mindful reader in the articles immediately foregoing; but because in certain cases the difficulty of the conclusion makes us forget the premises, I will contract this argument, and make it most evident to a single view. Every man has right to protect himself, as appears by the seventh article. The same man, therefore, has a right to use all the means which necessarily conduce to this end, by the eighth article. But those are the necessary means which he shall judge to be such, by the ninth article. He therefore has a right to make use of and to do all whatsoever he shall judge requisite for his preservation; wherefore by the judgement of him that does it, the thing done is either right or wrong, and therefore right. True it is, therefore, in the bare state of nature, etc. But if any man pretend somewhat to tend necessarily to his preservation, which yet he himself does not confidently believe so, he may offend against the laws of nature, as in the third chapter of this book is more at large declared. It has been objected by some: if a son kill his father, does he [do] him no injury? I have answered that a son cannot be understood to be at any time in the state of nature, as being under the power and command of them to whom he owes his protection as soon as ever he is born, namely, either his father's or his mother's, or his that nourished him; as is demonstrated in the ninth chapter.

Part Two: Dominion

Chapter 5: Of the Causes and First Beginning of Civil Government

1. That the laws of nature are not sufficient to preserve peace. 2. That the laws of nature, in the state of nature, are silent. 3. That the security of living according to the laws of nature consists in the concord of many persons. 4. That the concord of many persons is not constant enough for a lasting peace. 5. The reason why the government of certain brute creatures stands firm in concord only, and why not of men. 6. That not only consent, but union also, is required to establish the peace of men. 7. What union is. 8. In union the right of all men is conveyed to one. 9. What civil society is. 10. What a civil person is. 11. What it is to have the supreme power, and what to be a subject. 12. Two kinds of cities, natural and by institution.

1. It is of itself manifest that the actions of men proceed from the will, and the will from hope and fear, insomuch as when they shall see a greater good or less evil likely to happen to them by the breach than observation of the laws, they'll wittingly violate them. The hope therefore which each man has of his security and self-preservation consists in this, that by force or craft he may disappoint his neighbour, either openly or by stratagem. Whence we may understand that the natural laws, though well understood, do not instantly secure any man in their practice; and, consequently, that as long as there is no caution had from the invasion of others, there remains to every man that same primitive right of self-defence by such means as either he can or will make use of, that is, a right to all things, or the right of war. And it is sufficient for the fulfilling of the natural law that a man be prepared in mind to embrace peace when it may be had.

2. It is an old saying that all laws are silent in the time of war, and it is a true one, not only if we speak of the civil, but also of the natural laws, provided they be referred not to the mind but to the actions of men, by the third chapter, article 27. And we mean such a war as is of all men against all men, such as is the mere state of nature; although in the war of nation against nation a certain mean was wont to be observed. And therefore in old time there was a manner of living, and as it were a certain economy which they called λῃστρικὴν, living by rapine; which was neither against the law of nature (things then so standing), nor void of glory to those who exercised it with valour, not with cruelty. Their custom was, taking away the rest, to spare

life, and abstain from oxen fit for plough and every instrument serviceable to husbandry. Which yet is not so to be taken as if they were bound to do thus by the law of nature; but that they had regard to their own glory herein, lest by too much cruelty they might be suspected guilty of fear.

3. Since, therefore, the exercise of the natural law is necessary for the preservation of peace, and that for the exercise of the natural law security is no less necessary, it is worth the considering what that is which affords such a security. For this matter nothing else can be imagined, but that each man provide himself of such meet helps as the invasion of one on the other may be rendered so dangerous as either of them may think it better to refrain than to meddle. But, first, it is plain that the consent of two or three cannot make good such a security, because that the addition but of one, or some few, on the other side is sufficient to make the victory undoubtedly sure, and heartens the enemy to attack us. It is therefore necessary, to the end the security sought for may be obtained, that the number of them who conspire in a mutual assistance be so great that the accession of some few to the enemy's party may not prove to them a matter of moment sufficient to assure the victory.

4. Furthermore, how great soever the number of them is who meet on self-defence, if yet they agree not among themselves of some excellent means whereby to compass this, but every man after his own manner shall make use of his endeavours, nothing will be done, because that, divided in their opinions, they will be a hindrance to each other. Or, if they agree well enough to some one action, through hope of victory, spoil, or revenge, yet afterward, through diversity of wits and counsels, or emulation and envy, with which men naturally contend, they will be so torn and rent as they will neither give mutual help nor desire peace, except they be constrained to it by some common fear. Whence it follows that the consent of many (which consists in this only, as we have already defined in the foregoing section, that they direct all their actions to the same end and the common good), that is to say, that the society proceeding from mutual help only, yields not that security which they seek for, who meet and agree in the exercise of the above-named laws of nature; but that somewhat else must be done that those who have once consented for the common good to peace and mutual help may by fear be restrained, lest afterwards they again dissent

when their private interest shall appear discrepant from the common good.

5. Aristotle reckons among those animals which he calls politic, not man only, but divers others, as the ant, the bee, etc., which, though they be destitute of reason, by which they may contract and submit to government, notwithstanding, by consenting, that is to say ensuing or eschewing the same things, they so direct their actions to a common end that their meetings are not obnoxious unto any seditions. Yet is not their gathering together a civil government, and therefore those animals not to be termed political, because their government is only a consent, or many wills concurring in one object, not (as is necessary in civil government) one will.

It is very true that in those creatures, living only by sense and appetite, their consent of minds is so durable as there is no need of anything more to secure it, and by consequence to preserve peace among them, than barely their natural inclination. But among men the case is otherwise. For, first, among them there is a contestation of honour and preferment; among beasts there is none. Whence hatred and envy, out of which arise sedition and war, is among men; among beasts no such matter. Next, the natural appetite of bees, and the like creatures, is conformable, and they desire the common good, which among them differs not from their private. But man scarce esteems anything good which has not somewhat of eminence in the enjoyment, more than that which others do possess. Thirdly, those creatures which are void of reason see no defect, or think they see none, in the administration of their commonwealths; but in a multitude of men there are many who, supposing themselves wiser than others, endeavour to innovate, and divers innovators innovate divers ways, which is a mere distraction and civil war. Fourthly, these brute creatures, howsoever they may have the use of their voice to signify their affections to each other, yet want they that same art of words which is necessarily required to those motions in the mind, whereby good is represented to it as being better, and evil as worse than in truth it is. But the tongue of man is a trumpet of war and sedition: and it is reported of Pericles that he sometimes by his elegant speeches thundered and lightened, and confounded whole Greece itself. Fifthly, they cannot distinguish between *injury* and *harm*; thence it happens that, as long as it is well with them, they blame not their fellows. But those men are of most trouble to the republic who have most leisure to be idle; for they use not to contend for public places before they have gotten the victory over hunger and cold. Last of all, the consent of those brutal creatures is natural; that of men by compact only, that is to say, artificial.

It is, therefore, no matter of wonder if somewhat more be needful for men to the end they may live in peace. Wherefore consent or contracted society, without some common power whereby particular men may be ruled through fear of punishment, does not suffice to make up that security which is requisite to the exercise of natural justice.

6.   Since, therefore, the conspiring of many wills to the same end does not suffice to preserve peace, and to make a lasting defence, it is requisite that, in those necessary matters which concern peace and self-defence, there be but one will of all men. But this cannot be done, unless every man will so subject his will to some other one, to wit, either man or council, that whatsoever his will is, in those things which are necessary to the common peace, it be received for the wills of all men in general, and of every one in particular. Now the gathering together of many men who deliberate of what is to be done or not to be done for the common good of all men is that which I call a *council*.

7.   This submission of the wills of all those men to the will of one man or one council is then made, when each one of them obliges himself by contract to every one of the rest not to resist the will of that one man or council to which he has submitted himself; that is, that he refuse him not the use of his wealth and strength against any others whatsoever (for he is supposed still to retain a right of defending himself against violence) and this is called *union*. But we understand that to be the will of the council which is the will of the major part of those men of whom the council consists.

8.   But though the will itself be not voluntary, but only the beginning of voluntary actions (for we will, not to will, but to act), and therefore falls least of all under deliberation and compact, yet he who submits his will to the will of another conveys to that other the right of his strength and faculties. Insomuch as when the rest have done the same, he to whom they have submitted has so much power as by the terror of it he can conform the wills of particular men unto unity and concord.

9.   Now union, thus made, is called a city or civil society; and

also a civil person. For when there is one will of all men it is to be esteemed for one person; and by the word *one* it is to be known and distinguished from all particular men, as having its own rights and properties. Insomuch as neither any one citizen, nor all of them together (if we except him whose will stands for the will of all) is to be accounted the city. A *city*, therefore (that we may define it), is *one person* whose will, by the compact of many men, is to be received for the will of them all, so as he may use all the power and faculties of each particular person to the maintenance of peace, and for common defence.

10. But although every city be a civil person, yet every civil person is not a city; for it may happen that many citizens, by the permission of the city, may join together in one person for the doing of certain things. These now will be civil persons: as the companies of merchants, and many other convents. But cities they are not, because they have not submitted themselves to the will of the company simply and in all things, but in certain things only determined by the city, and on such terms as it is lawful for any one of them to contend in judgement against the body itself of the sodality, which is by no means allowable to a citizen against the city. Such like societies, therefore, are civil persons subordinate to the city.

11. In every city, that man or council to whose will each particular man has subjected his will so as has been declared is said to have the *supreme power*, or *chief command*, or *dominion*. Which power and right of commanding consists in this, that each citizen has conveyed all his strength and power to that man or council; which to have done, because no man can transfer his power in a natural manner [i.e. transfer his personal physical strength], is nothing else than to have parted with his right of resisting. Each citizen, as also every subordinate civil person, is called the *subject* of him who has the chief command.

12. By what has been said it is sufficiently showed in what manner and by what degrees many natural persons, through desire of preserving themselves and by mutual fear, have grown together into a civil person whom we have called a *city*. But they who submit themselves to another for fear, either submit to him whom they fear, or some other whom they confide in for protection. They act according to the first manner who are vanquished in war, that they may not be

slain; they according to the second who are not yet overcome, that they may not be overcome. The first manner receives its beginning from natural power, and may be called the natural beginning of a city; the latter from the council and constitution of those who meet together, which is a beginning by institution. Hence it is that there are two kinds of cities; the one natural, such as the paternal and despotical; the other institutive, which may be also called political. In the first the lord acquires to himself such citizens as he will; in the other the citizens by their own wills appoint a lord over themselves, whether he be one man or one company of men, endued with the command in chief. But we will speak, in the first place, of a city political or by institution, and next of a city natural.

Chapter 6: Of the Right of Him, Whether Council or One Man Only, Who Has the Supreme Power in the City

1. There can no right be attributed to a multitude out of civil society, nor any action to which they have not under seal consented. 2. The right of the greater number consenting is the beginning of a city. 3. That every man retains a right to protect himself according to his own free will, so long as there is no sufficient regard had to his security. 4. That a coercive power is necessary to secure us. 5. What the sword of justice is. 6. That the sword of justice belongs to him who has the chief command. 7. That the sword of war belongs to him also. 8. All judicature belongs to him too. 9. The legislative power is his only. 10. The naming of magistrates and other officers of the city belongs to him. 11. Also the examination of all doctrines. 12. Whatsoever he does is unpunishable. 13. That the command his citizens have granted is absolute, and what proportion of obedience is due to him. 14. The laws of the city bind him not. 15. That no man can challenge a property to anything against his will. 16. By the laws of the city only we come to know what theft, murder, adultery, and injury is. 17. The opinion of those who would constitute a city where there is nobody should have an absolute power. 18. The marks of supreme authority. 19. If a city be compared with a man, he that has the supreme power is in order to the city as the human soul is in relation to the man. 20. That the supreme command cannot by right be dissolved through their consents by whose compacts it was first constituted.

1. We must consider, first of all, what a multitude of men, gathering themselves of their own free wills into society, is; namely that it is not any one body, but many men, whereof each one has his own will and his peculiar judgement concerning all things that may be

proposed.[1] And though by particular contracts each single man may have his own right and property, so as one may say *this is mine*, the other *that is his*, yet will there not be anything of which the whole multitude, as a person distinct from a single man, can rightly say this is mine, more than another's. Neither must we ascribe any action to the multitude, as its one; but, if all or more of them do agree, it will not be *an* action, but as many actions as men. For although, in some great sedition, is it commonly said that the people of that city have taken up arms, yet is it true of those only who are in arms, or who consent to them. For the city, which is one person, cannot take up arms against itself. Whatsoever, therefore, is done by the multitude must be understood to be done by every one of those by whom it is made up; and that he who being in the multitude and yet consented not, nor gave any helps to the things that were done by it, must be judged to have done nothing. Besides, in a multitude not yet reduced into one person, in that manner as has been said, there remains that same state of nature in which all things belong to all men; and there is no place for *meum* and *tuum*, which is called dominion and property, by reason that that security is not yet extant which we have declared above to be necessarily requisite for the practice of the natural laws.

2.   Next, we must consider that every one of the multitude, by whose means there may be a beginning to make up the city, must agree with the rest that in those matters which shall be propounded by any one in the assembly, that be received for the will of all which the major part shall approve of; for otherwise there will be no will at all of a multitude of men whose wills and votes differ so variously. Now if any one will not consent, the rest, notwithstanding, shall among themselves constitute the city without him. Whence it will come to pass that the city retains its primitive right against the dissenter, that is, the right of war, as against an enemy.

3.   But because we said in the foregoing chapter, the sixth article, that there was required to the security of men, not only their consent, but also the subjection of their wills in such things as were necessary to peace and defence, and that in that union and subjection the nature of a city consisted, we must discern now in this place, out of those things which may be propounded, discussed, and stated in an assembly of men, all whose wills are contained in the will of the major part, what things are necessary to peace and to common

defence. But, first of all, it is necessary to peace that a man be so far forth protected against the violence of others that he may live securely; that is, that he may have no just cause to fear others, so long as he does them no injury. Indeed, to make men altogether safe from mutual harms, so as they cannot be hurt or injuriously killed, is impossible, and, therefore, comes not within deliberation. But care may be had [that] there be no just cause of fear; for security is the end wherefore men submit themselves to others; which, if it be not had, no man is supposed to have submitted himself to aught, or to have quitted his right to all things, before that there was a care had of his security.

4. It is not enough, to obtain this security, that every one of those who are now growing up into a city do covenant with the rest, either by words or writing, *not to steal*, *not to kill*, and to observe the like laws. For the pravity of human disposition is manifest to all, and by experience too well known how little (removing the punishment) men are kept to their duties through conscience of their promises. We must therefore provide for our security, not by compacts, but by punishments; and there is then sufficient provision made, when there are so great punishments appointed for every injury as apparently it prove a greater evil to have done it than not to have done it. For all men, by a necessity of nature, choose that which to them appears to be the less evil.

5. Now, the right of punishing is then understood to be given to anyone when every man contracts not to assist him who is to be punished. But I will call this right *the sword of justice*. But these kinds of contracts men observe well enough, for the most part, till either themselves or their near friends are to suffer.

6. Because, therefore, for the security of particular men, and, by consequence, for the common peace, it is necessary that the right of using the sword for punishment be transferred to some man or council, that man or council is necessarily understood by right to have the supreme power in the city. For he that by right punishes at his own discretion, by right compels all men to all things which he himself wills; than which a greater command cannot be imagined.

7. But in vain do they worship peace at home who cannot defend themselves against foreigners; neither is it possible for them to protect themselves against foreigners whose forces are not united. And

therefore it is necessary for the preservation of particulars that there be some one council or one man who has the right to arm, to gather together, to unite so many citizens, in all dangers and on all occasions, as shall be needful for common defence against the certain number and strength of the enemy; and again, as often as he shall find it expedient, to make peace with them. We must understand, therefore, that particular citizens have conveyed their whole right of war and peace unto some one man or council; and that this right, which we may call *the sword of war*, belongs to the same man or council to whom the sword of justice belongs. For no man can by right compel citizens to take up arms and be at the expenses of war but he who by right can punish him who does not obey. Both swords therefore, as well this of war as that of justice, even by the constitution itself of a city and essentially, do belong to the chief command.

8.   But because the right of the sword is nothing else but to have power by right to use the sword at his own will, it follows that the judgement of its right use pertains to the same party; for if the power of judging were in one, and the power of executing in another, nothing would be done. For in vain would he give judgement who could not execute his commands; or, if he executed them by the power of another, he himself is not said to have the power of the sword, but that other, to whom he is only an officer. All judgement, therefore, in a city belongs to him who has the swords; i.e. to him who has the supreme authority.

9.   Furthermore, since it no less, nay, it much more conduces to peace to prevent brawls from arising than to appease them being risen, and that all controversies are bred from hence, that the opinions of men differ concerning *meum* and *tuum*, *just* and *unjust*, *profitable* and *unprofitable*, *good* and *evil*, *honest* and *dishonest*, and the like, which every man esteems according to his own judgement: it belongs to the same chief power to make some common rules for all men, and to declare them publicly, by which every man may know what may be called his, what another's, what just, what unjust, what honest, what dishonest, what good, what evil, that is, summarily, what is to be done, what to be avoided in our common course of life. But those rules and measures are usually called the civil laws, or the laws of the city, as being the commands of him who has the supreme power in the city. And the civil laws (that we may define them) are nothing else but *the*

commands of him who has the chief authority in the city, for direction of the future actions of his citizens.

10. Furthermore, since the affairs of the city, both those of war and peace, cannot possibly be all administered by one man or one council without officers and subordinate magistrates, and that it appertains to peace and common defence that they to whom it belongs justly to judge of controversies, to search into neighbouring councils, prudently to wage war, and on all hands warily to attend the benefit of the city, should also rightly exercise their offices, it is consonant to reason that they depend on and be chosen by him who has the chief command both in war and in peace.

11. It is also manifest that all voluntary actions have their beginning from and necessarily depend on the will; and that the will of doing or omitting aught depends on the opinion of the good and evil, of the reward or punishment which a man conceives he shall receive by the act or omission: so as the actions of all men are ruled by the opinions of each. Wherefore, by evident and necessary inference, we may understand that it very much concerns the interest of peace that no opinions or doctrines be delivered to citizens by which they may imagine that either by right they may not obey the laws of the city, that is, the commands of that man or council to whom the supreme power is committed, or that it is lawful to resist him, or that a less punishment remains for him that denies than him that yields obedience. For if one command somewhat to be done under penalty of natural death, another forbids it under pain of eternal death, and both by their own right, it will follow that the citizens, although innocent, are not only by right punishable, but that the city itself is altogether dissolved. For no man can serve two masters; nor is he less, but rather more, a master whom we believe we are to obey for fear of damnation, than he whom we obey for fear of temporal death. It follows, therefore, that this one, whether man or court, to whom the city has committed the supreme power, have also this right, that he both judge what opinions and doctrines are enemies unto peace, and also that he forbid them to be taught.[2]

12. Last of all, from this consideration, that each citizen has submitted his will to his who has the supreme command in the city, so as he may not employ his strength against him, it follows manifestly that whatsoever shall be done by him who commands must not be punished. For as he who has not power enough cannot punish

him naturally, so neither can he punish him by right who by right has not sufficient power.

13. It is most manifest by what has been said that in every perfect city, that is, where no citizen has right to use his faculties at his own discretion for the preservation of himself, or where the right of the private sword is excluded, there is a supreme power in some one, greater than which cannot by right be conferred by men, or greater than which no mortal man can have over himself. But that power, greater than which cannot by men be conveighed on a man, we call *absolute*.[3] For whosoever has so submitted his will to the will of the city that he [i.e. the city] can, unpunished, do anything – make laws, judge controversies, set penalties, make use at his own pleasure of the strength and wealth of men, and all this by right – truly, he has given him the greatest dominion that can be granted. This same may be confirmed by experience in all the cities which are or ever have been. For though it be sometimes in doubt what man or council has the chief command, yet ever there is such a command, and always exercised, except in the time of sedition and civil war – and then there are two chief commands made out of one. Now those seditious persons who dispute against absolute authority do not so much care to destroy it, as to convey it on others, for, removing this power, they together take away civil society, and a confusion of all things returns.

There is so much obedience joined to this absolute right of the chief ruler as is necessarily required for the government of the city, that is to say, so much as that right of his may not be granted in vain. Now this kind of obedience, although for some reasons it may sometimes by right be denied, yet because a greater cannot be performed, we will call it *simple*. But the obligation to perform this grows not immediately from that contract by which we have conveyed all our right on the city, but mediately from hence: that without obedience the city's right would be frustrate[d], and by consequence there would be no city constituted. For it is one thing if I say, 'I give you right to command what you will,' another if I say, 'I will do whatsoever you command.' And the command may be such as I would rather die than do it. Forasmuch, therefore, as no man can be bound to will being killed, much less is he tied to that which to him is worse than death.

If, therefore, I be commanded to kill myself, I am not bound to do it. For though I deny to do it, yet the right of dominion is not frustrated, since others may be found who, being commanded, will not refuse to do it; neither do I refuse to do that which I have contracted to do. In like manner, if the chief ruler command any man to kill him, he is not tied to do it, because it cannot be conceived that he made any such convenant. Nor if he command to execute a parent, whether he be innocent or guilty and condemned by the law, since there are others who, being commanded, will do that, and a son will rather die than live infamous and hated of all the world. There are many other cases in which, since the commands are shameful to be done by some, and not by others, obedience may by right be performed by these, and refused by those; and this without breach of that absolute right which was given to the chief ruler. For in no case is the right taken away from him of slaying those who shall refuse to obey him. But they who thus kill men, although by right given them from him that has it, yet if they use that right otherwise than right reason requires, they sin against the laws of nature, that is, against God.

14. Neither can any man give somewhat to himself, for he is already supposed to have what he can give himself. Nor can he be obliged to himself, for the same party being both *the obliged* and *the obliger*, and the obliger having power to release the obliged, it were merely in vain for a man to be obliged to himself, because he can release himself at his own pleasure and he that can do this is already actually free.

Whence it is plain that the city is not tied to the civil laws, for the civil laws are the laws of the city, by which, if she were engaged, she would be engaged to herself. Neither can the city be obliged to her citizen, because if he will he can free her from her obligation, and he will as oft as she wills, for the will of every citizen is in all things comprehended in the will of the city. The city, therefore, is free when she pleases, that is, she is now actually free. But the will of a council, or one who has the supreme authority given him, is the will of the city. He, therefore, contains the wills of all particular citizens. Therefore neither is he bound to the civil laws (for this is to be bound to himself), nor to any of his citizens.

15. Now because, as has been shown above, before the constitution of a city all things belonged to all men, nor is there anything which any man can so call his as any other may not, by the same right, claim as his own (for where all things are *common* there can be nothing *proper* to any man), it follows that property received its

beginning when cities received theirs, and that that only is proper to each man which he can keep by the laws and the power of the whole city, that is, of him on whom its chief command is conferred.[4] Whence we understand that each particular citizen has a *property* to which none of his fellow-citizens has right, because they are tied to the same laws; but he has no property in which the chief ruler (whose commands are the laws, whose will contains the will of each man, and who by every single person is constituted the supreme judge) has not a right. But although there be many things which the city permits to its citizens, and therefore they may sometimes go to law against their chief, yet is not that action belonging to civil right, but to natural equity. Neither is it concerning what by right he may do who has the supreme power, but what he has been willing should be done; and therefore he shall be judge himself, as though (the equity of the case being well understood) he could not give wrong judgement.[5]

16. Theft, murder, adultery, and all injuries are forbid by the laws of nature; but what is to be called *theft*, what *murder*, what *adultery*, what *injury* in a citizen, this is not to be determined by the natural, but by the civil law. For not every taking away of the things which another possesses, but only another man's goods, is theft; but what is ours, and what another's, is a question belonging to the civil law. In like manner, not every killing of a man is murder, but only that which the civil law forbids; neither is all encounter with women adultery, but only that which the civil law prohibits. Lastly, all breach of promise is an injury where the promise itself is lawful; but where there is no right to make any compact there can be no conveyance of it, and therefore there can no injury follow, as has been said in the second chapter, article seventeen. Now what we may contract for, and what not, depends wholly upon the civil laws.

The city of Lacedaemon [i.e. Sparta] therefore rightly ordered that those young men who could so take away certain goods from others as not to be caught should go unpunished, for it was nothing else but to make a law that what was so acquired should be their own, and not another's. Rightly also is that man everywhere slain whom we kill in war, or by the necessity of self-defence. So also that copulation which in one city is matrimony, in another will be judged adultery. Also those contracts which make up marriage in one citizen do not so in another, although of the same city, because that he who is forbidden by the city, that is, by that one man or council whose the supreme power is, to contract aught has no right to make any contract, and therefore, having made any, it is not valid, and by consequence no marriage. But his contract which received no prohibition was therefore of force, and so was matrimony. Neither adds it any force to any unlawful contracts that they were made by an oath or sacrament, for those add nothing to the strengthening of the contract, as has been said above, chapter two, article twenty-two.[6] What, therefore, theft, what murder, what adultery, and, in general, what injury is, must be known by the civil laws, that is, the commands of him who has the supreme authority.

17. This same supreme command and absolute power seems so harsh to the greatest part of men as they hate the very naming of them, which happens chiefly through want of knowledge what human nature and the civil laws are; and partly also through their default who, when they are invested with so great authority, abuse their power to their own lust. That they may therefore avoid this kind of supreme authority, some of them will have a city well enough constituted if they who shall be the citizens, convening, do agree concerning certain articles propounded, and in that convent [i.e. gathering] agitated and approved, and do command them to be observed, and punishments prescribed to be inflicted on them who shall break them. To which purpose, and also to the repelling of a foreign enemy, they appoint a certain and limited return, with this condition, that if that suffice not, they may call a new convention of estates.

Who sees not, in a city thus constituted, that the assembly who prescribed those things had an absolute power? If, therefore, the assembly continue, or from time to time have a certain day and place of meeting, that power will be perpetual. But if they wholly dissolve, either the city dissolves with them, and so all is returned to the state of war, or else there is somewhere a power left to punish those who shall transgress the laws, whosoever or how many soever they be that have it, which cannot possibly be without an absolute power. For he that by right has this might given, by punishments to restrain what citizens he pleases, has such a power as a greater cannot possibly be given by any citizens.

18. It is, therefore, manifest that in every city there is some one

man, or council, or court, who by right has as great a power over each single citizen as each man has over himself, considered out of that civil state; that is, supreme and absolute, to be limited only by the strength and forces of the city itself, and by nothing else in the world. For if his power were limited, that limitation must necessarily proceed from some greater power. For he that prescribes limits must have a greater power than he who is confined by them. Now that confining power is either without limit, or is again restrained by some other greater than itself; and so we shall at length arrive to a power which has no other limit but that which is the *terminus ultimus* of the forces of all the citizens together. That same is called the supreme command; and if it be committed to a council, a supreme council, but if to one man, the supreme lord of the city.

Now the notes of supreme command are these: to make and abrogate laws; to determine war and peace; to know and judge of all controversies (either by himself or by judges appointed by him); to elect all magistrates, ministers and counsellors. Lastly, if there be any man who by right can do some one action which is not lawful for any citizen or citizens to do beside himself, that man has obtained the supreme power. For those things which by right may not be done by any one or many citizens, the city itself can only do. He therefore that does those things uses the city's right, which is the supreme power.

19.   They who compare a city and its citizens with a man and his members almost all say that he who has the supreme power in the city is in relation to the whole city such as the head is to the whole man. But it appears by what has been already said that he who is endued with such a power, whether it be a man or a court, has a relation to the city, not as that of the head, but as the soul to the body. For it is the soul by which a man has a will, that is, can either will or nill; so by him who has the supreme power, and no otherwise, the city has a will, and can either will or nill. A court of counsellors is rather to be compared with the head, or one counsellor whose only counsel (if of any one alone) the chief ruler makes use of in matters of greatest moment: for the office of the head is to counsel, as the soul's is to command.

20.   Forasmuch as the supreme command is constituted by virtue of the compacts which each single citizen or subject mutually makes with the other; but all contracts, as they receive their force from the

contractors, so by their consent they lose it again and are broken: perhaps some may infer hence that by the consent of all the subjects together the supreme authority may be wholly taken away. Which inference, if it were true, I cannot discern what danger would thence by right arise to the supreme commanders. For since it is supposed that each one has obliged himself to each other, if any one of them shall refuse, whatsoever the rest shall agree to do, he is bound notwithstanding. Neither can any man without injury to me do that which by contract made with me he has obliged himself not to do. But it is not to be imagined that ever it will happen that all the subjects together, not so much as one excepted, will combine against the supreme power. Wherefore there is no fear for rulers in chief that by any right they can be despoiled of their authority.

If, notwithstanding, it were granted that their right depended only on that contract which each man makes with his fellow-citizen, it might very easily happen that they might be robbed of that dominion under pretence of right. For subjects being called either by the command of the city, or seditiously flocking together, most men think that the consents of all are contained in the votes of the greater part; which in truth is false. For it is not from nature that the consent of the major part should be received for the consent of all, neither is it true in tumults; but it proceeds from civil institution, and is then only true when that man or court which has the supreme power, assembling his subjects, by reason of the greatness of their number allows those that are elected a power of speaking for those who elected them, and will have the major part of voices, in such matters as are by him propounded to be discussed, to be as effectual as the whole. But we cannot imagine that he who is chief ever convened his subjects with intention that they should dispute his right, unless, weary of the burden of his charge, he declared in plain terms that he renounces and abandons his government.

Now, because most men through ignorance esteem not the consent of the major part of citizens only, but even of a very few, provided they be of their opinion, for the consent of the whole city, it may very well seem to them that the supreme authority may by right be abrogated, so it be done in some great assembly of citizens by the votes of the greater number. But though a government be constituted by the contracts of particular men with particulars, yet its right depends not on that obligation only: there is another tie also towards him who commands. For each citizen compacting with his fellows says thus: 'I convey my right on this party, upon condition that you pass yours to the same'; by which means that right which every man had before to use his faculties to his own advantage is now wholly translated on some certain man or council for the common benefit. Wherefore what by the mutual contracts each one has made with the other, what by the donation of right which every man is bound to ratify to him that commands, the government is upheld by a double obligation from the citizens: first, that which is due to their fellow-citizens; next, that which they owe to their prince. Wherefore no subjects, how many soever they be, can with any right despoil him who bears the chief rule of his authority, even [i.e. especially] without his own consent.

Notes to Chapter 6

1. [What a multitude is.] The doctrine of the power of a city over its citizens almost wholly depends on the understanding of the difference which is between a multitude of men ruling and a multitude ruled. For such is the nature of a city that a multitude or company of citizens not only may have command, but may also be subject to command; but in diverse senses. Which difference I did believe was clearly enough explained in the first article; but, by the objections of many against those things which follow, I discern otherwise. Wherefore it seemed good to me, to the end I might make a fuller explication, to add these few things.

By multitude, because it is a collective word, we understand more than one: so as a multitude of men is the same with many men. The same word, because it is of the singular number, signifies one thing: namely, one multitude. But in neither sense can a multitude be understood to have one will given to it by nature, but to either a several; and therefore neither is any one action whatsoever to be attributed to it. Wherefore a multitude cannot promise, contract, acquire right, convey right, act, have, possess, and the like, unless it be every one apart, and man by man; so as there must be as many promises, compacts, rights, and actions as men. Wherefore a multitude is no natural person.

But if the same multitude do contract one with another that the will of one man, or the agreeing wills of the major part of them, shall be received for the will of all, then it becomes one person. For it is endued with a will, and therefore can do voluntary actions, such as are commanding, making laws, acquiring and transferring of right, and so forth; and it is oftener called the people than the multitude.

We must therefore distinguish thus: when we say the people or multitude wills, commands or does anything, it is understood that [it is] the city which commands, wills, and acts by the will of one, or the concurring wills of more; which cannot be done but in an assembly; but as oft as anything is said to be done by a multitude of men, whether great or small, without the will of that man or assembly of men, that is understood to be done by a subjected people – that is, by many single citizens together – and not proceeding from one will, but from diverse wills of diverse men, who are citizens and subjects, but not a city.

2. [The supreme power judges what opinions and doctrines are enemies unto peace.] There is scarce any principle, neither in the worship of God, nor in human sciences, from whence there may not spring dissensions, discords, reproaches, and by degrees war itself. Neither does this happen by reason of the falsehood of the principle, but of the disposition of men, who, seeming wise to themselves, will needs appear such to all others. But though such dissensions cannot be hindered from arising, yet may they be restrained by the exercise of the supreme power, that they prove no hindrance to the public peace. Of these kinds of opinions, therefore, I have not spoken of in this place.

There are certain doctrines wherewith subjects being tainted, they verily believe that obedience may be refused to the city, and that by right they may, nay ought, to oppose and fight against chief princes and dignities. Such are those which, whether directly and openly, or more obscurely and by consequence, require obedience to be given to others beside them to whom the supreme authority is committed. I deny not but this reflects on that power which many, living under other government, ascribe to the chief head of the Church of Rome, and also on that which elsewhere, out of that Church, bishops require in theirs to be given to them; and, last of all, on that liberty which the lower sort of citizens, under pretence of religion, do challenge to themselves. For what civil war was there ever in the Christian world which did not either grow from, or was nourished by, this root?

The judgement, therefore, of doctrines, whether they be repugnant to civil obedience or not, and, if they be repugnant, the power of prohibiting them to be be taught, I do here attribute to the civil authority. For since there is no man who grants not to the city the judgement of those things which belong to its peace and defence (and it is manifest that the opinions which I have already recited do relate to its peace), it follows necessarily that the examination of those opinions, whether they be such or not, must be referred to the city; that is, to him who has the supreme authority.

3. [That power, greater than which cannot be conveyed on a man, we call *absolute*.] A popular state openly challenges absolute dominion, and the citizens oppose it not. For in the gathering together of many men they acknowledge the face of a city; and even the unskilful understand that matters there are ruled by council. Yet monarchy is no less a city than democracy; and absolute kings have their counsellors, from whom they will take advice, and suffer their power, in matters of greater consequence, to be guided, but not recalled. But it appears not to most men how a city is contained in the person of a king. And therefore they object against

absolute command: first, that if any man had such a right the condition of the citizen would be miserable. For thus they think: he will take all, spoil all, kill all; and every man counts it his only happiness that he is not already spoiled and killed. But why should he do thus? Not because he can; for unless he have a mind to it he will not do it. Will he, to please one or some few, spoil all the rest? First, though by right, that is, without injury to them, he may do it, yet can he not do it justly, that is, without breach of the natural laws and injury against God. And therefore there is some security for subjects in the oaths which princes take. Next, if he could justly do it, yet appears there no reason why he should desire it, since he finds no good in it.

But it cannot be denied but a prince may sometimes have an inclination to do wickedly. But grant, then, that thou hadst given him a power which were not absolute, but so much only as sufficed to defend thee from the injuries of others (which, if thou wilt be safe, is necessary for thee to give) are not all the same things to be feared? For he that has strength enough to protect all wants not sufficiency to oppress all. Here is no other difficulty, then, but that human affairs cannot be without some inconvenience. And this inconvenience itself is in the citizens, not in the government. For if men could rule themselves, every man by his own command, that is to say, could they live according to the laws of nature, there would be no need at all of a city, nor of a common coercive power.

Secondly, they object that there is no dominion in the Christian world [which is] absolute. Which, indeed, is not true, for all monarchies, and all other states, are so. For although they who have the chief command do not all those things they would, and what they know profitable to the city, the reason of that is not the defect of right in them, but the consideration of their citizens, who, busied about their private interest, and careless of what tends to the public, cannot sometimes be drawn to perform their duties without the hazard of the city. Wherefore princes sometimes forbear the exercise of their right, and prudently remit somewhat of the act, but nothing of their right.

4. [*Property* received its beginning when cities received theirs.] What is objected by some, that the property of goods, even before the constitution of cities, was found in fathers of families, that objection is vain because I have already declared that a family is a little city. For the sons of a family have a property of their goods granted them by their father, distinguished indeed from the rest of the sons of the same family, but not from the property of the father himself. But the fathers of diverse families, who are subject neither to any common father nor lord, have a common right in all things.

5. [Citizens may sometimes go to law against their chief; yet such actions are not concerned with what he who has the supreme power has the right to do.] As often as a citizen is granted to have an action of law against the supreme, i.e. against the city, the question is not in that action whether the city may by right keep possession of the thing in controversy, but whether by the laws formerly made she would keep it;

for the law is the declared will of the supreme. Since, then, the city may raise money from the citizens under two titles, either as tribute or as debt, in the former case there is no action of law allowed, for there can be no question whether the city have right to require tribute; in the latter it is allowed because the city will take nothing from its citizens by fraud or cunning, and yet, if need require, all they have, openly. And, therefore, he that condemns this place, saying that by this doctrine it is easy for princes to free themselves from their debts, he does it impertinently.

6.   [It adds no force to any unlawful contracts that they were made by an oath or sacrament.] Whether matrimony be a sacrament (in which sense that word is used by some divines) or not, it is not my purpose to dispute. Only I say, that the legitimate contract of a man and woman to live together, i.e. granted by the civil law, whether it be a sacrament or not, is surely a legitimate marriage; but that copulation which the city has prohibited is no marriage, since it is of the essence of marriage to be a legitimate contract. There were legitimate marriages in many places, as among the Jews, the Grecians, the Romans, which yet might be dissolved. But with those who permit no such contracts but by a law that they shall never be broken, wedlock cannot be dissolved; and the reason is, because the city has commanded it to be indissoluble, not because matrimony is a sacrament. Wherefore the ceremonies which at weddings are to be performed in the temple to bless, or, if I may say so, to consecrate the husband and wife, will perhaps belong only to the office of clergymen; all the rest, namely who, when, and by what contracts marriages may be made, pertains to the laws of the city.

3   John Locke, *The Reasonableness of Christianity* (1695)

. . . .

It will here possibly be asked, *Quorsum perditio haec?* 'What need was there of a Saviour? What advantage have we by Jesus Christ?'

It is enough to justify the fitness of any thing to be done, by resolving it into the wisdom of God, who has done it; though our short views and narrow understandings may utterly incapacitate us to see that wisdom and to judge rightly of it. We know little of this visible and nothing at all of the state of that intellectual world, wherein are infinite numbers and degrees of spirits out of the reach of our ken or guess; and therefore know not what transactions there were between God and our Saviour, in reference to his kingdom. We know not what need there was to set up a head and a chieftain, in opposition to 'the prince of this world, the prince of the power of the air', etc., whereof there are more than obscure intimations in Scripture. And we shall take too much upon us if we shall call God's wisdom or providence to account, and pertly condemn for needless all that our weak, and perhaps biased, understandings cannot account for.

Though this general answer be reply enough to the fore-mentioned demand, and such as a rational man, or fair searcher after truth, will acquiesce in; yet in this particular case the wisdom and goodness of God has shown itself so visibly to common apprehensions that it has furnished us abundantly wherewithal to satisfy the curious and inquisitive, who will not take a blessing, unless they be instructed what need they had of it, and why it was bestowed upon them. The great and many advantages we receive by the coming of Jesus the Messiah will show that it was not without need that he was sent into the world.

The evidence of our Saviour's mission from heaven is so great, in the multitude of miracles he did, before all sorts of people, that what he delivered cannot but be received as the oracles of God, and unquestionable verity. For the miracles he did were so ordered by the divine providence and wisdom that they never were, nor could be, denied by any of the enemies or opposers of Christianity.

Though the works of nature, in every part of them, sufficiently evidence a Deity; yet the world made so little use of their reason that they saw him not where, even by the impressions of himself, he was easy to be found. Sense and lust blinded their minds in some, and a careless inadvertency in others, and fearful apprehensions in most (who either believed there were, or could not but suspect there might be, superior unknown beings) gave them up into the hands of their priests, to fill their heads with false notions of the deity, and their worship with foolish rites, as they pleased; and what dread or craft once began, devotion soon made sacred, and religion immutable. In this state of darkness and ignorance of the true God, vice and superstition held the world; nor could any help be had or hoped for from reason, which could not be heard, and was judged to have nothing to do in the case: the priests everywhere, to secure their empire, having excluded reason from having anything to do in religion. And in the crowd of wrong notions, and invented rites, the world had almost lost the sight of the one only true God. The rational and thinking part of mankind, 'tis true, when they sought after him, found the one, supreme, invisible God: but if they acknowledged and worshipped him, it was only in their own minds. They kept this truth locked up in their own breasts as a secret, nor ever durst venture it amongst the people, much less amongst the priests, those wary guardians of their own creeds and profitable inventions. Hence we see that reason, speaking never so clearly to the wise and virtuous, had never authority enough to prevail on the multitude, and to persuade the societies of men that there was but one God that alone was to be owned and worshipped. The belief and worship of one God was the national religion of the Israelites alone; and, if we will consider it, it was introduced and supported amongst that people by revelation. They were in Goshen, and had light, whilst the rest of the world were in almost Egyptian darkness, 'without God in the world'. There was no part of mankind who had quicker parts, or improved them more; that had a greater light of reason, or followed it farther in all sorts of speculations, than the Athenians, and yet we find but one Socrates amongst them, that opposed and laughed at their polytheism and wrong opinions of the deity; and we see how they rewarded him for it. Whatsoever Plato, and the soberest of the philosophers, thought of the nature and being of the one God, they were fain, in their outward professions and worship, to go with the herd, and keep to the religion established by law; which what it was, and how it had disposed the mind of these knowing and quicksighted Grecians, St Paul tells us, Acts 17: 22–29:

> Ye men of Athens (says he), I perceive that in all things ye are too superstitious. For as I passed by, and beheld your devotions, I found an altar with this inscription: TO THE UNKNOWN GOD. Whom therefore ye ignorantly worship, him declare I unto you. God that made the world, and all things therein, seeing that he is Lord of heaven and earth, dwells not in temples made with hands; neither is worshipped with men's hands, as though he needed anything, seeing he gives unto all life, and breath, and all things; and has made of one blood all the nations of men, for to dwell on the face of the earth; and has determined the times before appointed, and the bounds of their habitations; that they should seek the Lord, if haply they might feel him out, and find him, though he be not far from every one of us.

Here he tells the Athenians, that they, and the rest of the world (given up to superstition), whatever light there was in the works of creation and providence to lead them to the true God, yet they few of them found him. He was everywhere near them; yet they were but like people groping and feeling for something in the dark, and did not see him with a full and clear day-light; 'But thought the Godhead like to gold and silver, and stone, graven by art and man's device.'

In this state of darkness and error, in reference to the true God, our Saviour found the world. But the clear revelation he brought with him dissipated this darkness; made the one invisible true God known to the world: and that with such evidence and energy that polytheism and idolatry has nowhere been able to withstand it. But wherever the preaching of the truth he delivered and the light of the gospel has come, those mists have been dispelled. And, in effect, we see that, since our Saviour's time, the belief of one God has prevailed and spread itself over the face of the earth. For even to the light that the Messiah brought into the world with him, we must ascribe the owning and profession of one God which the Mahommedan religion has derived and borrowed from it. So that, in this sense, it is certainly and manifestly true of our Saviour, what St John says of him (1 John 3: 8): 'For this purpose the Son of God was manifested, that he might destroy the works of the devil.' This light the world needed, and this light it received from him: that there is but 'one God', and he 'eternal, invisible'; not like to any visible objects, nor to be represented by them.

If it be asked whether the revelation to the patriarchs by Moses did not teach this, and why that was not enough? [1] The answer is obvious; that however clearly the knowledge of one invisible God, maker of heaven and earth, was revealed to them; yet that revelation was shut up in a little corner of the world, amongst a people, by that very law which they received with it, excluded from a commerce and communication with the rest of mankind. The Gentile world, in our Saviour's time and several ages before, could have no attestation of the miracles on which the Hebrews built their faith but from the Jews themselves, a people not known to the greatest part of mankind, contemned and thought vilely of by those nations that did know them; and therefore very unfit and unable to propagate the doctrine of one God in the world, and diffuse it through the nations of the earth by the strength and force of that ancient revelation upon which they had received it.

But our Saviour, when he came, threw down this wall of partition, and did not confine his miracles or message to the land of Canaan, or the worshippers at Jerusalem; but he himself preached at

Samaria, and did miracles in the borders of Tyre and Sidon, and before multitudes of people gathered from all quarters; and, after his resurrection, sent his apostles amongst the nations, accompanied with miracles, which were done in all parts so frequently, and before so many witnesses of all sorts, in broad daylight, that, as I have before observed, the enemies of Christianity have never dared to deny them: No, not Julian himself, who neither wanted skill nor power to inquire into the truth, nor would have failed to have proclaimed and exposed it if he could have detected any falsehood in the history of the gospel, or found the least ground to question the matter of fact published of Christ and his apostles. The number and evidence of the miracles done by Our Saviour and his followers, by the power and force of truth, bore down this mighty and accomplished emperor, and all his parts, in his own dominions. He durst not deny so plain matter of fact, which being granted, the truth of Our Saviour's doctrine and mission unavoidably follows; notwithstanding whatsoever artful suggestions his wit could invent, or malice should offer, to the contrary.

2. Next to the knowledge of one God, maker of all things, a clear knowledge of their duty was wanting to mankind. This part of knowledge, though cultivated with some care by some of the heathen philosophers, yet got little footing among the people. All men indeed, under pain of displeasing the gods, were to frequent the temples, every one went to their sacrifices and services; but the priests made it not their business to teach them virtue. If they were diligent in their observations and ceremonies, punctual in their feasts and solemnities and the tricks of religion, the holy tribe assured them the gods were pleased; and they looked no further. Few went to the schools of the philosophers to be instructed in their duties and to know what was good and evil in their action. The priests sold the better penny-worths, and therefore had all the custom. Lustrations and processions were much easier than a clean conscience and a steady course of virtue; and an expiatory sacrifice, that atoned for the want of it, was much more convenient than a strict and holy life. No wonder, then, that religion was everywhere distinguished from, and preferred to, virtue, and that it was dangerous heresy and profaneness to think the contrary. So much virtue as was necessary to hold societies together, and to contribute to the quiet of governments, the civil laws of commonwealths taught, and forced upon men that lived under magis-

trates. But these laws, being for the most part made by such who had no other aims but their own power, reached no further than those things that would serve to tie men together in subjection; or, at most, were directly to conduce to the prosperity and temporal happiness of any people.

But natural religion, in its full extent, was nowhere, that I know, taken care of by the force of natural reason. It should seem, by the little that has hitherto been done in it, that 'tis too hard a task for unassisted reason to establish morality, in all its parts, upon its true foundations, with a clear and convincing light. And 'tis at least a surer and shorter way, to the apprehensions of the vulgar and mass of mankind, that one, manifestly sent from God, and coming with visible authority from him, should, as a king and lawmaker, tell them their duties, and require their obedience, than leave it to the long and sometimes intricate deductions of reason to be made out to them: which the greatest part of mankind have neither leisure to weigh, nor, for want of education and use, skill to judge of. We see how unsuccessful, in this, the attempts of philosophers were, before our Saviour's time. How short their several systems came of the perfection of a true and complete morality is very visible. And if, since that, the Christian philosophers have much outdone them, yet we may observe that the first knowledge of the truths they have added are owing to revelation; though as soon as they are heard and considered they are found to be agreeable to reason, and such as can by no means be contradicted. Every one may observe a great many truths which he receives at first from others, and readily assents to, as consonant to reason, which he would have found it hard, and perhaps beyond his strength, to have discovered himself. Native and original truth is not so easily wrought out of the mine as we, who have it delivered ready dug and fashioned into our hands, are apt to imagine. And how often, at fifty or threescore years old, are thinking men told what they wonder how they could miss thinking of? Which yet their own contemplations did not, and possibly never would have, helped them to.

Experience shows that the knowledge of morality, by mere natural light (how agreeable soever it be to it), makes but a slow progress and little advance in the world. And the reason of it is not hard to be found in men's necessities, passions, vices, and mistaken interests, which turn their thoughts another way. And the designing leaders, as well as [the] following herd, find it not to their purpose to employ much of their meditations this way. Or, whatever else was the cause, 'tis plain, in fact, that human reason, unassisted, failed men in its great and proper business of morality. It never, from unquestionable principles, by clear deductions, made out an entire body of the law of nature. And he that shall collect all the moral rules of the philosophers, and compare them with those contained in the New Testament, will find them to come short of the morality delivered by our Saviour and taught by his apostles: a college made up, for the most part, of ignorant, but inspired, fishermen.

Though yet, if any one should think that out of the sayings of the wise heathens before our Saviour's time there might be a collection made of all those rules of morality which are to be found in the Christian religion; yet this would not at all hinder, but that the world, nevertheless, stood as much in need of our Saviour, and the morality delivered by him. Let it be granted (though not true) that all the moral precepts of the Gospel were known by somebody or other amongst mankind, before. But where, or how, or of what use, is not considered. Suppose they may be picked up here and there: some from Solon and Bias in Greece, others from Tully [i.e. Cicero] in Italy; and, to complete the work, let Confucius, as far as China, be consulted; and Anacharsis the Scythian contribute his share. What will all this do, to give the world a complete morality that may be to mankind the unquestionble rule of life and manners? I will not here urge the impossibility of collecting from men so far distant from one another, in time, and place, and languages. I will suppose there was a Stobaeus in those times, who had gathered the moral sayings from all the sages of the world. What would this amount to, towards being a steady rule, a certain transcript of a law that we are under? Did the saying of Aristippus, or Confucius, give it an authority? Was Zeno a lawgiver to mankind? If not, what he or any other philosopher delivered was but a saying of his. Mankind might hearken to it or reject it, as they pleased, or as it suited their interest, passions, principles, or humours: they were under no obligation. The opinion of this or that philosopher was of no authority: and, if it were, you must take all he said under the same character. All his dictates must go for law, certain and true, or none of them. And then, if you will take any of the moral sayings of Epicurus (many whereof Seneca quotes with esteem and approbation) for precepts of the law of nature, you must take all the rest of his doctrine for such too, or else his authority ceases: and so no more is to be received from him, or any of the sages of old, for parts of the law of nature, as carrying with it an obligation to be obeyed, but what they prove to be so.

But such a body of ethics, proved to be the law of nature from principles of reason, and reaching all the duties of life, I think nobody will say the world had before our Saviour's time. 'Tis not enough that there were up and down scattered sayings of wise men conformable to right reason. The law of nature was the law of convenience too; and 'tis no wonder that those men of parts, and studious of virtue (who had occasion to think on any particular part of it), should by meditation light on the right, even from the observable convenience and beauty of it, without making out its obligation from the true principles of the law of nature and foundations of morality. But these incoherent apophthegms of philosophers and wise men, however excellent in themselves, and well intended by them, could never make a morality whereof the world could be convinced and with certainty depend on. Whatsoever should thus be universally useful, as a standard to which men should conform their manners, must have its authority either from reason or revelation. 'Tis not every writer of morality, or compiler of it from others, that can thereby be erected into a lawgiver to mankind and a dictator of rules which are therefore valid, because they are to be found in his books, under the authority of this or that philosopher. He that anyone will pretend to set up in this kind, and have his rules pass for authentic directions, must show, that either he builds his doctrine upon principles of reason, self-evident in themselves, and that he deduces all the parts of it from thence, by clear and evident demonstration; or must show his commission from heaven, that he comes with authority from God to deliver his will and commands to the world.

In the former way, nobody that I know, before our Saviour's time, ever did, or went about to, give us a morality. 'Tis true, there is a law of nature: but who is there that ever did, or undertook to, give it us all entire, as a law: no more nor no less than what was contained in, and had the obligation of, that law? Who ever made out all the parts of it, put them together, and showed the world their obligation? Where was there any such code, that mankind might have recourse to, as their unerring rule, before our Saviour's time? If there was not, 'tis plain, there was need of one to give us such a morality, such a law, which might be the sure guide of those who had a desire to go right, and, if they had a mind, need not mistake their duty; but might be certain when they had performed, when failed in it.

Such a law of morality, Jesus Christ has given us in the New Testament; but by the latter of these ways, by revelation. We have from him a full and sufficient rule for our direction, and conformable to that of reason. But the truth and obligation of its precepts have their force, and are put past doubt to us, by the evidence of his mission. He was sent by God: His miracles show it; and the authority of God in his precepts cannot be questioned. Here morality has a sure standard, that revelation vouches, and reason cannot gainsay, nor question; but both together witness to come from God the great lawmaker. And such an one as this out of the New Testament, I think the world never had, nor can anyone say is anywhere else to be found.

Let me ask anyone who is forward to think that the doctrine of morality was full and clear in the world at our Saviour's birth, whither would he have directed Brutus and Cassius (both men of parts and virtue, the one whereof believed, and the other disbelieved a future being) to be satisfied in the rules and obligations of all the parts of their duties if they should have asked him where they might find the law they were to live by, and by which they should be charged or acquitted, as guilty or innocent? If [he sends them] to the sayings of the wise, and the declarations of philosophers, he sends them into a wild wood of uncertainty, to an endless maze, from which they should never get out; if to the religions of the world, yet worse; and if to their own reason, he refers them to that which had some light and certainty, but yet had hitherto failed all mankind in a perfect rule, and, we see, resolved not the doubts that had risen amongst the studious and thinking philosophers, nor had yet been able to convince the civilized parts of the world that they had not given, nor could, without a crime, take away the lives of their children, by exposing them.

If anyone shall think to excuse human nature by laying blame on men's negligence, that they did not carry morality to an higher pitch, and make it out entire in every part with that clearness of demonstration which some think it capable of, he helps not the matter. Be the cause what it will, our Saviour found mankind under a corruption of manners and principles which ages after ages had prevailed, and must be confessed was not in a way or tendency to be mended. The rules of morality were, in different countries and sects, different. And natural reason nowhere had, nor was like to cure the defects and errors in them. Those just measures of right and wrong which necessity had anywhere introduced, the civil laws prescribed, or philosophy recommended, stood not on their true foundations. They were looked on as bonds of society, and conveniences of common life, and laudable practices. But where was it that their obligation was thoroughly known and allowed, and they received as precepts of a law, of the highest law, the law of nature? That could not be without a clear knowledge and acknowledgement of the lawmaker, and the great rewards and punishments for those that would or would not obey him. But the religion of the heathens, as was before observed, little concerned itself in their morals. The priests that delivered the oracles of heaven, and pretended to speak from the gods, spoke little of virtue and a good life. And, on the other side, the philosophers, who spoke from reason, made not much mention of the deity in their ethics. They depended on reason and her oracles, which contain nothing but truth: but yet some parts of that truth lie too deep for our natural powers easily to reach, and make plain and visible to mankind, without some light from above to direct them.

When truths are once known to us, though by tradition, we are apt to be favourable to our own parts, and ascribe to our own understandings the discovery of what, in truth, we borrowed from others; or, at least, finding we can prove what at first we learnt from others, we are forward to conclude it an obvious truth, which, if we had sought, we could not have missed. Nothing seems hard to our understandings that is once known; and because what we see, we see with our own eyes, we are apt to overlook or forget the help we had from others who first showed and pointed it out to us, as if we were not at all beholden to them for that knowledge, which, being of truths we now are satisfied of, we conclude our own faculties would have led us into without any assistance, and that we know them, as they did, by the strength and perspicuity of our own minds, only they had the luck to be before us. Thus the whole stock of human knowledge is claimed by everyone as his private possession, as soon as he (profiting by others' discoveries) has got it into his own mind: and so it is; but not properly by his own single industry, nor of his own acquisition. He studies, 'tis true, and takes pains to make a progress in what others have delivered; but their pains were of another sort, who first brought those truths to light which he afterwards derives from them. He that travels the roads now applauds his own strength and legs, that have carried him so far in such a scantling of time, and ascribes all to his own vigour, little considering how much he owes to their pains, who cleared the woods, drained the bogs, built the bridges, and made the ways passable; without which he might have toiled much with little progress. A great many things which we have been bred up in the belief of, from our cradles (and are notions grown familiar and, as it were, natural to us, under the Gospel), we take for unquestionable, obvious truths, and easily demonstrable; without considering how long we might have been in doubt or ignorance of them, had revelation been silent. And many are beholden to revelation who do not acknowledge it.

'Tis no diminishing to revelation that reason gives its suffrage too to the truths revelation has discovered. But 'tis our mistake to think that because reason confirms them to us, we had the first certain knowledge of them from thence, and in that clear evidence we now possess them. The contrary is manifest in the defective morality of the Gentiles before our Saviour's time, and the want of reformation in the principles and measures of it, as well as practice. Philosophy seemed to have spent its strength, and done its utmost; or if it should have gone farther, as we see it did not, and from undeniable principles given us ethics in a science like mathematics, in every part demonstrable, this yet would not have been so effectual to man in this imperfect state, nor proper for the cure. The bulk of mankind have not leisure nor capacity for demonstration, nor can carry a train of proofs, which, in that way, they must always depend upon for conviction, and cannot be required to assent to till they see the demonstration. Wherever they stick, the teachers are always put upon proof, and must clear the doubt by a thread of coherent deductions from the first principle, how long or how intricate soever that be. And you may as soon hope to have all the day-labourers and tradesmen, the spinsters and dairy-maids, perfect mathematicians, as to have them perfect in ethics this way. Hearing plain commands is the sure and only course to bring them to obedience and practice. The greatest part cannot know, and therefore they must believe. And I ask whether one coming from heaven in the power of God, in full and clear evidence and demonstration of miracles, giving plain and direct rules of morality and obedience, be not likelier to enlighten the bulk of mankind, and set them right in their duties, and bring them to do them, than by reasoning with them from general notions and principles of human reason? And were all the duties of human life clearly demonstrated, yet I conclude, when well considered, that method of teaching men their duties would be thought proper only for a few who had much leisure, improved understandings, and were used to abstract reasonings: but the instruction of the people were best still to be left to the precepts and principles of the Gospel. The healing of the sick, the restoring sight to the blind by a word, the raising and being raised from the dead, are matters of fact which they can without difficulty conceive; and that he who does such things must do them by the assistance of a divine power. These things lie level to the ordinariest apprehension; he that can distinguish between sick and well, lame and sound, dead and alive, is capable of this doctrine. To one who is once persuaded that Jesus Christ was sent by God to be a king, and a Saviour of those who do believe in him, all his commands become principles; there needs no other proof for the truth of what he says, but that he said it. And then there needs no more but to read the inspired books to be instructed; all the duties of morality lie there clear and plain, and easy to be understood.

And here I appeal, whether this be not the surest, the safest and most effectual way of teaching; especially if we add this further consideration, that as it suits the lowest capacities of reasonable creatures, so it reaches and satisfies, nay, enlightens the highest. The most elevated understandings cannot but submit to the authority of this doctrine as divine; which, coming from the mouths of a company of illiterate men, has not only the attestation of miracles, but reason to confirm it, since they delivered no precepts but such as, though reason of itself had not clearly made out, yet it could not but assent to when thus discovered, and think itself indebted for the discovery. The credit and authority our Saviour and his apostles had over the minds of men, by the miracles they did, tempted them not to mix (as we find in that of all the sects of philosophers, and other religions) any conceits, any wrong rules, anything tending to their own by-interest, or that of a party, in their morality: no tang of prepossession or fancy; no footsteps of pride or vanity; no touch of ostentation or ambition appears to have a hand in it. It is all pure, all sincere;

nothing too much, nothing wanting; but such a complete rule of life as the wisest men must acknowledge tends entirely to the good of mankind, and that all would be happy if all would practise it.

3. The outward forms of worshipping the Deity wanted a reformation. Stately buildings, costly ornaments, peculiar and uncouth habits, and a numerous huddle of pompous, fantastical, cumbersome ceremonies everywhere attended divine worship. This, as it had the peculiar name, so it was thought the principal part, if not the whole, of religion; nor could this possibly be amended whilst the Jewish ritual stood and there was so much of it mixed with the worship of the true God. To this also our Saviour, with the knowledge of the infinite, invisible, supreme Spirit, brought a remedy in a plain, spiritual, and suitable worship. Jesus says to the woman of Samaria, 'The hour comes when ye shall neither in this mountain, nor yet at Jerusalem, worship the Father: but the true worshippers shall worship the Father both in spirit and in truth; for the Father seeks such to worship.' To be worshipped in spirit and in truth, with application of mind and sincerity of heart, was what God henceforth only required. Magnificent temples, and confinement to certain places, were now no longer necessary for his worship, which by a pure heart might be performed anywhere. The splendour and distinction of habits, and pomp of ceremonies, and all outside performances, might now be spared. God, who was a Spirit, and made known to be so, required none of those, but the spirit only; and that in public assemblies (where some actions must lie open to the view of the world) all that could appear and be seen should be done decently, and in order, and to edification. Decency, order, and edification were to regulate all their public acts of worship; and, beyond what these required, the outward appearance (which was of little value in the eyes of God) was not to go. Having shut out indecency and confusion out of their assemblies, they need not be solicitous about useless ceremonies. Praises and prayer, humbly offered up to the Deity, was the worship he now demanded; and in these everyone was to look after his own heart, and to know that it was that alone which God had regard to, and accepted.

4. Another great advantage received by our Saviour is the great encouragement he brought to a virtuous and pious life: great enough to surmount the difficulties and obstacles that lie in the way to it, and reward the pains and hardships of those who stuck firm to

their duties, and suffered for the testimony of a good conscience. The portion of the righteous has been in all ages taken notice of to be pretty scanty in this world: virtue and prosperity do not often accompany one another, and therefore virtue seldom had many followers. And 'tis no wonder she prevailed not much in a state where the inconveniences that attended her were visible and at hand, and the rewards doubtful and at a distance. Mankind, who are and must be allowed to pursue their happiness, nay, cannot be hindered, could not but think themselves excused from a strict observation of rules which appeared so little to consist with their chief end, happiness, whilst they kept them from the enjoyments of this life; and they had little evidence and security of another. 'Tis true, they might have argued the other way, and concluded that, because the good were most of them ill-treated here, there was another place where they should meet with better usage: but 'tis plain they did not. Their thoughts of another life were, at best, obscure; and their expectations uncertain. Of manes, and ghosts, and the shades of departed men, there was some talk; but little certain, and less minded. They had the names of Styx and Acheron, of Elysian fields and seats of the blessed: but they had them generally from their poets, mixed with their fables, and so they looked more like the inventions of wit, and ornaments of poetry, than the serious persuasions of the grave and the sober. They came to them bundled up amongst their tales; and for tales they took them. And that which rendered them more suspected, and less useful to virtue, was that the philosophers seldom set on their rules on men's minds and practices by consideration of another life. The chief of their arguments were from the excellency of virtue; and the highest they generally went was the exalting of human nature, whose perfection lay in virtue. And if the priest at any time talked of the ghosts below, and a life after this, it was only to keep men to their superstitious and idolatrous rites, whereby the use of this doctrine was lost to the credulous multitude, and its belief to the quicker sighted, who suspected it presently of priestcraft.

Before our Saviour's time the doctrine of a future state, though it were not wholly hid, yet it was not clearly known in the world. 'Twas an imperfect view of reason; or, perhaps, the decayed remains of an ancient tradition, which rather seemed to float on men's fancies than sink deep into their hearts. It was something, they knew not what, between being and not being. Something in man they imagined might escape the grave; but a perfect complete life of an eternal duration, after this, was what entered little into their thoughts, and less into their persuasions. And they were so far from being clear herein that we see no nation of the world publicly professed it and built upon it; no religion taught it; and 'twas nowhere made an article of faith and principle of religion till Jesus Christ came: of whom it is truly said, that he at his appearing 'brought life and immortality to light'. And that not only in the clear revelation of it, and in instances shown of men raised from the dead, but he has given us an unquestionable assurance and pledge of it in his own resurrection and ascension into heaven.

How has this one truth changed the nature of things in the world, and given the advantage to piety over all that could tempt or deter men from it! The philosophers, indeed, showed the beauty of virtue: they set her off so as drew men's eyes and approbation to her; but leaving her unendowed, very few were willing to espouse her. The generality could not refuse her their esteem and commendation, but still turned their backs on her, and forsook her, as a match not for their turn. But now, there being put into the scales on her side 'an exceeding and immortal weight of glory', interest is come about to her; and virtue now is visibly the most enriching purchase, and by much the best bargain. That she is the perfection and excellency of our nature; that she is herself a reward, and will recommend our names to future ages, is not all that can now be said for her. 'Tis not strange that the learned heathens satisfied not many with such airy commendations. It has another relish and efficacy to persuade men that if they live well here, they shall be happy hereafter. Open their eyes upon the endless, unspeakable joys of another life, and their hearts will find something solid and powerful to move them. The view of heaven and hell will cast a slight upon the short pleasures and pains of this present state, and give attractions and encouragements to virtue which reason and interest, and the care of ourselves, cannot but allow and prefer. Upon this foundation, and upon this only, morality stands firm, and may defy all competition. This makes it more than a name, a substantial good, worth all our aims and endeavours; and thus the Gospel of Jesus Christ has delivered it to us.

5. To these I must add one advantage more by Jesus Christ, and that is the promise of assistance. If we do what we can, he will give

us his Spirit to help us to do what and how we should. 'Twill be idle for us, who know not how our own spirits move and act us, to ask in what manner the Spirit of God shall work upon us. The wisdom that accompanies that Spirit knows better than we how we are made, and how to work upon us. If a wise man knows how to prevail on his child to bring him to what he desires, can we suspect that the Spirit and wisdom of God should fail in it, though we perceive or comprehend not the ways of his operation? Christ has promised it, who is faithful and just, and we cannot doubt of the performance. 'Tis not requisite on this occasion, for the enhancing of this benefit, to enlarge on the frailty of our minds and weakness of our constitutions: how liable to mistakes, how apt to go astray, and how easily to be turned out of the paths of virtue. If anyone needs go beyond himself and the testimony of his own conscience in this point, if he feels not his own errors and passions always tempting, and often prevailing, against the strict rules of his duty, he need but look abroad into any age of the world to be convinced. To a man under the difficulties of his nature, beset with temptations, and hedged in with prevailing custom, 'tis no small encouragement to set himself seriously on the courses of virtue, and practice of true religion, that he is from a sure hand, and an almighty arm, promised assistance to support and carry him through. . . .

4 Bernard Mandeville, *The Fable of the Bees; or, Private Vices, Publick Benefits* (1714)

. . . .

Introduction to the *Remarks*

One of the greatest reasons why so few people understand themselves is that most writers are always teaching men what they should be, and hardly ever trouble their heads with telling them what they really are. As for my part, without any compliment to the courteous reader, or myself, I believe man (besides skin, flesh, bones, etc., that are obvious to the eye) to be a compound of various passions, that all of them, as they are provoked and come uppermost, govern him by turns, whether he will or no. To show that these qualifications, which we all pretend to be ashamed of, are the great support of a flourishing society has been the subject of the foregoing poem [The Fable of the Bees]. But there being some passages in it seemingly paradoxical, I have in the Preface promised some explanatory Remarks on it; which to render more useful, I have thought fit to inquire how man, no better qualified, might yet by his own imperfections be taught to distinguish between virtue and vice: and here I must desire the reader once for all to take notice that when I say men, I mean neither Jews nor Christians; but mere man, in the state of nature and ignorance of the true Deity.

An Inquiry into the Origin of Moral Virtue

All untaught animals are only solicitous of pleasing themselves, and naturally follow the bent of their own inclinations, without considering the good or harm that from their being pleased will accrue to others. This is the reason that in the wild state of nature those creatures are fittest to live peaceably together in great numbers that discover the least of understanding, and have the fewest appetites to gratify. And consequently no species of animals is, without the curb of government, less capable of agreeing long together in multitudes than that of man; yet such are his qualities, whether good or bad I shall not determine, that no creature besides himself can ever be made sociable: but being an extraordinary selfish and headstrong, as well as cunning, animal, however he may be subdued by superior strength, it is impossible by force alone to make him tractable, and receive the improvements he is capable of.

The chief thing, therefore, which lawgivers and other wise men that have laboured for the establishment of society have endeavoured, has been to make the people they were to govern believe that it was more beneficial for everybody to conquer than indulge his appetites, and much better to mind the public than what seemed his private interest. As this has always been a very difficult task, so no wit or eloquence has been left untried to compass it; and the moralists and philosophers of all ages employed their utmost skill to prove the truth of so useful an assertion. But whether mankind would have ever believed it or not, it is not likely that anybody could have persuaded them to disapprove of their natural inclinations, or prefer the good of others to their own, if at the same time he had not showed them an equivalent to be enjoyed as a reward for the violence which by so doing they of necessity must commit upon themselves. Those that have undertaken to civilize mankind were not ignorant of this; but being unable to give so many real rewards as would satisfy all persons for every individual action, they were forced to contrive an imaginary one, that as a general equivalent for the trouble of self-denial should serve on all occasions, and without costing anything either to themselves or others, be yet a most acceptable recompense to the receivers.

They thoroughly examined all the strength and frailties of our nature, and, observing that none were either so savage as not to be charmed with praise, or so despicable as patiently to bear contempt, justly concluded that flattery must be the most powerful argument that could be used to human creatures. Making use of this bewitching engine, they extolled the excellency of our nature above other animals, and setting forth with unbounded praises the wonders of our sagacity and vastness of understanding, bestowed a thousand encomiums on the rationality of our souls, by the help of which we were capable of performing the most noble achievements. Having by this artful way of flattery insinuated themselves into the hearts of men, they began to instruct them in the notions of honour and shame; representing the one as the worst of all evils, and the other as the highest good to which mortals could aspire: which being done, they laid before them how unbecoming it was the dignity of such sublime creatures to be solicitous about gratifying those appetites which they had in common with brutes, and at the same time unmindful of those higher qualities that gave them the pre-eminence over all visible beings. They indeed confessed that those impulses of nature were very pressing; that it was troublesome to resist, and very difficult wholly to subdue them: but this they only used as an argument to demonstrate how glorious the conquest of them was on the one hand, and how scandalous on the other not to attempt it.

To introduce, moreover, an emulation amongst men, they divided the whole species in two classes, vastly differing from one another: the one consisted of abject, low-minded people that, always hunting after immediate enjoyment, were wholly incapable of self-denial, and, without regard to the good of others, had no higher aim than their private advantage; such as, being enslaved by voluptuousness, yielded without resistance to every gross desire, and made no use of their rational faculties but to heighten their sensual pleasures. These vile, grovelling wretches, they said, were the dross of their kind, and having only the shape of men, differed from brutes in nothing but their outward figure. But the other class was made up of lofty, high-spirited creatures that, free from sordid selfishness, esteemed the improvements of the mind to be their fairest possessions; and, setting a true value upon themselves, took no delight but in embellishing that part in which their excellency consisted; such as, despising whatever they had in common with irrational creatures, opposed by the help of reason their most violent inclinations; and, making a continual war with themselves to promote the peace of others, aimed at no less than the public welfare and the conquest of their own passions. *Fortior est qui se quam qui fortissima vincit/ Moenia* ... [Stronger is he who conquers himself than he who breaches the strongest fortifications]. These they called the true representatives of their sublime species, exceeding in worth the first class by more degrees than that itself was superior to the beasts of the field.

As, in all animals that are not too imperfect to discover pride, we find that the finest and such as are the most beautiful and valuable of their kind have generally the greatest share of it; so in man, the most perfect of animals, it is so inseparable from his very essence (how cunningly soever some may learn to hide or disguise it) that without it the compound he is made of would want one of the chiefest ingredients: which, if we consider, it is hardly to be doubted but lessons and remonstrances so skilfully adapted to the good opinion man has of himself as those I have mentioned must, if scattered amongst a multitude, not only gain the assent of most of them, as to the speculative part, but likewise induce several, especially the fiercest, most resolute, and best among them, to endure a thousand inconveniences, and undergo as many hardships, that they may have the pleasure of counting themselves men of the second class, and consequently appropriating to themselves all the excellences they have heard of it.

From what has been said we ought to expect, in the first place, that the heroes who took such extraordinary pains to master some of their natural appetites, and preferred the good of others to any visible interest of their own, would not recede an inch from the fine notions they had received concerning the dignity of rational creatures; and, having ever the authority of the government on their side, with all imaginable vigour assert the esteem that was due to those of the second class, as well as their superiority over the rest of their kind. In the second, that those who wanted a sufficient stock of either pride or resolution to buoy them up in mortifying of what was dearest to them, [and] followed the sensual dictates of nature, would yet be ashamed of confessing themselves to be those despicable wretches that belonged to the inferior class, and were generally reckoned to be so little removed from brutes; and that, therefore, in their own defence they would say as others did, and, hiding their own imperfections as well as they could, cry up self-denial and public-spiritedness as much as any. For it is highly probable that some of them, convinced by the real proofs of fortitude and self-conquest they had seen, would admire in others what they found wanting in themselves; others be afraid of the resolution and prowess of those of the second class; and that all of them were kept in awe by the power of their rulers. Wherefore it is reasonable to think that none of them (whatever they thought in themselves) would dare openly contradict what by everybody else was thought criminal to doubt of.

This was (or at least might have been) the manner after which savage man was broke; from whence it is evident that the first rudiments of morality, broached by skilful politicians to render men useful to each other as well as tractable, were chiefly contrived that the ambitious might reap the more benefit from and govern vast numbers of them with the greater ease and security. This foundation of politics being once laid, it is impossible that man should long remain uncivilized: for even those who only strove to gratify their appetites, being continually crossed by others of the same stamp, could not but observe that whenever they checked their inclinations, or but followed them with more circumspection, they avoided a world of troubles, and often escaped many of the calamities that generally attended the too eager pursuit after pleasure.

First, they received, as well as others, the benefit of those actions that were done for the good of the whole society, and consequently could not forbear wishing well to those of the superior class that performed them. Secondly, the more intent they were in seeking their own advantage, without regard to others, the more they were hourly convinced that none were so obnoxious to them as those that were most like themselves.

It being the interest then of the very worst of them, more than any, to preach up public-spiritedness, that they might reap the fruits of the labour and self-denial of others, and at the same time indulge their own appetites with less disturbance, they agreed with the rest to call everything which, without regard to the public, man should commit to gratify any of his appetites VICE if in that action there could be observed the least prospect that it might either be injurious to any of the society, or ever render himself less serviceable to others; and to give the name of VIRTUE to every performance by which man, contrary to the impulse of nature, should endeavour the benefit of others, or the conquest of his own passions out of a rational ambition of being good.

It shall be objected that no society was ever anyways civilized before the major part had agreed upon some worship or other of an overruling power, and consequently that the notions of good and evil, and the distinction between virtue and vice, were never the contrivance of politicians, but the pure effect of religion. Before I answer this objection, I must repeat what I have said already, that in this *Inquiry into the Origin of Moral Virtue* I speak neither of Jews or Christians, but man in his state of nature and ignorance of the true Deity; and then I affirm that the idolatrous superstitions of all other nations, and the pitiful notions they had of the Supreme Being, were incapable of exciting man to virtue, and good for nothing but to awe and amuse a rude and unthinking multitude. It is evident from history that in all considerable societies, how stupid or ridiculous soever peoples' received notions have been as to the deities they worshipped, human nature has ever exerted itself in all its branches, and that there is no earthly wisdom or moral virtue but at one time or other men have excelled in it in all monarchies and commonwealths that for riches and power have been anyways remarkable.

The Egyptians, not satisfied with having deified all the ugly monsters they could think on, were so silly as to adore the onions of their own sowing; yet at the same time their country was the most famous nursery of arts and sciences in the world, and themselves more eminently skilled in the deepest mysteries of nature than any nation has been since.

No states or kingdoms under heaven have yielded more or greater patterns in all sorts of moral virtues than the Greek and Roman empires, more especially the latter; and yet how loose, absurd and ridiculous were their sentiments as to sacred matters: for without reflecting on the extravagant number of their deities, if we only consider the infamous stories they fathered upon them, it is not to be denied but that their religion, far from teaching men the conquest of their passions, and the way to virtue, seemed rather contrived to justify their appetites and encourage their vices. But if we would know what made them excel in fortitude, courage, and magnanimity, we must cast our eyes on the pomp of their triumphs, the magnificence of their monuments and arches; their trophies, statues, and inscriptions; the variety of their military crowns, their honours decreed to the dead, public encomiums on the living, and other imaginary rewards they bestowed on men of merit; and we shall find that what carried so many of them to the utmost pitch of self-denial was nothing but their policy in making use of the most effectual means that human pride could be flattered with.

It is visible, then, that it was not any heathen religion or other idolatrous superstition that first put man upon crossing his appetites and subduing his dearest inclinations, but the skilful management of wary politicians; and the nearer we search into human nature the more we shall be convinced that the moral virtues are the political offspring which flattery begot upon pride.

There is no man, of what capacity or penetration soever, that is wholly proof against the witchcraft of flattery, if artfully performed and suited to his abilities. Children and fools will swallow personal praise, but those that are more cunning must be managed with greater circumspection; and the more general the flattery is, the less it is suspected by those it is levelled at. What you say in commendation of a whole town is received with pleasure by all the inhabitants; speak in commendation of letters in general, and every man of learning will think himself in particular obliged to you. You may safely praise the employment a man is of, or the country he was born in, because you give him an opportunity of screening the joy he feels upon his own account under the esteem which he pretends to have for others.

It is common among cunning men that understand the power which flattery has upon pride, when they are afraid they shall be imposed upon, to enlarge, though much against their conscience, upon the honour, fair dealing, and integrity of the family, country, or sometimes the profession of him they suspect; because they know that men often will change their resolution, and act against their inclination, that they may have the pleasure of continuing to appear in the opinion of some what they are conscious not to be in reality. Thus sagacious moralists draw men like angels, in hopes that the pride at least of some will put them upon copying after the beautiful originals which they are represented to be.

When the incomparable Mr Steele, in the usual elegance of his easy style, dwells on the praises of his sublime species, and with all the embellishments of rhetoric sets forth the excellency of human nature, it is impossible not to be charmed with his happy turns of thought, and the politeness of his expressions. But though I have been often moved by the force of his eloquence, and ready to swallow the ingenious sophistry with pleasure, yet I could never be so serious but, reflecting on his artful encomiums, I thought on the tricks made use of by the women that would teach children to be mannerly.

When an awkward girl, before she can either speak or go, begins after many entreaties to make the first rude essays of curtsying, the nurse falls in an ecstasy of praise: 'There's a delicate curtsy! Oh fine miss! There's a pretty lady! Mama! Miss can make a better curtsy than her sister Molly!' The same is echoed over by the maids, whilst Mama almost hugs the child to pieces; only Miss Molly, who, being four years older, knows how to make a very handsome curtsy, wonders at the perverseness of their judgement, and, swelling with indignation, is ready to cry at the injustice that is done her, till, being whispered in the ear that it is only to please the baby, and that she is a woman, she grows proud at being let into the secret, and, rejoicing at the superiority of her understanding, repeats what has been said with large additions, and insults over the weakness of her sister, whom all this while she fancies to be the only bubble among them.

These extravagant praises would, by any one above the capacity of an infant, be called fulsome flatteries, and, if you will, abominable lies; yet experience teaches us that by the help of such gross encomiums young misses will be brought to make pretty curtsies, and behave themselves womanly much sooner, and with less trouble, than they would without them. It is the same with boys, whom they'll strive to persuade that all fine gentlemen do as they are bid, and that none but beggar boys are rude, or dirty their clothes; nay, as soon as the wild brat with his untaught fist begins to fumble for his hat, the mother, to make him pull it off, tells him, before he is two years old, that he is a man; and if he repeats that action when she desires him, he's presently a captain, a lord mayor, a king, or something higher if she can think of it, till, egged on by the force of praise, the little urchin endeavours to imitate Man as well as he can, and strains all his faculties to appear what his shallow noddle imagines he is believed to be.

The meanest wretch puts an inestimable value upon himself, and the highest wish of the ambitious man is to have all the world, as to that particular, of his opinion: so that the most insatiable thirst after fame that ever hero was inspired with was never more than an ungovernable greediness to engross the esteem and admiration of others in future ages as well as his own; and (what mortification soever this truth might be to the second thoughts of an Alexander or a Caesar) the great recompense in view, for which the most exalted minds have with so much alacrity sacrificed their quiet, health, sensual pleasures, and every inch of themselves, has never been anything else but the breath of man, the aerial coin of praise. Who can forbear laughing when he thinks on all the great men that have been so serious on the subject of that Macedonian madman: his capacious soul, that mighty heart, in one corner of which, according to Lorenzo Gracian, the world was so commodiously lodged, that in the whole there was room for six more? Who can forbear laughing, I say, when he compares the fine things that have been said of Alexander with the end he proposed to himself from his vast exploits, to be proved from his own mouth when the vast pains he took to pass the Hydaspes forced him to cry out: 'Oh ye Athenians, could you believe what dangers I expose myself to, to be praised by you!'? To define then the reward of glory in the amplest manner, the most that can be said of it is that it consists in a superlative felicity which a man who is conscious of having performed a noble action enjoys in self-love, whilst he is thinking on the applause he expects of others.

But here I shall be told that, besides the noisy toils of war and public bustle of the ambitious, there are noble and generous actions that are performed in silence; that virtue being its own reward, those who are really good have a satisfaction in their consciousness of being so, which is all the recompense they expect from the most worthy performances; that among the heathens there have been men who, when they did good to others, were so far from coveting thanks and applause that they took all imaginable care to be for ever concealed from those on whom they bestowed their benefits, and consequently that pride has no hand in spurring man on to the highest pitch of self-denial.

In answer to this I say that it is impossible to judge of a man's performance unless we are thoroughly acquainted with the principle and motive from which he acts. Pity, though it is the most gentle and the least mischievous of all our passions, is yet as much a frailty of our nature as anger, pride, or fear. The weakest minds have generally the greatest share of it, for which reason none are more compassionate than women and children. It must be owned that of all our weaknesses it is the most amiable, and bears the greatest resemblance to virtue; nay, without a considerable mixture of it the society could hardly subsist: but as it is an impulse of nature that consults neither the public interest nor our own reason, it may produce evil as well as good. It has helped to destroy the honour of virgins, and corrupted the integrity of judges, and whoever acts from it as a principle, what good soever he may bring to the society, has nothing to boast of but that he has indulged a passion that has happened to be beneficial to the public. There is no merit in saving an innocent babe ready to drop into the fire: the action is neither good nor bad, and what benefit soever the infant received we only obliged ourselves; for to have seen it fall, and not strove to hinder it, would have caused a pain which self-preservation compelled us to prevent. Nor has a rich prodigal that happens to be of a commiserating temper, and loves to gratify his passions, greater virtue to boast of when he relieves an object of compassion with what to himself is a trifle.

But such men as, without complying with any weakness of their own, can part from what they value themselves, and, from no other motive but their love to goodness, perform a worthy action in silence; such men, I confess, have acquired more refined notions of virtue than those I have hitherto spoke of; yet even in these (with which the world has yet never swarmed) we may discover no small symptoms of pride, and the humblest man alive must confess that the reward of a virtuous action, which is the satisfaction that ensues upon it, consists in a certain pleasure he procures to himself by contemplating on his own worth: which pleasure, together with the occasion of it, are as certain signs of pride as looking pale and trembling at any imminent danger are the symptoms of fear.

If the too scrupulous reader should, at first view, condemn these notions concerning the origin of moral virtue, and think them perhaps offensive to Christianity, I hope he will forbear his censures when he shall consider that nothing can render the unsearchable depth of divine wisdom more conspicuous than that man, whom providence had designed for society, should not only by his own frailties and imperfections be led into the road to temporal happiness, but likewise receive, from a seeming necessity of natural causes, a tincture of that knowledge in which he was afterwards to be made perfect by the true religion, to his eternal welfare.

. . . .

NOTES ON THE TEXTS

1. *Table Talk: Being the Discourses of John Selden, Esq.; or His Sense of Various Matters of Weight and High Consequence Relating Especially to Religion and State*, ed. R. Milward: First published in 1689. There were further editions in 1696, 1716, 1755 (Glasgow), 1786, 1797, 1798, 1818, 1819 (Edinburgh), 1821, 1847, 1854 (Edinburgh), 1856, 1868 (two editions), 1887, 1892, 1895, 1898, 1899, 1907, and 1927.

2. Hobbes, *Philosophicall Rudiments Concerning Government and Society* (1651): This is a translation of *De Cive*, which had appeared in a privately circulated edition in Paris in 1642. Two further editions (Elzevir, Amsterdam, 1647) appeared before the English translation and had included the explanatory notes which appear here. There have been a further twelve editions of the Latin text of *De Cive*. The English translation of 1651 is probably not the work of Hobbes himself, but of one 'C.C.' (R. Tuck, 'Warrender's *De Cive*', *Political Studies*, XXXIII (1985), pp. 308-15). It reappears in Hobbes's *English Works* (1839-45, reprinted Aalen, 1962); in part in *De Cive or The Citizen*, ed. S. P. Lamprecht (New York, 1949); in *Man and Citizen*, ed. B. Gert (Garden City, 1972); and in what is now the standard edition of *De Cive*, ed. H. Warrender (two vols., Oxford, 1983). It was translated once in whole and once in part into French in the seventeenth century, appearing in some five editions. It appeared in Dutch in 1675. In the twentieth century there have been three Italian translations, two German, and Spanish, Polish and Czech editions.

3. Locke, *The Reasonableness of Christianity*: 1695, with further editions in 1696 (two, one of them in French), 1731 (French), 1733 (German), 1785, 1791, 1834, 1836, 1843 (French), 1850, 1853, and 1976 (Italian). A substantial selection was edited by I. T. Ramsey (Stanford, 1958). It also appears in the thirteen editions of Locke's *Works* between 1714 and 1825.

4. Mandeville, *The Fable of the Bees:* In 1705 Mandeville published a poem, *The Grumbling Hive: or, Knaves Turn'd Honest.* In 1714 this was

published with additional remarks, including the present text (second
edition, 1714). In 1723 further additions were made (subsequently republished in 1724, 1725, 1728, 1729, 1732). These were insignificant as far
as the present text is concerned, with the exception of the expansion of the
passage concerning Alexander on p. 501 ('Who can . . . define then?'). In
1729 a second volume appeared, and this was republished in 1730 and
1733. Finally the entire work was published in 1733, reappearing in 1755
(two editions, one in Edinburgh and the other in London, dated 1734
(*sic*)), 1772 (Edinburgh), 1795, 1806, and in the standard edition, ed. F. B.
Kaye (two vols., Oxford, 1924). Selections have been published in 1934,
1962 (New York) and 1970 (Harmondsworth). French editions appeared
in 1740 and 1750, German in 1761, 1818 and 1914, and Russian in 1974.

FURTHER READING

With Locke and Mandeville we may be said to have reached the frontiers
of modern political theory. Three books that look backward from this
vantage point are Q. Skinner, *The Foundations of Modern Political Theory*
(two vols., Cambridge, 1978); R. Tuck, *Natural Rights Theories: Their
Origin and Development* (Cambridge, 1979); and B. Tierney, *Religion, Law
and the Growth of Constitutional Thought, 1150–1650* (Cambridge, 1982). One
that looks forwards is I. Hont and M. Ignatieff (eds.), *Wealth and Virtue*
(Cambridge, 1983).

Skinner has further developed the argument of his *Foundations* in 'The
Origins of the Calvinist Theory of Revolution', in B. C. Malament (ed.),
After the Reformation (Manchester, 1980). Skinner's arguments may, how-
ever, need correcting in the light of the following: J. H. Burns on Almain:
'*Ius Gladii* and *Jurisdictio*', *Historical Journal*, XXVI (1983), pp. 369–74;
R. Tuck on Buchanan, in *Natural Rights Theories* (Cambridge, 1979);
J. P. Sommerville on Suarez, 'From Suarez to Filmer', *Historical Journal*,
XXV (1982), pp. 525–40; D. Wootton on Althusius, in 'The Fear of God
in Early Modern Political Theory', (Canadian Historical Association)
Historical Papers 1983, pp. 56–80.

Tuck's very different account has been criticized by B. Tierney, 'Tuck
on Rights', *History of Political Thought*, IV (1983), pp. 429–41, by J. P.
Sommerville, 'John Selden, the Law of Nature and the Origin of Government', *Historical Journal*, XXVII (1984), pp. 437–47, and by P. Zagorin,
'Clarendon and Hobbes', *Journal of Modern History*, LVII (1985), pp. 593–
616.

A central problem in Tierney's book is the importance he attributes to
George Lawson. His approach seems to have been influenced by J. H.
Franklin, *John Locke and the Theory of Sovereignty* (Cambridge, 1978), which
has been criticized by J. H. Tully, 'Current Thinking about Sixteenth- and
Seventeenth-Century Political Theory', *Historical Journal*, XXIV (1981),
pp. 475–84, and by C. Condren in three articles on Lawson, in particular
'Resistance and Sovereignty in Lawson's *Politica*', *Historical Journal*, XXIV

(1981), pp. 673–81 (see also *Medioevo*, VI (1980) and *Journal of Religious History*, XI (1981)).

For introductions to the particular thinkers presented in this chapter, see: R. Tuck on Selden in J. Morrill (ed.), *Reactions to the English Civil War, 1642–49* (London, 1982); K. C. Brown (ed.), *Hobbes Studies* (Oxford, 1965); J. Dunn, *Locke* (Oxford, 1984); T. A. Horne, *The Social Thought of Bernard Mandeville* (New York, 1978); and M. M. Goldsmith, *Private Vices, Public Benefits* (Cambridge, 1985).

There is, of course, a vast literature on Hobbes and Locke, but, apart from Skinner's work referred to in the bibliography to Chapter Six, the last twenty years have been comparatively quiet ones in Hobbes studies. The same cannot be said for Locke, where major new studies have been appearing at a growing rate. The context in which the *Two Treatises* were written has been reassessed in a brilliant essay by R. Ashcraft, 'Revolutionary Politics and Locke's *Two Treatises*', *Political Theory*, VIII (1980), pp. 429–86. For their significance in the context in which they were published, see C. D. Tarlton, '"The Rulers Now on Earth"', *Historical Journal*, XXVIII (1985), pp. 279–98. And for their influence see R. Ashcraft and M. M. Goldsmith, 'Locke, *Revolution Principles*, and the Foundations of Whig Ideology', *Historical Journal*, XXVI (1983), pp. 773–800. Locke's rejection of previous styles of English political argument is discussed in D. Resnick, 'Locke and the Rejection of the Ancient Constitution', *Political Theory*, XII (1984), pp. 97–114.

Ashcraft has presented a new picture of Locke as a radical revolutionary. A major study attributing a radical rather than conservative view of property to Locke is J. H. Tully, *A Discourse on Property* (Cambridge, 1980). Tully's views should however be compared with those of: E. J. Hundert, 'The Making of *Homo Faber*', *Journal of the History of Ideas*, XXXIII (1972), pp. 3–22; K. I. Vaughn, *John Locke* (London, 1980); and I. Hont and M. Ignatieff in *Wealth and Virtue* (Cambridge, 1983).

Locke's theology has been reassessed by D. D. Wallace Jr, in 'Socinianism, Justification by Faith, and the Sources of John Locke's *The Reasonableness of Christianity*', *Journal of the History of Ideas*, XLV (1984), pp. 49–66.

Studies which bear on the secularization of political theory in the seventeenth and early eighteenth centuries are D. Gauthier, 'Why Ought One Obey God: Reflections on Hobbes and Locke', *Canadian Journal of Philosophy*, VII (1977), pp. 425–46; D. P. Walker, *The Decline of Hell* (Chicago, 1964); J. A. W. Gunn, *Politics and the Public Interest* (London, 1969); J. O. Appleby, *Economic Thought and Ideology in Seventeenth Century England* (Princeton, 1978); A. O. Hirschman, *The Passions and the Interests* (Princeton, 1977).

INDEX